THE CONCISE ENCYCLOPÆDIA OF
LIVING FAITHS

THE CONCISE ENCYCLOPÆDIA OF

Living Faiths

EDITED BY R. C. ZAEHNER

CONTRIBUTORS

A. L. BASHAM   H. A. R. GIBB
G. BOWNAS   A. C. GRAHAM
EDWARD CONZE   I. B. HORNER
T. CORBISHLEY   JOHN KENT
J. G. DAVIES   R. H. ROBINSON
H. FRANCIS DAVIS R. J. ZWI WERBLOWSKY
WERNER EICHHORN   R. C. ZAEHNER
NICOLAS ZERNOV

BEACON PRESS   :   BOSTON

First published as a Beacon Paperback in 1967 by arrangement with Hawthorn Books Inc., New York, and the author.

Published simultaneously in Canada by Saunders of Toronto,
Ltd.

Beacon Press books are published under the auspices of the
Unitarian Universalist Association.

Printed in the United States of America.

2c. "Christianity: St Thomas and Medieval Theology" *by* H.
Francis Davis, M.A., D.D.   Page 108

2d. "Christianity: the Catholic Church since the Reformation"
by T. Corbishley, S.J., M.A.   Page 150

Nihil Obstat: Richardus Roche, D.D., Censor Deputatus

Imprimatur: ✠ Franciscus, Archiepiscopus Birmingamiensis
Datum Birmganiae 4a Februarii 1959

CONTENTS

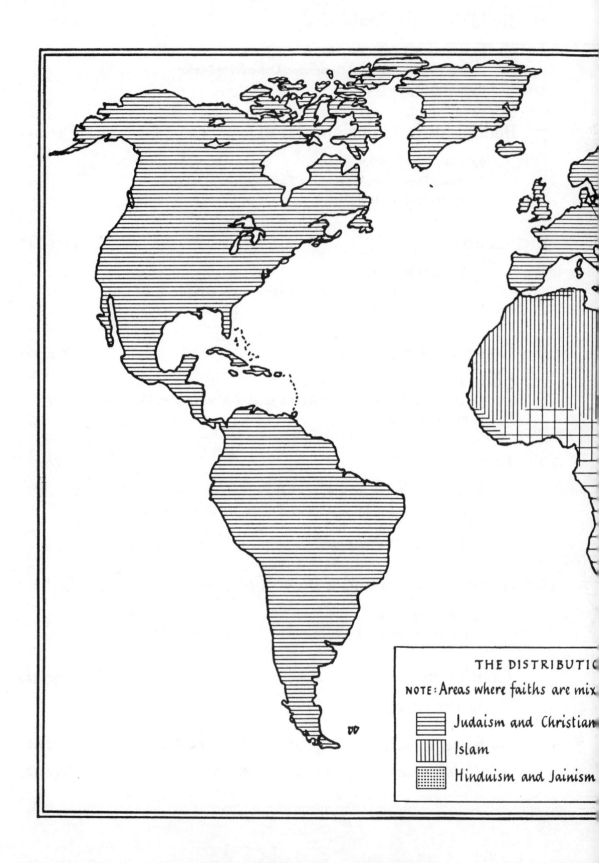

THE DISTRIBUTIO

NOTE: Areas where faiths are mix

Judaism and Christian

Islam

Hinduism and Jainism

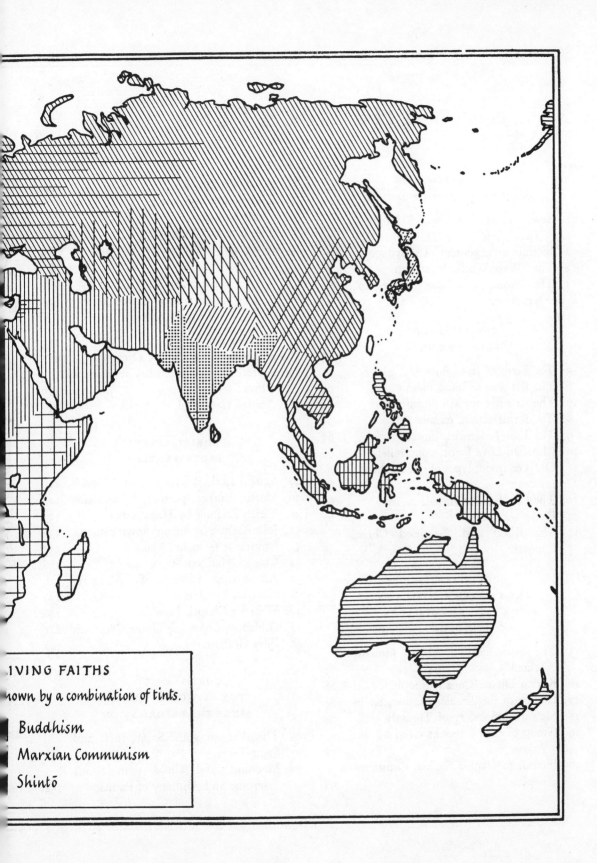

THE PLATES

THE CONCISE ENCYCLOPÆDIA OF LIVING FAITHS

ACKNOWLEDGMENT

The Publishers wish to thank Dr Frederic Spiegelberg,
Professor of Asiatic and Slavic languages,
Stanford University, California, for
his help with the text.

Introduction

by THE EDITOR

It has taken two wars of exceptional frightfulness to shake the "progressive" half of mankind out of its comfortable belief in progress itself which it inherited from the nineteenth century. Since the days of the French "Enlightenment" religion, and particularly Christianity, has been under constant and effective fire. The Darwinian theory of evolution was held to have exploded many a Christian myth, and religion itself was dismissed as mere superstition. The onward march of science and the triumph of reason over faith, it was confidently believed, would make religion outmoded, and religion itself would die a natural death. The Bolsheviks in Russia were more realistic; for, though they believed that religion, like the state, would "wither away", they were certainly going to take an active part in promoting the withering. But despite intensive persecution, religion in Russia has not withered away: despite severe disabilities, it still lives on and its death-throes seem to have been indefinitely postponed.

It is quite true that the rationalist attacks on religion have emptied the churches in Great Britain at least—though quite the reverse can be seen to be happening in the United States—yet even in Britain there is more interest in religion than there has been at any other period of this century. Much of this interest is amateur, and the present vogue for Zen Buddhism, for instance, probably signifies little more than an obscurely felt malaise at living in a world that has lost all meaning. For many Europeans and Americans, Christianity has been tried and found wanting, and so a new interest in Oriental religion has sprung up; for Oriental religion is obviously quite different from Christianity and does not ask you to believe what many regard as being impossible and incomprehensible things. Buddhism, for instance, does not even require you to believe in the existence of God, and for many post-Christians who are not at home in the desert of their unbelief and who still find it impossible to return to that particular "superstition", this is a great

relief. For such as these this *Concise Encyclopedia of Living Faiths* is primarily designed; for this is a book that attempts to describe in a brief compass those faiths which have withstood the test of time and which must, therefore, correspond to some fundamental need in man. It is for this reason that no account at all appears of the great religions of the past – either the national religions of departed cultures like ancient Mesopotamia and Egypt, or those religions, like that of the Manichees, which, though they once enjoyed a wide diffusion, nevertheless disappeared from the scene.

The living faiths of the world fall into two well-defined groups which appear to have little in common. This will become apparent to any student of this work who reads consecutively the chapter on the religion of Israel and the chapters on Buddhism. Both Judaism and Buddhism are commonly accounted "religions"; but what single common factor unites them? The one purports to give an account of God's dealings with his chosen people in history, both God and his people being treated as objective realities, whereas the other, in its early stages at least, has no consciousness of God as an external reality, assigns no importance whatever to history, sees no purpose at all in human life, but proclaims rather that salvation consists in individual escape from an intolerable existence into a state of being which is unconditioned, beyond space and time, and in which suffering and the deceptive joys which are but a mask for suffering are finally brought to rest. Between two such conceptions of man and the world in which he lives, there is, plainly, a gulf fixed.

In our conclusion we shall have something to say about the possible bridging of this gulf. Here we can do no more than draw attention to it, for the Eastern and Western ideas of religion are so utterly strange to each other that the very possibility of reconciling them in any one formula seemed hopeless unless a full-scale chapter were devoted to the problem.

The great bulk of the English-speaking world either is Christian or continues to act on Christian assumptions and to use Christian terminology. Religion is thus equated with the worship of God, and the belief in the existence of God as omnipotent, omniscient Lord is taken to be the hall-mark of religion. Thus freedom to conduct anti-religious propaganda, as provided for in the constitution of the U.S.S.R., is taken to mean freedom to undermine, refute, and confute the belief of other men in a Supreme Being who exercises sovereignty over the world. Marxian atheism, then, thinks of itself primarily as anti-religious, indeed as anti-God. To be anti-God, of course, implies logically a belief in the existence of God, but the matter is not quite as simple as this. The Marxian hostility to religion is in fact hostility to the *belief* in a Supreme Being for which the Marxist claims to see no warrant in reason. It is a frank acknowledgment of the tremendous power – not of God – but of the idea of God planted in the mind of man to influence him for good or ill. Yet the Christian idea of God can only provoke such hostility in people who take the idea seriously, indeed who take ideas as such with desperate seriousness. This has always been characteristic of the West.

The Eastern mentality as manifested in Indian and Far Eastern religion with which the second half of this book will deal, operates quite differently. At any rate since the rise of Christianity in the West, European civilization has been dominated by beliefs passionately held: toleration and "reasonableness" have been very late comers to the European scene, and even now, as the history of this century shows, their hold on our minds is at the most precarious. For better or for worse the European mind is possessed by the concept of Truth, the concept that the ultimate realities can be known at least in part, and that the possession of this truth is vital to man's well-being. Such is not, and rarely has been, the Indian or Chinese way of seeing things. Indian religion has always tended to regard different religious manifestations as being all in their own way aspects of one indivisible truth which cannot be seized in its essence because it is ineffable: each religion is the same truth seen from a different angle. If this is really so, then the endless trail of persecution which has defaced the history of the West, must seem not only wicked but incomprehensible. So the immense seriousness and awe with which the Jew or the Calvinist, for example, regards his God, must seem a trifle exaggerated to the Eastern mentality. So it is that persecution has been rare in the East since Eastern man does not see "error" as something particularly pernicious: when all is said and done, it is simply another way of looking at things.

THE TWO TRADITIONS

This sharp distinction between the "Indian" and "Judaic" conceptions of reality dictated the very arrangement of this book. The beliefs we are concerned with fell naturally into two well-defined halves. Each half is dominated by a basic way of thought, and this way of thought springs, in each case, from a given people. In each case what had been national religions gave birth, against their will, to universal faiths; and in each case there run parallel to the main streams of religious energy released by the two "chosen" peoples subsidiary streams in other lands which show a natural kinship to one or other of the main streams. This fact, and the fact that the subsidiary streams in each case form a geographical whole with the main stream, dictated the shape of the present volume.

What are these two main streams, and what are the subsidiary streams that run parallel to them? A glance at the map of the world religions will show that there is a fairly clear dividing line between the limit of extension of the two main religious traditions. "Western" religion, by which we in fact mean the religions originating in the Near East, owes its origin, directly or indirectly, to the Jews: "Eastern" religion either owes its origin to India or is profoundly influenced by Indian religious thought. In each case there is the parent stock from which the more widely diffused religions spring. In the West this parent stock is Israel, the Jews; in the East it is India. And just as Israel gives birth to Christianity and – less directly – to Islam, so does the national religion of India, Hinduism, give birth to Jainism and the two great form of Buddhism which now share betweenthem almost thes whole of South East Asia, China and Japan. In each case a religious genius appears among the "chosen" people: in the case of the Jews, Jesus Christ; in the case of the Indians, Gotama the Buddha. In each case there then springs up a new religion distinct both from the parent stock and from its great offshoot: in the one case, Islam, in the other Mahāyāna Buddhism which is so radical a transformation of early Buddhism as to constitute, almost, a religion in its own right. In each case again there are religions originating in lands adjacent to one of the two "chosen" peoples which are akin to and ultimately assimilable by the two great religious streams: in the one case Zoroastrianism, in the other Taoism. Here, however, the parallelism ends. The resemblances are of structure, not of content. It is in the matter of content that the two streams are so radically divided. Even a superficial comparison of the two halves of this book should make this point clear.

Let us, for our present purposes, take Judaism and Buddhism as the "types" of the two great religious traditions; and the radical difference between them will become immediately apparent. On the one side you find a God who appears as an objective reality, who chooses one people out of all the peoples of the earth and enters into an eternal covenant with them. The covenant works itself out in history: God is dealing with his people here and now, telling them what to do, legislating for them, encouraging them, chastising them, but leading them always on to their fulfilment at the end of time when there will be a new heaven and a new earth, and they will be in very truth his people and he will be their God. God, moreover, speaks to his people through men specially chosen out, the prophets: through them he makes his sovereign will known. It is for God to command, for man to obey. Though the gulf that separates man from God is immense, there is nonetheless a close and direct relationship between the two. "Religion" in the Jewish sense consists in the right relationship between God and man. It is a relationship between two parties, an "I" and a "Thou" in which the immense distance between the two is never blurred. God makes known his will, and it is for man to obey and humbly do that will. God must be worshipped as he commands, and not otherwise. To worship in any way that God has not commanded is to worship what is other than God. Idolatry is wrong because it puts man's subjective idea of God in place of the objective reality, the Living God who makes himself heard through the prophets. This is the type of "prophetic" religion, and the same accents are no less distinctly heard in the *Gāthās* of Zoroaster and in the Koran than they are in the Hebrew prophets. This is no place to point out the obvious anomalies that are liable to arise from utterances of prophets if and when these utterances do not appear to agree. The history of Semitic religion as a whole is commentary enough on that. For what is the situation that confronts us there?

For the sake of convenience I have spoken of two "chosen" peoples; and by this I have meant no more than that Israel and India have between them originated the religions that are practised by an overwhelming majority of the human race. In fact, between the two peoples there is all the difference in the world. Of the two it is Israel alone that claims to be God's chosen people; the Indians have never made any such claim, and it would sound utterly incongruous on their lips. Israel alone of all the nations of the earth has in fact made such a claim, and this *does* set her apart from all other nations, however much other nations may resent the claim. Whether the claim is true or false is quite another matter and cannot be allowed to detain us in this book. Similarly the Christian Church claims to be the new Israel, provided by God with a new covenant which supersedes the old. The Christian claim, however, is rejected by the Jews; and since Christianity claims to be the fulfilment of the old Law and of divine origin, and since the Jews categorically reject this claim, we are historically faced with two religions which both claim to be the one true faith revealed by God. Again, the situation is made no easier by the emergence of Islam, a religion which arose some six hundred years after Christ and which, in its turn, claims to be the final revelation of God to man, superseding both Judaism and Christianity. The three religions, however, though disagreeing on what they would themselves consider to be essentials, are united in one fundamental respect: each claims to be a direct revelation of the One True God to man. Moreover all three, despite the immense differences that divide them, agree in this: that God does make himself known by revelation, that his sovereignty is absolute, and that his will must be unhesitatingly obeyed. All three start with the premiss that God is an external, objective reality, the supreme and absolute ruler of the universe, who created it out of nothing. Further they agree that the human person was created one and indivisible, that bodily death, therefore, does not mean a final separation of body from soul, but that, in order that man's salvation shall be complete, his body must be re-united to his soul at the end of time. Thus the "prophetic" tradition, as I shall call it, is agreed on the nature of God as supreme ruler of the universe, its creator, sustainer and preserver; it is agreed that man was created for a purpose which will only be fully revealed at the end of time; and it is agreed that death, the result of sin, is not man's final condition but only a temporary separation. Man is composed of soul and body, and final beatitude must therefore include the re-union of man's severed parts: an immortal soul is only half a man, it is not the whole man. Moreover, the immortality of the soul, though it undoubtedly plays an important part in all three religions, is not quite central to any of them. Life on earth is regarded by all of them as being supremely important. This life is a time of testing, a preparation for life everlasting. Further, this life is unique: it is our only chance and can never be repeated. On it depends our eternal destiny of weal and woe. Earthly life, then, though only a preparation, is a preparation of immense importance: it is a deadly serious affair in which all is at stake, for – and here all three religions agree – we will be held to account by God, our sovereign Lord, for what we have done and left undone.

In all this the three religions which go to make up the prophetic tradition agree. What of the Indian tradition?

Here we immediately enter into a totally different religious climate. Indian religion, as it develops in history, starts with the Upanishads (pp. 227-8). These are "mystical" treatises the object of which is to discover what the common substratum of the universe is: they are primitive philosophical speculations and not by any means a direct confrontation of God and man. Man, rather, is groping towards God, and his groping leads him to experience the immortality of his own soul. At no stage does Indian religion have any clear conception of God as Lord and maker of all things out of nothing, as an essentially moral being who demands that man shall be righteous. From the time of Mahāvīra (p. 261) on, the principal preoccupation of Indian religion is "deliverance", and by this is understood the deliverance of the human soul, which is immortal, from the bondage of the body. Both Buddhism and Jainism regard this as being the essential core of religion – to realize a deathless condition in which space and time are transcended and in which all links with bodily life have been finally cut away. This, not the re-union of soul and body, constitutes salvation.

Further, both Jainism and Buddhism are originally atheistical creeds. This needs emphasizing, for this whole tradition is fundamentally indifferent to God as eternal law-giver who must be obeyed: in its extreme form it denies the existence of God altogether and puts its exclusive emphasis on the deliverance of the immortal soul from the body. Its attitude is throughout conditioned by an unquestioned and unquestioning belief in re-incarnation which it regards not as a desirable process but as the supreme evil. Human life is not God's greatest gift to man, it is a curse which inheres in the very nature of things. It is matter, the body as such, which is the persistent drag on the soul and from which the soul longs to be separated. Moreover, Indian religion in practically all its forms would go on to say that this deathless condition which is the soul's natural habitat is not something we take on trust from an external agency; it is something that, given the right dispositions and training, can be experienced here and now. Granted, then, that the *experience* of immortality is the *sole* object of religion, the very need for a divine revelation is done away with. This extreme emphasis on the experience of immortality, that state in which all differentiation falls away from the experiencing subject, led the more extreme supporters of the Indian Vedānta (pp. 237-8) to identify the human soul in this deep unity and isolation with the utterly undifferentiated source and ground of the universe: it identified the soul with the godhead, and claimed that once this condition is empirically realized the whole phenomenal world is seen to be an illusion. To the Western religious mind and particularly to the orthodox Protestant such an identification can only appear as blasphemy. Indeed it has been described by the great Neo-Calvinist theologian, Hendrik Kraemer, as a repetition of the Fall; so fundamentally different are the values of Israel and India.

It will be realized by now how immense is the gulf fixed between the two types of religion. For the one, man lives but once and it is his bounden duty to do the will of God who reveals himself to him and makes his will known: for the other, man is caught up in an endless cycle of re-births for which God (if he exists) or Nature is responsible, and it is his plain interest as well as his salvation to put an end to the whole ghastly and meaningless round. For the one, God and man confront each other as Lord and servant; for the other, there is either no God, or, if there is one, there is no essential difference between him and the human soul.

The contrasts I have emphasized are admittedly between extreme forms of the two types of religion, but they are nonetheless valid. That the Indian tradition, despite its frequent atheism, is ever again hankering after a more adequate concept of deity will become evident in the chapters devoted to Hinduism and Buddhism in this book; but I think it can scarcely be questioned that the overwhelming emphasis of Indian religion is, in the final analysis if not in the immediate manifestation, on the final realization of the soul of itself as immortal. The emphasis is always on experience, not on man's duty to God. The difference can perhaps be best stated thus: prophetic religion starts with God and his dealings with man here and now in this world of space and time; the Indian "mystical" tradition starts with the human soul and the manner in which its release *from* this world can be achieved. Salvation, whether it is achieved by one's own efforts or through the grace of a god, always means deliverance from the bond that links spirit with matter.

This brief account of the essential differences that separate the two great traditions seemed necessary if the reader is to understand the strictly oriental religions at all. It is largely for this reason that I have added a final chapter to this book entitled "A New Buddha and a New Tao" which deals with Jungian depth psychology and Marxian dialectical materialism; for both systems of thought bear an unmistakable likeness to much that is typical of oriental religion. The great monotheistic systems of the Near East, which the West has in part inherited, never tire of emphasizing the absolute distinction of God from the created order: God and Nature are not interchangeable terms as Spinoza maintained. In the oriental systems, however, the two are in fact never clearly distinguished: God is Nature and Nature is God. This is what brings the oriental religions so very close to both Jungian psychology and dialectical materialism at least as expounded by Engels. Jung quite rightly saw that much in oriental religion would more properly fall under the category of psychology than of religion, at least as the latter term is understood in the West, and he consequently draws frequently on oriental sources to substantiate his own psychological theories. Jung has in fact captured the essence of much in oriental religion and reduced it to purely subjective and psychological terms. Similarly Engels' whole philosophy of dialectical materialism with its interpretation of all existence as a perpetual and ever-changing flux superimposed upon fixed and immutable "Laws of Nature" is a re-statement in modern terms of a central doctrine of the Upanishads and of philosophic Taoism. Jung and Engels on the one hand, and the Indian tradition with its Chinese equivalent, Taoism, on the other, mutually illuminate each other. We shall have to speak of this again in our conclusion.

METHOD OF PRESENTATION

This book deals exclusively with living faiths; and it has therefore left out entirely any consideration of primitive religion or of the national religions of great cultures that have passed away. These are omitted not because they are not interesting or important but because they are of purely academic interest today and because, even though they have contributed to the formation of the still living religions, their inclusion would greatly increase the size of an already considerable volume. It may be asked why Zoroastrianism, a faith professed by a mere 100,000 souls today, should have found a place among the great faiths of the world. The answer is that Zoroastrianism, as a prophetic religion, is unique outside the Semitic fold, and the influence it has exercised on at least two of the Semitic religions is so great that some account of it seemed essential. Similarly Jainism has been included because it represents a real contribution to religious thought.

Since it is our contention that religions readily divide themselves into a "prophetic" and a "mystical" or "immanentist" type, the presentation and order of the contents offered no difficulty. In Part One which we have called "Prophecy" we present the prophetic tradition as represented by Judaism and the two world religions, Christianity and Islam, that derive from it. To these has

been appended that subsidiary stream to the great prophetic tradition, Zoroastrianism, which, though it arose in the Eastern provinces of ancient Iran, is nonetheless animated by the same prophetic spirit that informs the Semitic religions. In Part Two entitled "Wisdom" we turn to the "mystical" or "immanentist" tradition which is the great contribution of Indian thought to the general religious scene. We start with the primal form of this religion, the earliest stages in Hinduism, and trace the fortunes of that incredibly complex religious amalgam down to the present day. Next we come to Hinduism's lesser and greater offshoots, Jainism first and then Buddhism in its myriad manifestations. Then follows Shintoism, the national religion of Japan, which seemed to fit best into this position because of the intimate ties that it developed with Buddhism. Lastly we come to the subsidiary streams in the immanentist tradition, Confucianism and Taoism, China's peculiar contribution to the general picture.

Taoism certainly represents the same type of religion as the main Indian stream; but Confucianism stands alone, for it is rather a way of conducting one's worldly life than a religion or a belief. Some account of it seemed necessary, however, in order to make the total Chinese picture more intelligible.

The allocation of space to the various religions was no easy matter. It seemed right and inevitable that Christianity and Buddhism should receive the fullest treatment, for the one is the dominant religion of the West, the other of the East. Each in its own sphere is, or was, the dominant religious influence in one half of the world. That it should have been necessary to allot five sections of unequal length to Christianity seemed as necessary as it is deplorable, for of all the great world religions Christianity is still the most divided. I am well aware that the result has been that no clear picture of Christendom as a whole has emerged, but it is at least questionable whether such an overall picture in fact exists.

The exact treatment of each chapter has been left largely to the individual contributor who is in each case an acknowledged expert in his own particular field. This seemed inevitable as well as desirable, and editorial work has therefore been reduced to a minimum. I have already pointed out the totally different approaches adopted by the "prophetic" and "immanentist" religions, and this difference between them inevitably leads to a difference in treatment and emphasis. Only the expert in each given field is in a position to judge what is fundamental to the religion with which he is dealing, and what is not. In each individual case I have accepted the view of the contributor as final.

All the chapters in this volume are treated historically. This could scarcely be otherwise; for a living religion is, by the mere fact that it is alive, a growing thing, and it would be quite impossible to understand any given religion in its present-day manifestations without knowing the roots from which it has sprung. This applies as much to Indian religions, which are anything but historically minded, as it does to Christianity and Islam both of which emerge in the full light of history. It is, for example, quite impossible to understand the Hinduism of today without knowing both the primeval roots from which it grows and – quite as important – the foreign elements which have been grafted on to it in comparatively recent times. No religion is conformable to the pattern of any other, and if this work seems, at first sight, to be a bewildering jumble of irreconcilable beliefs, this is in the nature of the case. It has been our object all along to present each religion in its own context as it develops along its own necessarily individual lines. Buddhism, for instance, cannot be dealt with in Christian, nor Christianity in Buddhist terms. Basically the two religions are not dealing with the same subject-matter, and it is the function of the editor of a book such as this to see that each religion is presented against its own background, not against his.

Thus it is hoped to offer the general reader a truthful, scholarly and fair account of the faiths by which the world has for so long lived and, despite the onslaughts of secularism in modern times, continues to live. A word of warning must, however, be issued. The great majority of the religions treated in this book are complex growths, and much that will be found in the following chapters will appear strange to the reader who has no previous knowledge of the oriental religions. This, however, cannot be avoided, for the categories of thought in India are wholly different from those of the modern West. Indeed, we must go further, for whereas it seemed essential that a full account should be given of the development of Christian doctrine which crystallized in the Nicene Creed – a formula of belief that is accepted by all Christians who regard themselves as in some sense sharers in a common orthodox tradition – this account is bound to appear difficult and obscure to the modern man who, though calling himself a Christian, has never asked himself what he really does believe concerning the Holy Trinity and the Person of Christ. To omit these cardinal doctrines and the process that led to their formulation, however, would scarcely have been to present a true picture of Christianity, for difficult and indeed incomprehensible as they are, they are yet one of the few bonds that link Orthodox with Catholic, and Catholic with Reformed.

Yet strange though much of the country covered in this book may be, it is hoped that the reader will at least find it a fair guide to the incredibly diverse beliefs which still animate mankind. It is intended to be a kind of guidebook to the beliefs and religions of the world, but it is a guidebook in which the editor may not, in the interests of objectivity, assign stars to those religious structures which seem to him the most admirable. This is a task which, it is hoped, the reader will set himself.

Part One

PROPHECY

1. Judaism, or the Religion of Israel

by R. J. ZWI WERBLOWSKY

METHOD AND SCOPE

Of the great living religions of the Western world Judaism is the oldest. Its venerable age alone should give it a dignity sufficient to offset its numerical smallness when compared with Christianity and Islam. But its historical significance is enhanced by the fact that, in a way, it is the parent of these two religions. Together they constitute what are called the "monotheistic faiths", and the Christian Church in particular has always considered itself to be the successor and legitimate heir of the Biblical Israel.

However inspiring such a historical record may be, it gravely increases the difficulties in the way of any attempt at producing a satisfactory account of it. The writer has to choose between the historical method which traces the origins, growths and changes of religious life and thought in successive periods, and the systematic exposition which treats a specific religion as a closely-knit, integrated whole. Both methods, that of the "horizontal" and the "vertical" cross-section, have their advantages and their dangers. The systematic account is the only one to do justice to the integral meaning and functional totality of a religious configuration, but it invariably does so by more or less arbitrarily selecting one particular phase or stage in the history of the religion so described. The Islam of Muhammad was as different from that of Ghazālī as was the Christianity of the first apostles from that of the scholastics. Selection, of course, is not considered to be arbitrary by those who deny that religions grow and change in major respects, and who maintain that the one true religion (i.e. the one which the writer happens to subscribe to) sprang ready-made from God as Pallas from Zeus. But this view is no longer held by any reputable theologian, let alone by critical scholars. The historical approach, on the other hand, while faithfully chronicling developments and growth, may easily miss the full meaning and essence of a religious system in its totality.

There is a still graver difficulty inherent in the historical method. Once we admit that change can be profound and radical, we must next ask ourselves what constitutes the identity and continuity of a particular religious configuration. If a phenomenon keeps on changing, up to what point can we say that it is still "itself" and not something different? The question is of particular relevance to a correct understanding of Judaism. For Christians there is a straight line running from the Old Testament through the events recorded in the Gospels right up to the life of the Church today, and post-Biblical Jewish religion, which is then called "Judaism" in order to distinguish it from the religion of Biblical Israel, is considered as a sideline which branches off the main road at its most important juncture. For the Jewish consciousness, on the other hand, there is no break at all in the line leading from the Bible to the Scribes, Pharisees, Rabbis and later teachers of Judaism. But whatever the continuity or lack of continuity between one stage and the other, the important thing for a proper understanding of a religious faith is a correct appreciation of how the *believers themselves* conceive of the historical relation. It is precisely the way *they* experience their past which may be a decisive aspect of their religious attitude.

There is, however, still another side to the problem of change and continuity. The history of every religion is so rich and varied that we simply cannot take in all its manifestations and stages of development at one synoptic glance. Yet we often like to think that somehow all these are expressions of one underlying idea or type, variations as it were on one basic theme. There is a tendency to consider each religion as characterized by a specific structure, and then one proceeds to conceive of all its varied manifestations as stamped with this specific individuality and exhibiting its typical traits. Up to a point this procedure may be correct. Even if a religion were completely transformed by alien influences, we are still entitled to ask why a particular influence proved decisive in one case while other religions remained impervious to it. It often happens that a religion is truly enriched by the absorption of influences which we should be inclined to regard as utterly alien to it and all but incompatible with its essential nature. The influence of Pseudo-Denys on Christian mysticism, the history of Ṣūfīsm in Islam and the record of Kabbalah in Judaism are examples of the kind. They are mentioned here in order to indicate the necessity of avoiding dogmatic generalizations about the nature and character of any religion.

In order to give a really adequate account of a religious system, one would have to pay equal attention to its ideas, beliefs, hopes and expectations as well as to its life and practice (customs, morals, worship, ritual, etc.). These represent its inner and outer side as it were. Thus it is often said that liturgy or religious law is the manifestation or outward expression of the "faith", which is the "real" content or essence of religion. However the matter is not quite as simple as that. Although there are systems where the intellectual or philosophic elements dominate, there are few religions which start only from clear-cut expositions of ideas, teachings, dogmas and the like, and then proceed to illustrate or "express" these by symbolic acts of worship and practice. On the contrary, very often the so-called practical expressions are the chief material at our disposal and we have to work our way back to the "essence" by interpretative analysis which, needless to say, is often no more than guess-work. But even when authentic statements of faith are available in liturgy and creed, it would be wrong to say that religious practice merely "expresses" them. We might equally well have it the other way round by saying that theological statements are merely abstract, semi-intellectualized or conceptualized expressions of the true fullness of the religious life of worship and practice. One may get nearer to the heart of Catholicism by attending Mass than by reading theological manuals. The balance is particularly difficult to strike in an exposition of Judaism which abounds in minutiae of ritual and practice as well as in religious lore, but where the former only is fixed, codified and considered as absolutely binding. The non-legal part of religious teaching exists in a more nondescript or fluid state, accepted by a kind of tacit assent and hallowed by tradition, but unsupported by formal discipline or ecclesiastical authority.

This has led some authors to the palpably wrong assertion that Judaism has no theology but only laws. Other writers have erred in the opposite direction by presenting systematic theologies of Judaism which, of course, are nothing of the kind for the sole but cogent reason that an anthology of religious teachings and reflections, even if culled from the dicta of the most celebrated Rabbis, still does not make a theology. The truth of the matter is that the semantic value of the word "theology" has been determined by its use in the history of Christianity, and there it implies a divinely instituted *magisterium* or, at least, divinely revealed truths about salvation which can be made the object of systematic study. As will appear later, Judaism is focused on the revelation of the divine will whose manifestation in the "Law" has become the main object of systematic study. What we call Jewish theology is really the effort of Jewish teachers to understand the background, function and purpose of this divine will which is the Law of Israel. To use a felicitous expression of Leo Baeck, Jewish theology is the "reflection" upon Jewish history and tradition; as such it is a "theology of teachers", not that of a Church administering the symbols of the Faith. The "outer" side of Judaism is thus characterized by a relatively firmer authority, greater rigidity and fuller articulation than the "inner" side. Significantly enough, Hebrew has no exact counterpart to the term theology. The "Law" or rule of practice is called *halakhah* and the "inner" side *aggadah* (lit. "lore"); both are *Torah*.

Having mentioned some of the pitfalls inherent in the attempt to describe a religion, it is obvious that no writer can hope to avoid them all. What he can do is to fall into them with his eyes wide open. For our present purpose, which is a compressed account of Judaism, it must suffice to point out that we shall roughly take as our point of reference Rabbinic Judaism as it has existed for almost two thousand years and as it has crystallized in a rigid pattern of orthodoxy in the sixteenth to eighteenth centuries. However, this orthodoxy which exhibits the dominant or classical features of Rabbinic Judaism is our point of reference only, not the whole of Judaism. For purposes of convenience we shall divide our survey into five periods:

(*a*) The Biblical period.

(*b*) Post-Biblical developments and the consolidation of the type of Judaism that became finally enshrined in the Talmud.

(*c*) The Middle Ages with their peaks of religious philosophy and mysticism.

(*d*) The destruction of the unified medieval outlook towards the end of the eighteenth century and the major developments of the nineteenth century: emancipation, assimilation, reform, neo-orthodoxy and Zionism.

(*e*) (to be treated together with (*d*)): The climax of the preceding developments in the creation of the Jewish

PLATE I. The seven-branched candlestick is first mentioned in *Exodus* xxv, 31f. among the holy vessels of the Temple. The daily lightening of the perpetual light (cf. *Exodus* xxvii, 20–21 and *Leviticus* xxiv, 1–4) was among the duties of the priests (*Numbers* viii, 1–4). The candlestick varied with the times. This relief from Titus's Arch is supposed to represent the candlestick from the last Jewish temple, built by Herod and sacked by the Romans in 70 A.D. after the fall of Jerusalem. Opinions vary as to the reliability of the representation. The seven-branched candlestick is not to be confused with the well-known eight-branched candlestick used by Jews throughout the world for the eight-day festival of Hanukah, the festival of lights, commemorating the victory of the Maccabees in 165–4 B.C. and the subsequent re-dedication of the Temple. The seven-branched candlestick is not, at present, in liturgical use, which is traditionally reserved to the Temple, and only serves as a decorative symbol in Jewish art.

Photo: Maurice

PLATE 2. The interior arrangement of a synagogue varies according to the rite (Ashkenazi, Sephardi, etc.) and the tendencies (orthodox, conservative, reform, etc.) of the congregation. This picture represents an orthodox synagogue of the English type: the "Holy Ark", containing the *Torah*-scrolls (the Hebrew Pentateuch written on parchment scrolls) is on the east side, viz. "towards Jerusalem". On the steps leading to the Ark is the pulpit. On the *bimah* or *tebah* in the middle is the reading desk from which the minister, cantor or whoever leads the prayer, conducts the service. For the reading of the Law, the *Torah*-scroll is carried in procession from the Ark to the *bimah*. Orthodox tradition insists on the strict separation of the sexes in worship; the men, who alone can take an active part in the service, are on the ground floor, whereas the women sit in the gallery. In front of the Ark and above the pulpit is the lamp of the "perpetual light". (*Garnethill Synagogue, Glasgow*)

Photo: ATP Bilderdienst, Zürich

PLATE 3. The "West Wall", as it is called in Hebrew, is the remnant of the west wall of Herod's temple destroyed by Titus and all that remains of the oldest and most important Jewish sanctuary. It is held in particular affection by Jews everywhere as a token of their glorious past and as a reminder of the promised messianic future. It is consequently considered as a holy place. The term "Wailing Wall" was given it by gentile travellers who noticed the habit of pious Jews of visiting the wall in order to lament and weep there over the destruction of God's sanctuary, the exile and suffering of his people Israel and of the divine *Shekinah* (cf. page 44) and to pray for the advent of redemption. The wall is at present on the Jordanian side of Jerusalem, and the Jews are no longer allowed to go there.

27

Photo: Ruth P. Lehmann

PLATE 4. A series of old tombs hewn into the rocks at the outskirts of Jerusalem. The cave was probably used as a family-tomb. It contains about eighty burial chambers and this probably gave rise to the popular legend that these were the tombs of the Sanhedrin (the Supreme Jewish Court consisting of seventy members).

state and in the polarization of Jewish life in Israel and the Diaspora.

THE BIBLE

The corner stone of Judaism is the Hebrew Bible – that part of Scripture commonly known as the Old Testament – and it is in this sense that the word Bible is used throughout the present chapter. More particularly it is the first division of the Bible, the Pentateuch or Five Books of Moses, that is considered to be the direct and most fundamental revelation of God. Here we may note in passing that even if the Bible as an historical document does not permit a completely reliable reconstruction of events, its value is certainly unsurpassed as the literary expression of Israel's reaction to these events. Even reading the Bible as an historical text only we can find in it that which matters most for our present purposes – the testimony of a whole people telling of its experiences and responses in its intercourse with the divine. The implicit admission that the Bible, in spite of its universal import, is the book of a particular people or, to put it differently, is addressed to a particular people, enormously complicates our understanding of Judaism. It is a fact that Judaism has to this day remained the religion of one particular nation – Israel or the Jewish people. It is important to remind ourselves at the outset of this *historical fact* of national or group continuity, because it is often confused by the claim of the Christian Church to be the legitimate successor of Israel, viz. the "true" Israel. This claim, however, is a matter of theology only: it is not an historical fact and need not, therefore, concern us here.

It would be an interesting question whether this relation of near-identity between religion and nation exists of necessity or whether things might have been – or possibly have at times been – different. Although it appears that at some moments in its history Judaism was an actively missionary religion (cf. *Matthew* xxiii, 15) in the last resort it remained related to the Jewish people in a much more exclusive and intimate way than did the Christian Church to the English or Italian peoples for example (or even to Western civilization as a whole) or Islam to the Arabs. This ethnic limitation is undoubtedly a severe religious handicap in some respects, but on the other hand it has certainly added a touch of realism to Judaism. The Jews tended to translate every religious experience and value into terms of history and social reality. They could not, by any theological device, such as the distinction between spiritual and secular spheres, divorce religion from the concrete situations and realities of national and political life. Rightly or wrongly, the prophets and writers of Biblical history interpreted defeats, exile and suffering as results of the failure to implement God's will in society. Religion could never be separated from the concrete history, material *and* spiritual, of a real, historic people.

This national self-centredness can, in fact, become a valuable religious asset if it is set in a wider, universal perspective. This is precisely what the Bible has done with the history of Israel. Though mainly about Jews, the Bible begins with Man. The first chapters of *Genesis* tell us the Jewish myth of the world and man and man-in-the-world. To put it in slightly more modern terms: the world, in spite of its imposing appearance as a self-sufficient network of interconnections and causal laws, is a mystery hanging in the void. Whatever we can explain – and it is quite a lot – by definition only refers to relations *within* the world. The world as a whole remains mysterious, to some religions even divine or at least full of divine forces. Against this the Bible declares: it is God who is mysterious and the world is his creation. Man as a bio-physical organism, is part of creation; but he is also more than that. He is a more ambiguous creature than the rest. In spite of his organic unity with creation there is also a distance, a chasm which separates the two. Man as a biological being is immersed in the world, but he also confronts it in his consciousness, his conscience, his capacity for abstraction and language. To nature, that is, creation in the "raw" state, he opposes culture – creation transformed, and perfected.

The human response to the world is twofold. Like other animals, man is an integral and dependent part (or victim) of nature. But unlike the animals, he is actively and creatively responsive. He beholds the world and forms mental images, ideas and abstract concepts of it. The Greeks called this *theoria*. He also consciously and purposefully interferes with nature. To this end he, as it were, transcends nature by artificially prolonging his hands: he fashions tools for himself and becomes *homo faber*. In Biblical language all this would simply be expressed by saying that man is a link in the order of creation, that he was created together with the other animals on the sixth day, but that he also has in him the divine spirit. Created in the "image of God", he conceives of the specifically human quality in himself, of that which sets him apart, over and above the rest of creation, as his divine likeness. He is, in fact, a miniature God. Within his human limits he creates, like God. This is the true *imitatio Dei* or "imitation of God". By working, that is, by creating culture out of nature, man truly emancipates himself from his natural state. He is no longer victimized by nature, nor blindly preying upon

29

it; but in his hands, like primeval chaos in the hands of God, nature becomes a raw material to be fashioned according to an idea and a purpose. Whether man fashions a flint spearhead, or the first wheel, or a nuclear power plant, is immaterial in this respect. The danger besetting man here is self-destruction consequent upon the loss of his sense of human limitations. The Greeks who were afraid of this temptation more than of anything else called it *hybris*. There are various forms of it. Man may use nature for his own ends but forget that he himself is a piece of nature too which he – in the doubleness of his being – has to fashion and mould in accordance with a purpose. Failure to do so results in human chaos, fittingly punished, according to the Biblical myth, by a resurgence of primeval cosmic chaos. This is the story of Noah's flood. God punishes man who fails to let his own nature obey God's word by permitting the nature of the universe to deviate from the divine word of law and order. Another Biblical story concerns not chaos but the opposite – a highly organized human effort at unity and concerted action. The Tower of Babel is the symbol of a united humanity without obedience to God. But here God no longer needs to unleash cosmic chaos. He confuses man's tongues and historic chaos runs its own course. Divided humanity must work and hope for the divine order.

Here we have two examples of Biblical myth which, without necessarily providing exact historic records, tell us something of the way the old Israelites interpreted the human situation, encompassed as it is by nature and history. But this mythology, because of its exemplary humanity, is not concrete enough in a historic sense. It has to enter somehow the life of a historic group in order to become actual. Reverting to our aforementioned example we might say that one way of obviating *hybris* is exemplified by the Jew who herein acts vicariously for Biblical man: he ceases to be humanly creative every seventh day. By relating the rhythm of his life to the creation myth and by fully imitating the Creator God, man regains his true perspective as one creature among many. On the Sabbath the Israelite not merely rests but rather abstains from work: nature, *qua* raw material for human creativeness, becomes taboo. Human greed and lust for power are ritually suspended and man remembers his ambiguous nature. By ceasing to be fully human (i.e. creative of culture) he paradoxically becomes fully human again in the imitation of God. But the Sabbath of Israel is not based on this "mythical" perception of reality; it is based on the experience of the Exodus from Egypt and the subsequent divine command. It is significant that the creation story carefully avoids mentioning

the Sabbath; it consistently speaks of "the seventh day". But it gives us the anthropology, as it were, on which God's sign of the Covenant with Israel (*Exodus* xxxi, 13, 16–17) is later reared in connection with a concrete historical experience. As a sign of the Covenant, the Sabbath bears much resemblance to a similar major sign: the Covenant of Circumcision (*Genesis* xvii, 7 f). Like the Sabbath, circumcision limits or "circumcises" the sheer untrammelled expression of creative power and energy. Between godlike hubris and passive impotence, between Dionysiac intoxication and the asceticism of "castration" (*Matthew* xix, 12) the Covenant guarantees the permanence and growth of life as initiated by God in his creation. The alternative offered by the Covenant to self-forgetting hubris on the one hand and to ascetic negation on the other is the *sanctification* of life. The Biblical ideal of holiness expressed in the words "Speak unto all the congregation of the children of Israel, and say unto them, Ye shall be holy: for I the Lord your God am holy" (*Leviticus* xix, 2) is thus equally a negation of self-divinization and of self-annihilation.

The concept of a Covenant is central to the Israelite understanding of both the world (or nature) and man (or history). It implies that all life and existence are seen in social, that is, historical terms of relationship and mutuality. In fact, as clearly emerges from God's Covenant with Noahite humanity after the flood, the permanence of nature itself is the result of a "covenant", that is, a promise and a social bond. Whereas later philosophies attempted to derive society and morals from nature, the Bible sees nature as dependent on social, moral and historical categories. God's "Word" impinges on his twofold creation – the world of nature and the world of man. In the former this "Word" acts automatically; it is the kind of Covenant that later generations were to call the Law of Nature. In the specifically human world, however, God's Word appears as his will, appealing to the human will for fulfilment. The significant thing about all this is that existence is conceived as a dynamic turning of God to his creation and as his free entering into relations of mutuality and permanence. Created existence is the condescension of the Almighty God that grants apparent independence and selfhood to his creatures to the extent of admitting them as his partners, perhaps even to the extent of permitting them almost to frustrate his purpose.

With this background of ideas, what was the primordial experience of the Jewish people of God's dealings with them? To begin with, it seems that the old Israelites like some other Semitic peoples experienced the Divine as a very personal God who presided over the destinies of the group. But in their case the experience was of an extraordinary intensity, and God too was felt to be intensely personal. God was not just there and acting; he was turned towards man, asking for him and calling for his co-operative response. In fact, God was experienced as a calling God and hence the "Word" was his chief manifestation. He called man, and all that man had to do – although it may have been quite a lot – was to listen. To listen, however, means to obey. God wanted man or rather wanted something of man, and in spite of the obvious theological disclaimers it seems as if the purpose was not solely man's own benefit. God at least appeared to be somehow profoundly interested and involved in what would happen to man. To this end he called the ancestor out of Ur of the Chaldees, and his descendants, by now a small people, out of their bondage in Egypt. He made a solemn oath and covenant with them and told them what he would give them and what they were expected to do. Henceforth they were to walk in the way of the Lord, hearkening to, that is, obeying his voice.

This conception of the one Lord to whom they owed loyalty and allegiance turned out to be a grandly unifying one. Instead of succumbing to the atomizing variety of experience and expressing this variety in a polytheism of space (local gods in different places) and function (special gods for the various natural forces or various crafts), or in a moral and metaphysical dualism (two forces of light and darkness, good and evil), the Jews sensed the transcendent unity as the origin of all being. It was a slow and painful process by which they fully learned this lesson, but in the end a prophet could arise and declare that the one God was also the source of even darkness and evil (*Isaiah* xlv, 7)! But it was not only God's unity as such which they learned to know, it was rather the awareness that this unity was also unique, that it was the great mystery of God. Consequently the confession that "God is One" not only referred to his unity but also to his transcendence. "Hear, O Israel: Yahweh is our God, Yahweh is One" (*Deuteronomy* vi, 4) has become the central confession of Judaism; these words were on the lips of thousands of martyrs and are still repeated every morning and evening, as well as on his deathbed, by every practising Jew. Gradually the old Israelites learned to ascribe to Yahweh, their God, all the various epithets and functions which their pagan contemporaries attributed to other divinities. When the nomadic tribes of Israel settled in Canaan they were confronted by terrifyingly novel aspects of life – the power of the earth, the mystery of fertility and all the other realities and cultural patterns that go with a sedentary, agricultural

civilization. The struggle that ensued is recorded in the books of *Joshua*, *Judges*, *Samuel* and *Kings*, as well as in the collections of prophetic speeches. In the end the Israelites realized that Yahweh, the God of their fathers, whom they knew as having guided them in the desert, was in fact the same as the dispenser of fertility and rain. He was also the same that demanded justice and loving-kindness of a people that began to be increasingly influenced by the habits and morals of the ancient petty monarchies of the Near East. As time went on they had to learn that this God resented worship that was not backed by obedience and righteousness. In the end they were warned that if they would not learn their lesson in time they would have to learn it the hard way, in exile and suffering. It was true that they were a chosen people, but this chosenness was a double-edged sword (cf. *Amos* iii, 2). They were covenanted to God in a special relationship whose validity was everlasting, much like the similar covenant with nature (cf. *Jeremiah* xxxi, 34–5; xxxiii, 20–1, 25–6), and there was no escape or respite from the required loyalty. Even unfaithfulness could not dissolve the Covenant; it would only bring judgment. Israel was God's chosen spouse, as a favourite metaphor of the prophet put it; as such she could be neither widowed nor divorced but only corrected and invited to return God's love and to return *to* God's love. The doctrine of election did not so much proclaim a privilege (as the more easy-going often liked to think) as a glorious destiny and an ineluctable fate. Israel was to live as a nation much as the priests lived as a class and the prophets as individuals. Like priests they should serve God in the sanctuary of their lives; like prophets they should listen to God's word and respond to it.

Our account so far of Biblical religion may perhaps be summed up by saying that the encounter with the living and calling God means that Transcendence is experienced as addressing man and charging him with *responsibility*, that is, with the necessity to respond in hearing-obeying. The religious categories correlated to this type of experience are election, vocation and promise. This basic attitude of *listening* contrasts characteristically with another attitude, perhaps best portrayed by Greece, which may be described as *seeing*. Listening brought the Israelite to his goal – doing the will of God; seeing brought the Greek to his – knowledge. The decisive Biblical mode of intercourse with the divine was audition; for the mystery type of religion it was vision. Seeing-knowing or "beholding" reality appeals to reason, hearing-obeying appeals to the will. The former is more static and consequently looks to eternal and changeless reality; the latter is thoroughly dynamic and is directed towards events and the movement of history.

It has often been said that the contrast between static and dynamic is also expressed in the opposition of priest to prophet. There is undoubtedly a measure of truth in this observation in spite of the absurd exaggerations to which it lent itself in the hands of some nineteenth-century (and, one is afraid, also twentieth-century) writers. The purpose of the distinction was to use the institutionalized, ritual, and thus "lifeless" religion of the priests as a foil for the charismatic, inspired, moral and progressive character of prophecy. Today we have learned that distinctions are never quite so simple and convenient. There are false and inauthentic prophets no less than dishonest and self-seeking priests. The priesthood was mainly responsible for preserving the old religious tradition of Israel, and, conversely, the prophets were much more concerned with the Temple and its ritual than is generally realized. In his diatribe against Temple-attendance and sacrifice without purity of heart Isaiah also includes prayers (*Isaiah* i, 11–16); yet nobody ever thought of deducing from this that the prophets were all for abolishing prayer. The functions of prophecy and priesthood were complementary and both were engaged in an unremitting struggle against the paganizing, popular religion practised, so we must assume, by the majority of Israel. It is in this perspective that we must view the inordinate stress put by the writers of *Kings* and *Chronicles* on the centralization of worship in Jerusalem as the hallmark of true religion. The truth of the matter was that local cults practically meant the worship of local and pagan gods. The sole method of finally establishing the belief and worship of the one God was the insistence on the sole, unique and exclusive significance of his one sanctuary. Centralization of worship was indispensable to the strengthening of monotheism. But formal concepts like Covenant, Election and Law, and the existence of prophets, priests and a Temple ritual are merely the skeleton of Judaism. Its flesh and blood consists of a host of ideas and concrete beliefs. To describe them adequately one would have to review the whole Bible in detail and to examine the beliefs which it enjoins, combats or takes for granted, as well as the actions which it commands or prohibits. Thus there are symbolic acts which express the fundamental awarenesses of a group in the ways peculiar to ritual and myth. We have seen one example of this in the institution of the Sabbath. There are rites that regulate the relation of the group and of its individual members to God such as the annual ritual of Atonement. The bringing of first-fruits and similar customs belong to the same category; their purpose is to testify to the divine ownership of the national territory. The people hold their land from their liege lord, God (cf. *Leviticus* xxv, 23). There are feasts and fasts keeping alive the understanding of God's mighty deeds in history, and revitalizing the consciousness of historic solidarity with past and future. A splendid example is the annual Passover celebration of the Exodus. Originally perhaps of diverse origins – an agricultural festival and a nomadic rite – the Passover became charged with purely historic meaning and developed into the most intimate, moving and impressive Jewish home celebration. According to a later, Rabbinic formulation "every man in every generation should consider himself as if he had gone out of Egypt". On Passover the Jew re-lives the beginnings of his people as the revelation of the ultimate meaning of history as such: the liberation of slaves to the dignity of children of God and to the freedom which is a gift of God and a calling by God. For there is only one road from Egypt to the Promised Land: the road past Sinai. There are commandments fostering certain attitudes and values, and prohibitions designed to prevent a lowering of the moral or spiritual level. Among these are regulations prohibiting intercourse with the depraved pagan population of Canaan or the many food laws whose purpose it is to submit the whole of life, even on its purely vegetative level, to the discipline of sanctification (cf. *Leviticus* xi, 43–47; xx, 23–26). Even when eating, mating or dressing the Jew must realize that every part of his life and body is under a divine charge: it can be debased or hallowed. Other Biblical laws are more directly concerned with other objectives of the Covenant such as social justice, the love of one's fellow man and the like.

The essence of the Mosaic or Pentateuchal teaching can, perhaps, be reduced to three basic principles. The first is the inalienable value of the individual personality created in "the image of God". To teach this lesson, so the Rabbis later commented, Adam, the original man, was created alone and solitary. The "other" man is your "fellow" or "friend", not just an object. It is this relationship which Professor Martin Buber has so penetratingly analysed and termed the "I-Thou relationship"; it is expressed in its most general and obligatory form in the two great commandments. If men are "fellows" then slavery is impossible; in this respect too the Exodus is the foundation of Judaism. Because certain groups of men are always liable to be treated as "strangers", Mosaic law repeatedly warns that "a stranger hast thou been in the land of Egypt – thou knowest the soul of the stranger". The very notion of Prophecy and Revelation is based on the I-Thou relationship, a living intercourse and dialogue between God and man. It is not by accident that the same Hebrew word meaning "friend" or "fellow" is used of God's intercourse with Moses, the father of all prophets. No doubt this fact is connected with the character of Moses as the typical discoverer of the "fellow-man" (cf. *Exodus* ii, 11–12, 13, 17).

The second principle is that of the divine will as revealed law. Life is the effort to implement in history that part of the divine which is not immanent in the created world but which is engaged in a dialogue with human existence. Finally there is the specifically religious idea of holiness which prevents the system of law from disintegrating into a mere collection of laws and rituals. Holiness, which permeates the Law but goes beyond it, is the Jewish name for the commandment to imitate God (*imitatio Dei*). But this commandment is not addressed to individuals alone but to a whole nation *qua* nation.

Many other ideas and concrete beliefs – both popular and more sophisticated – were developed in course of time or were adapted and modified by dint of historical experience. Thus one of the greatest problems of later Judaism was the question why the chosen people was more persecuted and humiliated than any other. The problem is already adumbrated in the Biblical books. The answer, though it also includes the symbol of the Suffering Servant who represents Israel among the nations, was quite naturally related to the Messianic hope of a glorious future. A personal redeemer was probably unknown in early Israelite belief. This again gave rise to some crude popular notions concerning Israel's ultimate restoration. The "nationalist" aspect of Jewish belief was intensified by the extension, particularly in *Kings* and *Chronicles*, of the idea of a covenant with the people to that of an equally eternal covenant with the House of David. If, on the one hand, the prophetic books show how narrow nationalism was "debunked" by the message of divine judgment, then the *Psalms*, on the other hand, amply demonstrate how a religious feeling intensely focused on Zion, the Temple and the Davidic dynasty, could also produce a profound and almost mystical yearning for nearness to God, communion with him and peace in his sole presence. Still, as long as Israel existed as a more or less sovereign nation under its own king, this whole complex of political-social-religious life functioned, at least ideally, as an organic unity. Even when the people adopted local religious habits ("whoring after strange gods") and the kings followed the pattern of petty power politics set by the other Near-Eastern rulers, the consciousness was always alive that the nation was consecrated and covenanted to God, and

that his Law, as embodied in tradition and prophetic preaching, ought to be the valid norm of its life.

This unity was broken by the destruction of Jerusalem and of the Temple of Solomon by Nebuchadnezzar in 586 B.C. The people went into captivity to Babylon and henceforth the Jewish community lived under alien rule and alien law, neither of which could be considered as the ideal embodiment of the divine will. Jewish life was that of a minority enjoying greater or lesser autonomy and thus began to constitute itself on a religious basis in the narrower sense of the word. In principle, the idea of divine sovereignty and absolute rule was maintained; in practice it was recognized that Caesar's will ruled the world and that the traditional law of God could operate only as the private norm of a minority which increasingly conceived of itself as a religious community within the larger, ungodly, political state. The loss of the Temple with its priestly ritual also firmly established the Jewish custom of community meetings for prayer and instruction. This unheard-of innovation in the ancient world where worship and sacrificial ritual were inseparable, persisted even after the return to Zion and the rebuilding of the altar. Meeting Place (=Synagogue) and Temple existed side by side. Whereas the latter was the stronghold of the priesthood, the former was the forum of the lay teachers (Scribes, Pharisees, Rabbis) who, as a rule, had the following of the masses.

RABBINIC JUDAISM

Rabbinic Judaism thus took its beginnings from the seminal situation of the Babylonian exile. It crystallized only a few centuries later, after the second destruction of Jerusalem by the Romans (A.D. 70). For about five centuries the end of the Biblical age or "inter-testamentary" period (characterized by the composition of the apocryphal and pseudepigraphic books, most of which were excluded from the Hebrew Bible) and the beginning of the Rabbinic period can be said to overlap. During this time Judaism absorbed new ideas and faced new problems, mainly as the result of fresh historic experience and under the impact of continual warfare and great tribulations. It must suffice here to mention only the confrontation with other great cultures such as that of Persia and, particularly after the conquests of Alexander the Great, Hellenism. Very frequently alternative or even mutually exclusive ideas and beliefs existed side by side without anyone apparently bothering to arrange them in a logical and consistent system. A good example is the case of the doctrine of last things, or eschatology. Ideas and hopes were current about a glorious national restoration under a victorious military leader or through a miraculous intervention from above. The ideal redeemer would be a Davidic king, or a heavenly being referred to as "Son of Man". Redemption could thus mean a better and more peaceful world or the utter end and annihilation of "this age" and the ushering in, amid catastrophe and judgment, of a new era, "a new heaven and a new earth". The chaotic welter of these ideas is visible not only in the apocryphal books of the Bible, but also in the New Testament writings and particularly in their accounts of the diverse attitudes of the disciples and the various Jewish groups towards Jesus. The original Biblical tradition of thinking about the future in social, collective and historical terms was now further complicated by the absorption of new patterns of thought. The increasing preoccupation with the destiny of the individual, together with the demand for a satisfactory account of the ways of divine justice in meting out reward and punishment, produced the notion of the resurrection of the dead. This idea, in spite of its objectionable irrationality to modern, "enlightened" minds, has at least the advantage of implicitly safeguarding two fundamental Biblical beliefs. The one is the integral, total conception of the human personality as an animated body or flesh vivified by the Spirit. Resurrection of the body, if it means anything at all, can only mean that there is no way of talking about an eternal individual destiny unless we are prepared to define "individual" as this particular person with this particular body. The other point about the resurrection is that it keeps to the pattern of a final fulfilment as the consummation of the process of history: at the end of history God will inaugurate the New Era of his Kingdom.

The traditional doctrine of immortality as found, for example, in Greece and India, is opposed to the idea of resurrection in both respects. In the first place it tends to regard the "soul", a kind of independent spiritual substance, as the essential part of man. The body is merely its material clothing, a vile and inferior one at that. The body is a prison, and a considerable amount of philosophical ingenuity or mythopoeic imagination had to be spent in accounting for the "descent" or "fall" of the pure, spiritual and heavenly soul into this miserable body. It is obvious that on these premises the best hope that can be held out to the individual is the final separation – or rather liberation – of the soul from the body and its return to its celestial home. In fact, many systems of mystical contemplation or Yoga-like exercises are designed to anticipate death and to realize the liberation from the body already in this life. It would, after all, be a terrible thing for the soul to have to rejoin a body again at the end of time. The tension between these incompatible traditions is well expressed in the compromise solution which returns the soul to a so-called spiritual or glorified body. Moreover, the doctrine of immortality lifts individual eschatology out of the historical, Messianic context. The course of history as such becomes irrelevant to the fate and destiny of the individual. In the later development of Judaism the tension between the two tendencies remains discernible and, as we shall see, historic sense and Messianic fervour seem to be related in inverse ratio to the strength of the philosophic or mystical preoccupation with the spiritual soul.

We have thus at least three strands making up the thread of eschatology: (1) the Messianic era of national restoration, including the rebuilding of the Temple, (2) the new *aeon* of God's Kingdom, including the resurrection of the dead, (3) the celestial hereafter in which the soul eternally enjoys the blessed vision. In actual fact Jewish eschatology is a compromise which does not clearly appear as such because, as has been remarked earlier, theology has carefully been kept in a fluid, uncodified and unsystematic state. Compromise in this context therefore means that contradictory and supplementary traditions exist side by side, but the unconscious need to harmonize them, in spite of the absence of systematic dogmatics, has shaped their subsequent development in medieval theology. Thus the Messianic expectation became a kind of Millenarianism. The Messianic era will be followed by the Great Judgment, the Resurrection and the New Era. Meanwhile individual souls are provisionally judged after death and go to Heaven (also "Paradise") or, alternatively, to hell. From this discarnate state they will be called to the final judgment and resurrection.

I have dwelt somewhat at length on this one example among many for two reasons. In the first place it concerns an issue that is popularly held to be central to religious faith. Secondly, its relatively vague and unsystematic treatment is surely significant. This significance resides not so much in the apparent failure of Rabbinic theology to achieve dogmatic precision, but rather in the fact that it never occurred to the Rabbis that this was a failure at all. They were just not bothered by their lack of a *systematic* theology. Popular preachers, liturgical poets and apocalyptic writers gave free rein to their imaginations, but official Judaism refused to waste its time on such "trifles" as the details of eschatology. It was enough to know and to believe that there were "last things". Meanwhile one had to get on with the real business; how this real business was understood will become clear soon, so also will other important religious ideas. Eschatological ideas could be held in various combinations and forms and were discussed by the later teachers in a context of Platonic, Stoic and Gnostic notions that could be absorbed all the more easily because the Rabbis had developed a method of scriptural interpretation which permitted them to find new thoughts in the old texts. Whatever our modern objections to allegorical exegesis, the historian of religion has to admit that as a method it possessed a liberating and dynamic quality which allowed for creative adaptation.

Allegorical interpretation of Scripture reached its highest development in Alexandria where Jewish philosophers came profoundly under the influence of Hellenistic thought and piety. Under the impact of Greek philosophy they began to translate traditional Jewish symbols into abstract terms and thereby helped the monotheistic tendencies of philosophy (first cause, cosmic principle, ultimate reality, etc.) to crystallize. The coalescence of the two traditions which the successors of Philo of Alexandria initiated proved of far-reaching consequence for Western civilization. They were particularly exercised by the problem of the attributes of God (his goodness, strength, greatness, etc.) and by the outspoken anthropomorphisms of the Bible which seemed to model the idea of God rather too much on human forms of thought. They lifted these images to a higher spiritual level by stressing God's utter transcendence which cannot be grasped by discursive thinking but which can only be incompletely approached in the ecstasy of contemplation.

The Palestinian Rabbis, on the other hand, continued the Biblical tradition of boldly risking to speak of God in human, all-too-human terms. For only by adhering to anthropomorphic imagery is it possible at all to bring out the full, actual relevance and meaningfulness for our lives of the reality of God. On the one hand they used all sorts of circumlocutions for God (such as Heaven, the Power, the Holy One Blessed be He, etc.) to increase the awe of his Holy Name, but on the other hand they were at pains to bring God near to even the humblest heart and understanding. If necessary, Scripture could be made to show that God suffers together with his children in exile, weeps over the destruction of the Temple, rejoices over piety and good works, wears phylacteries, takes part in learned Rabbinic discussions about the niceties of ritual law, and eagerly looks forward to receiving prayers. More particularly he demonstrates moral values in order to teach his children the proper way of the "Imitation of God"; so we read: "even as he is merciful so be ye merciful, even as he visiteth the sick so go ye

and visit the sick". But whereas the various methods of scriptural exegesis served thinkers like Philo of Alexandria to turn the Bible into a system of Hellenistic philosophy, the Rabbis were stimulated by Hellenistic thought to adapt new ideas and concepts to the essential character of the Jewish tradition. In doing so they brought about on a spiritual and more permanent level what the Maccabean rising achieved less successfully on a political plane. However the terminology of Hellenistic or other philosophies was merely a vehicle which the Rabbis used for articulating their own understanding of the Jewish religious and historical experience. Their expositions lacked systematic elaboration and theological method; more often they moved on the level of popular homiletics, imaginative moralizing and the kind of half-mythical symbolic thinking whose inner coherence becomes evident (to us moderns) only after careful analysis. In this manner the Rabbis succeeded in expressing in simple but concrete language the apparent paradoxes of the Jewish religion: the unfathomable mystery of the godhead and its clear, ethical character; God's remoteness and his nearness; his forgiving love and the terror of his judgment, and many more "dialectical" polarities of this kind. Their theological thinking was thus unsystematic, which does not mean that it did not possess an organic, immanent unity of its own. But their intellectual and logical efforts were turned in a different direction.

The same method of scriptural interpretation which allowed the Rabbis to find the Jewish answer to the religious and intellectual questions of their time was employed to an even greater extent in their attempt to come to grips with such practical problems as were posed by new and changing economic and social circumstances. In this attempt they had no other guide but the divine law. Mention has already been made of the basic attitude of listening-obeying which is characteristic of the Bible. The concrete condensation, as it were, of this obedience under the covenant was the Law or *Torah*.[1] This explains how it came about that the central theological concept of "Revelation" has a very definite meaning in Judaism, namely "Law". For a Christian, e.g. the mysteries of revelation and redemption coincide: the supreme revelation of God, the incarnation, also brings man's salvation. For the Jew the two are quite

---

[1] As a matter of fact the translation 'Law' for the Hebrew *Torah* gives a lop-sided and misleading impression. *Torah* really means guidance, instruction, teaching, etc. The word can mean the Pentateuch, the Bible, Revelation or traditional religion as a whole. It is only against the wider background of the Jewish theology of the 'Word' as God's revealed Will that the translation 'Law' acquires a measure of legitimacy.

distinct. Salvation is the symbol of the "end", just as creation is the symbol of the "beginning". Between these two mythological poles or images of the limits there lies the daylight stretch of irreversible time that is called history. Perhaps the way of history is best compared to a suspension bridge with one-way traffic only, whose two bridgeheads are shrouded in mist. No doubt Jewish history knows of many outbursts of passionate yearning for salvation accomplished, and more than once have persecutions and pogroms led to Messianic "explosions" and to the proclamation of false saviours – the most notorious was, perhaps, Sabbatai Tsevi (1666). But always Judaism sobered up again and remembered that its business was not to testify to the end that had come, but to hope and to work for the kingdom that was still to come. In the long run it was the profound concern what to do, how to live, how to walk one's little bit of road along God's highway to salvation that determined Jewish religiosity. If history meant the co-operation of God and man in the Covenant, then man's sole business was the *bona fide* discharge of his obligations. Speculation about first and last things was discouraged by the Rabbis. The apocryphal writings which tended to take an exaggerated interest in these matters were excluded from the canon of Scripture. The Jew had his hands full doing his immediate job: listening and obeying.

The things to be done or to be left undone were of various kinds. There were symbolic acts expressing, in the ways peculiar to ritual and myth, the fundamental awarenesses and responses of the group. There were rites that regulate the relation of the group and of its individual members to God. There were feasts and fasts keeping alive the significance of God's mighty deeds in history and revitalizing the consciousness of historic solidarity with past and future. There were commandments fostering certain values and attitudes, and prohibitions designed to prevent a lowering of the moral or spiritual standard. There were provisions more directly concerned with the immediate objectives of the Covenant such as social justice and personal holiness. What all these have in common is that they are commanded and desired by God. To do them is to do God's will, to walk in his way, to further his purpose and thereby to achieve individual salvation and blessedness. It is obvious why the Jew, whose highest ideal and consuming desire was precisely this life of joyous obedience, developed a real passion for the business of ascertaining God's will in all things. From Scripture and traditional premisses, and by the accepted rules of interpretation and deduction, he was always engaged in discovering the specific applica-

tion of the divine law to each and every situation that occurred or might possibly occur.

As a result there emerged what seems to be one of the most characteristic features of Judaism. It is a religion less concerned with the developing and safeguarding of doctrine than with the formulation of norms and rules that will be able to relate human action to the revealed will of the Creator. The spiritual leaders or theologians of Judaism, the Rabbis, are thus essentially lawyers. The old institution known as the Sanhedrin was a legislative and judicial body halfway between a parliament and a supreme court. The adage that Judaism is not interested in orthodoxy (right faith) but in orthopraxis (right action), like most antithetic statements of this kind, is a dangerous half-truth. But it clearly brings out the main stress of Rabbinic Judaism which could, on occasion, go to extreme lengths. Thus the strenuous intellectual labour of *Talmud Torah* (the Study of the Law) became the ideal business of life and of supreme religious value in itself. The Rabbis seriously debated whether study of the Law or performance was to be preferred and decided in favour of study because only study (i.e. right knowledge) could lead to right action. Study tended to become a sort of sacramental activity to the Jew who saw in *Torah* the revealed word and *logos* of God. The negative side of this development was the hypertrophy of Rabbinic casuistry about legal and ritual minutiae which continued to proliferate as time went on and which often bordered on the absurd.

But however absurd in its extremes, any limit set to this development would have been even more absurd and arbitrary. If you are supposed to abstain from work on the Sabbath, then you must also define what constitutes work. Where is the thin line of division between harvesting, reaping and plucking ears of corn? There were thousands of problems of this kind because the whole of life had to be sanctified by being made subject to the Law. The house had to be a house of God, the table an altar, the market place an expression of justice. There is hardly an act which a practising Jew can do (including dressing or cooking a meal) to which some religious duty or prohibition is not attached. The Jew does not merely want to do the right and lawful thing and to avoid sin. He positively wants to do God's will and therefore desires that every act should be a divine commandment. The Hebrew word *mitsvah* which is used for "good deed" or "religious act" literally means "commandment". The Rabbis counted 613 positive and negative commandments (not counting their subdivisions and casuistic ramifications) which they related to the 613 parts of the body which their anatomy recognized. To make sure that all life was hallowed the Rabbis ordained blessings to be recited on all occasions: when eating, smelling a flower, putting on new clothes, seeing beautiful objects, receiving sad news, and so on. When the occasion is the performance of a positive commandment the blessing contains the words ". . . who has sanctified us by his commandments and commanded us to . . ."

This tremendous development of Rabbinic law and its decisive role for the practice of Judaism were made possible by the same use of Scripture that we found in the homiletic interpretation of the symbols of faith. By means of their rules of interpretation (hermeneutics) the Jewish teachers could develop, change and adapt the Law to new circumstances without realizing what they did, or rather in full consciousness of doing nothing but interpreting Scripture correctly. The legitimacy of the method flows from the profound rootedness of the Rabbis in the Biblical tradition and from their firm and unquestioning conviction that the divine word was an eternally valid guide to action. But validity, if it is to mean anything at all, must mean applicability. Refusal to adapt would have been tantamount to reactionary conservatism in social or practical matters. Alternatively it would have meant paying lip-service to the eternity of the *Torah* whilst, in fact, emancipating life from its authority. If the law is no longer applicable to certain spheres of life, then these are no longer subject to it and remain, to all practical intents and purposes, outside its competence and jurisdiction. This was, in fact, the attitude of the Sadducees who still flourished in New Testament times but later disappeared and left it to Pharisaism to stamp its character on the future of Judaism. Like the Sadducees, other sects and groups within Judaism dropped out of the picture. Some of them, like the Essenes, are known to us only by a few references and descriptions (not always very reliable) in the writings of Greek or Roman authors. Others, like the sect that lived near the Dead Sea (unless identical with the Essenes) are being discovered only now and show that Jewish religious life harboured a great number of attitudes and beliefs. It becomes increasingly clear that Pharisaism was only one movement in Judaism, albeit the most dynamic and viable force of them all. Of course the Rabbis would probably not have admitted that they were innovating. They believed that their rules of logic and interpretation were divinely authorized and that, moreover, there was a "tradition going back to Moses on Sinai", the so-called Oral Law, which was concurrent with Scripture and supplemented it. The task of Rabbinic learning, apart from the occasional enacting of new ordinances to meet

the needs of the moment, was the correlation by means of hermeneutic and logical rules of the "written" and the "oral" Law. It is thus in Rabbinic Judaism that the theory of tradition as a second vehicle of revelation parallel to Scripture was first developed.

In the century following upon the destruction of the Temple and the sack of Jerusalem by the Romans (A.D. 70) the creative phase of Rabbinic interpretation gradually came to an end. The centuries that followed were marked by an impressive labour of analysis and elaboration of detail. The results are embodied in the Talmud, the great compilations of Rabbinic (particularly legal) lore made in the Academies of Palestine and, more especially, of Babylonia. Whereas the *halakhah* (cf. p. 24) dominates the Talmud, *aggadah* figures more prominently in the collections of moralizing and edifying homilies known as *midrash*. The latter, quite in keeping with the Rabbinic stress on the Law as the embodiment of "what the Lord thy God requireth of thee", is considered as less authoritative and binding than the Talmud. Both together form the inexhaustible store-house of tradition, wisdom, guidance and instruction to which Judaism turns for elucidation of God's revelation. Theologically speaking, the Talmud as the "Oral Law" is second only to the Bible. But as a matter of fact it may almost be said to be primary since Rabbinic Judaism can view the Bible only *through* the Talmud whose categories of thought, theological perspective and legal interpretations are normative and determine the understanding of Scripture.

In conclusion of this section it may be useful to illustrate the Rabbinic method of defining both new and traditional laws or ideas by way of "interpreting" Scripture. The following example has been chosen at random and any other might have done as well; it presents a series of Talmudic comments on *Leviticus* xix, 26: "Ye shall not eat [anything] with the blood." As the "eating of blood", that is, the consumption of meat with the blood still on it is usually mentioned together with magic and pagan rites (cf. *Leviticus* xix, 26 and *Ezekiel* xxxiii, 25) we may assume the prohibition to be part of the Biblical legislation against idolatry and related practices generally. But the Rabbis used both the prohibition as such and the text for further teaching.

(1) A prohibition to eat any part of an animal whilst there is still life in it. The verse is thus made to mean: "Do not eat [any meat] with the life still in it." As respect for life does not imply vegetarianism in Jewish tradition it is expressed by a strict taboo on blood which is the seat of life (*Genesis* ix, 4 and *Leviticus* xvii, 14). Blood must be poured away on or near the altar; today it is poured out on the earth. Food is thus to be consi-

dered as a natural, metabolic activity and not as a magical rite in which man appropriates the "life" of the slaughtered animal. Life belongs to God – and therefore man must abstain from it. For that reason the Jewish method of slaughter is designed to drain the animal body as effectively as possible of blood. The Rabbis further extended the prohibition of blood by ordaining a further draining of blood after slaughter. In fact, eating meat with the fresh blood still on it seems to have been considered a heinous offence already at a very early date (cf. I *Samuel* xiv, 32). Up to this day meat is salted and allowed to drip for one hour in every practising Jewish household so as to draw out any blood still in the meat.

Connected with this prohibition is the law against eating parts of living animals. It is, in fact, one of the seven Noahite Laws considered to be binding on all men (cf. *Genesis* ix, 4).

(2) "Do not eat before you have prayed for your life." This interpretation is based on the double meaning: blood=life. By eating, man strengthens his life (=blood); therefore he should not eat before providing his life with that sustenance which is his one real necessity: divine assistance and favour. Thus the Rabbis establish the duty of praying first thing every morning, before breakfast. The more general duty to pray to God every day is derived by the Rabbis from another verse.

(3) "Do not eat [sacrificial meat] with the blood [still in the basin]." In the Temple ritual the blood that gushed out after cutting the animal's throat was caught in a basin and then sprinkled or poured out on or near the altar. It was only after concluding this essential "sacrificial" part of the ritual that the meat could be eaten by the priests or the owner of the sacrifice. Here we have a strictly ritual regulation based on our verse.

(4) "Do not eat [the meal of comfort] with the blood [of those slain in the course of justice]." A meal of comfort is given to mourners after the burial. This ceremony did not take place when the corpse was buried after execution for a capital offence. The Rabbis simply used this verse as a peg on which to hang a scriptural warrant for their tradition.

(5) "Do not eat [anything] with the blood [that you are lawfully shedding]." Members of the Sanhedrin, the Supreme Court, must observe a strict fast on a day when they pass a death sentence. Shedding blood in the course of justice is a divine command but no less an occasion of abstinence and penitence for those whose duty it is to administer justice.

(6) A warning to the "stubborn and rebellious son" (cf. *Deuteronomy* xxi, 18–21) who is an example how gluttony and drink (*ibid.* verse 20) can lead to a

violent end. The moralizing interpretation of our verse thus reads it as meaning "Do not eat [as a glutton and drunkard] with [that wicked intemperance that ultimately leads to the shedding of your] blood."

THE MIDDLE AGES

Whereas Judaism was shaped in the Biblical and Rabbinic periods, it was interpreted in the Middle Ages. The former period gave it most of its substance, the Middle Ages mainly sought to understand its meaning. The Midrashic preachers and Talmudic lawyers had developed and ramified the contents of religion, the medieval thinkers attempted to provide rational proofs. Of course the study of the Talmud and legal casuistry continued to flourish, but one of the most distinctive marks of medieval Judaism is its theology or, to be more precise, its philosophy of religion.

This philosophical effort was indebted to influences of various kinds. There was, first of all, the rediscovery and development of Greek philosophy by the Arabs. In the wake of the Muslim thinkers who examined their own faith in terms of the new philosophy, the Jewish theologians too began to discuss fundamental Jewish beliefs in the light of Aristotelianism or Neo-Platonism and with the rigorous discipline of philosophical logic. There was also the apologetic stimulus and the necessity of upholding one's own faith against competing religions which claimed equally divine and authoritative revelations as their basis. The only common ground on which the discussion could move was the neutral sphere of rational thinking and, if possible, of rational proof. There were, moreover, internal Jewish conflicts such as the one occasioned by the rise of the Karaite sect which pretended to recognize the authority of Scripture only and denied that of Rabbinic tradition. The Karaites could only be met by a systematic and convincing statement of the orthodox faith.

The problems which the Jewish philosophers faced and the categories in which they formulated their questions and answers were, as a rule, determined by the ascendant Aristotelian philosophy of the age, though some thinkers were more firmly rooted in the Neo-Platonic tradition. The nature of revelation, knowledge and faith and their relation to each other, the nature of the human personality and its relation to God, the existence of God and its rational proofs, the attributes of God, the eternity or createdness of the world, providence and theodicy – these were among the problems discussed with a profound religious seriousness but on the assumption that reason was not only competent to deal with them but was, in fact, required to do so as a religious duty. Reason was man's noblest part; through it alone he was the image of God and capable of communing with his Creator. The exercise of the rational faculty, that is, philosophy, thus became transfigured with the halo of religious contemplation. Many of the essentials of the Jewish faith were formulated with intellectual precision during that period, though it must be remembered that these discussions went on between philosophers and not between official theologians authorized to proclaim the truth or to pronounce anathemas. Thus even the formulations that were accepted by common consent never attained the same kind of binding authority enjoyed, for example, by a ceremonial law expounded or codified by a Rabbi on the basis of Talmudic texts.

Maimonides

The greatest and most influential of Jewish medieval philosophers, Moses Maimonides (1135–1204), also happened to be one of the most illustrious Talmudists, and his systematic code of Rabbinic law was more honoured in orthodox circles than his controversial philosophical *magnum opus* "The Guide of the Perplexed". As it happened, Maimonides was the one to formulate the thirteen articles of faith which are usually held to comprise the essential dogmas of the Jewish religion. Though other theologians disputed the number, the choice of dogmas and the very conception of binding articles of faith, they are important enough to be listed here:

1. The existence of God, the Creator of all things.
2. His absolute unity.
3. His incorporeality.
4. His eternity.
5. The obligation to serve and worship him alone.
6. The existence of prophecy.
7. The superiority of the Prophecy of Moses above all others.
8. The *Torah* is God's revelation to Moses.
9. The *Torah* is immutable.
10. God's omniscience and foreknowledge.
11. Reward and punishment according to one's deeds.
12. The coming of the Messiah.
13. The resurrection of the dead.

It is obvious that some of these articles are more rational, more capable of logical demonstration than others, and the list is, perhaps, more conventional than Maimonides' own thinking really was. Thus he would certainly have insisted that these things must be "known" and not "believed" (in the ordinary sense), except by those whose intellect was weak. He would also have had some difficulties about the immortality of these weaker brethren since it is the intellect alone which, if properly developed in contemplative knowledge, is man's immortal part. The belief in a Messiah who rebuilds the Temple and rules over an Israel restored to its ancient homeland does not, so one feels, form an organic part of this philosophical system. Maimonides really believed that the *Torah* or revealed law provided the kind of discipline most apt to assist the development of man's higher faculties (i.e. the rational faculty) and lead him to true contemplative knowledge of and communion with God. This stage of being lovingly united to God, the consummation of the *amor intellectualis Dei* or intellectual love of God is, according to Maimonides, the same as Prophecy. A Messianic world is one where peace, prosperity and orderly government prevent all distractions and render the undisturbed contemplative life possible.

Maimonides was particularly emphatic in his fight against anthropomorphism. His doctrine of divine attributes rules out everything that even faintly suggests corporeality or multiplicity. Maimonides believed, in accordance with Aristotelian logic, that positive attributes, that is, adventitious characteristics added to an *ens* or existent thing, implied a composite nature. Therefore God, whose nature is absolute *one*-ness, cannot have any attributes. Such innocent statements as "God is great, good, powerful", etc., are thus pregnant with heresy unless re-interpreted in terms of a "negative theology". In this important and truly impressive part of Maimonides' philosophy the almost unbridgeable gulf between the philosopher's God and the perhaps all-too-human God of the devout, simple believer becomes glaringly apparent.

Yehudah Halevi

We have dwelt on Maimonides because of his significance in many important respects. In the first place there is his outstanding importance as a philosopher and as the great orthodox theologian in the eyes of later thinkers. Of equal interest is the cry of heresy that was raised against the boldness of his thought still in his lifetime and, with increased violence, after his death. The battle between the supporters and opponents of Maimonides almost split Jewry into two camps. For our present purpose the main thing about Maimonides is the fact that he represents one of the extreme possibilities of which medieval Rabbinic Judaism was capable. The opposite possibility is illustrated by a thinker of a very different calibre who, as it happens, was also the greatest of all Hebrew poets. The poetry of Yehudah Halevi (1080–1141?) burns with the faithful love of the Community of Israel for its Lord and

Redeemer no less than with an intensely personal, mystic love of God and an individual longing for divine communion. This love does not recoil from paradox whenever paradox expresses truth more adequately than logical consistency:

> "Lord where shall I find thee?
> High and hidden is thy place;
> And where shall I not find thee?
> The world is full of thy glory."

(From *Selected Poems of Jehudah Halevi*, tr. Nina Salaman, Philadelphia, 1946.)

> "O Lord, before thee is my whole desire,
> Yea, though I cannot bring it to my lips.
> Thy favour would I ask a moment and then die –
>
> . . . . . .
>
> When far from thee, I die while yet in life;
> But if I cling to thee I live, though I should die." (*Ibid.*)

Or,

> "To meet the fountain of the life of truth I run;
>
> . . . . . .
>
> To see the face of my king is my only aim;
>
> . . . . . .
>
> Would I might behold his face within my heart!
> Mine eyes would never ask to look beyond." (*Ibid.*)

Halevi's philosophical book, the *Kuzari*, is cast in the form of a dialogue with the king of the Khazars and ends with the latter's conversion. The conversion of the Khazars to Judaism is, of course, an historical event (eighth century), but Halevi used it merely as a stage-setting for developing his own theology. The book is an all-out attack on the philosophers, in spite of its obvious dependence on their speculations and terminology. Centuries before Pascal, Halevi sharply formulated the difference between the God of Aristotle, who is at best a bloodless abstraction, a "first cause" or "prime mover", and the God of Abraham, who is the Living God experienced in personal relationship and in revelation. Religion is based not on speculative knowledge of causes but on miracles; it is faith and not knowledge – though Halevi is careful to point out that religion, even if it is not rational, is not for that reason anti-rational. Religion must never outrage reason. In a truly existential fashion Halevi's problem is not the quest of impersonal truth but that of the meaning of Jewish existence and Jewish history. Judaism is not based on universal reason but on the particular experience of a people: the call of Abraham, slavery in Egypt, the Exodus, the revelation on Sinai and so on. This experience is kept alive in the unbroken historic consciousness of the

Jewish people. Six hundred thousand Israelites (according to the Biblical story) witnessed the revelation on Mount Sinai; that is the foundation of the Jewish faith even in its most mystical inwardness:

> "And my heart seeth thee and hath faith in thee
> As though it had stood by at Sinai." (*Ibid.*)

But this experience includes not only the events recorded in the Bible, but also the actual situation of Israel in exile and, in it, the individual existence of the Jew, Yehudah Halevi. What do exile, suffering, persecution and – above all – constant humiliation at the hands of Ishmael (Islam) and Esau (Christianity) mean for Judaism? Halevi's answer places the mystery of Israel in the centre of his theodicy; it is a theology of the *ekklesia Israel*. Israel is a mystical community whose election and suffering are mysteriously and inextricably interwoven. It is the "heart of mankind", healthier than all and, at the same time, more sick than all. Its long "passion" in history is the very mark of its election. Israel's continued guilt is not the infidelity for which it was originally exiled but its failure to accept exile, suffering and humiliation gladly in the love of God. And Halevi, the liturgical poet, thus speaks to his Lord on behalf of the Community of Israel:

> "With all my heart, in truth, and with all my might
> Have I loved thee. In open and in secret
> Thy name is with me: how shall I go alone?
>
> . . . . . .
>
> Men have held me in contempt, knowing not
> That my shame for thy name's glory is my glory."

Or,

> "May my sweet song be pleasing in thy sight, and the goodness of my praise,
> O Beloved, who art flown afar from me, at the evil of my deeds.
> But I have held fast to the corner of the garment of love of him who is tremendous and wonderful."

and

> "Enough for me is the glory of thy name; that is my portion alone from all my labour.
> Increase the sorrow, I shall love but more, for wonderful is thy love to me." (*Ibid.*)

Even as God has chosen one particular people as the focus of his purpose with mankind, so has he chosen one particular country, the Holy Land, to be the territory of this people's religious fulfilment. With the personal consistency that behoves an "existential" thinker and the immortal poet of the moving "Elegies to Zion", Halevi left his native Spain for Palestine.

Maimonides and Halevi, each in his own way, are about half-way to two other significant though more extreme expressions of medieval Judaism. For Maimonides' ethics of intellectual contemplation, burning with an incandescent love of God, is merely the philosophical version of a pietistic, ascetic Judaism which combined Platonic and Ṣūfī (pp. 201-5) elements. Halevi's mysticism and his strong sense of the historical dimension of the religious bond of Israel and God finds an extreme expression in the Kabbalah. Both types of mysticism have profoundly influenced Jewish life.

Bahya Ibn Pakuda

The major representative of the first trend is Bahya ibn Pakuda (Spain, eleventh century). Himself a *dayyan* or judge at a Rabbinic Court, he was sensitive to the dangers of externalization and empty formalism inherent in a religion of works and ritual legalism. In his book *Duties of the Heart* he set himself to expound the principles of the religious life. Oddly enough, this book became the most popular and widely read treatise of edification, in spite of its extreme ascetic spirituality which one would expect to appeal to an élite only. Bahya's discussion of the fundamentals of the religious life, such as the existence and unity of God and similar subjects, moves in the familiar medieval Neo-Platonic tradition. But the ascetic piety based on this groundwork is definitely that of the Ṣūfīs, except where the weight of Jewish tradition inhibits certain extreme conclusions. Thus faith and trust in God are interpreted as complete and utter abandon; all worldly desires and activities are condemned. Desires must be discarded because they are "secret polytheism", that is, they admit other objects of intention and volition besides God. All activity is bad because it presupposes reliance on the permanence of nature and on the validity of causality. Ṣūfī piety considered the very admission of the reality of "secondary causes" as a breach in the immediate communion with the "First Cause", God. The practical duties and worldly activities which religion prescribes, such as working for a livelihood instead of begging, caring for one's family and dependants, etc., all of which involve man in the natural order of worldly illusions, are in fact useless and without intrinsic value. They have to be performed as tasks which God has laid upon us. The physician giving medicine and the patient taking it are bidden by God to behave *as if* medicine had curative virtues. To use them without the concomitant faith that God alone wounds and heals is, as we have seen, "secret polytheism". The ultimate goal has to be a complete indifference and equanimity towards the world, total abandon to God, humility and solitude. The treatment of solitude is a good example of the brakes which Bahya's orthodoxy applied to his Ṣūfī temperament. Solitude is meant negatively to help loosing man's bonds with the world; positively it is to prepare the consummation of the union of the soul with God or, as the Ṣūfīs used to call it, the "annihilation in unification". But how can one practise extreme solitude in a religion which strictly enjoins marriage, communal prayer three times a day, and a host of other corporate and social activities? In fact, how can the mystic lose himself in the raptures of union when he has to attend to fixed liturgical hours and other duties? As we shall see, the mystical union in its extreme, classical form is altogether excluded from the framework of Rabbinic Judaism. Bahya's formulations are therefore carefully qualified, but even so his demand for constant examination of conscience, repentance, solitude, humility and the practice of ascetic disciplines goes further than that of most other authors. The final aim should be the all-consuming love of God which is defined as "the longing of the soul and its yearning for the Creator, so that it may cleave to his supreme light". This intense, all-absorbing love presupposes the perfect state of indifference to worldly joys and sorrows and leads to supernatural knowledge so that the lover "sees but not with his eyes, hears but not with his ears, feels but not with his senses, understands without ratiocination, dislikes nothing and prefers nothing . . . makes his will dependent on the will of God, and his love on the love of God, loving only what God loves and rejecting what God rejects".

One of the remarkable features of Bahya's ascetic piety is the conspicuous absence of the historic values that loom so large in traditional Judaism. No doubt Bahya sincerely believed in the election of Israel, the coming of the Messiah and the ingathering of the exiles to the Holy Land; but in the dynamics of his system these hardly play any role. As happens frequently with great religious figures, the predominance of one particular idea or attitude pushes others into the background without explicitly denying them. For both Maimonides and Bahya the spiritual life of the individual was the one important subject.

The Kabbalah

It is different with the Kabbalists. To the outsider their thinking presents a curiously exotic and bizarre theosophic system. The difficulty of giving a correct and comprehensive synopsis of its tenets is sadly illustrated by the many uninformed and misleading accounts of it that have appeared. Of course Kabbalah is not the same as Jewish mysticism, of which it is merely one phase, though the most important and far-reaching in its effects. In spite of its name which means "[esoteric] tradition" and in spite of the Kabbalists' sincere belief that they only revived the old mystical teachings of Moses and earlier sages, there can be no reasonable doubt that the system as such evolved in the thirteenth century in Southern France and Spain. The developing Kabbalah could make use of the literature and traditions of earlier mystical movements, among which the *merkabah*-mystics deserve to be mentioned. For no doubt Jewish mysticism, as distinct from Kabbalah, goes back to early times; it may have had its beginnings in the esoteric teachings and speculations of certain sects like the Essenes, in the circles from which some of the apocryphal books have emanated and the group which has recently won international renown as the Dead Sea Sect. In early Talmudic times esoteric speculations were strongly tinged with Gnosticism; they were consequently viewed with misgiving and suspected of being apt to lead weaker spirits into heresy. In course of time a special, ecstatic kind of mysticism developed which taught its initiates ways and techniques of achieving visionary experience but *not* union with the divine glory or "throne", a concept which goes back to the vision of the divine chariot or throne in the opening chapters of *Ezekiel*. These mystics seem to have experienced ascensions of the soul, and the "perils of the soul" encountered during these ascents are described realistically and convincingly enough. The characteristic feature of this kind of mysticism is its stress on the transcendent, majestic, mysteriously tremendous and truly "numinous" aspect of the deity. The experience of loving communion, so common in later mysticism, is absent here. The initiate rises through spheres, worlds and heavens guarded by all sorts of terrifying angelic "guardians" until, at last, if he be worthy, he stands in awe and trembling before the supreme vision of the divine splendour. It was a mysticism of the *mysterium tremendum*. The esoteric teachings and practices of the *merkabah*-mystics have fallen into oblivion, but their mark on the liturgy has been permanent. The daily repeated recitation of the *trisagion* ("Holy, holy, holy is the Lord of hosts," etc.) and some of the most numinous hymns in the religious literature of the world are their contribution to the Prayerbook of the Synagogue.

However, the classical Kabbalah of the thirteenth and later centuries is a highly developed and complex system of mystical philosophy, and the student soon finds himself involved in fundamental and far-reaching problems. What, for example, is the relation of Judaism as described in the foregoing to mysticism? How can two such fundamentally different types of religion as the "pro-

phetic" and the "mystical" merge? Judaism seems, superficially at least, to be thoroughly extrovert: its relation to God is an objective I-Thou relationship, its main expressions are law and ritual, its major value is obedience to the divine will. On the other hand, mysticism is usually held to be turned inward. The mystic withdraws into his soul, he tends to despise ritual, his aim is not obedience but union with the divine. Is the typical *unio mystica* at all conceivable in a traditional Jewish framework? Can a Jew possibly echo Rūmī's desire "that all I's and Thou's might become one soul and at last be submerged in the Beloved"? Professor G. Scholem has demonstrated in recent years what the mystic transformation of Judaism really accomplished: it developed the mystical attitude of *communion* as distinct from *union*. Communion or *debhekuth* means a turning to God, an awareness of his otherness, a loving clinging or adhering to him which implies no loss of identity. But other, equally fundamental problems remain. The mythological element is extraordinarily strong in the Kabbalah. How must one explain the resurgence of myth in the midst of what is usually considered to be the mortal enemy of mythical religion? By what channels or mechanisms did mythical and Gnostic symbols reassert themselves in medieval Jewry? What is the relation of the old, Oriental Gnosticism and the almost explosive reappearance of similar ideas in the Kabbalistic systems of the thirteenth, and again of the sixteenth centuries? For our present purpose we can ignore these questions and concentrate instead on the essentials of the Kabbalistic doctrine.

The backbone of the Kabbalistic system is its rather startling doctrine of the deity. The starting point is the sharp distinction between two incompatible conceptions of the divine. There is the living, dynamic God of religion whose relevance to man resides precisely in his manifold vitality, and there is the conceptually purified God of philosophical theology. We have seen how, on a certain level of abstraction, monotheism can become "monolithic" and hence static. God was so much "one" that nothing could be said about him; even his attributes had to go overboard. But this philosophically unobjectionable non-anthropomorphic unity is bought at a price. The price is the sacrifice of the divine vitality; the divine has become a "state" and no longer a "process". The Kabbalists therefore distinguished between two aspects of the divine: the hidden and unknowable *Deus absconditus* and the manifest, self-revealing, accessible God of religious experience. Of the former, not even existence can be predicated; it is the paradoxical fullness of the great divine Nothing. The Kabbalists called it *En Sof*, the "Infinite". It is so hidden in the mystery of its nothingness that it is not even mentioned in the Bible, let alone addressed in prayer or accessible in contemplation. The Bible, God's Word, is by definition nothing but the revelation or self-manifestation of God. In fact, an existing God means a manifest, revealed and related God. The process of manifestation, i.e. revelation or developing relatedness is thus identical with the process by which God as it were comes into being. The text of the Bible, read superficially, seems to describe the creation of the world and God's first dealings with it; the Kabbalist's eye pierces through this layer of meaning to the esoteric level which is, to him, the ultimately significant one. What Scripture tells is the process of the divine becoming and of the inner-divine life. For in the depths of the divine hiddenness, all turned in upon itself, there occurs a primordial, initial wrench by which it begins to turn outwards, to unfold, to exist. Here existence is literally an *ex-stare*, a process of extroversion in the introverted *En Sof*. This initial movement is described in the *Zohar* (the most important Kabbalistic text) in a highly mystical passage as the concentration or crystallization of energy in one luminous point which bursts the closed confines of *En Sof*. The process of emanation has started.

Here we come to the second main feature of the Kabbalistic theology: its continual use of the term "emanation" instead of "creation". But although the term is obviously borrowed from Neo-Platonic tradition, its purpose is not to mediate between the spiritual One and the material many by introducing a number of intermediaries, but rather to describe the procession of the fullness of the divine Being from the hiddenness of the divine Non-Being or Nothingness. The World of Emanations is thus very godhead, its totality is described as a complex organism consisting of ten potencies or foci (*sefiroth*). These potencies are not ten gods but ten aspects, stages or manifestations of the deity revealing itself. The dynamic interrelations of the *sefiroth* make up the intensely dramatic inner life of the godhead which, in spite of its complexity, is essentially one. The Kabbalists could not or would not use categories such as "substance" and "persons" when wrestling with the conceptual difficulties of their symbols, yet one cannot but sympathize with their critics who felt that the *sefiroth* were even worse than attributes. Both the dualism between the hidden and the manifest God, and the doctrine of *sefiroth* looked dangerously like departures from strict Jewish monotheism, and the orthodox critics were quick to complain that the Kabbalists had substituted a tenfold God for the threefold one of the Christians. The Kabbalists, who had some of the greatest luminaries of orthodox Talmudic learning in their camp, replied that they were speaking of a profound mystery, and that the mystical understanding of the divine unity in all its manifestations was precisely their main concern. In fact, the emphasis on this unity grew more insistent as by the sheer inherent power of the Kabbalistic symbolism the various *sefiroth* became more and more personified.

There is one detail in this *sefiroth* symbolism which deserves to be mentioned because of its outstanding importance for Kabbalistic thinking and practice. This is the relation between the sixth *sefirah*, "*Tif'ereth*", and the tenth *sefirah* which is called "*Malkhuth*" or "*Shekhinah*". *Tif'ereth* is the central *sefirah*; it functions as the hub and pivot of the whole system. In the dynamic flow and give-and-take of the *sefiroth*, *Tif'ereth* receives the power or influx of the higher potencies and, harmonizing them, passes them on to the lower ones. It embodies the creative dynamism of the *sefiroth* and is conceived exclusively in male symbols – King, Sun, Bridegroom, etc. Standing at the lower end of the *sefiroth*-cluster is *Malkhuth*. As the last of the divine manifestations it is the point where the divine sphere contacts the non-divine. Standing at the lowest, receiving end of the system, *Malkhuth* is the receptive womb, the Moon, Bride and Queen. It is only in her relation to the nether worlds that *Malkhuth*, as that aspect of the deity which is nearest to them, acquires active, creative or even ruling characteristics. Then the "royal" aspect of her queenship is emphasized and the Bride is also Mother.

Now it is the frankly erotic quality of the relation between *Tif'ereth* and *Malkhuth* which is the most striking characteristic of Kabbalistic literature. The supreme and central mystery of the Kabbalah is the Holy Union or "sacred marriage" between these two aspects of the divine or, in other words, the unification of God. The greatest catastrophe that the Kabbalist can imagine is the destruction of the unity within the godhead, that is, the separation of the *Shekhinah* (as the tenth *sefirah* is also called) from her "husband". This was precisely the tragic consequence of Adam's sin. It is thus really the fate of God that is at issue in religion, and man's efforts, both in good works and in mystical contemplation, should be directed to the one end of promoting the wholeness of God, that is, the union of male and female within him. The gravity of sin is due to man's capacity to disrupt the divine union. *How* exactly man can operate this tremendous result cannot be considered here; it must suffice if we understand *why* he can do it. The reason is to be sought in certain common medieval ideas about the correspondence or analogy between microcosm and macrocosm. This blended well with the Biblical conception of man as the image of God, which was re-interpreted Kabbalistically to mean that the human frame reveals the same structure as the mystical divine "frame" of ten *sefiroth*.

The significant thing about all this is that both in the image of man (cf. *Genesis* i, 27; ii, 18, 24) and in the image of God totality and perfection are only achieved by the union of the male and female principles. Here we have a good example of how the Kabbalists added new, mystical layers to traditional Jewish doctrines; in this case to the doctrine that perfection was possible only in the married state. In fact, it seems that Kabbalah was the first system in the West to develop a mystical metaphysics of the sexual act.

There is one important consequence of this symbolism for Jewish mysticism that should not go unnoticed: erotic mysticism is limited to the sphere of the inner-divine (*sefiroth*) life, it has no place in man's relation with God. The Kabbalist knows no lover who ravishes him; he does not tell of the kind of experiences known to us from Christian or Ṣūfī literature. Instead of *union* with God, the Jewish mystic seeks *communion* and he achieves this by a kind of *imitatio Dei* by which his own integration follows the pattern and analogy of the divine. Contemplation of the divine, that is, of the *Shekhinah* in the first instance, thus leads to a communion whose ultimate purpose is mystical union *within* the godhead. It is the Kabbalist's task to promote this end by contemplative efforts and a holy life.

In the sixteenth century the Kabbalistic system underwent profound and far-reaching developments, of which the barest account only is possible here. According to the Kabbalistic "mythology" of Isaac Luria (1534–72) a cosmic fall or catastrophe took place long before Israel's exile, even long before Adam's fall, in the very heart of God's creation. The channels or "pipes" through which the creative light of God poured into Creation-in-the-making were said to collapse or break, and the divine sparks fell into chaos. Since then the history of the world, including the creation of Adam, is the drama of the struggle for restoration, with its ups and downs, its progress and setbacks. The two major setbacks were the fall of Adam and the destruction of the Temple. The decisive idea at the bottom of this system is that not only Israel or mankind are in desperate need of salvation but the whole cosmos. In fact, God himself is involved in the fall; every stone and every plant, as it were, shelters a fallen divine spark which yearns to return to its origin and, as it were, cries out for salvation.

What is the practical significance of this weird system in which Gnostic, Manichaean and traditional Jewish elements jostle one another? In the first place it created a religious world-picture in which God and man were bound together by much closer ties than in orthodox theology. In fact there was a community of fate and destiny between them: they needed each other. This well-known mystical motif is very different from the orthodox conception of a divine love for humanity which combines complete disinterested independence with a kind of condescending, paternal benevolence. God's interest and involvement in the history of mankind was more than once expressed by the Rabbis, but never with the near-heretical daring of the Kabbalists. In the second place Kabbalah fostered a new type of contemplative life and added a new layer of meaning to traditional Jewish practice. For the *ekklesia* of Israel, God's Bride, was the earthly counterpart of a mystical divine potency. The historical Israel was merely the symbol of some principle within the godhead, namely the *Shekhinah*; and everything in man corresponded to something in the divine *pleroma*. Israel's exile and suffering were merely the earthly reflection, the manifestation in the historical sphere of space-time of a more serious and tragic disruption – the exile of the *Shekhinah*, the divine Bride, and her separation from her divine Husband. Israel's fate has religious significance because it is a symbol of or pointer to essentially divine realities. The salvation or redemption which the Kabbalist works for is his own or that of Israel only in the second place. What he really means is the union of the divine. Kabbalistic life was based on the conviction that every human act, and particularly acts of contemplation and religion conforming to *Torah*, had a profoundly mystical significance and a direct bearing on the divine itself. Man was not merely a sinner dependent on divine grace, or a free agent working out his salvation. He was an active element in the cosmos, and his life and actions were vitally related to the inner life of the godhead itself. Lurianic Kabbalism, as we have seen, went even further in this direction and taught that man was created after the primeval fall as God's helper in the struggle for the restoration of the perfect order and the conquest of the "demonic" forces. Accordingly, the task of Israel consists in promoting and actually bringing about the salvation of the world (including matter) by a life of sanctity, mystical concentration and fulfilment of the divine Law which is mystically related to the structure of the cosmos. As long as the divine sparks are imprisoned in the "shells", in fallen matter and in fallen souls, God himself is, as it were, incomplete and unredeemed. God is redeemed, together with the souls and the world, in the great work of salvation in which he and man are united. The whole traditional Jewish system of life according to the Law was absorbed *in toto* into this framework. The *mitsvoth* (commandments, religious acts) had always been understood as the divine ordering of the world. But for the Kabbalist this was equivalent to saying that they were the mystical way by which the disturbed order of the cosmos could be restored and at-one-d. In Biblical times doing the will of God primarily meant conforming to the will of God as envisaged in the covenant, thereby ensuring blessing and long life. The Rabbinic concept of *mitsvah* meant an act of merit. The Kabbalistic life was a series of significant performances transformed into mystically redemptive acts by virtue of contemplative concentration.

Kabbalism was the dominant form of Jewish piety from the sixteenth century on, until it was severely shaken by outbursts of Kabbalistically inspired Messianism and, in their wake, antinomian excesses. Mysticism reasserted itself in the last great religious movement in Judaism. The movement, which is known as Hasidism, was initiated by Rabbi Israel Baal Shem Tob in the eighteenth century, flourished in Eastern Europe and still continues, albeit in a degenerate form, to the present day. Cleaving to God, the continual practice of the Presence of God, in some circles even ecstatic communion, were among the ideals cultivated by the Hasidim. It was only in modern rationalist Jewry that the Kabbalistic heritage was summarily dismissed as medieval superstition and fantastic obscurantism, and a new "enlightened" Judaism was preached.

Orthodoxy

However, before proceeding to an account of the developments and crises of modern Judaism, in which political, economic and cultural factors are inextricably intertwined, it may not be amiss to pause for a while and to look back at the beliefs of orthodox, Rabbinic Judaism as they had evolved by the end of the Middle Ages. To simplify the exposition it seems best to refer ourselves to the thirteen articles of Maimonides, in spite of their questionable authority and their admitted insufficiency.

1. The Existence of God

This article includes the faith in divine Providence and in God's continued sovereignty over and solicitude for his creation. The term "Creator" must not, therefore, be understood in a deistic sense, although "creation" has usually been held to imply the belief in a divine creative act at a particular date. Traditional Jewish chronology differs slightly from that of Archbishop Usher (A.D. 1959 corresponds to the year of creation 5719 according to the Jewish calendar) but the approach is essentially the same. The assumption of geological ages, evolution (in all its forms) and other cosmogonic hypotheses of modern science are still considered heretical by the orthodox. The Kabbalists tended to understand creation as a primeval, non-temporal or supra-temporal act. As such, creation is really eternal and is in no way similar to the construction of a clock or even to keeping it going. Modern theologians, who accept the relevance of the natural sciences in their own sphere, believe that dates are unimportant; they are merely a naïve but necessary concrete symbol of the faith in creation and the Creator. Here, one feels, modern Jewish theology is indebted to Kabbalistic concepts.

2. The Unity of God

The stress on unity has a theoretical and a practical aspect. Theoretically it excludes all types of polytheistic, dualistic and trinitarian beliefs and, according to Maimonides, all positive attributes. God's unity is an absolutely unique unity. For the Kabbalists the uniqueness of this unity actually means the mystery of the divine in its hidden, non-manifest aspect of *En Sof* and in its manifest, dynamic and creative aspect of the *sefiroth*. Divine unity is also usually defined so as to exclude all mediators. Nevertheless Kabbalism and folklore are full of angels, demons and spirits which, though never worshipped or adored, are nevertheless addressed and exorcized (by amulets, magic formulae, etc.) respectively.

3 and 4. The Incorporeality and Eternity of God

These two articles express among other things, the severely non-mythological character of God in Judaism. God has no form, no family, no history. In a way the two articles are corollaries of art. 2. The divine is beyond time (i.e. generation and corruption) and space (i.e. composite matter). As our language is derived from the world of our experience, it can never describe or adequately express the divine. Maimonides would probably have denied the possibility of a theology of analogy. Other thinkers did not go so far. The Kabbalists, whose thinking bears an unmistakably Platonic mark, would say that anthropomorphisms are legitimate because language as such (i.e. the Holy Tongue, Hebrew) is essentially a system of mystic symbols of the divine reality. It is only by derivation and by analogy that language is also applied to human conditions; essentially and ultimately it is "theomorphic". In modern philosophical and theological writing, the idea of God is treated either in orthodox, medieval-Aristotelian fashion, or else in accordance with the philosophical background (Kantian, Hegelian, existentialist or dialectical) of the various authors.

5. The Obligation to worship God alone

This article actually embodies the practical corollary of monotheism – the duty to serve God and God alone.

It not only excludes other divinities (already ruled out by the denial of their existence in art. 2) but forbids the worship of or even appeal to other powers, forces and intermediaries. The few instances in the liturgy in which angels are addressed and requested to bring our prayers before the throne of the Almighty have given rise to controversy. Thinkers like Bahya even denied the existence of intermediaries or "secondary causes".

In its simple and popular formulation the article merely states that God is the only object of prayer. It does not say anything about the nature, meaning, value or efficacy of prayer. Here again all sorts of views have been held, varying with the philosophical outlook and religious temperament of the authors concerned. The efficacy of petitionary prayer is usually taken for granted, in spite of the serious theological problems which it raises. Rabbinic tradition sees in prayer a divine *mitsvah* or commandment: God desires man to express his love of him, dependence on him and wish to commune with him in this form. In every prayer, then, there is the purest and most concentrated expression of what life as a whole, understood as the service of God, should signify. The Rabbis deduced the duty of daily prayer from the more generalized Biblical injunction "to serve him with all thine heart". "Which is the service of the heart?" they ask, and reply: "This is prayer". The order and character of prayer was regulated by the Rabbis so as to include praise, thanksgiving and petition. Both the proportion of these elements and their detailed contents varied with the individual worshipper, though for public worship a unified fixed liturgy developed. Jewish tradition insists on the value of public worship and, in fact, full liturgical proceedings are only possible in the presence of the "Congregation of Israel" which must be represented by a quorum of at least ten adult males. The Kabbalists considered prayer as the occasion of the most intense mystical meditation; in their inner life, "serving God" signified the mystical intention which turned every prayer or religious performance into a redemptive act. Later, modernist writers occasionally explained the meaning of prayer as "self-examination" and the like; in the place of the dialogue with God they put an edifying monologue.

6. Prophecy

This article is plainly meant as the methodological premiss of the validity of the actual, concrete Jewish religion. God communicates with man. Maimonides would even hold that prophecy is not a free divine *charisma* but is merely the technical term for the highest level of communion with God arrived at through the intellectual love of God. Other thinkers would distinguish between communion with God, various types of illumination and the very specific *charisma* of prophecy. According to Yehudah Halevi the capacity for prophecy is an innate hereditary characteristic of the Jewish people; his conception is almost biological, and involves the notion of a spiritual super-race. Modern liberal theologians tend to dilute the conception of prophecy to the rather vague idea of inspiration or "progressive revelation" or "working of the divine in the hearts of men". These concepts however belong to the history of modern liberal religion and to none of the great religions in their historic forms.

As the article stands it does not specify the nature and function of prophecy. It merely asserts that the words of the prophets, as handed down to us, are true. It does not even raise the question by what criteria true prophecy can be distinguished from false. This problem is treated in the Bible as well as in Talmudic and later literature.

7. The Superiority of the Prophecy of Moses

This is an intensification of the preceding article. It flows naturally from the position which the Pentateuch (the "Law") occupies in Judaism in relation to the other books of the Bible. Whereas the prophetic books are "inspired", the Pentateuch is God's very Word, literally spoken or dictated to "my servant Moses" to whom God did not speak, as to all prophets, "in a vision or a dream" but "mouth to mouth, even apparently and not in dark speeches" (*Numbers* xii, 6–8). For "the Lord spake unto Moses face to face, as a man speaketh unto his friend" (*Exodus* xxxiii, 11). On the revelation to Moses is based the authoritative and binding character of the Law. His superiority as a prophet safeguards the Law from the possibility of abrogation by claimants to greater authority.

8. The Torah is God's Revelation to Moses

This article guarantees the validity of the Law as actually known and practised at present. Jewish orthodoxy has therefore always staunchly upheld the theory of verbal inspiration in its extremest form – at least so far as the Pentateuch is concerned. "Higher Criticism" of the Pentateuch is flatly rejected and is considered a major heresy. The underlying assumption is that the whole fabric of traditional Judaism would crumble if its foundation, the notion of divine legislation to Moses, were to be exchanged for modernist ideas about historical growth and the composite nature of sacred texts. As a matter of fact Liberal and Reform Judaism once welcomed Biblical criticism for precisely that reason. They found in criticism a welcome ally in their struggle to get rid of the Law and to substitute for it a purely ethical (and so-called "prophetic") Judaism. Conservative Judaism, as distinct from Orthodoxy and Liberalism, is concerned at present with adapting itself to the climate of Biblical scholarship and with re-defining the meaning of the terms Law, Revelation, Mosaic teaching, etc., in a way that would conserve their significance and validity.

9. *The Torah is immutable*

The implications of this article are many and significant. On the surface it merely asserts the continued validity of Judaism against the claims of other religions, Christianity in particular, to have brought final and fuller revelations superseding or "fulfilling" the Jewish religion. On a deeper level the article depends on certain conceptions concerning the *Torah* as the divine *logos*. As the expression of God's eternal wisdom, *Torah* thus shares the immutability of God. A theology less indebted to a Greek evaluation of *ratio* and immutability may more easily admit the possibility of changes in the divine will and dispensation. Some mystical and Kabbalistic systems, bearing a certain resemblance to the ideas of Joachim of Fiore, allowed different manifestations of the same divine *Torah* in different world-cycles. But the "different" age *par excellence* is the Messianic *aeon* following upon the present era; consequently, the problem of the "new law" and the abrogation of the old became acute when Messianic movements claimed to have fulfilled the times. Towards the end of the Middle Ages Messianic movements were distrusted because they harboured the danger of antinomianism.

10. *God's Omniscience*

Divine omniscience is part of the complex of ideas that includes omnipotence and omnipresence; on the other hand it is a condition of the belief in a special providence and in individual reward and punishment (art. 11). Since God knows the heart and the innermost thoughts, purity of heart and holiness of thoughts are as significant as physical acts of omission or commission. On a more religious or mystical level the stress is less on God's knowledge of each individual than on the concomitant solicitude and readiness for personal communion. Thus the love of God, fear of God and practice of the presence of God become personal relationships instead of reactions to certain "attributes".

11. *Reward and Punishment*

The belief in individual reward and punishment is stated without explanatory details. The reference

is, however, clearly not to the Biblical idea of material prosperity or misfortune in this life, nor to the belief in a national, collective justice, but to the soul as the immortal part of the individual and to its fate in the hereafter. The traditional doctrine is that most souls are purged of their sins during one year of Purgatory; thereafter they are removed to Paradise. For the Kabbalists heaven and hell were too "static" as means of reward and punishment; they merely settled accounts, as it were, but did not allow for more dynamic change. They therefore accepted the belief in *gilgul* or the transmigration of souls which they regarded as a further manifestation of God's love for his creatures. Even after death God is prepared to give the sinner a fresh start and the possibility not only to expiate and repair his sins but also to acquire merits. According to most Kabbalists three times is the maximum number for *gilgul*. As in most religions, the rather lurid descriptions of hell to be found in medieval texts were understood more or less literally according to the degree of sophistication or religious temperament of the believer. Modern, nineteenth-century liberal theologians tried to explain hell and purgatory away but continued, with remarkable inconsistency, to cling to the belief in an eternal blessedness in one form or another. It need hardly be pointed out that this manifestation of modern religiosity merely bespeaks a total loss of understanding of the religious dimension of sin and guilt. Other attempts at mitigating the "crudity" of the idea of hell include its interpretation in a negative form. Hell or punishment thus means the exclusion from the positive bliss of the blessed vision.

12. *The Coming of the Messiah*

The meaning of Messianism is not explained nor is there any indication of what it is from which redemption is desired. In general it can be said that the historical, national reference of the Messianic faith has been preserved in most theological writings. Redemption, whatever else it may mean, always also means the actual, physical liberation of Israel from persecution and humiliation, its return to its ancient homeland, the restoration of the Davidic dynasty, the re-building of the Temple in Jerusalem and the recognition by all nations of Israel's election and calling. Whatever the spiritual significances attached to these hopes, they were never allowed to dissolve the concrete historical core into pure spirituality. The reality of Israel's historic consciousness and, we may add, the reality of anti-Semitism, saw to it that the spiritual or mystical "interiorizations" of Judaism never lost their touch with reality; redemption from evil and sin was always regarded as connected with the conquest of evil in the historical, that is, the political and social sphere. For some thinkers historical Messianism was a major concern; they obviously thought in terms of an historical salvation and the Kingdom of God. For others, including Maimonides, the Messianic kingdom was merely the background for the ideal contemplative life. In Lurianic Kabbalism the Messiah is no Redeemer at all in the normal sense of the word; his appearance merely signifies that Israel has achieved the great work of "restoration" and of repairing the primordial catastrophe or fall. For some of the eighteenth- and nineteenth-century Hasidim who sought communion with God almost to the point of the "annihilation of all being" and the ecstatic submergence of consciousness in the divine, historical categories were obviously irrelevant. Certain modern trends (democracy, socialism, Zionism) provided secular substitutes for the historical ideals of religious Messianism.

13. The Resurrection of the Dead

Since Pharisaic times the resurrection of the body was official doctrine. Rabbinic literature insists on it as an essential dogma. Its problematic relation to ideas of immortality and a hereafter has been discussed earlier. Here it must suffice to indicate that modernism has found this dogma to be one of the most unpalatable. Whereas orthodoxy still holds to it, the Reform Prayerbook has deleted all references to the resurrection of the body and substituted the apparently less objectionable and more "refined" expression "life eternal". Other theologians do not believe it necessary to have any hard-and-fast ideas on the subject and deem it sufficient to recognize the symbol as a confession of the value and significance of the total human personality (body-and-soul) in the divine scheme.

It is obvious that the thirteen articles omit much of what, according to our earlier account, must be regarded as essentially and fundamentally Jewish. Nobody could gain even a faint inkling of what Judaism actually is from a mere perusal of these so-called articles of faith. In fact they do not even give us the "inner" side of Judaism, its beliefs and ideas, as distinct from ritual and practice, but merely its formal pre-suppositions. For a really satisfactory and adequate account, the essence of Judaism must be made explicit from the teaching contained in the sources *and* from the meanings that can be derived from its laws, ethics and rituals. This means that no account of the beliefs of Judaism can hope to be adequate if it does not pay equal attention to the description and analysis of its "Law" and practice. This task, however, is beyond the scope of the present undertaking.

THE MODERN PERIOD

For Jewry the Middle Ages did not end until the eighteenth and nineteenth centuries. Until then they lived as social outcasts in ghettoes and under special laws. Their precarious existence, punctured by spasmodic persecution and accompanied by constant humiliation, did not permit them to notice the dawn of a new age. Their isolation was enforced from outside, but it had also been freely chosen by themselves long before ghettoes were legally established. They were a group held together by a religious tradition and by their faith in a common calling and destiny. Each local group knew of its identity with similar groups or "holy congregations" scattered all over the four corners of the earth. This cohesion and isolation produced a community that was national and international at the same time. Israel knew itself to be the chosen people, at home everywhere and nowhere, living *in* the world of nations and political states but not *of* them.

The relative integrity of this enclosed life crumbled together with the walls of the ghetto. The enlightenment and its secular human values, together with the emphasis on man as a "citizen" of his state, placed before the Jew a new chance and temptation. There was only one price to be paid for the right to human dignity, equality and emancipation: to cease to be different and to share in the cultural and civic values of society. Western Jewry took the chance, and Eastern Jewry, living under more benighted and despotic conditions, fought for it. Emancipation commended itself all the more as its ideals of equality and social justice seemed to accord so well with those universalistic, ethical aspirations of Biblical Judaism which even the most enlightened religion of reason could embrace. The ritual, irrational and particularistic elements were precisely those which the progressive temper of the age rejected anyhow. But instead of becoming the great chance of modern Judaism to reassert its vitality and adaptability in new and different circumstances, emancipation proved to be the great temptation to escape Judaism and the Jewish fate. The orthodox Rabbis opposed emancipation because they dimly sensed that anti-Semitism, pogroms and ghettoes, horrible as they were, were merely the other side of election. But modern Jewry desired neither the one nor the other.

In the more narrowly religious sphere this tendency came out clearly in the movement known as Reform Judaism. Rejecting the ritualism and particularism of orthodoxy, the reformers desired to formulate a Judaism that would be acceptable to the emancipated Jew trying to be the equal of his Gentile neighbour. They eagerly welcomed the new critical methods of historical research as these could be used as a weapon against orthodoxy to show that traditional religion, particularly the Talmud and Rabbinic law, had grown in time and was thus essentially a human creation. The new liturgy was modelled on the pattern of the German church service (organ, mixed choir, prayer in the vernacular, etc.), ritual laws which hindered free social intercourse were declared to be no longer binding, and "particularistic" or "nationalist" items such as the hope of a return to Zion were deleted from prayerbook and creed. An emasculated Judaism remained that was not much more than an exalted if rather vague sort of ethical monotheism.

Orthodoxy too reasserted itself after the first shock and, while developing a keener understanding of the problems and challenges of the new age, defended the validity and unbroken authority of the old way of life. But whereas the champions of the extreme views are in the minority, the bulk of twentieth-century Judaism, particularly in America, occupies an infinite variety of intermediary positions. Thus Reform Judaism shows signs of returning to a more positive appreciation of the *halakhah* and actually attempts to revive traditional symbols and ritual, whilst on the orthodox wing too there is a slowly growing awareness that neither all traditional ideas (e.g. that the whole Pentateuch was verbally dictated to Moses) nor all traditional rules (such as not riding a car on the Sabbath) are a *sine qua non* of a virile and authentic Jewish faith.

But perhaps the most decisive of all modern developments was Zionism. In principle Zionism is a secular movement, and in a way it duplicates on a collective, national level – no doubt inspired by the nineteenth-century nationalisms – the desire for emancipation which the reformers entertained as individuals. It may perhaps be said with some justice that Zionism was the reaction to the disappointment over the failure of social emancipation. Whereas the assimilationist believed that he was neither chosen nor different but a citizen of his country, the Zionist affirmed that the Jewish people as a whole was a nation like all the others. The reformers preached the religious mission of Israel and forgot that it was part of Israel's mission to live as God's *people*. The Zionists, on the other hand, stressed nationhood and denied that Israel was a people solely by virtue of its bond with God. There was, moreover, a group of religious Zionists who eagerly responded to the nationalist spirit but interpreted it as a Messianic chance by which Providence challenged Israel to live as a chosen people no longer in exile and dispersion but as a body politic. Present day

Israel has its orthodox extremists who ignore the ungodly, secular state and refuse their loyalty to it. To them the arrogation of the name "Israel" by a secular state is sheer blasphemy. On the other hand there is the secularist and nationalist majority, a large percentage of which still has some vague sentimental or purely social attachments to the "national" religion. There are also the religious Zionists. Like most dynamic historic movements with a profound appeal, secular Zionism has its roots in deeper layers of the soul than secularism, utility, expediency or similar rational considerations. These deeper motives may be classed as unconsciously religious, near-religious or pseudo-religious according to the observer's bias. But there seems little doubt that Zionism exhibits some, at least, of the dubious characteristics of other modern "secular religions" precisely because it refuses to relate its basic Messianic drives to the total pattern of Jewish theology (covenant, election, obedience under the law, serving through suffering, the imitation of God, etc.).

The religious situation of mid-twentieth-century Jewry is determined by two major historical events. One is the greatest "pogrom" in history – Hitler's systematic and cold-blooded extermination of about six million Jews under the eyes of a passive Christian civilization. The other is the emergence of the state of Israel amid toil, sweat and blood and in a confused tangle of justice, injustice and heroism. No Jew could fail to be touched to the quick by the existential significance which the age-old symbols of his faith had suddenly assumed – sanctification of the Name in martyrdom and the promise of a return to Zion, the depths of agony and the ingathering of the exiles, the freedom to build a society based on equality and justice and the opportunity to serve God as a chosen people in the promised "land which he has given thee". The dangers are obvious. Suffering may lead to self-righteousness and to injustice, faith in providence to arrogance, and Messianism to Chauvinism. Even religious Zionism is tempted to mistake for fulfilment what is really a trial and for accomplishment what is essentially another stage on the long road of Israel's Messianic destiny.

There seems to be a religious dimension to the sociological fact that Jewry has polarized in two centres – Israel and America. The two centres represent the two classical forms of Jewish life – the Judaism of the Diaspora and the Judaism of the nation in its homeland. Both are historical configurations which Israel has known as forms of the covenant. But instead of succeeding each other they now exist side by side in dialectical tension or – if we prefer biological metaphors – in symbiosis. Only prejudice or political dogmatism will exalt the one above the other. For the time being it seems that Judaism will re-formulate itself, as it always has done, by accepting the challenge of the historic moment and by adapting contemporary culture and thought to its unalterable essence. The essential framework and perspective of Judaism were given in the Bible. The elaboration of the detailed implications of obeying God's will and living as a holy people was provided by the Talmud together with the concomitant religious concepts. The first attempt at a philosophic clarification of the concepts involved was made by the medieval theologians whilst the Kabbalists added a mystical layer to the traditional ideas and practices of religion. The modern era suddenly burst the shell within which the Jewish people had lived, and placed it right in the midst of historic action and responsibility. The mystery of Israel appears to be complete now. Israel is the name of a state and of a minority religion, it is both *in* the world and *of* it, it is both national and international. The paradox of Judaism, its universalism and particularism, now manifests itself in a novel form. There is a Jewish state which must include Muslims, Christians and others as "Israeli" citizens, and a minority religion of Israelites which consists of loyal citizens of France, Great Britain or the United States.

What do Jews believe or what must they believe?

Does a Jew cease to be a Jew when he denies the existence of God, or the immortality of the soul, or the resurrection of the body? Must he desist from wearing a ready-made suit because it may contain a mixture of wool and linen (*Deuteronomy* xxii, 11), or abstain from riding in a bus on the Sabbath? Must he acquire an Israeli passport? Is he free to think what he likes provided he observes the traditional laws or may he adapt the law and compromise as long as he believes the central truths of God's transcendent unity and his revelation which requires of man to "do justly, love mercy and walk humbly with thy God"? How can he best become "holy even as the Lord your God is holy", or love God "with all thine heart and with all thy soul and with all thy might"? It would seem presumptuous to offer a clear-cut answer to such questions. But perhaps we do not go far wrong in suggesting that Judaism and Israel can at least be partly understood as a continuing historical process which is the result of and the response to God's charge to his servant Moses: "... for all the earth is mine. And *ye* shall be unto me a kingdom of priests and an holy nation. These are the words which thou shalt speak unto the children of Israel" (*Exodus* xix, 5–6). To which the Rabbis added the laconic comment: "These are the words – no more and no less."

2a. Christianity: the Early Church

by J. G. DAVIES

It was one of the charges levelled against the Christians of the second century that their "doctrine has but recently come to light". Christianity was a novelty, according to its pagan opponents, and therefore, so their argument ran, scarcely worthy of serious consideration in comparison with the ancient worship of the Greek and Roman gods. With a true sense of history and an accurate understanding of the origins of their faith, Christian Apologists replied that, so far from their religion having no roots in the distant past, it was in fact the fulfilment of an age-long process of preparation of which the records were contained in the Jewish Scriptures. What the Jews still hoped for, on the basis of the divine promises enshrined in the Old Testament, Christians now in large measure possessed through the realization of these promises in the Person and ministry of Jesus of Nazareth. In complete accord with this is the statement attributed to the apostle Paul, during his defence before Agrippa and Berenice at Caesarea: "I stand here to be judged for the hope of the promise made of God unto our fathers" (*Acts* xxvi, 6). Hence the primitive Christian message was: "how many soever be the promises of God, in him [Christ] is the yea" (II *Corinthians* i, 20). It is these promises, constituting the hope of Israel, that must be considered first if the nature of Christianity, at least as it is presented in the earliest written accounts, that is, in the pages of that part of the Bible known as the New Testament, is to be understood.

The theme of the Old Testament is that of God's dealings with Israel from the time when the twelve tribes were united under Moses to form a nation. This story is set within a universal context by the opening chapters of Genesis which recount God's creation of heaven and earth and of man "in his own image" (*Genesis* i, 27). Man, however, dissatisfied with his position of subjection to

God within the created order, rebelled against his Maker, and soon "all flesh had corrupted his way upon the earth" (*Genesis* vi, 12). God's method of dealing with this situation was to choose one man, Abraham, out of all the fallen mass of mankind, whose descendants were to form a nucleus of faithful people, and to be both the recipients of the divine blessing and the source of its mediation to all men.

It was these descendants who were delivered by God from bondage in Egypt, united to him in a Covenant, led into the promised land and provided with a King as the divine representative – a King who was at the same time the Messiah, which means the [Lord's] Anointed. Despite the warnings of the prophets, the Israelites did not persevere in the way of righteousness and so they were brought to the suffering of the Exile in Babylonia. Then, in penitence, hope revived and they looked forward to a restoration when the powers of evil should be overthrown, when God's Kingdom or rule should be set up, exercised either directly or through his promised Messiah, and a New Covenant should be established (*Jeremiah* xxxi, 31). Neither the events immediately succeeding the return from Babylon nor the short-lived independence of the Jews under the Maccabean house satisfied this hope, as successive foreign powers held them in submission, from the Persians in the sixth century B.C. to the Romans in the latter half of the first. But the hope did not die, and when St Luke, in the second chapter of his Gospel, referred to Simeon as a man "looking for the consolation of Israel", he was describing an attitude typical of the majority of the Jews of his day. The New Testament affirmation – and it is this that constituted it in the understanding of its first proclaimers as the Gospel or Good News – is to the effect that this hope was now in process of fulfilment through the mission of Jesus of Nazareth. Before however this interpretation by the first generation of Christians is considered, we must ask how far Jesus himself regarded his activity in this same light.

Jesus of Nazareth

"Jesus came into Galilee, preaching the gospel of God, and saying, The time is fulfilled, and the kingdom of God is at hand: repent ye, and believe in the gospel" (*Mark* i, 14–15). It is with this statement that St Mark introduces his account of the public ministry of Jesus, and while the saying is more probably to be regarded as a short summary by the evangelist of the contents of Jesus' message than as a verbatim record of his exact words, there is every reason to accept their substantial accuracy, since this is a theme that recurs constantly in the reports of Jesus' teaching. "Many shall come from the east and the west, and shall sit down . . . in the kingdom of heaven" (*Matthew* viii, 11). "There be some here of them that stand by, which shall in no wise taste of death, till they see the kingdom of God come with power" (*Mark* ix, 1). Thus the age to come is dawning and the inauguration of God's sovereign rule is imminent.

To the same effect is the teaching implicit in many of the parables. So those of the Mustard Seed and the Leaven tell of a veiled process which comes ultimately to fruition, as the ministry of Jesus is to issue in the coming of the Kingdom. Those of the Hidden Treasure and the Pearl of Great Price demand decisive action, involving the sacrifice of everything in view of the prize set before them – the impending Kingdom. Others again, like that of the Marriage Feast, relate to Israel's rejection of Jesus' proclamation of the Kingdom and the consequent summons to publicans and sinners. Inseparably connected with this are the miracles ascribed to Jesus, which can no longer be discarded, as in the hey-day of Liberal theology, as unnecessary embellishments of the simple Gospel record, rather they are to be understood as signs that the age of salvation is dawning. So Jesus declares: "If I by the finger of God cast out devils, then is the kingdom of God come upon you" (*Luke* xi, 20). His exorcisms mark the preliminary assault on the forces of evil preparatory to their final overthrow. This interpretation by Jesus himself or his works is again made plain by his reply to the question put to him by the disciples of John: "Art thou he that cometh, or look we for another?" "Go your way, and tell John what things ye have seen and heard; the blind receive their sight, the lame walk, the lepers are cleansed, and the deaf hear, the dead are raised up, the poor have good tidings preached to them" (*Luke* vii, 19, 22: cf. *Isaiah* xxxv, 5–6). Jesus thus intimates that *now* is the time of fulfilment, the miraculous healings being signs that the age of the promised Messiah is dawning. His works therefore intimate that the End is at hand, and they are consequently as much a part of his proclamation as his spoken words.

But if this be the burden of his proclamation, how did he conceive his relationship to the Kingdom whose approaching advent he was announcing? How did he interpret the nature of his mission and its connection with the realization of the hope of Israel? Was he no more than a herald, as John the Baptist before him, or was his activity an essential element in the process of fulfilment? Did he, for example, believe himself to be the Messiah, and, if so, how did he understand that office?

There can be little doubt that Jesus' choice of twelve apostles involved the claim, by symbolic action akin to prophetic symbolism, that he was to be the founder of a Messianic community which should replace the twelve tribes of the old Israel as the elect of God. There is also the further undeniable fact that he was executed as a pretender to the Messiahship (*Mark* xv, 2, 9, 26), which must have involved on his part the acknowledgement of some sort of Messianic claim. Whether or not therefore we accept as authentic Jesus' affirmative reply to the High Priest's question at his trial: "Art thou the Christ, the Son of the Blessed?" (*Mark* xiv, 61) we are bound to recognize that in some sense, still to be determined, Jesus did indeed interpret his mission in terms of the Messiah. Nevertheless, apart from his statement at his trial there is no recorded instance in the first three Gospels of Jesus making an explicit affirmation of Messiahship. When the demoniacs confess him as such, he bids them to be silent (*Mark* i, 25; iii, 11–12), and when Peter at Caesarea Philippi makes the same confession, he neither denies nor accepts its truth (*Mark* viii, 29–30). During the last fifty years it has been customary to explain this reticence in terms of the "Messianic secret", and although few would now accept this thesis in the form in which it was first propounded, many would hold that Jesus exercised this reserve because his own conception of the Messiah differed so radically from the popular expectation. There is however an alternative and more probable explanation.

The Jewish eschatological hope involved the belief that the Messiah himself would only be known and acknowledged as such when he had revealed his identity through his work of salvation. "According to Jewish thought," S. Mowinkel writes (*He that Cometh*, E. T. 1956, p. 303), "it is only then that he will become Messiah in the full sense of the term. Before that time we may say he is but *Messias designatus*, a claimant to Messianic status." If this be applied to Jesus, it means that during his ministry he is Messiah designate; only when he has accomplished his mission is he to be enthroned as Messiah. Alternatively it may be said that Jesus is only the Saviour when he has completed his work of salvation which involved not just his birth, but his death, resurrection and ascension. Here then is the probable reason for Jesus' refusal to declare himself; he could not claim full Messianic status until his work was complete. It is along similar lines that a further enigmatic designation is to be understood, that of "the Son of man".

Amongst the several passages in which this title appears, one that deserves particular notice is that in which Jesus clearly speaks of the Son of man as a being other than himself: "whosoever shall be ashamed of me ... the Son of man also shall be ashamed of him, when he cometh in the glory of his Father with the holy angels" (*Mark* viii, 38; cf. *Luke* xii, 8). Here it seems that Jesus in his earthly ministry is to be distinguished from the Son of man to come. Yet beside this statement must be set others in which the title is used by Jesus to designate himself even during his earthly ministry (*Mark* ii, 10, 28, etc.). The reconciliation of these two apparently divergent usages would seem to lie in the recognition that just as Jesus, while being Messiah designate, had yet to enter upon his Messiahship, so he had yet to become the Son of man while exercising, by anticipation, the functions appertaining to that glorified state.

The character of the decisive event, or rather process, by which he considered he would complete his mission, enter upon his Messiahship and become the glorified Son of man, is indicated by his immediate response to Peter's confession: "the Son of man must suffer many things ... be killed ... and ... rise again" (*Mark* viii, 31). That Jesus saw in his approaching Passion a divinely ordained necessity is evident from the use here of the word "must". This understanding of the divine purpose for him rests upon his own creative reinterpretation of the office of Messiah in terms of the Suffering Servant passages in the Book of *Isaiah* (xlii, 1–4; xlix, 1–6; l, 5–9; lii, 13–liii, 12). "He was despised and rejected of men ... he was wounded for our transgressions, he was bruised for our iniquities ... and the Lord hath laid on him the iniquity of us all ... when thou shalt make his soul an offering for sin. ... By his knowledge shall my righteous servant justify many: and he shall bear their iniquities. ... Behold, my servant shall deal wisely, he shall be exalted and lifted up." It is this series of statements that underlies the various predictions of the Passion (*Mark* viii, 31; ix, 12; x, 33–4). Jesus thus understands his mission as necessarily involving a vocation to suffering and to death.

He came "to minister, and to give his life a ransom for many" (*Mark* x, 45), to re-establish, therefore, the initial harmony between God and man which had been broken through sin, for this saying indicates that he thought of men as being in bondage to evil and of his own death as the means of securing their release. The ministry of Jesus then is not exhausted by his proclamation of the imminent Kingdom. This is further made plain by his sayings at the Last Supper.

"This is my blood of the covenant, which is shed for many" (*Mark* xiv, 24). These words, said in connection with the cup, have as their background both the ceremony of *Exodus* xxiv, when God brought his chosen people into covenant with him, and the prophecy of *Isaiah* xlii, 6, where it is stated that God will give the Servant "for a covenant of the people". Their primary meaning is that Jesus' death is an atoning or reconciling death and therefore a means of mediating a blessing to mankind, establishing the new and eternal communion of a humanity cleansed from sin with its God. Moreover, in the verse immediately following, in *Mark*, this saying is associated with the Kingdom. "Verily I say unto you. I will no more drink of the fruit of the vine, until that day when I drink it new in the kingdom of God" (cf. *Luke* xxii, 18). Thus the cup not only foreshadows the approaching death but heralds the joy of the Kingdom. Even under the threat of the cross Jesus is confident that the Kingdom will be inaugurated. "This can only mean that he believed his death to be a necessary step to the establishment of the Kingdom." Beyond his death, he saw his vindication through being raised from the grave, his consequent exaltation and his coming again as the glorified Son of man (*Mark* xiii, 26; xiv, 62).

There remains now one final aspect of what, without undue confidence, may be regarded as Jesus' own understanding of his task, and that is his conception of his relationship to God. While it is true, as A. J. Rawlinson points out (*The New Testament Doctrine of Christ*, 1926, p. 50), that he did not "indulge publicly in theological reflection with regard to his own Person," it is nevertheless clear that he did believe himself to stand in a unique relationship to God. Here the primary category is that of God as Father. Jesus did indeed affirm the Fatherhood of God, but it is important to notice that he is not represented as preaching publicly on this theme, but as speaking only occasionally of it within the confined circle of his closest friends and followers. The reason for this reticence lies in all probability in the fact that the Father was the supreme reality in Jesus' life. "His experience of the Father is something so profound and so moving that it will not bear to be spoken about except to those who have shown themselves to be fitted to hear" (T. W. Manson, *The Teaching of Jesus*, 1931, p. 113). So his prayer in the garden of Gethsemane, which there are no adequate grounds for doubting was audible to his disciples, reveals his absolute trust in and unquestioning obedience to the Father (*Mark* xiv, 36), whom he addresses, not in the normal fashion of an

Aramaic-speaking Jew as "*āhbi*", but as "*ăbbā*" which is the more familiar form used of one's earthly progenitor. It is only by means of a conviction of an intimate relationship of this kind that one can understand the effect that Jesus had upon certain of his contemporaries. "He taught" – and it amazed them – "as having authority, and not as the scribes" (*Mark* i, 22). Whereas the prophets spoke as the messengers of God and the scribes were content to cite tradition, Jesus spoke directly: "I say unto you." Moreover he asserted the right to supersede the Old Testament revelation in his own teaching (*Matthew* v, 21f, 27f, 33-7), to reject the accepted oral tradition (*Mark* vii, 6-9) and even to interfere with the conduct of the Temple concessions (*Mark* xi, 15f). Such a claim is scarcely intelligible except on the basis of that assurance of Sonship which the writers of the first three (Synoptic) Gospels associated with his Baptism: "Thou art my beloved Son" (*Mark* i, 11; cf. ix, 7).

In the light of these considerations, we may accept the statement of his Sonship, ascribed to Jesus in *Matthew* xi, 27 and *Luke* x, 22 as consistent with what we have seen above to be Jesus' own conception: "All things have been delivered unto me of my Father; and no one knoweth the Son, save the Father; neither doth any know the Father, save the Son, and he to whomsoever the Son willeth to reveal him." Jesus thus believed himself to stand in a unique filial relationship to God.

To sum up. Jesus regarded himself as the divine agent, as indeed the Son of God, sent to announce the fulfilment of the hope of Israel. As the Messiah designate who was to become, through death, the glorified Son of man, he proclaimed the approaching Kingdom. His own death he interpreted as the means by which the barrier of sin between God and man would be removed, since he believed that it would involve a victorious struggle over the powers of evil. Thus would be established the moral conditions in which the Rule of God could be perfected. He himself, in due course, would return for the final act of consummation (*Luke* xii, 40).

The Primitive Preaching

The preceding brief summary of Jesus' own understanding of his Person and mission will enable us to appreciate, when we turn to the beliefs of his earliest followers, that there is no essential contradiction between them; the main outlines of what Jesus believed being faithfully reproduced in the accounts of the apostolic preaching which we find in the Book of *Acts*. This preaching consists in the main of the proclamation of the facts of the death and resurrection of Jesus in an eschatological setting which gives them their significance. Thus

it is affirmed that the age of the fulfilment of the Old Testament prophecies has dawned (*Acts* ii, 16; iii, 18, 24), and that this has taken place through the ministry of Jesus, whose death was according to the "determinate counsel and foreknowledge of God" (ii, 23; iii, 13, 14). But death could not hold him and God has both raised him and exalted him (ii, 24-31; iii, 15; iv, 10), thereby making him "both Lord and Christ" (ii, 36), that is, the promised Messiah. The sign of his present power and glory is the Holy Spirit, now indwelling the Christian community (ii, 17-21, 33). The final consummation will shortly take place when the Christ, that is, Jesus, will return. Those who, on hearing this message, repent will receive forgiveness of sins and the Holy Spirit, "for to you is the promise, and to your children, and to all that are afar off" (ii, 39; iii, 19, 25-6; iv, 12).

The close parallels between this and Jesus' own message will be immediately apparent; it will also be noted that three new features have been introduced, namely, the statement that as a consequence of the resurrection and ascension Jesus has been made not only Christ but Lord, and the references to the Spirit and to the *imminent* return of Christ.

The first of these indicates an advance from the relationship of discipleship towards Jesus as Teacher to that of religious dependence upon Jesus as exalted Lord. There is however no necessary discontinuity between the two. Even during the ministry of Jesus there were some who regarded him as the Messiah, and to recognize him as such "was already to depend wholly upon him as the predestined Mediator of the religious salvation of Israel. The relation of religious dependence had already in that moment begun" (Rawlinson, *op. cit.*, p. 40). All that the resurrection and ascension did therefore was to re-establish this faith by the conviction that Jesus was exalted to the right hand of God – consequently "he is Lord of all" (*Acts* x, 36).

The second new feature is the reference to the Spirit, which is intelligible on the basis of an experience, subsequent to the mission of Jesus, whereby the primitive community was convinced that it was the recipient of divine power. This experience was interpreted quite naturally in eschatological terms – as yet another sign of the realization of the hope of Israel, in that it marked the fulfilment of Joel's prophecy (*Joel* ii, 28) that in the last days God would pour forth his Spirit upon all flesh.

The third feature, namely the speedy return of Christ, is less easy to understand, and it focuses attention upon a problem raised by the Gospel records which represent Jesus as both predicting his imminent return (*Matthew* xvi, 28; *Mark* xiii, 26) and refraining from giving any precise indication of when it would take place (*Mark* viii, 38; *Luke* xii, 40; xvii, 24). A possible solution of this problem may be that Jesus did indeed foretell his return, while disclaiming knowledge of its date, and that those passages which intimate the contrary are due to a reading back of a belief which first arose in the apostolic age. If this be correct, we must then seek an explanation of how such a belief could have come into being if Jesus himself had not given it countenance. There are four main factors which could have operated to transform a prophecy of a return into a prophecy of an *immediate* return. These are (i) the certainty, characteristic of apocalyptic literature, that what is predicted is close at hand: "the time will come and will not tarry" (*Apocalypse of Baruch*, xx, 6); "my salvation has truly drawn nigh, and it is no longer distant as formerly" (*ibid.* xxiii, 7; cf. *Revelation* i, 1); (ii) the influence of Old Testament prophecy with its eager expectancy; (iii) the rapid progress of the Gospel, which would suggest a speedy preparation of mankind for the Second Coming; (iv) the outbreak of persecution, which would lead to a quickened faith in the divine vindication, and in the revelation of Christ in glory to judge and punish the persecutors.

The Contribution of St Paul

Those who proclaimed the apostolic teaching in the first instance were Jews, but whether by force of circumstance or, depending upon one's point of view, divine guidance, they were soon unable to confine their preaching to their fellow countrymen. Yet the more Gentiles who heard and responded to their message, the greater was the danger that the Gospel would be paganized rather than the Hellenistic mind converted to Christianity. To prevent this it was necessary to preserve the Hebraic inheritance, but this could only be assured by the retention of the Old Testament, and this in turn could not be accepted by the majority of Gentile converts until two questions had been answered: (1) What was the purpose and meaning of the Law enshrined in the Old Testament? (2) What was the relation of Israel to the Christian community? These same two questions were the very ones that St Paul himself felt compelled to face as a consequence of his conversion to Christianity; by his answers he enabled not only Gentile Christians to accept the Old Testament as the basis of their Christian faith but also the Church to free itself from the narrow trammels of Judaism.

Paul of Tarsus, "a Hebrew of Hebrews", according to his own testimony, "as touching the law, a Pharisee . . . as touching the righteousness which is in the law, found blameless" (*Philippians* iii, 5, 6), was initially a persecutor of the Christians. To him their belief that the Messiah

had come to such folk – to people who were partly on the fringe of those who observed the Law and partly outside them altogether, was blasphemous. If God had given his Law as a revelation of truth, the Christians must be wrong. Their claim seemed to St Paul to involve an insult to God and subversion of the Law which he had himself bestowed. After his conversion, St Paul had perforce to evaluate the Law in a new light. He did so, not by denying that it was holy (*Romans* vii, 12), but by asserting that it was not an end in itself. Rather it was an interim dispensation which was to reveal sin in its true colours and convince men of their helplessness (*ibid.* vii, 13), thus serving as a preparatory discipline to make them ready for the coming of the Saviour. Its function therefore was to act as a "tutor to bring us unto Christ" (*Galatians* iii, 24). Having served its purpose, it was no longer authoritative and was to be regarded as occupying only a temporary place in the religious history of Israel.

It is at this point that we come to St Paul's answer to the second question that faced him, the relationship of God's chosen people, Israel, to the Christian community. In effect his reply was that the Church is the true Israel, that the Jews, who had failed to understand that they had been chosen by God not primarily for the enjoyment of privilege, but for the rendering of service, had been replaced, according to God's sovereign will, by the "righteous remnant", the New Israel, which is the Christian Church (*Romans* ix–xi). So the Christian community, composed of Jew and Gentile alike (*Galatians* iii, 28), may appropriate the Jewish hope. It is to the Church that the Jewish Scriptures belong by right (II *Corinthians* iii, 12–17), since its members are "Abraham's seed, heirs according to promise" (*Galatians* iii, 29). So the divine purpose, which ran through all the history of Israel from the call of Abraham onwards, has entered upon the final stages of its fulfilment. Christians are therefore those upon whom "the ends of the ages are come" (I *Corinthians* x, 11). They have been delivered "out of the power of darkness, and translated . . . into the kingdom of the Son" (*Colossians* i, 13). This, according to St Paul, is the outcome of the mission of Jesus Christ whose Gospel he had been commissioned to preach.

If however the contribution of St Paul to Christian belief is not to be misunderstood, it must be recognized that his proclamation of the Gospel, which is in all essentials identical with that of his contemporaries, was prior to the letters in which his beliefs have been preserved. These letters are attempts to answer questions, both practical and intellectual, such as the two considered above, which that proclamation had elicited. St Paul was neither a systematic theologian nor a barren intellectual, superimposing layer after layer of speculation upon a hypothetical simple Gospel; he was a missionary, concerned with the care of the churches, and, in what he had to say, drawing upon his own immediate experience of God's decisive action in Christ.

Paramount in that experience was a sense that it was God who had taken the initiative; the divine love thereby revealed never ceased to be an object of wonder to St Paul: "God commendeth his own love toward us, in that, while we were yet sinners, Christ died for us" (*Romans* v, 8). It is God's grace – his gracious, merciful act in Christ stemming not from sinful man's supposed merits but from the divine redeeming love itself, that is the ground of the Christian message. What God has done for man – and St Paul's concern that his converts should understand this needs no apology – was expressed by him in a variety of ways, but chiefly by the use of three terms which are the keywords of his theology – redemption, justification, and reconciliation.

Redemption means emancipation – the liberation of those that are enslaved. It was the term used in the Old Testament of the divine act of deliverance whereby Israel was set free from subjection to her Egyptian masters (*Deuteronomy* vii, 8). St Paul uses it to express his belief that through Christ the people of God have been delivered from their bondage to sin, to demonic powers and to the Law. Justification means acquittal – the passing of a verdict of not guilty. This, despite the fact that man, through his sinfulness, is indeed guilty, is not just a legal fiction, since justification only becomes effective insofar as man responds in faith to the divine act – and by "faith" St Paul means, not intellectual assent, but total self-committal or, alternatively, the humble acceptance of what God has himself accomplished. Reconciliation or Atonement means the bringing together of those who have been separated. It involves therefore the removal not only of past guilt but also of estrangement and misunderstanding. Always conscious of the divine initiative, St Paul is emphatic that this reconciliation is effected by God: it is not God who is reconciled, but God who is the reconciler, reconciling man to himself. So the believer has a new standing before him, which St Paul describes by the word "adoption". Redeemed, justified, reconciled, man is elevated from the status of slave to that of son, and becomes "an heir through God" (*Galatians* iv, 7) of the promised salvation.

So great is the difference between the Christian's present and former status, that St Paul can interpret God's saving act as one of new creation. "The old things are passed away; behold, they are become new" (II *Corinthians* v, 17). This transference from the old condition into the new corresponds to and is the outcome of Christ's own passage from death to life through his crucifixion and resurrection. St Paul indeed sees the cross as a necessary part of the divine plan. The old condition is one of sin, resulting both in spiritual death and in its outward expression, physical death (*Romans* vi, 23). Christ's death was due to sin – but not his own; God made his sinless Son "to be sin on our behalf" (II *Corinthians* v, 21), and this involved the outward expression of sin, physical death. Yet God's purpose was that his death should lead to life; "the death that he died, he died unto sin once: but the life that he liveth, he liveth unto God" (*Romans* vi, 10). So, freed from the world's sin by his crucifixion, he was transferred into the new condition of the Resurrection life, and that life out of death is now available for all men. The individual therefore, incorporated in Christ, is a new creature (II *Corinthians* v, 17), who is being progressively refashioned "until Christ be formed in" him (*Galatians* iv, 19). But this is no doctrine of solitary salvation. To be "in Christ" is, for St Paul, to participate in the solidarity of all Christians with one another and with their Lord: it is to be a member of the Church which is the Body of Christ (I *Corinthians* xii, 12), Christ himself being the Head. But the Church, in St Paul's thought, is inseparable from the Holy Spirit: "for in one Spirit were we all baptized into one body" (I *Corinthians* xii, 13).

St Paul, like his believing contemporaries, regarded the mission of the Spirit to the Church as the direct consequence of Christ's own mission. "When the fulness of the time came, God sent forth his Son . . . that we might receive the adoption of sons. And because ye are sons, God sent forth the Spirit of his Son into our hearts, crying, Abba, Father" (*Galatians* iv, 4–6). But close though the relationship between the Son and the Spirit is – exemplified by the phrase in this quotation "the Spirit of his Son"– they are not to be identified. The Spirit is not Christ nor is he conceived of as an impersonal energy but as a distinct personal being (cf. *Romans* viii, 26; I *Corinthians* ii, 11; xii, 11) whose activity complements that of Christ. The Spirit is the creative source of the new life, Christ its content. This means that the goal of the Christian life is conformity to the image of Christ, the forming in the believer of Christ, and this is the effect of the operation of the Holy Spirit. St Paul's advance upon his predecessors in this respect does not lie in any elaboration of doctrine, but in his belief that the Spirit is not primarily to be connected with the extraordinary but with the ordinary daily life of the Christian. To St Paul, the whole of Christian experience is within the sphere of his activity. Hence the Spirit is the ground of prayer (*Romans* viii, 26); he is the source of all spiritual gifts (I *Corinthians* xii, 11) which are not endowments for individual self-expression but the means of fostering the moral and spiritual health of the Body. It is the Spirit who guides and leads Christians, he himself being supplied to them by Christ (*Galatians* iii, 5). He is indeed the earnest of their final redemption (II *Corinthians* i, 22; v, 5), the pledge or guarantee that the work of salvation, already begun, will be carried through to its consummation. His indwelling is the assurance of final resurrection (*Romans* viii, 11).

So for St Paul there is no radical discontinuity between the present and the future; both are interpreted eschatologically by him, that is, with reference to the final consummation of all things; and his teaching concerning the "End" is central to his thought and not a mere appendage to it. His expectation can be briefly summarized as including belief in an imminent Second Coming, a final judgment, a resurrection of the righteous dead (possibly of all the dead), the transformation of those alive, and the final establishment of God's Kingdom when God will be all in all. Of these elements only his belief in resurrection requires further examination.

The Christianity to which St Paul was converted did not of itself require any other understanding of resurrection than that which he would already profess as a Pharisee. Here we must distinguish between popular Pharisaic ideas and those of the more spiritually minded. The latter, unlike the Greeks, refused to distinguish between soul and body – to them they are but two names for the same being seen from different points of view: the body is the person considered from the outside, the soul the same person considered from the inside. Consequently, the Pharisees believed in the embodied nature of the resurrection life; but rejecting any crass notion of physical reanimation, they understood this to involve transformation or transfiguration. St Paul propounds the same belief in I *Corinthians* xv. He begins his exposition with an analogy. A seed is placed in the ground where it ceases to be a seed and grows into a plant. The seed and the plant are in a sense identical, but between the two lies the critical point when the seed dies and is transformed into the growing plant. The link between them, according to St Paul, is the sovereign power of God: "He giveth it a body even as it pleased him." So, to apply the analogy, while the body of the believer is changed from flesh, which by its very nature decays, into glory, the personality, which has been displayed by the fleshly body, will by no means disappear. "It is sown a natural body; it is raised a spiritual body."

What, finally, of St Paul's conception of Christ? The apostle begins, as in all his thinking, with his experience of the divine initiative. "God was in Christ reconciling the world unto himself" (II *Corinthians* v, 19). To Christ therefore are to be ascribed the functions and dignities of godhead. He is indeed the "Lord", and Old Testament passages originally referring to Yahweh can be applied to him (I *Corinthians* i, 31; II *Thessalonians* i, 9). Moreover Christ is the Son of God. Whereas in some passages this title is used Messianically (e.g. *Romans* i, 4), in many it denotes a relationship which may be said to involve a community of nature between the Father and the Son (*Romans* viii, 3: *Colossians* i, 13). It was indeed St Paul's belief that Christ's redeeming work was of such a character that only a unity of life and being with the life and being of God could properly qualify him for it. So while to the original disciples the astounding paradox was that Jesus whose companion they had been and who died in shame was now exalted to the right hand of God, to St Paul the paradox was rather that the Exalted One, proved by the resurrection to be the Son of God, should have taken flesh and died on Calvary. He who was "in the form of God," that is, divine by nature, "counted it not a prize to be on an equality with God, but emptied himself, taking the form of a servant", that is, human nature, and "humbled himself, becoming obedient even unto death, yea, the death of the cross" (*Philippians* ii, 6–8). "Though he was rich, yet for your sakes he became poor" (II *Corinthians* viii, 9). Christ therefore was a pre-existent being; but he was not an angel; subordinate though he was to the Father (I *Corinthians* xi, 3), he was the ground and agent of creation; he who is "the image of the invisible God" created all "things visible and things invisible" (*Colossians* i, 15–16).

The passage just cited provides a valuable clue to the principal Pauline method of interpreting the relationship of God and his Christ, for the phrase "image of God" is used in the Greek Old Testament of the Divine Wisdom (*Wisdom* vii, 26); St Paul applies to Christ a description of one of the intermediaries which had been introduced in later Hebrew thought between the transcendent God and the world of his making. Moreover in one passage St Paul explicitly states that Christ is the Wisdom of God (I *Corinthians* i, 24, 30), and Wisdom in the Old Testament was both pre-existent (*Proverbs* viii, 23; *Ecclesiasticus* xxiv, 9) and the artificer of creation (*Proverbs* viii, 30; *Wisdom* ix, 2). A second intermediary was the divine Word who was equally creative (*Psalms* xxxiii, 6; *Wisdom* ix, 1), and while St Paul does not actually affirm an identity with Christ, it is probably implied in his statement that "in him all things consist" (*Colossians* i, 17), which would seem to be an echo of "by his word all things consist" (*Ecclesiasticus* xliii, 26). St Paul further identifies Christ with the power of God (I *Corinthians* i, 24), and in several passages seems to suggest that he is also the Glory of God – the *Shekhinah*, or vehicle of the divine presence. Hence while the apostle nowhere actually calls Christ God he can say that "in him dwelleth all the fulness of the Godhead bodily" (*Colossians* ii, 9).

The Epistle to the Hebrews

The author of the Epistle to the Hebrews shares St Paul's beliefs and expresses them in almost identical fashion. Christ is the pre-existent Son of God, and, in terms of Wisdom terminology, he is "the effulgence of his glory (*Wisdom* vii, 25–6) and the impress of his substance". He was the agent of creation and now upholds all things (*Hebrews* i, 2–3). Yet he who was superior to the angels was made a "little lower" than they (ii, 9) when he was "made like unto his brethren" (ii, 17), that is, when he became a partaker of flesh and blood (ii, 14), so identifying himself with those whom he had come to deliver from their sins. Christ, in his incarnate state, was thus God and man and as such the one Mediator.

The exposition of these beliefs is presented by the author as the prelude to the main part of his treatise which is concerned with affirming the finality of the Christian revelation given "at the end of the ages" (ix, 26). Since to him the heart of religion is worship, he seeks to demonstrate the incompleteness of the Jewish system and its fulfilment through Christ. The old sacrifices for sin, involving the offering of an unblemished life, were intended to remove defilement and so enable man to draw near to God and enter into communion with him: but in three ways these ordinances of the Old Covenant were imperfect. First, the victims were unblemished because they were incapable of sin, whereas only one who has conquered temptation could be the true sacrificial victim. Secondly, the animals were sacrificed unwillingly, whereas what was required was a free and perfect obedience to God in death. Thirdly, the animal sacrifices were on a subhuman level, whereas the life offered needed to be that of one who had overcome sin in man's own nature. In Christ we see the perfect victim and God-appointed priest in one and the same person. He was a man "that hath been in all points tempted like as we are, yet without sin" (iv, 15). He was obedient to the Father's will even unto death, which was thus the offering of a deliberately dedicated and consecrated will. Through his resurrection and ascen-

sion he has entered as our forerunner (vi, 20) into the divine presence, and as the great High Priest he now appears "before the face of God for us" (ix, 24), "wherefore also he is able to save to the uttermost them that draw near unto God through him, seeing he ever liveth to make intercession for them" (vii, 25).

It was in this way that the author accomplished for the Law as a system of sacrifice what St Paul had done for it as a system of commands: he vindicated its place in the Old Testament as a foreshadowing of that which was to come and declared its supersession through Christ.

The Fourth Gospel

In many respects the Fourth Gospel may be said to represent the summit of New Testament Christianity, but the exposition of its author's beliefs is rendered difficult by his consistent practice of making statements that intentionally have a double and sometimes a triple significance. This may be illustrated from the Prologue to the Gospel, which also contains the heart of the author's beliefs.

In the Prologue (i, 1–18) the writer speaks of the eternal Word of God who has become flesh. Two questions arise. What does he mean by the "Word"? At what point does he turn from the Word in his pre-incarnate state to the Word in his incarnate state? By "Word" the evangelist understands in the first instance the Old Testament "Word of God". With this meaning in view, he informs us that this Word existed substantially before the world and was the creative agent of all things. Manifested in the world as life and as the light of revelation, it was not recognized by mankind. Despite its mission to Israel through the prophets, it was accepted only by a minority who became thereby sons of God, until finally it was focused in an individual when "the Word became flesh". This is an intelligible statement against a Judaistic background, but further examination shows that it is not exhaustive, since a comparison with the Wisdom literature reveals that the "Word" of these verses possesses many features of Wisdom, and further a comparison with the writings of the Alexandrian Jew, Philo, shows that it is closely parallel with his conception of the "Word" which he had developed independently on the basis of the same Wisdom concept.

"Word" to Philo is not just the uttered Word of God but the plan or purpose of the universe, conceived as both transcendent and immanent. Thus the Prologue may bear a second meaning. The original principle of creation was immanent in the world and recognized by some, who thereby became children of God, generated by the creative divine will. But it was not accepted by all and so there took place what C. H. Dodd (*Interpretation of the Fourth Gospel*, p. 282) has called "the final concentration of the whole creative and revealing thought of God, which is also the meaning of the universe, in an individual who is what humanity was designed to be in the divine purpose."

According to both these superimposed layers of meaning, the evangelist speaks of the Word in his pre-incarnate state in vv. 1–13, and only in v. 14 refers to the Incarnation. But this again is not the complete story. It is also feasible to understand vv. 4ff as referring to the incarnate state, thus giving the meaning that the Word of life, which is the revelation of God, was not comprehended by men; indeed even his own people, the Jews, rejected him (v. 10), but a few received him and to them he gave the right to be children of God; in short, "the Word became flesh." The evangelist's consistent use of *double entendre* prevents an either/or solution of this problem and instead points the way to a synthesis which relates the Prologue to the Gospel as a whole. These verses are at the same time an account both of the relations of the Word with the world and of the ministry of Jesus Christ who reproduces those relations. So "the Prologue is an account of the life of Jesus under the form of a description of the eternal Logos [or Word], in its relation with the world and with man, and the rest of the Gospel an account of the Logos under the form of a record of the life of Jesus" (Dodd, *op. cit.*, p. 285). Hence Christ, the eternally pre-existent Word who became man, is God (*John* i, 1). He is the only-begotten, the unique Son of the Father with whom he enjoys the most intimate communion (i, 18).

The relation of the Father and the Son is then an eternal relation, not established in time (xvii, 10). Jesus does not stand within the temporal series of great men, such as Abraham; his is a different mode of being (viii, 58). He and the Father are one (x, 30); they mutually indwell each other (x, 38). All his authority derives from the Father. Because of this unbroken filial unity the knowledge he has, the power he exercises, the words he utters – these are all given him by the Father. So the earthly life of Jesus is the medium through which the Father is revealed: "he that hath seen me hath seen the Father" (xiv, 9).

Intimately associated with the Father and the Son is the Paraclete or Holy Spirit. Since "God is Spirit" (iv, 24), a living, powerful and life-giving reality, and since the Paraclete is also termed "Spirit of Truth", he must also be regarded as divine. In fact he came forth from the Father (xv, 26), his mission succeeding that of the Son (xvi, 7), and his task is to bear witness to Christ (xv, 26).

As the Spirit of Truth he is the guide to Christ (xvi, 13–15) who is the Truth (xiv, 6). He therefore glorifies Christ by revealing him to the believer as the only Way by which he can come to the Father, and by leading him along the way he initiates him into the Truth. So according to the Fourth Gospel, Christianity is a revelation made once and for all and ever renewing itself; the content of that revelation is the Incarnate Word, the agent of its renewal is the Spirit.

The purpose of the Incarnation was then in the first instance revelation – the giving of light – revelation of God and also of man as he should be according to the divine plan. Secondly, it was communication of life, eternal life, the life of the age to come (iii, 16). But in order that sinful man might respond to this the barrier of sin had to be removed: "God sent not the Son into the world to judge the world; but that the world should be saved through him" (iii, 17). Christ was therefore "the Lamb of God, which taketh away the sin of the world" (i, 29), thus bringing freedom to those in the bondage of sin (viii, 34–6) and voluntarily laying down his life that he might draw all men unto himself (xii, 32). Yet man is unlike God, for "that which is born of the flesh is flesh; and that which is born of the Spirit is spirit" (iii, 6). Consequently "except a man be born anew, he cannot see the kingdom of God" (iii, 3). This regeneration or transformation can only take place through the mediation of new life, and this in turn depends upon the knowledge of God through his Son. But this saving knowledge is not just an intellectual activity; to "know the Lord" is, according to the Old Testament, to trust in him, to serve him, to enter into harmony with his eternal will and purpose. So what St John calls knowledge is virtually identical with what St Paul calls faith, both implying a relationship of intimate unity. This unity is a fellowship of love (xvii, 26) and not something to be experienced in isolation – the flight of the alone to the Alone – but within the Church, the unity of which rests upon the unity of the godhead (xvii, 22) – an organic unity apart from which the individual is lifeless (xv, 1–6).

The beliefs formulated in the Fourth Gospel are the most highly developed in the New Testament, and yet, "behind all the theological interpretation we can discern the outline of the apostolic preaching, and beneath the whole structure of faith we can trace the foundation of the evangelic history of Jesus of Nazareth" (W. F. Howard, *Christianity according to St John*, 1943, p. 19). Nevertheless there is an unmistakable change of atmosphere between the first three Gospels and St John, and in particular, while the differences between them are often over-exaggerated, in the Fourth Gospel, while it is no less eschatological than its predecessors, the imminence of the end has ceased to be emphasized. St John in fact is concerned "with the age of the Church, the interval which lies between the adumbration of the end in Jesus and the end itself" (C. K. Barrett, *The Gospel according to St John*, 1955, p. 57). This is in part the explanation of his individual interpretation of Christian beliefs, beliefs which nevertheless in their main features were also the beliefs of those who had gone before him in the faith.

THE PERIOD OF THE FATHERS

The development of Christian belief in the Patristic period, which it is now our concern to trace in outline, involved "the elucidation of its unique subject matter in the light of its contemporary setting". This was the result of the interaction of elements both fixed and flexible. Amongst the latter must be included the change from the Hebrew technique of pictorial thinking to the more precise thought-forms of Greek metaphysics – a change which involved no radical alteration but rather the transposition of Christianity into a new key, traces of which are already discernible within the New Testament itself. Further there was the quest for exact terminology, for the invention of, and general agreement upon, technical terms for the use of Christian theology. Finally we shall have to consider the not insignificant differences of temperament, capabilities and approach of the individual theologians who did so much to clarify the formulation of Christian belief.

Amongst the fixed elements are to be found the practice of prayer and worship and the rule of faith, for if the forms of worship became more complex and the quasi-creedal formulae more stylized, their content remained much the same. There is also the acceptance of certain books as authoritative expressions of the Christian faith, a progressive acceptance which finally issued in the formation of a New Testament "canon" to be set beside that of the Old.

The Canon of Scripture

The use of the term "New Testament" hitherto has, of course, been an anachronism. The authors, whose beliefs we have been considering in the first part of this study, were not aware that they were writing Holy Scripture. But since their formulation of belief was accepted as authoritative by their successors, and therefore considerably influenced later development, it will be necessary to investigate the process by which these works were included in a sacred "canon".

The Bible of the early Church was the Old Testament in its Greek form, which consisted of what is now the Protestant Old Testament together with the Apocrypha. This, it was believed, was "God's book, the record of his ordering of history in preparation for his own coming to accomplish his purpose of salvation"– the key therefore to God's appearance on earth which had now taken place. It was the custom of the Church to read, during the course of worship, both from this book and from those Christian writings of which either the originals or copies were possessed (*Colossians* iv, 16). This led to the inference that the latter were in some sense as authoritative as the former, and so to the formation of a body of Christian Scriptures to be added to the body of Jewish Scriptures. Each local church had its collection, including some or all of the Epistles of St Paul (II *Peter* iii, 15–16) and, in course of time, the four Gospels. But the question inevitably arose, what should we include in our reading list? The answer would seem to have been determined by a combination of three main factors. First, whether or not the writing was deemed to have been by an apostle or by a close associate of an apostle. Secondly, whether or not it was accepted by the Church at large. Thirdly, whether or not its contents were generally edifying. So lists or "canons" were drawn up, the earliest known being that of the heretic Marcion, *c.* A.D. 150, to be followed shortly, *c.* 170, by the Muratorian Canon, which, though mutilated, gives the major portion of the books accepted at that date in Rome. There was considerable agreement on the main contents of these lists, but there were differences of detail from centre to centre and also between East and West; the East, for instance, long hesitated to accept the Book of Revelation and the West the Epistle to the Hebrews.

In the first decades of the fourth century Eusebius of Caesarea divided the New Testament writings into three classes: (i) acknowledged books; (ii) disputed; (iii) spurious. The combination of the first two produced the twenty-seven books of the New Testament as it is known today, and this combination appears in the *Festal Letter* of St Athanasius for the year 367, which secured the approval of St Jerome and St Augustine and was endorsed by synods at Hippo (393) and Carthage (397 and 419).

The reason for the inclusion in the New Testament canon of these twenty-seven books and no others is thus seen to lie in the historical process which defined it. But the final closure of the list does not mean that inspiration ceased with these works or that they were regarded as more inspired than writings of later days. Since Christianity is an historical religion, since its faith is founded upon the historic redemption which God wrought at a definite

PLATE 5. The Birth of Jesus: mosaic, twelfth century. (*Church of La Martorana, Palermo*)

PLATE 6. The Baptism of Jesus: mosaic in the dome, fifth century. (*Baptistry of the Orthodox, Ravenna*)

Photo: *Alinari*

PLATE 7. The Crucifixion: page from the Syriac Gospels of Rabula, sixth century.
(*Biblioteca Laurenziana, Florence*)

Photo: *Alinari*

PLATE 8. The Resurrection: mosaic, eleventh century. (*Church of the Convent, Daphne*)

Photo: *Alinari*

PLATE 9. The Last Judgment: mosaic, twelfth century. (*Cathedral, Torcello*)

Photo: Mella

PLATE 10. Christian Love Feast (*Agape*): sculptured relief behind the pulpit, ninth century. (*S. Ambrogio, Milan*)

PLATE 11. Old Testament types of the Eucharist (Abel, Melchizedek, Abraham and Isaac): mosaic, sixth century. (*S. Apollinare in Classe, Ravenna*)

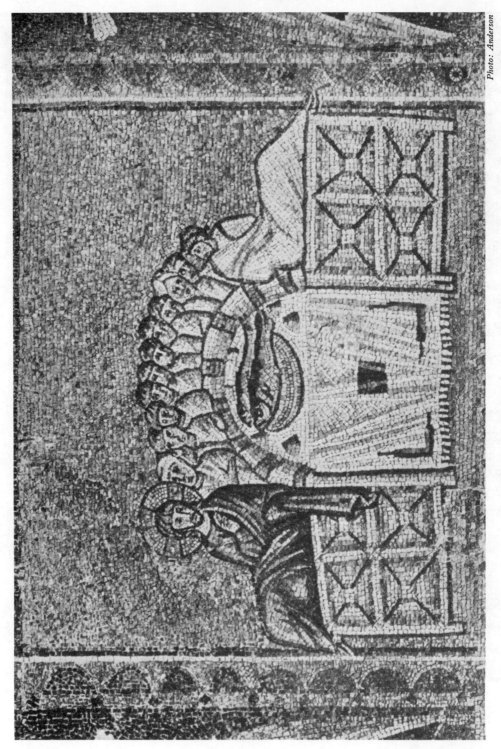

PLATE 12. The Last Supper: mosaic, sixth century. (S. Apollinare Nuovo, Ravenna)

time and place, the testimony to the historical reality of those events in which the redemption was accomplished is of basic importance. These writings are the primary witness to and interpretation of those events, and upon them all later re-writings and re-interpretations depend.

Even before the completion of the process that we have been examining the *idea* of a canon was accepted and the apostolic writings were regarded as authoritative for doctrine. It was this attitude that led to the defining of the canon, not the closure of the canon that generated this attitude. Consequently, in outlining Christian belief from the second century onwards the primacy of Scripture, that is, of Old Testament and apostolic writings, must be recognized. Christian teachers sought neither to replace those data nor merely to reproduce them photographically but to understand them, to interpret them and to draw out their implications. This quest for clarification centred, first of all, in the doctrine of the Trinity and only when this had received satisfactory expression in the latter half of the fourth century did interest shift to the doctrine of the Person of Christ which, in turn, reached more precise definition at the Council of Chalcedon in 451.

Belief in the Trinity

Into the relationship between Father, Son and Spirit the immediate successors of the apostles were not concerned to inquire. Beyond either directly affirming the divinity of the Son (e.g. Ignatius, *Ephesians* xviii 2; Justin Martyr, *Dialogue* 63; Irenaeus, *Heresies* iii, 6, 2), or indirectly implying the divinity of the Spirit, they did not attempt to proceed. Even when the proble m did present itself, they were content to use the Old Testament term inology already pressed into service by the New Testament writers. Typical of their statements in this respect is Justin Martyr's compendious ascription († 163–7) to the Son of the titles of almost every intermediary between God and man mentioned in the Old Testament. "God begat in the beginning before all creatures a certain rational power from himself, who is called by the Holy Spirit now the Glory of the Lord, now the Son, again Wisdom, again an Angel, and then Lord and Word; and on another occasion he calls himself Captain when he appeared in human form to Joshua the son of Nun. For he can be called by all those names, since he ministers to the Father's will, and since he was begotten of the Father by an act of will" (*Dialogue* 61).

In similar Biblical vein, St Irenaeus († *c.* 200) in opposition to the Gnostics who reduced the Son and the Spirit to mere emanations from God, refers to them as the "two hands of God" (*Heresies* iv, 20, 1), identifying the latter with Wisdom and the former with the Word. Of all these titles, however, it was that of the Word which received the most emphasis by the second-century writers. Their statements on this subject fall into three main groups. First, there are those in which the Word is regarded as the interpretative revelation of God. So Justin Martyr says that "the power sent from the Father" is called "the Word because he brings messages from the Father to men" (*Dialogue* 128). Secondly, there are those in which the Word is regarded as the principle of rationality; so the same author says: "He is the Word of whom every race of men were partakers; and those who lived with the Word (i.e. rationally) are Christians, even though they have been thought atheists" (*Apology* I, xlvi). Thirdly, there are those in which the Word is regarded as the active expression of the Father's will. So Hippolytus († 236) says that the Word "was the cause of all things" because he bore in himself the will of his Progenitor (*Refutation* x, 33, 2).

Valuable though this conception was, especially as a weapon in the hands of the apologists who strove to make Christianity intelligible to the Hellenic mind, it was not destined to prevail as a method of interpretation because it tended not only to obscure the personal element in the relations within the godhead, but also to subordinate the Son to the Father. This view arose from the two principal meanings of "Word" that we have already defined in examining the Prologue to the Fourth Gospel: it could mean either the immanent Word or the Word expressed. This led certain Christian thinkers to posit two stages in the Word's existence corresponding to these two senses of the term. From eternity he was regarded as indwelling the Father, as reason inhabits the mind; in the act of creation, of which he was the agent, he issued forth, as thought does when it is expressed in speech (Tertullian, *Against Praxeas* 5). This, in effect, was to make the Son an impersonal function of the Father.

This "subordinationism" persisted for a long period, albeit, owing to the great Alexandrian scholar Origen († 255), its character was changed. Origen sought to distinguish between creation and derivation. The Son is not a creature, but nevertheless he derives his being from the Father who is the fount of deity. Unfortunately as the terminology at his disposal was inadequate for his purpose, Origen failed to make his distinction clear, and so became the unwitting father of the later Arian heresy which carried the idea of subordination to the length of seeming to teach polytheism.

Side by side with speculation concerning the Word, other writers were advancing their tentative conclusions, and two such movements of thought found expression at the end of the second century and in the first decades of the third, namely Adoptionism and Modalism.

By this period the Church at large had accepted, on the basis of the rule of faith, the practice of prayer and worship, and the apostolic writings, three tenets: (i) God is one; (ii) Jesus is the Son of God and is to be worshipped; (iii) the Son is not identical with the Father. The "Adoptionists", whose leader, a certain leather worker named Theodotus, came to Rome in about 190, relinquished the second of these articles of belief in order to establish the first and third. So they taught that Jesus was a mere man, endowed with divine power at his Baptism and exalted to God's right hand because of his surpassing excellence. The "Modalists", on the other hand, whose principal leader, a cleric named Sabellius, reached the capital in about 215, relinquished the third point in order to establish the first two. So they taught that Father and Son are but two designations for one and the same person. The godhead is a monad which manifests itself in three different modes: in creation as Father; in redemption as Son; in sanctification as Spirit. God is thus one Person with three disguises; in other words, their teaching was essentially unitarian.

Adoptionism was never a great danger to the Church for it too plainly denied the divinity of Christ. Modalism, too, by identifying Father and Son, made nonsense of the intimate communion between Christ and the Father which is so predominant a feature of the Gospel records, and it involved the belief that God himself had been responsible for an unnecessary fiction in revealing himself under different names which corresponded to no eternal realities. But its strong emphasis on the oneness of God was not without its attraction and it called forth in answer Tertullian's *Against Praxeas* (c. 213) in which the great North African writer laid the foundations of the Western formulation of Trinitarian belief.

Tertullian's exposition is concerned with three matters: first, an examination of the Scriptural record to demonstrate that the Son is distinct from the Father: second, a reasoned argument from analogy to show that unity does not of necessity exclude plurality: third, a careful statement of the relationship of Father, Son and Spirit to safeguard both their unity and their plurality. He sums up his teaching on this last point in these words: "They are all of them one, namely by unity of substance, while nonetheless is guarded the mystery of that interior organization which disposes the unity into trinity, setting forth Father and Son and Spirit as three – three however not in quality but in sequence (*non statu sed gradu*), not in substance but in aspect (*non substantia sed forma*), not

in power but in its manifestation (*non potestate sed specie*), yet of one substance and one quality and one power, seeing it is one God from whom these sequences and aspects and manifestations are reckoned out in the name of the Father and the Son and the Holy Spirit" (*Against Praxeas*, c. 2). These three, as he states elsewhere, are persons, that is, beings conscious of themselves. Since therefore by "substance" he means "an existent thing", Tertullian holds that the godhead is one substance or object and three Persons or subjects. The one is compatible with the other, the unity with trinity, because there is a unity of origin and a unity of substance. The Son is "from the Father's substance" (*de substantia Patris*) and the Spirit is "from the Father through the Son" (c. 4). But these relations of origin do not imply any separation, since the Son came forth from the Father as a beam from the sun or a plant from the seed (c. 22), and in this unity the Holy Spirit participates. Hence Tertullian's formula: "I always maintain one substance in three who cohere" (*unam substantiam in tribus cohaerentibus*, c. 12). This is his expression of the "economy" or interior organization of the godhead. It was this formulation that was eventually accepted by the Western Church as a correct and intelligible expression of the Christian experience of the godhead. But before this could take place the excessive subordinationism, to which allusion has already been made and from which Tertullian himself was not free, was discarded in the course of the final and most radical Trinitarian controversy – the Arian debate.

Arius, a presbyter in charge of the church at Baucalis in Alexandria, first came into prominence in about 319. His teaching, which soon earned the censure of his bishop, was to the effect that the Son is a creature, the first and most perfect of God's creatures but nevertheless one that has been made by God. Moreover, pressing the analogy between human and divine fatherhood, Arius argued that as a human son is subsequent in time to his father, so the divine Son must be of later existence than the divine Father; hence "once he was not" since "before he was begotten he was not". This was to carry Origen's subordinationism to the extreme and to ignore his emphasis upon the Eternal Generation of the Son. This meant that since the Son was begotten in eternity, which by definition is outside time, there can be no before or after, no beginning or ending to the process. Arius indeed opened the door to polytheism since the worship of Christ, which he did not reject, was, on his interpretation, the worship of a creature, for whatever honour may have been offered to Christ, his complete divinity was denied. Arius' opponents were not slow to make themselves heard, and, in an endeavour to restore peace, the Emperor Constantine summoned a Council to Nicaea in 325.

The Council both condemned Arius and also produced a statement of faith which was intended to make the orthodox position plain. It therefore affirmed that the Son was "begotten not made" and that he was "of one substance with the Father". This term meant "of the same stuff" and it therefore involved the affirmation that what the Father is that the Son is also – fully divine. This left the problem of the divine unity unsolved, but then the framers of the Creed were only concerned to assert the complete and absolute deity of Christ against Arius. Yet "of one substance" could also mean "of one content", and in this sense it had a bearing on the relationship of Father and Son, as St Athanasius († 373), the great opponent of Arius, perceived. He used it to declare that Christ's complete divinity involved an identity of content of the divine Persons (e.g. *Of Synods*, 42, 51, 53); moreover he applied it also to the Spirit (*To Serapion*, i, 27), and so understood the unity of the Trinity to lie in the identity of substance. Hence God is one objective Being. Father, Son and Spirit are therefore not three equal Beings but substantially identical and so one Being.

St Athanasius had thus succeeded in providing an explanation of how Father, Son and Spirit can be regarded as one God. The Cappadocian trio, St Basil of Caesarea († 379), his brother St Gregory of Nyssa († 394) and their friend St Gregory of Nazianzus († c. 390), accepted his teaching and made a further step to explain how this one God is nevertheless at the same time three. They taught that the godhead is one Being, because of the identity of substance, but of this one Being there are three objective presentations – Father, Son and Holy Spirit. These three are to be distinguished from one another by their individual characteristics which are in fact modes of existence. The Father, as the fount and source of deity, is unbegotten – that is his distinguishing characteristic – the Son is begotten and the Spirit proceeding. This terminology is derived from the New Testament where it is stated that Christ is "the only begotten from the Father" (*John* i, 14) and that the Spirit is he "which proceedeth from the Father" (*John* xv, 26) – thus the relation of the Father to the Son is that the one begets the other, and the relation of the Spirit to the Father is that the one proceeds from the other. This implies no inferiority since these processes take place in eternity, where there can be no before or after, no beginning or ending. Consequently these modes of existence refer to the relations between the divine Persons and so express eternal processes continually operative within the divine Being. Hence from the point of view of internal analysis God is one Being, but from

the point of view of external presentation he is three Objects.

This subtle formulation of Trinitarian belief was in part misunderstood in the sixth and seventh centuries, but through the efforts of an anonymous writer, known as Pseudo-Cyril, whose work was incorporated by St John of Damascus († 749) in his *Of the Orthodox Faith*, the original meaning of the "Cappadocian Settlement" was recovered and became the standard of belief for Eastern Orthodoxy. But Pseudo-Cyril not only helped to preserve his predecessors' insights, he also pressed into service a further term to safeguard the Unity in Trinity. This term summed up one aspect of the Biblical record of which little notice had previously been taken. In St John's Gospel (xiv, 10), Jesus says: "I am in the Father, and the Father in me", thus the divine Persons are, as it were, coextensive; Pseudo-Cyril expressed this by the word "coinherence". So if one begins with the three objective presentations of the godhead, there is no danger of lapsing into tritheism because the doctrine of coinherence necessarily involves identity of Being.

But what meanwhile of the doctrine in the West? We have already seen that the assertion that Jesus is "of one substance with the Father" had not only ruled out Arianism but had also provided a means of expressing the divine unity. But the acceptance of this term at Nicaea was not due to the Eastern anti-Arians alone; we must also recognize the influence of the Western delegates, led by Hosius of Cordova, who regarded it as a convenient expression of their own beliefs. These beliefs as to the unity, identity and equality of substance were first propounded by Tertullian. His teaching was further expounded by the Roman presbyter Novatian in his *Of the Trinity* (c. 250): "The Father is manifested as the One God, true and eternal, from whom alone this power of divinity is emitted, and though transmitted to the Son and centred in him, it returns again to the Father through the community of substance" (c. 31). Identity of substance is also at the heart of the Trinitarian teaching of St Hilary of Poitiers († 367), which was enriched during his exile in Asia so that he became an intermediary between the theology of East and West. A similar role was played by St Ambrose of Milan († 397) who derived many of his ideas from St Basil, teaching that each of the divine Persons possesses in all its fulness the same one indivisible substance of godhead, and that each is distinguished from the other by his properties. St Augustine († 430), converted by St Ambrose and influenced by the writings of St Hilary, made no great advance upon their position and, apart from his emphasis on the procession of the Spirit "from the Father *and* the Son", his main importance lay in the numerous analogies which he propounded in an attempt to give some understanding of the Trinity. This body of Western teaching found its simplest formulation in the so-called "Athanasian" Creed, a semi-liturgical document which probably originated in Gaul towards the end of the fifth century. According to this, the Catholic Faith is "that we worship one God in Trinity, and Trinity in Unity; neither confounding the Persons nor dividing the Substance."

So the Latin and Greek beliefs, as finally formulated, differed in conception. To the Latins God is one Being in three Persons or centres of consciousness; to the Greeks he is one Being in three objects: as seen and thought he is Three, as seeing and thinking he is One. The Westerners were not unaware of this difference and St Augustine commented: "for the sake of speaking of things ineffable, that in some way we may be able to express what we are in no way able to express fully, our Greek friends have spoken of one essence and three substances, but the Latins of one essence or substance and three Persons." Either position is legitimate for "the transcendence of the godhead surpasses the power of ordinary speech" (*Of the Trinity* vii, 7). The doctrine of the Trinity is indeed an attempt to correlate and safeguard the truths of the Christian experience of God. It involves no rationalist claim to explain everything, for it is based upon analogy which must not be pressed in detail, since man cannot convey a complete account of what God is in his own perfect nature. "It is difficult," says St Gregory of Nazianzus, "to conceive God, but to define him in words is an impossibility" (*Orations* xxviii, 4).

The difficulty presented by the doctrine of the Trinity is how we can conceive of God to be both three and one at the same time, which is what the divine activity in history compels us to recognize. As long as we look at this problem from the point of view of arithmetic it remains insoluble, since mathematically, unity is defined by absence of multiplicity and moreover one plus one plus one will always equal three. But there are other unities than mathematical ones, unities which are multiple and in particular organic unities. An organism unifies various constituent elements in a single life and the higher the organism the more complex its unity, so that the unity of the human body is far more complex than the unity of an amoeba. The godhead may be understood from this point of view – its unity or oneness is that of a living organism and comprises three constituent elements – three objects according to the Greek way of thinking, three Persons according to Western thought. All existing earthly unities are but imperfect analogies of this divine unity and it is for this reason that the doctrine of the

Trinity, though strictly rational, surpasses our full comprehension.

Belief in the Person of Christ

As the doctrine of the Trinity was intended to state and safeguard the truths of the Christian experience of the godhead, so also the doctrine of the Person of Christ was concerned to preserve those factors upon which the Christian experience of salvation rested. Of this concern St Irenaeus' statement may be taken as typical: "Unless man had overcome the enemy of man, the enemy would not have been justly vanquished. And again: unless it had been God who had freely given salvation, we could never have possessed it securely. And unless man had been joined to God, he could never have become a partaker of incorruptibility. For it was incumbent upon the Mediator between God and men, by his relationship to both, to bring both to friendship and concord, and present man to God, while he revealed God to man" (*Heresies* iii, 18, 7). From this it follows that the Mediator must be both God and man – an affirmation that we have already met in the New Testament writings and in particular in the Epistle to the Hebrews.

The speculative bent of the Eastern Christians prevented their resting content with this simple statement. They wanted to know further in what sense Jesus was divine, and in what sense he was human. The Arian controversy was the occasion for propounding an answer to the first of these questions. Christology or the doctrine of Christ's Person was indeed an important element in the earliest form of Arius' teaching. He agreed that Christ was the Word Incarnate, and then argued that as, according to the Gospel record, he was capable of change and suffering, the Word must be regarded as mutable and therefore could not be equal with God. The outcome of this debate, as we have already seen, was the affirmation that Christ was "of one substance with the Father" and therefore completely divine.

It was partly, though not entirely, opposition to this Arian emphasis upon mutability that led Apollinaris of Laodicea († *c.* 390) to propound his doctrine of the Person of Christ, as a consequence of which the complete humanity of the Incarnate Lord came to be asserted. Accepting a tripartite conception of human nature as being made up of body, soul (the animal soul or principle of life) and spirit or mind (the rational soul or controlling principle), Apollinaris declared that as the last was the seat of sin it was not assumed by the pre-existent Word, who was therefore perfect and changeless. By this means Apollinaris believed that he also achieved a more complete understanding of the real union of the divine and human in the one Person of Christ. He considered that the admission of two complete natures would involve a dual personality, two natures meant two persons to him. Hence he taught that "the Word became flesh without assuming a human mind". He was condemned at the Council of Constantinople in 381 and the grounds for this sentence are succinctly expressed by St Gregory of Nazianzus: "If anyone has trusted in a man without a mind, he is indeed senseless and not worthy to be wholly saved. For that which is unassumed is unhealed; but that which has been united to God, this also is saved. If half Adam fell, half also is that which has been assumed and that which is saved. But if the whole Adam fell, he has been united to the whole of him who was begotten and is wholly saved. Let them not begrudge us a complete salvation, nor equip the Saviour with only the bones and portraiture of a man" (*Epistles* 101, 47–51).

Thus by the last quarter of the fourth century agreement had been reached that belief in Christ involved belief in his *complete* divinity and in his *complete* humanity. The further question then arose – one with which Apollinaris had been in part concerned – how are we to conceive of the relationship between the manhood and godhead? Two of the solutions that were put forward were immediately rejected, those of Nestorius († 451) and Eutyches († c. 453).

Nestorius, bishop of Constantinople, was a product of the Antioch school of Theology, which began from the unity of the godhead and laid its main stress on the reality of the two natures in Christ and on the moral character of the manhood. The opposing school of Alexandria, of which Apollinaris had been a representative, began from the plurality of the godhead and laid its main stress on the unity of the one Person of Christ and upon his pre-existent deity. The danger of the latter, as we have seen, is that the human nature may not be given its full stature: the danger of the former is that the one Person may be divided into two, and it was with this heresy that Nestorius was charged.

Nestorius drew a parallel between the creation of Adam and the creation of Jesus Christ, the Second Adam, in the womb of the Virgin. At the first creation God formed an animal mechanism and then breathed into it a living soul; at this moment of vivification God and Adam were united. This act performed, God withdrew himself, and Adam became a separate entity. At the second creation, God again formed an animal mechanism and vivified it, yet on this occasion he did not withdraw himself but remained permanently as at the moment of vivification. Thus while there never was a separate man Jesus, there was a potentially separate man, since God

could have withdrawn himself and so maintained an exact parallel with the creation of Adam.

St Cyril of Alexandria († 444), Nestorius' most implacable opponent, believed that this teaching involved the division of the one Person of Christ into two. So far from being an adequate explanation of the relation of the divine and human in Christ, it seemed to him a denial of true unity and the substitution for it of a juxtaposition or partnership of two individuals. Instead, St Cyril propounded a "hypostatic" or "natural" union. Using "hypostasis" in the sense of "person", St Cyril affirmed that the two substances of godhead and manhood, while retaining their distinctive properties, found their union in one Person, so that it is the Person who is "one" while the substances are "two". It was therefore a "natural" union because in Jesus Christ there was a "real" unification of godhead and manhood. Consequently, genuinely divine and genuinely human experiences belonged to the one Lord Jesus Christ. The experiencing Person was the pre-existent Son of God, and the manhood was his own and cannot be separated from him, as if one could think of it as "that of another existing individually beside him". This was to affirm that the union of godhead and manhood was so complete that the godhead shared in the names and properties of the manhood and the manhood in those of the godhead. Hence one may even say that "God was born" or that in Jesus Christ "God suffered" and "God died" (*Apology against Theodoret* xii).

The Nestorian solution of the relation of the divine and human in Christ having been condemned at the Council of Ephesus in 431, an alternative thesis was put forward by Eutyches, archimandrite of a monastery near Constantinople. Of the Alexandrian school and violently anti-Nestorian, he reacted to the opposite extreme. While he was prepared to acknowledge two natures before the union, he would only allow one after it; the human nature of Christ was, after the Incarnation, absorbed by the divine. This again was no adequate explanation of the unity, as it involved the denial of the permanence of Christ's manhood – absorption is the negation of unity – and so gainsaid the whole purpose of the Incarnation. Eutyches was condemned by the Council of Chalcedon in 451, but before we turn to the proceedings of this fourth Ecumenical Council, the thought of the Latin West, which had its contribution to make to the Definition of Faith promulgated in 451, requires a brief mention.

With its less speculative and more practical outlook, the Western Church had, from the earliest days, retained a firm grasp upon the essentials of Christological belief. Here, as is the case with the doctrine of the Trinity, Tertullian had been the pioneer. According to him "the primordial first-begotten Word" (*Apology* 21) had descended to earth and become man. But by this union with human nature the Word had not undergone any transformation, nor had the manhood lost its essential nature: "there remains unimpaired the proper being of each substance." So "we observe a twofold quality (*status*), not confused but combined, Jesus in one Person, God and man" (*Against Praxeas* 27). Here we may note the three basic factors in orthodox Christological belief: (i) The Incarnate Lord is one Person. (ii) He has two natures. (iii) These natures persist in their entirety unimpaired by their union with one another. Later teachers in the West had only to follow out the course already mapped by this African teacher, and indeed from Tertullian to St Leo († 461) we see a constant reiteration of these fundamental principles. Whether we examine the beliefs of a Novatian, a Hilary of Poitiers, an Ambrose or an Augustine, we find the same affirmations; while confessing the one Christ, they recognize in him the distinction of the two natures.

Turning now to the Council of Chalcedon it is important to note that its members were concerned to produce a definition of Christological belief that would not only rule out the errors of Nestorius and Eutyches but would also present a positive exposition of the insights of their predecessors. Thus they accepted St Cyril's *Letters to Nestorius* and St Leo's *Tome*, not just because the first condemned Nestorianism and the second Eutychianism but because they were considered to give an explanation of the Nicene faith, confirmed at Constantinople, and accepted by them as the essential basis of Christological definition. The most important section of this *Definition of Faith* reads as follows:

"Following, then, the holy Fathers we all unanimously teach that our Lord Jesus Christ is to us one and the same Son, the same perfect in godhead, the same perfect in manhood; truly God and truly man; the same (consisting) of a rational soul and a body; of the same substance as the Father as to his godhead, and the same of one substance with us as to his manhood; like us in all things, except for sin; begotten of the Father before ages as to his godhead, and in the last days, the same, for us and for our salvation, of Mary Theotokos as to his manhood; one and the same Christ, Son, Lord, only-begotten, made known in two natures (which exist) without confusion, without change, without division, without separation; the difference of the natures being in no way taken away because of the union, but rather the properties of each nature being preserved, and (both) concurring into one Person and one *hypo-*

stasis – not parted or divided into two Persons, but one and the same Son and only-begotten, the divine Word, the Lord Jesus Christ."

So at Chalcedon the unity of Christ's Person was affirmed and the principle of "recognizing" the natures was established. The godhead and the manhood, in St Cyril's phrase, are "two, though only in contemplation". In the one Person are "shewn forth" and therefore are "to be recognized" both natures, but it must never be forgotten that they "concur into one Person". Here the positive beliefs of both the schools of Alexandria and of Antioch, together with the consistent teaching of Western theologians from Tertullian onwards, find admirable expression.

Unfortunately the Council's findings were not universally accepted, largely due to a lack of agreement as to the meaning of the terms used. The representatives of the extreme Alexandrian tradition, who came to be known as "Monophysites" or believers in one nature only, understood "nature" to mean "person", and therefore when they read the Council's Definition with its reference to Christ "made known in two natures", they regarded this as affirming that in Christ there are two persons, which was in effect the Nestorian error. The debate that followed led to a clarification of belief and culminated in the work of Leontius of Byzantium († *c.* 543).

So far the relationship of the divine and human in Christ had not received satisfactory treatment. To say that Christ is human and divine immediately raises the problem how he can be both, and yet at the same time be only one Person. St Cyril had avoided splitting Christ into two persons by saying that his human nature was impersonal; but he had not given any explanation of what this meant. Leontius' importance lies in the fact that he faced this issue and provided a solution of abiding value. He begins from the pre-existence of the Son of God; before the Incarnation there already was in eternity a Person, the Second Person of the Trinity. At the Incarnation that Person created for himself a human nature and, uniting it to himself in the process of creating it, made it his very own. Consequently he was both human and divine; but his humanity had never had any existence previous to its being united with the godhead; it was not the human nature of a distinct human person but his very own. Thus the one Person of the God-man was the pre-existent Son of God and his humanity became personal in him: it was, to use Leontius' term, not impersonal but "*in-personal*" – personal *in* Christ, that is to say, because it has its personality *in* him. This teaching was endorsed by the fifth Ecumenical Council at Constantinople in 553. It was also included by St John of Damascus in his *De Fide Orthodoxa* (iii, 2; cf. iii, 11) in the following terms: "He took on himself the first-fruits of our flesh, and these not as having a separate existence, or as being formerly an individual, and thus assumed by him, but as existing in his own Person. For the Person of the divine Word itself became the Person of the flesh."

This insistence on the unity of the two natures in one Person did not mean that the essential properties of either were impaired; and at the sixth Ecumenical Council, also at Constantinople, in 680–1, it was laid down that in Jesus Christ there are

". . . two natural wills and two natural operations without division, without change, without separation, without confusion, according to the teaching of the holy Fathers. And these two natural wills are not contrary the one to the other . . . But his human will follows, and that not as resisting or reluctant, but rather as subject to his divine and omnipotent will."

This belief in two wills does not lead to a split personality, since, in St John of Damascus' words, the human will "wills of its own free will those things which the divine will willeth it to will" (*op. cit.*, iii, 18) – they are distinct and yet united. This involved the recognition of a single activity of redemption, the two natures and wills concurring into the one Person of the God-man. To this the medieval divines had nothing to add: belief in the Person of Christ had achieved its classic expression.

The Experience of Salvation

The doctrine of the Person of Christ, as we noted at the beginning of the last section, was concerned to preserve those factors upon which the Christian experience of salvation rested. How believers in the early centuries understood that experience it must now be our task to investigate.

The second century apologists, anxious to commend the faith to the educated pagan, affirmed that Christianity was the true philosophy. Christ is the Revelation of God and consequently redemption or salvation is illumination. "Through Jesus Christ God has called us from darkness to light, from ignorance to the knowledge of his glorious Name. Thou hast opened the eyes of our hearts that they may know thee" (I *Clement* lix, 2). Christ is thus the Teacher who brings the perfect knowledge of God, previously lost through sin. He is therefore the "example" whom we are called to imitate.

Thus understood, salvation is seen to issue in moral conduct, and it is important to remember that Christianity was not and is not primarily a system of beliefs to which intellectual assent is demanded but a way of life to be lived in total reliance upon God. In New Testament times Christianity was indeed known as the Way (*Acts* xix, 9), and those who followed it were required "to be dead unto sin, but alive unto God in Christ Jesus" (*Romans* vi, 11). This ethical note, which was an essential part of the inheritance from Judaism, is constantly sounded. "Like as he which called you is holy, be ye yourselves also holy in all manner of living; because it is written, Ye shall be holy; for I am holy" (I *Peter* i, 15–16). Conscious that he was united with God through Christ, and in him with his fellow believers, the Christian was to live constantly in the divine presence. His life was therefore to be characterized by joy, faith, love and hope, not just as internal dispositions of his spiritual life but expressed in outward behaviour. It was indeed this experience of salvation actualized in social relations that more than anything else converted the Roman Empire to Christ. "Loving God," says the author of the *Epistle to Diognetus* (? *c.* 200), "you will imitate his goodness. And do not wonder that a man can become an imitator of God. By the will of God he can. For happiness lies not in lordship over one's neighbours, nor in the desire to have more than one's weaker brethren, nor in being rich and coercing the more needy. Not in these things can any man imitate God. Nay, these things are outside his majesty. But whosoever takes upon himself his neighbour's burden, whosoever wishes to benefit another who is poorer in that in which he himself is better off, whosoever by supplying to those in want the things which he has received and holds from God becomes a god to those who receive them – this man is an imitator of God" (x, 4–6).

Righteous living, God-centred and no longer self-centred, should always be the outcome of the saving act of Christ, but to regard that act as consisting in no more than illumination was insufficient to convey the full richness of the Christian experience, and side by side with this interpretation, even in the second century, other aspects were being noted. Perhaps the most widely accepted of these was that which has been called the "classic" theory – the belief that salvation consists in freedom from the power of evil spirits and that consequently Christ's redeeming work is to be understood as a victory over Satan and his minions and over sin and death – a belief already enshrined in the New Testament writings.

In seeking to answer how this victory had been won the idea of the deceit of the devil was propounded. Hinted at by St Ignatius († *c.* 114, *Ephesians* 19), elaborated by Origen (*Commentary on Matthew* xvi, 8), it was very fully expressed by St Gregory of Nyssa: "The godhead was hidden under the veil of our nature, that, as is done with greedy fish, the hook of the godhead might be gulped down along with the bait of the flesh and thus, life being introduced into the house of death and light shining in the darkness, that which is contradictory to light and life might vanish away; for it is not in the nature of darkness to remain where light is present or of death to exist where life is present" (*Catechetica Oration* 17–23). So the devil, unsuspecting, swallowed the bait, represented by the humanity of Christ, and was caught on the hook of his godhead. Morally repugnant though this interpretation may be, it was a serious attempt to grapple with the problem of dualism which is bound up with this method of interpreting salvation; but it was certainly neither as cogent nor as compelling as the alternative teaching advanced by St Irenaeus in his theory of "Recapitulation".

The close connection of the theme of Christ Victorious with "recapitulation" is made very clear by St Irenaeus' statement that Christ "has therefore, in his work of recapitulation, summed up all things, both waging war against our enemy, and crushing him who at the beginning had led us away captive in Adam . . . in order that, as our species went down to death through a vanquished man, so we may ascend to life again through a victorious one" (*Heresies* v, 21, 1). Recapitulation means then "going over the same ground again." Christ placed himself in the same circumstances as Adam, but with the opposite result; where Adam yielded to temptation, Christ overcame. So the whole life of Christ, from birth to crucifixion, was a single process of redemption, in which he shared all the experiences of man, sin only excepted, and finally through his resurrection rose triumphant over death. But recapitulation also has the sense of "restoration into unity", and so the continuity between Creation and redemption is emphasized – God and man, divided by sin, are in Christ made one; he thus embodies in himself the whole of human history as purposed by God in his original creation. Consequently to experience salvation is to enter upon a life of unity with God and with one's fellows – a life characterized by a sense of freedom from the domination of sin and by a certainty of resurrection to eternal life.

St Irenaeus' teaching on the subject of salvation is not confined to recapitulation, although this undoubtedly receives his main emphasis; he also affirms salvation in terms of divinization: Christ "out of his great love became what we are, that he might make us what he is himself" (*ibid.*, v, Preface). This indeed became one of the principal features of the Alexandrian exposition of the meaning of salvation, and it is necessary here to recognize that, as the Church expanded, different emphases came to the fore in different parts of the Empire.

In the West, where the sense of order, of law and of imperial sovereignty was strong, Christians tended to place their emphasis on simple and clear definitions rather than on complex formulations. Consequently they interpreted salvation primarily in legal terms. Sin, to them, was a crime against God requiring satisfaction. But man is unable to offer the necessary satisfaction and is therefore under the divine condemnation from which there is no escape, unless God himself intervenes and both vindicates his law and pays the debt. This, according to the Westerns, is precisely what God has done in Christ; he is the one who has taken man's guilt upon himself, and, in willing obedience, offered himself as a sacrifice on man's behalf. Hence their main stress is on Calvary, on the meritorious death when the blood was freely given as the price of reconciliation to God. Christ, in St Augustine's words, is "both Victor and Victim, and therefore Victor because Victim" (*Confessions* x, 69). So salvation means essentially the forgiveness of sins mediated through the vicarious and sacrificial death of the God-man.

In the East the differing approaches of the schools of Antioch and Alexandria, patent in their Christological beliefs, are again to be noted. The former regarded man's state of mutability and corruption as the result of his disobedience to the divine will. To restore stability and order a new stage in the history of the universe was needed, involving the creation of a new Man who would live in perfect obedience to God. Since fallen man cannot achieve this alone, God must intervene and both create and unite to himself the new Man, thus re-establishing man in moral obedience to his will. At the Incarnation the Son of God did unite man to himself, and having consummated his lifelong obedience on the cross, triumphed over corruption and death through his resurrection.

If the West emphasized the cross, and the Antiochenes the resurrection, the Alexandrians concentrated upon the Incarnation. To this school of thought, which previous to the fourth century had found expression in St Ignatius, in St Irenaeus, in St Clement and in Origen, with differing physical, metaphysical and mystical overtones, the primary consequence of sin was the corruption of human nature with the corresponding loss of immortality. Salvation therefore meant the restoration of incorruption and for this the re-unification of God and man was necessary. In Christ God and man were made one, and so the divine Image, defaced but not effaced by the Fall, could be restored after the original, that is, after the divine

PLATE 13. Pieta. Handcolored woodcut. Master Michel South German. ca. 1460. William F. Worden Fund. (Courtesy, *Museum of Fine Arts, Boston.*)

PLATE 14. The Risen and Ascended Christ as Sovereign of the Universe: mosaic in the apse, 1132–40. (*Capella Palatina, Palermo.*)

Son himself who is eternally the Image of God. In St Athanasius' *Of the Incarnation*, this belief is given very full expression: "It was the part of none other than the Saviour himself, who in the beginning made all things out of nothing, to change the corruptible into incorruption; and it belonged to none other than the Image of the Father to recreate for man the likeness of God's Image; and it was the part of none other than our Lord Jesus Christ who is Life itself to make the mortal immortal" (c. 20). Hence Christ came into the world to effect man's deification: "He became man that we might become divine" (c. 53). By partaking of the eternal and incorruptible, man is made superior to death and decay, and, both grounded in Christ and rejoicing in the presence of the Spirit, he achieves at last the beatific vision. The process of deification therefore is undeniably ethical, and while it culminates in the Vision of God it does not lead to a monistic identification of man with God; Creator and creature remain distinct: "not that we become as the Father, for to become as the Father is impossible for his creatures who have been brought into existence out of nothing" (*Against the Arians* iii, 19). God, of his great condescension, stoops down to sinful man and enables him to attain his true end, not by transformation into godhead but by endowing him with immortality and with eternal qualities which the Creator himself possesses and, of his goodness, would bestow upon him.

Unlike Trinitarian and Christological belief, which crystallized in accepted formulae, no single way of interpreting salvation was deemed sufficiently comprehensive to enshrine the whole truth. The experience of atonement was too complex for any one theory to embody it satisfactorily and, while each preserved valuable insights, all were eventually considered necessary in the Christian understanding of redemption. And central to all Christian thinking was the Incarnate Lord, the Mediator of salvation and the object of devoted worship.

The Worship of the Community

Christian belief centred in Christian worship, by which, so it was held, the fruits of Christ's saving act were mediated. The twin poles of this cult were Baptism and the Eucharist, the former being administered to individuals once and for all, the latter being regularly repeated by the community as a whole. From the earliest days these two rites were essential features of Christian life. The Church was a worshipping community from the outset, and the central position occupied by its worship serves to emphasize the fact, already noted, that Christianity was not an intellectual system but a way of life, which began in self-committal to God in acceptance of his saving

act through Christ, progressed through corporate worship and private prayer, and expressed itself in ethical conduct and supremely in the loving service of mankind.

It has indeed been increasingly recognized that the New Testament writings themselves have in many instances a liturgical background. Thus much of the ethical teaching common to the Epistles would appear to derive from the primitive Christian catechism which was most probably used for the instruction of catechumens or candidates for Baptism within the context of divine worship. Certain, if not all, of St Paul's letters were written to be read out at the weekly gatherings (*Colossians* iv, 16). The Gospel of St Matthew was in all probability composed expressly for liturgical use. One of the purposes of the Fourth Gospel, so it has been argued, was to set forth the connection between contemporary Christian worship and the historical life of Jesus. The First Epistle of Peter may possibly be a primitive baptismal liturgy, while the Book of Revelation sees the whole drama of the last days in the context of the Lord's Supper on the Lord's Day.

The practice of Baptism in the Apostolic Age would seem to have rested in the main on the precedent of Christ's own Baptism by John in the river Jordan and also on the Jewish custom of baptizing proselytes. It consisted of immersion in water, followed possibly by the laying on of hands by a leading representative of the community (*Acts* xix, 5–6). Belief as to the meaning of this rite was expressed in a variety of ways, differing according to the particular conception of the Church which was consciously or subconsciously influencing the thought of the writer. Thus if one thinks of the Church as the chosen people, the New Israel, then Baptism is the means of initiation into it. Just as circumcision was the means whereby one became a member of the Israel of God and entered into the Covenant, so Baptism is spiritual circumcision whereby one becomes a member of the New Israel which is constituted under the New Covenant. "Ye were also circumcised with a circumcision not made with hands, in the putting off of the body of the flesh, in the circumcision of Christ; having been buried with him in baptism" (*Colossians* ii, 11–12). On the other hand, if the idea of the Church as the Temple or Sanctuary of the divine Presence is uppermost, then Baptism is the means whereby the individual is brought into that Presence in the Person of the Holy Spirit. So "ye are a temple of God, and the Spirit of God dwelleth in you" (I *Corinthians* iii, 16). Christians are then those who through Baptism "were made partakers (*metokhous*, sharers or partners in) of the Holy Ghost" (*Hebrews* vi, 4). So man is brought out of separation into unity and shares in the communion or fellowship of the Spirit (II *Corinthians* xiii, 14).

Again, if the Church as the Body of Christ is the primary category, then Baptism is the means of incorporating or grafting the individual into the living organism of the Church: "in one Spirit were we all baptized into one body" (I *Corinthians* xii, 13). But this unity in the Body of Christ involves sharing in his death and resurrection: "all we who were baptized into Christ Jesus were baptized into his death . . . that like as Christ was raised from the dead through the glory of the Father, so we also might walk in newness of life" (*Romans* vi, 3–4). So Baptism effects a death to sin and a rising to newness of life, and, through the Spirit, the neophyte partakes of the resurrection life, for God has "raised us up with him, and made us to sit with him in the heavenly places, in Christ Jesus" (*Ephesians* ii, 6).

If the Church is conceived of as the Bride of Christ, then Baptism is represented as the means of adopting or regenerating the individual whose mother the Church thereby becomes. "For ye are all sons of God, through faith, in Jesus Christ. For as many of you as were baptized into Christ did put on Christ" (*Galatians* iii, 26–27). This latter phrase – to put on Christ – is to be understood as implying a reference to Christ as the Image of God; so through Baptism one is invested with the Divine Image: the moral and spiritual character bestowed by God, which man bore at his creation and which became defaced by sin, is now renewed. "If any man is in Christ, there is a new creation: the old things are passed away; behold, they are become new" (II *Corinthians* v, 17). Hence, just as God in the beginning said: "Let there be light", now by an act of new creation he has "enlightened" the believer (*Hebrews* vi, 4), and invested him with a new righteousness which was embodied in Christ.

The formulated beliefs of the New Testament writers, which we have now briefly summarized, were so rich and, in many ways, so comprehensive, that later writers had little fresh to add. In the main they contented themselves with reproducing the same emphases. Thus, to give but two illustrations among many: St Basil, in his *Of the Holy Spirit* (c. 35) declares: "There are two ends proposed in Baptism: on the one hand, the destruction of the body of sin, that it may no longer bear fruit unto death; on the other, that it may live to the Spirit, and have its fruit unto sanctification. Now the water expresses the likeness of death, for it receives, as it were, the body into a tomb, but the Spirit is the source of the quickening power, by renewing our souls and bringing them from the deadness of sin into the life that was originally theirs." And, more briefly, from St John Chrysostom († 407):

"What the womb is to the embryo, the water is to the believer; for in the water he is fashioned and formed" (*Homily* 26 on *Gospel of St John*).

Although during the Patristic period baptismal belief was mainly expressed in the form of a reiteration of New Testament terminology, one practical problem arose which necessitated theological rethinking – the Baptism of infants. In the New Testament, faith is generally considered as the necessary condition for Baptism, and while this faith does not mean intellectual assent, but simple trust and self-committal, it would seem to imply a conscious decision which is obviously lacking in the case of infants. The matter came to a head in the course of the Pelagian controversy – Pelagius († ? 440) having denied the corruption of human nature and therefore, by implication, the necessity of infant Baptism. The answer propounded by St Augustine was that Baptism is the sacrament of faith. "Therefore, when, on behalf of an infant as yet incapable of exercising faith, the answer is given that he believes, this answer means that he has faith, because of the sacrament of faith. . . . Therefore an infant, although he is not yet a believer in the sense of having that faith which includes the consenting will of those who exercise it, nevertheless becomes a believer through the sacrament of faith. For as it is answered that he believes, so also he is called a believer, not because he assents to truth by an act of his own judgment, but because he receives the sacrament of that truth" (*Epistles*, xcviii, 9–10). St Augustine thus emphasizes that Baptism is a beginning and not an end; the effects predicated of it in the New Testament are bestowed on the infant by anticipation, as on the adult, but require to be progressively realized throughout the whole course of his life, as faith develops.

Apart from this reformulation, belief was constant, but ceremonial and structure were much elaborated. Rigid uniformity was unknown, since the rite developed differently in the principal centres. But there was sufficient similarity for a generalized description of the main features of the fourth-century liturgy to be reasonably accurate. After instruction during Lent, largely on the basis of a Creed, the candidates assembled on Holy Saturday night, that is, the night before Easter Day, in one of the chambers of the baptistery where, facing West, they renounced Satan and, facing East, declared their adherence to Christ. They then disrobed and were anointed with exorcized oil to dispel the powers of evil. After the bishop had blessed the water, the candidates were baptized. They descended three times into the font, symbolizing the three days' burial of Christ, and answered three questions – the baptismal interrogations – relating to their belief in Father, Son and Holy Spirit. The bishop then received them with the laying on of hands and/or unction; they were next clothed in white robes, as a sign that they had put off the covering of sin and put on the garments of innocence. Finally, each carrying a lighted taper, they proceeded to the church where they took part in their first Eucharist.

The origins of the Eucharist may be said to be twofold – the Last Supper on the one hand and the meals which Christ is said to have had with his disciples after his resurrection on the other. The earliest written account of the former is contained in St Paul's First Epistle to the Corinthians (xi, 23–25): "I received of the Lord that which also I delivered unto you, how that the Lord Jesus in the night in which he was betrayed took bread; and when he had given thanks, he brake it, and said, This is my body, which is broken for you: this do in remembrance of me. In like manner also the cup, after supper, saying, This cup is the new covenant in my blood: this do, as oft as ye drink it, in remembrance of me."

Even if we can no longer be quite certain of the exact words that Jesus used, there can be little doubt that he identified the bread with his body and the wine with his blood, thereby indicating that those who partake of them share in the redeeming power of his death. The early Christians also experienced the truth of Christ's statement: "Where two or three are gathered together in my name, there am I in the midst of them" (*Matthew* xviii, 20); that is to say, he shared their table fellowship, and so their union with their living Lord was renewed and perpetuated. Hence the predominating note of joy which characterized their gatherings (*Acts* ii, 46) – a joy which was eschatologically determined, for by this act they were anticipating the Messianic banquet or, to change the image, they were tasting "the powers of the age to come" (*Hebrews* vi, 5). For this very reason, because the Eucharist was believed to actualize the fruits of Christ's work of salvation, it became the focus not only of the Church's life but also of the Church's beliefs, since all that was said of Christ and his mission could be applied to it. The consequence is that Eucharistic belief in the early centuries was both rich and diverse.

If one thinks of the Church as the chosen people, as the New Israel, then just as Baptism is the means of initiation into it, corresponding to circumcision into the Old Israel, so the Eucharist is the means of reaffirming the covenant relationship, corresponding to the Passover whereby the people re-engaged to keep the Law. If the idea of the Church as Temple of the divine Presence is uppermost, then the Eucharist is the sacrificial action of the "royal priesthood" (I *Peter* ii, 9). It is a sacrifice in two main senses. First it is the *anamnesis* of Christ's sacrifice. This word, which is translated "remembrance" in the Revised Version of St Paul's account given above, implies more than the mental recollection of what is absent; it has the sense of making what is past present again "so that it becomes *here and now operative* by its effects" (G. Dix, *The Shape of the Liturgy*, 1945, p. 161). So the offering of the Eucharist in the Church is identical with the offering of Christ, not in the sense that that sacrifice is repeated nor that a re-immolation takes place but that the Eucharist offering is the *anamnesis* (re-presentation) of that perfect oblation by the Church. Secondly, it is a sacrifice in that it consists of the offering to God of bread and wine, under which forms the Church offers herself. "That poor widow the Church," says St Irenaeus (*Heresies*, iv, 17–18), "casts all her life into the treasury of God," and thereby identifies herself with the atoning act of Christ who offers himself in his members.

The sacrifice of the Church and of Christ in his Church is thus seen to be one with his eternal offering before the Father. The scriptural basis for this patristic belief was found in the Epistle to the Hebrews, where Christ is represented as ministering at the heavenly altar or rather still pleading his sacrifice, still offering himself to the Father. His atoning act therefore did not cease with the crucifixion, but continues even after his ascension, his self-oblation including not only his earthly life and death but also his ascended life. In his humanity he still offers himself to the Father, and there is thus in heaven a continuous worship of God into which the members of Christ are admitted, being included in the perpetual intercession of the High Priest. St Augustine formulates this belief in these words: "Thou art the priest, thou art the victim, thou art the offerer, thou art that which is offered. He is himself the priest who has now entered into the parts within the veil, and alone there of those who have worn flesh makes intercession for us. In the type of which things, in that first people and in the first Temple, one priest entered into the Holy of Holies, all the people stood without, and he who alone entered into the parts within the veil offered sacrifice for the people standing without" (*Psalm* 64, *Narration* 6).

Since, then, participation in the Eucharist mediates the fruits of Christ's sacrifice, it was believed to convey absolution or the remission of sins. "When the blood of the Lord and the cup of salvation have been drunk," says St Cyprian (*Epistles* lxiii, 11, † 258), "the memory of the old man is laid aside, and there arises an oblivion of the former worldly conversation, and the sorrowful and sad breast which before was oppressed by tormenting sins is eased by the joy of the divine mercy."

The third image of the Church, the Body of Christ,

CHRISTIANITY

serves to emphasize the corporateness of Christian worship by which the Church realizes its true nature: "If thou wilt understand what the Body of Christ is," says St Augustine in an often quoted passage (*Sermon* cclxxii), "hear what the apostle says to the faithful: 'You are the body of Christ, and severally his members.' Since, then, you are the Body of Christ and his members, it is your mystery that is placed on the Lord's table; it is your mystery that you receive. To the words that tell you what you are, you answer 'Amen,' and in answering you subscribe to the statement. For you hear the words: 'The Body of Christ,' and you answer 'Amen.' Be therefore members of Christ that your 'Amen' may be true." In other words: "If you have received well, you are that which you have received" (*Sermon* ccxxvii). But the Eucharist is not only creative of the Church, it is also the means of perpetuating the unity between the Body and its Head. "As through the second birth [i.e. Baptism] and through the Holy Spirit all of us become one Body of Christ, so also by the one nourishment of the Holy Sacrament, through which the grace of the Holy Spirit feeds us, all of us are in one fellowship with Christ our Lord" (Theodore of Mopsuestia, *To the Baptized*). To be united with Christ is to be united with one another in him, so that "we, who are many, are one bread, one body: for we all partake of the one bread" (I *Corinthians* x, 17). Hence the Eucharist is rightly termed "the sacrament of unity".

The Church is, fourthly, the Bride of Christ and consequently the mother of believers, in which case the Eucharist is to be understood as the means of providing sustenance for those who have been born again in Baptism. "It behoves us," says Theodore of Mopsuestia († 428, *op. cit.*), "who have received a sacramental rebirth in the death of Christ our Lord, to receive the sacramental food of immortality in this same death, and to feed ourselves in the future from where we had also received our birth." One of the effects of this spiritual nourishment deserves special notice: it was believed to renew the image of God in man, that moral and spiritual likeness which had been defaced through sin. So according to St John Chrysostom (*Homily* 46 on *Gospel of St John*): "it causeth the image of the King to be fresh within us, produceth beauty unspeakable, permitteth not the nobleness of our souls to waste away, watering it continually and nourishing it." Here the Christ-centred nature of the Church's worship is apparent, for man can only be renewed in the divine image insofar as he is united with it, and this union is effected through the Eucharist when Christ, who is "the image of the invisible God" (*Colossians* i, 15), comes to the fellowship of believ-

ers. "I am the food of grown men," declares the heavenly voice to St Augustine (*Confessions* vii, 10), "grow and thou shalt feed upon me; nor shalt thou convert me, like the food of thy flesh, into thee, but thou shalt be converted into me."

This schematized presentation of Eucharistic belief, while simplifying exposition, tends to obscure the development which certainly took place in the early centuries – a development which centred in three main topics – sacrifice, consecration and presence. Concerning the first of these, to which reference has already been made, Christians in the period before Nicaea were quite emphatic that the Eucharist was a sacrifice; they did not however attempt to define exactly in what sense it could be regarded as such. The main clarification of this is to be found in the writings of St Ambrose and St Augustine who, on the basis of the Epistle to the Hebrews, connected the offering of the Church on earth with the eternal self, oblation of Christ in heaven. Beliefs as to consecration are less easy to disentangle, but the earliest theory would seem to have been adopted from Jewish practice; it was that consecration was dependent upon a blessing of the bread and the wine with a thanksgiving in gratitude for a particular divine act. God was thus thanked for his inestimable love in the Redemption of the world through Christ, and the elements thereby became holy. An alternative theory, which eventually made its way to the fore, was to the effect that the bread and the wine were blessed by the imposition of the "Name" of God – God was directly invoked to do something to the bread and the wine. It involved therefore a calling down of divine power upon the elements and this issued ultimately in the "Epiclesis" of the Eastern rites by which God is asked to send his Holy Spirit that the sacramental species may be "made" or "transformed" into the Body and Blood of Christ. Here we touch upon belief in the Real Presence. Statements on this subject fall into three groups in the Ante-Nicene period. There are first those passages which describe what is bestowed in the Eucharist in terms denoting a spiritual gift without defining its specific nature. There are others that refer to the bread and the wine as "symbols" or "figures" of the Body and Blood. There are finally those which describe the consecrated elements as the Body and Blood of Christ. In the Post-Nicene period these complementary views persisted, but there was an increased emphasis on the identification of the species with the Body and Blood although little attempt was made to explain the relationship between them.

As belief about the Eucharist developed, so its setting was elaborated and this in turn had its effect upon belief. In the apostolic age the Eucharist would appear to have

82

consisted in a repetition of the Last Supper *in toto*. It involved therefore seven actions, four before and three after the meal: (1) taking the bread; (2) blessing it; (3) breaking it; (4) distributing it. Then came the meal proper and at its conclusion: (5) taking the cup; (6) blessing it; (7) distributing it. The lax behaviour which, on occasion, accompanied the meal (I *Corinthians* xi, 17–34) led to the discontinuance of this pattern. The meal was taken out and, provided with its own grace in the form of an initial breaking and blessing of bread, continued until the fifth century as a separate observance with the name of the *agape* or lovefeast. Its removal however brought the ceremonies of the bread and of the wine together and so the seven actions were reduced to four, and this became henceforth the normal shape of the Liturgy: (1) taking of bread and wine together; (2) blessing of both; (3) breaking of bread; (4) distribution of both. Whatever elaborations were introduced, this simple structure underlay all Eucharistic rites, the four actions corresponding respectively to what are now called the Offertory, the Consecration Prayer, the Fraction and the Communion.

From the earliest days there was added, by way of introduction, a Ministry of the Word, largely based upon the worship of the Synagogue with which so many of the first Christians had been familiar. This consisted of readings from the Old Testament and the apostolic writings, together with a sermon on these readings. As only those who were full members of the Church were allowed to be present at the Eucharist proper, the first part became known as the Mass of the catechumens to distinguish it from the succeeding Mass of the faithful.

The Mass of the faithful began with the Offertory, and here an important difference between Eastern and Western practices requires notice as it led eventually to a difference of belief. In the West the members of the congregation brought their own bread and wine to the altar; their offerings were received by the deacons who took part of them for the celebration, the rest being blessed and put aside for distribution to the poor. In the East the offerings of the people were handed in before the service began, and as much as was required was carried in at the Offertory by the deacons alone. From this developed the whole rite of the "Prothesis", or preparation of the elements in the vestry beforehand. This elaborate symbolic action culminated in the slaying of Christ in a figure by piercing the bread with a miniature lance. At the Offertory, or Great Entrance, it was believed that the dead Christ was carried in to undergo resurrection through the Spirit at the Epiclesis or invocation. It will be evident how different this ritual action is from its Western counterpart – a difference which, as a result of the Great Schism

between the Eastern and Western Churches which forms the subject of the next chapter, was destined to continue without the possibility of the two separate traditions cross-fructifying.

The Crystallization of Belief in Creedal Formulae

Christianity, so it has been affirmed, is a revelation given once and for all and yet ever renewing itself. Consequently, the history of its beliefs is the record of the fruitful tension between the original deposit of the faith and its continual elucidation in each succeeding age. In this development canonical Scripture, ecclesiastical tradition and the use of right reason are all involved. From the earliest days of the Church factors were at work to distinguish the fundamentals of belief, essential and common to all who profess themselves Christian, from those more speculative items concerning which a certain difference of opinion was not only legitimate but to be expected. These formulations came to be expressed in succinct formulae known as Creeds, and it is the purpose of this final section to examine the influences leading to their production and the process by which standardization was achieved.

In New Testament times there was quite evidently no creed in the sense of an official and textually determined formula. The legend, for which the first indubitable evidence comes from the fourth century, that the Apostles held a committee meeting at which they settled on an agreed norm for their future preaching has nothing to recommend it. But this is not to say that the beliefs of the early Church were vague and nebulous. A considerable number of passages in the New Testament indicate that there was a recurring pattern of belief. Thus we have references to "the faith which was once for all delivered unto the saints" (*Jude* 3), and to "the pattern of sound words" (II *Timothy* i, 13). The Thessalonians are bidden to "hold the traditions which ye were taught" (II *Thessalonians* ii, 15), and the Romans (vi, 17) are reminded that they "became obedient from the heart to that form of teaching whereunto ye were delivered." This emphasis upon the transmission of an authoritative body of doctrine is to be expected, for the early Church was a believing, confessing and preaching Church with its own distinctive ideas, some inherited from Judaism and others determined by its response to God's action in Christ.

The tasks of preaching the Gospel, of preparing candidates for Baptism, of requiring a confession of faith at Baptism, together with the rite of exorcism and the Liturgy itself, comprising hymns and praise, all these were factors which worked upon the recognized body of teaching to crystallize it into conventional summaries.

The New Testament contains a large number of these in the form of liturgical tags, catch-phrases and quasi-creedal affirmations – statements having sometimes one, sometimes two, sometimes three members. The first type is patently Christological, declaring that "Jesus is the Christ" (I *John* ii, 22), "Jesus is Lord" (I *Corinthians* xii, 3), or "Jesus is the Son of God" (I *John* iv, 15). Occasionally these are elaborated by the addition of selected material from the history of redemption, e.g.,

"Christ Jesus that died, yea rather, that was raised from the dead, who is at the right hand of God, who also maketh intercession for us" (*Romans* viii, 34; cf. I *Corinthians* xv, 3ff).

The two-membered formulae associate the Father and the Son, e.g.,

"To us there is one God, the Father,
of whom are all things, and we unto him;
and one Lord, Jesus Christ,
through whom are all things, and we through
him" (I *Corinthians* vii, 6).

Finally there is the triadic scheme:

"The grace of the Lord Jesus Christ,
and the love of God,
and the communion of the Holy Ghost,
be with you all" (II *Corinthians* xiii, 14).

In the second century the situation remained very much the same. There were plenty of semi-formal summaries, the one-, two- and three-membered forms continuing to be used side by side. So we find in Justin Martyr (*Apology* I, xlii, 4):

"But Jesus Christ,
who came in our times,
was crucified, and
died,
rose again,
has ascended into heaven and has reigned."

In addition to these short and fragmentary declarations there also came into existence a form of baptismal interrogation – a series of three questions put to the convert at his initiation to which he was required to give his assent. The framework of these questions was provided by the command to baptize, found in *Matthew* xxviii, 19, and the candidate was asked whether he believed in the Father, in the Son and in the Holy Spirit. By the middle of the third century, and even before, it was possible to speak of "the customary and established words of the

interrogation" (Firmilian in Cyprian, *Epistles* lxxv, 10–11).

This development preceded the framing of formal creeds and at the same time stimulated it. These found their origin in the catechetical instruction for which concise summaries were required, but since this preparation was to culminate in Baptism with its threefold immersion in the threefold Name, it was inevitably cast in the Trinitarian mould, and its verbal content was largely borrowed from the baptismal interrogations, enlarged by the insertion either of clauses descriptive of the three Persons or of additional items of belief. The increasing influx of converts from paganism necessitated careful organization on the part of the Church to prevent its being swamped by large numbers of folk with false notions of the content and meaning of Christianity. This was the main impetus which finally produced stereotyped formulae, and these were connected with special ceremonies in order to emphasize their importance. These were the *traditio* and the *redditio*. The first, the handing over, was the disclosure to the catechumens of the content of the Christian faith in the form of a creed. The second, the handing back, marked the solemn occasion when the creed was repeated to the bishop after it had been memorized and in part explained.

It will be evident from the above that the original and positive function of creeds was to set forth the faith – any anti-heretical purposes were secondary in the period before Nicaea – and this is expressed very clearly by St Cyril of Jerusalem (*Catechetical Lectures* xviii, 32) in words which in all probability he himself used at the *traditio*.

"In learning the Faith and in professing it, acquire and keep that only which is now delivered to you by the Church, and which has been built up strongly out of all the Scriptures. For since all cannot read the Scriptures, some because they are illiterate and some because they have not the leisure, in order that the soul might not perish through ignorance, we comprise the whole doctrine of the Faith in a few lines. This summary I wish you both to commit to memory when I recite it and to rehearse it carefully among yourselves, not writing it on paper but engraving it by memory on your heart. . . . I wish you also to keep this as a provision through the whole course of your life, and beside this to receive no other, neither if we ourselves should change and contradict our present teaching, nor if any adverse angel, disguised as an angel of light, should wish to lead you astray. So for the present listen while I simply say the Creed, and commit it to memory; but at the proper season expect the confirmation out of Holy Scripture of each part of its contents. For the articles of the Faith were not composed as it seemed good to men, but the most important points are collected out of all the Scriptures to make up one comprehensive summary of the Faith. And just as the mustard seed in one small grain contains many branches, so also this Creed has embraced in a few words all the knowledge of godliness in the Old and New Testaments."

Typical of these pre-baptismal declarations of belief is that which is known as the Apostles' Creed. In origin this was a local creed, the product of the church at Rome, which may be traced back to at least the early third century, but it did not assume the precise form familiar at the present day until the sixth or seventh century. In all probability this took place in South West France, whence, under the influence of Charlemagne, it began to spread throughout the Frankish dominions until its wording entirely replaced that of the Old Roman Creed and it was accepted as authoritative by the whole Western Church. This however does not complete the history of the Creeds, for in the fourth century began the issuing of declarations of faith drawn up by Church Councils.

In the year 325 the Emperor Constantine summoned a council to Nicaea with the express purpose of bringing an end to the Arian controversy. Taking an Eastern Baptismal Creed of uncertain origin, the bishops inserted several phrases intended to rule out the Arian teaching, and assent to this formula was required from all present. Thus began the Age of Synodal Creeds, during which formula followed formula in rapid succession until finally in 381 at Constantinople the Arian controversy within the Empire was brought to an end and a further Creed was issued which was in fact that which is usually known today as the "Nicene" Creed. In the East this Creed was incorporated into the Eucharistic liturgy in the fifth century, first by the Monophysites, apparently in order to affirm their adhesion to the Nicene faith and their refusal to accept the findings of Chalcedon. Their example was soon followed by the Eastern Church as a whole. In the West it was not until the sixth century at the Council of Toledo in 589 that the Creed was ordered to be said at Mass, and at first this practice was confined to Spain. Gradually it spread further afield, reaching Ireland in the eighth century, then passing to England. In the early ninth century it was adopted throughout Gaul to combat a revival of Adoptionism (p. 70), but it was not until 1014 that Benedict VIII, persuaded by the Emperor Henry II, accepted it at Rome.

Since this is the only one, of all existing Creeds, for which universal acceptance can be claimed, it is quoted here, in the form in which it was first promulgated, as a convenient summing up of all that has gone before:

"We believe

in one God the Father almighty, maker of heaven and earth, of all things visible and invisible;

And in one Lord Jesus Christ, the only-begotten Son of God, begotten from the Father before all ages, light from light, true God from true God, begotten not made, of one substance with the Father, through whom all things were made, who for us men and for our salvation came down from heaven, and was incarnate from the Holy Spirit and the Virgin Mary and was made man, and was crucified for us under Pontius Pilate, and suffered and was buried, and rose again on the third day according to the Scriptures, and ascended into heaven, and sits at the right hand of the Father, and will come again with glory to judge living and dead, of whose kingdom there will be no end;

And in the Holy Spirit, the Lord and life-giver, who proceeds from the Father, who with the Father and the Son is co-worshipped and co-glorified, who spoke through the prophets; and in one holy Catholic and apostolic Church. We confess one Baptism for the remission of sins; we look forward to the resurrection of the dead and the life of the world to come.

Amen."

2b. Christianity: the Eastern Schism and the Eastern Orthodox Church

by NICOLAS ZERNOV

THE SCHISM BETWEEN THE CHRISTIAN EAST AND WEST, AND ITS CONSEQUENCES

The history of the Christian community is marked by three major schisms. The first occurred in the fifth century and split Eastern Christendom in two; the second took place in the early eleventh century and ended the fellowship between the Latin and Byzantine Churches. The third was the Reformation of the sixteenth century in Western Europe from which Protestantism arose in direct antagonism to the Church of Rome. The first and third were similar in character, both being suddenly tense and dramatic. They separated Christians, who, before these schisms, had shared the same teaching and types of worship and had accepted the same ecclesiastical administration.

The Eastern and Western Christians were alienated under different circumstances. It was a long and confused process, beginning in the ninth century and only reaching its final stage in the middle of the fifteenth. One of the characteristics of this separation was the uncertainty which accompanied each step. The more it is studied, the less convincing does the traditional description and chronology appear. Such questions as why the rift occurred, who the chief instigators were, what motives prompted them and how much responsibility for the disruption of Christian unity is theirs, still await satisfactory answers. But if the previously accepted verdicts of historians are increasingly contested, the far-reaching consequences of schism gradually become more distinct, and the connection between the separation of the Byzantine and the Latin Christians and some of the landmarks in world history is now convincingly established. This link is most clearly apparent in the fall of the Eastern Roman Empire, the failure of the Crusades, the growing antagonism of Islam to Christianity, the growth of the Papacy and the

Protestant reaction against it, and finally the rivalry and suspicion between Russia and Western Europe. Even the wars of the last hundred and forty years can be traced back to the schism between the Christian East and West. The Napoleonic campaign of 1812, the Crimean war of 1853–5, the Balkan wars of 1878 and of 1912, and the world wars of 1914 and 1939 all aimed at the control of Constantinople, and can thus be seen as part of the aftermath that followed the disruption of communion between the Orthodox and the Western Churches.

As the result of the schism two distinct cultures developed within Christendom, each holding the conviction that it alone was the legitimate expression of their common religion. Many Eastern and Western Christians no longer regard each other as being participants in the same Covenant. They have tried either to ignore each other's existence or to enforce submission of the one to the other. In consequence both have become victims of their one-sidedness and bitter rivalry. Their unity once provided Christendom with a solid basis for its growth and expansion, but their subsequent disunity has greatly damaged the prestige and vitality of the Christian religion.

There are two different explanations of the split between Rome and Constantinople. The first ascribes it to doctrinal differences; the second to the political struggle between the Byzantine Empire and the Christian West. It has been a long-established Christian custom to treat heresy as the only legitimate cause for suspending fellowship with other members of the Church. On these grounds the Greek-speaking Churches excommunicated the Oriental Christians in the fifth century, for they held that the Syrians and Copts of Egypt had distorted the Orthodox belief in Jesus Christ as true God and perfect man.

The Western split of the sixteenth century was also justified on the ground of doctrinal errors. Salvation by

PLATE 15. The Annunciation: early fifteenth-century ikon of the Moscow School, attributed to Andrei Rublev (*c.* 1370–1430), one of the greatest of the Russian ikon painters. The veil hanging over the Virgin's head is the conventional device of Byzantine iconography to indicate that the scene depicted is inside a building.

Photo: Cecil Stewart

PLATE 16. Karieh Djami, Constantinople, a typical example of Byzantine architecture at its best.

Photo: Society for Cultural Relations with the U.S.S.R.

PLATE 17. The Church of the Transfiguration at Kizhi, on the Onega Lake, built in the eighteenth century, showing wooden Russian architecture of the extreme north.

Photo: D. M. Nicol

PLATE 18. One of the Meteora monasteries of Thessaly, the so-called monasteries "in the air": some thirty of these were built on the precipitous rocks, accessible originally only by rope chair, but now only five are still in use. This is the Monastery of the Visitation.

Photo: "Mont Athos – Montaigne Sainte", Jacques Lacarrière, Editions Seghers, Paris

PLATE 19. A group of Greek monks from the Holy Mount of Athos. No women have been allowed here for the last thousand years.

Photo: *Exclusive News Agency*

PLATE 20. Haghia Sophia, Constantinople, formerly the chief cathedral of Eastern Christendom. It was built by the Emperor Justinian in the sixth century, turned into a mosque by the Turks after their conquest of Constantinople in the fifteenth century and is now a state monument.

PLATE 21. This plate represents the Uniate Church which, although it follows the Eastern Rite, is under Roman Obedience and has incorporated several western motifs – thus the picture of the Virgin is typically Italian while the priest represents the East. He stands before the screen which separates the sanctuary from the nave. (*Greek Uniate Church, Cargèse, Corsica*)

Photo: Edinburgh University Press

PLATE 22. The Virgin and Child: fourteenth-century ikon of the Byzantine School, painted in Macedonia. The style, with the face in strong light, is characteristic of the earlier fourteenth century. (*Macedonian State Collection, Skoplie, Yugoslavia*)

faith alone and the Papal headship of the Church were in the centre of the dispute which provoked the disruption of Western Christendom. There is, however, no similar agreement concerning the doctrinal causes of the suspension of communion between Rome and Byzantium.

Photius, the learned Patriarch of Constantinople (858–86), was the first to draw up a list of what the Byzantines considered to be Latin errors. In this catalogue of heresies he included certain irregularities in the observance of Lent, the compulsory celibacy of the clergy, the denial of the power of priests to administer Confirmation, and finally the most serious error of all, a false teaching concerning the Holy Spirit contained in the addition to the Nicene Creed (p. 85) of the words "and from the Son", the so-called *Filioque* clause.

The Latin theologians took up the challenge and produced their own list of Greek omissions and additions. Gradually the number of these items was increased by both sides, and in the heat of the controversy in the course of the next three centuries, as many as fifty points of incrimination were listed by the Greek and Latin divines. These included some doctrinal questions, the most important of which concerned the mode of the Procession of the Holy Spirit (p. 70ff). The East maintained that the Holy Ghost proceeded from the Father (*John* xv, 26), while the West insisted that the Holy Spirit proceeded from the Father *and* the Son (the *Filioque* clause). Another important theological controversy centred on the belief in Purgatory, which was taught by the West but repudiated by the East.

These disagreements concerning the tenets of the faith, however, played a comparatively minor part in the arguments between the Greeks and the Latins. Their main attention was concentrated upon those irregularities which they claimed to discover in the ritual, customs and even manners of their opponents. The celibacy of the clergy, the use of leavened or unleavened bread at the Eucharist, Baptism by immersion or by sprinkling, the different rules of fasting – all these points were subjected to sharp criticism. Even such small details of custom as the wearing of rings by Western bishops, or the shaving of beards by the clergyan d the introduction of instrumental music into worship, were condemned by the East as unlawful departures from the Apostolic tradition.

When, however, the Byzantine Empire was approaching its end and the leaders of the Orthodox Church and State, in their desperate attempt to secure Western help and so save their realm from the impending Turkish onslaught, opened their last theological debate with the Roman representatives at the Council of Florence in 1439, only four points were chosen for deliberation. The rest of the alleged heresies were dropped as being either irrelevant or trivial. These four points were:

(*a*) the prerogatives of the Papal See,
(*b*) the *Filioque* clause,
(*c*) the doctrine of Purgatory,
(*d*) whether leavened or unleavened bread was to be used at the Eucharist.

Those theologians who attribute the schism between East and West to doctrinal causes, have usually followed the line of approach taken by the Council of Florence, and adhere to the list of doctrinal differences there drawn up. Few of them today, however, would ascribe the same significance to the questions of Purgatory and the type of bread used at the Eucharist as was assigned to them in the fifteenth century. There remain, therefore, only two important items of disagreement: the teaching concerning the Holy Ghost and the limits of Papal power.

The "Filioque" Controversy

The origins of the *Filioque* controversy present one of the unsolved mysteries of Church history. No one has so far discovered when, how and by whom the words "and from the Son" were added to the Creed, the text of which had been solemnly approved both by the East and West as their common confession of faith at the first four Ecumenical Councils (p. 105). It appears that the addition was made in Spain some time in the sixth or in the seventh century, but the circumstances under which this change occurred have so far not been discovered. From Spain the *Filioque* clause spread gradually to neighbouring Gaul, and from there to England, Germany and Italy. At first the Roman pontiffs were opposed to it, and Pope Leo III (795–816) even ordered the original text of the Creed to be inscribed on silver shields and hung in St Peter's. Charlemagne and his successors, however, were determined to uphold the legitimacy of the addition, for it provided them with a handy weapon against Byzantium. In accusing the Eastern Christians of heresy, the Western rulers found a convenient excuse for aggression. The refusal of the Orthodox to accept the Spanish addition to the Creed thereby became a pretext for the conquest of territories belonging to the Eastern Empire. Under political pressure Rome withdrew its opposition to the *Filioque* clause, and in the next century, at the coronation of the Emperor Henry II (1002–24) in 1014, the Creed was solemnly intoned in St Peter's, complete with the offending addition.

The difference between the two texts of the same Creed

has provoked one of the longest and most confused theological disputes in the annals of Church history. Yet in spite of so many volumes published on this subject no common agreement has been found as to the nature of the offence. Some theologians insist that the insertion or omission of the *Filioque* clause constitutes a radical difference in the matter of an all-important Christian dogma, namely the nature of the Holy Trinity. Other scholars, however, consider the *Filioque* controversy to be not so much the question about the Holy Spirit as about whether the Pope has the right to alter the Creed. These theologians believe that both the Eastern and Western wordings of the Creed can be reconciled, and that the addition made first in Spain does not substantially affect sound Christian doctrine.

For theologians of this school the *Filioque* controversy was of secondary importance: the one serious disagreement which came to separate the Orthodox from the Roman Catholics was that of the Papal prerogatives. According to this school of thought the dispute concerning the constitution of the Church made communion between the Christian East and West impossible. The Romans conceived the Church as a monarchy, the Greeks as a federation of self-governing or autocephalous bodies. The Latin ideal of a Pope uniting in his person the universal jurisdiction of the entire episcopate stood in open contradiction to the Orthodox teaching that all believers were entrusted with the power and duty of guarding the true faith and seeing the sacramental life of the Church properly preserved and ordered. Nevertheless the actual suspension of communion between Rome and Constantinople, which took place in the eleventh century, was, strangely enough, not connected with the Papal controversy. The year 1054 is the traditional date from which the schism between East and West is supposed to have started, and the unusual circumstances which accompanied it therefore deserve special attention.

The Schism of 1054

In the spring of 1054 an embassy sent from Rome reached Constantinople. Pope Leo IX (1049–54) and the Emperor Constantine Monomachus (1049–55) were both menaced by the growing power of the Normans, who had seized Sicily and were determined to extend their hold over the rest of Italy. The Papal legates, headed by Cardinal Humbert (1010–61), were warmly received by the Emperor, but they soon found themselves involved in a bitter altercation with the Patriarch Michael Cerularius (1045–58), a determined opponent of the use of unleavened bread at the Eucharist. The Patriarch, an ex-civil servant, was a man of narrow mind and hot temper.

Cardinal Humbert was no less hard-headed and aggressive. The Emperor's attempts to cement the friendship between Rome and Constantinople were constantly thwarted by the exchange of incriminations between these two proud prelates. In the midst of these uneasy negotiations the news reached Constantinople that Pope Leo had died on May 16, 1054. The Patriarch at once suspended his contacts with the Papal legates, declaring that, with the death of the Pontiff, their credentials were null and void. Cardinal Humbert thought differently. He treated the vacancy of the Papal throne as an opportunity to inflict a final blow upon his opponents, and on July 16, 1054, he laid upon the altar of St Sophia a letter excommunicating the Patriarch and all his associates. This document contained a long enumeration of Michael's alleged transgressions. Among these was his supposed omission from the Creed of the *Filioque* clause. This accusation was inaccurate, for the Eastern Church had never accepted the Western addition. The other charges were equally misinformed, trivial or baseless. The Cardinal protested, for instance, against Michael's unwillingness to baptize women in labour, against the Greek prelate's supposed refusal to give communion to men with shaven beards, and against the disregard for Mosaic Law; the question of the Papacy was not mentioned. The Patriarch, on his side, lost no time in convoking a council of bishops. He returned the excommunication to Humbert and denounced him as an impostor who had no right to act as the spokesman of the Roman Church.

Such was the rupture of relations between Rome and Constantinople. No one at that time took it seriously, and the Emperor dispatched the Cardinal back to Rome with presents, hoping that the next Pontiff would be of a more amenable disposition than the envoy of his predecessor, and that peace would soon be restored.

These expectations, however, were not fulfilled. The Normans prevented the Popes from resuming negotiations with the Byzantine Emperors and although for a long time after 1054 the Eastern and Western Christians continued to treat each other as members of the same Church, communion between the two leading Sees, those of Rome and Constantinople, was never restored, although the excommunication pronounced by Cardinal Humbert in the name of the dead Pope has never been confirmed or repudiated by any of the later Pontiffs. This survey of the doctrinal side of the schism shows the difficulty in fixing its causes on any one clearly defined theological difference. The Eastern and Western controversialists were never sure about it, and they constantly shifted the ground of their polemics from one point to another.

Political Rivalry between Rome and Constantinople

Such lack of agreement as to the exact heresy which made suspension of communion necessary strengthens the argument of those who seek the true explanation of the rift in political rivalry. Historians of this school of thought emphasize that the separation between the Eastern and Western Christians was slowly but irrevocably widened by the competition between the Byzantine Empire and Western Christendom. They fix the start of their quarrel on Christmas Day 800, when Pope Leo III (795–816) crowned Charlemagne (768–814) as the rival Western Emperor in the old basilica of St Peter in Rome without the consent of the Byzantine sovereign. The next act of the same drama occurred in the middle of the ninth century when Rome and Constantinople became engaged in fierce competition for the control of the newly converted Tsar of Bulgaria, Boris (852–89). It was during that controversy that the Patriarch Photius drew up his list of Western heresies in order to persuade the Bulgarian ruler to accept the Eastern rather than the Latin form of churchmanship. The Photian schism ended with a Byzantine victory, since the Bulgarians accepted the Eastern tradition; but Roman resentment caused by this defeat flared up in the eleventh century when Humbert on his side declared that Greek customs were infested with heresy. Nevertheless the sense of unity was so strong among the members of the Church that they continued to recognize each other. It was the sack of Constantinople on Good Friday 1204 that made any further fellowship between the two wings of Christendom impossible.

The story of this assault upon their fellow Christians launched by the Crusaders, whose avowed aim was to fight against the infidel, is one of the most tragic in the history of Christendom. The great Eastern capital, which for ten centuries had stood as a stronghold against the "barbarians", and which contained within its walls innumerable treasures of classical and Christian civilization, was mercilessly pillaged by the Western aggressors, who for three days were allowed to kill, burn and destroy at their pleasure. Nothing was spared; palaces and humble dwellings, churches and libraries, monasteries and convents, all were sacrificed to the fury of a drunken soldiery. The sacred city of the Christian East was ruined for ever by the Christian warriors of the West. This act of wanton destruction, sacrilege and revolting cruelty created an abiding resentment and hatred of Rome in Eastern Christendom and fixed a gulf between the two halves of the Christian world.

Theologians and statesmen on both sides still continued their negotiations for some time after this disaster. The Councils of Lyons in 1274 and of Florence in 1439 even reached some temporary doctrinal agreement, but these were only paper reconciliations. The majority of Eastern and Western Christians ceased to recognize each other as members of the same community, and this estrangement has lasted right up to the present time. Animosity between them was so strong that in the last days of the Byzantine Empire many Orthodox looked upon the Turkish advance as a lesser evil than submission to the Papacy. Even the fall of Constantinople in 1453 was regarded by many Eastern Christians as a divine punishment for the acceptance of Italian supremacy by the Emperor and the Patriarch at the Council of Florence in 1439.

Such is the story of the Schism between the Christian East and West. The two most popular explanations of it, however, do not go to the bottom of the problem, for both theological disagreements and political rivalry had their roots in deeper strata of the corporate life of the people involved in this drama.

The study of controversial writings reveals the bewilderment and irritation experienced by the Greek and Latin contemporaries of the Schism. Both parties considered the behaviour and the customs of their opponents unreasonable and almost perverse. They were unable to explain the motives behind this strange conduct and con-fined themselves to an indignant enumeration of the wrong things done by other members of the Church.

The Causes of the Schism between the Christian East and West

It is only in our own time that some of the reasons for this antagonism have been discovered. In this new light the whole story of the Schism, instead of being an incomprehensible manifestation of human folly and bigotry, acquires another character, that of a fratricidal conflict between two partners united in professing the same faith, but separated by their different interpretations of the nature of the Church and of her mission.

The root cause of the Schism lay in the different mentality of the Christian East and West. Geographically it is impossible to draw any clear-cut line of demarcation between the two; some regions, such as Southern Italy, Dalmatia or Galicia have been contested between them since the time of their christianization. At the same time it is impossible to deny the existence of two types of outlook within Christendom which can be defined as Eastern and Western. The Oriental Churches, namely the Armenians, Copts, Ethiopians, the Orthodox of South India and the Churches of the Byzantine tradition, that is the Greeks, the Russians and the Balkan Christians, represent the Christian East, while the Roman Catholics, Anglicans and Protestants form the Christian West. Both Roman Catholics and Protestants might be surprised at being classified under the same rubric, for they are acutely aware of their divergences; but seen from the Eastern angle they have a similarity, in that both start from the same premises, and although at some points they arrive at opposite conclusions, nevertheless they are nearer in mentality to each other than to the Eastern Christians.

There are, however, some Christians who form a bridge between East and West; these are the Uniates, or Roman Catholics who follow the Byzantine or Oriental ritual in their worship, and a smaller body of Western Christians who, having retained their own liturgy, have joined the Orthodox Church. The existence of these minorities indicates the possibility of eventual reconciliation between the divided halves of Christendom, but also complicates their relations, which are affected by the cross-currents and tensions within each of these sections of the Church.

It is also significant that two main actors in the drama of separation, the Greeks and Italians, have more in common with each other than other representatives of Western and Eastern outlooks, and it is useful to be reminded that the rupture of communion between Pope and Patriarch took place when Germanic influence was predominant in Rome. Cardinal Humbert, who took it upon himself to excommunicate the Byzantine Patriarch, was a native of Lorraine, while it was the Normans who made it impossible to restore communion between the two leading sees of Christendom. Moreover, the soldiers of the Fourth Crusade, who sacked Constantinople in 1204, were mostly recruited from Northern France, Flanders and the Rhineland.

The Russians, who had no part in the original quarrel, moreover, played a decisive role in its later stage, for it was the repudiation by the Muscovite Prince Basil II (1425–62) of the terms of agreement made in Florence in 1439 that destroyed the last hope of Eastern and Western reunion. The most typical manifestations of Western Christian mentality are found on this side of the Alps and not in Italy, while the Russian Church today represents the largest and most conservative bloc of Byzantine Orthodoxy.

It is not easy to define the differences between the Eastern and Western approach to religion, for it is more instinctive than rational, and it is seldom clearly grasped by Christians themselves; for they take it for granted that their own reactions are the only ones possible and are therefore universally valid.

In two spheres of Church life this opposition between Eastern and Western outlook is outlined particularly sharply; these are the inter-relations between community and individual, and between spirit and matter. Orthodoxy starts with community, and sees an individual as a member thereof. Western Christianity begins with the individual, and interprets the community as an outcome of a decision made by individuals to act together. The Western mind, being more analytical, approaches spirit and matter as distinct and even opposite entities, whereas Orthodoxy conceives matter and spirit as two interdependent manifestations of the same ultimate reality. These two attitudes are not contradictory but complementary to each other; yet in their own way they colour every aspect of Church life, and, as a result, the same terms are differently understood by the Christian East and West. Their buildings for worship are architecturally distinct; the movements of their liturgies have their own rhythm, and their interpretations of authority, of the Church, of the sacraments and even of salvation, do not coincide.

An example of this is the word "Catholic", which in the West has acquired the meaning of universal in the sense of the geographical extension of the Church throughout the world, so that all nations are included in its orbit. In the East "Catholic" means "integral" or "whole"; the word signifies the inner quality of the true Church as opposed to heresies or sects which present one-sided or even distorted versions of Christianity. A Western Christian sees the Church from the standpoint of an individual, and therefore to some extent, from outside it. Thus he tends to identify catholicity with universalism. The more corporately minded Eastern Christian looks upon the Catholic Church from inside, and to him it is a community enjoying harmony and unity in freedom.

The same difference in interpretation applies to the word "Orthodoxy". In the West this word stands for "correct doctrine"; in the East it is also interpreted as "right praise", for the Eastern mind links teaching with worship, and considers that only those Christians who pray to God in the spirit of love and humility have proper access to Orthodox belief and profess it in the right way. It is significant that "Orthodoxy" is translated in all Slavonic languages by the word *Pravoslavie* which means "right praise", the purely doctrinal element being thereby eliminated. "Orthodoxy" is translated in a similar fashion into Arabic and other oriental languages. In the past this divergence in interpretation of the same familiar words often escaped the attention of theologians, leading to many confused and bitter disputes and increasing antagonism.

The same dissimilar approach to their common religion is contrasted by the internal arrangement of the buildings used for worship by the Eastern and Western Christians. In the West, churches have a central focus, either the altar or the pulpit, visible to the whole congregation. In the East, a solid screen, called the *Ikonostasis*, divides the sanctuary from the rest of the building, hiding the Communion Table and the celebrants from the worshippers.

The majority of Western Christians, in order to take part in corporate worship, act in uniformity with their fellow worshippers, and they experience a sense of unity because everyone is doing the same thing together. For this reason a Western congregation requires a single priest or minister to lead the laity or to act on its behalf. His central position which is visible to all is a characteristic feature of Western services.

An Eastern Christian has a much stronger sense of identity with the community. He is able to act in unison with others even while retaining the freedom of his own movement; he does not depend upon any single person for the orderly conduct of worship, and in the East the priest remains hidden behind the screen, only occasionally appearing in a procession before the congregation.

The shape of the liturgy is also different in the East and West. The Eucharist of the Western Christians reflects to some extent their differentiation between spirit and matter. In the Catholic rite the culminating point is the Consecration, in which the spiritual breaks through into the material world in a revolutionary manner. According to the doctrine of Transubstantiation, the consecration of the elements changes their material substance into the Body and Blood of Christ, so that only in appearance do they remain bread and wine. This tendency to oppose spirit and matter is carried still further in some of the Protestant rituals, where the culminating point is reached when the believer communicates. The more consistent Protestants omit the Consecration of bread and wine altogether and regard the material elements as being outside liturgical action. They treat the soul of man as the only worthy recipient of divine grace.

The Anglicans combine both these views, and for this reason Consecration and Communion are brought as closely together as possible in the rite of the 1662 Prayer Book.

Since the early Middle Ages the West has tried to minimize the material side of sacramental life. Baptism has been administered by pouring instead of by immersion, unleavened bread has been used in the Eucharist by Catholics, and the Church of Rome withdrew the Chalice from the Communion of the laity. These steps in the evolution of the Western ritual surprised and irri-tated the Orthodox, who could not understand their underlying motives. The last stage in this development was reached by those Protestants who dispensed altogether with Baptism by water and with Holy Communion, interpreting the sacraments as having spiritual significance only and as having a direct divine action upon the soul of the believers.

The Eastern approach is from the opposite angle. The Eucharist is seen by the Orthodox Christians as the revelation of the divine Presence in the material world. Their rite has no single culminating point, but represents a gradual unveiling of Christ's mystical presidency over the assembly of the faithful. Thus the communion table is called the "Throne". The screen, with its doors which are open and shut at different stages of the service, is essential for their presentation of the Eucharist, which is based on the idea that matter is spirit-bearing, and that it is not only the souls of the participants but also their bodies and the fruits of the earth transformed into bread and wine by their labours, which are sanctified and brought into sacramental union with the risen Christ in his glory.

Eastern Christians regard the physical framework of man as a worthy recipient of sacred mysteries. The Holy Eucharist is treated as a feast both for the soul and the body. A communicant in the East does not kneel after he has consumed the consecrated elements, for his entire being is sanctified by divine grace.

This Eastern outlook explains the traditional Orthodox preference for leavened bread, and for red wine to which hot water is added before the act of communion, as an integral part of the Holy Liturgy. The members of the Orthodox Church treat sanctified matter as an essential element of the New Covenant. They therefore baptize through complete immersion in the water which has been previously blessed by special prayers. They confirm by Chrism or sacred oil, elaborately prepared at a ceremony presided over by the chief hierarch of each self-governing church; they anoint their sick with oil, and they bless fruits, animals and plants, invoking upon them the grace of the Holy Spirit.

THE AUTHORITY OF THE CHURCH

The corporate sense of the Eastern Christians has helped them to develop an attitude to the Church and to its authority, which is equally distinct from the Roman and from the Protestant doctrine. The more individualistically minded Western Christian is confronted with the question of how to discern between truth and error in his own and in his fellow Christians' beliefs. The Roman answer is that in the person of the Bishop of Rome, Christians possess an organ of infallibility, and every individual can find an answer to his quest for the revealed truth by appealing to that final authority. Protestants adopt as their criterion of truth the text of the Bible or even the writings of the Reformers, or the articles of religion composed at the time of their separation from the Roman Church.

The Eastern Christians approach the question of authority from another angle. The four Oriental Patriarchs, in their epistle addressed in 1848 to the Roman Pontiff, declared that the guardian of truth in the East is neither a single hierarch, nor the clergy as a whole, but the entire body of the faithful. The Orthodox Christians believe that the Holy Spirit guides and protects the Church from all error. He speaks to each member, and every Christian has to search his own heart for the right answers; but in order to distinguish between the voice of the Heavenly Master and his own opinions or imagination, a Christian is expected to compare his experience with that of other members of the Church, especially with those men and women whose purity of heart and soundness of judgment have been testified to by the rest of the community in listing them among the recognized saints of the Church. In practice this means that only those decisions and opinions which have been accepted unanimously by the whole body of the Orthodox have the divine sanction for the Eastern Christians. Any teaching which is only partially upheld or taught fails to carry conviction with them.

The doctrine of salvation is also affected by the same difference in outlook. In the West it is predominantly interpreted as the release of the individual from the bondage of sin (p. 76). Christ's death on the Cross is regarded as the culminating point of this act of forgiveness. In the East salvation is seen as the gift of immortality and holiness, bestowed by the Holy Spirit upon regenerated mankind, as the consequence of Christ's victory over the powers of darkness by his glorious Resurrection. Accordingly the Catholic West prefers the crucifix, and the East the empty Cross, as their traditional symbol of faith. Even on Good Friday, the Eastern service reverberates with a note of triumph, while that of the West concentrates upon Christ's agony and death which he voluntarily accepted for the redemption of sinners.

This more tragic approach to salvation, with its emphasis on sacrifice, finds its visible manifestation in the architectural designs of Western churches. Their grey stone walls and strong towers suggest confidence in the ultimate victory of good, but only after long and costly struggle. Their spires point worshippers to the realm of spirit, but they remind them also of the sorrow of earthly life. This instinct to conquer the heaviness of matter is most powerfully expressed in the medieval Gothic. The cathedrals and churches of that period are a perfect artistic expression of this attitude towards the material world, which by the creative spirit of men is lifted up to the throne of their Creator.

In the East, ecclesiastical architecture expresses the opposite idea, that of the Holy Spirit descending upon earth, and sanctifying and transforming the material world by his redeeming action. Accordingly, the churches are built with domes, which in Russia have a distinctive shape, becoming brightly coloured cupolas, crowned with golden eight-pointed crosses, symbolic of Christ's victory over death. Many Eastern churches are painted blue, red or green; they are richly adorned with frescoes which sometimes cover even their outer walls. The congregation of Eastern Christians gathered for worship is treated as one community, in which the living and the departed form one indissoluble whole. Their liturgical action and prayer sanctify both their souls and their bodies, and hallow the material world brought by men into this divine-human encounter. The cathedral or parish church thus becomes part of the transfigured earth which has glimpsed celestial light and fire, reflecting it in design and colour.

The special popularity in the East of such festivals as the Baptism of Christ (Epiphany) and his Transfiguration are further examples of the same mental approach. The Orthodox ascribe cosmic significance to Christ's Baptism, for the Incarnate Lord sanctified water by his sacramental washing in Jordan. The same idea is associated with the feast of the Transfiguration, commemorating the vision seen by the disciples, not only of the glorified Christ, but also of the transfigured Mount, which revealed the sacred beauty of the universe.

The Christian East believes that the final destiny of matter is not its annihilation, but its transformation into a perfect and obedient instrument of the Spirit. This confidence in the goodness of matter has inspired the Eastern Christians to make generous use of material elements in the administration of all their sacraments.

The number and purpose of the sacraments have often been disputed among Christians. Since the Middle Ages the West has reduced their number to seven. The Reformers went further and retained only two, Baptism and the Eucharist. The Orthodox Church offers to its members a greater number, but the seven most important are Baptism, Confirmation, Confession, Holy Communion, Ordination, Matrimony and the Anointing of the Sick.

Sacraments

Baptism represents for the Orthodox the incorporation of a newly born Christian into the community of those who believe in Jesus Christ as their Lord and Saviour. Chrismation or Confirmation is the sacrament of Pentecost. Through it a Christian receives the gift of the Holy Spirit, which places him in the position of a lay co-celebrant in the administration of all the other sacraments. In practice it means that all confirmed, or chrismated, Christians are treated as members of a special order and as such have their right and duty to teach, to preach, and to take part in the government of the Christian community.

An important difference between the Eastern and Western liturgical practices is the Orthodox custom of joining together the sacraments of Baptism and Chrismation. This means that Eastern Christians start their life as communicants at a much earlier date than is the custom in the West. The majority of the Orthodox receive the Sacrament when they are still infants, and they therefore feel a deep attachment to their Church, for they are initiated into its sacramental life from the very beginning of their lives. At the age of seven the first confession, preceded by instruction, marks the first stage of moral responsibility. After this stage has been reached, children, like their parents, approach the Sacrament fasting and prepare themselves for its reception by self-examination and confession.

The Sacrament of Confession, like all other sacraments, is conceived of by the Orthodox in accordance with the corporate teaching of their Church. The person who intends to make this act of repentance is expected to be reconciled first with all those who might be grieved or offended by his actions. Only when forgiveness and reconciliation with his neighbours have been achieved, does an Orthodox Christian go to the priest and make his confession in his presence.

In the Roman Church the role of the priest in the confessional is that of a judge. The priest occupies the seat of judgment and the penitent kneels beside him. The priest has the power to absolve the penitent and he assigns to him a penance in reparation for the sins he has committed. In the East the priest is not a judge, but a witness. He stands by the side of the penitent and in his introductory prayers reminds him that every penitent has come to a hospital where Jesus Christ is the only healer. The priest is a fellow-member of the Church whose help and brotherly advice can facilitate the act of repentance. At the end of confession the priest in his prayers asks God to reconcile the sinner to the Church and to pardon all his offences. In the Russian Church the taking of Holy Communion is always preceded by confession. Among other Orthodox groups confession is less frequently used.

The same corporate spirit manifests itself also in the administration of the laying on of hands. There are two opposite traditions in the West in regard to Ordination. According to the Catholic teaching only a bishop in the Apostolic succession has the right to make valid priests and deacons, while for the Protestants the inner call to the ministry is generally regarded as being the essential part of this special dedication to the full-time service of the Church. The imposition of hands by other ministers only confirms the decision made previously by the candidate, and the bishop's participation in it is not required. The Orthodox differ from both of these Western approaches. According to their teaching the local congregation starts the process of ordination, but the bishop alone, in the name of the Church Universal, can complete this action. He does it by the imposition of his hands upon the person being ordained.

The service is performed in the following manner. The candidate is brought into the middle of the congregation by subdeacons, who ask the assembled Christians to authorize the ordination. A unanimous sanction is indispensable if the ordination is to be proceeded with. Only when such approval is given first by the laity and then by the clergy, does the bishop lay his hands on the person in question and invoke divine help upon him after ordination. The united prayers of the whole Church are essential for this sacrament. Only one person of the same grade can therefore be ordained at the same service.

Marriage in the Orthodox Church is called "the Crowning". During the ceremony the couple who are being married wear crowns of glory. Neither bridegroom nor bride give any promises during the service, but merely express their consent to marry each other. Ideally the unity thus achieved excludes any second marriage; but the Orthodox Church nevertheless allows divorce and re-marriage. Such a practice does not seem to Eastern Christians to be incompatible with their belief in that sanctity of the union between man and woman which links the mystery of human love with the love which Jesus Christ has for his bride, the Church. The Orthodox consider that it is undesirable to force all their members to adhere to the ideal of a single wedlock. A divorce is granted, therefore, to those whose family life has been destroyed either by the disappearance of one of the partners, or by a life sentence passed on them for some crime, or by insanity or by unfaithfulness. The second marriage is, however, a different service from the glorious crowning. It contains an element of penitence for the failure to maintain the original intention. Widows and widowers, if they want to re-marry, are treated in the same way as divorcees. A married man will be accepted for ordination in the Orthodox Church, provided that he has not been married twice, or to a widow or a divorcee.

Holy Unction is the sacrament of healing. It has lately been increasingly used, especially in the Russian Church, as a divine help to those who are afflicted either by bodily or psychological troubles and who need strengthening, purification or greater stability.

Besides the seven sacraments which the Orthodox share with the Western Catholics, they regard their Church as a source of sanctification and blessing for all aspects of their life and work. Special services are frequently held either in church or at the homes of the faithful. These mark happy or unhappy events, such as a special blessing received, or illness, starting on a new job, or on an intended journey. All these occasions find their reflection in the services of the Orthodox Church, whose prayers and supplication accompany its members from the day of their birth to their final rest in the grave. Houses, gardens, crops, fruits and domestic animals are blessed by the Church and are in this way included in the sacred ring of its liturgical actions.

The home life and the Church life of the Eastern Christians are closely inter-related, and whilst the services of the Church are often held in the houses of the parishioners, their personal and family needs are mentioned during public worship. A very important part in the prayer life of Eastern Christians is played by the commemoration of the Saints and by the loving remembrance of the departed. The Church for the Orthodox is one great family, and those members of it who have departed from this life are not treated as though they have lost all contact with it. Eastern Christians therefore pray for the departed and ask for their prayers, believing that the power of love is stronger than the power of death.

The Orthodox do not, however, define the exact status of the departed, nor do they claim to know the effect of their prayers on their destiny. They place Mary, the Mother of the Incarnate Word, above all the Saints. She is *Theotokos* or God-bearer (the Mother of God) and her name is invoked in public and private prayers.

The special reverence shown by Eastern Christians for the bodies of the departed can again be explained by their view on the sanctification of matter. The relics of the Saints are venerated as a part of the material world which has received the permanent imprint of the purified and regenerated personality of a man of God.

Ikons

The cult of ikons is also the expression of the same Eastern belief that matter is spirit-bearing, and that re-demption signifies not the liberation of the spirit from its dependence on the material world, but the transfiguration of the latter. The final act of Christian history is the resurrection of the body which will bring about a perfect harmony between spirit and matter.

The ikons, or pictures representing Jesus Christ, his Mother, the Saints and scenes from the Old and New Testaments, occupy a prominent place in the public worship and private devotions of the Orthodox. An ikon is usually a picture painted on wood; sculptures and carved figures are only in exceptional cases used by the Eastern Christians. The art of the ikons is distinct from Western religious paintings, and its appreciation requires some understanding of the realm of ideas lying behind it. The aim of the ikon is to help the worshipper to realize his dependence on the spiritual world and to assist him in his efforts to attain harmony between his body and soul. Men and women depicted on the ikons represent those Christians who gave up their selfish and self-centred existence and entered into the wider and inspiring world of loving fellowship with their Creator and their fellow-men. Such an achievement required struggle, self-discipline and sacrifices. The Saints therefore are represented on the ikons as ascetics, whose movements are restrained and whose bodies bear the signs of voluntary privations, but their robes are shining and their faces are turned towards the new world of joy and freedom. Their triumph is expressed by their eyes, and the contrast between the immobility of their bodies and the intense aliveness of their glance emphasizes their reconciliation with their Creator and the perfect control over matter which they have achieved.

The ikons which adorn the homes of the Eastern Christians remind them of the invisible bond which links them with the triumphant departed. Ikons are particularly numerous in places of worship, the most important of them being placed on the *ikonostasis*, that is, the screen which divides the Eastern part of the church from the rest of the building. This screen symbolically represents the line of demarcation between heaven and earth. The ikons of the Incarnate Lord, together with his Mother and the Saints, when seen on the *ikonostasis*, teach the worshippers that man is both the link and the cause of the partition between the two realms, that of the spirit and that of the flesh. The *ikonostasis* has three doors leading into the sanctuary. The central one, called the Royal Door, is decorated with pictures of the Annunciation and of the four Evangelists. This expresses the belief of the Orthodox that only the Incarnation opened the door into the divine realm for redeemed mankind by removing the stain of sin from its members. Only the celebrant, who

PLATE 23. The Life of Christ. Artist unknown. Scenes from the life of the Virgin and from the life and passion of Christ. Russian, late 17th–18th century. Turner Sargent Collection. (Courtesy, *Museum of Fine Arts, Boston.*)

PLATE 24. Novgorod Miracle Workers. Ikon. Russian School. Gift of Vladimir G. Simkhovit. (Courtesy, *Museum of Fine Arts, Boston.*)

represents the Redeemer during the service, can pass through the Royal Door, and he brings to the worshippers through that door the book of the Gospels and the Holy Gifts of the Eucharist.

It is the custom of the Orthodox to put lighted candles in front of the ikons during the service. This action indicates their warm affection for the Saints and their recognition of the interdependence of all human beings, both living and departed.

THE CONSTITUTION OF THE ORTHODOX CHURCH

The Orthodox Church today consists of fourteen autocephalous or self-governing Churches, each of which enjoys complete independence, though bound to the others by the same belief and by the same type of worship.

The faith of the Orthodox Church is expressed in the words of the Nicene Creed, the only one used by the Eastern Christians. Other doctrinal definitions accepted by all of them are contained in the decisions of the first seven Ecumenical Councils (Nicaea 325, Constantinople 381, Ephesus 431, Chalcedon 451, Constantinople 553 and 680, and Nicaea 787).

Five of these Churches date from the time of the Byzantine Empire. They are the Patriarchates of Constantinople, Alexandria, Antioch, Jerusalem and the Church of Cyprus; six other Churches represent the nations where the majority of people are Orthodox. These are the Patriarchates of Russia, Rumania, Yugoslavia, Bulgaria, the Catholicate of Georgia and the Church of Greece. Three more autocephalous Churches belong to the countries where only a minority profess the Eastern tradition. These are the Churches of Albania, Poland and Czechoslovakia. The Monastery of Sinai occupies a unique position, for it too claims an ancient privilege of independence.

Besides these autocephalous Churches, the Eastern Orthodox federation also includes other Churches, which depend on some other ecclesiastical authority for their administration. Such are the Churches of Finland, Japan, Hungary, the Orthodox Churches in North and South America and in Australia, and finally the Church of the Russian emigrants in Western Europe.

Each of the Eastern Churches is divided into dioceses governed by a bishop. A diocese is further subdivided into parishes. A priest, or sometimes several priests, assisted by deacons, is placed in charge of each parish. Bishops are unmarried, but the parochial clergy are married. The bishops of the Orthodox Church have different titles such as Patriarch, Catholicos, Metropolitan, Archbishop, Exarch. These names only indicate the degree of their seniority and honours, for otherwise they are all equal to one another in the exercise of their pastoral functions within each of their dioceses.

Clergy and Laity

The Church for the Orthodox is the community of the redeemed gathered round the Holy Eucharist. Each member is responsible for all others, and has his appointed role in the worship of the community. Clergy and lay people are co-celebrants in the administration of the divine Mysteries, the purpose of which is to assist them in the process of their spiritual growth and to increase the power of love among them. Christian love is interpreted as a desire for perfect unity among independent persons. Only where freedom is unimpaired is it considered that love can grow into its fullness. The Orthodox Church therefore lays great stress on freedom as an indispensable condition for the proper functioning of the Church organism.

This means that laymen play an active part in the life of the Eastern Churches, and so it is that many of the best known theologians of Eastern Orthodoxy are laymen. Every chrismated (confirmed) member of the Eastern Church can be a teacher if he has a special gift or training for such a calling. The educational, philanthropic and missionary work of the Eastern Church is usually carried on by clergy and laity in close collaboration. Some of the best known Orthodox missionaries in modern times were lay people. Laymen also take part as elected representatives at church councils, national, diocesan or parochial.

Monasticism

A special role in the Eastern Church is assigned to monks and nuns. These men and women, who choose a life of celibacy, poverty and obedience, dedicate themselves entirely to prayer and the service of the Church. Eastern monks have no orders, but different communities specialize in different types of work. Most of them, however, consider prayer as the main service a religious can offer to the rest of the community. The majority of Eastern monks remain laymen, only a few of them being ordained priests and deacons. Monasteries and convents also serve as places of retreat for the rest of the community who can stay in them for varying periods of time, and receive training and help in their spiritual life.

Worship in the Orthodox Church was moulded into its present form by the monastic communities, and such offices as Matins or Vespers still clearly preserve the marks of their origin. The major portion of them is sung and recited by the laity. The centre of Eastern monasticism is Mount Athos in Greece. That peninsula is inhabited exclusively by monks of different nationalities who live in large and small communities, each following its own rules.

The first settlements of religious were founded on that isolated and most beautiful spot as early as in the ninth century, and since that time until our own days the Holy Mountain has been the abode of men who seek solitude and contemplation. For more than a thousand years no women have been allowed to cross the frontier of this monastic republic. The territory of Mount Athos is divided nowadays among twenty self-governing monasteries which, by common consent, govern the peninsula through their representatives. Their churches and libraries contain some of the finest specimens of Byzantine art and learning, and they attract the increasing attention of scholars and artists from all parts of the world. Every visitor receives free hospitality for three days at each of the religious houses.

Some of the monasteries follow the strict rules of community life, and every monk has to give up all his earthly possessions to the monastery; others are organized along more individualistic lines, each monk living according to his own rule. Some inhabitants of Mount Athos prefer to build their own cells and remain quite independent. Most of the monasteries are Greek, but some of them are Russian, while a few are Serbian, Bulgarian or Rumanian.

CHURCH AND STATE IN THE CHRISTIAN EAST

The relations between Church and State have taken a different course in the East and West. In the history of the Byzantine Christians of the Middle Ages there was nothing similar to the struggle between the Popes and the Emperors. The Church and Christian State were conceived of in Byzantium as two independent but closely related guardians of the Christian people. They were neither identical, nor was one considered superior to the other. The task of the Christian State was defined as safeguarding order and justice. The Church's aim was to help its members towards eternal salvation. The Church was organized piety, the State organized pity. At times there were clashes between the Emperors and the representatives of the Church, but they were always temporary and personal. The harmonious collaboration between Church and State, based on respect for the autonomy of each in its own sphere, remained intact until the end of the Empire.

It was popular at one time to describe the Orthodox Church as subservient to the secular power and incapable of defending its independence, but the latest historical research has done much to dispel this misconception and discredit the term Caesaropapism, coined by the Western opponents of Byzantium.

After the Turkish conquest of the Byzantine Empire in 1453 the Moscow Tsardom assumed the leadership of the Christian East. Its capital became known as the Third Rome, and the same peaceful collaboration was maintained there until the beginning of the eighteenth century when Peter the Great (1682–1725) imposed state control over the Russian Church as a part of his policy of Westernizing the country. From 1700 until 1917 the Russian Church was deprived of self-government and subjected to oppressive bureaucratic supervision, the organ of which was the Synod shaped by Peter in imitation of similar institutions in Lutheran countries.

In 1917, after the fall of the Empire, the Russian Church convoked its Council and restored its independence. This event, however, was followed by the Communist attack on the Church which ushered in a long period of acute suffering for the Russian Christians. Since 1943 the Russian Church has once more been governed by its Patriarchs and recovered the possibility of training its clergy for the conduct of public worship, the only activity allowed to Christians by the Communist regime.

The Orthodox Churches in the Balkans have regained their freedom of action after the liberation of their people from the Turkish yoke. During the nineteenth century their relations with their states have been regulated by constitutions which differ in detail, but adhere to the same principle of treating each Church as an autonomous unit, the life of which is directed by its own elected organs in which both clergy and laity take part.

The history of the Western Church since its alienation from the Orthodox East is full of dramatic events, such as the spectacular growth of the medieval Papacy, the intellectual achievements of scholasticism, the successful rebellion of the Reformation against the Papacy and the swift and effective reaction of the Counter-Reformation, the driving force of Puritanism, the spread of rationalism followed by Liberalism and modernism, and of the latest reaction to those tendencies known as Neo-Orthodoxy. To the Orthodox the Western Christians seem to move from one extreme to the other, and Eastern ecclesiastical history may seem monotonous when compared with the West. For even such calamitous events as the Mongol invasion of Russia in the thirteenth century, the fall of Constantinople, the subjugation of the Balkan Christians to the Turks in the fifteenth century, or the collapse of the St Petersburg Empire in 1917, have not altered in any radical way the character of the life of the Eastern Church, which is distinguished by steadfast adherence to the same tradition.

Its apparent uneventfulness, however, does not exclude the possibility of development in a new direction. The Church has to perform its mission under constantly varying conditions and within an environment which is never the same. Individual Christians or groups of Christians are called upon to seek for solutions of current problems; they experiment, they try new methods. Some of these are eventually adopted by the rest of the body and become a part of the tradition; others are rejected, and drop out of Church life. There is a constant process of growth and change in the East as in the West, but the Western evolution is full of sharp turning points, jolts and upheavals, whilst the history of Eastern Christianity represents a gradual movement in which no radical breaks with the past have ever taken place, and where the sense of uninterrupted continuity has been lovingly preserved. It is in the fellowship with the Saints that the Eastern Christians find their best guarantee against hasty decisions leading to the one-sided twists in the life of the Christian community. Both wings of the Church need each other. The stability of the East and the dynamic qualities of the West are complementary elements of Christian history, equally required for the proper exercise of its universal mission.

The Christian East and West possess different gifts and can learn much from each other. The Orthodox Church has maintained balance and harmony in its doctrines and worship, but compared to the West, its organization and driving power is deficient. Centuries of rivalry have made the Eastern and Western Christians suspicious and critical of each other, and it is time for both to meet and work as friends in the same field of Christian life and action.

The distinctive Eastern and Western approach to their common religion does not destroy the fundamental unity which exists among the principal branches of contemporary Christendom. They share the same Bible and the same belief in Jesus Christ as the Saviour of mankind. They recognize the same sacraments, with Baptism and the Eucharist occupying a special place of honour in their life and worship.

At present the Eastern Church is not in communion with any of the Western Churches. Several Orthodox Churches, however, are members of the Ecumenical Movement and one of the Vice-Presidents of the World Council of Churches is usually chosen from the hierarchs of the Orthodox Church.

Since the First World War and the establishment of Communist dictatorship in Russia and other neighbouring countries, the Eastern Christians have been exposed to the relentless pressure of a godless campaign sponsored by totalitarian governments. The Orthodox Church has suffered some grievous losses, but it has survived in spite of its hard trials, and has now emerged as a community capable of enduring under the most unfavourable circumstances. One of the great lessons it has learned is the necessity for unity.

2c. Christianity: St Thomas and Medieval Theology

by H. FRANCIS DAVIS

I have avoided the term "scholastic" because of the depreciatory meanings and emotive overtones that this word has acquired during the last three centuries. Yet the word is innocent enough in its origins, and most admirers of St Thomas and his contemporaries have been content to use it themselves to describe the professors and writers of our first Western universities. There are still many associations in Oxford which remind us that *schola* and its derivatives were once ordinary words to denote some connection with a home or institute of learning. Scholastics were simply those who taught or studied in the Schools.

But it cannot be denied that there is a tendency for words indicating scholarship to acquire a depreciatory sense. The same fate has occasionally befallen even such highly dignified words as "professorial", "speculative", and "intellectual". The greatest living authority on medieval philosophy, Etienne Gilson, in spite of his enthusiasm for things medieval, does not love the word "scholastic". To him it connotes a philosophy which ends in itself, instead of in reality. He concludes that a Thomism worthy of the name is not rightly called a scholasticism. "Philosophy," he writes, "degenerates into scholasticism the moment when, instead of taking the existing concrete as object of its reflections in order to study it deeply, penetrate it, throw more and more light upon it, it applies itself rather to the statements which it is supposed to explain, as if these statements themselves and not what they shed light on, were the reality itself" (*The Christian Philosophy of St Thomas Aquinas*, 1957, pp. 366–7). He agrees that Thomism itself could degenerate into scholasticism if it were to forget that it is only concerned ultimately with the real concrete existing world. But, he adds, this is not true of St Thomas.

The word has also been used frequently for the scientific, as opposed to the literary, method of exposition in theology or philosophy. In a very special sense it refers to the scientific methods that were popular in the Middle Ages, such as the method of lecturing in the form of a comment on a set authoritative text, or the method of systematic formal disputation on a series of questions, afterwards to be gathered together into an organized *summa*.[1] Such a method has its advantages and disadvantages, but neither would be sufficiently outstanding to justify for its users a special place in the history of beliefs. If the medieval theologians have a special place in the development of Christian thought, it is for the content of their theology and philosophy rather than for their method of exposition.

It will be best in this chapter to confine our remarks mainly to the golden period of medieval thought, that of the thirteenth century, and above all to its greatest representative, St Thomas Aquinas. A full historical account would have to cover the many centuries from the end of the patristic period to the Reformation. Even the more limited era which has frequently been called "Scholastic" extended from the end of the eleventh century until the fourteenth. It has been customary to distinguish three periods. *Early* scholasticism would extend from the late eleventh century to the early thirteenth, and would include St Anselm, Lanfranc, Abelard, St Bernard, Peter Lombard, Grosseteste, and the schools of St Victor and Chartres. The *golden* period would cover the middle and late thirteenth century, and

---

[1] *Summa* was the medieval term for a summary treatise containing a brief and lucidly reasoned statement of the important doctrines of Christian theology. It was divided into questions and articles. Each article began with objections against the view defended, continued with an exposition and defence of the thesis, and concluded with answers to the original objections. Readers unacquainted with the method have to beware of confusing the objections with the defence. It has happened that St Thomas has, through such a confusion, been quoted as declaring: "it seems that there is no God. . . ."

would include Alexander of Hales, St Albert the Great, Roger Bacon, St Thomas, St Bonaventure, Siger of Brabant, and John Duns Scotus. The *late* or *decadent* period would include Durandus, Aureolus, William of Ockham and the later Nominalists, as well as a distinctive group of mystics, separated from the philosophical tradition, found mainly in the north of Europe.

The early period was influenced, apart from the Scriptures and general Church tradition, chiefly by St Augustine, and in a lesser degree by several Christian Neo-Platonists, as well as, through Boethius, by the logical works of Aristotle. There can be distinguished both a strong *logical* tradition, fully Catholic, yet deeply confident of the power of reason, and, on the other hand, a more *mystical* tradition occasionally somewhat distrustful of the logicians. St Anselm would be the greatest name in the first tradition, and St Bernard in the second. By these two traditions, and also by a third strong tradition of *humanism* of which perhaps John of Salisbury is the most illustrious representative, the twelfth century was itself to provide some of the most powerful forces influencing the development of theology in the following period. But in many other ways the field of study was to be widened incomparably during the thirteenth century. In the sphere of theology, there was to be added during the mid-century to the influence of St Augustine that of Greek patristics through the newly translated works of St John of Damascus (p. 75). Perhaps equally important was the new scientific spirit that was introduced when a whole new world of philosophy was revealed to the West with the discovery of the complete works of Aristotle. These were made available first through the Arabic translations, and afterwards in direct translations from the Greek. With Aristotle came the works of the Arabian commentators and philosophers, and also the medieval Jewish philosophy (p. 39). The characteristic, on the other hand, of the final period of decadence was rather to divide and delimit these influences, so that the fourteenth-century scholastics and mystics fell into separate and often individualistic groups, sometimes more anxious to search for a superficial originality than to pass on a constructive view of truth.

If this book were to be a survey of medieval history, rather than of Christian and other beliefs, some might question the propriety of concentrating on St Thomas. Though he is the finest flower of medieval theology, he is not perhaps its most typical representative. Yet the Middle Ages have the right to claim him, just as ancient Greece could claim Plato and Aristotle, or sixteenth-century England Shakespeare. Of St Thomas's contemporaries some followed their own brand of theology

which was eclectic in a way he would not approve, while others went to the extreme of condemning important parts of his theology or philosophy. Within a few years, in fact, of St Thomas's death, the bishop of Paris and two successive archbishops of Canterbury, one of the latter a Dominican like St Thomas himself, had drawn up from his works lists of propositions to be condemned. Most of the Franciscans and several illustrious Dominicans of the century after his death were vigorous opponents of Thomism. The Nominalists of the fourteenth century rejected the whole theology and philosophy of the thirteenth century. Yet it would be false to pretend that there was not, during all this time, a steady increase of followers of St Thomas among the rank and file of Dominican and other Catholic thinkers. When it came to the division of Western Christendom at the Reformation, Catholics, now conscious that the values they stood for had been undermined or betrayed by the Nominalists, almost instinctively rediscovered, and preferred above his fellows, St Thomas Aquinas. The only significant exceptions to this were the Franciscans, who were more attracted to Duns Scotus.

Yet for several centuries after the Renaissance and Reformation the influence of St Thomas remained greatly restricted. The new Humanists, thrilled by their "rediscovery" of Greek and Roman literature, and apparently ignorant both of medieval literature and poetry and of the school of Chartres,[1] dismissed the many centuries since the fall of Rome as barbaric. One might have expected them to recognize the philosophic importance at least of writers like St Thomas and Scotus, and even of St Bonaventure and Siger of Brabant, and the scientific progressiveness of Roger Bacon and St Albert. But they had been blinded to all this by the mainly destructive criticism of the fourteenth-century Nominalists.

It is not clear whence Luther acquired such a special antipathy to St Thomas, whose writings he hardly knew, with the result that he bequeathed his contempt to centuries of Continental Protestants. He made the somewhat contradictory accusations against St Thomas both of using Aristotle alongside the Bible, and of failing to understand a single chapter of that Greek philosopher.

---

[1] There was an important humanistic renaissance in the school of Chartres during the eleventh and twelfth centuries. John of Salisbury was its greatest representative. He was a devotee of Cicero, Virgil, Ovid, Horace, Juvenal and Seneca. In his philosophy he might be called a Christian Platonist. Just as thirteenth-century science was almost to anticipate the modern rise of experimental science, so did twelfth-century humanism almost anticipate the Renaissance. This early humanism was to succumb to the late medieval interest in pure metaphysics. *See* Frederick B. Artz, *The Mind of the Middle Ages*, New York, 1953, chapters ix and x.

He doubtless picked upon St Thomas from the time he saw that his Catholic opponents were using the latter as the chief defence of their own position.

St Thomas and the Scholastics suffered the nadir of contempt at the time of the French Encyclopaedists, who had no good word for any writer between the fifth and fifteenth centuries. Scholasticism, they said, degraded philosophy, obscured truth and was a scourge of the human mind.

Yet, in spite of so long a period of neglect in so great a part of the Christian and philosophic world, St Thomas has during this century become known and respected in the world of thought more than at any previous period. Not even in the countries where Existentialism has been the fashion has St Thomas been without influence, especially since several modern Thomists have plausibly claimed that the aspect of Existentialism which leads to its insistence on the concrete existing object is also a distinctive aspect of Thomism.

What is it that has drawn so many of our modern age to look to St Thomas for inspiration? Perhaps one should put first his great sense of responsibility for the truth, from which follows his instinctive reverence for all great thinkers of every age who have spent their lives in its sincere search. If St Thomas had not the advantage of modern critical scholarship when dealing with his sources, he had something that perhaps by and large is more important. He had a deep sympathy and understanding of the principles on which those sources were based, and which they were trying to express. Thus, as a commentator of St Paul, St Thomas would often have to yield to a modern critic for the interpretation of a phrase here and a word there, but few of our modern Scripture commentators would disagree with St Thomas's understanding, for instance, of the basic argument underlying St Paul's Epistle to the Romans. Moreover, though from St Thomas's day until the present there is division of opinion as to the true interpretation of Aristotle, St Thomas's theistic interpretation has never been proved untenable. As a modern English philosopher said, "If St Thomas's interpretation of Aristotle is not the true one, so much the worse for Aristotle."

St Thomas's sense of responsibility is closely connected with what some of his opponents might call his conservatism or traditionalism, but which could with more justice be called his universalism. Traditionalism is an unsatisfactory name, because St Thomas did not merely record tradition. No one was a stronger believer in theology, which means the use of reason to analyse and synthesize, and penetrate more deeply, the truths handed down by tradition. Thomism could justly be called universalism,

because in its search for help from every quarter towards the understanding of its subject it cut clear from both locality and time, and invited all comers seriously to make their contribution. There was in the thirteenth century nothing of what C. S. Lewis has called chronological snobbery, nor was there national or racial snobbery. National feeling, as between theologians and philosophers, hardly existed. Scholars from England, Germany, France, Spain and Italy met on an equal footing in the universally recognized intellectual metropolis, Paris. Christians and Arabs met on an intellectual equality in the universities of Spain. Whatever the "Scholastics" said in support, or in criticism, of Avicenna, Averroes or Maimonides (pp. 39, 45-8), the nationality or religion of these latter altered not a whit the respect with which they were treated. What was true of contemporary Muslims and Jews was true across the ages of the ancient pagan classical writers. There was never any question of an *a priori* rejection of pagan or Muslim thought on the sole grounds of the doctrine of Original Sin, as was to be the case with some of the Protestant Reformers. All writers were judged on their philosophical merits. If they were refuted, St Thomas insisted that they should be refuted by their own philosophical weapons, not by an appeal to Christian revelation.

St Thomas's reverence for other sincere thinkers is such that he rarely contradicts them. When he disagrees with them, he appears to be defending them from perverse interpretations. "What Boethius says must be understood in this way"; "Dionysius is here defining God in so far as God is a cause"; "Augustine is here speaking after the manner of Plato"; "When Gregory of Nyssa says that all sadness is evil, he is speaking from the point of view of the person who rejects it." Such is the courteous way in which St Thomas corrects his medieval opponent without involving the ancient revered authority. St Thomas was able to adopt his universalist attitude of sympathy towards other sincere thinkers because of his deep conviction of the unity of truth. If there is a lesson he taught us more clearly than any other thinker, it is this.

There were both historical and doctrinal reasons for this conviction. Historically, the Christians of the West had found themselves in an entirely new situation of responsibility. No longer was the Christian community the "little flock" gathered together from out of a great hostile world. With the destruction of the Roman Empire and the withdrawal of the Byzantine Emperors, Western Christianity suddenly found itself left with the responsibility not only of converting, but also of civilizing, its world. They had no other idea of laying the foundations of a new culture than by the preservation and promulgation of the only culture they had known, that of the Hellenistic world. Hence throughout the Middle Ages it went without saying that Christian libraries would be furnished and maintained with a collection of all that had been preserved from the ancient culture. But since Christians were first and foremost Christians, and since Christianity, as well as, to a degree, ancient Greek and Roman thought, claimed to contain the truth, sooner or later Christians had to learn to fit the truths of one world into those of the other. Not that anything was sacrificed of the Christian revelation. But, however greatly the latter was valued, it could not survive in the human mind in a compartment utterly separated from that which still profited by the classics. The new must learn to live with the old, and the old with the new. The health and progress of Christianity in its world demanded that long process of assimilation and synthesis, which gained momentum until it reached the wide and deep sense of unity that characterized the high Middle Ages. Like all movements of human thought, it had its dangers. Writers like Abelard and Siger of Brabant were suspected of adulterating Christianity with one or other form of naturalism. The achievement of the greatest minds was so to baptize hellenistic thought that it was able to become Christian without ceasing to be, say, Aristotelian or Platonic.

The chief doctrinal reason which compelled a synthesis was, of course, the Christian doctrine of God's unity and universal creatorship, as well as the doctrine of the universal redemption by Christ. Man, with all that is good in man, even apart from grace, comes from the Creator. Man, with all his perfections, is destined for God. If there is any good in the pagan world – and good there must be, since the pagans are also God's creatures – to God be the glory! And if the Christian revelation through Christ also comes in a specially direct way from God, this is in a higher sense divine.

To St Thomas, to reject either would be unthinkable. It would be unthinkable that we should refuse to listen to the Christian revelation, or even forgo to find out whether there be such a revelation, in the name of philosophy, which only means a love of wisdom. How can one love wisdom and refuse to seek it when there are grounds to believe that God may have spoken! On the other hand, on what grounds will one refuse to consider the voice of God in our reason, if one reveres the voice of God in revelation?

It will be seen from this that there was in St Thomas in common with his greatest contemporaries a balance and moderation that many would call common-sense optimism. All that God made was good, whether it were

matter or spirit, body or soul, nature or grace. Not even sin could essentially destroy God's creation. The sinner's intellect and will still remain capable of good, though they can no longer act in a Christian way without special graces. St Thomas was never tempted to call the virtues of pagans "splendid vices", to recall a famous Augustinian phrase. He agreed that, without grace, man's capacity for virtuous action was much curtailed. Fallen man without grace could no longer act as the son of God, and so would never reach God's destiny for him. But he was still capable of much natural good. St Thomas's respect for the body, which is of course in full harmony with Hebrew thought (p. 34), was part of the basis of his preference for Aristotle over Neo-Platonism. Yet it was again characteristic of his universalism and his moderation that he could still learn from the Platonic tradition. It must not be thought that he was an eclectic. He did not pick and choose doctrines from here and there and everywhere. But he was capable of recognizing that a sound coherent "Christian" philosophy could be Aristotelian without ceasing to owe many important debts to Plato. One at least of St Thomas's arguments for the existence of God – the one that people find hardest to understand, the fourth "way"[1] – as well as most of his arguments in favour of the created nature of everything material, are much more Platonic in inspiration than Aristotelian. It was perhaps because St Thomas's Aristotelianism was so Platonic that he failed to be able to recognize as genuine the pantheistic Aristotelianism of some of his contemporaries.

This common-sense optimism of St Thomas is the more remarkable in that there was a pessimistic line of thought running through the Middle Ages. It could be traced back to St Augustine's dark views on Original Sin, it was reflected sometimes in a general distrust of philosophy, as with St Peter Damian, sometimes in an almost morbid distrust of man's power to lead a good life in the world even with God's grace. True enough, this pessimism was frequently offset by deep and sincere spirituality, which was offended by undeniable scandals. This doubtless is the explanation of the pessimism of St Peter Damian and the writer of the *Imitation of Christ*. But in the long run the optimism of St Thomas was recognized as more in harmony with the joyous faith in the Incarnation and Redemption that is the mark of Christianity.

The troubled history of thought since the Reformation, with the exaggeratedly critical attitude of most modern

---

[1] *The Fourth Way.* The fourth of St Thomas's five arguments for the existence of God. It starts out from the existence of different grades of perfection in the world to that of an all-perfect first cause.

philosophies and the consequent destructive tendency of modern thought, has perhaps been one of the greatest influences in turning men's minds back to a more peaceful and more constructive age. Is the truth to be found by a distrust of all common-sense metaphysics, as the logical positivists would persuade us? Or is it not rather to be found by a return to a saner and more natural view of the world, which has the advantage of being readily harmonizable with Christian revelation? It has often been discussed whether Thomist philosophy can be called a Christian philosophy. Most Thomists have thought that St Thomas would have rejected such terms, since he always maintained that philosophy, though it could help theology, was in its principles and arguments self-sufficient. Recently one of our greatest Thomists has defended the term "Christian" as appropriate to describe Thomism. He argues that, while it is true that St Thomas does not introduce any arguments into his philosophy other than those of pure reason, yet we must admit that there are certain philosophical truths taught by Christianity which, together with Aristotle and Plato, formed part of St Thomas's sources, even in philosophy. However we decide this question, there is one sense in which St Thomas's philosophy remains eminently Christian. It commends itself to the Christian as a system of thought, of which the principles have been found by the long experience of Christians to be such as in no way undermine the distinctive truths of Christian revelation. The same could not be said either of logical positivism or of the Sartre form of existentialism.

But St Thomas's theology also commends itself for its emphasis on the supernatural, without any distrust of the natural. St Thomas inherited something of the devotional atmosphere of the mystical tradition. His *Summa*, with all its simplicity and prosaic appearance, has yet the dignity of prayer. Those who have studied St Thomas deeply find it easy to believe the tradition that he learnt much of his theology at the feet of the Crucified.

PLATE 25. The *Disputa* by Raphael (1483–1520): Heaven and Earth follow the discussions of medieval theologians on the Eucharist. Above are the apostles and prophets with Christ, below are the hierarchy, doctors and laity of the church. (*Vatican, Rome*)

PLATE 26. St Thomas Aquinas by Andrea Orcagna (*c.* 1308–68), from the Strozzi Altarpiece: the Church present St Thomas to Christ, who gives him power to open the Book of the Seven Seals and a "wise and discerning mind". The scroll quotes *Revelations* v, 9 and 1 *Kings* iii, 12. (*Santa Maria Novella, Florence*)

PLATE 27. Twelfth-century representation of Pentecost: the Spirit of wisdom comes down upon the Church. (*Bavarian State Library, Munich*)

Photo: Exclusive News Agency

PLATE 28. Façade of Amiens Cathedral, begun in 1220: "the noblest church that the hand of man ever built to God" (John Buchan).

2d. Christianity: Protestantism

by JOHN KENT

THE PRINCIPLES OF THE REFORMATION

Martin Luther (1483–1546) began the Reformation, and any proper account of Protestantism must start with him. It was his upside-down conception of a sinning saint whose hold on Heaven was, in the last resort, never more than humility prostrated upon the sustaining Christ which shocked and pained some of his most sincere contemporaries and seemed like the revelation of a new religious universe to others. Luther describes his own discovery quite clearly in his comment on *Galatians* v, 17:

"When I was a monk I thought by and by that I was utterly cast away, if at any time I felt the concupiscence of the flesh: that is to say, if I felt any evil motion, fleshly lust, wrath, hatred, or envy against any brother. I essayed many ways, I went to confession daily, etc., but it profited me not; for the concupiscence of my flesh did always return, so that I could not rest, but was continually vexed with these thoughts: this or that sin thou hast committed; thou art infected with envy, with impatiency, and such other sins; therefore thou art entered into this holy order in vain, and all thy good works are unprofitable. If then I had rightly understood these words of Paul: 'The flesh lusteth against the spirit, and the spirit contrary to the flesh,' etc., and 'These two are one against the other, so that ye cannot do the things that ye would do,' I should not have so miserably tormented myself, but should have thought and said to myself, as now commonly I do: Martin, thou shalt not be utterly without sin, for thou hast yet flesh; thou shalt therefore feel the battle thereof, according to that saying of Paul: 'The flesh resisteth the spirit.' Despair not therefore, but resist it strongly, and fulfil not the lust thereof. Thus doing thou art not under the law. . . ."

Luther recognized the danger of what he was saying and saw that when his insight was taught to people unskilled in religious matters, it might lead them to be careless, negligent and slothful. He complained bitterly that if he emphasized the necessity of faith, ordinary men and women neglected everything else and thought goodness unimportant, whereas if he began to emphasize the necessity of keeping the law of God, they took it that nothing else mattered and their faith suffered instead. Even so, his deep sense of religious truth compelled him to make such forceful statements as this:

"Hereby we may see who be very saints indeed. They be not stocks and stones (as the monks and schoolmen dream) so that they are never moved with anything, never feel any lust or desires of the flesh: but as Paul sayeth, their flesh lusteth against the spirit, and therefore they have sin and can sin." (*Comm. on Ep. to Galatians*, ed. P. Watson, 1953, pp. 504–8.)

The apparent simplicity of such a passage leads to very real difficulties, and Protestantism still follows Luther from afar. It is against popular Protestantism rather than against Luther's own teaching that criticisms such as the following have some force. It was written by John Keble (1792–1866) in the early days of the Oxford movement:

"The tradition which goes by the name of justification by faith and which in reality means that one who has sinned and is sorry for it, is as if he had not sinned, blights and benumbs one in every limb, in trying to make people aware of their real state. And this is why I so deprecate the word and idea of Protestantism, because it seems inseparable to me from 'Every man his own absolver'; that is, in other words, 'Peace where there is no peace' and mere shadows of repentance."

The perfect reply to this may be found in the writings of the Elizabethan divine, Richard Hooker (1553–1600):

"It is a childish cavil wherewith in the matter of justification our adversaries do greatly please themselves, exclaiming, that we tread all Christian virtues under our feet, and require nothing in Christians but faith; because we teach that faith alone justifieth; whereas we by this speech never meant to exclude either hope or charity from being always joined as inseparable mates with faith in the man that is justified; or works from being added as necessary duties, required at the hand of every justified man: but to show that faith is the only hand which putteth on Christ to justification; and Christ the only garment, which being so put on, covereth the shame of our defiled natures, hideth the imperfections of our works, preserveth us blameless in the sight of God, before whom otherwise the very weakness of our faith were cause sufficient to make us culpable, yea, to shut us out from the kingdom of heaven where nothing that is not absolute can enter."

This theological insight inspired what was best in the Reformation. In the light of it Luther and Calvin set out to reform, not to re-create, and still less to destroy, the existing Catholic church in the West, its doctrines and institutions. They believed that church to be of divine origin, and they drew on its traditions and theologians in advocating their own positions. When the reforming movement failed to win over the ruling hierarchy, it was a measure of the earnestness of the leading Reformers that they allowed separate ecclesiastical bodies to come into existence wherever the secular power was willing to accept and foster them. These bodies grew up as an affirmation that primitive Christianity could be faithfully re-expressed (not invented for the first time) without the authority of the Pope, without various aspects of the cult of the Blessed Virgin Mary, without the invocation of saints and the systematic use of indulgences and masses for the dead, without monasticism and compulsory auricular confession, though not without confession at all, and without the Sacrifice of the Mass as commonly interpreted. Worship was to be conducted in the everyday language of men, the social aspect of the Eucharist restored, and salvation from sin seen above all as the unmerited gift of God. One must emphasize how completely the Reformers agreed on a programme of this kind; they did not dispense with the historic creeds, dismiss dogma or exalt the right of private judgment. The fact of private judgment is as much medieval as modern; no one has ever accepted a religion purely on authority.

The extreme advocacy of the right of private judgment in Protestantism belongs to a later period. The sixteenth-century Protestants were not disposed to exaggerate the importance of the individual, nor was the idea of toleration developed until the following century. Authority was one of the aspects of Catholicity which the Reformers sought to re-affirm.

All this does not make Protestantism simply a parasitic body, with no positive ground for its existence beyond the reformation of alleged Roman abuses. At first sight it might seem that the attempt of the Roman Catholic Church to reform itself at the Council of Trent (1545–63) (pp. 154-5) cut away the ground on which Protestantism stood. To begin with, no Protestant would agree that the reforms of the Council of Trent were satisfactory. For evidence of this we may turn to a nineteenth-century Anglo-Catholic, Edward Bouverie Pusey (1800–82). Pusey can hardly be regarded as a witness prejudiced in favour of what is commonly called Protestantism – he cheerfully repeated Keble's dismissal of the popular doctrine of justification by faith as "every man his own absolver" – but when John Henry Newman left the Church of England for the Roman obedience in 1845, Pusey, one of the most convinced Tractarians, remained behind and found it necessary to make these broad criticisms of the Roman position. They occur in a letter of 1846 which gives his reasons for not following the example of his friend, and they are interesting as examples of Protestant and Anglican argument.

Pusey claimed that the authority of the Pope which the Reformation set aside was human and not divine. The sentence of the Pope in excommunicating unjustly Queen Elizabeth and her adherents had not been confirmed in Heaven, as the event showed. There had been real corruptions at that time, as Roman Catholics confessed, which the Anglicans had set themselves to reform by themselves, whether it was the wisest course or not. He thought that, in so doing, they had not contravened any decision of the Church or ruled anything contrary to the Faith. He claimed that the Anglican Church, having the Apostolic Succession, had also the sacraments, and, being neither heretical nor schismatic, had their grace and "the power of the keys". Having all these, it had all things necessary to salvation, and those who would be saved anywhere would be saved in the Church of England. He thought that since the Anglican Church had the Apostolic Succession it was the Catholic Church in England, that is, the church which God planted there for man's salvation, and that those who had been placed by God in that church had no right to choose another for themselves:

"There are very serious things in the Roman Communion which ought to keep us where we are. I would instance chiefly the system as to the Virgin Mary as the Mediatrix and dispenser of all blessings to mankind. (I think nothing short of a fresh revelation could justify this.) Then the sale of Masses as applicable to the departed, the system of indulgences applied to the departed, the denial of the cup to the laity . . . I cannot think that all this, so different from all that one finds in the early centuries, can be right. It goes far beyond the Council of Trent; yet however hereafter in a reconciliation of the churches those decrees might be ruled so as not to authorize this, an individual cannot act thus. He will not separate the letter from the practical system." (H.P. Liddon, *Life of E.B.Pusey*, 1893, vol. ii, pp. 505–6.)

Pusey's attitude is neither negative nor parasitic: if the criticisms are justified, the position must be held by someone as a matter of duty, as a positive act, as a continuing declaration of what Protestantism – whether Pusey liked the word or not – conceived the true Church of the Gospel to be. Pusey wrote, moreover, before the Vatican Council and before the promulgation of the dogmas of the Immaculate Conception and of the Bodily Assumption of the Blessed Virgin Mary. Pusey is in line with the Reformers when he does not attempt to say that Rome is devoid of Christianity. "The Lord there wondrously preserves some remains of his people," Calvin observed a trifle patronizingly in the fourth book of the *Institutes*, "though miserably torn and scattered, and inasmuch as some symbols of the Church still remain."

Nor was there anything purely negative in the Reforming attitude to the central act of Christian worship, the Eucharist. The sixteenth-century Reformers shared a determination to root out from the Mass any suggestion of a repetition of the atoning act of Jesus Christ. This did not necessarily involve reducing the Eucharist to an occasional memorial of the tragic yet ennobling death of a hero. Luther could have accepted the language of a recent writer:

"The primitive idea was not so much that Christ is brought down to be mystically immolated on the church's altars, as that the worshipping church herself is, in and through the liturgical action, caught up into the heavenly places and enabled there, through her intimate union with her Head, to participate in the eternal oblation of the Lamb slain from the foundation of the world." (N.P.Williams, *Northern Catholicism*, 1933, p. 194.)

The Reformers also agreed – and one gathers that the modern Roman liturgical movement is moving in the same direction – on the restoration of the Eucharist as a Communion service. It is worth remembering that, while the Eucharist has not been celebrated as often as the sixteenth-century Reformers would have liked in some Protestant traditions, the actual service has never lost this social character of the people of God sharing in the means of Grace.

Protestant worship suffered more than Protestant theology from a violent reaction from Roman Catholicism. By the end of the eighteenth century it had stripped itself of most visible reminders of the supernatural. The plain woodwork of the Independent meeting-house was not meant to reflect the glory of God, but to fall into the background as the worshippers concentrated on God's presence. This was the atmosphere that made, and was meant to make, New England new, a seventeenth-century Protestant Utopia, worthy in its crabbed and covenanted way to stand with Athens and Florence as an example of what a comparatively small community can achieve. Here was a radically new society, for neither the land itself nor the children of the Pilgrim Fathers had ever known a monk, a nun, a friar or a political bishop. The New Englanders invoked no saints and knew nothing of burning candles before altars; for them church authority was contained in the local congregation which was Christ's catholic church in that place; they thought of the confessional as did the Anglican Dean who said that it made men women and women worms, and they were innocent of the attractive power of a celibate community. In the Church of England the furniture was not so completely changed because Archbishop Laud (1573–1645) had attempted to restore a more elaborate form of worship. It had been obvious as early as the reign of Edward VI that many Englishmen had a natural leaning towards extreme severity of taste in worship, and Laud found that many of his contemporaries preferred war to what they were too prone to regard as the "rags of popery". Laud's attempt did however prevent any simple identification of the Church of England with the Puritan tradition. For Protestantism in general the impact of this stripping away of symbolism before 1800 on the society outside the church was very great; it may have had more to do with Protestant contributions to science and capitalism than any other variations from the medieval norm.

On worship, this fear of images had far-reaching effects. It is well known that neither Luther nor Calvin actually intended what came to be. Luther's attitude, indeed, was extremely tolerant. He wrote to the Dean of Berlin in 1539:

"If your Lord, the Margrave, desires it, let his Grace leap and dance at the head of the procession, with harps, drums, cymbals, and bells, as David danced before the Ark of the Lord when it was carried into Jerusalem. I am fully satisfied, for none of these things (as long as no abuse is connected with them) adds anything to the Gospel or detracts from it. Only do not let such things be regarded as necessary to salvation, and bind the consciences of men." (*Luther's Letters of Spiritual Counsel*, ed. T.G. Tappert, 1955, pp. 306–7.)

He added that the Dean might elevate the Sacrament in the Mass if the Margrave strongly requested the ceremony.

Calvin wanted to remove from worship whatever the Scriptures did not positively ordain, and might have found it difficult to understand Luther's not altogether serious advice. He did, however, personally favour both set prayers and frequent communion, and it is important to note that even his prestige in Geneva was apparently not sufficient to persuade the citizens to accept his ideas. The Lutheran churches never developed the variety of objections to ceremonial found in contemporaneous Puritanism, which was egged on by the Separatists, but it is significant that the history of Lutheran worship follows the same pattern. As time went on more and more Protestants found themselves uncomfortable if they were asked to worship to fixed liturgies, with elaborate instrumental music, in ornate chapel, led by richly-dressed clergy. Such a situation involved a breach with habits of religious practice of more than Christian antiquity, which is why its importance cannot be over-emphasized. Its advocates upheld its "spiritual" nature, but all the Calvinist stress on the sovereignty and mystery of the Triune God was needed to stem the leakage of awe and wonder.

Recent evidence of all this can be found in the report "Ways of Worship" which was prepared for the World Council of Churches in 1952. It says of German Lutheranism that during the periods of Pietism and the Enlightenment the traditional orders of worship frequently underwent abbreviation and alteration or even took an altogether new form, according to the type of piety or the intellectual attitude represented by local pastors. Such isolated and independent alteration produced by the end of the eighteenth century a great variety in the shape of the church service and in hymnody. Preaching absorbed the liturgy so that even now "the Holy Supper is celebrated as a rare appendix, combined with a kind of general confession, for those few who stay behind 'after the church service'" (*Ways of Worship*, ed. F.R.

Maxwell, 1952, p. 82). This confession is what survives of the practice of individual confession which had survived into the seventeenth century. Of Swedish Lutheranism the Report says that, in reaction against the prevailing Roman practice, it became the custom in the Reformed church of Sweden, as elsewhere, not to celebrate the Eucharist without the participation of the congregation in the Communion. This resulted in the reduction of the number of celebrations, which in turn led to the development of a Sunday service without the Sacrament. Provision was made in the Kyrkoordnung of 1571 for just such a service – a preaching service of a very simple nature. American Lutheranism has the same tradition of simple worship centred on the preaching of the Word. In Switzerland "it is the great predicament of the Reformed Churches . . . that for them the normal service consists of preaching taken out of the communion setting, the communion having become a rare, and for the members, an unfamiliar occasion" (*ibid.*, p. 130). Professor Julius Schweizer traces this service back to a fifteenth-century special preaching service which appeared alongside the Mass in South Germany and Switzerland. This, he argues, formed the basis for the development of the new Reformed liturgy. From a practical point of view this is no doubt true, but the widespread movement elsewhere in the same direction shows that this new type of service was peculiarly able to satisfy whatever devotional, doctrinal or communal demands the early Reformed congregations made on worship. It is significant, for example, that by the eighteenth century the Anglicans, in spite of their quite different tradition, were content to lapse into celebrating the Communion once a quarter in most parishes. As late as 1854 an Anglican archdeacon regrets passionately that there are still "numerous parishes" where that was true. "What a departure this from that early precedent, when the Disciples at Troas came together weekly to break bread!" he exclaims.

Describing the situation in reformed Scotland in the same report, Professor W.S. Maxwell says that the first edition of the *Scottish Book of Order* (1562) directed that the Holy Communion should be celebrated monthly. This was never obeyed, and Maxwell suggests that one important reason was the sixteenth-century shortage of clergy in Scotland, which helped to bring about the custom of celebrating from once to four times a year. The lack of ministers was a fact, but as has already been explained, local conditions were not all-important. Maxwell also says that the infrequency of communion was a reversion to Scottish practice before the Reformation. This point is often made and transfers the responsibility for this state of affairs to the laity. The infrequency of communion in the Reformed churches can be exaggerated: the Presbyterian tradition was always, apparently, four times a year, but seventeenth-century English Baptists and American Independents probably administered the rite once a month. Although the Independent service was more frequent, it was only a brief addition to the service of the Word. The deacons took bread and wine to the people seated in their pews. The minister blessed the bread and wine separately, a double consecration which went back to the earliest Independents' exact following of the Gospel narrative. The congregation simply ate and drank and meditated. The intention was a bare, almost silent, re-presentation of the scene in the Upper Room. Fear of idolatry had eliminated almost every scrap of interpretation, fear of the printed word left the prayer to the occasion and the pastor.

The most probable explanation of all this is that the sixteenth-century Reformers succeeded in filling their flocks with utter horror of the Sacrifice of the Mass, but failed to convince them of a positive case for the frequent use of this means of grace. Indeed the interpretation of the Supper given by Zwingli (1484–1531) almost required infrequent celebration: an act whereby we commemorate the death of Christ and testify our reverence for his memory cannot be repeated at short intervals without, as most Protestants have felt, gradually cheapening the effect. The failure, then, was theological, and therefore in the last resort ministerial, as it was in Switzerland. This becomes more apparent when we remember that the many sixteenth-century schemes for the union of the Protestant groups on a conciliar basis usually broke down over the radically different interpretations of the Eucharist clung to by some of the most prominent leaders. Uncertainty about the meaning of the rite hampered the growth of any Puritan system of devotion centred upon it.

THE IDEAL OF RELIGIOUS FREEDOM

A hopelessly entangled process links this diminution of religious symbolism with the rise of religious individualism. It is often supposed that individualism was a nineteenth-century invention, but individualism hardly needs a century to invent it; and it was characteristic of the piety of both Roman and Reformed churches in the seventeenth century. In Protestantism, Lutheran Pietism and English Puritanism both pulled in the same direction. In Germany, Philip Jacob Spener (1635–1705) and August Francke (1663–1727), the Pietist leaders, based their hopes of regenerating Lutheranism on the theory of the priesthood of all believers. They taught that the Christian laity not only possessed the right to offer God the sacrifice of prayer, but could also exercise their priestly office at home or among friends, edify one another from the Bible, especially under the guidance of their pastor, and both ask and answer questions in devotional meetings. Nothing in Pietist teaching suggested that the laity had any right to administer the sacraments or to preach in church, but such developments were implicit and would come. Spener, indeed, seems to have had to struggle all his life to prevent some of his more intense followers from seceding from the Lutheran Church. The one major event of this kind was the consolidation of the remnants of the Bohemian Hussites into the Moravian community by Count Zinzendorf (1700–60), himself thoroughly trained in the Pietist school. It was similar tendencies that had led in England to the temporary collapse of the Elizabethan Church Settlement from 1642 to 1662 and the permanent organization of sects outside the State church after the Restoration.

Pietism was a layman's movement which transferred the centre of religious life from the church building to the home. A similar transfer was made in England by the early Methodists, who did not expect to become a permanent body and for years conducted most of their meetings either in the open air or in the houses and cottages of sympathizers. The Pietists made this jump because of an inner conviction that the institutional church was a failure and was likely to remain one, hardened as it was in the shell of confessional orthodoxy which, in the later seventeenth century, it had humped round itself in terror of the anti-Christian philosophy of the day. The ruthlessness of the Reformation had left the layman with few objective channels into which to pour his devotion. Monasticism had gone, and the seventeenth-century Archbishop of Glasgow, Robert Leighton, was not the only one who regretted at this time that "The one great and fatal error of the Reformation was, that more of those houses and that course of life, free from the entanglement of vows and other mixtures, was not preserved: so that Protestant churches had neither places of education, nor retreat for men of mortified tempers." The layman was expected to accept the church as something given and the minister as the expounder of perfectly defined Confessional truth. Driven in upon themselves, the Christians of the Western Protestant tradition sought within themselves the objectivity or "assurance" which was no longer mediated to them in any other way. The Pietist disapproved of cards. dancing, theatregoing and, essentially, every action which could be seen as a concession to "the world". In the small local group so characteristic of this type of religiosity, men and women came to know each other intensely, encouraged one another in their devotional life, came directly under the influence of powerful personalities, and shared together the private prayer-meeting which was the dynamo of the system. This fervent common pursuit of holiness usually failed when men returned hopefully to the official cult to try to reproduce there the fierce excitement which burned in the domestic assemblies. Public worship retained what seemed to them a formal atmosphere, partly because the symbolic element had never quite passed away and could not easily be fused with the vivid, individual, vocal methods of this kind of movement.

Thus the gradual change inside Protestantism came to full flower in the early nineteenth century, by which time the heavy "catholic" element in the teaching of Luther and Calvin had been forgotten or deliberately regarded as superseded. Nor did people really understand the complicated pattern which lay behind the voyage of the Pilgrim Fathers to America. They underestimated the passion with which the seventeenth-century Puritan believed that he was called by God to set up on earth, perhaps only very shortly before the appearance of Our Lord, the ideal community of the saints, from which all unbelief and all that was evil and unelect had been banished. No modern "protestant catholic" can outdo the Pilgrim Father in his belief in the divine society, for he meant Massachusetts to show to an astonished Europe the image of that society, separated for ever from the "rags of popery" and at last completing the work of the Reformers. The seventeenth century saw the death of all these hopes. The saints lived on and the world remained unredeemed; the bewildered survivors subsided into half-hearted Calvinism much as English nonconformity flirted, in equal despair, with Unitarianism. Continuity has profound truth, but so has discontinuity: in one sense the Reformation ended in 1689, when the Toleration Act proclaimed that the Puritans had abandoned hope of either reforming or replacing the Church of England.

There emerged from all this, in the nineteenth century, a type of Protestantism which had little in common with the sixteenth-century Reformers, but which, as we shall see, was not representative of the whole of Protestantism. According to this radical point of view, the Reformers stopped too soon. They had only purged the medieval church of such errors as transubstantiation and the cult of the saints and the Blessed Virgin Mary. Their effort to recover the essence of the primitive church had been carried no further back than to the church of the fourth

century; and once the first excitement had died away, the Reformed and Lutheran churches had stiffened into a positively idolatrous confessionalism. Already in the seventeenth century early radicals had condensed this critical standpoint into the famous statement that "The Lord hath yet more light and truth to break forth from his word". This principle had been held to require the rejection of creeds (though not necessarily, it should be remembered, of what they said), of bishops and other symbols of government from above, and of what came to be called "ritual". George Fox (1624–91) arrived at the conclusion that the Lord forbade him to put off his hat to any, high or low. The tradition remains unbroken: a recent Baptist statement said, "Our forms of worship are in the Reformed tradition and are not generally regulated by liturgical forms. Our tradition is one of spontaneity and freedom" (*The Nature of the Church*, ed. R.N.Flew, 1952, p. 162). In the nineteenth century the position was carried to the point of actually seeming to identify Protestantism itself with individualism, the right of private judgment and intellectual freedom. Yet even in the liberal nineteenth century the general principles of "spontaneity and freedom" could be combined with a fervent version of the "old-time religion".

THE DEMAND FOR CERTAINTY IN RELIGION: SOME EARLY ANSWERS

From one point of view there was nothing extraordinary about this tradition. The demand for freedom from authority recurs in each century, though rarely with such confidence as was sometimes the case in the nineteenth. In its Liberal metamorphosis it became one side, and one only, of the Protestant attempt to make Christianity a convincing solution to the problems of modern man. There is nothing sectarian about these difficulties: they plague the would-be Roman Catholic or Greek Orthodox just as much as the would-be Protestant. When one studies the history of the church since 1600 one senses that these difficulties have become sharper, and that the answers once accepted cheerfully enough have again and again had to be taken back to the workshop and improved. At times one has the impression that Western Christendom has been very much on the defensive within Western culture for about three hundred and fifty years. Few books have proved more significant in the long run than the *De Veritate* of Lord Herbert of Cherbury, which was published in 1624. This was the first shot in the Deist controversy, a controversy which only became general with the close of the religious wars and the success of the early ventures with scientific method. Text-books still sometimes repeat the comforting statement that the Deists were put to flight by the combined assault of Bishop Butler (1692–1752) and John Wesley (1703–91); Butler's *Analogy* crushed them intellectually and Wesley's Evangelicalism made sin and salvation facts of experience which logic and mockery could not assail. It is true that Wesley's zeal rescued generations from unhappy unbelief, but the victors in the intellectual contest were the sceptics, and their attack, combined with greater attention to historical method, had already made inroads into conventional Christianity before 1789. What took place between 1789 and 1815 was the explosion of forces which had been pent up with difficulty for generations behind the cracking ramparts of the *Ancien Régime*. The explosion had parallel effects on the Roman church, which had to face demands for sweeping reforms in Austria and Germany and a series of bitter anti-clerical revolutions which followed one another throughout the nineteenth century in the Romance countries and in South America. Behind it all lay a growing demand for certainty in religion: certainty about accepting it, as in the Wesleyan and Ultramontane movements, or certainty about rejecting it, as in the case of the German and French successors of the English Deists or of sceptics like Hume. Compulsory confessional religion, with the minutest points of faith over-defined and under-experienced, had failed to satisfy and so had the accommodating Latitudinarianism which in England and Switzerland, for example, had worked out a version of Christianity from which anything that a purely rational man was unlikely to believe had been removed. In Geneva this pale and sickly Christianity faced the French Revolution without a convincing doctrine of the divinity of Christ.

Above all we must realize that the moment of crisis was in the early nineteenth century and not in its closing decades. In the French Revolutionary period men caught a glimpse of their own deep dissatisfaction with the conventional demonstrations that God is living and personal. Nothing else can explain the fantastic burlesque of Christianity which took place in Revolutionary Paris but the most profound religious malaise – and that glimpse of the depths helps to explain why European society, even though it consciously disbelieved much of what it superficially accepted, struggled desperately after 1815 to hold back a progress which seemed to contain diabolical forces. In primitive communities men could demonstrate the existence and goodness of the gods by pointing to their protection of the community, its crops, its ships, its soldiers; but eighteenth-century Western man had already begun to transform agriculture and industry by

subtly changing the way in which he thought about them. Fertilizers and mechanical inventions had already started to close the area in which men expected direct answers to prayer. Primitive man prayed for victory in war, modern man was beginning to argue that God ought not to permit war at all. In the late seventeenth and eighteenth centuries another popular way of demonstrating the existence of God was to point to an allegedly providential interference in the normal course of events. A favourite tale in Evangelical magazines was about a drunkard who one day cursed the parson and within a week was killed as he stood on the same spot by a falling roof-tile. George Fox included in his personal Messianism the conviction that those who resisted him received a speedy rebuke from God. This was the argument that Voltaire ridiculed so grimly when he heard of the Lisbon earthquake.

Altogether more important in the eighteenth century was the demonstration afforded by Wesleyanism. The violent experiences of conviction of sin and justification found among the early followers of John Wesley are often misunderstood. One sees it said, sometimes with approval, that the Wesleys taught people to *feel* their religion. This is to see the eighteenth-century revival out of context through the eyes of the following century. The Wesleys did not teach ordinary people to feel religion. "The sense of sins forgiven", for which Charles Wesley prays in his hymns, is thought of as an objective fact of religious experience which can be sought and found through prayer and the use of the means of grace, worship, searching the Scriptures, sharing in the Eucharist. A bishop might confuse this with enthusiasm (dismissed by Wesley himself as "wanting the end without the means"), but it was irrelevant to confuse the main, sane Wesleyan tradition with the sheer individualism of groups which claimed peculiar direction by the Holy Spirit. Wesleyanism's real connections with the seventeenth century were with John Alleine's *Alarm to the Unconverted* and the pattern of Grace in life recorded by John Bunyan. The early Wesleyans did not question the reality or the immediate divine origin of their conviction of sin and knowledge of pardon, but none of this involved a claim to any fresh revelation. John Nelson, one of John Wesley's earliest lay preachers, says of his justification: "Jesus Christ was as evidently *set before* the eyes of my mind as crucified for my sins, as if I had seen him with my bodily eyes; and that instant my heart was set at liberty from guilt and tormenting fear, and filled with a calm and serene peace." One may compare this with the experience of another Wesleyan itinerant, Thomas Taylor, when in his experience of justification "the

Lord appeared in a wonderful manner, as with his vesture dipped in blood. I saw him by the eyes of faith, hanging on the cross; and the sight caused such love to flow into my soul that I believed that moment and never since gave up my confidence." He adds, very significantly for those who know the Puritan psychology, "I had not then any particular promise applied" – no verse of Scripture, that is, had entered his mind. If one had, he would have believed absolutely that God had put it there. Wesley encouraged his people to pursue and trust this evidence of divine activity, and at the level of English society at which the revival took place, such events were self-authenticating and were never thought of as subjective or emotional. The same could be said of the New England revivalism directed by Edwards and Whitefield. The tradition died hard; a country clergyman, Augustus Jessopp, who knew the Victorian country labourer very well, gave this account of a Primitive Methodist Camp Meeting in Norfolk at the end of the nineteenth century.

" 'Three times I've felt it; twice I've seen it,' said one of the speakers, his voice dropping in awe and amazement, the pupils of his eyes dilated as though some dread vision was present before him; 'I can't tell what it was, I can't tell how it was. There was a light as blazed, and I tell you I saw it, as sure as I'm a living man; and I knowed it was the Lord, and I've felt it since, I have, I know I have. Talk to me of not believing as I'm saved – you might as well try to tell me as this ain't a cart and I ain't a standing on it.'" (A. Jessopp, *Arcady for Better or Worse*, 1890, pp. 78-9.)

For various reasons this manner of demonstrating the existence of God seemed less convincing in the nineteenth century, and in descriptions of evangelism of the new American type there often occurs the claim that the meetings were not "emotional". This did not mean that emotion was absent: in fact the methods of Finney, Moody and Billy Sunday involved a more conscious exploitation of the emotions than had ever taken place before. But men were no longer so certain that the emotions could serve as the direct vehicle of divine action, and they hesitated to affirm that prostrations, tears, visions and suggested texts were authentic "signs and wonders". In the 1859 revival these and similar phenomena were frequent in Northern Ireland and Wales but rarer in England where their final appearance may have been at the Salvation Army's Holiness Meetings. When a woman started to shriek in one of Moody's English meetings he simply stopped and said "We'll stand up

and sing *Rock of Ages* and the ushers will please help that friend out of the hall." All this was the result partly of the changed attitude to the Scriptures, partly of the increasing self-consciousness of a more educated public and partly of the rapid wastage of converts in the later revivalism.

LIBERALISM: A NINETEENTH-CENTURY SOLUTION

At this time there was taking place a change in the moral climate of Europe. Men now openly rebelled against the doctrines of double predestination and eternal punishment. This sensitivity to the idea of a vengeful God may have been in part a result of Christian teaching about the love of God, but it was also a part of the long humanistic tradition which went back to the Renaissance. In this context what the nineteenth century called Liberalism meant a criticism of the Scriptures by moral standards not directly taken from them, combined with the assumption that the Bible was an historic document like any other. This moral protest against the ethical values of orthodoxy paved the way for the easy acceptance of the evolutionary attitude to the Bible, since this provided a means of preserving it from total disrepute. Indeed, if the geologists and the Darwinians shocked the orthodox on the one hand, they also provided them with an answer which could be used against the older critics. They were further assisted by Friedrich Schleiermacher's shifting of the defence of Christianity from the ground of reason to the ground of religious experience rightly interpreted. From Schleiermacher (1768–1834) to the present-day theologian, Bultmann, a line of theologians have taught that Christianity must be accommodated to the post-eighteenth-century world, even if that means saying, as Schleiermacher cheerfully said, that the phrase "Original Sin" did not refer to a primary sin actually committed by Adam and Eve, but to the fact that the human race was visibly and incontrovertibly sinful. In the sharp reaction which followed the French Revolution there was a brief renaissance of pure Calvinism, notably in Geneva, where from 1817 a revival spread slowly but firmly across France into the Low Countries. In England the Evangelicals, led by Charles Simeon, enjoyed another generation of power in the established church. But any chance that orthodoxy would have an easy passage disappeared as the new century piled up a heap of scientific facts which men knew they must believe. It was the inexorable evidence that the world was of fantastic age and that the origin of man was almost unbelievably complicated that made men so willing to accept the comparatively mild suggestion that Moses did

PLATE 29. Portrait of Martin Luther. Woodcut by Lucas Cranach, Sr. (Courtesy, *Museum of Fine Arts, Boston*)

IN SILENCIO ET SPE ERIT M · L FORTITVDO VESTRA

Photo: Alinari

PLATE 30. Martin Luther (1483–1546): portrait by Lucas Cranach (1472–1553). The artist was a friend of Luther. (*Uffizi, Florence*)

not write the whole of the Pentateuch at the dictation of the Holy Spirit. Indeed, one's impression is that Biblical criticism mattered less to most Christians than is often supposed until the Liberals began to attack the traditional theories of the Atonement. "At last," Benjamin Jowett wrote, "the question has arisen, within as well as without the Church of England: How the ideas of expiation, or satisfaction, or sacrifice, or imputation, are reconcilable with the moral and spiritual nature either of God or man?" (*Theological Essays of B.Jowett*, ed. L.Campbell, 1906, p. 250.) The Liberals seemed to want to say no more than that the object of the suffering and death of Christ was to draw men's hearts to God by the vision of redeeming love. The ordinary Christian had never felt that his salvation depended on theories about the Bible, but his hold on Christianity itself seemed to be slipping when the clear explanation of how he was saved from his sins was taken from him. When Liberalism reached this point, the reaction in favour of orthodoxy set in. Even so, when Adolf von Harnack (1851–1930) summed Christianity up in the 1890s as the Fatherhood of God and the Brotherhood of Man, he was expressing a whole theme of nineteenth-century Protestantism.

It is to Harnack that we may turn for the clearest summary of the Liberal position. In his book *What is Christianity?* he said (E.T., 1901, pp. 275–7):

"Protestantism reckons–this is the solution–upon the Gospel being something so simple, so divine, and therefore so truly human, as to be most certain of being understood when it is left entirely free, and also as to reproduce essentially the same experiences and convictions in individual souls. . . . And when we are reproached with our divisions and told that Protestantism has as many doctrines as heads, we reply. 'So it has, but we do not wish it otherwise; on the contrary, we want still more freedom, still greater individuality in utterance and doctrine; the historical circumstances necessitating the formation of the national and free churches have imposed only too many rules and limitations upon us, even though they be not proclaimed as divine ordinances; we want still more confidence in the inner strength and unifying power of the Gospel, which is more certain to prevail in free conflict than under guardianship; we want to be a spiritual realm and we have no desire to return to the fleshpots of Egypt; we are well aware that in the interests of order and instruction outward and visible communities must arise; we are ready to foster their growth, so far as they fulfil these aims and deserve to be fostered; but we do not hang our hearts upon them, for they may exist today and tomorrow give place, under

other political and social conditions, to new organizations; let anyone who has such a Church have it as though he had it not; our Church is not the particular church in which we are placed, but the *societas fidei* which has its members everywhere, even among the Greeks and Romans.' That is the evangelical answer to the reproach that we are divided, and that is the language that the liberty which has been given to us enjoys."

It is a measure of how irrelevant Liberalism has become that such language would be used by hardly anyone today. Harnack's account of Liberal Protestantism may be compared with the criticism of Protestantism itself made by a friendly Roman Catholic critic, Yves M.J.Congar, O.P. Father Congar says (*Divided Christendom*, p. 35): "The principles of secularism, of naturalism, of rationalism, which to us were from the first implicit in the Reform, have grown into a movement which has ended in liberalism and the reduction of Christianity to an aspect of the moral consciousness of mankind. This it is which has come to be called worship in spirit and in truth. By comparing dogma, forms of worship and of church order to the letter which killeth, a religion of the Spirit is arrived at in which religious sentiment passes for faith, God in conscience for revelation, and private judgment for the interior witness of the Holy Spirit." Father Congar adds that these are but speculative matters and that the real life of souls and parishes only follows theological extremes from afar.

Such criticism confuses with Protestantism a very real and terrible secularization of the European spirit which has taken place since the sixteenth century, and confuses the effect of that revolution on a part of Protestantism with Protestantism as a whole. Father Congar wrote twenty years ago, and in the meantime it has become clear that Liberalism has not swallowed up the entire Protestant tradition. The modern Biblical theology, which cuts across denominational barriers, and is especially associated with Karl Barth and Emil Brunner, takes as its starting-point the assumption that Liberalism was wrong to assert that the Bible must simply be treated like any other document.

Harnack's answer to the modern problem – which was really to gamble everything on individual sincerity – was neither the only nor the best approach for the Protestant tradition. There were two other important answers. One was the intensification of the evangelical tradition, by altering its evangelical methods and by adapting its theology: not entirely distinct from this, though it helped to preserve the unity of the church by being more than this, was nineteenth-century missionary enterprise. The other was the emergence within Protestantism of the Anglo-Catholic solution.

ANGLO-CATHOLICISM

If the major problem of modern Protestantism has been how to counter the gradual disappearance of religious certainty, then Anglo-Catholicism was clearly a major answer to the problem. A major answer because Anglo-Catholicism was able, thanks to the strange nature of the Episcopal Church of England in which the movement appeared in the 1830s, to call back into "Protestant" use the traditional symbolical sacramental side of Christianity at the very time when such a revolutionary development must have seemed most unlikely. Anglo-Catholicism could only have happened initially in a church which had survived the sixteenth century without too radical a transformation; and although the Church of England had almost laid aside her sacramental character in the eighteenth century, no irreparable breach had occurred. The Anglo-Catholic was able to offer an implicit faith in the Christ of the Sacraments to those who could not find elsewhere the objective religious reality which satisfied them. The success of the return to sacramental worship amazed the radicals, but many men must have felt that they had been shown the way out of a nightmare. At a moment when the general fashion of Protestant worship was still for bareness, sincerity and the preached word, the new form of Anglicanism shifted the centre of worship from the priest to what the priest did, to the symbolic, and staked everything not on individual sincerity but on God's willingness to act through the traditional symbols profoundly believed in. What Anglo-Catholicism meant to the pioneers can be seen from a letter which was written by a famous parish priest of the movement, Arthur Stanton, to his mother in 1866. Controversy about the introduction of elaborate ceremonies into a few London churches was then at its height, and Stanton's mother disapproved of her son's position.

"I believe in the Church of England [he wrote] because if A means A and B means B she declares that she possesses priests . . . I know that you don't believe what I do. I know more – that the very doctrines I love so much, which at Oxford and Cuddesdon, and ever since I have been here, I have with tears and entreaties offered to others, are the very ones from which you recoil most instinctively: (1) the Adorable Mystery of the Altar; (2) Confession to a Priest. They are much dearer to me than all the incense,

vestments, music in the world; they are my hope o salvation, for one is to me Jesus Christ, and the other pardon in his most precious Blood." (G. W. E. Russell, *Arthur Stanton*, 1917, pp. 89–90.)

One can understand, but hardly go all the way with, the contemporary critics who denounced the Confessional automatically as "popery". The practice of confession was upheld on the ground that it increased a man's horror of sin, which popular Protestantism was thought to diminish. Lutheranism never forbade the practice officially, nor did the Church of England; moreover the new school did not teach that confession was compulsory or that it necessarily involved spiritual direction – there was no question of simply repeating the Latin theology of the practice. Similarly, no one could prove that a belief in the Real Presence of Christ at the Eucharist was forbidden to an Anglican. In fact theology was less important than people's experience of the new habits. In the Confessional, in the presence of the priest, the penitent was filled with a new awareness of the awfulness of sin; while the priest's absolution brought him a new certainty of divine forgiveness, a new sense that God was really there, offering and bestowing the pardon of the sinner. For the leaders of the movement there was no question of the confessional fostering the casual attitude towards sin that thorough-going Protestants assumed it must; the need of personal holiness, one of the themes of the group, was quickened, as it seemed to them, through the habit of confession. In the Eucharist, the Anglo-Catholic felt a renewed conviction of the power of God as he took the symbols and used them in unfamiliar yet traditional ways; he felt compelled to adore Christ in the Eucharist because of his sense of the reality of Christ's presence. This has never been put better than by Frank Weston, the Bishop of Zanzibar, when he told the Anglo-Catholic Congress in 1923:

"If you are prepared to fight for the right of adoring Jesus in the blessed Sacrament, then you have got to come out from before your Tabernacle and walk, with Christ mystically present in you, out into the streets of this country and find the same Jesus in the people of your cities and your villages. You cannot claim to worship Jesus in the tabernacle if you do not pity Jesus in the slum. Mark that: that is the Gospel truth. . . .

"You have got your Mass, you have got your Altar, you have begun to get your Tabernacle. Now go out into the highways and hedges. Go out and look for Jesus in the ragged, in the naked, in the oppressed and sweated, in those who have lost hope, in those who are struggling to make good. Look for Jesus. And when you see him, gird yourselves with his towel and try to wash their feet. . . ." (H.A.Wilson, *Received with Thanks*, 1940, pp. 119–21.)

Bishop Stubbs, the great medieval historian, saw accurately the truth about the ritual of Anglo-Catholicism. He defended it on the ground that superstitious reverence for holy things was not a danger of the nineteenth century; idolatry and superstition had been snares for the unwary in former times, but now what tempted man was pride in the human intellect and pride in human freedom. To those who understood Anglo-Catholicism at its best, what mattered was its sacramentally mediated conviction "Christ is here" – a conviction which dispersed the doubt and melancholy of the darker side of the Victorian spirit – that side which, haunted by the terrible theory of the survival of the fittest, and dogged by the conviction that no one was really fitted to survive, was appalled by the spectacle of increasing wealth going hand in hand with the growth of teeming poverty in heartless cities. The same doubts and melancholy attracted them to Carlyle, Browning, Tennyson and Henry George.

In considering Anglo-Catholicism, one is bound to consider its relationship to the popular idea of Protestantism. As is obvious in the letter by Pusey quoted at the beginning of this chapter (p. 119), the Anglo-Catholic shared the traditional Protestant distrust of Papal authority. It is true that a wing of the movement always hoped for some kind of *rapprochement* with Rome; actual conversations took place between Anglicans and Roman Catholics with this end in view as recently as 1925, but the importance of this can be exaggerated, especially in view of the firm Papal pronouncement in 1896 "that ordinations performed according to the Anglican rite have been and are completely null and void".

This decision was in accord with, though not of course affected by, the attitude which Cardinal Newman took in 1850 in *Anglican Difficulties*, in which he tried to persuade his former friends that Anglo-Catholicism had no natural place in the established Church of England, which was not a church at all:

"Anglo-Catholic teaching is not only a novelty in this age, (but) while it is a system adventitious and superadded to the natural religion, it is, moreover, not supplemental, or complemental, or collateral, or correlative to it, – not implicitly involved in it, nor developed from it, – nor combining with it, – nor capable of absorption into it;

– but on the contrary most uncongenial and heterogeneous, floating upon it, a foreign substance, like oil upon water." (*Difficulties Felt by Anglicans*, 1850, p. 31.)

He besought the Anglo-Catholics, in view of all this, "to seek those principles in their true home . . . you cannot change your Establishment into a Church without a miracle . . . If you would make England Catholic, you must go forth on your mission from the Catholic Church" (*Ibid*, p. 57).

Of course if Anglo-Catholicism had been nothing more than a Romanizing party within the Church of England, Newman's position would have been logical; but this was exactly what Keble, Pusey and their followers did not admit. One wonders if Newman ever realized how much of his earlier success as a leader of the group within the English Church had depended upon his ability to stir within the breasts of Anglican clergymen an excited proud feeling of belonging to a Body which was the divine, historic Catholic church planted by God in Britain. His converts did not lose this precious conviction just because Newman himself lost faith in his own arguments. Individual Anglo-Catholics might choose to accept much that was Roman, not least in ritual; but such personal action was quite distinct from obedience, and had more than a touch of that claim to the right of private judgment which became so horrid in a "Protestant". In any case such freedom was never based on a denial of the reality of the Church of England.

As always, much depended on definition. What "Protestantism" meant to any nineteenth-century Anglo-Catholic was a kind of vulgarized Wesleyanism, known at second hand. The way in which they talked about the Reformation often gave great offence: for example, George Campbell Ommanney, one of the better-known parish priests of the movement, told his Sheffield parishioners in 1883, when he had only known them for a few months, that there was a choice between two religions, the Catholic religion of the Church of England, and the Protestant religion begun only three hundred years before:

"The choice is between a religion of eighteen hundred years' standing, and a new religion of three hundred years; between the religion of Jesus Christ – for he is the Founder and Head of the Catholic Church – and a religion of men, founded by men whose characters would hardly bear examination. The choice is between the religion that formed the saints and martyrs of old, and the religion which appeared to produce no change in the lives of those professing it." (*Memoirs of G.C. Ommanney*, ed. F.G.Belton, 1936, p. 81.)

Writing his autobiography many years later, Ommanney said that he could not see what there was in this to cause great excitement. He was a pioneer whose career typified that of many others. From the time he went to Sheffield in 1882 he heard confession and used the mixed chalice; in 1886 he began to wear the Eucharistic Vestments and put many stained-glass windows into his church; he started High Mass in 1889; and he began the Reservation of the Blessed Sacrament in 1898. This last step led to a guerrilla war with the episcopal bench which lasted until 1931, shortly before his death. Ommanney said that the Canon Law of the Catholic Church enjoined reservation, and that a bishop could not authorize him to break the rule.

To men like this "Protestantism" seemed to consist only of Liberals and Evangelicals. They could not be expected to sympathize with Liberalism: in Holland, for example, at the time when Ommanney wrote the above, doubts were once again raised about the historic existence of Jesus. English Evangelicals, on the other hand, seemed to the Anglo-Catholics to preach an indulgent doctrine of self-justification, to hold views on the Eucharist which made the rite little more than a commemoration of a dead hero, to emphasize "conversion" almost to the exclusion of the remainder of the Christian life, and to comprehend all this in a vague though charitable conception of the Church with minimizing definitions of ministry and membership. The years between 1840 and 1870 were a period of low vitality among the Anglican Evangelicals, deeply wounded by the combined attack of scientific and Biblical critics. In the same years, unfortunately, English Methodism was dissipating its strength in the dissensions which had produced a schism in 1849. This disaster spelt the defeat of a view of the authority of the ministry somewhat similar to that of Anglo-Catholicism, though neither group seems to have recognized the kinship. This was partly because Pusey in the 1840s accused Wesleyanism of heresy, only to be told roundly that his own doctrine of justification was that of the Council of Trent. Jabez Bunting, the Wesleyan leader, spoke for the Evangelicals as a whole when he said in 1841 that "unless the Church of England will protest against Puseyism in some intelligible form, it will be the duty of Methodism to protest against the Church of England". As late as 1891 the Congregationalist historian Charles S. Miall dismissed Anglo-Catholicism as an unnatural revival of medievalism. In practice the Free Churches usually

encountered Anglo-Catholicism through its least appealing feature, its reassertion of the traditional Anglican requirement of episcopal ordination for ministers; Evangelical ministers whose ordination was presbyterian felt outraged when their pastoral status was called in question. It was hardly surprising that just as the Anglo-Catholic refused to be called a Protestant, so the Evangelical did not want to call him one.

Nevertheless a very important aspect of Anglo-Catholicism has been its long-term effect on other Protestant bodies. The movement's most striking triumph has been in its complete transformation of the worship of Anglican parish churches, a change so drastic as to refute in itself Newman's assertion that the movement was alien to the Church of England. Over the last hundred years this increase in sacramental devotion has at once irritated and stimulated Protestantism as a whole. We have already described the way in which the preaching service came to dominate Protestant piety. A counter-revolution has been taking place, very slowly and quietly, for the last century. In many denominations a new positive value has been put on formal liturgy. Read prayers have been greeted with less suspicion. A new importance has been attached to the Eucharist as the central act of Christian worship, and in some quarters the rite has grown more elaborate. Beautiful music and architecture, even pageantry, have seemed more appropriate to Protestants than they did in past days. This gradual indirect action shows that nothing could be more misleading than the view that Anglo-Catholicism was a reactionary flight from nineteenth-century reality, confined to a small group of intense clerics in an Oxford senior common room. In fact, it is clear that the general religious crisis was compelling a revolution of this kind. A similar movement followed its own course in America and on the Continent the same development took place, especially in the Lutheran Churches of Germany and Sweden. In recent years a new emphasis has been put on worship by the Iona Community in the Reformed Church of Scotland, and the French Reformed have established a monastery at Cluny. The total context of this new interest in worship is wider than Protestantism. Since the late eighteenth century a liturgical renaissance has gradually developed in the Roman Catholic Church. Its leaders have been anxious to deepen the religious life of the laity by making them more aware of the meaning of the Mass, and by impressing on them the corporate nature of the liturgy; the problem of religious individualism faced the Roman Church also in the nineteenth century. All this corresponds to a growing awareness among Protestants that the sixteenth-century Reformers did not intend to separate so sharply the Word and Sacrament, and that sacramental worship may become perfectly admissible to Protestants if it is properly understood. As we shall see in the conclusion, this gradual progress towards a common kind – though not a common order – of worship is vital to the modern Ecumenical Movement; for worship, far more than doctrine, divides present-day Protestant denominations.

EVANGELICALISM AND THE REVIVALIST TRADITION

One of the main reasons for the disappearance of the older, hard-shelled denominationalism was the dissolving influence of Evangelicalism. If the advanced forms of Liberalism were really Continental and the sacramental reaction was predominantly English, the mainspring of nineteenth-century Evangelicalism was American. The great continent filled up slowly, and from the first the frontier was the home of the revivalist. After 1865 the problem cities of the industrial period provided a second, urban frontier, where the revivalist worked at the vital meeting-point of the traditional and the new economy and the cultures which they underlay. The original frontier conditions allowed America to evolve a new theology of revival, and in this environment Methodists and Baptists were far more successful than they had ever been in England.

Against this background, the fate of the Protestant Episcopal Church – American Anglicanism – was instructive. This body could trace back a strongly High Church tradition to 1722, when at Yale seven ministers staggered the Independent and Calvinist establishment of New England by expressing a voluntary preference for the Church of England. This tradition produced its own fruit without any great help from England; indeed American Anglicans were keener to preserve the episcopal succession after the War of Independence than the Church of England was to provide it. As the new nation settled down, a local Anglo-Catholicism made its appearance. There is evidence that confessions were occasionally heard before the eighteen-thirties. Henry Hobart, Bishop of New York, visited England in 1824, and met Newman at Oxford; at this time Hobart was much more of an Anglo-Catholic than Newman. Monastic experiments – such as the Nashotah Community of 1842 – were less surprising in the United States, which was then a favourite proving-ground for Utopian community schemes, but Nashotah was not inspired by any English examples, such as Newman's similarly unsuccessful attempts at Oxford. When an American edition of *Tracts for the Times* came out in 1839,

the American editor said that because of influences from the English Non-jurors (the small high church schism from the Church of England which survived after James II left the throne), and because the American Episcopal Church had no connection with the State, "some of the leading doctrines of the Oxford divines relating to the constitution of the Church and of the ministry have been better preserved in America than in the English Establishment". The monastic movement failed to grow: it is significant that no new and permanent monastic house was set up in America for men until J.D.S. Huntington founded the Order of the Holy Cross in New York in 1881. For one thing, the internal opposition was intense, culminating in secession by a small number of extremists in 1873, led by G.D.Cummins, Assistant Bishop of Kentucky. Writing in the Centenary volume, *Northern Catholicism*, in 1933, E.H.Hardy felt bound to say that "with the single exception of architecture . . . we have scarcely touched the life of the country . . . The Episcopal Church has at times been fashionable, but the Movement has not" (N.P.Williams, *op. cit.*, p. 116).

This in itself is proof of the powerful hold of Evangelicalism on the American religious world. There were other reasons for the failure of the Episcopal Church to seize the initiative as it did in England. Stout colonial resistance to the introduction of episcopal control from any point nearer than London had hampered the growth of a homogeneous body. After the War of Independence the Church lacked almost all the advantages that the English Establishment had for the spread of ideas. In England, persistent propaganda in one of the two universities could transform Anglicanism in a generation, but no similar way existed of influencing the long line of colonies. As it was, there had been difficulty in persuading the High Church North and the Evangelical South to unite as a single body. Faced with the unfamiliar conditions of a country expanding rapidly and absorbing people of many different nationalities, the Episcopal Church showed less adaptability than the Methodists or Baptists, whether in church system or in preaching style. Moreover Roman Catholic immigration challenged the easy assumption that America was by definition a Protestant country; and one result was an anti-Roman Catholic crusade which lasted until the Civil War, and hardly made the atmosphere favourable to Protestant experiment with liturgical worship. Perhaps as important was the moral question of slavery, which gave the American churches an objective religious issue around which to divide.

The strength of Evangelicalism did not depend upon

CHRISTIANITY

the weakness of Anglo-Catholicism. Evangelicalism, even after 1865 when the sects began to settle down into denominationalism, drew its self-confidence from the frequent recurrence of large-scale revivals which came fairly regularly throughout the century. The individual conversions during such an outburst seem to have become less important than the actual spectacle of masses of people being drawn into the revivalist's orbit: this became a new objective justification of the tenets of both Evangelicalism and Christianity. The churches renewed in the revivals their conviction that what would work for their ancestors would still work now, despite everything in modern culture that militated against religion. It was significant that the revivals were said to produce the "old-time religion". America was haunted by the spectre of Jonathan Edwards and the Northampton Revival of 1735, just as in England men felt that John Wesley's success proved that the same could be achieved now if only men had faith.

In fact the kind of revivalism associated in the early nineteenth century with men such as Charles G. Finney (1792–1875) differed in important ways from the Evangelicalism of the previous century. When a revival broke out in the eighteenth century its origin was attributed absolutely to the free hand of God; no man could foresee, evoke, control or perpetuate a revival, God did everything. The English editors of Edwards' *Account of the Northampton Revival* (one of whom was Isaac Watts) even emphasized that "there was no storm, no earthquake, no inundation of water, no desolation by fire" to provide a natural explanation of why people should turn to religion, but the revival began because the Lord poured out his Spirit upon the people. Between Edwards and Finney came the great camp-meeting revivals of the late eighteenth century, and the effort to maintain the tradition finally made a breach in these underlying assumptions. The influence of Methodist theology also explains the change. Once men believed that God offered salvation to all – and more than Methodists came to believe it – the emphasis of the word "revival" began to shift from the older sense of an actual outbreak of religious conviction to that of an attempt to offer the gospel to people. It became more important to make the offer, and the idea grew up that revivals in the old sense came in answer to prayer, and that, the more people there were who prayed, the more likely the answer was to come swiftly. The new school of revivalists now started to plan the revival ahead, on the ground that hard preparatory work, the prayer of faith together with the skill and experience of the devoted revivalist would receive the divine blessing.

To this was added the new passion for big-scale organization, which became more important in the post-Civil War period when the industrial cities were the principal targets, and D.L.Moody (1837–99) perfected the techniques which Finney had roughed out. Finney had coined the dangerous phrase that "God Almighty may use any method, or means, or individual that he pleases in order to promote a revival" (quoted by W.G. McLoughlin, *Billy Sunday was his Real Name*, 1955). One very important result of this attitude was a final break with the Puritan tradition of disliking music linked with religion. Methodism had already popularized hymn-singing; now the hymn itself was popularized. Moody's partner, Ira Sankey, playing his American organ and singing "Where is my wandering boy tonight?" touched many a heart that Moody could not reach. The logical conclusion was the massed choir singing softly in the background as the evangelist made his appeal in the specially constructed tabernacle of the Billy Sunday era.

The theology of the Revivalists was Protestantism simplified; their aim was to bring people to the experience of conviction of sin and then lead them on to obtain forgiveness of their sins through justification by faith. Most revivalists held the Methodist belief that all men might be saved if they would. The most unusual aspect of this theology was a revival of interest in the doctrine of holiness. John Wesley had taught that a Christian should not rest content with his first Christian experience, but take as the final goal of the Christian life perfect holiness. Wesley said that God gave holiness in answer to faith: like Luther, he did not depreciate good works, but said that the actual eradication of sin was God's work alone. Many of the early Methodist preachers speak of seeking this gift. Some describe a distinct experience of being filled entirely with the love of God, utterly separated from all sinful desires. They do not normally speak of continuing in this state for long, but they claim more than the brief ecstasy of the mystic. Wesley's teaching was carefully guarded against the obvious dangers of talking about perfection at all; but the nineteenth-century holiness movements, most of which had a Methodist background, did not always keep their balance. Although Finney kept a doctrine of holiness in the forefront of his preaching, the main renewal of interest seems to have begun in America in the 1860s, where it took the form of holiness camp-meetings. The movement was in part a reaction against the penetration of the older bodies by Liberalism, and led in the 1890s to several small secessions from American Methodism which finally combined in the Church of the Nazarene. The teaching was brought to

England by Robert Pearsall Smith, a revivalist of great power, in 1873, at the time of the first Moody and Sankey campaign. Hitherto, the older Evangelical bodies had shown marked coolness to American revivalism, and had been taken a little by surprise by the revival which spread to the United Kingdom from America in 1859. At least one Anglican Evangelical leader, Handley Moule, Bishop of Durham, thought that his own church missed a great chance to form a popular movement at that time. In the end, the sheer necessity of preaching the Gospel to the increasing multitudes outside the churches changed this attitude of suspicion, and in 1873 a tremendous impetus was given to the English Evangelicals by the Moody and Sankey campaign. The activities of Pearsall Smith were perhaps more important because they were the basis of the Keswick Convention. This was not a new sect, but an interdenominational movement, largely Anglican Evangelical in origin. Its emphasis on the doctrine of holiness has continued, but the Convention never quite answered to the hope that it would enable the Anglican Evangelicals to recover the initiative from the Anglo-Catholics. The holiness revival was also indirectly responsible for the separate emergence of the Salvation Army in 1878, which laid great stress on "holiness meetings" in its first generation.

The underlying reasons for the growth of a new, highly organized revivalism become clearer when one notices that its rise in importance and intensity runs parallel with the spread of Liberal theology and the building of industrial cities. In the great revival meetings men caught a glimpse of the universal church which they were too often denied as they took their seats in the little local chapel, where every man knew his brethren and sisters far too well. The social element preponderated, and the social element was what was in danger of disappearing from life, as well as from over-individualistic Protestantism. The audience came to the meetings in carefully arranged parties and was packed together into a vast multitude gripped by expectancy and excitement. There was something sacramental, in a sense, in the moment when the revivalist made his final appeal and men and women streamed down to the front to kneel or shake hands with the preacher. Was there reflected here the same demand for more elaborate ritual, a more generous use of music and drama, that was also finding expression in Anglo-Catholicism? Superficially, the revivals played a great part in the earnest attempt of later nineteenth-century Protestantism in England and America to reach the masses of people who never entered any kind of church. In fact, in so far as these people were touched at all, it was probably through the ordinary steady work of the settled denominations, aided by the new techniques worked out to combine religion with social work in the new city missions, institutional churches, the Y.M.C.A., the Brotherhood Movement and many other organizations of a similar kind. What Christians wanted to see in the great revivals was the fact that conversions still took place, that the "old-time religion", on which their own spiritual experience depended so entirely, had not lost its power or its meaning, and that the Biblical critics must be wrong, because the revivalists were right. This meant that at times revivalism united with the new, self-conscious Fundamentalism which began an organized existence in America about 1910, and which actually succeeded for a while in preventing any instruction in the Darwinian hypothesis in the public schools of some American States. The wider effect was to keep Protestant confidence alive until the turning of the theological tide, which came earlier than is sometimes suggested.

SOCIAL AND ECONOMIC TEACHING

The history of the social and economic teaching of Protestantism suggests once more the small degree to which one can think of a separate Protestant history, or of a Protestant effect on history. The period 1500–1850 saw the almost entire emancipation of economics and politics from religious control, the secularization, in other words, of European society. The folklore of modern capitalism, to use Thurman Arnold's striking phrase, is, like its diplomacy, non-religious. Of course, decisions on public and economic policy had always included a large element of national and private interest, but human society had been assumed to aspire to a divinely-ordained, theologically-interpreted pattern. This radical change in the sanctions applicable to human motives is another example of how increasingly difficult it has become to bring Christianity, Protestant or not, into fruitful contact with a totally new era. The disappearance of the simple medieval world of the farmer, the local craftsman and shopkeeper and the moneylender, together with the enormous expansion of international trade and the growth of the financial system necessary to make it run smoothly, left the spokesman of the church with little to say which fitted the world in which men believed that they lived. Just as there is little in the nature of a new Protestant social or business ethic, so there is no truth in the picture of Protestantism acting as a catalyst to release an economic individualism which destroyed an ideal "Catholic" social order. Christianity, to a surprising extent, simply suffered its own re-making in the image of industrial men; neither Latin nor Lutheran piety in the seventeenth century could avoid the individualism of the age. One may reasonably speak of Capitalism and the decline of religion; there was within the economic order a dynamic of change which carried men along with it, revolutionizing Europe through a combination of increased mechanical and financial skill and the deep human impulse to possess material objects. India and China are suffering a similar dramatic development in our own day.

Nothing could have been more medieval than the economic ideas which the Pilgrim Fathers took with them to New England, or more complete than the contrast of these modest, self-sufficient, congregational villages with the fiercely competitive capitalism of the United States in the Reconstruction period. It is perhaps not unfair to quote as an example of the slow rate of change of Christian thought about economics that in the heart of the post-Civil War years, when the unemployed of Boston came to D.L.Moody, himself firmly in the Calvinist tradition, and asked his advice, he could only make two suggestions: one was that they should return to the farms of the West, advice economically impossible, the other the argument that if they lived honestly Christian lives an employer was bound to find them work. Moody still clung rather pathetically to the feeling that their unemployment was their own responsibility, as it probably would have been in the medieval period, or even in the eighteenth century. His attitude resembles that which Henri Talon points out (*John Bunyan*, English Translation, 1951) was the attitude of the representative Puritan writer, John Bunyan (1628–88). For Bunyan at the close of the seventeenth century the economic virtues were still honesty, thrift, the "just" price, the well-made product – local economics, in a world where the tailor still came to the country house and stayed to make the clothes. Talon makes the interesting observation that, when one compares the social teaching of Bunyan with that of John Wesley, it is clear that a new world is being created. He suggests that while the prayer "Give me not riches" still has a full and medieval meaning for Bunyan, to Wesley, on the other hand, money has been re-interpreted, as was to be expected in the mid-eighteenth century, as an excellent gift of God. In the sermon in which he sums up his economic theory Wesley says "Gain all you can, Save all you can, Give all you can." This advice, and above all the opening phrase, would have horrified Bunyan, who would have emphasized the certainty that a man would forget the injunction to charity and remember the encouragement to

accumulate. The surviving element of more primitive thought in Wesley came out in his later denunciations of wealthy Methodists, who he roundly declared would be the end of the societies, but his own attitude had helped both the temptation and the fall. In his old age Wesley said that he ought to have imitated Quakerism and devised sumptuary laws for the Wesleyan societies: this is more in keeping with his first plans for the Revival when he was under the influence of Cave's "Primitive Christianity" and the example of German Pietism, and dreamed of the reproduction of the communal life which is described in the Acts of the Apostles.

Apart from such gradual accommodation as this, which made the ascetic tradition more and more remote from the realities of economic life, the traditional system of social ethics became increasingly strained. Honesty and corporations hardly met; the problem of poverty rose to a size which seemed only mocked by private charity, despite the tremendous quantities of money redistributed in this way in the first half of the nineteenth century. In the sphere of national policy, the theory of the "just war" looked more tattered after every fresh application of it to the steadily worsening conflicts of the modern nation states. Nor had tradition much to say about such matters as the ethics of advertising, which at times seemed to verge on anti-social activity. The main elements of Western society wanted the secularization of economics and politics; they cannot fairly blame the Christians for not preventing it from happening. Indeed, much was done in the way of private charity and individual regeneration to avert the worst consequences of European folly. A great deal has been written about the alleged stumbling-blocks put in the way of British education by Protestant denominationalism; much more will have to be written about the dubious results of what has amounted to the secularization of education.

After about 1870, some Protestant thinkers began to admit that poverty – the point at which economic facts were hurting the conscience of society – could not be solved by the goodwill of Dickensian millionaires. A report to the Convocation of Canterbury in 1907 made this quite typical statement:

"We feel that the existing methods by which the Church relieves the poor – that is, the administration of 'charity' by the Church, as by Christian bodies generally – has been shown in its results to be singularly unproductive of permanent good. . . . On the other hand, the existing system is responsible for much alienation from

Photo: *Exclusive News Agency*

PLATE 31. Ulrich Zwingli (1484–1531): portrait by Hans Asper (1499–1571). (*Public Library, Zürich*)

PLATE 32 . John Calvin (1509–1564): this portrait, by an unknown artist, is considered
to be the best portrait of Calvin. (*Public and University Library, Geneva*)

Photo: United States Information Service

PLATE 33. Church at Camden, Maine: Puritanism was not bound to be either black or ugly.

PLATE 34. Charles Haddon Spurgeon (1834–92): nineteenth-century Protestantism – the preacher.

Photo: Sheila Harrison

PLATE 35. All Saints' Church, St Margaret Street, London: nineteenth-century Protestantism the return of the altar.

Photo: *Exclusive News Agency*

PLATE 36. Chapel built in 1777: before Methodist architecture was corrupted by the Gothic Revival.

Photo: Jarrolds and Sons Ltd

PLATE 37. Gildencroft Meeting House, Norwich: built in 1699 and destroyed during the Second World War. (*Society of Friends, London*)

Photo: *Keystone Press Agency Ltd*

PLATE 38. Billy Graham conducting his first open-air meeting in England, Trafalgar Square, April 3, 1954

the Church, and from religious worship, of self-respecting workers, who are afraid of being supposed to come "for what they can get". . . . We have to go deeper to the grounds of existing misery and want and unemployment; and, while we do our best to deal with the present distress, direct our chief attention towards furthering the re-organization of Society on such principles of justice as will tend to reduce poverty and misery in the future to more manageable proportions."

In the United States the same point of view was held by W.Gladden and Walter Rauschenbusch. If taken seriously, this was Socialist doctrine, and it is not likely that many Christians, as Christians, have ever accepted it; there was no question in the Report itself of the Church of England becoming an agency for the Socialist Party.

Here lay the difficulty of the Protestant churches. If individual action was not enough, then the churches must become agents for some kind of collective action. This was not beyond the horizon of the evangelicals. Slavery had been abolished largely by collective Christian action, and in the later nineteenth century popular Protestantism had found another important common objective in teetotalism. Prohibition was obtained in the United States and changes made in the law in many countries. Such organized campaigns as these did not require prior agreement about the re-organization of society; they were popular partly because they by-passed political divisions. The question of re-organizing society, however, had been taken out of Christian hands and become a political matter. The secularization of economics and politics had gone so far that throughout the world the Labour Movements had been able to steal from the churches their former primacy in moral issues. The root of the Socialist appeal was ethical; men believed less in the practical details of a Socialist programme than in the demand for a drastic alteration in the basis of human economic relationships. The emergence in non-Christian hands of a political theory which used ethical but not Christian terms meant that Christian leaders, who now accepted the need for a radical transformation of society, found that in effect they had surrendered the initiative to secular minds. Socialism was so much "in the air" that it paralysed the Christian capacity to produce a picture of a more deeply Christian alternative.

A generalization that the Anglo-Catholics and the Liberals followed the path of collective action while the Evangelicals favoured the more traditional methods –

individual regeneration and private charity – would go too far, but points in the right direction. In the long run, perhaps, the traditional answer worked better. From the early days of the Inner Mission in German Lutheranism, deaconess orders began to appear in Protestant bodies parallel to the more monastic Anglican Sisterhoods. Orphanages, hospitals, schools and similar institutions were built in great numbers; brilliant attempts were made to combine relief work with evangelism in the Methodist Central Halls, of which S.F.Collier's Manchester Mission (1885–1921) was perhaps the most famous; and in such departures as the Settlement Movement something was done to close the gap which Marx and poverty were widening between the classes. All these activities – and Protestantism has probably never been more earnestly or sincerely active in doing good – looked like palliatives in a period when many believed in bolder, more radical solutions.

The collective action favoured by a smaller group meant in practice political action, and this demanded more agreement than it was possible to obtain. A great deal of discussion took place, especially in such bodies as the Christian Social Union, which was founded in 1889, but the direct political effect was small. In the meantime the working class acted for itself. In a period when capitalism greatly multiplied the wealth of the Western world the trade unions could increase the wages, decrease the working hours and advance the political power of the working classes. The organized churches, conscious of much goodwill and hard work on their own part, have been unable to realize that the working class has not felt that it owed the improvement of its condition of life to Christianity. The American trade unionist, Samuel Gompers, said in 1898 that his associates had come to look upon the church and the ministry as the apologists and defenders of the wrong committed against the interests of the people. His attitude could be paralleled throughout Europe. The Welfare State, which has appeared in various forms in most countries, represents the final secularization of social morality: it was the inevitable result of the failure of organized Christianity to sustain a Christian civilization, and it has made much of the charitable work of the churches superfluous.

For Protestantism the inner problem remained the same, though the nature of the poverty with which it had to deal altered dramatically in some parts of the world from the material to the spiritual. The church could work essentially through the regeneration of the individual – the Barthian opposition to the social gospel was a paradoxical revival of this classical approach – or it could seek the reconstruction of ordinary society on Christian lines, which meant trying to obtain collective action, or it could try to make of the church a redeemed society visibly different from its environment. There have been signs that the World Council of Churches, building on the foundations laid by the Life and Work Movement which held ecumenical conferences at Stockholm in 1925 and Oxford in 1937, still wants to find a way to the second. The most remarkable fruit of this tradition was this famous statement by the Amsterdam Meeting of the World Council in 1948:

"The Christian churches should reject the ideologies of both communism and laissez-faire capitalism, and should seek to draw men away from the false assumption that these extremes are the only alternatives. Each has made promises which it could not redeem. Communist ideology puts the emphasis upon economic justice, and promises that freedom will come automatically after the completion of the revolution. Capitalism puts the emphasis upon freedom, and promises that justice will follow as a by-product of free enterprise; that too, is an ideology which has been proved false. It is the responsibility of Christians to seek new, creative solutions which never allow either justice or freedom to destroy each other."

This is the most important economic statement produced by modern Protestantism; but how socially effective the World Council can be in view of the progressive secularization of Western culture remains to be seen. It is unlikely that any change of spirit will arise from the simultaneous conversion of masses of men; past experience suggests that small groups are the usual source of creative change. There has certainly never been any serious suggestion of a Protestant equivalent of the Roman Catholic trade union organizations and other political groups. In the period since 1929 the retreat from Socialism as a social expression of Christianity has become almost complete: it was a clue to the way in which many Christians, especially ministers, approached the modern world that, in the 1920-39 period, St Francis of Assisi enjoyed a new and obviously symbolic popularity, not only in High Church circles. But as it becomes clearer that the modern crisis is not one of poverty, but of the collapse of any feeling of community in the great industrialized nations, Protestantism needs to become more aware than hitherto that Christian social thinking ought to be able to start from a living, visible Christian community, offering at least some contradiction to the limp standards of the time, and finding the centre of its common life in the reality of the Eucharist. Anglo-Cath-

olic monasticism has been no more than a gesture in this direction, because celibacy removes the religious community from convincing contact with the social order. Utopian experiments are out of fashion; it is on the housing estates of the Western world that the battle for Christianity is being fought.

OVERSEAS MISSIONS

The idea of a visible Christian community has been implicit in the methods of much missionary enterprise. In China or India a sharp contrast inevitably appeared during the nineteenth century between Christianity and its environment, even though the contrast was to some extent forced on the Christians by the attitude of the locally established faiths. In the spectacle of comparatively isolated mission-posts proving the truth of Christianity by service and sacrifice could be seen another kind of objectivity, enforced by such gestures as the erection of the Cathedral of Zanzibar on the site of the former slave-market. Sometimes the contrast was very striking indeed. "I am about to die for the Baganda, and have purchased the road to them with my life," said Bishop James Hannington to his captors shortly before they killed him near the shores of Lake Victoria Nyanza in 1885. That was part of the glamour which the nineteenth-century Protestant churches loved to throw round missionary work, and which caused a bishop of Lahore to say that "one death in the mission-field is worth six lives at home". The mission worship, the schools, the hospitals, the advice about farming and other crafts, the undeniable proof that men of one colour were trying to do something essentially generous for men of another, formed a set of objective facts to which the Western churches could turn more and more in their perplexities. Gains in a new world seemed to balance losses in an old, and the simple faith of the converted savage was compared favourably with the complicated doubts of highly-civilized man. It was sufficiently impressive that Christianity could make inroads into countries which had followed faiths of their own for centuries.

Protestant missionary work may be divided into two periods, before and after the French Revolution. The second period began with the foundation of the Baptist Missionary Society in England in 1792. The impulse ran strongly among the Evangelicals, and when the London Missionary Society was founded in 1785 it was meant to include all of Evangelical sympathies, though in practice it depended largely for its support on the English Congregationalists. The Anglican Evangelicals established their own society, the Church Missionary Society, in 1799 after two further groups had been created in Scotland in 1796. Missionary work always seemed to call out more than purely denominational effort, and in 1799 the Religious Tract Society was formed to draw on as wide a range of Christian literature as possible. In 1804 there followed the British and Foreign Bible Society, intended to centralize the work of publishing Bibles at a low cost and of obtaining new translations of the Scriptures. The sign of the entry of the United States into this field was the setting up of the American Board of Commissioners for Foreign Missions in 1810. The Wesleyan Methodist Missionary Society was organized in 1817–18 on a connectional basis, but Jabez Bunting had been preparing the way since Thomas Coke died on his way to start a Wesleyan mission in Ceylon in 1814. Less commonly linked with all this was the somewhat self-confident attempt of the Evangelicals in England to spread the revival to the Continent. At the close of the French Wars Wesleyanism had some success, especially in the South of France, where this drive to find a foreign audience for Arminianism encountered a second movement, this time a Calvinistic one, coming from Geneva. There Robert Haldane, a Scottish Baptist, had helped to touch off what is still called the Reveil in 1817. English money helped to pay for the itinerant preachers who carried this reborn classical Calvinism through Switzerland and France and into Holland. In the long run new missionary societies and missionaries were the result of this endeavour.

One is bound to ask what factors caused this period of very considerable missionary expansion. One can hardly suggest that the principal aim of the missionaries was to persuade Europe of the truth of Christianity by a demonstration of its successful application to Africa. On the other hand, the question is not quite fair if it suggests that this was the beginning of Protestant interest in spreading the Gospel outside Europe and America. This would be to accept too lightly the nineteenth century's own view of the matter and to exaggerate the extent to which most people cared about missions – the shift of interest was in a small group. In fact those European nations which had acquired overseas possessions had made some attempt from the first to fulfil their obligations to their colonists and subjects. The Spanish and Portuguese, ahead in the race, had done this in South America and the Far East, although the amazing initial success of Roman Catholicism in Japan was almost completely lost in the sixteen-thirties, after which time Japan was closed to European influence until the middle of the nineteenth century. China was widely evangelized, despite serious

setbacks in the eighteenth century. Naturally enough, in the French, Spanish and Portuguese colonies and trading stations no Protestant missionary work was done.

The Protestant trading stations were by no means entirely neglected, however. In the Dutch East Indies a state Reformed Church grew up in which the Bible was translated into Malay; this had at least 65,000 members in 1815. In the eighteenth century Pietism and its offshoot, Moravianism, inspired most of what was attempted. Two Germans from Halle began operations in the Danish trading post of Tranquebar in Southern India in 1706, and the Lutheran community which they established has continued with Danish and Anglican support to the present day. India only fell under the political control of the British in the later part of the century and not until 1813 was the British East India Company compelled to allow missionaries to enter its territories. In the North, Hans Egede went to Greenland in 1721 and began an Eskimo mission which was supplemented by Moravians who arrived in 1733 and who attacked Labrador in the 1750s. Zinzendorf, the Moravian leader, also sent a mission to the negroes of the Danish West Indies in 1732. In the thirteen colonies the number of Germans grew steadily in the eighteenth century, and by 1742 Halle found it necessary to send H.M.Muhlenberg to organize them into a proper religious community. Throughout this period the Church of England, like other state churches, tried to fulfil its duties to the colonists and natives of the growing Empire. The Society for the Propagation of the Gospel had been founded in 1701 and was on corresponding terms with the Lutheran leaders. Its main responsibility was to find the chaplains to work in the colonies. It is worth remembering that when John Wesley sailed for Georgia in 1736 he was thinking of evangelizing the American Indians. At the Southern tip of Africa there was a small Dutch trading post, and a small Reformed community emerged here, helped by another Moravian who worked among the Hottentots from 1737 to 1743. In the north of Africa a vigorous Muhammadanism blocked the natural route into the interior. Nineteenth-century missions had little success in penetrating Muslim countries and recent reports have suggested that the initiative in West Africa might easily pass to Islam.

Despite all this, the opening years of the nineteenth century have generally been credited with seeing the beginning of Protestant foreign missionary enterprise. Perhaps there is less need to criticize adversely the comparatively small-scale effort of the first missionary period – which reflects an era, from 1500 to 1750, in which the expansion of Europe was dominated by France, Spain and Portugal – than to underline that in this same period Protestant countries took a large share in the slave trade from Africa to America and at the same time showed little sympathy in their contacts with the American Indians. The revulsion from this tradition was of marked importance in the history of Christianity. The Evangelical battle with the slave-owners stamped the missionary societies, which were also evangelical in the first years, with this authentic note of the gospel: those who rejected slavery could offer a Christianity free from ultimate dependence on the economic standards of the West. Frank Weston stood in this tradition when, as Bishop of Zanzibar, he crusaded against the use of African forced labour in East Africa after the First World War.

One must not exaggerate either the depth or the suddenness of the transformation. Theologically, the change had been taking place at least since the point in the mid-seventeenth century when Richard Baxter (1615–91) began to modify the classical creed of Calvin. It has become the fashion to talk as though Calvin hardly mentioned the doctrine of predestination in the *Institutes* and to emphasize that his theology turns on a vivid sense of the awful and unquestionable sovereignty of God. A case can be made for this, but it remains historically true that the seventeenth and eighteenth centuries understood the Genevan tradition in another way, and their long preoccupation with Calvin's thought was very much concerned with his grim insistence on the terrible decrees. These were still a living force in the lives of the early Methodist preachers, many of whom, as they struggled from conviction of sin to justification, spent long periods wondering whether in fact their names were written in the list of those damned from eternity to eternity. The assumption that God, if he wanted to save Indians and Chinese, would do so in his own good way, was useful to many who perhaps really wanted to oppose missions for other reasons. The danger of believing that God could confine whole races of men to specific fates in this fashion can be seen in South Africa at the present day. But from the time that Charles Wesley wrote such lines as "For all, for all, my Saviour died" – and the word "my" was not the least surprising to his contemporaries – his hymns lived a life of their own and played a large part in modifying the general Evangelical theology.

Too much has been made of the idea that Protestant missionary work hung fire because of the lack of monastic orders. The Protestant equivalent, the missionary society, proved just as effective. These organizations were a typical example of the passion which the nineteenth century had for centralizing and systematizing philanthropy. A society existed for every kind of good work, with a committee experienced in raising money on a national scale, in writing, publishing and distributing propaganda, in finding and training workers and in running political campaigns, if necessary, on behalf of the desired objects. Everything depended on the steady increase in wealth in Britain and the United States, for the missionary society expected the missionary ideal to loosen the purse-strings of the laity.

This confidence in the power of organization went hand in hand with a natural, if tragic, confidence in Western civilization. The Protestant missionary found himself at a crisis in modern history, the meeting-point of very dissimilar cultures. It must be insisted that the crisis took place in the early part of the century – Westerners have tended to feel that there was no crisis until mutiny or rebellion challenged their power. The assumption in the minds of most of the Evangelicals, as they commenced their work, was that Indian, Chinese and Japanese cultures were either static or declining, and that the African was hardly cultured at all. Robert Moffat wrote of the latter: "Evangelization must precede civilization: nothing less than the power of divine grace can reform the heart of savages: after this the mind is susceptible." One must not forget that the missionaries were conscious of the great and recent improvement in public order and decency which had been made in Europe between 1750 and 1850. The missionaries were perfectly and evangelically sincere; armed with the material and spiritual benefits of the West, they did their best for both their converts and their culture, striving to combine them under the Cross of Christ. Their assumption was doubly wrong. The Eastern cultures had sufficient vitality to absorb the scientific, industrial and educational advantages of the West without accepting Christianity. They began to reform their old culture rather than reject it, so that Christianity entered upon a period of uncertain toleration. On the other hand, in some parts of Africa there has been a terrible interim in which the tribal system, so often misinterpreted by governments as well as missionaries, has been shattered without any new system taking its place. Nevertheless the missions have achieved more than can be measured statistically. Apart from founding churches, the missionaries taught the East to set a new value on human life and sympathy, and they prevented Africa from passing simply from the tyranny of superstition to the tyranny of economics.

PROTESTANTISM

THE ECUMENICAL MOVEMENT

Nineteenth-century missionary enterprise did Protestantism in general a great service by bringing home how serious the divisions of Protestantism really were. The old reproach that there was some fatal flaw in Protestant principle which made division and sub-division inevitable, and that in the end there would be as many sects as Protestants, looked appallingly true on the mission-field. In 1807, when the London Missionary Society became the first Protestant body to enter China, the Roman church had already worked there alone for three hundred years. By 1900, Protestant missions had multiplied so rapidly that thirty-three American, twenty-three British and twelve Continental missionary societies had missions there. In some countries questions of colour and local patriotism soon caused new sects to spring up: there are, for example, at least eight hundred independent Bantu churches in South Africa. It has been shown already how in Liberalism, Evangelicalism, Anglo-Catholicism, missionary enterprise, and social thinking, Protestantism has tried to meet the strains of the modern world. It now remains to consider these developments in relation to the Ecumenical movement, the effort to bring the churches together again which will probably be Protestantism's greatest contribution to Christianity in this century. The first triumph came in 1948 when all the most important Protestant bodies, together with a number of the Orthodox churches, formed at Amsterdam the World Council of Churches whose chief function is to promote the ecumenical consciousness of Protestantism.

Liberalism undoubtedly helped to dissolve the theological barriers between the churches. The official basis of the World Council – which is not a world church – is a fellowship of churches which accept our Lord Jesus Christ as God and Saviour. This is not vague; but a hundred and fifty years ago much more would have been necessary to bring together some of the member churches. Liberalism crossed all denominational frontiers; the reaction against it has also been general, which means that everywhere Protestants share an interest in the return to a theology which accepts the assumptions of the Scriptures and takes a new interest in what the sixteenth-century Reformers actually said. This change of attitude entails a fresh encounter with some of the Biblical problems which Liberalism was designed to solve. and it will be interesting to see how long the theological common front is maintained. What will not happen is a return to the purely denominational theological pattern, and this is an enormous gain for the future.

The social and economic role of the church has always been a prolific source of divisions. In the Reformation tradition one church often became identified with the ruling class and even used the powers of the state to make any dissent from the official body illegal. Much was done to remedy this situation in the nineteenth century, and this has eased the friction between, for example, the Church of England and the English Free Churches. This was not a purely Protestant problem: in Russia, Orthodoxy has struggled with dissent since the seventeenth century, and the anti-clericalism of intellectuals in some Roman Catholic countries fulfils a similar function. The increasing secularization of the modern state has thrown Protestantism on its own resources. It is denied the support, if not always the interference, of the state and there is little prestige to be gained from the adherence of particular social groups. As a result the Protestant churches have become more independent in the social and economic sphere. Reference has already been made to the World Council's pronouncement on Communism and capitalism. In the same vein the Council noted that, since modern nation states claim to be a law unto themselves, Christians needed to become more aware of the tension between the moral claims of a sovereign God and the political claims of a sovereign state. Such statements do not lead to action by individual churches, but they modify the conduct of individuals. From the ecumenical point of view, what is coming into being through the World Council is a general body of opinion on social policy, broader in its sympathy than any single group could attain. This has lessened the need for divisions on social issues, though it is necessary to remember that matters such as the colour question are not settled by resolutions.

The Evangelical contribution to the reunion movement in Protestantism has been very great. The historian of the united Church of South India, Bengt Sundkler, traces its origin straight back to the Evangelical revival of the eighteenth century which brought home the fact that evangelism was a world-wide task laid upon all the churches. The work of the Wesleys left, in the Methodist societies, a body not permanently committed to either the Presbyterian or the Episcopal tradition and able to act as mediator between the two. The generous theology of the revival, preached and sung by every nineteenth-century evangelist, penetrated everywhere, especially through the new hymn-books which drew their contents from the whole of Christendom. This common Evangelical tradition is, however, less helpful when one comes down to actual discussion of ways of reuniting the church. Reunion would mean the joining together of denominations whose ways of thinking about the nature of the church differ considerably. In the past many Protestant communions have held that the ideal pattern of church order, to which all Christian bodies must conform, was set out in the Scriptures. Seventeenth-century Independents and Presbyterians took this view, and some do still. Baptist churches would normally regard adult Baptism and local church autonomy as being quite as essential to a united church as Anglicans would episcopacy. Early nineteenth-century Wesleyans, though they did not share the dissenting desire to disestablish the Church of England, could still on occasion suggest that Methodism possessed the perfect combination of freedom from the state and the true, primitive episcopacy. Some Lutheran bodies of which the American Lutheran Church (Missouri Synod) is one, take an extremely restricting view of the Church's freedom to vary doctrinally from the Lutheran interpretation of Scripture. The impact of all the forces we have been discussing, and of the new Revivalism in particular, on all this was to give greater prominence to the idea of freedom. Unity was held to lie more in the Christian fellowship which comes from sharing in the life of Christ than in dogmatic agreement. From this point of view what mattered was that one should be free to preach the gospel of redemption from sin through the Cross of Christ, and that men and women should be given the chance to surrender themselves to the saving truth; men who shared this passion for souls could find ways of working together. This position is distinguished from Liberalism by a strong doctrinal element.

The belief that Christian men and women were united by a common faith in Christ seemed dangerously sentimental to many nineteenth-century Anglo-Catholics, who were more inclined to seek church unity by magnifying than by minimizing the importance of church order, and who first thought that, by doing so, they would make possible a greater understanding with Rome. They felt that the movement for unity had arisen because Evangelicals and Liberals did not take the doctrine of the Church and the ministry seriously, and thought the only result was a vagueness worse than unbelief. They thought that the Church of England should be content with the fresh measure of unity which the world-wide Anglican community had discovered since 1867 in the decennial meetings of the bishops at Lambeth Palace, the London home of the Archbishop of Canterbury. This attitude was maintained until the end of the century, when a change took place which may have been due in part to the firm Roman Catholic refusal to recognize the validity of Anglican orders. The fact that Anglo-Catholic repre-

sentatives attended the Edinburgh World Missionary Conference in 1910 marked a new era. From this conference the modern Ecumenical movement really stems. The attendance of the Anglo-Catholics, who had not shared in such gatherings before, has usually been regarded as the work of the Student Christian Movement. (Here the lines of history cross again in a fascinating way, for the S.C.M. can be traced back to Dwight L. Moody, whose campaigns among students led in 1886 to the formation of the Student Volunteer Movement for Foreign Missions, about which it has been said that no voluntary movement has done more to bring the churches together.) The Edinburgh Conference did not meet consciously to plan a world council of churches, but the Anglo-Catholic decision enabled the Church of England to enter the Ecumenical movement without internal dissension. The Anglo-Catholics did not modify their doctrinal position, but they admitted to a possible future within Protestantism. This meant in the long run the further admission that terms such as "Protestant", "Catholic" and "Evangelical" no longer correspond to easily definable bodies or groups, and that much of what they have traditionally stood for has passed across the denominational frontiers.

Many detailed accounts of the Ecumenical movement are available. There is space here only to return to the mission-field for the movement's most striking achievement, the foundation of the Church of South India in 1947. In this church were reconciled five Anglican dioceses, the Methodist Church of South India, and the South India United Church, a union, dating from 1908, of most of the Congregational and Presbyterian missions of South India. Here for the first time a church with the historic succession of the episcopate has entered into corporate union with non-episcopal bodies.

CONCLUSION

There is no useful brief definition of Protestantism. The difficulty of maintaining a balance between the claims of the church and the individual soul is inherent in Christianity. At times Protestants have stressed the importance of the individual and have emphasized the danger that primitive Christianity may be swallowed up by "the church". The Word of God has been exalted above everything else on the ground that the one true safeguard against the worship of institutions is the constant return to the Bible read in humility and the Holy Spirit. No particular body, from the Roman church to the Quaker meeting, has ever expressed all the riches of Christianity, and the disintegration of Protestantism in the post-Reformacion period was an honest attempt, which had to be made, to explore those riches more fully.

On the other hand, the idea that Protestantism is a man's right to define Christianity for himself, believe it for himself and build a private chapel in which to preach his own sermons is an extravagant parody. The corporate idea has never been without a witness, whether Puritan, Anglican, Methodist or in the Ecumenical movement. At the present time the emphasis on the Church is stronger than ever before, as may be seen in the renewed interest in this aspect of the theology of the Reformers, and in the widespread liturgical experiments which are giving the denominations a better understanding of different types of worship. It may be that in these movements Protestantism will achieve lasting reconciliation of these two sides of Christianity, personal salvation through justification by faith and the practice of a corporate Christian life in the Church.

2e. Christianity: the Catholic Church since the Reformation

by T. CORBISHLEY

In the last four centuries the religious consciousness of the Western world has been so dominated by the experience of the Reformation that there is some danger of exaggerating its importance in an account of the Catholic Church in modern times. Grave as that experience was, profound as are its consequences, it was, it should be remembered, only one amongst a number of not dissimilar incidents in the life of the Church. Whereas the history of the various Protestant groups as distinct entities does not begin before the sixteenth century, the Catholic Church remains fully aware of the fifteen hundred years of history which had already moulded her outlook. To her, Lutheranism and Calvinism are numbered amongst the long list of heresies which have sought to wrest the truth of Christ away from its universal validity to serve the interests of a party. In a famous phrase, W.G.Ward described the condition of the Church since the rise of Lutheranism as a "state of siege". There is a sense in which the description is useful. But the expansion of the Church outside Europe and the immense effort she has put into her missionary endeavour in every corner of the globe must be borne in mind to correct the impression of a body desperately seeking to defend herself against extinction.

The justification of Ward's description, in so far as it is valid, must be sought for in the fact that the chief intellectual and theological activity of the Church is centred in Europe, where the effects of the Reformation have been most marked. In a volume which tries to state the faiths of different religious bodies the main interest will, necessarily, be theological and philosophical. Yet the Church is not and never was concerned with theology primarily and for its own sake. Her mission is to teach the truth of Christ so that men may come to believe in him, and believing may find salvation. Her reaction to the Reformation, as it has always been to heresy, was to reject what she considers to be its errors, because to imperil the truth of salvation is to imperil truth itself.

In the chapter dealing with the early Church the account of Christian beliefs was very largely the story of the progressive development of a body of theological doctrine. When we turn to consider the contribution made by the Catholic Church since the Reformation, the discussion is complicated by a number of factors. Hitherto, despite the recurrence of heresy and the reality of schism between East and West, the main stream of development has been clear and the essential unity of Christendom sufficiently widely accepted. Henceforward we are faced with the problem of a divided Christendom, with different bodies claiming to represent, in their different ways, the authentic Christian tradition. Side by side with this development, and to some extent stemming from it, has gone the widespread decline in religious belief of any kind. The result has been that the Catholic Church has been attacked on two fronts. On the one hand, she is accused, generally by non-Christians, of being obscurantist, clinging to outworn dogmas, unprogressive in outlook. On the other hand, many Christians accuse her of having obscured the primitive truths of Christ's teaching by adding to it doctrines for which there is no warrant in Scripture, dogmas irresponsibly promulgated, ideas which are the outcome of uncontrolled human speculation. The fact that such contradictory criticisms can be made is testimony to the dual role which the Catholic Church claims. She believes that she is the custodian of a body of truths, entrusted to her care by Christ, truths which are yet living and therefore growing. She must be conservative; she must be progressive. This tension in the intellectual life of the Church is exemplified most

Photo: National Gallery of Art

PLATE 39. The Virgin with Saint Inés and Saint Tecla: painting by El Greco (1541–1614). (*National Gallery of Art, Washington, D.C. Widener Collection.*)

PLATE 40. Madonna and Child with Saints Jerome and Anthony of Padua. Lorenzo Lotto. Charles Potter Kling Fund. (Courtesy, *Museum of Fine Arts, Boston*.)

clearly in this post-Reformation period. As she sees it, the Reformation itself was an attack upon her right to teach the whole truth progressively revealed by Christ. Against such an attack she had to defend herself by re-stating old truths, justifying her teaching and where necessary clarifying. Yet the whole intellectual development which has taken place in the world during the last four centuries, not least in the field of the natural sciences, the change in men's political and social outlook, the opening up of new vistas in so many disciplines, has meant that the Church has had to adapt herself to a constantly changing situation. She believes that the basic doctrines she has always taught are permanently valid. She is equally aware that thought, even theological thought, does not stand still.

Any attempt, then, to outline the principal developments which have taken place in Catholic thought since the beginning of the sixteenth century must begin with an emphatic reminder that these developments are to be judged in the light of all that went before. The work of the great Councils of the Church, depending largely on the writings of the Fathers, is the permanent basis for further speculation. Just as the achievement of the medieval Schoolmen was to reduce to order the disparate strands of tradition, so the speculations of modern theologians and the dogmatic pronouncements of the Popes are to be seen as elucidations of ideas already accepted. The ground-plan of the grand structure of Catholic theology was laid down in the beginning; the building which has arisen during the succeeding centuries has not strayed outside that plan. Whatever shifts of emphasis may have occurred, these have referred to some already existing feature, illuminating, elaborating, completing.

Never in the history of Christendom has there been such profound and such widespread theological activity as has taken place during the four centuries under review. In the earliest centuries the tools of the new science were being slowly forged; in the medieval period, speculation, vigorous as it was, concerned itself largely with domestic issues. In the modern age, in addition to the continuing theological debate within, the Church has constantly had to face new challenges from outside. In view of all this variety and multiplicity, it is difficult to be certain which are the essential developments, and which, in course of time, will fall into the background. What follows is an attempt to single out for comment and explanation those features of the Church's history which, since Luther first went into action, seem to have had the most lasting effect. Let us begin with some account of the historical situation which produced the Reformation and of that which resulted from it.

THE REFORMATION

"Martin Luther and Ignatius Loyola did what they did, and we are what we are, because Leo X was short of money." In this challenging sentence Dr Pullan, in the 1923 Bampton Lectures, sought to sum up the causes of the Reformation. Without wishing to deny that, as a matter of historical fact, it was Luther's attack on the prevailing abuses in the Church's practice concerning Indulgences which precipitated the cleavage within Western Christendom which is called the Reformation, we must remind ourselves that history is rarely as simple as that. Luther applied the match to an explosive mass: there might well have been others to produce a similar effect. In the complex social, economic, political and religious situation of the late Middle Ages, it seems all too probable that some major upheaval was inevitable. The lethargy which perpetually menaces all settled institutions had not spared the Church; careerism and indolence corrupted the higher levels of the clergy; the lower ranks of the clergy contained far too many ignorant and easy-going priests; the great religious Orders had declined from their ancient ideals of austerity and unworldliness. The involvement of the temporal interests of the Papacy with current political struggles made it inevitable that the Church's policy should be invariably suspect in the eyes of the great powers now emerging into full national self-consciousness.

The marvel is that the Church should have already survived the recurrent shocks of the Avignon exile and the Great Schism, the hostility of all the powers in turn, the abiding threat from the Turks, the profligacy and ambition of her most exalted rulers. Why did Luther's revolt result in that rending of Christendom which tore from the control of Rome great provinces in the North of Europe? The answer is to be found far more in the political situation of the time than in any purely religious factors. The rival ambitions of Charles V of Spain (elected Emperor in 1519) and Francis I who succeeded to the throne of France in 1515, the aggressive policy of the Turks under Suleiman the Magnificent (1520–66), the autocratic temper of Henry VIII of England (1509–47), the independent spirit of the German princes and the commercial designs of the Venetian Republic, all conspired to defeat the Church's attempts to preserve religious unity. It is true that a more vigorous religious spirit in the Christian rulers and peoples would have prevented the worst effects of political disunity. But even granted this, it is wrong to ascribe the success of the Reformation to purely religious factors.

It would, of course, be idle to deny that there was need

of thorough-going reform. The Popes themselves were aware of this and time after time sought to convene a General Council to produce a remedy for the different diseases weakening the Church. As early as 1523 Adrian VI determined to convene such an assembly, but his own death and a variety of political and other considerations postponed the realization of his plan for another twenty years. Finally, on 13 December, 1545, the Council of Trent was formally opened. It had before it two main tasks. One was to study and legislate for the removal of abuses in the Church; the other was to restate the orthodox view on those points of doctrine which had been attacked by Luther and his associates. The work of the Council was spread over some eight years, though with two interruptions, one from 1549 to 1551, and a much longer one from 1552 to 1563.

It is impossible to discuss in any detail the progress of the Council, but some indication of its main achievements must be given, for its importance in the life of the Catholic Church during the last four centuries is absolutely fundamental. It may be asserted with confidence that the general level of moral and religious observance in all levels of the clergy was raised to a height perhaps unknown since the early centuries of Christianity. The duties of bishops – in particular the obligation of residence in their dioceses and the unlawfulness of holding several benefices – were clearly defined and strictly enforced; steps were taken to ensure that an educated and edifying clergy should be trained in the Church by the establishment of seminaries for their proper formation; abuses in religious orders were dealt with by appropriate measures. In his closing address delivered to the Council on 3 December, 1563, an Italian bishop spoke as follows:

"Henceforth ambition will no longer usurp the place of virtue in the sacred ministry. The word of God will be more frequently delivered and with greater care. Bishops will remain among their flocks. Henceforth those privileges which were a cloak for vice and error and greed are abolished, idle clergy are swept away. Sacred things will cease to be sold for money and we shall no longer be afflicted by the scandalous commerce of professional mendicants. Ministers bred from youth in the service of the Lord will be taught to worship him in greater purity and more worthily. Provincial synods have been re-established and strict rules laid down for the granting of benefices and spiritual charges. Church property may no longer be devised as a family inheritance, excommunications are restricted within narrower bounds, a strong brake has been applied to the cupidity, the licence and the luxury of clergy and the laity alike...."

This might have been little more than the empty rhetoric of insincerity. It has in fact proved to be a true forecast.

On the doctrinal side, the Council dealt with some of the fundamental questions which had been raised by the Reformers. Of these by far the most important was the problem of "Justification" – the relative role of human nature and divine grace in the work of man's salvation and sanctification. Luther had maintained and taught with all the vehemence of his tempestuous spirit that human nature had been so corrupted by the Fall that it was henceforth impossible for man to do anything but evil. Therefore, all that mattered was that, believing firmly in the redemptive merits of Christ, he should surrender to God not only the whole initiative in the work of his salvation, but should confess that it was impossible for any human being to play any active part in that work. Mankind as such was damned; only a favoured few had been chosen by God irrespective of any merits of theirs, to be saved.

Luther claimed that this doctrine was plainly contained in the teaching of Scripture (notably in the Epistle to the Romans), and he went on to accuse the Church of having withheld the Bible from the faithful and of having erected a whole system of ideas and practices at variance with the obvious sense of the inspired Word of God. Other Reformers, applying their own minds to the same source, propounded doctrines which were not only at odds with the Church's traditional teaching but were often rejected by Luther himself. Calvin, for example, whilst working out Luther's ideas on predestination into a coherent logical system, nevertheless rejected his teaching on Justification by Faith alone. In his 1553 Catechism occurs the question: "Can we believe in order to be justified without performing good works?" To which the explicit answer is given: "It is impossible. For the belief in Jesus Christ means receiving him as he offers himself to us. Now he promises us not only to deliver us from death and restore us in the grace of God, the Father, through the merits of his innocence, but also to regenerate us by his Spirit to make us lead holy lives."

In such a welter of theological opinion, the Council assumed the traditional role of formulating explicitly the teaching of orthodoxy. It began by insisting on the fact that the Church had always regarded the Bible, together with the teaching of the Apostles, as the source of all doctrinal and moral truth. It is not without interest that, in laying down the canon of Scripture, the Council includes several books which are treated in official Protestant versions as apocryphal, such as the First and Second Books of Maccabees. Moreover, whilst recognizing as the Church's official text the version that is known as the

Vulgate, the Council nevertheless urged that a carefully revised text should be produced. What the Council did insist on was that private interpretations of Holy Scripture, rejecting the long-standing traditional views supported by the learning and wisdom of generations of scholars, could not be tolerated.

The Council then turned to consider the topics of Original Sin and justification. Whilst maintaining, on the one hand, the truth of the doctrine that Original Sin is universal in its effects, so that Baptism is necessary for all, the Fathers of the Council stated with equal firmness that such Baptism is completely effective in removing all the guilt of such sin. It is, again, relevant to mention that in arguing its case the Council quotes freely from the Bible, not least from Luther's favourite Epistle to the Romans. It should also be added that the Council explicitly excluded the Blessed Virgin from the scope of its decree on the universality of Original Sin.

The next step in the theological discussions of the Fathers of the Council was to consider the meaning of "justification" – the process whereby the sinner is restored to the favour of God, his virtues developed, his salvation achieved. In a lengthy statement, carefully argued with reference to contemporary errors and based solidly on scriptural references, they agreed that natural virtue and the fulfilment of the Law of Moses could not, of themselves, give man supernatural life, which could come through Christ alone. But such life is not the result of any mere confidence in Christ. Faith is complete only when united with hope and charity, nor is justification independent of morality. Text is piled on text to refute a view which Luther claimed to have found in Scripture. One alone might well have sufficed – the passage not from St Paul but from St Luke, where Christ himself says: "if you wish to enter into life, keep the commandments".

What the Council was in fact doing was to defend against a radically pessimistic view of human nature the dignity of the human spirit. True as it is that man needs the grace of God in order to attain sanctity of life and the eternal joys of heaven, this grace is no mere cloak hiding a corrupt nature; it is a force which intrinsically affects that nature, and makes it more capable of free action. Once again the balance of the Church's outlook was manifested, as she steered a middle way between the extremes of an unrealistic optimism, which believes in a natural perfectibility of human nature, and the Lutheran view described above.

In the Church's teaching grace is conferred by means of the sacraments, and it was logical that the Council should next turn to consider in some detail the Catholic doctrine concerning the sacramental system. One of the most important achievements of the Council was undoubtedly its discussion of this topic, and in particular its luminous exposition of Eucharistic theology, an exposition which has been the starting-point for so much fruitful speculation in succeeding centuries. Reference may be made in particular to one of the most important theological treatises produced in modern times, Père de la Taille's magisterial volume *Mysterium Fidei* which may be said to continue and almost to complete the work begun four hundred years ago at Trent.

THE SOCIETY OF JESUS

But it is not by means of legislation or theological formulation alone, or even primarily, that reformation is achieved, and the work of the Council of Trent might well have proved sterile had it not been supported by vigorous action on the part of a number of remarkable men who arose in the Church at this time. It is a commonplace of historians to ascribe the success of the Catholic "Counter-Reformation" to Ignatius Loyola and the Society of Jesus which he founded; and due place must be given to their contribution. But it would be unhistorical and unjust to claim that there were not already energetic champions of reform in the Church before Ignatius appeared on the scene.

However gross or frivolous the lives of too many prelates had become, there had never been completely wanting saintly and conscientious men who saw the needs of the time and laboured to meet them. Already in 1517, the year in which Luther declared open rebellion, a new religious order, the Theatines, was beginning to take shape in Italy. It was the first organized attempt to introduce the spirit of reform into the ranks of the clergy. Significantly, the Theatines sought to counteract the spirit of worldliness so prevalent in the higher clergy by an unusually strict vow of poverty. One of their number was Bishop of Verona, and the example of his life and the vigour of his reforming zeal turned his diocese in the generation before Trent into something approaching the ideal which that Council was later to strive to realize throughout the Church. In the same period a reform within the great Franciscan Order produced the Capuchins, who also sought to practise to the full the ideal of evangelical poverty which had inspired St Francis of Assisi himself. Not least surprising was the foundation of a new order of women, the Ursulines, destined to become world-famous as educators of girls.

At the time, therefore, the establishment in 1540 of the Society of Jesus, consisting of Ignatius Loyola and ten companions, can have caused little stir. This small group had met in the University of Paris, stimulated by the example of the Spanish hidalgo – turned ascetic and apostle – to dedicate themselves to the service of Christ in whatever situation might present itself. They had thought at first of a life of work and prayer in the Holy Land, a new sort of crusade against the infidel. Events were to turn their energies in other directions; but their ideal remained unaltered.

It has been so frequently stated that the spirit of the Church since the Reformation has been largely moulded by the work of the Society of Jesus that some attempt must be made to estimate the extent of this influence. And it is necessary to begin by removing certain misconceptions about the nature of "Jesuitry" and the spirit animating the Society of Jesus.

The ground plan of the ideals of St Ignatius himself is laid down explicitly in his *Spiritual Exercises*, a work which has shaped the minds and aspirations of generations of his sons. It is at once a compendium of Christian doctrine and a manual of Christian asceticism. Starting from the fundamental principle that man's purpose in life is the worship of God through a right use of God's creation, Ignatius emphasizes the disasters which have resulted from a refusal to put into practice this principle. Natural calamities, psychological dislocations, physical sufferings, are to be traced to deliberate refusal to accept the law of God as the law of creation. Sin is the supreme evil; had there been no sin, the world would have been a paradise of delights.

Yet, for all its rebelliousness, man's nature is not hopelessly corrupt, nor has God left man to go from bad to worse. At the centre of the Christian story is the crucial event in human history – the Incarnation of the Son of God. Ignatius makes no original contribution to Christian theology; he is content to accept the traditional teaching on this subject. The Incarnation is the supreme act whereby God intervened in human history to restore man's nature to its original integrity. The whole of human history is to be seen as the struggle between the powers of evil – created spirits, angelic and human, resisting the divine purpose – and the powers of good, with Christ, the great Captain, at their head. The challenge is stated squarely in a famous meditation on the Kingdom of Christ. In a romantic scene we are shown the preparations which Christ is making to launch a crusade against the powers of evil. He is calling for volunteers, appealing to the chivalrous instincts of those who will not be deterred by the hardships which they will have to share with their Leader.

The immediate appeal is to the emotions. But much of what follows in the text of the *Exercises* is a process of will-training, based on a recognition of the splendour of the ideal to be pursued and the matter-of-fact way in which success will come. So the "exercitant" is encouraged to study with prayerful attention the life of Christ himself, the every-day activities of the artisan of Nazareth, the benevolent humanity of the wonder-worker of Galilee, the steadfastness with which he pursued his mission to the people, the integrity with which he faced his inquisitors, the lonely courage of Calvary.

It is unnecessary here to enter into any great detail about the method of the *Exercises*. What has been said should suffice to show the spirit which Ignatius wished to inspire in those who would distinguish themselves in the service of Christ. For that, and that alone, was the purpose which he himself followed single-mindedly to the end. One of the most outstanding expressions of this ideal is to be found in some words written nearly half a century later by Edmund Campion, Oxford scholar, Jesuit priest and finally a martyr to the cause of truth as he saw it. In an open letter to the Privy Council of Queen Elizabeth, he writes:

"... And touching our Societie, be it known to you that we have made a league – all the Jesuits in the world, whose succession and multitude must overreach all the practices of England – cheerfully to carry the cross you shall lay upon us, and never despair your recovery, while we have a man left to enjoy your Tyburn, or to be racked with your torments, or consumed with your prisons. The expense is reckoned, the enterprise is begun; it is of God, it cannot be withstood. ..."

It would be idle to pretend that all Jesuits have been of the temper of Campion, and dishonest to deny that there have been worldly Jesuits, men who relied over-much on political intrigue or other unworthy methods. But their number is infinitesimal compared with the thousands of patient scholars, devoted schoolmasters, missionaries in remote lands, parish priests and curates in towns and cities in more settled countries. Whatever their interests, they have pursued them with a single-mindedness that springs in no small measure from the broad foundation of the *Spiritual Exercises*.

It has been necessary to insert this *apologia* for a much misunderstood body of men because it is impossible to estimate their influence on the development of Catholic thought unless we clear our minds of the fatuous picture of a group of sinister and Machiavellian intriguers. They have, as a body, sought to serve the interests of Christ, sincerely, honourably, disinterestedly. Wherever the need has been greatest there have they been found.

The chief intellectual needs of the Church since the Reformation have been first, to defend and clarify those doctrines which were called in question by the Reformers; secondly, to ensure that the education and formation of Catholic clergy and laity alike should keep pace with the growth of learning in the modern world; and thirdly, to present, to a world grown increasingly impatient of religious belief, a statement of Catholic truth which might win their respect if it did not command their allegiance.

Something has been said already of the work of the Council of Trent in the reformulation or amplification of Catholic doctrine in the light of Protestant attacks. But the definitions of the Council did not end the controversies. On the contrary, the work of the theologians at Trent initiated a period of theological activity which, despite serious setbacks, has gathered strength down the centuries. At first, the chief debates were concerned with the subject of grace and free will, the central issue, as we have seen, raised by Luther and Calvin. For close on two hundred years the topic was thrashed out by theologians of different schools. First of all, Michael du Bay (more commonly known as Baius) taught a doctrine of extreme pessimism. Amongst the many propositions of his condemned as false (1567) are the following: "All the works of unbelievers are sinful, and the virtues of philosophers are in fact vices." "No sin is of its nature venial; every sin merits eternal punishment." "Free will, without the help of divine grace, is capable of nothing but sin."

These errors, revived some fifty years later by Jansenius and preached by his disciples, were to plague the Church for many years to come, and even though the theological errors in their extreme form were abandoned, the rigorist mentality, characterized as Jansenistic, was to affect the spirit of Catholic asceticism and devotion almost to contemporary times. The Jesuits, who from the first set their faces against these ideas, came in for the brunt of the attack from Jansenist writers, the most famous onslaught being contained in Pascal's *Lettres Provinciales*. Singling out for his attention some admittedly extravagant examples of casuistic evasion, Pascal implied that the whole Society was corrupted by a laxity of moral teaching which, had it been a fact, would have discredited all Jesuits in the eyes of right-thinking men. Unfortunately, the brilliance of Pascal's pen, though employed in an unworthy cause, had an effect entirely unjustified by the facts of the situation.

Meanwhile, the topic of grace and free will provided a new theme of debate between Jesuits and Dominicans. In their attempt to explain how man's will could be free, even under the influence of divine grace, some Jesuit writers (notably Molina) were alleged by their Dominican opponents not merely to have abandoned the traditional teaching of the Church as expounded by Aquinas, but to have imperilled the truth of God's omnipotence. The Jesuits, on their side, complained that the Thomist (or Bannesian) view, so called from the Dominican theologian Banes, rendered man's free will meaningless. In 1598 Pope Clement VIII set up a commission *De Auxiliis* to decide the question as between the two groups of disputants, but the commission was suspended in 1607 and both views were permitted to be taught.

Whilst, then, the vexed question of predestination has not received complete clarification, and what may be called the mechanics of grace still remain a mystery, the upshot of all this debate has been to remove some of the misconceptions (to which, it must be admitted, the writings of the great Augustine have made their contribution) about Original Sin and the reality of the part which man plays in the work of his own salvation. However that work is achieved, at least man is no mere sleeping partner. Important as is the "Thomist" emphasis, it remains true that room must be found for a doctrine which insists that the moral struggle is not an illusion.

To this reassertion of a fundamental Christian and indeed human ideal, the contribution of Jesuit thinking was all-important. In this the members of the Society were faithful to the spirit of their founder, with his strong practical sense. Whilst they resisted the antinomianism to which Lutheranism logically tended and the scarcely less dangerous rigorism of the Jansenists, they were not less alive to a threat from another quarter. During the seventeenth century the healthy development of mystical theology, so successfully reinvigorated in the sixteenth by Teresa of Avila and John of the Cross, began to be infected by the creeping paralysis of Quietism. Unlike Jansenism which preached the inability of man to do anything good, the Quietists taught that it was unnecessary for the "perfect" to act at all. All initiative must be surrendered to God. The cultivation of the virtues, the practice of mortification, even, in the last resort, positive resistance to temptation were unnecessary and undesirable. The two major figures in this controversy were Bossuet and Fénelon, both men of great ability. Of the two Fénelon would seem to have been the more attractive character. It may well be that he supported the teachings of Mme Guyon because he saw in them an antidote to the poison of Jansenism. But he went too far. It is to his great credit that when his ideas were officially condemned he withdrew them unreservedly.

It seems not unjust to claim that the support which the Society of Jesus lent to the new devotion to the Sacred

Heart of Jesus which was now coming into prominence through the preaching of St John Eudes (1601–80), who was not a Jesuit, and the Visitation nun, Margaret Mary Alacoque (c. 1680), was inspired by the realization that in this devotion was to be found the reply to both dangers. On the one hand, emphasis on the human affections of God-made-man would serve to offset the terrors of the Jansenist presentation of God's anger, whilst, on the other, the demands made by the devotion on the need for an active participation in the redemptive sufferings of Christ would counteract the enervating tendencies of the Quietist doctrine. The immense success of the devotion at the popular level is the best witness to its basic humanity.

THE CHURCH OUTSIDE EUROPE

Important as was all this work of theological definition and elucidation, it would give a wholly misleading impression of the achievement of Catholicism during this period to leave unmentioned the immense efforts that were made to bring the faith of Christ to the new lands beyond the seas whose discovery and conquest was one of the great events of the sixteenth and seventeenth centuries. In a characteristic decision, Ignatius Loyola, as early as 1542, sent Francis Xavier, one of his most valuable subjects and dearest companions, to work in the Portuguese possessions in the Indies. Over a period of years he worked his way down the coast from Goa to Cape Comorin, on to Malacca and Cochin, and finally established Christian communities in Japan itself. His great desire was to spread the truth as he saw it within the vast Chinese Empire, but he died a lonely death before his wish could be granted. Nor was his work ephemeral in its effects. Not only did he establish the work of the Society in India on lasting foundations, but even in Japan, which was later closed to Christian priests, Christian communities were still in existence when missioners returned in the nineteenth century.

There is little need here to go into any detail about the work of the Church in these lands, though mention should be made of certain outstanding figures such as Robert de Nobili, who sought to win souls to Christ by himself adopting the way of life of a Brāhman; of the mission which penetrated China, and not least the brilliant Ricci, whose mathematical, astronomical and technical skill won for him a hearing at the court of Peking; of the heroic deaths of Europeans and Japanese alike in the savage persecutions which later broke out; of the incidental contributions to learning which the missioners made, such as the Jesuit brother who, single-handed, explored the overland route from India to China. It is pleasant to record that the camellia derives its name from a German lay-brother, Georg Kamel.

On the other side of the world a similar story is to be told. In North America, whilst Spanish Franciscans were making their way up the West coast, a group of intrepid Frenchmen were doing pioneer work amongst the Indians. In the South, the story of the devoted care of St Peter Claver amongst the slaves pouring into the port of Cartagena brightens the dark history of that appalling traffic. The most remarkable achievement of all was perhaps the establishment in Paraguay of the famous Reductions – an experiment in practical Christianity which has no parallel in history. Cunninghame Graham's *A Vanished Arcadia* tells in sympathetic fashion the tale of this attempt to rescue the native Indians from their own primitive habits and from the greater threat of enslavement by European landowners. For a century and a half the work went on, to be brought down in ruins when the Society of Jesus was suppressed in 1773.

In neighbouring Brazil an immense missionary effort went side by side with the Portuguese conquest. The fact that both Spain and Portugal had remained largely unaffected by the Reformation meant that in this, the heyday of their imperial history, the growth of the Church in the lands they acquired more than offset her losses in Europe. Today, in fact, considerably more than half the population of the American continent is Catholic, and though it must be confessed that the Catholic life in some of the Latin American countries leaves much to be desired, in North America the picture is one of healthy and vigorous development.

THE "AGE OF REASON"

With the end of the seventeenth century, the great impulse given to the Church by the Reformation had more or less worked itself out. Theologians and apologists continued to debate the issues raised by Luther and Calvin and the rest, but little constructive work was done. If Catholicism had not succeeded in routing its enemies completely, these latter had at any rate reached the high-water mark of their success. At the end of the Religious Wars, Europe remained divided into two camps, uneasily content to leave matters as they were. But so preoccupied were the Protestants and Catholics with their disagreements, so concerned were Catholic theologians with their domestic disputes that they were ill-prepared to meet a new and even more serious threat to the very foundations of Christian belief. This was the movement of thought, characteristic of the eighteenth century as a whole, which, beginning in England with the free thought of Locke and the scepticism of Hume, swept through France and Germany. It was the Age of Enlightenment. Reason occupied the throne of Religion. Side by side with this attack on the very validity of all religious truth went an attack on the central authority or the Church. The spirit of Gallicanism, already stirring in the seventeenth century, had gathered strength and threatened to disrupt the structure of ecclesiastical government.

The attack was as much political as ecclesiastical. Not only did the French bishops, as a body, seek to assert their independence of the Papacy, but they were supported in this by the government, which sought to bring the Church of France completely under its control. Nor was the movement confined to France. In Germany and Austria the same centrifugal tendencies were at work. It is against this background that we must see the mounting attacks on the Society of Jesus, culminating, in 1773, in its suppression, forced on a reluctant Pope under threat of worse evils. The century ended with the Revolution which swept away so many familiar landmarks in France, and initiated a series of political and social upheavals of which we have not yet seen the end.

In such a situation the intellectual life of the Church seemed to reach its lowest ebb. The Society which had been the chief educational force within the Church for two hundred years was practically destroyed, and with it much of the theological, philosophical and pedagogical achievement which had been its greatest contribution to the cause of Catholic truth. In France itself, other religious orders were swept away and throughout Europe the revolutionary wars brought in their train a dislocation of the settled ways of life which are essential if learning is to flourish. Yet, despite these appalling disasters, not only did the Church survive, but she entered upon one of the most fruitful phases of theological and philosophical development. Fortunately, weakened and impoverished as it was, the system of clerical training established by the Council of Trent survived. However inadequate the quality of the teaching, however remote from the burning issues of the time much of that teaching may have been, priests continued to be trained and ordained, and gradually an improvement set in.

The recovery began in France itself. In the first quarter of the nineteenth century a handful of remarkable men produced works which have had a significant effect on Catholic thought. Voltaire and the Encyclopedists, with their triumphant mockery, had almost laughed religion out of court in the eyes of intellectual Europe. It was the layman, Chateaubriand, who produced one of the most effective retorts. His *Génie du Christianisme* (1802), instead of arguing in the traditional way that Christianity must be true because it is revealed by God, presented the sceptic with a picture of Christianity in all its majesty and beauty, its humane and civilizing power, the inspiration it has afforded to the greatest poets and artists, the reality of its appeal to the deepest human aspirations. The book is not a masterpiece of theological statement, nor a closely argued philosophical treatise; but in its generation it proved to be a most effective defence of Christian truth.

But the corrosive influence of eighteenth-century rationalism continued to be felt at a more strictly philosophical level for many years. Even more pernicious than the out-and-out Rationalism which overreached itself by the very extravagance of its scepticism was the attempt of Immanuel Kant (1724–1804) to safeguard ultimate truth by removing it from the sphere of pure reason. Where Aquinas had sought to base his whole theological system on the findings of reason, in such a way that both religious faith and moral practice should be seen as entirely in accordance with the conclusions of metaphysical speculation, Kant, having denied to the ordinary processes of thought any access to an ultimate truth lying beyond the sphere of the phenomenally perceptible, was reduced to making the notion of God's existence a postulate of the practical reason. In the climate of the time this was suspiciously similar to Voltaire's aphorism that, if God did not exist, it would have been necessary to invent him. Nor does all Kant's awe in face of the moral imperative do anything to commend it to the average man. In the end the Kantian critique, dissolving away the rational basis of faith and moral obligation, was an even more powerful solvent of faith and morals than the most radical attacks of the out-and-out sceptic.

In the void thus created attempts were made to discover a fresh justification for believing in divine truth. Another layman, the Vicomte de Bonald (1754–1840), tracing not merely the irreligion of his day but also the political radicalism, which produced and was developed by the French Revolution, to the doctrine of private judgment taught by Luther, sought to re-establish religious orthodoxy and political stability by an appeal to tradition. According to him the only valid explanation of religious faith and political authority is to be found, not in the reasoning of the individual but in a general reason, analogous presumably to Rousseau's general will. This general reason is the custodian of a primitive revelation. This primitive revelation, on which depends the well-being of society at large, is preserved and handed on by society, generation after generation. The fundamental truths, which man could not discover for himself, he could not re-discover if they were to be lost. Moreover, it is clear that society could not survive without a knowledge of the principles essential to its preservation.

Tradition, then, preserves and promulgates the fundamental truths of the primitive revelation. Furthermore, society, which is the matrix within which this body of truths is safeguarded, is the sovereign and infallible authority, since there can be no superior power to judge or correct it. Nor can any individual presume to criticize it. Society is greater and wiser than any single individual. To go against it is to go against nature.

The Abbé de Lamennais (1782–1854) accepted the same basic theory, though supporting it with different arguments. Man cannot of himself prove fully any single truth; he will always be haunted by the fear that he may be mistaken. Equally he cannot live without assenting to certain truths. Hence "he must either live by faith or perish in the void". Now this faith, not depending on reason, is a kind of instinct, springing in the end from the general feeling of mankind. For the basic truth on which all certainty depends is the existence of God, a truth which cannot be rationally demonstrated but must be accepted on the universal testimony of men. Such an idea led straight to Fideism, the doctrine that faith is independent of reason and can neither be defended nor defeated by it. Others such as Bonnetty (1798–1879) and Rosmini (1797–1855) sought to find the idea of God in some direct intuition.

In Germany, where the impact of the Kantian critique was more immediate, the first important attempt to defend Catholic truth against it was made by a priest, Georg Hermes. Having for a time suffered acutely from an inability to justify his faith in the face of Kant's denial of any possibility of proving transcendental truth, he eventually satisfied himself and many of his co-religionists that he had found the answer. Starting, like Descartes, from a position of universal doubt, he concluded that certain truths were necessary and indubitable. It is impossible to reproduce here the steps of his argument. It is sufficient to say that his conclusions were incompatible with orthodox Catholic teaching since he did, in effect, maintain that revealed truth could be established by a process of pure reason. Even before his death, which occurred in 1831, his teaching had been attacked as erroneous and despite the immense reputation which he enjoyed his writings were eventually condemned in 1835.

THE VATICAN COUNCIL

It has been necessary to dwell at some length on these various attempts to repair the harm done by eighteenth-century rationalism and by the philosophy of Kant as they form part of the general situation which the Vatican Council was convoked to deal with. The two main topics discussed by the Council (1869–70) were first the nature and the content of faith in Catholic teaching and secondly the nature and powers of the Church.

In the first place, the Council asserted, as against materialism, pantheism and deism, the existence of a Supreme Being, distinct from the universe of matter and from all finite spirits, creating that universe by a free act. In a famous sentence, which has been much scrutinized by contemporary philosophers, the Council also asserted that the existence of God can be known with certainty by the natural powers of human reason, through his creation. The Council re-affirmed the inspired nature of the canonical books of Scripture, as laid down by the Council of Trent. Steering a middle course between the semi-rationalism of Hermes on the one hand and the position of traditionalists and fideists on the other, it stated categorically that reason is not the sole guide in matters of faith, in which the authority of God, the revealer, must be accepted as the final guarantor of their truth. Nevertheless, reason has an important part to play in the development of faith, since it is reason which justifies us in accepting divine revelation as credible. Yet reason is not fully autonomous. It cannot claim to sit in judgment on the truths of faith.

This latter assertion calls for some elucidation. Clearly, the process whereby certain dogmatic conclusions are arrived at is largely a rational process. The methods of scholastic argument, the investigations of exegetes and historians into the meaning of Scripture and the teaching of the Fathers, constitute a rational activity. But once reason has brought a man to the point of seeing that a certain truth has been revealed by God, it becomes his duty to accept that truth as God's truth. Reason can continue to work at further elucidation; but it would clearly be illogical for a finite mind to claim that its discoveries can overthrow that truth. Nor does this mean that the believer is in danger of insincerity or "double-thinking". Knowing as he does that revealed truth and empirical truth cannot be at variance, he realizes that, where some apparent discrepancy emerges, this is simply because he has failed to grasp the full meaning either of the truth he has discovered for himself or the truth which has been revealed to him.

As we turn to consider the pronouncements of the Council on the nature of the Church we may recall the historical situation in which the discussions were taking place. Apart from the survival of Gallican ideas, after their explicit condemnation by Pius VI in 1794, the very independence of the Papacy was actively threatened by the events of the *Risorgimento*. Yet it would be a mistake to conclude from this that the definition of Papal Infallibility was a kind of retort to the Liberal politicians of the time. As we shall see, and as is invariably true of dogmatic definitions, the subject had long been debated amongst theologians and was almost universally accepted in practice by clergy and laity alike.

In the first place, the infallibility which, according to the teaching of the Catholic Church, is the personal prerogative of the Pope from an *ex cathedra* point of view, is to be seen as a function of the guarantee originally given to his Church by Christ. As Christianity developed and spread throughout the world, as different minds and different temperaments applied themselves to the task of interpreting afresh the teachings of Christ, it was inevitable that there should arise sectional disagreements, as St Paul himself had foreseen (1 *Corinthians* xi, 19). If the essentials of Christ's teaching were not to be altered out of all recognition, there must be some central control, some permanent guiding authority, preserving that truth to all generations.

The Protestant view is that this is performed by the Holy Spirit operating in all the members of Christ's Church. The Catholic view, whilst believing in the absolute necessity of this continual operation, insists also that such inspiration must be effected in a clear and recognizable way, through a definite, authoritative *teaching*. The Church claims that this consciousness of authority to teach, under the guidance of the Holy Spirit, was present in her from the beginning. The most striking expression of this early conviction is to be found in the pronouncement of the Apostles at the Council of Jerusalem, less than twenty years after the death of Christ: "It is the Holy Spirit's pleasure and ours" (*Acts* xv, 28).

From the beginning, too, when there was any uncertainty about the authentic doctrine of Christ, it was to the Apostolic tradition, and specifically to the teaching of Peter and Paul, that local Churches turned for enlightenment. Jerusalem passed away; Rome became the great centre of Christian teaching and Christian jurisdiction. Even when, as usually happened, for historical reasons, the great Councils were held in the East, the approval of the Western Church, and particularly of the See of Rome, was recognized as necessary for validity.

For a fuller study of the development of the doctrine of infallibility in general and Papal Infallibility in particular, it would be necessary to consult the writings of the great theologians. In the post-Reformation period, the first important name is that of the Dominican, Melchior Cano (1509–60), to be followed by that of the Jesuit Bellarmine

(1542–1621). However much Jesuits and Dominicans might be at variance on the subject of Grace, they were at one in their view of the nature of the Church.

The growth of Gallican tendencies in certain European countries did little to affect the Church's teaching on Infallibility. The decline of theological activity in the eighteenth century did not mean that, in the nineteenth, this particular topic had to be rethought. Theologians simply took up the position which had been established in previous centuries, and, on the eve of the Vatican Council, whilst there was much debate as to the opportuneness of a formal definition, there was substantial agreement on the nature and extent of the Papal prerogative. In effect, the definition amounts to little more than the assertion that, when speaking as the Church's official mouthpiece, the Pope enjoys all the freedom from error which Christ promised to his Church.

THE BLESSED VIRGIN

The most interesting single historical event which preceded and perhaps led up to the formal definition of Papal Infallibility was the Pope's personal act when, on 8 December, 1854, he declared the doctrine of the Immaculate Conception of the Blessed Virgin Mary to be an article of faith. Before we go on to consider this and other modern developments in Mariology, it may be useful to examine this particular pronouncement as an example of Papal Infallibility in action. We have already seen (p. 155) that, in treating of justification, the Council of Trent explicitly excluded the Virgin Mary from the scope of its decree on the universality of Original Sin. The question of Mary's freedom from all sin, even from the first instant of her conception, had been a subject of theological debate in the Middle Ages, and the ultimate definition of the dogma is to be seen as the culmination of this whole movement of clarification, ending in general agreement. The Pope in 1854 was not inventing a new doctrine. He was merely declaring that this was, in fact, what the Catholic Church believed.

It is not unnatural to ask, at this stage, why a formal definition should be necessary or even desirable. To understand the answer to this question is to understand the Catholic's attitude to his faith. The Catholic, then, believes what he does believe on the authority of God. He believes, that is to say, that just as he acquires most of his information at the natural level, not by thinking things out for himself, but by listening to those who are in a position to know, so, at the level of religious truth, he realizes that he must be prepared to accept information from the best accredited source. The evidence of history satisfies him that God has spoken through Christ, and that Christ founded a Church to preserve and teach his message. This Church he believes to be the historical Catholic Church and no other. So he is prepared to listen to the Church's experts, as he is prepared to listen to experts in other fields. He listens to his religious experts with the greater confidence, because he believes not only that they have received from Christ a commission to teach, but that Christ is present to prevent them from teaching error.

Not, of course, that the Catholic sees his religion as exclusively or even primarily an intellectual affair. But, as an intelligent being, he is aware that his service of God must be an intelligent affair. He serves God in this world not least by using his brains about it. Yet he realizes that what is chiefly important about this present life is that it has eternal implications. He believes that in his Church he is given authentic information about those implications. The doctrine of the Incarnation has a significance going far beyond the technically theological. The idea that Jesus Christ, whose human history can be written as can that of Socrates or Gandhi, was in the completest sense also divine is the final assurance to him that human history possesses a meaning that transcends time and space.

He believes, that is, that the life of Christ is at once a pattern of ideal human behaviour and also an experience enriching all human behaviour, because linking it somehow to the life of God. Therefore he finds in the circumstances of Christ's earthly life not merely an inspiration; he finds there an analogue of eternal life. To take an example from Christ's teaching about the Eucharist. Since Christ described himself as the bread of life, the Catholic realizes that earthly food and drink are a kind of symbol of the life-giving power of God-in-Christ. He realizes, in fact, that, if he is to make sense of this life, he can do so only by seeing it in relation to the next. Nor does this mean that he feels, with Plato, that this life is a kind of mirage, or with the Buddhist that he must aim at a *nirvāṇa* of complete disinvolvement. Whilst it is true that we in this life see "a confused reflection in a mirror" (I *Corinthians* xiii, 12), it remains a reflection of eternal truth. It is the medium in and through which that truth is revealed to him.

That is why he is glad to feel the support of a coherent framework of "defined" truth. Just as the scientist or mathematician is helped, not impeded, in his investigations by a solidly established body of principles and formulae which provides the basis for his further investigations, so the intelligent Catholic regards the body of dogmatic pronouncements as a kind of skeleton giving shape and intelligibility to life.

All this is highly relevant to any attempt to appreciate the place of Mariology in the Catholic view of life. It is sometimes said, even by some who would claim to accept Catholic traditional teaching in its entirety, that recent pronouncements about the Virgin Mary have destroyed the balance of this skeletonic framework by an emphasis on purely secondary doctrines, which have been made to assume a significance out of all proportion to their true importance. The fact is that these doctrines are of importance precisely because they illustrate and illuminate the primary truths. They present Our Lady as the supreme achievement of God, after and through the Incarnation, in the order of nature and grace. It is as though the Church, having completed the working out of a theology of the Incarnation and Redemption, now wishes to show what, in the ideal case, Redemption means. It means that the creature who is completely redeemed by the grace of Christ is thereby caught up into the divine order so absolutely that, even in this world of space and time, intimations of eternal life can be glimpsed.

Thus, in believing the doctrine of the Immaculate Conception, the Catholic holds that at no stage of her earthly existence was the Virgin Mary ever anything but completely subordinated to the purposes of God. At no stage was she ever under the influence of any power that might alienate her in any degree from that manifestation of perfect goodness and truth which is man's assimilation to God. Similarly in accepting the Church's teaching about the Assumption the Catholic holds that even the physical body of Mary, the body which played such an important part in the economy of the Incarnation, was preserved from the corruption which is the normal lot of man's mortality. By a sort of anticipation of Christ's work of restoration, which enables Christians to believe in the resurrection of the body, Mary's body and soul were not divided even in a temporary separation.

The position of Mary in Catholic theology is not to be thought of in isolation. It cannot indeed be understood except with reference to the work of her Son. The suggestion that Catholic theology has somehow belittled Christ by emphasizing the dignity of Mary is similar to the accusation that the Catholic doctrine of the Mass derogates from the significance of Calvary. The Mass is of supreme importance because and only because it links us directly with Calvary; Mary's dignity is due solely to her role in the great work of man's Redemption.

This seems to be the place to add a few words about the Church's teaching concerning the title Co-redemptrix, which, though not officially defined, is spoken of by some theologians as "definable". It is by no means certain that the doctrine will be defined in the near future, if at all, but it needs to be made clear that the doctrine and the title do not mean that she and her Son are to be seen as equals in the work of Redemption. The constant teaching of the Church has been that the Redemption is essentially the unique achievement of Jesus Christ. At the same time, the continuation in history of the redemptive activity of Christ, the redemption of individual Christians, calls for the co-operation of the members of the Church he founded. The whole meaning and purpose of the sacramental system, the fundamental purpose of the priesthood, cannot be appreciated except in terms of that continuing activity. Now, in the divine plan, the whole work of the redemption depended in a special way on Mary's co-operation. The title Co-redemptrix is to be seen in the light of that unique contribution. If the doctrine is ever defined it will inevitably be defined in accordance with the Church's traditional teaching about the Redemption itself, though the terms of the definition may well cast further light on this basic truth.

We have here in fact a good example of the sort of thing that is meant when theologians talk about the development of doctrine. This idea, which finds its fullest and most explicit formulation in Newman's celebrated *Essay on the Development of Christian Doctrine* (1844–5), has become increasingly prominent in Catholic thinking during the last century. It is not a little strange that it was not until the middle of the nineteenth century that this idea received full expression, and that by one who, when he wrote his *Essay*, had not yet made his final submission to the Roman Catholic Church. It is, of course, implicit in the Church's appeal to tradition as one of the sources of the doctrines she professes; nor should it come as any surprise to anyone with more than a superficial acquaintance with the very earliest centuries of Christian history. For between the writing of the New Testament in the first century and the Council of Nicaea in 325 the seminal ideas of the first Christian writers had borne a richer fruit than some of those writers themselves probably foresaw. The Church insists, therefore, that what may seem to those unfamiliar with her theological experience "new" doctrines, are no more than corollaries of doctrines long formulated. There is a real parallel between the individual's growth in appreciation of the faith he has held since he was first baptized into the Church and the Church's own growing awareness of the full riches of the original deposit. In both cases we see exemplified the truth of Christ's promise to his Apostles: "I have still much to say to you, but it is beyond your reach as yet. It will be for him, the truth-giving Spirit, when he comes, to guide you into all truth. . . . He will make plain to you what is still to come" (*John* xvi, 12–13).

POSITIVE THEOLOGY: THE SCRIPTURES

This account of theological development in the Catholic Church since the Reformation would not be complete without some reference to the growth in recent centuries of what is known as positive theology, as distinguished from speculative theology. During the Middle Ages theological progress had been mostly achieved by an examination and elucidation of dogmatic truths largely in the light of certain metaphysical ideas which had been pressed into service to justify and explain the content of the faith. The great achievement of Aquinas and the Schoolmen generally had been the construction of an all-embracing synthesis in which, starting from certain basic axioms arrived at by reason, a coherent logical system was presented, embracing every aspect of human life, scientific, ethical and religious. At its best, such activity was of great value; but with the general decline of intellectual vigour in the later Middle Ages a certain ossification had set in. Catholic theology became a kind of self-perpetuating, self-justifying entity, independent of historical criticism and in danger of losing contact with historical reality. One of the great benefits conferred on the Church by the attacks of the Reformers was that they emphasized the need for re-examining the historical, traditional basis of the faith.

The historical and patristic studies of the sixteenth and seventeenth centuries may seem to modern eyes almost crude. Yet it is not too much to claim that they laid the foundations on which later generations have built. The revival of classical studies which the Renaissance had stimulated led logically to a similar revival in scriptural and patristic learning. Amongst the foremost names in this field must be mentioned that of the Jesuit Petau (better known under the Latin form Petavius) who lived from 1583 to 1652. The breadth of his scholarship and the vigour of his mind entitle him to rank with the best exponents of the positive method in theology. It was an age when, it is not too much to say, the Fathers were being scientifically studied for the first time. Texts were critically edited, commentaries produced, lexicons compiled, and, in general, a careful and systematic use of historical method and of sciences such as archaeology and other disciplines ancillary to history was being developed. The result was a re-invigoration of theology in the Church, and incidentally an equipping of Catholic controversialists to enable them to refute the arguments of heretics, drawn from an inadequate presentation of scriptural or patristic authorities. The Church claimed, and justified her claims in action, that the great medieval synthesizers had, for all the imperfections of their methods, built on a sound tradition, which went back to the teaching of the Fathers and, through them, to the Scriptures themselves.

Of the Catholic attitude to the Scriptures it will be necessary to write at some length, if only because this again has been the subject of some misunderstanding. This misunderstanding is due to two historical situations. In the first place, in the period preceding the Reformation, when men such as Wyclif were making use of Scripture texts in a tendentious manner, it was necessary for the Church to forbid the use of versions of the Bible which were not authorized by her. It is not true, as is sometimes alleged, that she always opposed the use of vernacular renderings of the sacred books. It should be borne in mind that until the Renaissance period most people who could read at all were sufficiently familiar with Latin to make translations into the vernacular largely unnecessary. When the need became felt, she was not slow to meet it. Thus the standard Catholic translation of the Bible into English, the Douai version, appeared before the Protestant Authorized Version, which indeed shows evidence of having made use of the Catholic rendering. Medieval churches with their stained-glass windows and mural paintings, the old mystery plays and similar compositions, show that the essentials of the Bible story were kept before the minds of the faithful. The Church can scarcely be blamed for having refused to allow uncontrolled discussion of the more difficult theological passages, whose understanding required specialized training.

In more modern times the chief criticism brought against the Church in this regard is that her scholarship is reactionary and unprogressive. Such truth as there is in this assertion must be seen against the contemporary background. At a time when much Protestant activity was devoted to a radical type of criticism which almost succeeded in destroying men's appreciation of the special character of the sacred books (pp. 124, 127), the Church maintained and continues to maintain that there are truths contained in the Bible which are of more fundamental importance than niceties of textual criticism or speculative historical reconstructions. The more extreme form of the Higher Criticism did little to deepen our appreciation of what the Bible stands for. At its worst it merely played into the hands of the sceptical and the irreligious. Whilst Strauss and Bauer and the Tübingen school generally were casting doubt on the historical value of the New Testament documents, Catholic scholars believed that it was their first duty to defend the scriptural basis of Christian truth, even if this meant that their scholarship must seem somewhat old-fashioned. They have been proved right. It is the Higher Criticism which now seems

old-fashioned, and once again a conservative approach to the Bible is coming back into favour. It is a sardonic commentary on the mutability of human opinion that the Church, which in the sixteenth century was accused of not making enough of the Bible, should, in the nineteenth, be laughed at for taking it too seriously.

In fact, to those who are familiar with it, the history of Catholic Biblical scholarship is a story of genuine if gradual progress. The great commentaries of men like Maldonatus, Knabenhauer, and Cornelius à Lapide still contain much that is of value, whilst in the present century, the work of a Lagrange will bear comparison with the best Protestant scholarship. Nor is it without significance that, in the last ten years, some of the most essential, if not necessarily the most spectacular, work on the Qumrān Scrolls has been carried out by Catholic scholars, notably Père de Vaux and his fellow-Dominicans of the Ecole Biblique in Jerusalem. It is easy to represent the work of the Biblical Commission in Rome as a mere brake on progress. In effect it has been and is no more than a salutary reminder that speculation should not be allowed to outstrip solid proof and that the best criticism is not always that which is prepared to relinquish traditional views without understanding them.

In attempting to appreciate the attitude of Catholic authorities to questions of scientific discovery in any field, it should be borne in mind that they regard it as their first duty to protect the spiritual interests of a flock which is overwhelmingly non-intellectual. The ill-considered presentation of new truths may disturb the minds of those who are unable to assimilate them to long-cherished beliefs. There are often many old truths to be defended, and this can sometimes be done effectively only by being slow to give public hearing to the latest claim. It is this principle which explains the Church's caution in the face of the more extreme positions taken up by Scripture scholars. It explains her condemnation of the Modernists in the Church in the first decade of the present century. It is not possible here to enter into a detailed study of this complex question, and those who wish for further information must be referred to the works mentioned in the bibliography. But the sad story of that episode makes it all too clear that the chief "victims" of the Church ban were men whose intellectual zeal had outrun their pastoral duty. Had they but remembered the restraint of their Master who said: "I have still much to say to you, but it is beyond your reach as yet" (John xvi, 12), had they but remembered that the divine mysteries are not to be solved by human reasoning alone, but can be appreciated only by a slow process of reasoning illuminated by faith, they would have benefited themselves and the Church much more than they did by their impetuous criticism.

So far we have concerned ourselves with specifically theological doctrines or disciplines. But there are two major fields of human interest which are very much the Church's concern, in so far as they affect man's well-being in this world and have, directly or indirectly, important theological implications. These are the recent advances in scientific discovery and the political and sociological development of modern times.

THE CHURCH AND SCIENCE

Turning to the sphere of the physical sciences, we may begin our discussion with some brief comments on the story of Galileo. (For a fuller treatment reference should be made to the *Life of Robert Bellarmine* by James Brodrick, S.J., 1928.) That the story of Galileo is not simply a story of scientific enlightenment struggling with ecclesiastical obscurantism should be clear from the fact that the heliocentric theory, which had been propounded by Copernicus, a Catholic cleric, in 1540, was at first freely accepted by the Church. As a purely scientific doctrine it did not particularly concern her, and had it not been for the aggressiveness of the Italian scientist there need have been no conflict on this point between the Church and the astronomers. It is not irrelevant to mention that the Copernican theory was much more bitterly denounced by Protestant divines than it ever was by Catholic authorities. When Galileo began to "interfere", as the latter thought, in the realm of theology, they felt they had to take action. Their action was not as wise as it should have been, and Galileo was handled with something less than tact (though scarcely with the brutality which is sometimes alleged). In the climate of the time, when the Church was beginning to recover from the worst assaults of the Reformers, it was perhaps inevitable that heresy should be suspected where there was no more than a combination of arrogance and a desire to make theological capital out of a scientific discovery. There were undoubtedly faults on both sides. But it is quite unhistorical to base on this incident a wholesale condemnation of the Church as always and necessarily opposed to scientific progress. She was actuated as usual primarily by a desire to safeguard revealed truth.

Whenever there has arisen a tension between "the Church" and "Science", it will generally be true to say that the hostility has been between certain scientists and certain individual Catholic authorities. It is probably fair to claim, too, that the hostility has generally originated from the side of science. It is regrettably true that the whole eighteenth-century movement which called itself the Enlightenment was, for reasons not always purely rational and scientific, bitterly opposed to religion in general and the Catholic religion in particular. True as it is that the remarkable advances which the physical sciences have made in modern times have coincided with a decline in religious belief, it is both illogical and unhistorical to argue that therefore these advances could not have come about without that decline. If the Schoolmen made no important scientific discoveries, they did at least preserve for posterity what was of value in the scientific tradition of the ancients. Their own genius was directed to other fields. The Church's chief duty in the realm of culture was to tame and civilize Goth and Vandal, Saxon and Dane. Had there been no medieval Church there might well have been no Renaissance, and the history of modern Europe would have been a very different affair. It is as idle to accuse the Church because there were no great scientists in the thirteenth century as it would be to express surprise that the great flowering of Greek culture which took place in the fifth century B.C. did not occur two or three centuries before. The laws governing the movement of man's thought are more mysterious than those which control the annual cycle of seed-time and harvest.

What is certain is that the Church has never been hostile to scientific advance. Apart from the positive contributions made by Catholic men and women, both clerical and lay, especially in the field of astronomy and biology, the study of the various scientific disciplines forms a regular part of the educational programme which she lays down for her ecclesiastical students as well as in those centres of higher learning which she establishes or controls in so many countries.

For the Church knows that all genuine progress in empirical knowledge is a stage in that discovery of the full truth which is the revelation of God. As was said above, some tension arises from time to time when the enthusiasts for some scientific discovery present it in a way which suggests that it is opposed to religious truth or when theologians are nervous about its possible repercussions in their domain. One of the difficulties inherent in the religious situation is that the transcendental truth which the theologian claims to possess is necessarily stated in terms of a philosophical or scientific system which must be more or less inadequate to express it. As philosophical theories develop or scientific concepts change, there will inevitably be a certain time-lag before the theologian can readjust himself to the new situation.

The classical example of such a tension is to be found in the Biblical account of Creation. Until recent times the traditional interpretation of the early chapters of *Genesis* was the *prima facie* obvious one. God created heaven and earth in a week, in the order given in those chapters. A Protestant archbishop was bold enough to date this event as occurring in the year 4004 B.C. The impact on this attitude of mind which was made by the advances in biological and geological science in the last century is too well-known to need describing. For a time many Christians felt that the "evidence of the rocks" must be unreliable because it was obviously in conflict with the plain truth of Scripture, whilst the theory of evolution seemed not merely to contradict the story of the creation of Adam and Eve but even to threaten the reality of the divine agency altogether. This not unnaturally satisfied the already sceptical scientist that he had succeeded in disproving the truth of Christianity. He was certain – perhaps over-certain – of the validity of his inferences; if they were incompatible with revealed truth, so much the worse for the latter.

Both parties to the dispute seem to have forgotten (and there was less excuse for such forgetfulness on the part of the theologians) that St Augustine had already met this problem and laid down the lines of a solution over fourteen hundred years earlier. In his *De Genesi ad Litteram* and other writings he had recognized the fact that even in his day certain scientific theories were incompatible with a literal interpretation of the scriptural account of the origins of the world. He laid down the important principle that where some established fact, whether of science or history, is at variance with what would seem to be the natural interpretation of some Biblical passage, then it will be necessary to reject the natural interpretation.

Today this sort of problem no longer troubles the theologian. He recognizes the fact that just as the author of the Biblical account was expressing a fundamental truth in a way which would impress it on the minds of the primitive folk to which that account was addressed, so is he prepared to see in the scientist a collaborator and not an enemy. The picture of the origins of the universe which the astronomer, the geologist, the physicist and the biologist have produced is on a scale so much more impressive than is the simple anthropomorphic scenario sketched out in an era of crude thinking that it seems to him much more expressive of the majesty of the Creator. Far from diminishing the value of religion it actually increases the sense of awe and mystery which is at the heart of all worship. Just as, in the famous dictum of the Schoolmen, philosophy is the handmaid of theology, so can even the most dramatic discovery of the scientist make its contribution to a deeper understanding of divine truth.

SOCIAL TEACHING

The other major development which has affected human life is the change in political and social outlook which has occurred since the later Middle Ages. At the time of the Reformation feudal ideas were still prevalent and the notion of a social hierarchy with a more or less absolute monarch at its head was all but universally accepted. For all his insistence on the rights of private judgment in religious matters, Luther's attitude to the peasants in their revolt against the princes shows that, in politics at least, he was markedly authoritarian. Now, in strict theory, the Church's concern with politics, like her concern with science, is merely indirect. That is to say, she has no "theology" of politics, and in practice, is prepared to accept any type of government, provided only that certain fundamental human rights, necessary for man's development as a free and responsible agent, are secured. At the same time, she cannot but be involved in political questions, and that for two main reasons.

In the first place, even her spiritual mission is exercised in a particular concrete situation, her members are the subjects of a hundred different national states, tribal organizations, ethnic groupings, political confederations. The political allegiance of a Catholic is not in itself any concern of his Church. But his moral welfare is. Political activities of one sort or another not infrequently involve moral issues on which the Church may have a duty to pronounce. Such pronouncements, some of which we shall study in a little more detail, are not to be seen as an attempt to interfere with political regimes as such. They are concerned with morals. But morals and politics cannot be separated. To that extent the Church must concern herself with politics.

Moreover, for all her basic spiritual nature, the Church is necessarily an organization. She will be found in a more or less well developed form in all the countries of the world. Hence arise those sporadic instances of tension between "Church and State". Fortunately, with the decline in the temporal power of the Papacy, purely political considerations no longer exacerbate a difficult situation, but nevertheless the Church needs to insist on the necessary freedom of action in, for example, the appointment of bishops, the nature of the education given to her children, to say nothing of the corporate worship which is essential for the survival of the religious life of her members. On the whole, in the modern world, relations between the Church and the democracies have been reasonably good, making all allowances for the bigotry and suspicion which still prevail in many countries which have been affected by the propaganda of the

Reformation. In the totalitarian regimes the Church has always been an object of some form of persecution, at times going beyond the worst savageries of the Roman Empire.

Nor is this surprising. Not because the Church is, as is sometimes suggested, just another totalitarian regime. This is simply not true. The Church does not claim to control man's whole life. All she does say is that man, in all his activities, has an allegiance to God which transcends all earthly loyalties. But in asserting this truth she is, in fact, asserting a great principle of human freedom. It is just because the totalitarian regimes, in their most thoroughgoing forms as found in Nazism and Communism, have thought to enslave man by preaching a doctrine that he has no loyalty higher than that of loyalty to the State or the Party that a headlong collision was inevitable. In Nazi Germany attempts to subordinate the Church to the ideology of the Party broke down in face of the profoundly religious temper of the people as a whole. But the number of priests and prominent Catholics who, along with other Christians, suffered and often died in concentration camps, are some measure of the ruthlessness of those attempts.

In countries which have been conquered by Communism persecution has been just as persistent, though generally carried out with more cunning. It is no coincidence that in Yugoslavia, Hungary, Poland and Czechoslovakia the most important members of the Catholic hierarchy have suffered longer or shorter terms of imprisonment, whilst the number of priests and nuns who have died in labour camps or been executed by the authorities throughout the Communist-controlled world, though not known with certainty, is known to be formidable. These Christians have not suffered and died on behalf of any political ideal. They have borne witness to their faith in man's right to freedom of thought as expressed in freedom of worship.

It is a remarkable tribute to the essential wisdom of the Catholic system of theology that at a time when, in the name of Liberalism, the new doctrines of Socialism and Communism were being preached for the first time in Europe, the Church found it necessary, on theological grounds, to condemn these doctrines. It should be pointed out that "Socialism" here does not mean any political system which merely aims at a more equitable distribution of wealth; such a doctrine clearly must command the sympathy of any genuine Christian. What the Church condemned and still condemns is the idea that private property itself is against the common good, and that society must be so radically re-shaped that all wealth will remain in the hands of the state, the citizens being no more than pensioners of the government. Such an idea, the Church declares, is contrary to the nature of things, contrary to human dignity and to that measure of independence which is required if a man is to live a human life. Wealth in the hands of private individuals is undoubtedly a grave responsibility and, as Christ himself has warned us, a great moral danger. Nor does the Church seek to deny that the state has the right and the duty to control the distribution of wealth in the interests of the general good. What she will not permit is the doctrine that the general good is best served by depriving men of the right to own at least that minimum of property which, in normal circumstances, is necessary for their true development as responsible members of society.

The doctrine which the Church condemned on theological grounds in 1849, is now condemned by the "free world" in general on political and practical grounds. The combination of a misconceived economic system with a mistaken philosophy of dialectical materialism has brought into the world the most inhumane political system which it has known since the Church civilized the barbarian. Once again, it has to be admitted that, when Marx and Engels wrote *The Communist Manifesto*, there were present in the structure of Western society grave abuses which cried aloud for remedy. It may be true that the conscience of Europe needed to be goaded into action by the threat of violent revolutionary explosion. At the same time, it is unreasonable to suppose that the Church was in any position to deal with those abuses herself. Apart from the severe blows inflicted on her authority by the Reformation, the eighteenth-century *philosophes* and the preachers of the doctrine of progress, the growing secularization of public life and the determination of the politicians to keep the Church out of their affairs, all meant that the Church's role was reduced to one of warning, exhortation or advice. These were given frequently in Papal pronouncements and the pastoral utterances of the clergy, face to face with the social evils of the time. That they went largely unheeded is unfortunately true; but their value and their timeliness cannot be doubted.

One of the most important documents to state in clear and unmistakable language the Church's teaching on social justice is Pope Leo XIII's encyclical *Rerum Novarum*, published in 1891. Its analysis of the dangers of the time and its boldness in prescribing remedies make it worthy of more than a passing reference here. After indicating briefly the causes of the social problem as it existed at the end of the nineteenth century, the Pope goes on to condemn the remedy proposed by the Socialists who "working on the poor man's envy of the rich, are striving to do away with private property and contend that individual possessions should become the common property of all, to be administered by the State or by municipal bodies. They hold that by thus transferring property from private individuals to the community the present mischievous state of affairs will be set right, inasmuch as each citizen will then get his fair share of whatever there is to enjoy." Not only is this remedy rooted in injustice, since every man has a right to own property, but it would inflict hardship on the very class it is meant to help. "Socialists therefore by endeavouring to transfer the possessions of individuals to the community at large strike at the interests of every wage-earner, since they would deprive him of the liberty of disposing of his wages and thereby of all hope and possibility of increasing his resources and of bettering his condition in life."

The encyclical then goes on to examine the true remedies for the existing social evils. Whilst insisting that there can be no lasting remedy without religion, and claiming that the Church, as history shows, has in fact worked for the transformation of society, the Pope suggests various specific means. The function of the State is shown to be to protect the interests of all classes, amongst which the poor have a special claim. Fundamental to the welfare of the worker is the payment of a living wage and the establishment of certain standards in the equipment of factories, etc. The interests of the worker will best be protected by institutions such as Trade Unions and similar associations, which are commended by the Pope. "It is gratifying to know that there are actually in existence not a few associations of this kind consisting either of workmen alone or of workmen and employers together; but it is greatly to be desired that they should become more numerous and more efficient.... To sum up then, We may lay it down as a general and lasting law that working-men's associations should be so organized and governed as to furnish the best and most suitable means for attaining what is aimed at, that is to say, for helping each individual member to better his condition to the utmost in body, soul and property.... The condition of the working classes is the pressing question of the hour; and nothing can be of greater interest to all classes of the State than that it should be rightly and reasonably settled. But it will be easy for Christian working-men to solve it aright if they will form associations, choose wise guides and follow on the path which with so much advantage to themselves and the common wealth was trodden by their fathers before them...."

As the encyclical says, it is impossible to enter into detailed discussion of particular problems and remedies which vary so much from country to country; but a reading of the document shows that the Church not only appreciated the gravity of the danger but, in her approach to a solution, showed genuine wisdom and impartial sympathy.

What Leo had asserted in 1891 was reasserted with no less emphasis forty years later by Pius XI in *Quadragesimo Anno*. Not that these two documents are alone amongst the Catholic utterances on the social and economic problems of our age, but they are more than enough to refute the suggestion that the Church, in social and political matters, is always on the side of reaction. Her enemies point to the so-called Catholic countries and complain that they are economically and politically backward, compared with the countries where the Reformation triumphed. The complaint is based on a failure to appreciate the complex historical factors of the situation. The position of the Church in the Mediterranean lands is by no means one of supreme control, as anyone with a knowledge of the history of these regions during the last two hundred years must admit. Nor is it easy to substantiate the thesis that the prosperity of the United States, Great Britain or the Scandinavian countries is to be traced directly to the success of the ideas of the Reformers.

And indeed, in the Protestant countries themselves the contribution of the Catholic body is becoming increasingly significant. In the United States of America, where the Catholic population now numbers approximately 30 million, Catholics are to be found fully active in the political, cultural and economic life of the country. It must always be borne in mind that there, as well as in Britain, the largest proportion of Catholics is to be found in the less wealthy and therefore the less well educated classes, a fact which explains the relative weakness of Catholic representation at the highest levels. Perhaps the most impressive single fact is that whereas, in the early years of the twentieth century, it is probably true to say that Catholicism was regarded with something approaching contempt by the intelligentsia of these two countries, today its appeal to intellectuals is beyond question.

Moreover, at the level of the less well-to-do or less intellectual, one of the most significant developments of modern times has been the emergence of a well-developed Catholic social and political consciousness. One of the most dramatic features of post-war Europe has been the part played by Catholic politicians and their parties in Germany, France and Italy. The Christian Democrat party in Germany, although not a strictly confessional party in that members of other Christian bodies provide an important part of its membership, nevertheless derives its inspiration from and owes no

PLATE 41. The Council of Trent by Titian (c. 1477–1576). The scene seems to owe much to the artist's imagination, since it combines some of the features of a religious ceremony with the actual business of theological debate. The bishop seen on the right below the pulpit is addressing the assembled prelates, but it is unlikely that they wore mitres during the ordinary sessions. The presence of the lay attendants and soldiers is unaccountable. (Louvre, Paris)

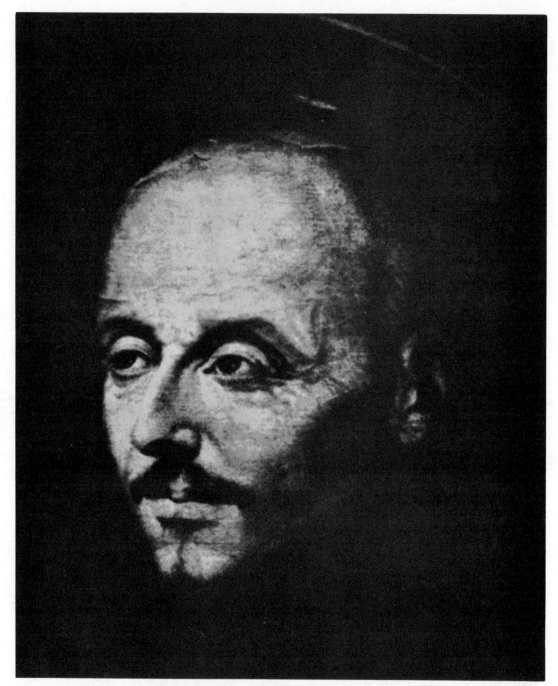

Photo: Hechos y Dichos, Zaragoza, Spain

PLATE 42. St Ignatius Loyola, founder of the Society of Jesus, by Sanchez Coello (1513 or 15–1590). The original was destroyed in 1931, when the mob sacked the Jesuit Professed House in Madrid. A few copies survive. St Ignatius and the Society which he founded played an outstanding part in the Counter-Reformation.

Photo: from "Peking" by Monsignor A. Favier, Paris 1902

PLATE 43. Matteo Ricci (1552–1610) and Johann Adam Schall von Bell (1591–1666). These are the most famous of the Jesuit missionaries who worked in China. Their use of Chinese dress was one of the many ways in which they sought to accommodate the ideas of the Christian West to the Oriental mind.

Photo: David Moore

PLATE 44. Rivers of light formed by the candles carried in procession at night at the opening of the centenary of the apparitions to Bernadette at the grotto of Lourdes in 1858. This centre of devotion, pilgrimage and, as many believe, miraculous healing has become world-famous.

172

Photo: Keystone Press Agency Ltd

PLATE 45. Pope John XXIII, wearing the Triple Crown, blesses the City and the world, from the balcony of St Peter's, Rome, after his coronation on 4 November, 1958. The world-wide interest in and appreciation of the position of the Papacy today suggest that much of the hostility aroused at the time of the Reformation is disappearing.

PLATE 46. Statue of Christ on Corcovado Peak overlooking Rio da Janeiro Harbour. The construction of this huge figure is an expression of the faith of South America, an area comprising some of the largest Roman Catholic populations in the world.

small part of its success to that great Catholic and great European, Konrad Adenauer. In Italy, the threat of Communism, acute as it still is, has been held at bay very largely through the efforts of the Christian Democrats, whilst in France, where the picture is too complex to be adequately discussed here, the Catholic inspiration of the M.R.P. party has been impressive and valuable.

In Holland, once the very symbol of the Protestant achievement, the role played by Catholics in public life calls for special mention. The proportion of Catholics to the total population is rather more than a third, they have their own political party, formed over fifty years ago, and now controlling about a third of the seats in parliament. This means, of course, that there has never been a Catholic government in Holland, but in coalition with other parties the Catholic party has made an important contribution. The Catholic university of Nijmegen, founded some thirty years ago, whilst it clearly cannot yet claim to rival older foundations, is nevertheless playing a more and more important part in the cultural life not only of the Catholic body but of the country at large. Of the contribution of Dutch Catholics to the well-being of the Church as a whole it is enough to say that their profound religious sense allied with a sturdy common sense and a tenacious loyalty afford an example of Catholicism at its best.

It is in the United States that the most spectacular growth has taken place. Of the 170 millions constituting the total population, about one fifth are Catholics, many of them bringing with them the European tradition in which their forebears were reared. Yet there is something specifically American about the Church in the United States. It is often thought of as merely a large, well-organized and wealthy body. But this is to take a very superficial view. Wisely the hierarchy and the superiors of religious orders have made immense efforts and immense sacrifices to ensure that the Catholic body receives an education comparable with that of their fellow-countrymen, and the American achievement in this field is solid and enduring. It is due more, perhaps, to the climate of opinion in the United States that the Church does not yet make the appeal to the intelligentsia which it appears to make in England, but intelligent Americans are beginning to realize more and more the contribution which the Church makes to stability and loyalty in a world of shifting values. Despite the bigotry raised on occasion by the activities of Catholics in public life, despite the fears of a Paul Blanshard that Catholicism is as big a threat to the American way of life as is Communism itself, the clear fact emerges that the very growth of the Church in America and the contribution it makes

to that country's development show that genuine Catholicism can flourish in a democratic milieu as well as anywhere.

Nor is this in any way surprising to a Catholic, who knows that some of the most important contributions to a philosophy of democracy were made by Catholic writers, not least by Suarez at the beginning of the seventeenth century. Francis Suarez, a Spanish Jesuit, who lived from 1548 to 1617, was a versatile and voluminous writer. The most important of his works for our purpose was his *De Legibus* published in 1612. In it he argues that political authority resides ultimately in the people. He argues that this truth springs from a consideration of man's nature. Since the formation of political organizations is necessary for man to lead a human life, the root of that authority without which such organizations cannot survive is to be found, not, as our own James I sought to argue, in some Divine Right given to the monarch as such, but in something like a Divine Right given to man to be ruled for his own good. The sovereign is, in the end, the people's delegate. Whilst Suarez held that monarchy was in fact the best form of government, he insisted that political power does not belong to any individual, except in so far as it is delegated to him from the community.

THE CATHOLIC CHURCH AND MARRIAGE

By many people the Catholic Church is thought of primarily, perhaps almost exclusively, as holding very strict and inhumane views on such matters as marriage and divorce, contraception and, indeed, on sexual morality in general. It is perhaps necessary to begin by making it clear that the Church does not claim to make special laws on this subject for those who are Catholics. She maintains that what she teaches is simply the universal law of God. She says that marriage is, of its nature, indissoluble; that divorce is, therefore, forbidden not just to Catholics but to all men and women, whatever the law of the land may be; that contraceptive practices are, in themselves, an interference with natural processes and therefore against that moral law which lays down how man must behave in the use of the different elements which go to make up "Nature".

To state the whole case for the Church's teaching would be impossible within the necessarily narrow limits of the present chapter, but it seems necessary to insist that such teaching springs, not from a morbid disapproval of sex or a puritanical flight from enjoyment, but, on the contrary, from an exalted view of marriage and of all that pertains to it and from a profound conviction that human happiness depends, in the end, on having the sort of joy that the laws of nature provide for and, at the same time, control. The laws of nature are to be understood here as applying not merely to the physical laws governing the course of nature but all those physiological, psychological and spiritual laws which describe the nature of man at all levels.

An analysis of the whole of that nature shows that the union of man with woman in marriage is only fully and perfectly fulfilled where the instinctive urge on the part of each to make the other partner the object of a lasting and absolute devotion is reinforced by the deliberate life-long mutual dedication which the marriage contract is. One of man's abiding temptations is to look on sexual activity as a superficial and relatively trivial affair. The Church teaches that man's human dignity as a person is involved in such activities, which are to be taken seriously and treated as, in a literal sense, vitally important.

It is also necessary to point out that the Catholic Church does not require her members to have large families. It is sometimes suggested that the Church's teaching on contraception is simply dictated by a desire to increase her membership. This is plain nonsense. After all, if such were the Church's policy she would hardly impose a law of celibacy on her clergy. Nor would she exalt virginity as a state of perfection. The Church is, in principle, not concerned with the size of a family. All that she does say is that married people must not use unnatural means to limit the number of their children.

In this context some reference needs to be made to a violent debate which took place a few years ago as the result of a pronouncement made by Pius XII on a problem of obstetric practice. When the Pope said that it was wrong to kill a child in process of being born, in order to save the life of the mother, it was apparently inferred by some that he meant that it was better, in such cases, to kill the mother. The Pope's point was, in fact, the perfectly simple one that the child is a human being and has its own right to life. To deprive it of life by a deliberate act is just as wrong as it would be to deprive the mother of hers.

In general, about the Church's moral pronouncements, this much may be stated with assurance. The Church does not invent laws to make life more difficult. She is not unaware of the immense problems – psychological, economic, physical – involved in being married and in having children. She simply says that, in the end, mankind will not be better off if individuals take the moral law into their own hands instead of obeying the law of God.

THE CATHOLIC CHURCH TODAY

To say that the Church has "recovered from the effects of the Reformation" is to say at once too little and too much; too little, because the Church will always be conscious of failure; too much, because it implies that the Church thinks of herself primarily as one amongst a number of comparable bodies, struggling for supremacy. She claims to be the one fully authenticated agency for the salvation of mankind, the one fully accredited teacher of the truth of Christ. So long as there are divisions amongst Christians she knows that the work of salvation is being impeded. No one, therefore, desires unity more than she does. Why then, it will be asked, is she so intransigent in her attitude to other Christian bodies? The answer is that her attitude is not one of arrogant and self-satisfied disregard for their feelings; it is based on the simple conviction that the fulfilment of Christ's prayer for unity amongst his followers (" . . . that they may all be one . . . as thou, Father, art in me, and I in thee", *John* xvii, 21) cannot be brought about by a general spirit of compromise and an agreement to differ. If Christ, in his own life, had shown a readiness to compromise there would have been no need of a crucifixion; but there would have been no redemption.

So long then as men look for Christian Unity through some surrender by the Catholic Church of some of her firmest beliefs, they are looking for the impossible. She believes that loyalty to Christ demands that she maintain in its integrity the truth committed to her from the beginning, the truth from which, in this or that respect, men have constantly fallen away into what she calls heresy. She cannot see how the interests of Christ are likely to be served by the pretence that heresy is not heresy, error not error. As her Master came to "bear witness to truth" even at the cost of his life, so she holds that she has the same mission, even at the cost of vituperation and persecution and the loss of large regions over which she once exercised jurisdiction.

At the same time, she has never been unwilling to permit variations of ritual and custom, of ecclesiastical discipline and other matters of secondary importance. The existence within the one Catholic Church of the various Uniate Churches, to which no one has given greater encouragement than Pope Pius XII, the permission of widely differing liturgical forms, generally in some vernacular manner, the toleration of married clergy in some localities – all this shows that the Catholic Church is not opposed to variety in itself. She is equally prepared to co-operate with other groups where such co-operation is not likely to be misinterpreted as a surrender of her central Christian sovereignty.

Yet there is no doubt that any sincere attempt at re-union will meet with sympathy and appreciation from Catholics. At the same time, it must be borne in mind that the Church does not see it as looming so large as others do. The very universality of her commitments, the ever-growing needs of Asia and Africa, the remarkable development of a native clergy and hierarchy in India and the Far East, in central and southern Africa, the fact that less than half the Church's membership is to be found in Europe – all these factors mean that, important as the question of re-union is, it is not one of the major pre-occupations of the Church.

She sees herself, as she saw herself in the days of the barbarian invasions, as charged with the mission of safe-guarding those fundamental human values and Christian truths which are menaced above all by the threat of atheistic materialism, as preached and practised most violently in Marxism. In the work of that mission she will welcome whatever allies are to be found amongst men of good will. But her chief source of strength is to be found in her own organization: in a hierarchy which is, in integrity of life and devotion to Christ, unmatched in the history of the Church since Apostolic times; in a clergy, professionally trained, and, as a body, devout and industrious; in a vast army of religious men and women, belonging to orders and congregations, some of which are of recent origin, others stretching back to the life-time of St Benedict himself, and with traditions deriving from an earlier age still; in a laity increasingly aware of the active part it is called upon to play in the life of the Church, through the liturgy, through various organizations loosely grouped under the heading of Catholic Action, and not least through the contribution they can make, owing to their firm grasp of Christian principles, to a healthy political and social life in their various countries.

Since, in a study of the Church since the Reformation, the Society of Jesus has come in for special mention, it is necessary, in giving a picture of twentieth-century Catholicism, to insist on the value of the contribution made by the clergy as a whole and by the various religious orders. Whilst the immense task of maintaining a vigorous parochial life – the foundation of a healthy Church – is very largely in the hands of the secular clergy, the work of education at the higher levels and of theological and philosophical activity is largely, though by no means exclusively, in the hands of the Orders. In England, Benedictines, through their schools at Ampleforth and Downside, have come to challenge the pre-eminence enjoyed during the nineteenth century by Stonyhurst; whilst the education of girls in the many convents wins high praise. In the United States of America, of the 250 Colleges and Universities and the 2,500 High Schools established for the education of Catholics, much the larger proportion are directed and to a large extent staffed by religious of almost every Order, ancient and modern. And in this work of education in modern times special mention should be made of the work of the Salesians, founded by St John of Bosco in the early nineteenth century, and now playing a formidable part in the education of boys not only in Don Bosco's native Italy but in many distant lands as well.

There is much more that ought to be said to give a complete picture of the Church as she is today. But this must suffice. If this chapter has concentrated largely on theological activity, this is because of the theme of this book. But Catholic life is much more than theology. It is to be hoped that enough has been said to suggest those wider interests and activities which form, for the average Catholic, the chief element in his faith. For he sees himself not so much committed to holding a body of doctrine as sharing in a way of life. The dogmatic structure is, as it were, the skeleton holding together the body of which he is a member. He leaves it to the anatomist to study that skeleton; he is content to know that he belongs to a body which, growing and developing, yet remains recognizably the same as that which on the first Pentecost, gathered in the Upper Room, received the Spirit of God and was charged with power to go forth and teach all nations.

3. Islam

by H.A.R. GIBB

Islam is the proper name of the religion traditionally called *Mohammedanism* in the West. In its origins the religion is based on the revelations uttered by the Prophet Muhammad (Mohammed) in Arabia in the seventh century of the Christian era, and collected shortly after his death in the volume called the Koran (Arabic *Qur'ān*). From this work, supplemented by statements and rulings traced back to the Prophet, there were derived in the following centuries a system of law and a theology; these combined with elements from other sources to form a distinctive Islamic civilization, which has continued to exist into modern times. The term *Islām* is applied in the Koran to denote the characteristic attitude of its adherents, in "surrendering" or "committing themselves" to the will of God; the adherents themselves are called Muslims (Arabic *Muslimūn*) or "Believers" (*Mu'minūn*).

The religion of Islam was spread by the conquests of the Arabs in the seventh century A.D. over Western Asia and North Africa, and in the eighth century A.D. into Central Asia, Sind and Spain. From the eleventh century A.D., under Turkish leadership, it spread into Southern Russia, India and Asia Minor, and under negro leadership in the Niger basin. In the fourteenth century A.D. it became politically dominant in the Balkans under the Ottoman Turkish Sultans, and in India under the Sultans of Delhi; and spread, largely by missionary endeavour, into Indonesia and China. On the other hand, it was receding in Spain, whence it was finally expelled at the end of the fifteenth century A.D. In the nineteenth and twentieth centuries A.D. it has lost ground in the Balkans, where it survives only in local communities (especially in Bosnia and Albania), but continues to advance in East and West Africa, and is represented by groups of immigrants in South Africa and in North and South America. The total number of Muslims in the world is estimated at about three hundred and fifty millions.

MUHAMMAD AND THE KORAN

Apart from casual allusions in the Koran, the history of Muhammad's life is known only from the oral traditions of his followers, subsequently collected and written down in biographical works of the eighth and ninth centuries A.D. The substantial accuracy of these biographies is authenticated by internal evidence, in spite of a tendency towards schematic treatment and a growing accretion of pious legend. According to the received dating, Muhammad was born about A.D. 570, in Mecca, then a prosperous centre of the caravan trade between Southern Arabia and the Mediterranean countries. He was himself engaged in the caravan trade, and married a well-to-do widow named Khadīja; from this marriage three daughters survived into his later years. In middle life he developed contemplative habits, and in his fortieth year received the call to proclaim the worship of the One God (*Allāh*) against the prevailing polytheism and idol-worship of his Meccan fellow-citizens and the majority of Arabs in North and Central Arabia.

For ten years his preaching made slow headway against accumulating opposition in Mecca, and succeeded in winning over only a few prominent citizens, amongst whom were Abū Bakr and 'Umar, who were later, after his death, to launch the Arab armies on the expeditions that led to the expansion of Islam. At this juncture he was invited by a group of citizens of Yathrib (later called al-Madīna) to move to their city, then a group of agricultural villages with a mixed population of Arabs and Jews. After prolonged negotiation he sent his Meccan converts on to Yathrib and himself joined them there in September 622. This was the celebrated *hijra* (Hegira) or "Emigration", with the year of which the Muslim calendar begins. Shortly after his arrival, he began to organize the emigrants and the citizens of Yathrib as a political community, and to open attacks on the Meccan caravans. Hostilities continued for seven years; during this time the

Jewish tribes in Yathrib (who had become irreconcilable opponents) were expelled, and the bedouin tribes of Western and Central Arabia were gradually incorporated in the Muslim community. In 630, in face of a massed attack, Mecca capitulated, was purified of its polytheistic idol-worship, and its ancient sanctuary was rededicated to Allah and reconstituted as the central pilgrimage shrine of Islam. During the next two years adhesions were received from, and missionaries and political agents sent out to, tribes in all parts of Arabia. In 632 Muhammad died and was buried in the hut of his wife 'A'isha, at the edge of the Mosque ("place of worship") which he had constructed in al-Madīna. After a brief moment of confusion, the community at al-Madīna elected Abū Bakr as his "Successor" (khalīfa, caliph) in the political and religious headship, and on Abū Bakr's death two years later he was succeeded by 'Umar in the same office.

The personality of Muhammad, as it is presented in the Koran and the earliest stratum of tradition, is that of an ordinary human being who was charged with a special mission from God, to which he thenceforth unremittingly devoted himself. In conformity with the insistent argument of his revelations for the sole divinity of Allah, he denied any suggestion of supernatural character attaching to himself, admitted himself to be, as a man, liable to error, and disclaimed the power to work miracles. The Koran itself was the sole "miracle" which demonstrated his prophetic mission, and he was no more than the mouthpiece of its revelation to men. Orthodox Islam has consistently maintained the humanity of Muhammad, and formally rejects, as worse than heresy, any kind of worship addressed to him.

Nevertheless, the impact made by Muhammad on the life and thought of Muslims could not be wholly satisfied by an ordinary human figure. From early times the popular imagination seized on hints and allusions in the Koran and elaborated them into miracles (as, for example, the splitting of the moon to confound his Meccan adversaries) or other supernatural interventions in his life. The most famous is the lengthy narrative of the "Night-journey" (isrā') to Jerusalem, followed by an "Ascension" (mi'rāj) to paradise in the course of a single night, when, under the guidance of Gabriel, he is said to have met and talked with the Prophets who had preceded him and to have been granted the ineffable Vision of God. The theme, repeatedly retold and illustrated in Muslim literature, was accepted as an article of orthodox belief and played its part in later controversies. At the same time, with the intense absorption of the early Muslims in the events of the Last Judgment, Muhammad had become an eschato-

logical figure, and more especially the privileged intercessor for the whole community of Muslims on that day. With the development of Ṣūfism and saint-worship, he became the chief of the saints; and as Ṣūfism worked out its own theosophical construction of the universe the mystical cult of the Prophet was linked with the Koranic theme of the "Covenant" (p. 200 below). The pre-eternal essence of Muhammad was the link between God and all creation, as the human Muhammad was the intermediary of God's revelation to men: "All the lights of the Prophets proceeded from his Light; he was before all, his name the first in the Book of Fate; he was known before all things and all being, and will endure after the end of all" (Al-Ḥallāj, Kitāb al-Ṭawāsīn, ed. L.Massignon, 1913, p. 11).

The Koran in its finished form is a book of medium size, divided into 114 chapters called suras, and arranged roughly in order of length, from chapters containing over 200 verses to chapters of three to five short verses at the end. The first, called "The Opening" (al-Fātiha), is a brief invocation, widely used by Muslims in diverse circumstances and held by many Muslim divines to comprehend all the essentials of Muslim belief:

"In the name of the One God, the Compassionate One, the Merciful.
Praise be to God, the Lord of the Universe –
The Compassionate One, the Merciful –
The Ruler on the Day of Judgment.
Thee do we worship, and from thee do we seek aid.
Guide us into the straight path –
The path of those to whom thou hast shown mercy –
Not those who have incurred thine anger, nor those who go astray."

Most of the other 113 suras are a mosaic of passages of revelation, uttered by Muhammad at different times and on different occasions, somewhat unevenly compiled from oral and written records. It seems possible that the work of compilation was begun in his lifetime, but it was completed only some years after his death. The third of the Caliphs, 'Uthmān, had an authoritative recension prepared about 650; copies of this were sent to the chief cities and quickly superseded the unofficial private recensions which were already beginning to circulate. As a result of this measure the consonantal text of the Koran was stabilized for all time. But since the Arabic script was not yet supplied with a vowel notation, it was still read in different centres with minor differences in vocalization. Seven of these systems of "readings" were accepted as orthodox, and are still studied; but practically all modern texts of the Koran reproduce only one of these, which is in consequence all but universally followed by Muslims today. The doctrine of the verbal inspiration of the Koran is an article of belief of all Muslims and has seldom been questioned; its verses when quoted are introduced by the phrase "God has said", the Prophet's part being understood to have been wholly passive.

In analysing the contents of the Koran, Muslim as well as non-Muslim students have always distinguished between Meccan and Madinian passages. There are marked differences in both subject and style between the earlier and the later revelations. The Meccan *sūras* begin with short staccato oracles in rhymed prose, like that which the tradition asserts to have been Muhammad's first call to the prophethood:

> "Recite, in the name of thy Lord who created
> Created man from a clot!
> Recite, for thy Lord is the Most Bountiful
> Who taught by the Pen,
> Taught man what he knew not!"
>
> (96. 1–5)

The themes which are stressed in the early passages are God's mercies to man, man's ingratitude and misuse of God's gifts, the evidences of God's creative power in nature, the resurrection of the dead and the Judgment, the joys and bliss of Paradise, the terrors of Hell, the missions of former Prophets and the punishment that followed their rejection by their fellow-citizens. Later revelations expand these themes in greater detail in the context of argument against the idolatry of the Meccans, and indicate an increasing acquaintance with Biblical and post-Biblical materials. At al-Madīna, on the other hand, the revelations are directed chiefly to the guidance and instruction of the new Muslim Community in the vicissitudes of its existence, together with controversy with the Jews, the Christians and the "hypocrites", the dissident elements among the Arabs. The religious obligations of prayer, alms, fasting, and pilgrimage are laid down, the basic social institutions of marriage, divorce and inheritance are defined in detail, and a general structure of law adumbrated.

The Koran as a whole thus reflects the evolution of Islam in Muhammad's lifetime. In Mecca, it is still essentially a personal religion, not tied to any specific social structure and organization. With the establishment of the community at al-Madīna Islam asserts itself as a religious system, distinct from Judaism and Christianity (both of which, in its own view, it completes, purifies from accumulated errors, and supersedes), and carrying with it a complex of divinely-ordained social institutions. Further-

more, by virtue of the repeated injunction to "strive in the path of God, until allegiance to God is victorious over all other allegiance", the community is invested with a duty and a power of expansion, universal in aim. So far as lies within the organized capacity of Muslims, idolatry is not to be tolerated; Jews and Christians, on the other hand, are not to be molested provided they acknowledge the supremacy of the Muslim state and pay the stipulated tribute, a concession subsequently extended to Zoroastrians also.

THE CONSOLIDATION OF THE ISLAMIC STATE AND THE RISE OF POLITICAL SECTS

The first consequence of the establishment of the Muslim Community at al-Madīna was that when Islam emerged from Arabia and conquered Western Asia and Egypt, it did so as an organized and coherent political institution which was able to set up a regular administration in the conquered provinces under the supreme government of a Caliph, whose religious authority gave him a means of control over the traditional tendencies of the Arab tribes to anarchical independence. But too rapid a success brought its own nemesis. Neither the Koran nor Muhammad himself had laid down rules for the government of the Muslim Community. The election of Abū Bakr as Caliph had been an action of the Community itself. This established a precedent, without defining the authority so created. Rulership was simply a personal function of supervision over operations of external war and defence and internal maintenance of the religion and institutions of Islam. No distinction was drawn between the religious and the political aspects of the Community, and even in the later theory of Islam they have always remained bound up with one another. At no time has it recognized a "church" as an organized religious institution, within and distinct from the political institution called the "state".

It was due to this fact that political discontents in Islam have always assumed a religious character, and that within thirty years of Muhammad's death the Community was involved in a civil war that gave rise to the three sects into which Islam remains divided to the present day. The basic factors were resentment on the part of the Arab tribal garrisons in Iraq and Egypt at the controls exercised by the third Caliph and his governors, and rivalries among the Meccan mercantile aristocracy as a result of the conquests. The civil war began with the murder of the Caliph by the tribesmen, and ended with the restoration of imperial unity under a new dynasty of Meccan Caliphs, ruling from Damascus. But it left deep divisions within the Community. The largest group was composed of those who placed above all else the unity of the Community, and were willing to recognize the authority of those political chiefs who were able to maintain it, by force of arms if need be. This was the origin of the majority party, called *Sunnīs* or followers of the *Sunna* (practice) of the Community at large. Opposed to them were two dissident groups: one which maintained the sole legitimacy in the headship of the Community after Muhammad's death of his cousin and son-in-law 'Alī and his descendants, and held that the Community had erred in electing Abū Bakr and his two successors – these were called the *Shī 'at 'Alī* ("partisans of 'Alī") or *Shī'a*; the other which rejected both the Sunnī and Shī'a positions and maintained not only the right of the Community to elect its own head but also its duty to depose him if he were found guilty of sin – these were called the *Khārijites* (*Khawārij*) or "Seceders".

During the century that followed, the division of feeling between these parties was reinforced by the repeated suppression of armed revolts. Later on, when (as noted below) the main currents of Islamic activity were diverted from the political arena to the field of theology, law and other intellectual activities, each of the dissident parties developed and expounded its own positions in terms of opposition to or distinction from the doctrinal or legal positions of the Sunnī majority and vice versa, thus becoming religious sects in the strict sense of the word. It should be added that these parties were all in origin divisions between and amongst the Arabs, and that all of them gained adherents at different times among non-Arab converts, in roughly the same proportions as their bodies of Arab supporters, the Sunnīs therefore predominating almost everywhere. There is no historical justification for the view, often expressed by writers on Islam, that the development of Shī'ism was due to the impact of Persian culture on Islam, and that Shī'ism was more particularly favoured or adopted by Persians. The imposition of Shī'ism as the state religion of Persia dates only from the beginning of the sixteenth century A.D. The Khārijite sect was always limited in its appeal by its intransigence, and survives only in the moderate form called *Ibādī*, in Oman, Zanzibar, and southern Algeria.

THE GROWTH OF PROPHETIC TRADITION AND THE CONSOLIDATION OF ISLAMIC LAW

The second consequence of the community structure of Islam was that the practical problems involved in the life of the Community took precedence as the main field of religious studies over the elaboration of a theology.

The basic social institutions had been, as already noted, laid down in detail in the Koran, together with a few other definite rulings relating to murder, vendetta, theft, and the like, and a variety of ethical injunctions. In daily life, Caliphs and governors in the first century A.H. supplemented the Koranic rulings by drawing on traditional Arab practice and their own judgment. In the chief cities of the empire, however, small groups of students of the Koran were beginning to elaborate legal systems, supplementing the Koran by drawing on rulings and traditions handed down from first-generation Muslims (the "Companions of the Prophet") and by reasoning based on these and the rulings of the Koran. By the second century A.H. the divergences between these schools of law and the infiltration of speculative reasoning (partly influenced by Roman Law) in some schools, alarmed religious circles. The means which they adopted in order to counteract such divisive tendencies was to engage in an intensive search for Traditions, authentically transmitted from Companions of the Prophet, in which these eye-witnesses recorded actions done or statements made by Muhammad on legal points not defined by the Koran. Where such Traditions were found to exist, it was held, the rulings they contained, explicitly or implicitly, were decisive and mandatory for all Muslims. The *sunna* (practice) of the Prophet obviously superseded all other *sunnas*, and still more any speculative reasoning.

This argument (elaborated by the jurist al-Shāfi'ī, d. 820) was so clearly unchallengeable that it was perforce accepted in principle by all the schools of law. By the third century A.H., therefore, the theory of Islamic law (called the *Sharī'a* or "Highway") took final shape. The law, not for Muslims only, but for all mankind, is given by God, and is of necessity mandatory, universal, and immutable except by his decree. The means chosen by God to transmit his law to men is by sending prophets, the last being Muhammad, whose revelation conveys the final and definitely immutable commands of God in the "clear Arabic language" of the Koran. Thus the Koran is not strictly the "basis" of the *Sharī'a*, but in principle contains the whole of the *Sharī'a*. It requires no supplementing in substance, but only clarification or elaboration of its texts in respect of method, interpretation or application – for example, it prescribes the payment of an alms-tax, but nowhere defines how much or on what possessions. This clarification is supplied by the record of Muhammad's statements and actions, reliably transmitted from Companions who heard and saw them. But Muhammad may not be called a "lawgiver" except in the sense of "the channel of transmission from God" and the only fully qualified or implicitly inspired interpreter.

This scheme is philosophically underpinned by a further argument. The purpose of law is to define the Good, and to define and prohibit the Evil. Good and Evil are known only to God, and hence cannot be defined by the exercise of an inherently fallible human reason. The Koranic commands and prohibitions are of course absolute, and cannot be questioned without incurring the guilt of sin, unless they are qualified in some way by the Koran itself. So also are the definite and unimpeachable commands and prohibitions in the Traditions of the Prophet. But a large number of human actions are legally indifferent (though not necessarily morally indifferent in all circumstances). When there is no formal pronouncement in Koran or Tradition, men are free to follow customary usages or to apply their own reason; and one of the legitimate uses of reason is to discover whether any of the actions not explicitly mentioned in Koran or Tradition are implicitly covered, through parallel circumstances or conditions, by Koranic or Prophetic commands or prohibitions. (For example, the Koran explicitly prohibits the drinking of wine made from grape juice – does this implicitly include other fermented drinks?) This process, called "analogy", thus supplies a third source of legal rulings.

While all the schools of Law, however, formally adhered to these principles, they did not produce a fully unified system of Islamic Law. For it was found that the Traditions which satisfied the conditions required for authenticity (namely, transmission through a reliable chain of authorities) not only had, by the end of the second century A.H., run into several thousands, but also contained many contradictory rulings. In spite of the elaboration of a science of Tradition-criticism, each of the established schools of law, starting from the same unqualified commands and prohibitions in the Koran, adopted as normative on minor matters somewhat diverse Traditions and "analogies" in supplementation of them. The Shī'a went further in refusing to accept Traditions not transmitted through 'Alī or one of his descendants. The final outcome of this situation was parallel to the decision concerning the different "readings" of the Koran. On the principle of "Consensus of the Community" (ijmā'), authenticated by a Tradition that "My Community will never agree upon an error", the rulings within each school were unified and consolidated by a "particular ijmā'", and the different Sunnī schools, by a "general ijmā'", recognized all these rulings as acceptable and authoritative within the system of that school. The Shī'a, on the other hand, rejected entirely the doctrine of ijmā', holding that the Law could be interpreted only by the Imāms of the House of 'Alī, and

their system was in return excluded from the ijmā' of the Sunnī schools.

The result of the operation of this principle was to squeeze out the minor schools, and leave within the Sunnī community four equally orthodox and recognized schools – the old Iraqi school, called Ḥanafī; the school of al-Madīna, called Mālikī; a "reformed" Mālikī school, called Shāfi'ī; and a later Iraqi school, called Ḥanbalī, which in principle rejected both "analogy" and the wider extension of ijmā'. Each school has its own systematic text-books, and applies only its own rulings in courts of law. Their systems, however, are not "codes" of law in the Western sense, although they resemble Western codes in some respects – as in the distribution of materials between religious, personal, contract and penal law, and the provision of fixed penalties for the neglect of formal obligations or breach of formal prohibitions. They are rather classifications of acts, laying down standards of conduct and defining the moral qualities of particular actions (obligatory, recommended, indifferent, reprehensible, or forbidden), without necessarily attaching civil penalties to the disregard of the legal norm; and they offer a further contrast to Western law in including religious obligations.

To regard the Sharī'a, however, as merely a complicated system of legal rules and discussions is entirely inadequate. It is the constitution of the Muslim Community, the pattern of its communal order. As the political government of the Community more and more manifestly failed to fulfil its original function by its divisions and its growing secularization, it became the task of the religious leaders to make or re-make the communal life and order of all Muslims, in every land and under every form of government, in the image of its true pattern, and thus to preserve and to reinforce the unity of the Muslim Community in the terms of its divine constitution, homogeneous in social practice and ethical ideals. And it is the fact of this millennial and never-completed endeavour, in the face of long-established and resistant local custom among the diverse Muslim populations, which has given the Muslim world that psychological unity which it continues to display down to the present time, and which, in their common Koranic basis, embraces (if more loosely) the Shī'a and the Khawārij as well as the four Sunnī schools.

For the accomplishment of this task, the authority and finality of the Sharī'a gave powerful assistance to the religious leaders; but remarkable as their achievement has been, it almost inevitably brought some concomitant disadvantages. Both the Muslim theory of Law and the pursuit of unity implied a fixation and a degree of formal rigidity which gave little room for flexibility. In the age of the formation of the schools it was still open to jurists to apply themselves to critical studies of the sources and the formulation of rulings (technically called *ijtihād*), but from the end of the third century A.H. every jurist and judge (*qāḍī*) was bound to "acceptance on authority" (*taqlīd*) of the rulings ratified by the *ijmā'* of his school. At most, a recognized "professional jurisconsult" (*muftī*) might, within the limits of the principles and methods of his school, authorize some adaptation to new circumstances. But if his permissible field of action was small, so also was the demand for social adaptation. The kin-system and social traditions of practically all the populations who adopted Islam were sufficiently like those of the Arabs to be, in most cases, readily adaptable to the basic legislation of the Koran in matters of family law (marriage, permission of polygamy and divorce, inheritance), the vendetta, slavery and manumission.

It was moreover in these fields (with that of the religious institutions proper) that the *Sharī'a* was most consistently and universally applied. When even in them, however, the external rigidity of the juristic formulations often gave the *Sharī'a* the character of an ideal system or counsel of perfection, in other fields it became increasingly a theoretical construction, divorced from actual practice. Particularly in criminal cases and public administration, and to some extent in commercial practice, the governments of the Muslim countries steadily encroached on the prerogatives of the *Sharī'a* courts by setting up rival jurisdictions. These derogations were partially justified, at least, by the defective methods of procedure and excessive scrupulosity of the *qāḍīs'* courts in criminal cases, and by the changing systems of land tenure and public finance in administration. But the final result was to establish two distinct and separate systems of justice in almost all Muslim societies, based on different authorities and sanctions. Only the first, to be sure, was truly lawful and authoritative; the second was accepted only by the sanctions of power, and as the nemesis of the degeneration of the Muslim Community and its abandonment of the true bases of its proper constitution.

To the non-Muslims in the Muslim state the *Sharī'a* was not automatically applicable except in mixed cases. This was, of course, the logical conclusion from the Muslim concept of revelation and law; each protected religious community was therefore governed by its own law, administered by its own ecclesiastical leaders, unless, exceptionally, both parties should desire their case to be judged in a *Sharī'a* court and the *qāḍī* concerned consented to act.

THE DUTIES OF THE BELIEVER

In contrast to the organized institutions of Islam described above, the religious life of the Muslim was placed by the Koran and essentially remained on a personal and individual basis. The Koranic dictum "No burdened soul shall bear the burden of another" (17.16) is held to imply the personal responsibility of the Believer and the rejection of any spiritual hierarchy. As already noted, Islam does not admit the concept of a "church" and has rigorously excluded from its religious leadership any of the spiritual functions and prerogatives of a priesthood. Even when, as will be seen later, it admitted in Shī'ism and Ṣūfism the existence of special spiritual vocations, these in no way derogated from the duties laid upon the individual in virtue of his personal creaturely relation to his Creator.

The basic conception of the politico-religious Community of Islam carried the corollary that none but Muslims could be "citizens" of it. But the social function to which we give the name of "citizenship" had in Muslim society a special connotation, and the term corresponding to "citizen" betrays the legal and religious point of view from which it was envisaged. This term is *mukallaf*, one on whom is laid full responsibility for the performance of his religious duties and observance of the *Sharī'a*. All human beings stand towards God in the relation of the slave towards his master. Slaves as such have no rights. But God has made known through prophets the precise demands which he makes upon his slaves. To the individual who accepts and fulfils these demands in full, God in his mercy grants certain privileges, which then become in a sense "rights" of the Believer. One who does not accept God's demands in full cannot enjoy these privileges in full. Thus the "rights" of free Muslims are derived from acceptance of the responsibility of fulfilling them.

The duties laid on the individual Muslim "citizen" or *Mukallaf* are called "the Pillars of the Faith" and are five in number. None of them, however, is validly performed unless, on each and every occasion of performance, the Believer expressly or inwardly prefaces them by a statement of sincere "intention" (*nīya*).

(1) Confession of Faith by repetition of the Word of Witness (*Shahāda*): "There is no God but the One God, Muhammad is the Apostle of God" (*Lā'ilāha 'illa 'Llāh, Muḥammadun rasūlu 'Llāh*). The first phrase is the explicit repudiation not only of polytheism in its current sense, but of the sin of associating any creature with the creative and sustaining power of God (*shirk*). The second phrase implies, not the rejection of any other prophetic

183

missions (for Islam recognizes a sequence of prophets since the creation of the world, including Adam, Abraham, Moses and Jesus), but that Muhammad, the "Seal of the Prophets", is the bearer of the final and perfect Revelation in the Koran. In the view of Sunnī Islam, no person who repeats the *Shahāda* may be called an infidel or excluded from the Community of Muslims.

The other four obligations are disciplines, by which the Muslim is assisted to live the "good life":

(2) Regular performance of the ritual of Prayer (*ṣalāt*) at the five appointed times. It is by this repeated act that the Muslim publicly avows and demonstrates his citizenship in the Muslim Community. The ritual consists of a series of seven movements, with their appropriate recitations, collectively termed a "bowing" (*rak'a*), and each *ṣalāt* is made up of a fixed number of "bowings". The *rak'a* is performed as follows: (i) recitation of the phrase *Allāhu akbar*, "God is Most Great", with the hands open on either side of the face; (ii) recitation of the *Fātiḥa* (see p. 179 above) and another passage or passages of the Koran, while standing upright; (iii) bowing from the hips; (iv) straightening up; (v) gliding to the knees and a first prostration with the face to the ground; (vi) sitting back on the haunches; (vii) a second prostration. The second and later *rak'as* begin with the second of these movements, and at the end of each pair of *rak'as* and the conclusion of the whole prayer the worshipper recites the *Shahāda* and the ritual salutations, then sitting with upraised finger makes his private prayers.

The set times of prayers are at daybreak (2 *rak'as*), noon (4 *rak'as*), mid-afternoon (4 *rak'as*), after sunset (3 *rak'as*), and in the early part of the night (4 *rak'as*). If possible, they should be performed congregationally in a mosque, the worshippers standing in rows behind the prayer-leader, the *imām*, all facing in the direction (*qibla*) of the Sacred Mosque at Mecca, marked by a niche (*mihrāb*) in the wall of the mosque. But they may be performed individually on any clean ground or a rug, in the direction of the *qibla*. Additional or "supererogatory" prayers are frequently recommended, especially during the night.

The noon prayer on Friday is the principal congregational service of the week, and is distinguished by a formal address (*khuṭba*) in two sections, partly invocations of blessings on the Prophet, the Companions, the sovereign, etc., and partly sermon, delivered by a preacher (*khaṭīb*). Similar congregational services are held on the two major festival days, the day of the Breaking of the Fast after the fast of Ramaḍān (see no. 4 below), and the Feast of Sacrifice at the Pilgrimage (see no. 5 below).

The hours of prayer are announced by a caller (*mu'-adhdhin, muezzin*) from the minaret of the mosque. The "Call to Prayer" is chanted as follows: "God is Most Great, God is Most Great. I bear witness that there is no god except the One God, I bear witness that Muhammad is the Apostle of God. Come ye to the prayer. Come ye to the Good. Prayer is better than sleep. God is Most Great. God is Most Great. There is no god but the One God." Before entering the prayer-hall or praying elsewhere the worshipper is strictly required to perform an ablution of face, head, arms, feet and ankles; for this purpose every mosque is furnished with a water-tank. The Shī'a add to the Call to Prayer (after "Come ye to the Good") "Come ye to the best deed", and also have a special ritual of ablution. As so often, these minor differences have in the course of centuries assumed an entirely disproportionate significance in sectarian controversy and popular attitudes.

(3) The "giving of *Zakāt*" is repeatedly conjoined in the Koran along with the observance of prayer. The term is usually translated by "alms", but is distinguished in Arabic from free-will offerings, and in early times was regularly assessed as a tax on the possessions of Muslims. In principle, however, it is not a tax, but a "loan" made to God in the form of a regular percentage (normally one fortieth, of annual revenue, made over to the local authorities for the relief of the poor and needy, the freeing of slaves and prisoners and other religious objects. At most times and in most countries it has been left to the conscience of the individual Muslim to tax himself for charitable purposes, and, though it remains a personal obligation, no civil penalties are prescribed for the evasion of it, nor for the neglect of the *ṣalāt*.

(4) Observance of the fourth "pillar", the annual Fast, has always been more exigently demanded by public opinion, if not by the Law. The Koran makes it obligatory on all *mukallaf* Muslims to fast during the hours of daylight for the whole of the ninth month of the lunar year, called *Ramaḍān*. In Muslim practice, fasting involves total abstinence from food and drink of any kind. Those who are sick or on a journey at this time are exempted, but are required to make compensation by fasting an equal number of days later. Food may be consumed in any quantities during the hours of darkness, and special additional prayer services are held after the night prayer. Since the lunar year is eleven or twelve days shorter than the solar year, the incidence of Ramaḍān moves through all the seasons of the year in cycles of approximately 33 years – in 1957 it corresponded to April and in 1960 will correspond to March. The fast ends with a feast (popularly called *Bairām*) on the first day of the following month.

(5) The disciplines in the three preceding obligations – the surrender to the service of God of a daily portion of time and personal interests, of a portion of wealth, and a season of bodily comfort – are all included at a higher level of intensity in the fifth obligation. At least once in his lifetime (if he possesses the necessary means and the physical possibility) the Muslim should make a Pilgrimage to the Sacred Mosque at Mecca, in the twelfth month of the lunar year, called Dhu'l-Ḥijja. The Pilgrimage consists of a series of ceremonies. After visiting the mosque and going seven times in circuit round the Ka'ba, the pilgrim runs between two small eminences outside the sanctuary, called Ṣafā and Marwa; on the ninth day of the month he joins in the assembly at the hill of 'Arafa (about 12 miles east of Mecca) for the afternoon service there; this is the essential act which constitutes a valid pilgrimage. On the following day, which is the Feast of Sacrifice, he offers sacrifices of sheep or camels at Minā on the way back to Mecca. Other traditional rites included in the Pilgrimage are the kissing of the Black Stone set in one of the corners of the Ka'ba, and the stoning of pillars representing the Devil in the vicinity of Minā. The visiting of the Prophet's Mosque at al-Madīna is not included in the Pilgrimage, but is frequently combined with it. There is also a "Lesser Pilgrimage" (called 'Umra), which may be performed at Mecca at any period of the year.

Just as the worshipper must be ritually clean before praying, so also, before making either the Greater or Lesser Pilgrimage, the pilgrim must be in a state of ritual consecration (iḥrām). For this, the head is shaved and the pilgrim discards his ordinary clothing before entering the territory of Mecca, putting on instead two plain unsewn sheets (also called iḥrām) which leave his head and face uncovered. Women, however, keep the head covered as usual. From the time of putting on the iḥrām the pilgrim is required to abstain from using perfume and from sexual cohabitation, but need not fast. After the sacrifice of Minā he resumes his normal clothing and habits of life.

The significance of the Pilgrimage in maintaining the spiritual vitality and the communal life of Islam has been incalculable. The hardships (and frequently even dangers) which it involved for the ordinary Believer, the personal spiritual experience and the sense of community reinforced by participation in common rituals and worship with a multitude of fellow-Muslims from many lands – all these gave a new dimension to his understanding of and personal identification with the Faith, besides earning him the coveted title of al-Ḥājj or Ḥajji.

Over and above these five duties, certain other obligations are laid on the Muslim by the Koran. He is forbidden to drink wine, to eat swine's flesh, to gamble or to practise usury, in addition to the normal prohibitions of unethical conduct, such as perjury or slander. Above all, it is implicit in the Confession of Faith that he accept the Sharī'a as both system of law and rule of life, setting out the ethical ideal to which he should conform. For it is also the Sharī'a which confirms to him, as a Muslim "citizen", those personal rights of liberty, property and function given to him by God, which frees him from the capricious restrictions and classifications of a purely secular society. But he achieves all this only through his status as a member of the Muslim Community and in so far as he maintains that status and its obligations. The self-consciousness of the individual as a free agent and his enjoyment of his rights can be realized in practice, therefore, only in so far as the Community as a whole is conscious of and faithful to its collective life and functions. This fact, that the ultimate guarantee of the liberty of the Muslim is that the collective self-consciousness of the Community remains vigorously alert, confronts him with his final and most difficult obligation. The common interest of the Community requires him to join with all those of its other members who are similarly aware of their responsibilities to "strive in God's path" for its defence against external and internal enemies.

This "Holy War" (jihād fi sabīl Allāh) has naturally taken different forms in different ages. In the primitive Muslim Community of al-Madīna its dawning self-consciousness in a hostile environment dictated the policy of expansion which, combined with the warlike instincts of the Arab tribesmen incorporated into it, touched off the wars of conquest. Since the wars of expansion continued under their own momentum during the crucial first century A.H. of Islam, in which the classical formulations of Islamic institutions and the foundation of the Sharī'a were being shaped, the consequence was to concentrate the legal formulation of jihād almost exclusively on its external aspect, to the neglect of its inner aspects. These were, on the other hand, stressed by the Khārijites (see p. 181 above), but the crude violence of their methods provoked a reaction among the Sunnīs, which narrowed down and finally inhibited the active expression of this responsibility in regard to the political government of the Community. But because the dignity of Muslim citizenship was inherent in the concept of Islam itself, its exclusion from the purely political sphere did not destroy the obligation to strive for the collective self-realization of the Muslim Community, but only diverted it into other spheres of action. This became the "inner jihād" – to make Islamic society more truly Islamic and its social institutions conform to the law and ethic of Islam. It was through the continuing and conscious effort of the common body of Muslims, under the leadership of their religious teachers, that the social institutions of Islam were preserved and strengthened, despite the secularism and dismemberment of its political institutions, and that eventually, in the Ṣūfī movement (see p. 202 below), the "inner *jihād*" developed its own corporate forms of organization.

SOCIAL INSTITUTIONS

In view of its long history and the wide range of peoples who entered into the Muslim community, it is obvious that there has at all times been a greater or lesser variety in the institutions of different Muslim peoples, that the practice of the Muslims of Indonesia, for example, will in many details diverge markedly from those of Morocco, and vice versa. The institutions to be considered in this section, however, will be limited to those which are laid down, mostly in outline in the Koran and which have been developed in great detail in the *Sharī'a* – furthermore only to those which have remained within the purview or jurisdiction of the *Sharī'a* courts. As already pointed out, these were confined almost exclusively to family law, including marriage, divorce and inheritance, with the addition of certain related matters such as slavery and the vendetta. Owing to the fact of their elaboration and regulation by the *Sharī'a*, these institutions were universally regarded as included in the Revealed Law of God and were for the most part rigorously observed by all Muslim communities; and even when the common practice of one or other group diverged in certain respects from the *Sharī'a* norms or rules, the latter still continued to be looked upon as ideal.

The constitution of the nuclear family-group (husband, wife, or wives, and offspring) with mutual rights and obligations was an Islamic innovation (or at least regulated by Islam for the first time) in Arabia. The prevailing Arab system was that of the kin-group, in which all property was held in common under the general control of the patriarch. In the second place, Islam created a system of individual rights and obligations towards all other individual Muslims, in place of the tribal system, in which the interests of the clan imposed obligations upon members of the same clans, none towards other tribal groups. To a large extent, therefore, the Muslim was freed from tribal controls in respect of individual rights and responsibilities and possession of property, but the articulation of society in tribes and clans was preserved, and the continuing claims of the kin-group upon the individual were recognized, more particularly in respect of inheritance and the vendetta.

The Law endeavours to maintain a balance between the competing claims of the family-group and the kin-group, but in its final formulations (perhaps owing to the reinforcement of the tribal system resulting from the Arab conquests) leans towards the side of the kin-group. Thus it tends to strengthen the position of the husband as against the wife (who continues to belong to her father's, not her husband's, kin-group) and that of the male kin generally. But where the honour of the kin-group is concerned (and also because adultery, if proved, is a capital offence) it also protects the wife by providing the widest possible limits within which the legitimacy of children born in wedlock is recognized. A divorced mother retains the right of guardianship of her children up to the age of seven; over that age the legal schools have adopted different rulings, most of them transferring the guardianship of sons to the father and some schools that of daughters as well. Management of the property of minors, on the other hand, belongs exclusively to the father, or failing him, to other male kinsmen. Islamic law permits the adoption of children, but distinguishes them sharply from true kin, especially in the matter of inheritance.

The outstanding survival of the *patria potestas* in Islam is the right recognized to the father of giving a virgin daughter in marriage to whomsoever he pleases, and of contracting marriage for a son below the age of puberty. This power was, in all probability, an extension of the practice of arranging marriages between paternal cousins. So customary was (and still is) this form of endogamous marriage among the Arabs that (besides providing the theme of innumerable romances) a young man is regarded as having an unchallengeable first claim to marry his *bint 'amm* (father's brother's daughter), and she in turn can be divorced only at the cost of considerable scandal. In all marriages, however, the formal contracting parties are not the bridegroom and bride but the father or other male relative of each; the marriage of a woman in particular, without the intervention of a qualified male relative as *walī*, "next of kin", is invalid, and in default of a male relative the office is filled by the *qāḍī*. Marriage is prohibited between a man and his mother, daughters, sisters, aunts, nieces, son's wives, foster-sisters, foster-mother, and with a mother and her daughter or niece at the same time; but a Muslim man may marry a Christian or Jewish woman or a slave other than one belonging to himself or to his son. A Muslim woman, on the other hand, may not be married to a Christian or a Jew. The schools of law lay stress also on the principle of "equality" of the two parties, i.e. parity of rank and position, and a woman who has been married by her *walī* to one whom she regards as an unsuitable husband may institute a suit for annulment. No marriage with a free woman is valid without the securing of a dowry (*mahr*) to the bride; the lawbooks lay down a small sum as the minimum, but allow that only a portion need be paid over to her on marriage, the balance being held over until the husband dies or divorces her. As regards the legal age of marriage, the rules (or rather recommendations) of the law-schools generally agree on the attainment of puberty as the minimum age for consummation, although marriages may be contracted before then. In Sunnī Islam no limitation or time may be specified in the contract of marriage, all marriages being in principle for life, but the Shi'ites permit "temporary" marriage for a fixed period (*mut'a*), with dowry but without right of inheritance.

In family life, husband and wife retain individual rights and responsibilities. The husband is alone responsible for the maintenance of the wife (or wives) and children. The wife remains in sole possession of any property she may possess (including her dowry and her slaves), and is not required to admit her husband to any control over it, or to contribute to the household expenses, but may employ it as she will (as, for example, in trade). On the other hand, she is obliged to obey her husband's commands in matters of public and private conduct, provided that they accord with the recognized usages of her class and place of residence.

The economic independence of the wife and sole responsibility of the husband for the upkeep of the household are derived not from explicit legislation in the Koran, but as logical consequences of two privileges accorded to husbands by the Koran. One of these is his right to marry more than one wife at a time, the other the right to divorce his wife by repudiation. The Koranic sanction for the former is the verse: "If ye fear that ye may not do justly by the orphans, then marry of the women who are lawful to you in twos or threes or fours" (4. 3). The permissible limit of simultaneous marriages was thus fixed at four, this interpretation of the verse being confirmed by the practice of the Muslims of the Prophet's own generation. In the classical legal literature polygamy is represented as not merely permissible but commendable, the sole restriction being that the husband is required to place all his wives on a strictly equal footing and treat them all alike. A husband may in addition take his own female slaves as concubines, any children born to him by them being freeborn and inheriting from him on a parity with the children of his regular wives.

The right of a husband to repudiate a wife (*talāq*) by mere declaration, without the intervention of any judi-cial authority, is affirmed in passages several Koranic, none of which explicitly requires any assignment of reasons or justification. It would, in consequence, have been difficult for the later jurists to restrict this right in any way, even if they had wished to do so. But the tendency was rather in the other direction. The Koran lays down a definite procedure for repudiation, which appears designed to allow time for a reconciliation. After a first repudiation the wife may not remarry within a period of time of from three to four months (this is called her '*idda*, or period of waiting); during this period the husband may revoke the repudiation, and the marriage is resumed without a new contract, or he may remarry her later with a fresh contract. The same procedure applies after a second repudiation. But after a third repudiation the divorce is irrevocable and the marriage may not be resumed unless the divorced wife has in the meantime been married to and divorced by another husband. Shortly after the Prophet's death, however, the Caliph 'Umar (according to the received tradition) ruled that a triple repudiation made at one and the same time constituted a final and irrevocable divorce, and this ruling is accepted by all the legal schools. After an irrevocable divorce the husband remains responsible for the maintenance of the divorced wife during the period of her '*idda*, or, if she is pregnant, until her child is born.

The rights of the wife in the matter of divorce are much more severely restricted. She may not repudiate her husband by declaration, but may by agreement with him have the marriage rescinded (*khul'*) on payment of compensation to him, usually by return of her dowry. (The Mālikī school is apparently alone in holding compensation to be invalid if the cause of dissolution of the marriage is injurious treatment of the wife by the husband.) Otherwise she may apply to the courts for annulment of the marriage (*faskh*) on certain specified grounds, such as her husband's incurable disease, or failure to pay the dowry or to maintain her, or second marriage with a slave-girl, but this provision seems to have been largely inoperative. One method for the protection of the wife, very commonly adopted in modern times, was to insert in the marriage contract various stipulations, on any breach of which the husband bound himself to divorce her. A stipulation that the husband should not marry another wife, however, though nowadays regarded as valid, was by the classical jurists held to be invalid, on the ground that it contravened a right expressly granted by the Koran.

Closely bound up with the whole subject of marital rights is the practice of the seclusion and veiling of women. The Koran (33. 59) commands the wives and daughters of the Prophet and the wives of Believers to wear veils out of doors in order that they may not be exposed to molestation, but a later passage (24. 31) does not explicitly require "believing women" to veil their faces. The law-schools generally prescribe veiling, since what was commanded for the Prophet's wives could clearly be regarded as the desirable practice for all married women. But to some extent the question of "recognized usages" also entered in, and while in certain countries these might prohibit a married woman from even leaving her house without her husband's permission, or from shopping in the public bazaars even if veiled, in other places or among other peoples or classes the veil might be partially or wholly discarded. On the whole veiling was most rigidly observed in the cities, where public order and morality were seldom of the highest, and seems to have been as much insisted on by the women themselves, as a means of protection and mark of respectability, as demanded of them by orthodox opinion. The rules of inheritance are among those which are laid down with the greatest precision in the Koran. They are somewhat complicated, and provided later Muslim lawyers with an intricate field for legal specialization. The main principle is that the inheritance is equally divided among the sons and daughters (each daughter receiving half the share of a son), after the subtraction of certain "obligatory quotas" (*farā'iḍ*) to father and mother and wife or wives, and payment of debts. Failing sons, it passes to son's sons, brothers, and other agnatic relatives. Daughter's sons and cognate relatives are admitted only by the Shī'ites. No person may alienate by will more than one third of his property, excluding debts, nor may any portion of this third be willed to a legal heir (with some exceptions in Shī'ite law). Muslims may not inherit from Jews or Christians, and vice versa. The prescriptive rights of agnatic kin are further protected by the rule that they may, on application to the courts, restrain a spendthrift or unbalanced relative from dilapidation of his property.

With inheritance is associated also the constitution of endowments (*awqāf*; sing. *waqf*). These are in principle assignments of immovable property of all kinds to charitable objects, from the upkeep of mosques and *madrasas* or religious schools (for which no responsibility was assumed by the State) to the paving of streets and the provision of corn for birds. They must be constituted in perpetuity and registered in the courts; the founder may devote to them any portion of his property that he wishes during his lifetime, but only the disposable third if they are constituted by testament, and he is entitled to appoint the superintendent of the endowment, who enjoys a portion of the income. Since, however, the founder's family was included among legitimate charitable objects, a large number of endowments were in fact family trusts, by which the fortunes of the family were protected to some extent from seizure, and the strict provisions of the law of inheritance were evaded. In later times, lands could be bestowed only with the permission of the sovereign; nevertheless, in different periods and countries the snowball-like growth of charitable and family *waqfs* so clogged the natural economy that the balance could be restored only by periodical confiscation or abolition of all *waqfs*.

Since the Koran, like the other Scriptures, recognizes the institution of slavery, the status, duties and rights of slaves were also regulated by the schools of law. The Koranic basis of their regulations amounts to little more than a few casual phrases, and the liberalizing tendency which they generally exhibit is more frequently ascribed to traditions and recommendations of the Prophet. It was, however, again 'Umar who established the principle that no Muslim could be enslaved, thus abolishing the practices of selling children for debt and of enslaving captives taken in war, unless they were unbelievers. The only persons, therefore, who could be legally enslaved were non-Muslims captured in hostile territory. In Islamic legal theory all men are presumed to be free, except such captives and the children of slave parents. The slave is the absolute property of his master, who may sell him, give him away, or bequeath him, and whose permission he requires to marry. But the law lays great stress on manumission, whether by his owner's free act, or as an expiation for misdeeds, or by contract (whereby the slave may earn money by handicraft or in business and buy his freedom). On emancipation, the freed slave and his descendants become "clients" of his late master, i.e. remain attached to his kin-group, this relationship carrying with it certain mutual rights and duties.

The great majority of slaves, both male and female, were household slaves, although industrial and agricultural slavery were not uncommon. The most remarkable slave-institution in Islam, however, was the slave-army, constituted usually of white slaves (*mamlūks*) and mainly of Turks from Central Asia. After passing through a rigorous training (religious as well as military), the military slave was manumitted as he rose to higher ranks, and the most successful were appointed to governorships and high administrative offices. Not infrequently they became independent and founded dynasties of their own, of which the most famous were the slave kings of Delhi and the *Mamlūk* Sultanate in Egypt (1258–1519). The same system was followed by the Ottoman Sultans in their recruitment of the celebrated Janissaries (*Yenicheri*) from their Greek subjects in the Balkans. From the sixteenth century A.D. no Ottoman Sultan was married to a free woman.

Finally there are two other institutions which are more or less regulated by the *Sharī'a*. Male circumcision (*ṭahāra*), though not mentioned in the Koran, has from early times been regarded by Muslims as one of the essential symbols of adherence to Islam, presumably because it was not practised by Christians, Persians or Indians. The Shāfi'ite school is the only one which makes it obligatory; nevertheless, it is universal except among a few outlying groups. It was customarily performed before boys reached the age of puberty, the occasion being one of much ceremony and festive celebration on the part of the family. Female circumcision, although regarded by the law-schools as commendable, has been much less universally practised and almost, indeed, confined to Arabian, Egyptian and African Islam, where it accords with or reinforces traditional usages.

The vendetta (*tha'r*) was a tribal institution of great antiquity and of immense strength, since it alone made human life possible in the desert. The Koran explicitly recognizes that fact, but sets limits to its operation. The male next-of-kin (*walī*) of a slain person has the right to avenge his killing, but only upon the actual slayer, and the Koran adds (as often in its legislative passages) a recommendation to mercy. There was consequently disagreement among the legal schools as to whether a *walī* might or might not accept blood-money in the case of deliberate homicide. The Ḥanafī school alone maintained in principle the doctrine of a life for a life (except when the person slain is son or slave of the slayer); the other schools recognized degrees of standing, so that vengeance could not be exacted upon a Muslim for the murder of a non-Muslim or a slave. Accidental slaying, however, should in no case give a claim to retaliation, but only to blood-money (*diya*), for payment of which a certain group of the slayer's agnatic kindred are collectively responsible. The value of the blood-money for a free man was assessed on the basis of a hundred camels or a thousand sheep, and for other persons on a comparative scale. The same principle was applied to compensation for mutilations and minor injuries, if the right of retaliation should be forgone by the injured person or was inapplicable. For crimes against property, the Koran prescribes amputation of the hand of the thief, whether male or female. Though this rule could not be formally rescinded, the Ḥanafī school, at least, in later times permitted the substitution of monetary penalties for theft also. For most other infractions of the law, the prescribed penalty is beating,

often supplemented by discretionary punishments on the part of the authorities. Only for proven adultery and apostasy was the death penalty mandatory.

THEOLOGY AND DOGMATICS

The elaboration of doctrine and a scholastic theology was a relatively late development in Islam. Simple unspeculative piety and fear of God (*taqwā*), together with the performance of the ritual obligations, sufficed the earlier generations, and even through later centuries a succession of influential religious teachers continued to disapprove of and to discourage all speculative and scholastic theology. What is explicitly stated in the Koran is to be accepted "without asking 'How?'" (*bilā kayf*). The themes which it stresses again and again are the Oneness of God, the sole divinity in relation to man, one in his nature, the only Real and Eternal, his unlimited sovereignty over his entire creation, especially the human creation, his omniscience and omnipotence, his mercy, forgiveness and beneficence, and the imminence of the Day of Judgment on which God, as Judge, will assign, in his sovereign will, mankind to Heaven or Hell, the joys and pains of which are portrayed in vivid imagery. The angels are his celestial servants and messengers, and the prophets through whom he conveys his revelation to men are but mortal men. But although in his revelation he uses in relation to himself terms applicable to human beings and their actions (such as face, hands, speaking, hearing, sitting on the Throne), these are not to be understood in their human meanings and contexts – "there is nothing that is like unto him" (*Koran*, 112. 4). His nature is inaccessible to men and his acts are inscrutable. He is "the First and the Last, the Manifest and the Hidden" (*ibid.*, 57. 3) yet he is "closer to man than his own neck vein" (*ibid.*, 50. 15), and "the light of the heavens and of the earth" (*ibid.*, 24. 35). He creates by the command "Be!" (*ibid.*, 6. 72, etc.). He "turns astray whom he will and guides aright whom he will" (*ibid.*, 16. 95, etc.) and gives authority to the leader of the evil spirits, *Shaiṭān* or Satan, to seduce those of mankind who reject his signs (*ibid.*, 15. 42).

It is in keeping with what has been said above on the origins of the sects that the first issue of dogmatics that arose in Islam related to membership of the Community. The Khārijites maintained that the Believer who committed a sin and did not repent became thereby an unbeliever, an apostate, and was excluded from the Community. The more extreme groups of the Shī'a held that only those were true Muslims who recognized the true Imām of the House of 'Alī. The beginnings of dogmatic theology among the Sunnīs are almost all confined to a statement of the "orthodox" positions against such sectarian views and opinions. But in the second century A.H., in consequence largely of the confrontation of Islam with the Hellenistic culture and popular Gnosticism of Western Asia, these same issues led straight into the heart of the theological problems.

Already there had arisen the problem of faith and works. Granted that the Khārijite insistence on the sole criterion of works is to be rejected, is faith alone sufficient, irrespective of works? This was the teaching of the political conformists, the *Murjī'a*, who held that the dividing line between believer and unbeliever was known to God alone, and must be left to his decision at the Judgment, because the Koran declares that all man's actions are predestined and created by God. Does God then create evil actions in men, and punish or reward them for the actions which he himself has created in them? The more puritan wing pointed to a string of Koranic verses which proclaim human responsibility and declare that men will be recompensed at the Judgment according to their works and their deserts; man is therefore free to choose for himself, and does so by the power which God has created in him. This was the doctrine of the Qadarites, the "Abilitarians", as against the absolute Predestinarians.

At the beginning of the second century A.H. (about A.D. 720), a group of Qadarites "separated themselves" to take up a neutral position on the question whether a Muslim who committed flagrant sin was a believer or an unbeliever; he was, they held, not to be described by either term, but as a "reprobate". From their "separation" they acquired the name of *Mu'tazila*, and it was in their circle that the beginnings arose of an apologetic or scholastic theology, called in Arabic *Kalām* or "discussion". The origins of the *Kalām* are not yet clear, but it seems evident that it was primarily directed against two kinds of opposition. On the one hand, it aimed at asserting the unity and creatorhood of God against non-Muslim opponents, dualists of various kinds, sceptics, and the Hellenistic philosophy which maintained the eternity of the world. On the other hand, it maintained and developed the Qadarite doctrine of human freedom against its Muslim opponents, and seems to have aimed, in principle at least, at closing the gap between Sunnīs and Shī'ites. The Mu'tazila therefore called themselves "the supporters of Unitarianism and Divine Justice".

It was probably in connection with the Mu'tazila, and to serve the needs of their apologetic, that the work of translating Greek philosophical works was begun. A considerable impulse was given to this work by the Caliph al-Ma'mūn, who not only declared himself in favour of the Mu'tazilite doctrine but gave it the support of the civil power, and who set up a "House of Wisdom" (*Bait al-Ḥikma*) in Baghdad about A.D. 820 in order to organize the production of translations. Inevitably, however, the Mu'tazilites themselves became increasingly influenced by Greek philosophy in their *Kalām*, and all the more easily since many of their materials were derived, not from the original works of the Greek philosophers, but from the later commentaries and interpretations of the philosophical schools of Egypt and Asia, which had already harmonized philosophy with Christian theism.

The first objective of the new *Kalām* was to prove by rational argument the existence of God and his sole Creatorship. On this they stood on the universal Muslim positions. The Koran is at one with reason in asserting the contingent and temporal nature of the universe; from this reason deduces the necessary existence of a Creator, eternally self-subsistent. The impossibility of postulating more than one Creator is based on the unity and order of the universe, reinforced by the Koranic argument that this order would be destroyed if there were more than one God. But when it came to defining the nature of God's unity, the Mu'tazila found themselves compelled to oppose the anthropomorphism of the ordinary Muslim, in respect of God's attributes. The Koranic passages which refer to God's hands or bodily movements must be interpreted figuratively, and the attributes of hearing, seeing, etc., are not to be accepted as separate realities, but are "identical with his essence". The concept of God must be purified from every shadow of createdness or occasionalism – otherwise the attributes may be expanded into separate hypostases, and the unity of God endangered.

It seems reasonably clear that the Mu'tazila, taking their philosophical rationalism seriously, were fully aware of the real problems involved in a thoroughgoing monotheism. The only way, however, by which they could meet them was by such processes of interpretation or negation; and by the traditionalist theologians these were regarded as emptying the concept of God of all positive content, in striking contrast to the doctrine of the Koran. The controversy between the two schools inevitably declined from the high philosophic plane to concentrate on two attributes, those of "visibility" and "speech". The former involved the question of interpretation, the latter the question of the nature of the attributes.

The Koran declares that among the rewards enjoyed

Photo: Exclusive News Agency

PLATE 47. The Sultan Hasan Mosque and Madrasa, Cairo, with a sugar cane market outside its walls.

PLATE 48. Marble inlay and lattice work from the tomb of Ittimad-ud-Dowlah, Agra, India.

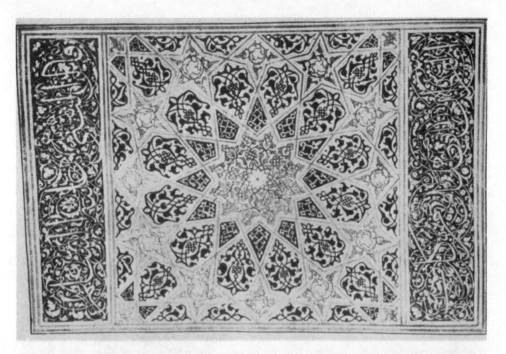

Photo: Arthur Upham Pope

PLATE 49. Decorative pages from sections of a Koran: written by ʿAbd Allah ibn Muhammad ibn Mahmūd al-Hamadhānī in Hamadan for Oljeitu Khudābanda, 713 H. (1313.)(*Royal Egyptian Library, Cairo*)

193

PLATE 50. Miniature of a preacher in a mosque: Muhammad preaching his farewell sermon, from al-Athār al Bāqīya by Al-Bīrūnī, dated 707 H. (1307–8 A.D.). (*Edinburgh University Library, Edinburgh*)

PLATE 51. Miniature of the Annunciation, Persian School of painting: in Rashīd-ad-Dīn, Jāmi ʿat, Tawārikh, dated 714 H. (1314 A.D.). Folio 9, Koran III, 42–47. (*Edinburgh University Library, Edinburgh*)

Photo: Edinburgh University Library

PLATE 52. A Mihrab in the Alhambra, Granada.

Photo: Austrian National Library

PLATE 53. Title page of Panegyric of the prophet by Al Busīri.
(*Austrian National Library, Vienna*)

PLATE 54. Islamic slip-painted vase. (*Victoria and Albert Museum, London*)

by the blessed in Paradise will be the joy of seeing their Lord. Simple believers accepted this, as they accepted all the other descriptions of Paradise, in the literal sense of seeing God with their own eyes. But to the Mu'tazila any belief of this kind constituted the climax of gross anthropomorphism, since it involved representing God as an object situated and bounded in space. The Koranic passage could not, in their view, be so interpreted, and the words must be taken as metaphorical imagery, the literal phrase "looking at their Lord" therefore meaning "looking for the bounty of their Lord".

The second problem, relating to the attribute of Speech, was complicated by the doctrine of the verbal inspiration of the Koran. If the Koran is the Speech of God, how is it to be related to God's eternal Being? Since it had been revealed in time, the Mu'tazila placed it among the "contingent" attributes, and regarded it as a "created" Speech, corresponding to God's "contingent" knowledge of the free actions of men.

To both of these Mu'tazilite positions the pious orthodox reacted violently. The Vision of God and the Uncreated Koran became and remained the slogans of anti-Mu'tazilite polemic, but it took nearly a century before the orthodox realized that reasoned arguments must be met not by slogans but by reasoned arguments on the other side. Early in the fourth century A.H. (about A.D. 920) there emerged the beginnings of an "orthodox *Kalām*", associated with the names of al-Ash'arī of Baghdad and al-Māturīdī of Samarqand. Methodologically it took over, as was inevitable, many of the bases of the Mu'tazilite *Kalām*, but it rejected the Mu'tazilite claim to establish human reason as the ultimate criterion of religious truth. True, the blessed will not see God in Paradise as a spatially-defined Being, but they will see him nevertheless, in some manner which human reason and experience cannot specify. True, the Koran, as a written book and as recited by human agency, is created, but its quality as the Speech of God is the same as that of the other attributes, existing in his Essence and therefore uncreated. True, there are in the Koran a number of anthropomorphic metaphors, but they express actions or attributes of which we, as human beings, can know neither the nature nor the manner, and they are not to be wished away by simple or laborious philological exercises or conceits.

Much of this early orthodox theology, it will be seen, still remains on the traditional ground of "without asking 'How?'". Even so, however, it was bitterly assailed by large sections of the Muslim populace, who distrusted its element of intellectualism and clung to the old unspeculative faith. The "followers of al-Ash'arī" and the "followers of Ibn Ḥanbal" became rival factions in Baghdad, to the extent of public demonstrations and riots, and for some two centuries it seems probable that the *mutakallimūn*, the practitioners of the *Kalām*, were confined to relatively small schools in different centres. In such circumstances it would be vain to expect any great elaboration or development of theological activity, but little by little, especially through controversy with the *falāsifa* or followers of Greek philosophy, the philosophical expression of orthodox theology was refined and improved, more particularly in respect of the problem of the attributes (which, in opposition to the Mu'tazila, all orthodox schools defined as existing "in" the divine Essence, although with some differences on their relation to the Essence).

The principal Mu'tazilite thesis, however, the affirmation of human freedom, had still remained without an orthodox refutation on the plane of theological argument. The Mu'tazila, it will be recalled, had asserted that the concept of divine justice requires, as its corollary, a power in men to choose their actions. This power, in their developed view, was created by God in man once and for all, not occasionally, and God's knowledge of men's actions is therefore contingent. Furthermore, good and evil exist in the nature of things, and can be known by reason before any revelation of the divine Law; also, since God has created the universe with a fixed order, reason can distinguish a chain of secondary causes which produce effects according to that natural order. God does not will evil, nor does he order it (his will and command being identical), but evil is willed and done by men; and some of them went so far as to assert that God is bound by his own nature to do always that which is best.

To the orthodox the whole of this argument seemed to relegate God to the position of an impersonal "First Cause". Does not the Koran insist, again and again, that nothing escapes the power of God, that he bestows his favour on whom he will, that he "guides whom he wills and turns astray whom he wills", and that it is he who created men and creates all that they do? Is it not presumptuous to seek to justify him and his doings in terms of human reason, or to assert that he is bound by human ideas of good and evil? In their reaction the pious believers, followed by the Ash'arites, swung towards an extreme insistence on the absolute omnipotence of God. Nothing whatsoever exists, or can exist, save by his Will and Decree. The moral qualities of good and evil are determined by him and known to men only through his revelation; if he chooses to reverse them, reversed they would be. To ascribe to men power over their own acts would involve recognizing a creative agency other than

God's and capable of opposing God's will. Similarly, there can be no secondary causes which effectively produce results of themselves; the so-called result is created anew by God on each and every occasion. The whole creation is discontinuous, not a coherent fabric but recreated at every instant of time. Its appearance of continuity and regularity and the consequent assumption that certain events will follow upon other events is due to God's mercy in establishing a regular "custom", which, according to the Koran, he does not change – but which he may on occasion modify, as when he allows "miracles" to occur as the proof of the missions of his Prophets. Most Ash'arites went on to underpin this doctrine by expounding an atomistic theory, according to which everything is no more than a concourse of "atoms", continually reconnected and readjusted by the Divine Decree.

The bearing of the whole Ash'arite argument on the question of human freedom is obvious. Since everything is existentialized in its momentary form only by God's creation, the idea that anything can come into existence as a "consequence" of human action is an illusion. Every action and its so-called "consequence" exists only by God's decree, which brings into being in the realm of time that which he had determined from all eternity according to his eternal will. Belief and unbelief, piety and impiety, are predestined and come from God. What room, then, is left for the repeated Koranic teaching that in the future life every man will be rewarded or punished in the measure of his works? To meet this dilemma, the Ash'arite school, following, apparently, a hint dropped by al-Ash'arī himself, fastened on a Koranic phrase: "Every man will be retributed for what he has acquired" (52. 21). Every man, therefore, will indeed be rewarded or punished according to his predestined actions, but in virtue of his participation in them by "acquisition" (kasb). In so far as this is more than a merely verbal accommodation, it would seem to imply that on the psychological level man continues to act as if he were free, and thus, though in reality acting of necessity, "acquires" the responsibility for his acts and their attribution to himself.

This has remained ever since the official doctrine of Sunnī Islam. Many theologians, it is true, were dissatisfied with it, some shifting the ground of predestination from God's will to his knowledge and interposing a created "capacity to act" (istiṭā'a) before the "acquisition" of the action, some seeing in human disobedience an "abandonment" by God of man to himself. But the common body of Muslims, whether scholastic theologians or simple believers who opposed or looked with

suspicion on the introduction of intellectual reasoning into matters of faith, continued and still continues to hold firmly to the belief in predestination, while at the same time acting as if they were free agents, with the power to choose and the responsibility for what follows on their choice. The Ash'arite doctrine, in the last resort, is simply an attempt to rationalize the common attitude, and owes to this fact, not to its superior demonstrative force, its victory over the Mu'tazilite argument.

At the same time the Ash'arite theology preserved, in agreement with the intuitive feeling of the ordinary Muslim, the element of mystery inseparable from the reverent acceptance of the will of God. The Mu'tazilites had tried to explain too much. The visible world and its "laws" were not everything; there was also an invisible world outside time and space, where events took place which prefigured and conditioned events on the human scale, and where the apparent contradictions of the latter were resolved. So the whole theme of human responsibility was bound up with the scene of the "Covenant" (mīthāq) related in the Koran, in which the race of men in a pre-eternal existence bound themselves to the worship of and obedience to God:

"And when thy Lord took from the children of Adam, from their loins, their seed, and made them testify concerning themselves, 'Am I not your Lord?' they said, 'Yea, we testify'." (7. 171.).

To the Mu'tazila this was a metaphor, but to the orthodox a firm unchallengeable reality, even if situated outside historical time; and for the later Ṣūfīs in particular the theme of the "Covenant" and its implications were to prove of the greatest significance.

Orthodox theology might well have remained at this stage had it not had other opponents with whom to contend. These were, on the one hand, the Shī'ites, more especially the extreme Shī'a, the Ismā'īlīs or Bāṭinīs (followers of the esoteric interpretation of the Koran), and on the other hand the falāsifa, the disciples of Hellenistic philosophy, represented especially by Avicenna (Ibn Sīnā) and Averroes (Ibn Rushd). Their argument with the former related largely to the spiritual, as well as temporal, government of the community, but also became involved with cosmology, as a result of the connections between Ismā'īlī theology and Neo-Platonist philosophy.

Apart from the philosophical issues already raised in the controversy with the Mu'tazila, there were three theses maintained by the falāsifa (with more or less diversity in detail) which more especially offended pious

Muslim sentiment. In briefest outline these were (in ascending order of offence) the eternity of the world, the denial of the resurrection of the body, and the exaltation of philosophy over prophecy. The first, although not necessarily excluding the doctrine of creation for the philosophical mind, to the ordinary Muslim detracted from the uniquely eternal Being of the One God. The second, in maintaining that only through the soul does the individual personality survive death, ran counter to the explicit teaching of the Koran; but what more probably incurred the deepest wrath of the theologians was the condescending attitude of the philosophers to the Koranic descriptions of Paradise and Hell. The only real happiness of the blessed in the hereafter is in the exercise of intellectual contemplation; as for the "baser sorts of celestial happiness", they are only images which correspond and appeal to base souls, although no doubt they furnish the only means by which the mass of mankind may be moved to the pursuit of virtue. So likewise the "torment of the grave", the common Muslim belief (although without explicit Koranic authority) that the souls of men are questioned in the tomb by the two angels Munkar and Nakīr, and recompensed by physical torment or ease until all are summoned on the Day of Judgment – this too was explained by the *falāsifa* as a parabolic expression for the experience of the soul after death.

The third of the philosophers' theses went far towards undermining the whole foundation of Muslim theology and law. If, as they claimed, prophecy and divination were connected with an innate imaginative faculty in the human soul, not the product of inspiration by a supernatural power, if prophecy were no more than auxiliary to the rational faculty, then the final and unique authority of revelation was destroyed. The arguments presented by the philosophers themselves pointed in the same direction; they might possibly, and did, cite the Koran and argue that, when properly understood and applied by qualified scholars, there was no contradiction between reason and revelation; but the theologians could see clearly enough that for them the Koran took second place to the postulates of Greek philosophy. Their God was not the perpetually active Will which at every moment governs the universe and the actions of men, but a remote intelligence, from which, through the intermediary of the Active Intellect, the world is necessarily produced and governed by a series of successive emanations. At this point the heresy of the philosophers linked up with the heresy of the Ismāʿīlīs; although the philosophers for their part rejected any union of the human mind with the Active Intellect, the

Ismāʿīlīs, in taking over the theory of emanations, developed it along Gnostic lines, and with much use of far-fetched esoteric interpretation of the Koran, to bring their Imāms into direct connection with the Active Intellect and to confer on them a divine authority.

So far as classical theology was concerned, the decisive counterblast to both philosophy and Ismāʿīlism was delivered by the great theologian al-Ghazālī (d. 1111). Point by point, in his scathing "Incoherence of the Philosophers" (*Tahāfut al-Falāsifa*), he displays the conjectural and discordant bases of their theories, and re-establishes the faith on the reasonableness of the Koranic revelation, in so far as human reason may be admitted into the controversy. It was more probably, however, less by the brilliance of his refutation that philosophy and esotericism were overcome than by the simultaneous development and expansion of a new and organized system of Sunnī education, which gradually dried up the roots of free intellectual activity, and congealed Islamic theology in a stereotyped orthodox scholasticism. The new type of *madrasa*, the first example of which was founded by the vizier Niẓām al-Mulk in Baghdad about 1070, spread rapidly through Western Asia and thence into all the Muslim lands. By the fourteenth century A.D., these colleges were numbered by the dozens in all great cities, and they monopolized the higher education of the upper classes who manned the bureaucracy, as well as of the members of the religious profession. Their programmes of studies were practically uniform, and confined to Arabic philology, Koran and Prophetic Tradition, orthodox law and theology, all based upon standard textbooks.

Yet the grip of the *madrasa* was not total, and two sectors of Islamic life and thought in particular remained beyond its control. One of these was the surviving body of Shīʿites, not now of the more extreme Ismāʿīlī wing, but of the more moderate Imāmī and Zaidī sects. The former, called also the *Ithnāʿasharī* or "Twelver" Shīʿites, had, since the disappearance of the twelfth Imām, a descendant of ʿAlī in the tenth generation, about 874, regarded him as the "awaited Mahdī" who will reappear in the latter days. In the interval the leadership of the Imāmī community was invested in the heads of the religious profession, called *Mujtahids*. Under their guidance, Shīʿite law and theology developed independently of the Sunnī community; first formulated in a group of standard works about the year 1000, they were given final form after the establishment of Shīʿism as the state religion of Persia in 1500 and the development of Shīʿite *madrasas* in Persia and Iraq. The Zaidīs, who have maintained themselves in the highlands of Yemen for the last thousand years, differ from the Imāmīs mainly in their belief in the existence of a continuing visible Imāmate in the house of 'Alī.

On the main heads of theological doctrine neither the Imāmīs nor the Zaidīs differ greatly from the Sunnis, except on the one subject of human freedom and responsibility. Both of them stand in this respect somewhat closer to the Mu'tazila. Human reason is competent to determine good and evil, except in such matters of religious obligation as are defined by revelation. Men do not themselves possess the power to create actions, which belongs to God alone, but they are invested by God with a volition whereby they may choose to do good or evil actions, and thus become liable to reward or punishment in the future life.

SŪFISM

The second, and much larger, group in Islamic society which escaped almost wholly from the domination of the *madrasa* were the Ṣūfīs. Since Ṣūfism is essentially the pursuit of spiritual experience by bodily discipline and mystical intuition, it is peculiarly resistant to any kind of systematic treatment. Especially is this the case in respect of the early Ṣūfīs, who were isolated or small groups of individuals, not necessarily associated with any of the rival legal or theological parties in Islam, and often indeed in open or latent opposition to them.

There can be little doubt that in its origins, Ṣūfism was influenced by the traditions of monastic asceticism and mysticism in Western Asia and Egypt. (The name itself is derived from the monastic tradition of wearing garments of wool, *ṣūf*.) It would not be strange, therefore, to find that the content or ideas of many mystical vocations were equally influenced by Christian, Gnostic, Hermetic, or Buddhist traditions. Yet all this was clearly secondary. The main impulse arose out of primitive Islamic asceticism, governed by the eschatology of the Koran and the fear of Hell, and passing into a positive search for God, then into the quest of the mystical experience of oneness with God. This too could find and claim Koranic sanction in a number of passages in the Sacred Book, which asserts, for example, that God is "closer to man than his own neck vein" (50. 15) and presents him as saying:"I am near to answer the call of the caller when he calls to me" (2. 182). But the characteristic tendency of the mystic to disregard outward conformity with the rules of law, and the theopathic utterances of some in the state of trance made mysticism as such obnoxious or even detestable to the orthodox. In 922 an example was made by the execution (for his

assertion "I am the Truth") of the most notorious of the theosophists, al-Ḥusain ben Manṣūr al-Ḥallāj, who became in consequence the patron saint of a whole school of Persian Ṣūfīs.

Not all Ṣūfīs, however, shared these extravagances. In Baghdad especially a movement of orthodox Ṣūfism, initiated about the same time by al-Junaid, insisted that no man could be a true Ṣūfī unless he held firmly to the Koran and the *sunna* of the Prophet. It was through the tradition of this school that the eventual reconciliation of Ṣūfism with orthodoxy was achieved, chiefly through the influence of the same al-Ghazālī who had delivered the decisive blow against the philosophers. Convinced by his own experience that mere intellectual apprehension of the truths of religion was insufficient, al-Ghazālī placed himself under the discipline of the Ṣūfī "path" and found in it the gateway to true knowledge of God. At the same time, his second experience as a Ṣūfī novice warned him of the greater dangers of purely imaginative intuition; without the guidance of sound orthodox learning, the mystic, instead of attaining the true goal, might sink in a morass of fantasies. For the simple believer, therefore, the orthodox path of obedience to the Law was the safer one.

But already it was too late to attempt to impose on Ṣūfism the kind of control which could be exerted through the *madrasa* on intellectual heresy. The encouragement of Ṣūfism among the masses had become, perhaps only half consciously, the policy of the orthodox authorities as the means of weaning them away from Shī'ite and other heresies; and the transference of political authority from the Persian and the Arab to the Turk and the Berber favoured the introduction into the heart of Islam of their traditional religious institutions under a thinly Islamic guise. These two factors went far towards changing the whole character of Ṣūfism. Hitherto, as has been noted previously, it was the vocation of a relatively small number of individuals. The original mystic was usually a solitary, frequently taking up his abode in the corner-chamber (*zāwiya*) of a mosque. He taught his spiritual discipline or "path" (*tarīqa*) to a small number of disciples, who in due course initiated others. Thus there grew up a number of "chains" of spiritual affiliation (*silsila*), by which the doctrine taught to the postulant (*murīd*) was authenticated by its transmission through an unbroken series of *shaikhs* back to the original teacher, and behind him (more artificially) through a further series of early Muslim personalities back to one of the Companions of the Prophet, most frequently to 'Alī. The theological content of this doctrine was usually small (being for the most part formally identical with pious, but not scholastic, orthodoxy), and its especial feature was its method of spiritual discipline and the particular formula of invocation (*dhikr*) to be employed by the disciples in solitary meditation or when they met together for religious exercises. Already before the time of al-Ghazālī, various adjuncts had been introduced into many of such seances for the purpose of intensifying the psychological effect of continual repetition of the *dhikr* and inducing the absorption of the participants into the Infinite. Of these adjuncts, the one which roused the strongest opposition of the orthodox was the use of musical instruments, and the lawfulness of the "spiritual concert" (*samā'*) continued to form the subject of a violent polemical literature for many centuries – without, however, affecting the attitude and practice of the Ṣūfīs in any way.

When, therefore, it became the policy of the authorities to encourage the spread of Ṣūfism, most of the institutional ingredients were already present. Together with and often alongside the new *madrasas*, Sultans, viziers and other wealthy persons built and endowed convents for the housing of Ṣūfī *shaikhs* and their disciples, and notable *shaikhs* built their own out of the gifts that poured in on them from every side. These convents, still called by the name of *zāwiya* or by the Persian term *khāngāh*, were often of immense size; out of their revenues some could maintain not only the initiates themselves but also their wives and families (for the adoption of the mystical way in no way implied the practice of celibacy, even if many were celibate from choice). They became the centres of spiritual life not only for the inmates but for the whole district or region in which they were situated, attracting to themselves a numerous following amongst all classes of the population.

The wide diffusion of Ṣūfism almost of itself involved the next development. Unlike orthodoxy, which sets all Believers on the same level and makes each individual responsible for his own spiritual life and salvation, Ṣūfism from the first was a form of Gnosis, the transmission to initiates of a particular doctrine, not necessarily or in principle esoteric, but by which its practitioners were distinguished from the general body of the Community. Each Ṣūfī group constituted an *ekklesia*, a "church", and its organization was of necessity hierarchic, the disciple or *murīd* surrendering himself wholly to the will and direction of his *shaikh*. Each new *khāngāh* had as its *shaikh* an initiate who had been a disciple, at first, second or third remove, of some celebrated *shaikh*, and followed his *tarīqa* ("path"). Gradually, therefore, as *khāngāhs* were multiplied, they were enrolled as offshoots

or daughter-houses of the mother-convent, the original convent of the *shaikh* who had initiated the *tarīqa*, and remained under the obedience of the "prior" of the mother-convent, himself frequently a lineal descendant of the founder. By the thirteenth and fourteenth centuries A.D. "regular" Ṣūfism was represented by the convents and "lodges" of affiliates of a few great *tarīqas* (usually translated as "orders" or "brotherhoods"), with branches in many different countries. In course of time, as they spread ever more widely, most of the "orders" were divided into "sub-orders", founded by eminent *shaikhs* who modified in some respect the original rituals of their parent "orders". The most widely spread was the Qādirī (named after 'Abd al-Qādir al-Gīlānī of Baghdad, d. 1166), followed by the Rifā'ī (from Aḥmad al-Rifā'ī of Iraq, d. 1183), the Shādhilī in North Africa, Egypt and Arabia (from Abu'l-Ḥasan al-Shādhilī of Morocco, d. 1258), the Suhrawardī (from 'Umar al-Suhrawardī of Baghdad, d. 1234) and Chishtī (from Mu'īn al-Dīn Chishtī of Sīstān, d. 1236) in Persia and India, the Naqshbandī (from Bahā' al-Dīn Naqshband, d. 1389), and the Mevlevi (from the Persian mystic and poet Jalal al-Dīn al-Rumī, called *Maulānā*, d. 1273) in Turkey. Of the hundred or so of later "orders" and "sub-orders", the most notable were the Khalwetī in the Ottoman Empire, the Tījānī in North and West Africa, and the Shī'ite Ṣafavī order, which established the rule of the Safavid Shāhs in Persia in 1500.

But the "regular" orders by no means represented the whole extent of the Ṣūfī movement. Outside the range of the urban centres, and especially among the nomadic Turks and the Berbers, as well as among the rural population generally, local preachers created their own congregations of followers; some of these, favoured by circumstances, also acquired a vast, though still localized, range of influence. The most famous is the Bektāshī order (named from an obscure Ḥājjī Bektāsh), to which the Janissaries were affiliated in the Ottoman Empire. The most marked characteristic of the "rustic" orders was not so much in their deviation of ritual from the "regular" orders as in the extent to which they reflected or admitted inherited customs or traditional beliefs of the rural populations and the converts from other religions in the more recently acquired Islamic territories in the Balkans, India, and South-East Asia. However much the orthodox might deplore their superstitions, they were as a rule too powerful or too deeply rooted in their regions to be forcibly reformed, and the only recourse open to the orthodox was to rely upon the gradual influence of Muslim education and environment in the course of successive generations. In North-West Africa, the Berber tradition expressed itself in another deviant form. The efficient principle in all forms of Ṣūfism was the veneration or "worship" of saints as intercessors, but whereas elsewhere the saints were so "worshipped" only after death, it was a particular feature of Berber Islam to venerate their "holy men" (marabouts) during their lifetime.

The term Ṣūfī (generally replaced in later centuries by faqīr, "poor brother", or its Persian equivalent darwesh/dervīsh) applied strictly only to the shaikhs and their initiated disciples. In addition to these, however, the convents and local branches of the orders served as centres for the religious instruction and spiritual exercises of the surrounding population. These were the "affiliates" already referred to, who might be called "lay members" of the respective orders. By a process not yet fully clear, lay-membership of particular orders was often integrated, especially in the cities, with the guild organizations of the different crafts and occupations, the local members of each guild forming a "lodge" affiliated to their own order. The social consequences of this coordination of economic and religious organizations were immense. The orthodox religious institutions, particularly the services in the mosque, were, to be sure, regularly observed; but the vital force of Islam as a religion was largely, and in some regions wholly, diverted into the channel of the rival Ṣūfī institutions.

For, notwithstanding the "reconciliation" effected by al-Ghazālī, rivals they continued to be in almost everything but outer form, and probably only the simple native piety of the masses prevented the recurrent polemics between theologian and mystic from leading to open breaches. With the recognition and growing domination of the Ṣūfīs, the theosophical elements which had persisted among them from the beginning began to find freer and more audacious expression. Not all Ṣūfīs were theosophists; the Qādirīs and Shādhilīs in particular remained on the whole closely attached to orthodoxy and even cultivated the kalām. But the commoner tendency was to regard the kalām, with its intellectualism and logical arguments for the truth of theological doctrines, as an obstacle to the attainment of direct spiritual experience. Al-Ghazālī's warning of the dangers attendant on imaginative intuition, when not corrected or held in balance by sound orthodox learning, was disregarded and the consequences that he feared soon began to show themselves. What was called taṣawwuf, the practice of the purgative "way" of the Ṣūfīs, became a doctrine, or rather a group of doctrines, taught in the convents and with a growing literature of their own, hardly to be reconciled with orthodox theology.

Of these new systems of Ṣūfī dogmatics, the one which gained the widest circulation and ultimately came to be the Ṣūfī doctrine par excellence was that called Waḥdat al-Wujūd, "the oneness of all existence". At its basis lay the Neo-Platonic monism, with its apparatus of successive emanations, which had been adopted by the Ismāʿīlīs for the purposes of their cosmological scheme; one might even say that, by the transference of this doctrine into Ṣūfism, the Ismāʿīlīs revenged themselves on orthodox Islam for their suppression. Even al-Ghazālī himself had not been immune from its influence; it has been pointed out that the Ashʿarite doctrine of the contingency of all human being and action in face of the sole reality and creative Power of God might well, at a further stage of mystical intuition, lead to the belief that all empirical existence is an illusion. The Ṣūfīs went further still; the human spirit, being a direct emanation from the divine Command, is therefore an emanation from God himself, and could find its highest aim only in the obliteration of its illusory selfhood and absorption into the Eternal Reality. The supreme mystical experience is thus achieved in union with God, even if only momentarily, and for the justification of this bold claim it fell back on yet another Ismāʿīlī legacy, the allegorical and Gnostic interpretation of Koranic texts.

The most elaborate, if not wholly consistent, exposition of this doctrine was given by the Spanish-Arab mystic, Ibn al-ʿArabī (d. in Damascus 1240), in an immense output of prose and verse works. Its wider diffusion, however, was due to its adoption by the great galaxy of Persian poets of the thirteenth and the two following centuries A.D., and especially by Jalal al-Dīn al-Rūmī, whose huge Maṣnavī has been called the Bible of later Ṣūfism. Through them, it spread into the Ottoman Empire and India, the madrasa-trained theologians themselves yielded to its fascination, and in spite of a few attempts to stem the tide, the main effort of theological activity in the later centuries was directed to the combination and reconciliation of orthodox Ashʿarite theology with the near-pantheism of Ibn al-ʿArabī.

Even so, there remained many to whom the idea of unification with God himself was wholly inconsistent with the teachings of Islam, if not indeed blasphemous. These found a less obnoxious goal of mystical striving in the doctrine of "the Perfect Man", the microcosm, created by God out of nothingness before the creation of the world as a kind of mirror-image of himself, in which his love found for itself an external reflection. By Ibn al-ʿArabī this being was identified with the Active or First Intelligence of the philosophers, through whom "God's consciousness is manifested to himself in creation", and this in turn with the pre-eternal essence of Muhammad. Here again, a doctrine of Gnostic origin could be linked up with a tendency already current in orthodox Islam, developing out of the natural veneration for Muhammad as, in one sense or another, the intermediary between God and man, and again won an enthusiastic reception in the prevailing atmosphere of mystical speculation. It was a wholly legitimate aim to strive to become a perfect man by mystical union with "the Perfect Man", the perfect image of God, the essence (*ḥaqīqa*) of Muhammad.

Yet another system went back for its imagery to the light-doctrine, angelology and myths of ancient Persia and the Zoroastrian Avesta, elaborated on a Platonic basis and in conscious opposition to philosophical monism. At the summit of being is the "Light of Lights", from which emanate or are effused the hypostatized lesser "lights" in hierarchical order. By interior discipline the soul attains through ascending degrees of "illumination" or "light-dawning" (*ishrāq*) and increasing abstraction from itself of dark matter to the presence of the "Ultimate Presence". This *Ishrāqī* philosophy was elaborated by Yaḥyā al-Suhrawardī (executed in 1191) and found acceptance, as might be expected, chiefly in Persia; in modified form it entered the doctrine of the order called after his namesake 'Umar al-Suhrawardī, and later schools of Persian philosophy.

In a movement so extensive and uncontrolled as Ṣūfism became, no "system" as such could remain exclusive, and in practice elements of all the three preceding cosmologies mingled with one another and with elements from yet other sources. The survival of an ancient Asiatic tendency to Gnostic syncretism had already shown itself in aberrant forms of Ismā'īlī extremism, two of which still exist in the Nuṣairī sect in Northern Syria and the Druze sect in Central Syria and Lebanon. During the period when the Ṣūfī cosmologies were being elaborated, other syncretist sects also were forming in the remoter regions, such as the *Ahl-i Ḥaqq* and the Yezīdīs in Kurdistan; these may well be regarded as aberrant forms of the same general movement, favoured by the disorganization and removal of all Islamic political controls which resulted from the Mongol invasions of Western Asia in the thirteenth century A.D.

It would, however, be entirely erroneous to leave the impression that the great body of members and affiliates of the Ṣūfī orders concerned themselves in any way with the speculations and systems described above. Just as the mass of pious Believers had left the elaboration of theology to the scholastics, so now, in their relations with the Ṣūfī *shaikhs*, they remained unconcerned with the emanationist or illuminationist theories which these

spiritual directors might privately profess. What they looked for was primarily intensity of religious devotion and intuitive understanding, and help in the problems and difficulties of daily life. In times of need, or of disorder and oppression, the *shaikhs* were looked to for refuge and support, and at all times for true exemplars of the Islamic ideal and the interiorization of the *jihād*. Popular concern with the supernatural, on the other hand, could not fail to induce a large element of superstition into their attitudes towards the *shaikhs*. They expected to find evidences of their sainthood in the production of those lesser miracles which, it was believed, God granted as "graces" (*karāmāt*) to his saints: the power to foretell the future, to discover the unseen, to transport themselves great distances in the twinkling of an eye, to produce material objects out of nothing. Not only the popular literature of edification and hagiography, but also the writings of learned scholars and theologians of the later centuries, abound with narratives of this kind. Leading saints were ranked in a mystical hierarchy, culminating in the *Quṭb*, the "Pole" of the Age, who with his lesser subordinates governed the affairs of this world, although the exact composition of the hierarchy was supposed to be known only to those included in it. It is not to be wondered at that, alongside much genuine purity of religious life, later Ṣūfism came to be shot through and through with charlatanry and popular magic, and that impostors and half-wits of all kinds exploited the credulity of the masses, even if themselves not guilty of shameless immorality.

MODERN ISLAM

It was precisely with a reaction against the excessive lengths to which superstition had entered into and corrupted the primitive faith that the movement of Islamic revival began. As in most reactions of this kind, it swung at first violently to the other extreme, under the leadership of an Arabian *shaikh* named Muhammad ibn 'Abd al-Wahhāb (d. 1787). He and his followers, known as *Wahhābīs*, called for a return to the doctrines and practices of the early generations, the "ancestors" (*salaf*), as they had been transmitted by the tradition of the rigid Ḥanbalite school; in particular, they denounced the veneration of "saints" or any other persons, alive or dead, and systematically destroyed all buildings or monuments erected over tombs. Saint-worship was equivalent to ascribing partners to God, i.e. to apostasy, and was therefore to be punished by death; the more extreme held that the other schools, Ḥanafites, Shāfi'ites and Mālikites, as well as the Shī'ites, were equally guilty of perverting

Islam and therefore apostates and infidels. Armed with this doctrine, they made war under the princes of the house of Su'ūd on all their neighbours in Arabia and built up an empire which was destroyed only by a Turco-Egyptian campaign in 1818. The Wahhābī movement survived, however, and even in defeat exercised a steadily widening influence in the other lands of Islam, an influence which showed itself in various ways and in combination with other factors in the course of the nineteenth century A.D.

Most immediately it contributed to the building up of a strong current of hostility to Ṣūfism and the Ṣūfī brotherhoods in orthodox circles. Political factors also entered into this movement, ascribing the "decadence of Islam" to the fatal influence of superstition, as well as the revival of earlier scholasticism in the madrasas, particularly the college of al-Azhar in Cairo. A vigorous campaign for the "purification of Islam", led by the reformer Jamāl al-Dīn al-Afghānī (d. 1897; he was the protagonist of Pan-Islam, the political adhesion of all the Islamic countries to the Caliphate of the Ottoman Sultans) and his disciple Shaikh Muḥammad 'Abduh of Egypt (d. 1905), by stimulating Muslim self-consciousness and revivalism, reopened the discussion of issues long since regarded as closed. New schools of thought grew up in Egypt and in India, the most conservative of which naturally gravitated towards Wahhābism, to form "neo-Wahhābī" or Salafīya movements. Ṣūfism thus steadily lost ground; it disappeared from the madrasas altogether, and in the cities the old brotherhood guilds, simultaneously weakened or disrupted by economic factors, began to die out. The great ṭarīqas, however, still survive in most Muslim countries, and even retain, as in North Africa, considerable strength and importance. But they too, it would appear, have become more orthodox; the Gnostic or pantheistic philosophies of Ibn al-'Arabī and others no longer command any significant following. The fraternity has resumed in large measure its original function of an association of pious Believers for the promotion of personal and collective obedience to the Law of Islam.

Even before this, orthodox revivalism had found expression in new brotherhoods, organized on the pattern of the Ṣūfī brotherhoods, but directed towards missionary activities in Africa, India and Indonesia. Most of them were in principle pacific, but could and did in specific circumstances develop a militant attitude, as among the Tījānīs in Morocco and West Africa, and the Sanūsīs in Cyrenaica and Central Africa; others, like the so-called "Indian Wahhābīs" in the Punjab and the Mahdists in the Sudan were organized for the military jihād from the beginning. The continuing effort to create new organizations remains a characteristic feature of modern Islam to the present day, perhaps in an unconscious attempt to find a substitute for the social solidarity of the Ṣūfī brotherhoods. These range from upper- and middle-class clubs, such as the Association of Muslim Youth (a kind of Muslim counterpart of the Y.M.C.A.), through various local associations, to widespread popular movements like the Muslim Brotherhood (al-Ikhwān al-Muslimīn) in Egypt and Syria. But unlike the Ṣūfī brotherhoods, which operated in a society in which Islamic tradition and Muslim values were supreme and unquestioned, the new associations have as their main object the defence and consolidation of Islam against the invasion of foreign influence and ideas, whether these are represented by Westerners themselves or by the westernized intelligentsia in the Muslim countries.

This invasion is the second main factor which distinguishes modern Islam from its classical civilization and culture. Though carried into the Muslim countries in the first instance by Europeans employed in administration, education and commerce, their wide extension (in the Near and Middle East, at least) was due to the adoption of Western systems in all these fields by the Muslim rulers and governing classes themselves, and the rise of new professional classes—civil servants, doctors, lawyers, journalists—trained in Western schools and in various parts of Europe, reaching to a climax in the rise of nationalism and the introduction of parliamentary institutions.

A development such as this must inevitably affect every sector of Muslim life, thought and institutions, except in the few and remote areas which have remained, so far, isolated from its impact. In economic activities, in social habits and organization, in the aims and content of education, and the structure and conduct of law no less than of government, it has brought into existence a series of new problems to which Muslims must find the answers within the framework of Islam. The effects of all this upon the classical religious structure of Islam can be estimated only in general terms, and in relation to those sectors of the Muslim world in which contact with the West has been most sustained and profound. It must not be forgotten that there are some Muslim countries in which the traditional habits of thought and social conduct have been, at most, only superficially touched by these new forces. In almost all the other countries differences of local customs and traditions and in national psychology, which were overlaid by the classical Islamic culture, have created a variety of reactions to them; and even in these countries the rural populations largely retain their inherited institutions and attitudes. It has therefore been, as was to be expected, in the urban societies that the consequences of the Western impact have been the most apparent, and from the cities that they have radiated, in proportion to the influence exerted by the urban population over the countryside.

The traditional structure of religious education in the *madrasas* also was more strongly influenced by the orthodox revival described above than by contemporary movements in Muslim society. For this reason, rather than because of "conservatism" in the narrow sense, the orthodox scholastic system of theology appears to have remained outwardly unaffected, but beneath the external conformity to the traditional formulations lie concealed subtle changes of emphasis. It is doubtful whether any modern Muslim theologian could now reproduce in a work on dogmatics the type of argumentation employed by al-Ghazālī and the early scholastics, although the basic propositions would remain the same. The most perceptible change, probably, has taken place in regard to the Ash'arite doctrine of absolute predestination and human responsibility, about which many theologians are uneasy, and which is indeed openly disputed by those who call themselves "neo-Mu'tazilites" and uphold some degree of human freedom. On the other hand, modern philosophies are occasionally called in to support Islamic positions; modern atomic theory, for example, is commonly held to support the doctrine of continuous recreation and to have undermined the classical Western doctrine of causation.

Nevertheless, although an official or unofficial censorship often hampers open discussion of theological issues, some attempts have been made, mostly in lay circles, at a bolder "reconstruction" or revaluation of Muslim dogmatics. Their success, so far, had been limited. The average attitude of the intellectuals appears to be one of suspension of active interest in theology. For some, the dividing line between Islam and Muslim nationalism is a thin one; for all, the basic assumption is that the medieval formulations have no relation to modern life, and that there is and can be no conflict between Islam, properly understood, and any experientially verified truth.

In the area of Islamic social institutions the attitude and assumptions of the intellectuals are basically the same; but in this field the argument, because it is concerned with contemporary social problems, is more vigorous and intense. Both the procedures of the *Sharī'a* courts and the rulings of the schools of law have been under sustained attack for half a century. The former have been gradually assimilated to the new Civil Courts set up in the nineteenth century A.D., and the current tendency is to transfer their functions entirely to the Civil Courts, although only in the Turkish Republic has the jurisdiction of the *Sharī'a* been completely abolished in favour of legislated civil codes. In other countries, following on the introduction of national legislatures, the *Sharī'a* structure continues to be preserved in outward form, but with an increasing movement towards substituting for the traditional rulings of the orthodox schools new legislated codes to be applied in the *Sharī'a* courts. The new codes profess to follow the established methodology for the derivation of legal rulings from the Koran, the Traditions of the Prophet, and decisions reported on the authority of early jurists, but depart from it by leaving the legislators an entirely free hand in the choice of Traditions and juristic decisions from any and every school, including the Shī'a, or if necessary to disregard all school decisions and replace them by new provisions which are held to "conduce to the public welfare".

Although the general underlying principle has been to establish new legal systems in closer conformity to modern Western codes of personal status, the result has been to superimpose on the common substratum of Ḥanafī law more or less divergence in the rules actually applied in different countries. All of the new codes, however, introduce restrictions in the contracting of marriages, lay down minimum ages for legal marriages, restrict the customary freedom of the husband to repudiate his wife, and grant wives certain rights to demand judicial annulment or dissolution of the marriage. The practice of polygamy is hedged round with conditions, but only in one or two countries prohibited outright. In some codes also modifications have been introduced in the rules of inheritance and bequest, reducing the rights of the agnatic kin in favour of lineal descendants.

At a deeper level, however, this process brings into question the two basic principles upon which the unity of the Muslim Community was built up. In rejecting the principle that every ruling, to become valid, must be endorsed by a general consensus (*ijmā'*), and resorting instead to an eclectic choice of rulings, it introduces into the hitherto catholic structure of Islam what may be called a "protestant" principle. The Community, it is true, has always admitted, in secondary matters and under safeguard of its recognized methodology, diversity in interpretation of its constitutional documents, the Koran and the Traditions of the Prophet, and consequent diversity of rulings in their application. But the inner function of *ijmā'*, as the instrument by which the Community regulates its spiritual life, is to secure and to preserve the integral spiritual unity of all Muslims (not excluding even the Shī'ites) as a spiritually governed society, and not merely in the sense of a common external profession of Islam.

In the second place, it represents the culmination of the process by which the state has asserted its independent legislative authority. Previously, as has been noted above (p. 183), the state contented itself with establishing a parallel system of rulings and jurisdictions in the field of public administration. It has now claimed an exclusive right of legislation, overriding the *Sharī'a* even in face of an established *ijmā'*, and binding upon all Muslims under its political jurisdiction, irrespective of the legal schools to which they individually adhere. This claim may be sustained, in Islamic terms, by the argument that the social developments of the last century have modified both the traditional social economy and the general body of social ideas within the national group, that a democratic parliament is an authentic mouthpiece of the *ijmā'* of the national group, and that its legislation is a legitimate means of overcoming, at a time of rapid social changes, the time-lag inherent in the traditional method of validation of new rulings by a general *ijmā'*.

Both questions thus resolve themselves finally into an argument over the true character and function of *ijmā'*, and the exercise of its complementary principle of *ijtihād*, or formulation of rulings on the basis of a critical study of the sources. On the one hand, the *ijtihād* of the state may be regarded as merely an anticipation of a future general *ijmā'*; as, for example, the abolition of slavery in the nineteenth century A.D. by the administrative decree of Muslim governments has been validated by universal assent, in spite of some opposition at the time and the sporadic survival of slavery in Arabia. So also legislation restricting polygamy, although not necessarily reflecting a general consensus of Muslims at the present day, may serve to consolidate an increasingly powerful trend which may become a general *ijmā'* in the next generation. On the other hand, the claim of a political institution to express the *ijmā'* even of a national group remains open to question, since, leaving aside the character of the institution itself, there can be no *ijmā'* of any small segment of Muslims, but only "innovation". Any innovation, propounded by a particular group and made binding by the secular power, is a usurpation of the spiritual rights of Muslims, and carries with it the danger of disrupting the *Sharī'a* and consequently of destroying the peculiar and divinely-ordained constitution of the Muslim Community. The question for the future is whether Islam will remain, what it has been in the past, a comprehensive culture based on a religion, or become a "church", a religious institution accepted by larger or smaller bodies of adherents within the framework of a secular civilization.

4. Zoroastrianism

by R. C. ZAEHNER

The religion of Zoroaster has today almost vanished from the face of the earth, and is now professed by perhaps no more than 120,000 faithful souls. Why, then, should it be included in the present volume which is devoted to the *great* faiths of the world?

Zoroastrianism, like Judaism, is – or rather was – a national religion: from the third to the seventh century A.D. it was the national religion of the Persian Empire. When, however, it collapsed before the onslaught of the Muhammadan invader, Zoroastrianism lost its privileged position in its native land and became the religion of a barely tolerated minority. In the course of the centuries during which a number of the adherents of the old faith migrated to tolerant India, where they now form the prosperous and respected community of the Parsees, Zoroastrianism was gradually reduced numerically to a tiny fraction of what it had once been.

The importance of Zoroastrianism, however, like that of Judaism, lies not in the number of those who profess it, but rather in the influence it has exercised on other religions, and particularly on Christianity, through the medium of the Jewish exiles in Babylonia who seem to have been thoroughly impregnated with Zoroastrian ideas. Christianity claims to be the heir of the prophets of Israel. If there is any truth in this claim, it is no less heir to the Prophet of ancient Iran, little though most Christians are aware of this fact.

THE PROPHET

Zoroastrianism is a prophetic religion: its founder, Zoroaster – or Zarathushtra, to give him his proper name – was a prophet, or at least conceived himself to be such; he spoke to his God face to face. Until recently scholars found it impossible to agree either about the time or the place in which he flourished. Recently, however, agreement seems to have been reached that there is no good reason why we should not accept the date tra-

ditionally preserved by the Zoroastrians themselves. The date they assign to their Prophet is "258 years before Alexander"; and for the Persian or Iranian the name "Alexander" meant the extinction of the first Persian Empire and the death of the last of the Kings of Kings, Darius III. This occurred in 330 B.C. Zoroaster's date, then, would be 588 B.C., and this date we may take to refer to the beginning of his prophetic mission when, at the age of thirty, he is said to have received his first revelation. Since he is traditionally said to have lived seventy-seven years, his dates would be 628–551 B.C. The region in which he proclaimed his message was probably ancient Chorasmia – an area comprising what is now Persian Khorasan, Western Afghanistan and the Turkmen Republic of the U.S.S.R.

About the Prophet himself we know almost nothing that is authentic. In his own country he had no success and was forced to flee (*Yasna* 46.1) in search of a prince who would protect him and accept his religion. Such a prince he found in Vishtāspa, possibly the paramount ruler in Chorasmia. Under the protection of this ruler his religion was able to establish itself.

The sacred book of the Zoroastrians is called the Avesta, of which only a fraction survives today. Apart from fragments this section contains three main parts – the *Yasna* which constitutes the liturgy, the *Yashts* or sacrificial hymns addressed to specific deities or angels, and the *Vidēvdāt* or "Law against the Demons" which concerns itself mainly with matters of ritual purification. Into the *Yasna*, the great liturgical text, are inserted a series of *Gāthās* – "songs" or "hymns" – and these, since they are written in the first person, must be the work of Zoroaster himself. These *Gāthās* are, then, our principal, indeed our only, source for the doctrines actually proclaimed by the Prophet.

All living religions are liable to change, expansion and growth; but few religions have known such vicissitudes as has the religion of Zoroaster. For it seems to have been the great achievement of the Iranian Prophet that he eliminated all the ancient gods of the Iranian pantheon, leaving only Ahura Mazdāh, the "Wise Lord", as the One True God, and this monotheism is central to his doctrine. Yet very soon after his death, it would appear, many of the ancient gods infiltrated their way back into his system and although they did not, when so restored, ever challenge the supremacy of Ahura Mazdāh, they nevertheless figure prominently as *yazatas* or "worshipful beings" – angels, if you like, who often came precariously near to usurping the functions of absolute deity. Again when Zoroastrianism became the official religion of the second great Persian (Sassanian) Empire, we find two forms of Zoroastrianism existing side by side, the one neatly dualist in that it makes the principle of evil independent of Ahura Mazdāh and co-eternal with him, and the other tentatively monotheistic in that it raises Infinite Time to the status of the mysterious origin of all things from which the twin principles of good and evil severally proceed. Neither of the systems, perhaps, represented the authentic teaching of the Prophet. What, then, was this teaching?

His Teaching concerning God

Zoroaster was a prophet – speaking to God and hearkening to his reply. He is "the Prophet who raises his voice in veneration, the friend of Truth" (*Yasna* 50.6), God's friend (*Yasna* 46.2), a "true enemy to the followers of the Lie and a powerful support to the followers of the Truth" (*Yasna* 43.8). As a prophet he is chosen by God in the beginning (*Yasna* 44.11), and as he is chosen, so does he choose. "O Wise Lord," he exclaims, "Zarathushtra here chooses for himself thy Spirit which is the most holy." The relationship, then, between God and his Prophet is one of freedom: Zoroaster is not constrained, as the Hebrew prophets sometimes are; he rather sees God's holiness and, having seen it, he chooses it. In this free interchange between God and his Prophet is reflected the general relationship of the deity to the human race. Man is not, as in Judaism or Islam, a servant or a slave; he is a free man, master of the awful freedom to choose between good and evil. This is the religious situation with which Zoroaster confronted his hearers.

If, then, man is thus made conscious of his freedom to choose and of the awful responsibility that such choice entails, what did the Prophet who flung down this challenge understand by good and evil? The short answer to this is that he understood as "good" that which his God revealed to him – a new religion which recognized no god but Ahura Mazdāh – and as "evil" the old national religion which recognized a plurality of gods, those who

persisted in following that religion despite his warnings, and the sanguinary practices that that religion appears to have encouraged.

What the old religion was we can only infer from Zoroaster's own denunciation of it, from the texts of the *Rig Veda* (p. 226) which was the sacred book of the Indian branch of the Indo-Iranian family, and from the *Yashts* of the Avesta itself in which some of the ancient Indo-Iranian gods are once again invoked in defiance of the fact that the Prophet had either denounced them or passed them over in silence. From the earliest Indian and Iranian texts it is clear that the united Indo-Iranian peoples recognized two classes of deity, the *asuras* or *ahuras* on the one hand and the *devas* or *daēvas* on the other. The two different classes of deity met with a very different fate in the sister civilizations: for whereas, in India, the *asuras* were gradually reduced to the status of demons and the *devas* alone retained their divinity, in Iran it was the *ahuras* who retained their divine character and the *daēvas* who were reduced to demonhood. It was Zoroaster himself – or so we must suppose – who dethroned the *daēvas* completely and who, among the *ahuras*, retained only Ahura Mazdāh, the Wise Lord, as the One True God. It is, then, the *daēvas* specifically whom Zoroaster attacks, not the *ahuras* whom he prefers to ignore except once only when he declares that "Truth is to be invoked, and the Wise One and the (other) lords (*ahuras*)" (*Yasna* 31.4) – an important qualification since it may well indicate that Zoroaster, monotheist though he certainly was – we shall be considering his dualism later – did not utterly dethrone the other "lords" from beside the "Wise Lord". In all probability he considered them to be God's creatures and as fighters on his side. In any case he concentrated the full weight of his attack on the *daēvas* and their worshippers who practised a gory sacrificial ritual and were the enemies of the settled pastoral community to which the Prophet himself belonged.

Zoroaster was a Prophet: and prophets tend to see things in black and white. On his side was Truth and Righteousness (*asha*), on the other only the Lie (*druj*). His community was a community of settled husbandmen who tended and reverenced their kine; his enemies were no husbandmen (*Yasna* 31.10) and oppressed, carried off, sacrificed, and consumed these beneficent and (to the Zoroastrians) sacred beasts. This struggle between a pastoral community whose riches consist in cattle on the one hand and a predatory nomadic and tribal society which raided the settled cattle-breeders on the other forms the constant background to Zoroaster's preaching. The first are the "followers of Truth or Righteousness", the second the "followers of the Lie": there can be no peace or concord between the two until one or the other is converted. "The follower of the Lie, ill-famed and reprobate by his deeds, would prevent the supporters of Righteousness from making their kine to prosper in their district or their land. Whoso deprives him of his sovereignty or life shall, leading the way, tread the path of the good doctrine" (*Yasna* 46.4). For Zoroaster there is no more question of doing good to one's enemies than there was for the Jews when they entered the promised land. If they will not be converted, they must be attacked. "He who, by word or thought or with his hands, works evil to the follower of the Lie or converts his comrade to the good, such a man does the will of the Wise Lord and pleases him well" (*Yasna* 33.2). The follower of the Lie must be opposed with every weapon.

Asha and *druj*: Truth and Falsehood, Righteousness and wickedness, order and disorder – these are the basic opposites in the *Gāthās* of Zoroaster. They apply to every sphere of activity, whether human, cosmic or divine. Zoroaster did not invent this basic distinction since it appears in the ancient Indian tradition as well, but he brought it right into the foreground and made it basic to his whole view of the universe. On the purely social plane this basic antinomy exhibited itself in the contrast between the settled communities and the lawless nomads; on the religious plane it manifested itself in the unbridgeable gulf that separated the religion of the Truth revealed by the Wise Lord to his Prophet from the traditional religion of the Iranian race which, as its adherents must have claimed, had been handed down from time immemorial and had been instituted by the primal ancestor of the race, Yima, son of Vivahvant – Yima, that is, the child of the Sun. This religion was false: and Zoroaster does not hesitate to attack the great ancestor himself, Yima, who had introduced animal sacrifice and the unseemly rites that accompanied it; for, the Prophet exclaims, "among these sinners, so tradition holds, was Yima, son of Vivahvant – (Yima) who, to please mortal men, gave our people of the flesh of the ox to eat. As to these, O Wise One, I leave the decision to thee" (*Yasna* 32.8). "The followers of the Lie', it is who "destroy life" and "strive with all their might" to deprive husband and wife of their inheritance and would sever the followers of Truth from the Good Mind (*Yasna* 32.11). They, on their side, recognize the danger that this Prophet represents for them and they do everything in their power to destroy him; and to this purpose they continue to offer bulls in sacrifice to the accompaniment of the fermented *Haoma* juice – a rite which they had practised since remote antiquity. For Zoroaster the whole cult with its bloody sacrifice and ritual drunkenness is anathema – a rite offered to false gods and therefore a "lie". How long will the Wise Lord tolerate this state of affairs? the Prophet wonders. "When will the warriors come to understand (my) message?" he demands: "When wilt thou strike down this filthy drunkenness with which these priests evilly delude (the people) as do the wicked rulers in full consciousness (of what they do)" (*Yasna* 48.10).

Thus on the purely religious plane the enemy is the old "pagan" cult which must be utterly abolished in favour of the new religion of righteousness and truth. Each man must choose between the two sides for himself (Yasna 30.2) just as the Prophet made his choice and thereby publicly adhered to the "Most Holy Spirit" (Yasna 43.16) of Ahura Mazdāh.

Truth and the Lie, righteousness and wickedness, good and evil, and the choice that all must make between the two – always we come back to this. God himself as well as his "Most Holy Spirit" must make this choice: and here we come to the all-important question of Zoroaster's dualism. How far was he, in fact, a dualist, and how far did he go in setting his Wise Lord, Ahura Mazdāh, on a pinnacle which evil could not touch? Let us consider the two crucial dualist texts.

The first describes the two primeval Spirits who can never agree. "I will speak out," the Prophet proclaims, "concerning the two Spirits of whom, at the beginning of existence, the Holier spoke to him who is Evil: 'Neither our thoughts, nor our teachings, nor our wills, nor our choices, nor our words, nor our deeds, nor our convictions, not yet our souls agree' " (*Yasna* 45.2). Or again, as the Prophet says elsewhere "in the beginning the two Spirits who are the well-endowed(?) twins were known as the one good and the other evil in thought word and deed. Between them the wise chose the good not so the fools. And when these Spirits met they established in the beginning life and death that in the end the evil should meet with the worst existence, but the just with the Best Mind. Of these two Spirits he who was of the Lie chose to do the worst things; but the Most Holy Spirit, clothed in rugged heaven, (chose) Righteousness (or Truth) as did (all) those who sought with zeal to do the pleasure of the Wise Lord by (doing) good works." But "between the two the ancient godlets (*daēvas*) did not choose rightly; for, as they deliberated, delusion overcame them so that they chose the Most Evil Mind. Then did they, with one accord, rush headlong unto Wrath that they might thereby extinguish(?) the existence of mortal man" (*Yasna* 30.3–6).

Here, then, is the primeval tragedy, the Zoroastrian counterpart to the Christian doctrine of Original Sin.

Two primeval Spirits meet, the Holy Spirit and the Evil One. Yet they are holy and evil, it appears, by *choice* rather than by nature. The Holy Spirit is the Most Holy Spirit of Ahura Mazdāh (*Yasna* 43.16), but is not identical with him; indeed we read elsewhere that he is his son (*Yasna* 47.2–3). This means that both the Holy and the Evil Spirits proceed from Ahura Mazdāh, the Wise Lord, who is God. It seems, then, that Zoroaster, the founder of "Zoroastrianism", which is generally regarded as the classic example of a dualist religion, was not himself a dualist, if by that term we mean one who posits two first principles, not one, and makes the Evil One co-eternal with God and independent of him. On the other hand his monotheism never went so far as to attribute evil directly to God: *his* God could never have said to him: "I form the light and create darkness: I make peace, *and create evil*: I the Lord do all these things" (*Isaiah* xlv, 7), as Yahweh said to the second Isaiah. To Zoroaster such an idea would have seemed blasphemous, for, to him, God is revealed as both powerful and all-good.

We have seen that the Holy and Evil Spirits are referred to as *twins* and that Ahura Mazdāh is called the father of the first of these. In strict logic, then, he must also be the father of the Evil Spirit. Zoroaster, however, was a prophet, not a theologian; and prophets, in their direct apprehension of deity, are liable to leave all manner of loose ends for the theologians to tidy up later. The theologians were, indeed, much exercised by these texts as we shall see, and except in the late Sassanian and early Muhammadan periods they never seem to have agreed. Zoroaster's own view, however, seems to have been that Ahura Mazdāh, the supreme God, "generated" two Spirits, one of which *chose* righteousness and the other of which *chose* "to do the worst things". The second of the Spirits is, then, evil by choice, not by nature; for so tremendous is the Prophet's emphasis on the freedom of the will that not even God escapes. Ahura Mazdāh himself must, by an act of will, choose the good as against evil.

"Family and village and tribe, and the godlets too (the *daēvas*), like me, asked bliss of the Wise Lord (saying): 'Let us be thy messengers that we may keep at bay those who hate thee.' To them did the Wise Lord, united with the Good Mind and in close companionship with Truth, make answer from his Kingdom: 'Holy and good Right-mindedness do we choose; let it be ours'" (*Yasna* 32.1–2).

Here God himself is represented as making the great choice which all must make between good and evil. United with the *Good Mind* and in close companionship with the Truth or Righteousness, God chooses the good

and utterly condemns the old religion which he identifies with evil.

"But you, you godlets," he exclaims, "and whosoever multiplies his sacrifice to you, are all the seed of the Evil Mind, the Lie, and Pride: doubtful(?) are your deeds for which ye are famed throughout the seventh part of the earth. For ye have so devised it that men who do what is worst should be called the favoured of the 'gods' (*daēvas*) – men who depart from the Good Mind and break away from the will of the Wise Lord and from Righteousness. So would you defraud man of the good life and immortality, even as the Evil Spirit (defrauded you), you godlets, by the Evil Mind – a deed by which, with evil words, he promised dominion to the followers of the Lie" (*Yasna* 31.3–5).

God's relation to the Evil Spirit or Devil is here made clear, for the old gods, the *daēvas* or godlets, are themselves represented as approaching him in supplication, thereby acknowledging his supremacy. But they have already made their choice, deceived, as they were, by the Evil One, who was the first to choose wrongly. The fact, however, that these minor "godlets" or spirits should approach Ahura Mazdāh at all shows that they account him the supreme arbiter to whom even the Evil Spirit (the Ahriman of later Zoroastrianism), the first to choose evil, is subject.

That Zoroastrianism deeply affected the Jewish sect of the Dead Sea Scrolls has long been recognized, and it is in the *Manual of Discipline* that this influence is most clearly seen. Here we find a type of dualism that seems to be almost identical with what appears to have been that of Zoroaster himself rather than with the extreme and formal dualism of later Zoroastrianism. The idea has, of course, been clothed in Jewish dress, but it is clearly recognizable.

God "created man," we read, "to have dominion over the world and made for him *two spirits*, that he might walk by them until the appointed time of his visitation; they are the spirits of *truth* and of *error*. In the abode of light are the origins of truth, and from the source of darkness are the origins of error. . . . And by the angel of darkness is the straying of all the sons of righteousness . . . and all the spirits of his lot try to make the sons of light stumble; but the *God* of Israel and his *angel of truth* have helped all the sons of light. For he created the spirits of light and of darkness, and upon them he founded every work and upon their ways every service. *One of the spirits God loves* for all the ages of eternity, and with all its deeds he is pleased for ever; as for the other, *he abhors its company, and all its ways he hates for ever*" (see Millar Burrows, *The Dead Sea Scrolls*, 1956, p. 374).

Here we find reproduced in a Jewish setting an exact counterpart of the Zoroastrian two Spirits which sprang from God. There is, however, one crucial difference. In the Jewish account God creates one of the Spirits evil and, most illogically, hates his own handiwork. With Zoroaster, however, it is implied, though never explicitly stated, that the Evil Spirit derives from God; but this Spirit is evil by choice and was not created evil. As in Christianity it is God's gift of free will and the misuse of it by creatures that brings evil into the world.

How, then, did Zoroaster understand his God? He is Ahura Mazdāh, the Wise Lord, "the Creator of all things by the Holy Spirit" (Yasna 44.7). We have met this Holy Spirit before and have seen how he came into conflict with the Evil Spirit at the beginning of time. For Zoroaster, however, he is not identical with the Wise Lord; indeed, he is once called his son (*Yasna* 47.3). Yet, as in the Christian Trinity, the two are in some sense one as their subsequent identification in later Zoroastrianism shows. The "generation" of the Holy Spirit is necessarily spiritual or mental, for God is a pure spirit and operates through other spirits who are at the same time in some way identical with himself. Beside the Holy Spirit there are also "the Good Mind", "Righteousness" or "Truth", and "Right-mindedness" (*ārmaiti*), paternity of which is again ascribed to the Wise Lord (*Yasna* 31.8; 44.3; 45.4; 47.2). These "children" of the Wise Lord are at the same time aspects of himself or faculties through which he operates. Similar to them are three other entities – the "Kingdom", "Wholeness", and "Immortality", the last two being more especially regarded as God's gifts to man. In later Zoroastrianism these entities were to become "archangels" separate from the Wise Lord and created by him, but in the *Gāthās* this is not so: they are rather faculties through which he operates.

The Wise Lord is all-powerful for he "rules at will" (*Yasna* 43.1); he is the Creator of all things (*Yasna* 44.7) and his creation is "thought" by him into existence (*Yasna* 31.7, 11): it is, then, a creation out of nothing. As we have seen, he chooses Righteousness and utterly condemns the evil, because the evil, both among spiritual beings and among men, have become what they are by choice. For their right or wrong choices he rewards or punishes them (e.g. *Yasna* 45.7), for they were created free and responsible beings. In a series of rhetorical questions Zoroaster paints a magnificent picture of his God:

"This I ask thee, Lord, answer me truly: Who is the first, the father of Righteousness through (generation and) birth? Who appointed their paths to the sun and stars? Who but thou is it through whom the moon waxes and wanes? This would I know, O Wise One, and other things besides.

"This I ask thee, Lord, answer me truly: Who set the earth below and the sky (above) so that it does not fall? Who the waters and the plants? Who yoked swift steeds to wind and clouds? Who, O Wise One, is the Creator of the Good Mind?

"This I ask thee, Lord, answer me truly: What goodly craftsman made light and darkness? What goodly craftsman sleep and wakefulness? Who made morning, noon, and night to make the wise man mindful of his task?

"This I ask thee, Lord, answer me truly: Who created Right-mindedness venerable with the Dominion? Who made the son dutiful in his soul towards his father? Recognizing thee by these (signs) as the Creator of all things through thy Holy Spirit, I (go to) help thee" (Yasna 44.3–5, 7).

To sum up: for Zoroaster there is only one God, Creator of heaven and earth and of all things. In his relations with the world God acts through his main "faculties" which are sometimes spoken of as being engendered by him – his Holy Spirit, Righteousness, Good Mind, and Right-mindedness. Further he is master of the Kingdom, Wholeness, and Immortality, which also form aspects of himself. Righteousness or Truth is the objective standard of right behaviour which God chooses, as against the "Lie", wickedness or disorder which, in its turn, is the objective standard of all that strives against God, the standard which the Evil Spirit chooses at the beginning of existence. Evil imitates the good creation: and so we find the Evil Spirit operating against the Holy Spirit, the Evil Mind against the Good Mind, the Lie or wickedness against Truth or Righteousness, and Pride against Right-mindedness. Evil derives from the wrong choice of a free being who must in some sense derive from God, but for whose wickedness God cannot be held responsible. Angra Mainyu or Ahriman, the Devil, is not yet co-eternal with God as he was to become in the later system: he is the Adversary of the Holy Spirit only, not of God himself.

Other Teachings

Zoroaster's teachings reflect the milieu in which he worked, a milieu in which the settled herdsman had constantly to strive against the depredations of the marauding nomad. His religion is identified with the former; the traditional religion which offered sacrifices to lesser deities or *daēvas* with the latter. Primarily, Zoroaster seems to have been interested in establishing the Kingdom of Righteousness here on earth. So then, just as his division of human society into "the followers of the

Truth" and "the followers of the Lie" reflects an actually existing state of affairs in the society in which he lived so do his views on the after-life start from a concrete earthly situation. Because his God had chosen Truth and Righteousness from all eternity, he believes that he must chastise the wicked and reward the righteous; and he believes further that a day will come when the Kingdom of Righteousness will be set up here on earth. "Declare to me, O Wise One," the Prophet asks, "the best words and deeds. Through Righteousness and the Good Mind declare the debt(?) of praise (we owe thee). Through thy Kingdom make existence excellent (*frasha*) according to thy will" (*Yasna* 34.15). This perfecting or renewal of existence Zoroaster had hoped to achieve himself, for he prays that "it may be *we* who shall make existence excellent . . . when (all) minds shall agree (even) among those for whom false teaching prevails" (*Yasna* 30.9). This hope was, however, soon to vanish and the Prophet then looks forward to a "second existence" which the followers of the Lie will be unable to corrupt (*Yasna* 45.1). Meanwhile the good will be rewarded with immortality and the evil will be visited with eternal punishment. Unambiguously the Prophet proclaims:

"I shall speak out the word which the Most Holy One declared to me – the best of all words for men to hear: 'Whoso shall hearken even unto him (my Prophet) for my sake, shall attain to wholeness and immortality by (performing) the works of the Good Mind.' (Thus spake) the Wise Lord . . . from Whom all men who live (today), who have been or are yet to come, shall receive their lot of weal (or woe), for he apportions both. Powerful in immortality shall be the soul of the follower of Truth, but lasting torment shall there be for the man who cleaves to the Lie. So does the Wise Lord dispose through his sovereign power" (*Yasna* 45.5, 7).

Man, then, meets his judgment after death: the righteous are rewarded with heaven, "the best existence", and with immortality and wholeness; united with the Good Mind (*Yasna* 28.8; 46.12, 14), they rejoice in "the House of Song" (e.g. *Yasna* 51.15). The wicked, on the other hand, will be afflicted with "lasting torment", feeding on foul food (*Yasna* 31.20; 49.11) in "the House of the Lie" (*Yasna* 49.11; 51.14). Life after death, then, is seen as a prolongation of life on earth in which some sort of body is involved; because for Zoroaster and his followers survival meant survival in soul and body, and in order to make this survival a reality Zoroaster's followers looked forward to a resurrection of the body at the end of time. The actual individual judgment after death is, however, mentioned by Zoroaster himself. It takes place at the "Bridge of the Requiter" (*Yasna* 46.10–

11; 51.13) where the souls are tested in molten metal and fire (*Yasna* 51.9) – a form of ordeal to which the first Zoroastrians probably appealed on earth (*Yasna* 32.7). The judgment over, the righteous and the wicked depart to their respective destinies – the first to eternal bliss but the second to enduring misery. Such judgment was decreed from the beginning and seems to have been regarded by Zoroaster as final, for the essence of his message to man is that the freedom bestowed on him by God is an awful thing, and its misuse could only lead to eternal woe. To quote our Prophet for the last time:

"Then did I realize, Wise Lord, that thou wast holy
When I saw that in the beginning, at the birth of existence,
Thou didst ordain that deeds and spoken words should meet with (just) requital –
Evil for the evil, but good reward for whoso is good
At the last turning-point of this created world.
  So far doth thy power extend" (*Yasna* 43.5).

ZOROASTRIANISM AFTER THE PROPHET

Eschatology

Such would appear to be the principal doctrines enunciated by Zoroaster himself. One of the main teachings which was later to become an integral part of his religion was only faintly adumbrated in his own work – the doctrine of the resurrection of the body and life everlasting. This doctrine centres around the figure of the Saoshyant – a word which is usually translated as "Saviour" but which might be better rendered as "he who will bring good fortune". In the *Gāthās* the word occurs many times, but it seems either to refer to Zoroaster himself (e.g. *Yasna* 45.11; 48.9) or to a secular ruler who would establish his religion on earth. The Kingdom of Righteousness on earth, however, did not materialize, and gradually the coming of the Saoshyant was looked forward to only at the end of the world, when the powers of evil would be finally defeated. Then "the victorious Saoshyant and those others who help him . . . will make the world most excellent, unageing, undecaying, neither passing away nor falling into corruption; for ever shall it live and for ever prosper, (each man) ranging at will. The dead shall rise again and the living shall be visited by immortality, and (all) existence shall be made most excellent in accordance with its will. . . . The material world will no more pass away . . . and the Lie shall perish" (*Yasht* 19.89–90).

This eschatological doctrine which is so typical of Zoroastrianism probably arose in the Achaemenian period – though this cannot be proved – and it is largely

Photo: Exclusive News Agency

PLATE 55. The so-called Kaʻba of Zoroaster. A Zoroastrian Fire-temple.

Photo: "The Rock Sculptures and Inscriptions of Darius at Behistun", L. W. King, and R. C. Thompson, British Museum

PLATE 56. Figure of the god Ahura Mazdāh from the great rock relief of Darius I at Behistun.

PLATE 57. Archangel. End of the 14th century. Persian painting. Francis Bartlett Donation. (Courtesy, *Museum of Fine Arts, Boston*.)

PLATE 58. Dervish. Signed, Mohammad Yusuf. 1645. Persian painting. Francis Bartlett Donation. (Courtesy, *Museum of Fine Arts, Boston.*)

developed in the later literature. It introduces a new element into Zoroaster's teaching, for the drama ends with the final release of all sinners from Hell and their admission to eternal bliss (see *The Teachings of The Magi*, by R.C.Zaehner, 1956, pp. 139–150). The *Frashkart* or final Rehabilitation of Creation, however, does not correspond to the Christian Last Judgment. Souls are individually judged at death and sent to heaven or hell in accordance with their deserts. When creation is finally rehabilitated at the end of the cosmic year of 12,000 years, the Saoshyant, born miraculously from the seed of Zoroaster, appears and raises the bodies of the dead. These are re-united with their souls, and all are plunged into a sea of molten metal which purges them from all remaining stain of sin. After this final purgation the whole human race will enter paradise where they will rejoice for ever and ever. "All men will become of one voice and give praise with a loud voice to the Wise Lord and the Bounteous Immortals" (*ibid.*, p. 148) and "the material world will become immortal for ever and ever" (*ibid.*, p. 150). Ahriman, the Devil, and his hosts will be cast into hell where they are either totally annihilated or made powerless for all time.

Theology

We saw, when we were dealing with the Prophet Zoroaster, that he recognized two Spirits, a holy and an evil one, who at the beginning of time made their irrevocable choices between good and evil. Ahura Mazdāh, who is God, was in some sense identified with the Holy Spirit and declared himself against the Evil One. About the origin of the Evil Spirit, however, the Prophet is mute. It is true that the elements of a total dualism are present in germ in the *Gāthās* since Ahura Mazdāh is always associated with the Holy Spirit and Righteousness and categorically denounces the Lie and all its works. This does not, however, mean that Zoroaster believed that there were two separate principles responsible for the universe; it means that, for him, God rejected and combated evil from the very moment it arose.

In the *Gāthās*, then, Ahura Mazdāh and the Holy Spirit are intimately connected but not identical. Indeed in one passage the first is spoken of as the father of the second. What was God's relationship to the Evil Spirit, Angra Mainyu or Ahriman as he was later to be called? This was a subject about which Zoroastrian theologians were to argue right up to, and long after, the Muhammadan conquest of the Persian Empire. The situation was complicated by the fact that at an early date the Holy Spirit was wholly identified with Ahura Mazdāh and

simply became another name for him. Now it is stated in the *Gāthās* that the Holy Spirit and the Evil Spirit are twins. If, then, the Holy Spirit is simply another name for Ahura Mazdāh, that is God, then it would follow that God and the Devil, Ahura Mazdāh and Angra Mainyu, or Ohrmazd and Ahriman as they were later called, were twin brothers; and if they were twins, they must have a common progenitor. So it came about that a sect of the Prophet's followers posited a principle above Ohrmazd and Ahriman – *Zurvān i akanārak* or Infinite Time, which thereby became the first principle from which the good and evil Spirits arose. Alternatively the offending Gāthic passage was either ignored or mistranslated, and the purely dualist position was promulgated according to which Ohrmazd and Ahriman, God and the Devil, were co-eternal principles, the one wholly good and the other wholly evil. When Zoroastrianism was revived as the state religion of the Sassanian Empire (A.D. 226–652), these two views seem to have alternated, the completely dualistic position being finally adopted as the official and orthodox doctrine probably under Khusraw I (531–578). After the Muhammadan conquest this rigid dualism remained the orthodox Zoroastrian faith: it is the religion that was transmitted through the so-called Pahlavi books which, although they were mainly written in their present form in the ninth century A.D., certainly represent the views of the theologians of the last century of the Sassanian Empire. Zoroastrianism and dualism thereby became two words for one thing, and it is only during the last century that the surviving remnant of the Prophet's faith, the Parsees in India, have thought fit to question this rigid dualism. There can scarcely be any doubt that this change was motivated by the influence of Christianity as understood by the British in India and by an uneasy feeling among the Parsees themselves that somehow dualism was not quite respectable. In some ways this is a pity, for the "classic" dualism of the Pahlavi books is perhaps the most rational solution of the problem of evil ever devised.

For the orthodox Zoroastrians of the Sassanian and early Muhammadan periods, however, there were two first principles, not one. "I must have no doubt", their catechism reads, "but that there are two first principles, one the Creator and the other the Destroyer. The Creator is Ohrmazd who is all goodness and all light: and the Destroyer is the accursed Ahriman who is all wickedness and full of death, a liar and a deceiver" (*ibid.*, pp. 22–23). These two principles were conceived of as existing the one on high in the light and the other down below in the darkness: they were separated by the

Void (*ibid.*, pp. 34–35). Ohrmazd, God or the good principle, realized that once his enemy knew of his existence, he would attack him "because his will is to smite" (*ibid.*, p. 36), and he therefore created the spiritual and material worlds as a means of self-protection. At one stroke, then, "classical" Zoroastrian dualism not only solved those two hoary mysteries – the origin of evil and the reason for creation – it drained them of all their mysteriousness. If evil is a separate principle, then its origin is no mystery. Creation too ceases to be a mysterious overflowing of the Godhead and becomes simply the means by which God protects himself from his eternal enemy: God creates because, out of pure self-interest, he has to. Moreover, there is a certain poetic justice in the whole affair; for the Evil One, being by nature chaotic and stupid, is instrumental in destroying himself. He invades the world and brings death, disease and sin into it, but, although his capacity for hurting God's creatures is enormous, the inner compulsion that drives him to his own destruction is greater still; for once he has entered the world, he becomes a prisoner in it and, like a trapped beast, lashes around to his own certain and overwhelming ruin. His dilemma is admirably expressed in the following words:

Ohrmazd "is like the owner of a garden or a wise gardener whose garden noxious and destructive beasts and birds are intent on spoiling by doing harm to its fruit and trees. And the wise gardener, to save himself trouble and to keep those noxious beasts out of his garden, devises means whereby to capture them, like gins and snares and bird-traps, so that when the beast sees the trap and strives to escape from it, it is ensnared inside it, not knowing its nature. It is obvious that when the beast falls into the snare, it is caught not because of the superiority of the snare [itself] but because' [of the superiority] of the maker of the snare. The man who is the owner of the garden and maker of the snare knows in his wisdom how great the beast's strength is and for how long [it can hold out]. The strength and power which the beast has within its body is neutralized by its own struggles and is expended in the proportion that it has enough power to trample on the snare and to rend the gin and to strive to destroy it. Since its strength is insufficient, its power to resist diminishes and it is put out of action. Then the wise gardener, putting his plan into effect and knowing [the needs of] his own produce, drives the beast out of the snare; and the beast's substance remains but its faculties are put out of action. And the gardener returns his snare and gin undamaged to his store-house where he will refit it" (*ibid.*, pp. 49–50).

Creation, then, is the snare in which the Devil is trapped and man is in the forefront of the battle. More powerful than man, however, and more directly concerned with this cosmic battle are the angels. The "angels" or "gods" are created spirits much as are the angels in Judaism, Christianity and Islam. Six of them are derived from the *Gāthās* where, however, they are rather faculties of the one God – the Good Mind, Righteousness, the Kingdom, Right-mindedness, Wholeness and Immortality. In later Zoroastrianism these became separate entities, what we might call archangels, and have a fully personal existence. In addition some at any rate of the old gods whom Zoroaster had either ignored or demonized, reappear as powerful angels fighting on the side of Ahura Mazdāh or Ohrmazd. The greatest of these is Mithra who was to enjoy so astonishing a career in the early Roman Empire. These spiritual creatures conduct unceasing war against Ahriman and all his demonic creation.

Man too has to play his part in the struggle against evil, and this he does primarily by thinking good thoughts, speaking good words and doing good deeds, by reproducing himself and by making the earth fruitful; for life, being the creation of Ohrmazd, must be preserved against death which was introduced into the world by his enemy Ahriman. The material world, too, is the creation of Ohrmazd and is therefore good. Thus the Zoroastrians have never had any use for asceticism in any form, since the contempt for physical life which it implies appears to them nothing short of blasphemy. For them evil is not, as it was for the Manichees, synonymous with matter. Far from it: matter is essentially good, and evil is a spiritual principle inimical to the material creation as well as to God. Hence the Zoroastrians' reverence for physical things, particularly in their simplest form, that is, the elements, and among these especially fire and water.

Fate and Free Will

We saw that freedom of the human will was perhaps the prime dogma enunciated by the Prophet himself. This dogma is in the main maintained in the "medieval" period, and it is characteristic of this religion that God does not put man in the world to fight against the Evil One without first obtaining his free consent. Rather "he took counsel with the consciousness and pre-existent souls of men and infused omniscient wisdom into them, saying: 'Which seemeth more profitable to you, whether that I should fashion you forth in material form and that you should strive incarnate with the Lie and destroy it, and that we should resurrect you at the end, whole and immortal, and recreate you in material form, and that you should eternally be immortal, unageing and without enemies; or that you should eternally be preserved from the Aggressor?' And the pre-existent souls of men saw by that omniscient wisdom that they would suffer evil from the Lie and Ahriman in the world, but because at the end they would be resurrected free from the enmity of the Adversary, whole and immortal for ever and ever, they agreed to go into the material world" (ibid., p. 41).

Every religion, sooner or later, is involved in the controversy of free will *versus* determinism. Zoroaster took his stand firmly on the absolute freedom of the will, but this did not prevent fatalism from creeping into his religion in the Sassanian and post-Sassanian period. As an extreme example of this we may quote the following. "When fate helps a slothful, wrong-minded, and evil man, his sloth becomes like energy, and his wrong-mindedness like wisdom, and his evil like good: and when fate opposes the wise, decent and good man, his wisdom is turned to unwisdom and foolishness, his decency to wrong-mindedness; and his knowledge, manliness and decency appear of no account" (Mēnōk i Khrat, 51).

This, however, is a serious aberration from the Prophet's teaching, and the orthodox view is more faithfully reflected in the following statement of the case: "The things of this world are divided into twenty-five parts: five are through fate, five through action, five through nature, five through character, and five through heredity. Life, wife, children, sovereignty and wealth are through fate. Membership of the castes of the priests, warriors and husbandmen, virtue and vice are through action. Going in to one's wife, satisfying one's natural needs, eating, walking and sleeping are through nature. Friendship, respect, generosity, righteousness and humility are through character. Body, stature, understanding, intelligence and strength are through heredity" (Pahlavī Texts, p. 82).

Ethics

Zoroastrian morality is summed up in the words: "good thoughts, good words, and good deeds". If Zoroastrianism early became completely dualist, it was because Zoroaster's God was so completely identified with goodness and righteousness that it became unthinkable that he could be even indirectly responsible for evil. We have seen that the six most prominent "aspects" of Ahura Mazdāh in the Gāthās – the Good Mind, Righteousness, the Kingdom, Right-mindedness,

Wholeness and Immortality – later became archangels in their own right. As attributes or qualities, however, they are common to God and man; for wholeness and immortality are the destiny for which God intended man whereas righteousness and goodness of mind and intention are those divine qualities that man must strive to imitate. In the medieval period, however, "righteousness" was interpreted as being the "mean". There can be no doubt that this idea was borrowed from Aristotle, but so greatly did the Iranians take to it that they claimed it as their own. "Iran has always commended the mean," we read, "and censured excess and deficiency. In the Byzantine Empire the philosophers, in India the learned, and elsewhere the specialists have in general commended the man whose argument showed subtlety, but the Kingdom of Iran has shown approval of the (truly) wise" (Dēnkart, Madan, p. 429).

Zoroastrian ethics were elaborated largely during the Sassanian period when Zoroastrianism was the state religion. It is not surprising, then, that they should bear an aristocratic stamp. The Zoroastrian ethic is essentially gentlemanly: and even after the overthrow of the Persian Empire by the Muhammadans and the gradual substitution of Islam for Zoroastrianism throughout the Iranian lands this aristocratic ethic perpetuated itself in the new religious climate and survived long after the Iranian Prophet's religion had crumbled before the onslaught of the followers of another prophet from barbarous Arabia.

The Zoroastrian is expected to reproduce himself as a religious duty and to render the earth fertile. He should be contented with his lot and always do good, not rendering evil for evil (ibid., p. 113); and the maxim that one should "not do to others anything that does not seem good to oneself" is as true for the Zoroastrian as it is for the Christian, the Buddhist or the Confucian.

The Zoroastrian ethic can be compared to that of the Book of Proverbs or Ecclesiasticus. It is essentially an ethic of moderation: it is urbane. Drinking, for example, is encouraged in moderation, but the abuse of this good thing is reproved. The world is neither a prison nor an exile as in so many religions; it is a transitory abode in which there is much that is good and enjoyable, and it is the reverse of sinful to make the most of the good things it has to offer while we are still here. "Do in holiness anything you will" is the golden rule. Zoroastrianism detests paradox, and we will therefore not find any of the great paradoxes that characterize Christianity and Buddhism in this religion. There is no demand for heroic self-sacrifice or that one should love one's enemy, since one's enemies should in any case be the "followers of the

Lie" and the Lie is the fountain-head of all sin. Rather, "do not make a new friend of an old enemy, for an old enemy is like a black snake which does not forget old injuries for a hundred years." It is true that the Prophet's fire no longer glows in the ethics developed in his name during the Sassanian period, but the worldly wisdom they display has remained part and parcel of the Iranian inheritance right up to the present day when, for the average Iranian, Zoroaster, in many ways Iran's greatest son, is little more than a name.

Sacrament

The central rite of the Zoroastrians is the *Yasna*, a word which literally means "sacrifice". Zoroaster, as we have seen, vehemently attacked the old sacrificial rite in which a bull was slain and the fermented juice of a plant called *Haoma* consumed; yet it is precisely the drinking of this *Haoma*-juice which has for time immemorial constituted the central act of the Zoroastrian ritual. Whether the rite, in some form, was indeed tolerated by Zoroaster or whether it was later introduced contrary to his intention, it was never disputed by any party at any later time. Zoroaster had promised immortality to his followers, and in the rite of the *Haoma*-juice lies the elixir which confers immortality. The *Haoma* (cf. the Indian *soma*, p. 226) is not only a plant: it is also a god, and the son of Ahura Mazdāh. In the ritual the plant-god is ceremonially pounded in a mortar; the god, that is to say, is sacrificed and offered up to his heavenly Father. Ideally *Haoma* is both priest and victim – the son of God, then, offering himself up to his heavenly Father. After the offering, priest and faithful partake of the heavenly drink, and by partaking of it they are made to share in the immortality of the god. The sacrament is the earnest of everlasting life which all men will inherit in soul and body in the last days. The conception is strikingly similar to that of the Catholic Mass.

Zoroastrianism has practically vanished from the world today, but much of what the Iranian Prophet taught lives on in no less than three great religions - Judaism, Christianity and Islam. It seems fairly certain that the main teachings of Zoroaster were known to the Jews in the Babylonian captivity, and so it was that in those vital but obscure centuries that preceded the coming of Jesus Christ Judaism had absorbed into its bloodstream more of the Iranian Prophet's teaching than it could well admit. It seems probable that it was from him and from his immediate followers that the Jews derived the idea of the immortality of the soul, of the resurrection of the body, of a Devil who works not as a servant of God but as his Adversary, and perhaps too of an eschatological Saviour who was to appear at the end of time. All these ideas, in one form or another, have passed into both Christianity and Islam. Only one of the typically Zoroastrian doctrines was wholly rejected – a doctrine which became the corner-stone of the whole system, but which seems not to have been the doctrine of the Prophet himself – the doctrine of the two co-eternal principles of good and evil. This doctrine which accords with reason but which runs counter to a deep religious instinct in man, was rejected by Jew, Christian and Muslim alike, as it is by the modern Parsees: and on the balance of the evidence it would seem that it might well have been rejected by Zoroaster himself at least in the rigid form it was later to assume.

Zoroaster was one of the greatest religious geniuses of all time, a Prophet who believed he held colloquy with God. He was ill served by his successors who not only re-introduced into his system those deities which he had dethroned, but also reduced his prophetic utterance to an arid dualism which quite distorts his magnificent conception of God as the Holy, Righteous and Good. Yet the Zoroastrianism of the Sassanian period, even if it distorted the Prophet's message, adhered, nevertheless, to the essential teaching of the Prophet, namely that God, despite all appearances to the contrary, is utterly and completely Good.

Part Two

WISDOM

5. Hinduism

by A. L. BASHAM

ESSENTIAL CHARACTER

There are probably over 300 million Hindus in the world, most of them in India, but also many in other parts of Asia, and in Africa and the West Indies. Though they form one of the largest and most important religious groups of the world, their faith is indefinable in a few words. It is possible to define the Christian or Muslim as the man who attempts to follow what he believes to be the teachings of Christ or Muhammad respectively, but Hinduism had no such single founder. Some modern sociologists have defined Christians and Muslims as those who consider themselves such, but a similar definition cannot be applied to Hindus, for probably most of them have never even heard the word Hindu, and have no name for their own religion. It was once said that anyone might be considered a Hindu who respected the Brāhman and the cow, and maintained the rules of caste, but this definition would exclude many of the most earnest of modern Hindus, as well as a number of unorthodox Hindu groups of earlier times. We can perhaps best briefly describe a Hindu as a man who chiefly bases his beliefs and way of life on the complex system of faith and practice which has grown up organically in the Indian sub-continent over a period of at least three millennia.

Thus Hinduism is a very ancient religion, in which many primitive aspects survive beside highly developed philosophical systems. Broadly speaking, it is a religion of an ethnic character, unlike the more recent missionary religions of Buddhism, Christianity and Islam; like Judaism, Hinduism is the faith of a single cultural unit, and it has not in the past made any special attempts at attracting the support of people outside that unit. Together with Buddhism and Jainism, which bear to Hinduism somewhat the same relationship as Christianity and Islam bear to Judaism, Hinduism is sharply distinguished from the religions of the West by its belief in transmigration; the great religions of the world may broadly be divided into two main groups by this criterion, and Hinduism is the oldest and most enduring of the Eastern group, which maintains that the soul inhabits many bodies in its journey through the cosmos, until it reaches its final goal, which is described in varying terms by different sects. The corollary of this doctrine is that all life, whether supernatural, human, animal, insect, or with some sects even plant, is governed by the same law. Whereas Western religions generally teach that man is a special creation, possessing an immortal soul which is denied to the lower animals, Hinduism maintains that all living things have souls, which are essentially equal, and are only differentiated through *karma*, or the effect of previous deeds, which conditions the integuments of subtle and gross matter imprisoning the souls and thus leads to their successive re-births in different types of body. This doctrine of *samsāra* has given a very distinctive character to much Hindu thought and philosophy.

A further characteristic feature of Hinduism, at least in its higher manifestations, is its tendency to reduce all apparent differences to a single entity or principle. It is not true to say that monism is universal in Indian religious thought – there are sects which maintain that spirit and matter are eternally different and separate, and others which hold that the soul can never become one with God – but it is monism that gives Indian thought much of its characteristic flavour, and monistic ideas continually appear in many guises in the thought and writing of Hindus – for instance in Rāmakrishna's famous dictum that "all religions are one".

EVOLUTION

The earliest civilization of India, that of the valley of the Indus, which flourished some two thousand years before Christ, had a religion possessing several features which appear again in later Hinduism. The people of the first Indian cities revered a mother goddess, such as was worshipped in many ancient civilizations; they also had a male divinity, depicted in one of the typical attitudes of the later Indian Yogī, and surrounded by animals, suggesting the Hindu god Śiva in one of his aspects; they revered phallic emblems; certain animals, such as the bull, were held sacred, as well as certain trees, such as the *pīpal*, which is still holy in both Hinduism and Buddhism; they appear to have laid much stress on ritual ablutions. There is little more that we can say here about the religion of the Indus people, which has been the subject of much speculation on the part of many scholars, but about which our knowledge is really very small, since the brief seal inscriptions, which are almost the only written remains of the civilization, cannot be read, and without written sources only the barest outlines of a vanished religion can be reconstructed. There is enough to show, however, that features of the Indus religion survived the Āryan invasion and reappeared in later Hinduism.

Around the middle of the second millennium B.C. the Indus civilization disappeared, overwhelmed by chariot-eering invaders who came through the passes of the North-West. Among these groups of invaders, some, if not all, called themselves *Ārya*, and spoke a language akin to those of classical Europe. Like the early Greeks, Romans and Teutons, they were a patriarchal people, and their most important divinities were male. They worshipped these gods with great sacrifices, at which the sacred *soma* (=Avestan *haoma*, p. 222) was pressed and its inebriating juice was drunk. The Āryans were a wild, martial people, but they had an important class of priests who were very skilled in composing hymns for use at the sacrifices and in memorizing the hymns composed by others. Though they had no knowledge of writing, the memories of these priests were so good that the hymns have survived without appreciable corruption to this day, in the oldest and theoretically most sacred book of Hindu scriptures, the *Rig Veda*.

The religious system of the *Rig Veda* is not that of Hinduism, and many of its most important gods are today practically forgotten by the ordinary Hindu. The great war-god of the Āryans, Indra, has degenerated into a mere rain-god, who is little worshipped; Varuṇa, the king who once sat in his palace on high and surveyed all the acts of men, visiting punishment upon the sinner, has become a sort of Indian Neptune, who is rarely remembered. Sūrya, the sun-god, still receives some honour, as does Agni the god of fire and the sacrifice. On the other hand two comparatively insignificant gods

of the *Rig Veda*, Vishnu, a divinity connected both with the sun and with the sacrifice, and Rudra, who later became known as Śiva ("the Auspicious"), a fierce mountain-god, have become the chief gods of Hinduism.

There is no complete unanimity among scholars about the date at which the hymns of the *Rig Veda* were composed, but it seems probable that the collection was virtually complete by about 900 B.C. In the latest hymns of the *Rig Veda* there is evidence of a development in the religious outlook. Some of the older gods are already beginning to fall into the background, and a vein of mystical speculation appears, which is characteristic of all later Indian religions. The authors of the later hymns are very much concerned with the problem of the origin of the universe. They suggest that the world emerged from a golden embryo at the beginning of time (*Rig Veda*, x. 121). They declare that a primeval urge which they call "desire" (*kāma*), acted upon chaos and produced the universe (*R.V.*, x. 129, 4). They regretfully decide that really nobody, not even the gods themselves, knows certainly how creation came about (*R.V.*, x. 129, 7). Among the most significant of these cosmogonic hymns of the last book of the *Rig Veda* is the "Hymn of the Primeval Man" (*Purusha-sūkta*), where it is said that the whole world appeared as the result of a great sacrifice performed at the beginning of time, when a mighty primeval person (*purusha*) was sacrificed by the lesser gods to himself, and, mystically surviving his own dismemberment, produced from the different parts of his body the various features of the universe, including the four great classes of society which are here mentioned for the first time (*R.V.*, x. 90).

The Hymn of the Primeval Man marks the transition to a new stage of Indian religion. Sacrifice had always been among the most important elements of the Āryan cult, but now its significance increased a hundredfold. New Vedas appeared, the *Sāma Veda*, a collection of verses taken from the *Rig Veda* and rearranged for chanting at sacrifices; the *Yajur Veda*, a collection of prose utterances with instructions, to be used by the officiants who performed the manual part of the ceremony; and the *Atharva Veda*, chiefly versified spells for achieving such varied ends as the curing of diseases, the expulsion of rival wives, victory in war and success in law-suits. The Vedas were expanded by the addition of lengthy supplements, called *Brāhmaṇas*, which elaborately explained the sacrificial rituals, finding symbolism in even the smallest feature of the ceremonies. The sacrifices, in fact, were now conceived of as repetitions of the first great sacrifice at which the world was created, and by their regular performance the creative

HINDUISM

process was symbolically repeated and the universe renewed. The gods themselves were dependent on the
sacrifice, and the sacrifice was dependent on the priests
who alone could perform it properly. If every rite was
not carried out with complete accuracy, the sacrifice
would do nothing but harm, and bring disaster on those
who participated in it; on the other hand, if correctly
carried out, it sustained the cosmos, and the whole
community benefited. The emphasis on sacrifice in the
later Vedic period, roughly from 900 to 500 B.C., had
as its corollary the great increase in the power and prestige of the priestly class, which claimed full immunity
from all temporal law and implicit obedience and respect.
There is good evidence that such obedience was not
always forthcoming, and many of the more pretentious
passages in the *Brāhmaṇas* are almost certainly the result
of wishful thinking, but in general this period was
certainly one in which the priest began to exert the
immense influence in Indian society which he has still
by no means wholly lost.

In this, its final form, the Vedic sacrificial cult was a
rather sterile thing. The large sacrifices which the
Brāhmana literature enjoined were exceedingly expensive, and could only be supported by kings or chiefs.
The ordinary man needed some less wasteful method of
achieving religious merit. Moreover, by this time Āryan
culture had spread farther into India. The *Rig Veda*
seems to have been composed chiefly by people whose
main habitat was the Punjab, and who knew little about
the valley of the Ganges. The later Vedas and the
Brāhmaṇas are centred on the land between the Jumna
and Ganges rivers (the *Doāb*) and the region to the west
of the Jumna around the modern Delhi. In the next
phase, that of the *Upanishads*, which overlaps with that
of the *Brāhmaṇas*, Āryan culture had penetrated farther
to the east, and had reached the borders of modern
Bengal. It was now that new doctrines appeared, perhaps
borrowed from the indigenous inhabitants of the Ganges
plain; most important of these new doctrines was that
of transmigration. First there appears the belief that one
is liable to death even in heaven. Then it is declared that
even the gods themselves must ultimately die, to be
replaced by new gods, and that all beings must be re-born
over and over again, in an endless cycle.

The doctrine of transmigration brought with it a new
attitude of mind. The sacrifices of the *Rig Veda*, though
they had much mystery and awe about them, seem on
the whole to have been cheerful ceremonies, at which
the gods feasted with men and rewarded them with
increase of cattle, strong sons and success in battle. The
religion of the *Brāhmaṇas*, though hag-ridden by ideas

of sympathetic magic, was still chiefly interested in life
on this side of the grave; the purpose of the sacrificial
cult at this period was in part to ensure re-birth in
heaven for its patrons, but also to gain them temporal
benefits, and, most important of all, to maintain the cosmos in good working order. But with the appearance of
the doctrine of transmigration it was felt by many
thoughtful souls that the aims of the orthodox religion
of the day were really rather trivial ones. What was the
use of re-birth in heaven if it was only one more link
in an endless chain of further re-births? What was the
point of maintaining the cosmos if it merely meant the
monotonous repetition of the same dreary pattern *ad
infinitum*? Something more was wanted, something
which would carry the soul out of the cycle of transmigration altogether, to a state of complete security.
For the first time the need was felt for release (*moksha*)
from the bonds of earthly existence, and, for that matter,
from those of heavenly existence also.

The way out was found, to their own satisfaction at
least, by men who had taken to lives of asceticism. It
would seem that, with the spread of the belief in transmigration, thoughtful men, often Brāhmans, but including people of all ranks, took to leaving their homes
and dwelling austerely in huts in the forests, where they
meditated on the problems of the universe, disputed one
with the other, and often subjected themselves to severe
self-mortification in the belief that thus they might
escape from the bonds which tied them to the cycle of
birth and death and re-birth. Other ascetics wandered
about the land, begging their bread, and teaching and
disputing as opportunity offered. The latter class, the
wanderers (*parivrājakas*), produced many thoroughly
heterodox teachers, who denied the inspiration of the
Vedas and the validity of Brāhmanic pretensions, and
claimed to have discovered systems which by-passed
Vedas, sacrifices, and Brāhmans alike, and led straight
to the ultimate truth and full salvation. These heretics
included some of the greatest religious teachers India
has produced, such as Buddha (p. 279ff.) and Mahāvīra
(p. 261), the founder of Jainism. The forest hermits, on
the other hand, were more orthodox, and admitted the
relative value of the sacrifice and the inspiration of the
Vedas, though they claimed to have reached a spiritual
stage which transcended both. Thus they were found a
place in the Brāhmanic fold and their mystical doctrines
were gradually made a part of Hinduism. Records of
their teachings and discussions are contained in a series
of texts called *Upanishads*. These beautiful texts, though
they differ in many particulars, contain one chief theme,
the unity of the individual soul (*ātman*) with the one

227

impersonal and absolute World-Soul (*Brahman*),[1] which pervades and underlies the cosmos. From the time of the earliest *Upanishads*, perhaps about 600 B.C., to the present day, this has been the basic doctrine of the most important school of Hindu mystical philosophy – the unity of all things in the one Absolute Being, and the necessity of fully realizing this unity within the soul of the individual in order to escape from *samsāra*, the round of birth and death, and to achieve the highest bliss, in which personality is lost in that which both underlies and transcends it. From this time, too, mystical experience has been a cardinal point of Indian religion. Every religion had found room for mystics, but their importance has varied from religion to religion, and from period to period. In India, from the time of the *Upanishads* onwards, mysticism has been fundamental to all religious systems, and detailed courses of mental and physical training have been devised to induce mystical experience, on the data of which the many schools of philosophy have been based.

In the latter centuries of the first millennium B.C. the great sacrifices of the earlier age became less and less popular owing to the opposition of the new religions of Buddhism and Jainism which spread *pari passu* with the growth of new classes of the population. The rising class of merchants wanted a form of religion which did not involve extravagant ceremonies and which would give them a place in its system comparable to their importance. The new religions in part met these requirements, but the changing character of Indian civilization, together with other factors, gradually produced many modifications in the religion of the Āryans. By the second century B.C. the old gods such as Indra and Varuṇa had largely lost their importance to other divinities, who were worshipped not so much with animal sacrifice as with reverent devotion. Chief of these new deities were Vishnu and Śiva, both of whom had played a part in the old Vedic cult, though only a small one. For reasons which cannot yet be fully established their characters changed greatly, and they became the chief gods of Hinduism, absorbing features of non-Āryan origin. By the early centuries of the Christian Era what we may call classical Hinduism was established in something like its final form, with temple worship and most of the salient characteristics of the religion of India as it existed when the first factories of the East India Company were founded.

[1] The reader should not confuse *Brahman*, the impersonal World-Spirit, which is neuter, with *Brahmā*, the creator-god or demiurge, who is masculine. The derivative *Brāhmaṇa* means either a sacred text of the type discussed on p. 226 or a member of the priestly class; in the latter sense it is here given in its modern form, *Brāhman*.

The texts which show us this early Hinduism are numerous. Oldest and most important are the great epics, the *Mahābhārata* and the *Rāmāyaṇa*. The former, which has the dubious honour of being the longest poem in the world, is based on an old martial story of a great battle between the Pāṇḍavas and the Kauravas, two related families of the Kuru tribe, but this legend, looking back to shadowy events which took place perhaps a thousand years before Christ, has been enlarged beyond measure by the inclusion of other stories and episodes, and by the addition of many long didactic sections, giving instruction on politics, ethics, morality and religion. Thus it has virtually become an encyclopedia of early Hinduism. The *Rāmāyaṇa* has been similarly developed round an old heroic tale, but here the story itself has been altered considerably, and the interpolations are somewhat fewer. In both these stories the god Vishnu appears in human guise as one of the chief characters. As Krishna in the *Mahābhārata* he is the friend and mentor of the heroes, the five Pāṇḍava brothers. As Rāma (in modern Indian languages, Rām), the hero of the *Rāmāyaṇa*, he is the brave prince who, obedient to his father's command, suffers voluntary exile, gallantly rescues his devoted wife Sītā from the demon king of Ceylon who has captured her, and finally returns to rule wisely and benevolently in his ancestral kingdom. The cult of the incarnate divinity, worshipped with intense devotion, had by now become part of Hinduism. The mythology of classical Hinduism was further developed in the *Purāṇas*, a series of lengthy versified texts of the medieval period, in which many old legends were refurbished and new ones developed, and the cosmology, theology and religious practices of Hinduism were enunciated.

With the Middle Ages various strange and often unpleasant practices were incorporated into orthodox Hinduism. Schools performing esoteric magical rites which were thought to result in union with the divine, arose in many parts of India, but especially in Bengal and Assam. Later there took place a great development of pietistic mystical theism, with the appearance of devotional hymnodists, whose songs in honour of their favourite manifestation of God were composed and sung in the current regional languages, in place of the learned Sanskrit in which the epics, *Purāṇas*, lawbooks (*dharmaśāstras*) and philosophical commentaries (*bhāshyas*) were written. In every regional language of India there exists an enormous collection of such devotional hymns, many of them of high literary quality and of deep spirituality, and these beautiful songs are probably nowadays the most truly influential religious literature of

India, being known and sung by everyone. Devotional hymnody of this type seems to have begun in the Tamil land, where the local language was developed in literary form long before the regional tongues of the North. Still very popular in South India are the many hymns of the *Nāyanārs* who sang in praise of Śiva, and of the *Āḷvārs* who were devotees of Vishnu; the earliest of these probably dates from the seventh century A.D. In the Middle Ages every language of India produced its hymnodists and religious poets, greatest of whom are Kabīr, Tulsī Dās and Sūr Dās in Hindī, the numerous followers of the great reformer Chaitanya in Bengālī, Nām Dev and Tukārām in Marāthī, and Vemana in Telugu. The form of religion propagated by these singers was generally a simple devotional theism with a strong moral element. Most of them sang of human brotherhood and of the futility of the distinctions of caste and sect which divided one man from another, but they appear to have had little effect on social conditions, so deeply ingrained were the old ideas.

With these hymns we enter on the final phase of Hinduism, before it began to reform itself as a result of influences from outside India. Features of all the many strata that we have traced are still to be found in India today, and many of them are likely to remain indefinitely. Thus we describe orthodox Hinduism before briefly considering the more recent developments which are rapidly altering the character of the religion.

THE HINDU WORLD-VIEW
AND THE GODS OF HINDUISM

The traditional cosmology of the Indians differs very considerably from that of the Jews and ancient Greeks, on which the world-view of earlier Christianity was based. While in the Western religions, at least until comparatively recently, it was thought that the universe was geocentric, comparatively small in dimensions and brief in time, the Indians have for well over two millennia believed that such was not the case, that the universe was not geocentric, and that it was immensely large and immensely ancient and would endure for a very long time, if not for ever. Though there are differences in many details, the three religions of India – Hinduism, Buddhism, and Jainism – would all agree to these propositions. Here is a further point on which the Eastern religions differ from those of the West, and which has also helped to produce certain differences between the outlook of the people of India and that of Europeans.

Those old-fashioned Hindus whose ideas have not been influenced by modern astronomy still believe that the universe is shaped like an enormous egg – the "Egg of Brahmā". It is divided into twenty-one zones, of which the earth is seventh from the top; above earth are six heavens, and below it is a series of seven netherworlds (*pātāla*) where snake-spirits (*nāgas*) and other supernatural beings dwell; these nether-worlds are not places of torment, but rather are thought of as realms of mystery and magic, containing many hidden treasures. Below the seven nether-worlds are seven hells (*naraka*), or rather purgatories, where beings suffer long periods of torment in expiation of sins committed in the middle zones of the universe.

It is believed that the world passes through cycles within cycles through all eternity; in the most usual version of the creation myth of Hinduism these cycles are said to be connected with the life of the god Vishnu. The basic cycle is the *kalpa*, the "day of Brahmā", lasting 4,200 million earthly years. In mythological terms it is said that at the beginning of each cosmic day Vishnu lies asleep upon the enormous thousand-headed cobra *Śesha*, a symbol of endless time, who is in turn cradled by the primeval cosmic ocean. From Vishnu's navel grows a lotus, and from the unfolding petals of the lotus is born the god Brahmā, the demiurge. It is Brahmā who creates the world, after which Vishnu awakes and governs it throughout the *kalpa*. At the end of the *kalpa* Vishnu once more sleeps, and the universe is absorbed into his body. The cosmic night is equal in length to the cosmic day. Three hundred and sixty such days and nights form a "year of Brahmā", and the life of Vishnu lasts one hundred such years. He is now believed to be in his fifty-first year. When the hundredth year of Brahmā is completed, Vishnu, and the potential universe contained within him, will merge with Brahman, the impersonal Absolute which is the ultimate entity of the universe, until once more the World-Soul develops a personality, a new Vishnu is born, and the process is repeated.

Within the basic cycle of the "day of Brahmā" are lesser cycles, most important of which are the great aeons, or *mahāyugas*. There are 1,000 of these in the *kalpa*, each divided into four aeons or *yugas*, called *kṛta*, *tretā*, *dvāpara*, and *kali* respectively, each marking a progressive decline in the virtue, longevity and happiness of men. We are at present in the *kali-yuga*, which is believed to have begun in 3102 B.C., at the end of the great war of the *Mahābhārata*, and the total duration of which is 432,000 years. At the end of this period, according to earlier Hindu texts, the world will be destroyed by fire and flood; but an alternative view was put forward that, thanks to the intervention of Vishnu in incarnate form, there will be a fairly smooth transition to a new age of gold. The similarity between the Indian doctrine of the four *yugas* and the four ages of classical mythology has often been noticed.

The world is presided over by a High God, on whom it depends, and it is governed by him, with the aid of many lesser gods, who are thought of by the theologians as manifestations of him in his various aspects or as emanations from his being. Thus Hinduism is fundamentally monotheistic, and, from the point of view of the educated Hindu at any rate, the lesser gods have much the same status as the saints and angels of Catholic Christianity; for the ordinary believer, however, the gods have considerable independence, and the more popular legends about them often depict them as disagreeing with one another rather in the manner of Homer's Olympians.

Hindus may be divided into three broad groups according to their views on the name and nature of the High God. These are generally known as *Vaishṇava*, *Śaiva* and *Śākta*, and maintain the supremacy of Vishnu, Śiva, and the *Śakti*, or female and active aspect of Śiva, respectively. Members of all three groups have generally lived side by side without friction, and though their doctrines and practices often differ considerably they have been roughly harmonized, each believing that the views of the others are erroneous, in attributing to a secondary manifestation of the Deity the functions of the chief one, but not so perverse as to merit persecution. Cases of mild persecution, especially by Śaivites, have occurred here and there, but Hinduism has on the whole a very good record of solving its theological differences in a tolerant spirit. All three branches are to be found in every part of India, but there are regional differences in their numerical strength. Thus the Tamil land in the South and Kashmīr in the North have long been strongholds of Śaivism. Vaishnavism in one or other of its forms is the most popular form of Hinduism in most other parts of India. Śāktism is now nowhere predominant, but it is strongest in Bengal and Assam. Families are by long tradition supporters of one sect or another, but in most cases there is no sharp division on this account as there is on account of caste. A man of a Vaishṇava family will occasionally worship at a Śaiva shrine, and vice versa, without any consciousness of having betrayed his traditions. If, in its social aspect, Hinduism has in the past tended to divide and exclude, in matters of doctrine it has preferred to assimilate; and the believer sees no inconsistency in the fact that he may generally worship Vishnu as the creator and preserver of the universe, but occasionally attribute the same functions to Śiva. For the educated Hindu the two gods are merely different ways of looking at the same God; from the point of view of the simple peasant they may be distinct, and one may be greater than the other, but both are mighty and beneficent and therefore worthy of worship.

The fundamental monotheism of Hinduism has arisen, not, as in Judaism, through the exclusion of all gods but one, but through the assimilation of many local divinities to one or other of the great gods. Hence it is possible, within a single all-embracing system, for many apparently opposed beliefs to exist side by side, and indeed even to be held by the same individual. Synthesis is part of the Indian genius. The position is well expressed from the Vaishnava angle in the *Bhagavad Gītā* (vii. 21–2), a text to which we shall frequently refer; here Krishna, the incarnation of Vishnu himself, declares:

"If any worshipper do reverence with faith
    to any god whatever,
I make his faith firm,
        and in that faith he reverences his god,
    and gains his desires,
        for it is I who bestow them."

Similarly in the *Śivañānasiddhiyar* (i. 47), the chief text of Tamil Śaivism, we read:

"Whatever god you accept, he (Śiva) is that god.
    Other gods die and are born, and suffer and sin.
They cannot reward,
        but he will see and reward your worship."

These two passages are not to be thought of as mutually exclusive. From the point of view of the Hindu both are true, because, on ultimate analysis, Śiva is one with Vishnu, and Vishnu with Śiva. In medieval Hinduism a syncretistic god, called *Harihara*, was devised, combining characteristics of both divinities, and temples of Harihara are still frequented in the Telugu and Canarese districts of the Indian peninsula; but Harihara never became really popular, and Hindus have generally accepted the two gods without trying to combine them.

Of the three chief gods Vishnu is generally worshipped in the form of one of his incarnations. After his awakening from sleep and the creation of the world by Brahmā, Vishnu is believed to take up his abode in Vaikuṇṭha, the heaven over which he presides, where he sits enthroned beside his wife, the goddess Lakshmī or Śrī, patroness of good fortune and temporal blessing. But, in his intense concern for the world, he descends from time to time in the form of an incarnation (*avatāra*). Incarnations of Vishnu may be either full or partial, and the latter are very frequent; in fact any great or good man is often thought of by Hindus as a partial incarnation of the divine, and religious teachers of special sanctity are worshipped as such. There must be hundreds of Yogīs and ascetics all over India at the present time who are believed to be partial divine incarnations by the circle of their followers. But the full incarnations of Vishnu are much rarer and more important. According to the general classification there have been only nine such incarnations in this *mahāyuga*, and there is one yet to come. In each case the god descended to earth when the world was in dire danger of being overwhelmed by the ocean of chaos or of perishing from the attacks of demons. The first six incarnations, though the legends about them are still popular, have very little religious value at the present day – they are the Fish, the Tortoise, and the Boar, in each of which incarnations the god appeared in the form of a gigantic animal to save the world from the flood; the Man-lion, and the Dwarf, in which he saved the world from destruction by demons; and Paraśurāma, the god's incarnation as a human hero to destroy the warrior class, which had become aggressive and arrogant, and to establish the supremacy of the Brāhmans.

Much more important than these first six incarnations are the seventh and eighth, when Vishnu descended in the forms of the heroes Rāma and Krishna respectively, for it is in these guises that he is today chiefly worshipped throughout the length and breadth of India. We have seen that these two incarnations began as heroes of the epic stories. The legend of Rāma was never developed beyond the story in the Sanskrit epic as we have it, though it was rewritten in all the major regional languages of India in versions emphasizing its religious element more strongly than the original. To the tale of Krishna, on the other hand, many legends have been added to those contained in the original story, adapted from various popular sources. In the finished form of the Krishna myth the hero appears as a prince of the tribe of the Yādavas of Mathurā. He is often worshipped as an infant and is thus depicted as a plump baby, crawling on all fours; in this form he is very popular with Indian women, and many stories are told both of the wonderful miracles and of the lovably naughty pranks performed by the divine child. Next, as a youth, a fugitive from his wicked cousin Kaṁsa, the ruler of Mathurā, Krishna dwells among the cowherds of Vṛndāvana (in modern languages Brindāban), where he charms the hearts of the wives and daughters of the cowherds (*gopīs*), and accompanies their moonlight dances with his flute. This aspect of Krishna, that of the divine flute-player, is perhaps the most important and popular. It has been the subject of much erotic verse and painting, but the many stories of Krishna's amours and of his relations with his favourite mistress Rādhā have always been interpreted by the Hindus in a religious and mystical sense, in the same way as Jews and Christians have interpreted the Song of Songs in the Old Testament. Finally Krishna emerges as a mighty hero, a leading character in the Mahābhārata legend, preaching the *Bhagavad Gītā* to his friend Arjuna before the great battle and destroying demons and wicked kings throughout India. In these three main phases he is still the chief object of worship among the ordinary folk of India – a divinity of remarkable psychological completeness, standing to his worshippers not only in the relation of father, friend and elder brother, but also of lover and husband, and even of son.

The ninth incarnation of Vishnu, added only in the Middle Ages, is a surprising one – Buddha. As Buddhism declined in India, Hindu propagandists began to maintain that Buddha had been in fact an incarnation of Vishnu. There was some disagreement as to the god's motive in taking the form of one who denied the Vedas and even the transcendent nature of the gods themselves. One of the earliest explanations was that Vishnu became incarnate as Buddha in order to put an end to animal sacrifice, but later it was generally stated that he did so in order to lead wicked men to deny the Vedas and thus to ensure their destruction. In any case the Buddha incarnation was never very important, at least within the framework of orthodox Hinduism. The final incarnation, known as *Kalkin*, is yet to come. At the end of this dark age Vishnu will descend once more, this time as a mighty warrior mounted on a white horse, with a flaming sword in his hand, and in this guise he will finally destroy the wicked and restore the age of gold, the *kṛta-yuga*. Christian parallels have been found for this incarnation, and it is not beyond the bounds of possibility that the doctrine of the Kalkin was influenced by Nestorian Christianity; but it is equally or more possible that the inspiration comes from Zoroastrianism, for the Kalkin has much in common with the *Saoshyant* (p. 214) of old Persian myth.

Śiva, the second great god of Hinduism, is of a character rather different from that of Vishnu. The latter is wholly beneficent, but Śiva has a dark and grim side to his nature. He derives in part from the fierce Vedic god of mountain and storm, Rudra, and he is often described as lurking in horrible places such as battlefields and cremation-grounds. Sometimes he is depicted in sculpture as wearing a garland of skulls and surrounded by evil spirits as he dances the grim dance with which he destroys the world at the end of the *kalpa*. In this form he is the personification of destroying time, bringing all things to an end. Śiva is also thought of as the great ascetic, wrapped in continual meditation on the slopes of Mount Kailāsa in the Himālayas, his head covered with matted hair, in which the crescent moon is fixed and from which the sacred river Ganges flows. By his meditations the world is maintained, and thus for his devotees he takes over the preserving function of Vishnu. Evidently the characteristics of an agricultural and pastoral fertility-god have been merged in the personality of Śiva, for he is often known as "Lord of Beasts" (*Paśupati*), the patron of procreation in men and animals. As well as in the form of an image he is commonly worshipped in his emblem, the *linga*, a short cylindrical pillar with rounded top, which is quite evidently phallic in origin, though it is said that the ordinary Śaiva worshipper does not recognize it as such. Unlike Vishnu, Śiva is not generally believed to incarnate himself for the welfare of the world, but he is said to have manifested himself temporarily in many disguises in order to help his devotees or for other worthy purposes. Despite his malevolent aspects in popular mythology Śiva has been the object of some of the most exalted religious poetry of India. Certainly his cult has sometimes developed unpleasant features, such as animal sacrifice, and, among ascetics, psychopathic self-mortification of the type which has gained Hinduism a bad name with those who do not understand it; but most of the Śaiva sects look on their deity as a god of love and grace. The literature of Tamil Śaivism describes him in very exalted terms and with strong moral emphasis:

"In his love the Lord punishes,
　　that the sinner may mend his ways
and follow the right.
　　All his acts flow from his love.

. . . .

"Goodness, love, grace and gentleness,
　　courtesy, friendship and modesty,
honesty, penance and chastity,
　　charity, respect, reverence and truthfulness,
purity and self-control,
　　wisdom and worship –
all these together are perfect virtue,
　　and are the word of the loving Lord."
(*Śivañānasiddhiyar*, ii. 15, 23.)

In the finished form of Tamil Śaivism all the capricious and harsh elements of the old Śiva have practically disappeared, and the god has become the compassionate father of all things living, who cares for them in his love and justice and defends them from evil. Some authorities would claim that Tamil Śaivism is the highest form of Hindu devotional religion.

Durgā or Pārvatī, the wife of Śiva, is considerably more important than Lakshmī, the wife of Vishnu, who usually takes a comparatively humble place beside her husband. Known in her fierce form as Durgā or Kālī, and in her mild form as Pārvatī or Umā, or often referred to simply as "the Mother", she is worshipped as a secondary divinity by most orthodox Hindus and as the major divinity by the Śākta sects. The fully developed cult of the Mother Goddess appeared comparatively late in orthodox Hinduism, and is not attested definitely until the fifth century A.D.; but it has very ancient roots and was certainly practised in India millennia before this time among simple people on the fringes of Āryan society, ultimately to be found a place in the capacious system of Hinduism.

An interesting theological doctrine was developed to give respectability to the Mother Goddess cult. With the growth of Śāktism it was declared that the High God was essentially inactive and transcendent; but before creation he developed the will to activity, and this active energy (*śakti*) of the divinity is personified as his wife. The act of creation is thought of as the intercourse of the god and his spouse, and this has led to much sexual imagery and often to orgiastic rites in some sects of the Śāktas.

Durgā, as the active aspect of the divinity, is thus a more accessible and practical object of worship than Śiva. From the point of view of the Śākta the god in his male aspect does not need worship and is not active in the world. Hence the Mother Goddess is to all intents and purposes the supreme divinity. In her fierce form she is often depicted as a repulsive hag, sometimes bearing an assortment of weapons in her many arms, and trampling on a demon. In her milder form she appears as a beautiful young woman. From the point of view of her devotees, however, her fury is only unleashed upon sinners, and she is generally thought of as loving and benevolent; but to this day her worship is often accompanied by animal sacrifice, and in earlier times human sacrifice to Durgā was not unknown.

As well as these three great gods many lesser deities are worshipped, most of them associated with Śiva. All over India Śiva's son, the elephant-headed Ganesh (Sanskrit Ganeśa) is revered as a bringer of good luck, and prayers are said to him at the commencement of every new venture; his great popularity and his quaint theriomorphic form have made his image very well known throughout the world, and those who have no knowledge of Hinduism often imagine that the worship of this pleasant and harmless luck-bringer is the best and highest that the religion has to offer. Another son of Śiva is Kārttikeya, also called Skanda and Subrahmaṇya, usually depicted with six heads and twelve arms and riding on a peacock. Theoretically a war-god, leader of the army of the gods against the demons, he seems, in the South, where he is chiefly worshipped, to have acquired the features of an agricultural fertility deity; this character was probably borrowed from an indigenous Tamil god Murugan who was identified with the Northern Kārttikeya at a very early date.

Sūrya, the sun-god, whose history can be traced back to the *Rig Veda*, is still honoured. A further important divinity is the beautiful Sarasvatī, patroness of art and learning, who is regularly worshipped by students and teachers at the beginning of school and college sessions. Hanumān, the monkey-god, is closely associated with Vishnu's incarnation as Rāma and is much revered by peasants, especially in Northern India. Sītalā, a goddess of uncertain ancestry who came late into the pantheon, is worshipped by mothers as the protectress of children from smallpox. As well as these, the numerous gods of earlier days, Brahmā, Indra, Varuṇa and many others, are still members of the Hindu pantheon, but they play little part in the devotions of the ordinary Hindu and in most cases have been virtually in eclipse for centuries.

Still very important, however, is the host of local divinities and demigods, whose total is enormous and who play a great part in the life of the peasant and the ordinary man. While the great gods are thought to be busied with important affairs and chiefly accessible in temples, these often nameless godlings are always available to help the villager in his troubles. Moreover divinity inheres in many beings and material objects. The cow, for instance, is virtually divine in her own right and one of the best known deities of Hinduism. The cult of the cow seems to have developed in India quite early, but its history cannot be clearly traced. Indian apologists declare that the cow became sacred and inviolate because of her great economic value as the producer of milk and butter and of bullocks for draught purposes. This explanation is, of course, a rationalization; the cow is not revered and respected because of her value, but because she is thought to be holy as the representative of Mother Earth herself. As such she should never be injured or killed, but should be cherished, humoured and petted in all circumstances. The bull is also sacred as the vehicle of Śiva who rides the humped bull Nandi, who in most Śiva temples has a shrine to himself. There is no cow-goddess, however; the cow is holy in her own right. Anyone who has visited Benares or Calcutta, where sacred cattle are particularly numerous, will realize how deeply the cult affects Indian life. To the average modern Hindu, even when he has given up many of his older taboos and has taken to many of the ways of the West, the killing of unwanted or worn-out cattle seems almost if not quite as reprehensible as the killing of elderly or infirm human beings.

Many other living creatures are sacred in various degrees. Monkeys, the living representatives of Hanumān, who helped the incarnate god Rāma so loyally in his need, are generally respected and are not normally killed, though they cause great damage to the crops. Snakes too are holy, and if it is necessary to kill one in self-defence a penance should be performed. Not only are animals sacred, but also many trees and plants. The banyan and the *pīpal* are particularly respected, and every village has at least one sacred tree which must never be cut down or injured. Among smaller plants the *tulasī*, a variety of basil, is very holy as the emblem of Vishnu, and many Indian homes have in their courtyards fine *tulasī* plants, which are tended with great care and treated with much respect. All mountains and rivers are in some measure divine, and some of them, notably the Ganges, are especially so. Large or strangely shaped rocks receive honour from the villagers dwelling in their vicinity. In fact the divine is to be found everywhere, not only in a single transcendent deity, or even in a number of deities and superhuman beings, but in human beings, in animals, in trees, even in rocks and rivers. The Hindu conception of divinity is thus much closer to that of classical Europe than to that of early Judaism, which has much influenced both Christianity and Islam and which postulated a God absolutely unitary and transcendent, and so awe-inspiring and holy that even his name might not be uttered. The Hindu rubs shoulders with godhead in every field and in every street; he is on comparatively familiar terms with the divine both in its friendly and in its awful manifestations. He will use the same word, *pūjā*, for the worship he renders to his gods and the honour he pays to his parents and teachers. Indeed parents and teachers are themselves gods to the child or youth as the husband is to the wife. Brāhmans and ascetics are often referred to as *bhūdevas*, or gods on earth. In the words of Krishna in the *Bhagavad Gītā* (x. 36, 38–40):

"I am the dice-play of the gamester,
I am the glory of the glorious,
I am the victory, I am courage,
I am the goodness of the virtuous . . .
I am the force of those who govern,
I am the statecraft of those who seek to conquer,
I am the silence of what is secret,
I am the knowledge of those who know,
and I am the seed of all that is born . . .

There is nothing that can exist without me.
There is no end to my holy powers . . .
And whatever is mighty or fortunate or strong
springs from a portion of my glory."

Thus God is to be found in all that has any merit, strength or value. At its highest this aspect of Hinduism leads to a nature-mysticism or pantheism reminiscent of the ideas of Wordsworth, a poet who is very popular with educated Indians, or to the mystical philosophy of the great doctors of Hinduism. In its humbler manifestations, among the peasants and the illiterate, it has much in common with primitive animism, seeing spirits behind every bush and looking on all unusual occurrences as the work of the supernatural. But even among simple villagers there is some realization that the spirits and demigods which inhabit the world are all servants and manifestations of the High God, by whatever name he is known.

PHILOSOPHY AND THEOLOGY

We have seen that philosophical and religious speculation began in India very early, perhaps even before it began in Greece and China. In the older *Upanishads*, which are still some of the most important texts of Hinduism, there is much thought about the relation of the soul to the highest reality, usually conceived in impersonal terms and explained by analogy:

" 'Put this salt in water, and come to me in the morning.' The son did as he was told. The father said: 'Fetch the salt'. The son looked for it, but he could not find it because it had melted. 'Taste the water from the top,' said the father. 'How does it taste?' 'Of salt,' the son replied. 'Taste from the middle. How does it taste?' 'Of salt,' the son replied. 'Taste from the bottom. How does it taste?' 'Of salt,' the son replied. Then the father said: 'You don't perceive that the one Reality exists in your own body, my son, but it is truly there. Everything which is has its being in that subtle essence. That is Reality! That is the Soul! And you are that, Śvetaketu!' "
(*Chāndogya Upanishad*, vi. 13.)

Often, however, especially in the more recent *Upanishads*, the ultimate is thought of in terms which suggest a personal God:

"He encircles all things, radiant and bodyless,
   unharmed, and untouched by evil.
All-seeing, all-wise, all-present, self-existent,
   he has made all things well for ever and ever."
(*Īśā Upanishad*, 8.)

In nearly all the later speculation and philosophy of India one of these two tendencies appears – to conceive the Absolute either as an impersonal entity or as a personal deity. The two doctrines have produced numerous distinct schools of philosophy, which have taught and meditated side by side without undue acrimony for centuries, each admitting the qualified truth of the others. From the point of view of Western logic one or other doctrine must be wrong – the ultimate power in the universe, if such a power exists, is either a superhuman personality or an impersonal entity – it cannot be both at once. Hinduism, with its propensity for assimilating disparate notions, has never found much difficulty in harmonizing the two doctrines. For the strict monist the personal God is the highest manifestation of the impersonal Entity, while for the theist the impersonal Entity is really the personal God rather inadequately understood.

We have seen that, for the religiously minded Indian, the main spiritual quest for at least 2,500 years has been to rise above the cycle of transmigration and to achieve union or close contact with the ultimate Being. According to most of the Upanishadic sages and many of the philosophers who followed them this amounted to complete identification, with the total loss of individual personality in the divine, but there were many schools which rejected this view. The aim might be achieved in various ways. It was generally agreed that sacrifices and good works were not enough, but would merely result in a very lengthy residence in one of the heavens, a desirable enough goal for the ordinary worshipper, but not possessing that finality which the truly spiritual soul desired. Various schools of philosophy emphasized different means of achieving the supreme goal and gave different interpretations of the experiences of the mystics on which the whole theory of salvation was based. By tradition there were six such schools, all of which were in existence by the beginning of the Christian era. Some of them seem hardly to qualify as schools of salvation, but all have been somehow fitted into the scheme. The six schools are:

(i) *Nyāya* ("Analysis"), the Hindu school of logic, which taught a system of syllogistic argument, apparently quite independent of that of Aristotle. Though it was brought into the scheme by the admirable doctrine that clear and logical thinking was an essential preliminary to salvation, its most characteristic teachings are from our point of view rather secular than religious and will not be treated here.

(ii) *Vaiśeshika* ("the School of Individual Characteristics"), a school closely linked with Nyāya and noteworthy for its atomism. Unlike Vedānta, it postulated a dualism of matter and soul and taught that salvation depends on the soul's fully realizing the difference between

PLATE 59. Siva as Natataja. 16th century. Southern. Copper. Marianne Brimmer Fund. (Courtesy, *Museum of Fine Arts, Boston.*)

PLATE 60. The Hour of Cowdust. Late 18th century. Kangra, Pahari, Rajput. Indian painting. Ross Collection. (Courtesy, *Museum of Fine Arts, Boston.*)

the two. The matter in the universe is composed of eternal atoms of the five elements – earth, water, air, fire, and space – and souls are involved with the atoms in such a way that they become incarnate and are liable to re-birth and suffering. Only by freeing themselves from matter and realizing their complete independence of it can souls find ultimate bliss, not, incidentally, in union with the deity, but in complete self-sufficient detachment. This school was essentially atheistic, and its basic doctrines had much in common with those of Jainism. The texts of Vaiśeshika are now largely museum pieces and have little or no effect on the general religious life of India.

(iii) *Sānkhya* ("the Count") was likewise fundamentally dualist and atheist. It taught, in its classical form, that the universe contains two types of entity – matter (*prakṛti*) and souls (*purusha*). The two are completely independent of one another, for the universe does not evolve through their interaction, but solely through the inherent nature of matter. At the beginning of the *kalpa*, matter, without the intervention of a god, develops within itself intelligence and self-consciousness, whence evolve the five elements and the organs of sense and action; last to appear in the process of cosmic evolution is mind, which also is thought to be independent of the soul. It is conceivable, on the Sānkhya hypothesis, that a universe might exist completely like the present in every apparent respect and yet be devoid of any soul whatever, for personality and intellect are attributes not of spirit but of matter. Yet, though souls are essentially independent of matter, the two become involved with one another. It is suggested that the relation of the soul and matter is like that of a lame man and a blind one, matter carrying the soul and giving it the opportunity of varied experience. In any case the union of spirit and matter, however explained, is liable to delude the soul and enmesh it in the toils of transmigration. By meditation the difference between the two may be fully realized in the inmost being; then the soul is no longer subject to the bondage of matter, and is finally released.

An interesting aspect of Sānkhya is its doctrine of the three qualities (*guṇas*) – virtue (*sattva*), passion (*rajas*), and dullness (*tamas*). It is these three, in their different permutations and combinations, which give matter its character. Though the term is usually translated "quality" these *guṇas* are in fact thought of as substances, which compose matter rather as the atoms of different elements compose the molecules of a chemical compound. Virtue predominates in everything that is wise, beautiful or good, passion in that which is active or fierce, dullness in whatever is dark, stupid or ugly. The doctrine of the three qualities occurs in its earliest surviving form in the *Bhagavad Gītā*, and, though the Sānkhya school made it

especially its own, it is to be found in much of the religious thought of other schools. Similarly the original Sānkhya doctrine of soul and matter was taken over by the more theistic sects of the Middle Ages and given a new look. The inactive *purusha* or soul was identified with God, and *prakṛti*, or matter, with the active Mother Goddess, his wife; ideas of this kind were particularly common among the medieval Śākta sects.

(iv) *Yoga*. This term, well known in the West, has both a narrower and a broader meaning. It is cognate with the English word "yoke" and has the connotation both of submission to discipline and of union. Probably "spiritual discipline" is the best translation of the term. In its narrower sense it refers to a school of philosophy, traditionally founded by the sage Patañjali, whose *Yoga Sūtras* form an important text of Hinduism, and in its broader sense it implies religious exercises and discipline and is thus the property of all Hindu schools and sects. The metaphysical teachings of the Yoga school are closely akin to those of Sānkhya, but it allows the existence of a God of sorts, a specially exalted soul which has never been enmeshed in matter and serves as an example to the others. But the chief distinguishing feature of the Yoga school is its carefully planned and graduated course of spiritual exercises, which, variously adapted, are now a common feature of all the higher manifestations of Hinduism. We have no space here to discuss Yoga in its broader sense, the Hindu technique of meditation, or the interesting physiological doctrines with which it is often associated.

(v) *Mīmāṁsā* ("Enquiry") was originally a school of Vedic exegesis which defended the complete authenticity of the Vedas against heretics and other critics, claiming that these texts were self-existent and eternal. The doctors of Mīmāṁsā developed interesting theories of logic, epistemology and semantics, but the school lost much of its importance with the growth of the sixth school of philosophy, which is by far the most significant at the present time.

(vi) *Vedānta* ("the End of the Vedas") was the school which gave organized and systematic form to the teaching of the *Upanishads*. While the other schools are almost or wholly extinct, Vedānta is still very much alive, for nearly all the great Hindu religious teachers of recent centuries have been Vedāntists of one branch or another. The basic text of the school is the very elliptical *Brahma Sūtras* of the sage Bādārāyaṇa, but the shining light of Vedānta is Śankara (often referred to as Śankarāchārya or "Doctor Śankara"), a Malabar Brāhman who taught in the early ninth century. Śankara was able to his own satisfaction to harmonize the many apparently contradictory statements of the *Upanishads* into a consistent system. His main contribution to Hindu philosophy was a concept which he probably adopted from Buddhism, that of a double standard of truth. As a pious orthodox Brāhman Śankara could not deny that all the Vedic literature, including the earlier texts with their emphasis on sacrifice, was sacred and true. But the truth of the Vedas was mainly truth on the ordinary pragmatic level, true with the truth of such affirmations as "trees grow upwards and their roots downwards". On this level of truth, according to Śankara, the world was produced from a divine personality by a system of evolution similar to that of Sānkhya, and went through interminable cycles according to the general teachings of Hinduism. But in the higher level of transcendent truth, which was that of the *Upanishads*, the world was not real.

Ultimate analysis shows that all our knowledge of the ordinary pragmatic type is shot through and through with inner contradictions; that which appears to be a snake may turn out on closer examination to be a rope, and who can say that all our perceptions of the world are not similarly deceptive? In fact the world, on the higher level of truth, is little different from a dream, a figment of the imagination; it is like the deceptive appearances produced by a conjurer, brought about by *māyā*, the magic art of the Absolute. Only the Absolute is wholly and truly real – the neuter *Brahman*, which permeates the whole universe, and is identical with the *ātman*, the soul of the individual. When this identity is fully realized, not merely as a logical proposition but as a fact of one's inmost consciousness, the soul is raised above the illusions of this transitory world and is lost for ever in the one final Truth. Like the Upanishadic sages Śankara describes this ultimate entity chiefly in negative terms. It is without qualities or parts, unbounded, without action, having no consciousness of "I" or "thou", eternal and immutable. Its only characteristics are three, a trinity often repeated in Hindu religious writings – existence (*sat*), consciousness (*cit*), and bliss (*ānanda*). Around the soul, on the lower level of truth, is a series of sheaths, the outer one being the physical body of the individual. The sheaths are conditioned by *karma*, the results of actions in this life or a previous one; hence arises the idea of individuality and the illusion that the world is made up of innumerable separate beings and things. When, by long practice of virtue, piety and meditation, the sheaths are one by one peeled off, like the successive layers of an onion, the illusion is fully recognized as such, and the one Entity possessing true Being, Consciousness and Bliss (*Saccidānanda*), the Supreme Soul (*Paramātman*) is known to be all that truly exists.

Śankara was a brilliant dialectician, and his teaching soon became the standard philosophy of intellectual Hinduism. It is not without reason that his work has been compared to that of St Thomas Aquinas in Catholicism. But the system of Śankara did not go unchallenged, and there are many sub-schools of Vedānta which reject it. Though very impressive, the monism of strict Vedānta is not without logical difficulties and loose ends which are hard to explain away. If the one ultimate Being is perfect existence, consciousness and bliss, there seems no reason why it should evolve the great mesh of illusion from its own essence, for it is by definition complete and perfect in itself and has no need of anything else. Moreover the attribution of consciousness to the Absolute creates problems. If the Absolute is conscious, it must be conscious either of itself or of something other than itself. But by definition nothing but the Absolute truly exists. Therefore the Absolute must be self-conscious. But if it is self-conscious, it must in some sense have personality, which it is said to transcend. Moreover self-consciousness is hardly conceivable without consciousness of that which is not self. Logical arguments such as these were used by numerous theistic philosophers of the Middle Ages to attack the *Advaita* ("Non-dualism", strict monism) of Śankara. There seems little doubt, however, that, prior to the logical arguments of these theistic schools, was an intense psychological dissatisfaction with Śankara's intellectual approach to religious experience, which allowed only a qualified validity to *bhakti* or devotion to a personal deity, since according to Śankara's system the High God himself was merely the primary illusory manifestation of the Absolute and thus only real on the lower or pragmatic level. For Śankara devotion and piety were merely the first rungs of the spiritual ladder; full salvation could only be achieved by the knowledge born of meditation. Other philosophers, however, strongly disagreed with him.

Greatest of the theistic philosophers was Rāmānuja, a Tamil Brāhman who taught in the eleventh and twelfth centuries. Where Śankara proclaimed "the way of knowledge" (*jñāna-mārga*) Rāmānuja proclaimed that of devotion (*bhakti-mārga*), declaring that Śankara's way leads to a state of bliss below the highest, which is only to be gained by intense devotion to God, until the worshipper fully realizes that he is but a fragment of God and wholly dependent on God; salvation is also to be gained by completely abandoning oneself into the hands of God and humbly waiting for his grace, which will never be refused. For Rāmānuja the Absolute has personality. For Śankara creation was conceived of as a sort of sport (*līlā*) on the part of the Absolute; for Rāmānuja it was an expression of the personality of God, of God's primeval need to love and be loved by that which was in some sense other than he. The individual soul, though made out of God's own essence, is never completely identical with him; in the state of highest bliss it is permanently joined to God but is never wholly one with him, and therefore retains some degree of individual self-consciousness; for if it lost self-consciousness, it would cease to exist as an individual soul, and it can never perish, for it is a part of the divine essence and shares the eternity of the divine. Thus the emancipated soul is one with God, but yet separate; hence the system of Rāmānuja is known as "qualified monism" (*Visishṭādvaita*).

There were many other theologians who developed systems along the lines of that of Rāmānuja and taught that the ultimate entity was not an impersonal Absolute, but a God full of grace and love for his creation, with whom the soul might find final peace through intense devotion. Here we have only space to mention one of them, the thirteenth-century Canarese theologian Madhva, whose system is of particular interest to Western students. This teacher went a step further than Rāmānuja and maintained a doctrine of dualism (*dvaita*). God, souls and matter, according to Madhva, are eternally distinct. Salvation is not thought of as union with God, but as drawing close to him and dwelling for ever with him in the contemplation of his glory. God saves souls entirely by his grace, without which even the intensest devotion and strictest morality are of no avail. But grace is only bestowed on those who live righteous lives and is unfailingly granted to those who deserve it. Evil souls, who become so weighted down by *karma* that they cannot rise, will be expelled from the universe to a state of eternal damnation, which is thought of as infinite remoteness from God. Such a doctrine is unique in Hinduism, which generally teaches that all souls, even the most reprobate, have the chance to rise again. Many lesser features of Madhva's theology, as well as many of the legends that are told about this teacher, show that his system was influenced by Christianity, no doubt through the church of Malabār. Madhva's is the only branch of older Hinduism in which Christian influence is almost certain. Many students have claimed to find traces of such influence elsewhere in Indian religion, but few of these traces are so striking that they cannot be explained as coincidental similarities.

Though the school of Śankara is very much alive at the present day and all Indians revere his memory, we believe that the devotional theism of Rāmānuja and his successors has been far more influential in the long run than the intellectual monism of Śankara. Most educated Hindus declare that there is no conflict between the two systems, which are complementary; but in fact it is theism which has been the real inspiration of most of the great Hindu reformers and which continues to inspire them. *Pari passu* with the theologians who appealed to the learned and wrote chiefly in Sanskrit, many hymnodists, singing in the current languages, carried the message of devotion to the masses. The simple Hindu peasant may never have heard the name Śankara and has no real understanding of the very sophisticated system of metaphysics which Śankara devised, but he understands the doctrine of salvation through faith and devotion, which he heard at his mother's knee, conveyed through beautiful religious songs sung in his regional language. It was the hymnodists, and not Śankara, who prepared the way for the great changes in Hinduism which have taken place in the last hundred years.

Rāmānuja, like Śankara before him, is said to have travelled and taught all over India. Among the greatest of his successors was Rāmānanda, who taught at Benares in the early fifteenth century. This teacher strongly opposed the rigidity of caste and founded an order of ascetics which still survives. He is specially revered in Uttar Pradesh. Among Rāmānanda's followers was Kabīr, by tradition a poor weaver, who was one of the great religious poets of India and the world. Kabīr lived at a time when most of Northern India was dominated by Muslims, who looked with the utmost abhorrence on much that was essential to orthodox Hinduism, especially image worship. Kabīr's chief aim seems to have been to convince Hindu and Muslim alike that they were both children of the same Father and were thus brothers in their common humanity. For this reason his hymns disparage many of the practices of both religions which tend to divide the two faiths – caste, idol-worship, pilgrimage, reverence for sacred buildings, legalism and ritualism. The hymns of Kabīr are still sung throughout Northern India, many of them even by Muslims and Christians, for their contents are so undogmatic that there is little in them that any theist could object to, while their message of trust in God and brotherly love is one of which few religions would not approve. Kabīr, in fact, was so unsectarian that many Muslims claim that he was not a Hindu at all, but a rather unorthodox Muslim *pīr*.

"O servant, where dost thou seek me?
  Lo! I am beside thee.
  I am neither in temple nor in mosque: I am neither
    in Kaaba[1] nor in Kailash:[2]

[1] The shrine of the Black Stone at Mecca.
[2] A mountain of the Himālayas thought to be the abode of Śiva (p. 232).

Neither am I in rites and ceremonies, nor in Yoga
and renunciation.
If thou art a true seeker, thou shalt at once see
me: thou shalt meet me in a moment of time.
Kabīr says, 'O Sādhu![1] God is the breath of all
breath'.

"There is nothing but water at the holy bathing
places; and I know that they are useless, for I
have bathed in them.
The images are all lifeless, they cannot speak; I
know, for I have cried aloud to them.
The Purāṇa and the Koran are mere words; lifting
up the curtain, I have seen.
Kabīr gives utterance to the words of experience; and
he knows very well that all other things are untrue.

"I laugh when I hear that the fish in the water is thirsty;
You do not see that the Real is in your home, and
you wander from forest to forest listlessly!
Here is the truth! Go where you will, to Benares
or to Mathurā; if you do not find your soul, the
world is unreal to you.

"If God be within the mosque, then to whom does
this world belong?
If Rām be within the image which you find upon
your pilgrimage, then who is there to know what
happens without?
Hari (Vishnu) is in the East: Allah is in the West.
Look within your heart, for there you will find
both Karīm[2] and Rām;
All the men and women of the world are his living
forms.
Kabīr is the child of Allah and of Rām: he is my
Guru, he is my Pir."

(Tr. Rabindranath Tagore, *One Hundred Poems of
Kabīr*, nos. i, xlii, xliii, lxix.)

Among those much influenced by the teachings of
Rāmānanda and Kabīr was a Panjābī hymnodist, Nānak,
who was born in 1469. The keynote of Nānak's message,
like that of Kabīr's, was that "there is no Hindu and no
Musalman (Muslim)" in the sight of God. Nānak organized a body of followers who were called *Sikhs*, or
"disciples", and this continued under the leadership of a
succession of *Gurus* or teachers, ever growing in numbers
throughout the sixteenth century. In the seventeenth
century the Sikhs became somewhat involved in politics
and earned the displeasure of the ruling Mughal dynasty

through their support of rival claimants to the throne.
The bigoted Emperor Aurangzeb (1659–1707) caused
one of the *Gurus* to be unjustly imprisoned and executed.
As a result of this persecution the Sikhs, who had been
becoming more closely knit and martial in character for
some generations, reorganized their "church". The tenth
and last *Guru*, Govind Singh, gave Sikhism the military
character which it still possesses.

Throughout the Middle Ages there were many other
hymn-singers in all parts of India, including men of all
classes, and even a few women such as Mīrā Bāī in
Rājasthān and Lāl Ded in Kashmīr. Though there are
many variations in emphasis in the poems of these singers,
they have also much in common. All teach ecstatic devotion as the chief and best means of salvation. All are fundamentally theistic, and though a few references may here
and there be made to the doctrines of monism and *māyā*
(p. 238), the strict monism of Śankara is usually ignored
and occasionally positively opposed. The God of the
hymnodists is a being distinct from man, though always
very near to him. The theology of these singers is rather
that of Rāmānuja than that of Śankara.

The hymnodists discouraged the rigidity of caste, if
they did not wholly oppose it, as did Kabīr. Thus
Vēmana, the shadowy author of fine Telugu gnomic
verses in the typical vein of the period, writes: "Why
should we constantly revile the Pariar? Are not his flesh
and bloodthe same as our own? And of what caste is he
who pervades the Pariar?" (L.D.Barnett, *The Heart of
India*, p. 112). As well as this emphasis on brotherly love,
the devotional poetry of the Middle Ages shows a very
wide range of religious experience, which often reminds
us of that of the mystics of Christianity. Perhaps the closest
resemblance to Christian mysticism is to be found in the
poems of the Marāthā singers, who seem in many cases to
have had a livelier sense of guilt and inadequacy than do
the poets of most other parts of India, and who often felt
the loneliness and despair of temporary loss of the divine
vision and separation from God, known to Spanish mystics as "the dark night of the soul". These characteristics
are well illustrated by a hymn of the seventeenth-
century Tukārām, one of the greatest poets of India.

"With head on hand before my door,
    I sit and wait in vain,
Along the road to Paṇḍharī
    My heart and eyes I strain.

"When shall I look upon my Lord?
    When shall I see him come?
Of all the passing days and hours
    I count the heavy sum.

---

[1] A Hindu ascetic.
[2] "The Bountiful", an Arabic word used by Muslims as an
epithet of Allah.

"With watching long my eyelids throb,
  My limbs with sore distress,
But my impatient heart forgets
  My body's weariness.

"Sleep is no longer sweet to me;
  I care not for my bed;
Forgotten are my house and home,
  All thirst and hunger fled.

"Says Tukā, Blest shall be the day –
  Ah, soon may it betide! –
When one shall come from Paṇḍharī
  To summon back the bride."
(Nicol Macnicol, *Psalms of Marāṭhā Saints*,
                                    pp. 58–9.)

But the general tone of these singers was one of happy confidence and love. They could express this feeling with a childlike simplicity, sometimes reminiscent of the less obscur everses of William Blake. Again we quote Tukārām:

"Holding my hand thou leadest me,
  My comrade everywhere,
As I go on and lean on thee,
  My burden thou dost bear.

"If, as I go, in my distress
  I frantic words should say,
Thou settest right my foolishness
  And tak'st my shame away.

"Thus thou to me new hope dost send,
  A new world bringest in;
Now know I every man a friend
  And all I meet my kin.

"So like a happy child I play
  In thy dear world, O God,
And everywhere – I, Tukā, say –
  Thy bliss is spread abroad."
                                    (*ibid.*, p. 71.)

Not every devotional teacher was as great as those whom we have mentioned, and some were of doubtful value. One important example of the latter class was Vallabhāchārya, born in 1479, who taught the easy-going doctrine that salvation could be gained by the simple worship of Krishna while indulging to the full in all forms of worldly pleasure. Vallabhāchārya established what amounted to a fully organized "church" within Hinduism, with himself as its head, and this survives to the present day with its headquarters at Mathurā. The

Mahārājas, as the chiefs of the Vallabha sect are called, are still treated with a devotion rare even in India where the tradition of honour and respect for the priest and ascetic is so strong. At one time it was considered right that the lay members of the sect should give to the *Mahārāja*, as the incarnation of Vishnu upon earth, the full use of all their possessions, including their wives, but a number of unpleasant scandals in the last century led to reforms within the Vallabha community, and it is no longer open to such accusations of immorality.

Numerous other teachers of the type of Vallabha existed in Hinduism, and they probably still exist – either downright charlatans or sincere men deluded by spiritual pride. In general, however, the medieval teachers were great forces for the good. Unable themselves so to influence the structure of Hinduism as to destroy the old caste prejudices and make it a universal system of salvation, they nevertheless helped to lay the foundations of the great reforms which were to take place in the nineteenth and twentieth centuries, by their doctrines of theism, simple but intense devotion to God, brotherly love and equality. It is through these men, rather than the learned doctors of the school of Śankara, that Hinduism has retained its vitality and is now finding the basis on which to adapt itself to the demands of the twentieth century and the resurgent nationalism of modern Asia.

IN PRACTICE

We have written enough already to show that Hinduism is not merely a matter of belief but also of action. For a Hindu of the old-fashioned type it is not a question of great concern whether a man believes in one god or several, or indeed in no god at all; what is really important is that he should believe in the Hindu way of life, and follow it to the best of his ability. And the whole life of the Hindu is punctuated at frequent intervals by ritual acts which are incumbent upon him if he attempts to maintain the Āryan *Dharma*, as the traditional way of life of the Hindu is often called. Here we can only give a very brief survey of the ceremonies, sacraments and social customs of Hinduism, though from many points of view they form its most important aspect.

The old Vedic rites which had no images have largely disappeared except in connection with such sacraments as marriage and cremation. The large-scale animal sacrifices of the Brāhmaṇas have completely ceased, though some old-fashioned Brāhmanic families still try to keep up the very ancient custom of the five daily sacrifices of the householder, which do not involve the killing of animals but only the pouring of ghee upon the domestic fire and the recitation of Vedic verses. In place of the old sacrificial worship have arisen ceremonies connected with an image or symbol, which, in the rite of *pūjā*, is worshipped on human analogy. The sacred image is treated in the home as an honoured guest, in the temple as a great king. In the larger temples, where there are many officiants of various ranks, the god is awakened at dawn in his bedroom where he has been sleeping with his wife, ceremonially conducted to his throne in the shrine-room, washed, dried and dressed, propitiated with flowers, incense and swinging lights, and fed. He eats the immaterial part of his meal, and the rest is distributed to his worshippers, or in many temples to the poor. Throughout the day he is often fanned by attendants and music is played before him. In the past, if he dwelt in a large temple, he had his troupe of dancing girls who performed before him, and just as an earthly king might temporarily bestow one of his dancers upon a guest visiting his court, so the god might temporarily bestow a *devadāsī* on the male worshipper who paid a suitable fee. This form of religious prostitution, well known in the ancient Middle East, was once very prevalent, especially in South India, but it has now been done away with.

The part played by the temple in Hinduism is perhaps not quite as important as that of the church in Christianity, the mosque in Islam or the synagogue in Judaism. In orthodox Hinduism there is no corporate worship or liturgy in which a congregation takes part. *Pūjā* may be performed individually in the temple, and on festival days a large gathering of worshippers may watch the ceremony being conducted by a professional *pūjārī*; but only in some of the reformed sects has congregational worship developed, on Islamic or Christian analogy. Yet, though it is theoretically possible to be an orthodox and pious Hindu without entering a temple during the course of one's life, and though all the most important rites of Hinduism are performed not in the temple but in the home, the average Hindu looks on his temple as the centre of his religious life. The larger temples contain many shrine-rooms and courts, usually richly adorned with sculpture and painting; they are not only places of worship, but also centres of social life, and some are the objects of pilgrimage for the devout throughout India. In the past the temples often maintained schools, and they still give religious instruction.

Though animal sacrifice of the large-scale Vedic type disappeared long ago, another form of such sacrifice arose in the Middle Ages and still continues in some temples, though much disparaged by many educated Hindus. This sacrifice usually involves the decapitation of the victim, often a goat or cockerel, before the sacred image in such a way that some of the blood falls upon it. Animals are still often sacrificed thus to Durgā and less often to Śiva. Animal sacrifice to Vishnu in his various incarnations is virtually unknown. The sacrificed animal is normally eaten by the worshipper who provides it, often offering the blood to the divinity and a choice portion of the meat to the officiating *pūjārī*; in this way it is possible for the Hindu to eat meat occasionally without infringing the rule of non-violence, for the soul of the slain animal is believed to pass straight to heaven, and thus, according to those who still believe in it, the sacrifice bestows a great blessing on the victim and is in quite a different moral category from the mere slaying of an animal for food. There is no doubt that in the past human sacrifices often took place; at these the victims were usually criminals provided by the king for the purpose, or volunteers, who took their own lives in fulfilment of a vow or in the hope of gaining heaven thereby.

The most important religious acts of the Hindu are performed within the home. The life of the individual is hedged round with sacraments of all kinds, which accompany him not merely from the cradle to the grave, but even from conception to long after his death; for rites are performed while an unborn child is still in the womb to ensure its safety, and an ancestor is cared for in the after-life by special ceremonies performed by his descendants. There are some forty sacramental rites (*saṁskāras*) which the orthodox high-class Hindu should perform or have performed on his behalf at various stages of his life. Many of these rarely take place nowadays except perhaps in a few old-fashioned Brāhman families. Most of them are very ancient in origin, and many features of the sacraments may be paralleled in similar rites of early Greece and Rome, and thus apparently survive from prehistoric days, when the Indo-European peoples had not yet divided.

No less than three rites are prescribed for performance during the mother's pregnancy. Immediately on birth, before the cutting of the umbilical cord, a short ceremony is performed. Another takes place ten days later when the child and his mother cease to be ritually impure, and the baby is given his name. His first sight of the sun, in his fourth month, is also the occasion of a ceremony, as is his first feeding with solid food. The ritual tonsure, performed only in the case of high-class boys, takes place in the child's third year.

Very important in traditional Hinduism is the rite of initiation (*upanayana*), which roughly corresponds to confirmation in Christianity and makes the child a full member of the Āryan community. This ceremony has always normally been confined to boys of the three highest classes, though there are cases of girls receiving initiation in very ancient days. Nowadays it is rarely performed except by Brāhmans. The chief feature of the ceremony is the investiture of the boy with the sacred thread (*yajñopavīta*), which is hung over his right shoulder and under his left arm, and which he must wear throughout his life, keeping it free from all defilement. In theory it is only after this ceremony that a boy is entitled to hear, learn and recite the Vedas. Nowadays the Vedas have been published and are available to anyone, whatever his class or sex, but probably many old-fashioned village Brāhmans still try to keep the sacred texts from uninitiated eyes and ears. At this ceremony the boy is also taught the *Gāyatrī*, a verse of the *Rig Veda* which is thought particularly sacred, and is repeated on many occasions, playing a part in Hinduism somewhat like that of the Lord's Prayer in Christianity or the *Fātiḥa* (p. 179) in Islam. The verse refers to a Vedic solar divinity, Savitṛ, but is generally interpreted as applying to the Supreme Deity:

"Let us think of the lovely splendour
of the god Savitṛ,
that he may inspire our minds."
(*Rig Veda*, iii. 62, 10.)

The ceremony of initiation makes the boy a full member of the Āryan community, and with it he enters on the first of the four stages (*āśrama*) of the life of the Āryan, that of the celibate student (*brahmacārin*).

According to very ancient tradition the initiate, whose age might vary from eight to twelve, was expected after this ceremony to undertake a long course of study at the feet of a *guru* or master, leaving his parental home for the master's house, where he lived a life of austere frugality, learning how to perform the domestic devotions of the Brāhman, and studying the Vedas together with some of the sciences ancillary to them. The authors of the *Dharma-śāstras*, the ancient texts on the Āryan way of life, seem to have expected all male members of the priestly, warrior and mercantile classes to go through this long course of Vedic training, but it is certain that such was not the case, even with the Brāhmans. However, it is no doubt thanks to the Brāhmanical system of education that the Vedic texts have been transmitted orally from one generation to another without serious corruption. Though India has been literate for two and a half millennia, in ancient times the Vedas were never committed to writing.

On completing his course the student, now a young

man, returned home to his parents and married. Though provision is made for the perpetual celibate in the Hindu scheme of things, it is generally thought that marriage and the production of one or more sons is a religious duty, and to this day there are few old bachelors or old maids in India except those who become ascetics in early life. In Hinduism the family, rather than the individual, is the unit, and marriage is necessary not only for the continuation of the family but also, as we shall see, for the welfare of its dead members in the other world. Thus the wedding ceremony is one of the most solemn and complicated rites of Hinduism.

Some of the earliest texts dealing with Hindu law make a distinction between religious and civil marriage, but in orthodox Hinduism all marriage is religious. The kernel of the wedding ceremony is the circumambulation of the sacred fire by the couple hand in hand and their taking seven steps together. Though the Hindu Code recently introduced by the Indian government allows divorce, which was certainly sometimes possible in ancient times, Hindu marriage for the orthodox is completely indissoluble once the seven steps have been taken. The ceremony magically links the couple together in a bond which no power on earth can break and which continues in the after-life if the two are faithful and true to one another. In this respect Hinduism goes even further than Catholic canon law, for while the latter declares that the sacrament of marriage does not become fully effective until the union is consummated, and thus, if there is no cohabitation, may be annulled, Hinduism makes no such provision. In the days when Hindu marriages were performed in childhood this often led to much unhappiness, for girls might be left widows before reaching puberty, to spend the rest of their lives in a state of asceticism, fasting and praying for the welfare of the soul of a husband whom they had scarcely seen.

Traditional Hindu society is strongly patriarchal, though there are exceptions in certain classes and castes, for instance in the Nayyar caste of Malabār, where a matrilinear system of inheritance and polyandrous marriage prevailed until quite recently. Normally the wife is definitely subordinate to her husband. In fact it is said in more than one sacred text that a woman cannot in any circumstances be independent; in her childhood she is subject to her father, in maturity to her husband, in old age to her sons. She can own no property except jewellery and similar personal possessions. It is her duty to wait on her husband in every possible way, rising before him and going to bed after him. Even a neglectful or wicked husband should be obeyed implicitly. In

Northern India women of the higher classes were often kept in confinement and never allowed in public except when escorted and veiled, and this custom has by no means completely disappeared. Though at all times the Hindu wife was expected to maintain a very high standard of decorum and modesty in her relations with men other than her husband and relatives, there is no evidence that such strict confinement of women was regularly practised before the coming of the Muslims at the end of the twelfth century, and we must attribute it to Islamic influence. In the South, where Muslim influence was less, the movements of women were never so restricted, and veiling was never insisted on.

Hinduism permits polygamy, though recently it has been forbidden in India by law. The members of ruling families have always maintained large harems of wives and concubines, and many of the wealthier men of all classes were polygamous. But on the whole polygamy has been disapproved of, except in special cases. The ideals of Hindu marital relations are to be found in the famous legend of Rāma and Sītā, who were wholly constant to one another. Society frowned on the man who took a second wife without good reason. On the other hand if his first wife was childless or produced only female children, it was his positive duty to take a second wife in order that the family might continue and the ancestral rites might be performed after his death.

Though the woman is definitely inferior to the man in nearly every respect, she is not without honour. All Hindu codes of morality urge that women, especially wives, should be treated with kindness and respect. As a mother, woman is particularly honoured.

A man, once he has completed his training and married, enters the second stage, that of the householder (grhastha). In this his life is spent in the pursuit of the "Three Aims" – religious merit, wealth and pleasure. This threefold classification is mentioned very frequently in the Hindu lawbooks, which declare that the claims of the first should override those of the second, and the claims of both those of the third, but that all are legitimate and desirable for the ordinary man. Old age, however, should be spent very austerely. The third stage, that of the hermit (vānaprastha), should commence when a man's hair begins to turn grey and he sees his children's children. Then the ideal Hindu should abandon his home, and, accompanied by his wife, should take up residence in a hut in the forest, to devote his life to penance and religious exercises for the welfare of his soul. The fourth and final stage is even more rigorous – as an aged man, when all his last worldly attachments are sundered, the ideal Hindu should become a homeless

religious beggar (sannyāsī), wandering the length and breadth of the land, owning nothing, attached to nothing.

> "He should not wish to die,
>   nor hope to live,
> but await the time appointed,
>   as a servant awaits his wages. . . .

> "He must show ño anger
>   to one who is angry.
> He must bless the man who curses him. . . .
>   He must not utter false speech.

> "Rejoicing in the things of the spirit, calm,
>   caring for nothing,
> abstaining from sensual pleasure,
>   himself his only helper,
> he lives on in the world,
>   in hope of eternal bliss."
>   (Laws of Manu, vi. 45ff.)

It is improbable that more than a small proportion of Hindus have at any time strictly followed the scheme of the four stages of life, but it has provided a framework of ideals in which ordinary Hindus have lived their lives for millennia. Even today, after busy lives devoted to the affairs of the world, elderly men often give up all comforts and luxuries and take to a life of religion, devoting the rest of their days to meditation and worship.

From the time of the Rig Veda the dead have normally been disposed of by cremation, though small children and ascetics are often buried, and some low castes also generally bury their dead. A corpse, and all the relatives of the dead man or woman, are looked on as ritually impure, and for ten days after the funeral the mourners are secluded from society while daily ceremonies are performed to provide the naked soul of the dead man with a new spiritual body with which it may pass on to the next life. If these funeral rites, which involve the offering of balls of rice (piṇḍa) and vessels of milk, are not properly performed the soul is liable to remain a ghost, miserably haunting the scenes of its past life and often causing trouble to its living kinsmen. This is the main reason why the orthodox Hindu desires a son, for only sons can perform the funeral rites. Though there are theoretically means whereby the sonless man may obtain a happy re-birth, these, in the mind of the orthodox Hindu, are at the best less certainly effective than the regular antyeshṭi ceremonies, presided over by a true son rather than an adopted substitute. After the tenth day, though the soul can now pass on to a new life and

Photo: Press Information Bureau, Government of India

PLATE 61. Popular Hinduism: effigies of the demon Rāvaṇa and his two brothers, to be ceremonially burned at the festival of Dasahra.

245

PLATE 62. Kālī as demoness playing cymbals; bronze statue from South India, seventeenth century A.D. (*Victoria and Albert Museum, London*)

Photo: *Press Information Bureau, Government of India*

PLATE 63. Ganesh, the god of good luck: medieval sculpture from Varanasi (Benares).

Photo: Press Information Bureau, Government of India

PLATE 64. Worship: devotees in a temple at Varanasi (Benares).

Photo: Press Information Bureau, Government of India

PLATE 65. The great temple of Jagannāth, Puri, Orissa, twelfth century A.D.

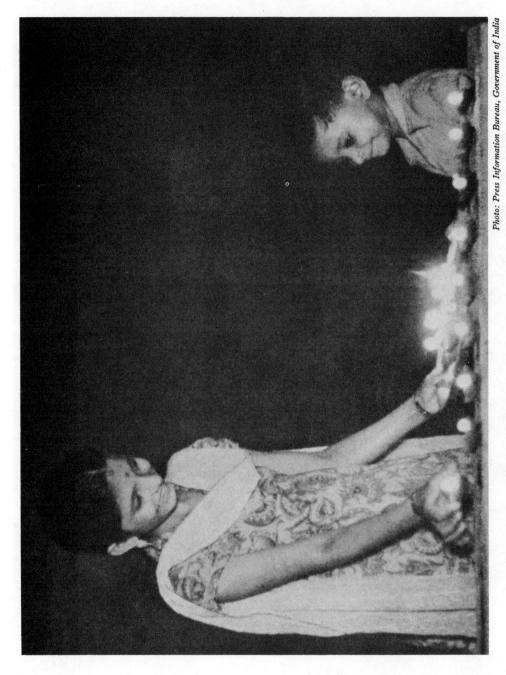

Photo: Press Information Bureau, Government of India

PLATE 66. Domestic Hindu rites: lighting the lamps at the annual festival of Dīvālī, in honour of the goddesses Lakshmī and Durgā.

Photo: T. Gelblum

PLATE 67. Pilgrims at a bathing *ghāt*, Varanasi (Benares).

PLATE 68. Colossal rock–cut image of the Jaina saint Gommateśvara, from Śravaṇa Belgola, Mysore, tenth century A.D.

the mourners are once more purified from the contagion of the corpse, further offerings are made periodically and are thought to nourish the souls of the ancestors in the after-life. These regular memorial offerings to the ancestors, called *śrāddha*, are probably based on rites going back to the early Indo-Europeans and, like the ancestor-cult of the Chinese, are a most potent force in maintaining family solidarity.

Hinduism has in the past gained some notoriety on account of the rite erroneously called *satī* or suttee, a word which in fact means "a virtuous woman". Often in ancient and medieval India a high-class widow would be burnt alive on her husband's funeral pyre. Though this sacrifice was in theory voluntary and was never demanded of the mother of young children, family and social pressure were often so strong that the widow had little choice in the matter. The inducements to the *satī* were tremendous – by dying thus she would expunge both her own and her husband's sins and the pair would enjoy millions of years of bliss together in heaven. On the other hand the widow who did not die on her husband's pyre had little but misery in store for her. According to sacred custom she was expected to spend the rest of her days in asceticism, with shaven head and devoid of all the jewellery, cosmetics and fine clothes which Indian women delight in, in continual prayer for her husband's spiritual welfare. In practice she was often a household drudge, inauspicious to all who came into contact with her and neglected by everyone. Provision for the remarriage of widows in certain cases, and for the levirate of childless widows, occurs in some very early lawbooks, but from well before the Christian era a widow of good class could not remarry and had nothing in life to look forward to. Hence it is not very surprising that *satī*s were quite numerous before widow-burning was stamped out early in the last century.

From our brief account of the life of the Hindu it will be seen that domestic ritual marks every stage. The rites of the Āryan continually remind him that he is a member of a divinely ordered society, in which each member has his part to play. As the family is more important than the individual, and the individual is not a whole man except as part of a family, so families are subsumed in castes, castes in the four great classes, and these in the whole of Āryan society. It is society and not the state which is looked on as fundamental. Classical Hinduism recognized the existence of the state and even ascribed divinity to kings, but, in theory at least, the only function of government was to preserve society from the chaos and anarchy which, in this benighted period in the

evolution of the world, would inevitably supervene without government based on force. For Hinduism society transcends the state and the state is the handmaid of society. The general ethics of Hinduism are based on the needs of a functional social order, the purpose of which is to further the Three Aims – the religious merit, the prosperity, and the pleasure, of its members. These Three Aims are in turn subordinate to a fourth long-term aim, which overrides them all – the winning of salvation (*moksha*) from the bonds of transmigration. Thus all social activities, all governmental activities, in fact all the activities of the individual, are fundamentally religious activities, and there is no aspect of life which can be divorced from *Dharma*.

This term is virtually untranslatable. Generally it implies the idea of an eternally fixed and divine standard of conduct, a sacred law which is never to be altered, but only to be interpreted by legislation or by social reform. It is for the preservation of the *Dharma* of the *varṇas*, the four great classes of society, and of the *āśramas*, the four stages of life which we have already described, that society and the state exist, and it is the fact that Āryan society maintains this *Dharma* in comparative purity which distinguishes it from the impure societies of the *Mlecchas*, or outer barbarians. There is a general *Dharma*, incumbent upon all men alike, and there are special *dharmas* for each class of society. For instance it is good for a Brāhman to study and repeat the Vedas; for a low caste man to do so is a heinous sin. On the other hand the man of low class may drink liquor, which is a great sin for a Brāhman. Thus each class of society has its own special functions and its own standards of conduct to go with them.

The idea that all men are fundamentally equal is to be found in Buddhism and in the work of the medieval hymnodists, but it is quite foreign to classical Hinduism. Āryan society is divided into four great classes, which were established at the creation of the world and are absolutely immutable. At the head of the social hierarchy the Brāhman studies and teaches, performs religious ceremonies and exhorts the members of the lower orders. The *kshatriya* or nobleman, next below him, maintains law and order and preserves the land from external foes and internal troubles. The third class, the *vaiśya*, theoretically comprises the merchant and peasant, while the fourth, the *śūdra*, consists of the menials and labourers who serve the three higher classes. This division of function has usually been ideal rather than real, and we have record even of *śūdras* becoming kings, but the system of the four classes has set the tone of Hindu society for perhaps as long as three millennia. The four classes are looked on as absolutely separate species, not normally intermarrying or having meals together; their rights and responsibilities differ, and they form a hierarchy within society, each recognizing its place and function and willingly accepting it. The mild equalitarianism of some of the medieval hymn-singers made little impression on even their immediate followers, and, until well into the last century, no influential body of Hindu opinion seriously criticized the stratified order of society, which even tended to impose itself on other religious communities of India such as the equalitarian Muslims and Christians.

The classes are not the same as castes, though they are often loosely referred to as such. The thousands of castes in India are said by tradition to have resulted from the miscegenation of the four great classes, and thus to be subdivisions of them, but it seems that the systems of caste and class have different origins, and the latter was artificially imposed on the former. Class divisions probably existed among the Āryan tribes even before they invaded India; caste, on the other hand, arose within India as a result of the mutual contact of many tribal and other groups with endogamous and craft-exclusive traditions. The sacred texts of Hinduism say much about the four classes, but little about the castes, which are usually taken for granted. In the life of the ordinary man, however, caste is very important, but class makes little difference for the non-Brāhman.

In every region of India there exists a complex hierarchy of castes, each of them normally endogamous and maintaining comparatively distant relations with the other castes. Their respectability or otherwise is conditioned partly by their trade and partly by their habits. Certain crafts and trades, such as scavenging, leatherworking, liquor-distilling, butchering and so on, are thought to be essentially impure, and thus the castes following these trades are untouchable. Their members must avoid all close contact with those of the higher castes, and in some parts of India social custom still ordains that members of certain untouchable castes shall remain a specified number of paces distant from Brāhmans, lest the latter be polluted by their very proximity. But, however pure their profession, castes which have retained old customs, such as widow remarriage, meat-eating and post-puberty marriage of girls, have usually sunk very low in the social scale. On the other hand castes have been known to rise by adopting habits more closely in conformity with higher class standards.

It seems that for the last thousand years until new ideas began to affect the Indian social situation, caste regulations have tended to grow stricter, and the many taboos of Hinduism to become more rigid and numerous. Yet we must not disparage the traditional Hindu social order unduly. For all its apparent strangeness the system of class and caste has much in common with the social order of the European Middle Ages, likewise stratified and likewise claiming divine sanction. It is wrong to judge an ancient social system by the standards of the twentieth century, however deeply we may believe in them. Moreover Hindu society, for all its apparent injustice, was by no means as harsh as many societies of antiquity. In ancient India slavery was mild, and slaves comparatively few in number. As in medieval Europe, all men, whatever their class or caste, had a place in society, and the caste organization, like the European guild, gave a degree of social security, for in most cases local caste councils cared for their members in trouble and for the widows and children of those who died in straitened circumstances. Where in most other societies loyalty was felt to nation or state, in India it was often felt to the caste. Hence Hindu society maintained its integrity against successive invaders, for the castes, independent of any government but possessing the very definite sanctions of social ostracism and disapproval, succeeded in maintaining the social order even in the face of alien governments which were strongly opposed to it. The old order is now rapidly changing, and class and caste in India may soon become things of the past; but it would be wrong to assert that they have never fulfilled a useful function.

It is in the framework of the social order of family, caste and class that we must read the *Bhagavad Gītā*, one of the most influential texts of Hinduism. The main theme of this great religious poem is one of moral conflict. Arjuna, the second of the five Pāṇḍava brothers of the *Mahābhārata* story, stands in his chariot awaiting the great battle which is the main subject of the epic. Beside him is his friend Krishna, who has agreed to act as charioteer, and whom Arjuna does not know to be the incarnate Vishnu. In the opposite camp are many great and good men, relatives of the Pāṇḍavas, teachers and friends. Surely, thinks Arjuna, to take up arms against them, even in a just cause, is wrong; it would be better to let his cousins keep the kingdom which was not theirs by right than to cause such carnage. Arjuna turns to Krishna and tells him of his misgivings – and the main body of the poem contains Krishna's answer. There is much theology and philosophy in it, but its kernel is ethical. Krishna dispels Arjuna's doubts first by explaining that he is a *kshatriya*, a man of the warrior class, and as such it is his duty to fight in a just battle. Fighting is his function and he should therefore fulfil it:

"For there is more joy in doing one's own duty badly
    than in doing another man's well.
It is joy to die in doing one's duty,
    but doing another man's duty brings dread."

                         (*Bhagavad Gītā*, iii. 35.)

"You are concerned with the deed, not with its results" (*ibid.*, ii. 47), says Krishna, and this is the *leit-motiv* of the whole poem. There is an intrinsic rightness in some actions and a wrongness in others, in no way connected with their outcome – the end does not justify the means. And the guiding principle of all action should be *Dharma*, the eternal divine law which has decreed that warriors should fight, just as Brāhmans should study and *śūdras* should serve their betters. A man, if he earnestly follows his *dharma*, may leave the results of his actions to God, whose concern they are. Just as God works unceasingly to maintain the cosmos, and yet rises above it and is not essentially involved in it, so man should labour without attachment, "seeking to establish order in the world" (*ibid.*, iii. 25). There is no great merit or virtue in the inactive life of the recluse. Rather a man should work continuously for the welfare of the world, caring nothing for himself, but doing all things for the glory of God in the knowledge that he is striving to fulfil the eternal law which is the will of God.

This, the highest flight of Hindu ethics, has been the inspiration of many of the reformers of modern Hinduism. More than by any other text the equalitarian and pacifist Mahātmā Gāndhī was inspired by the *Bhagavad Gītā*, for, though it appears to support the class system and militarism, it has a message which can be adapted to all systems and ideologies, a timeless value which makes it one of the greatest religious poems of the world.

"Do the work that you have to do,
    for work is better than inaction.
You cannot even keep your body alive
    if you are wholly inactive. . . .

"Do the work you are ordained to do
    always without attachment,
for the man who works without attachment
    reaches the supreme. . . .

"There is nothing in the three worlds which I need,
    nothing I do not own,
nothing which I must get –
    and yet I labour for ever.

"If I did not always work unwearying . . .
    men would follow my ways.
The worlds would perish if I did not work –
    I should bring back chaos,
and all beings would suffer. . . .

"Cast all your acts upon me,
    with your mind on the highest Soul.
Have done with craving and selfhood.
    Throw off your terror, and fight!"

                (*ibid.*, iii. 8, 19, 22–4, 30.)

MODERN DEVELOPMENTS

The system of belief and action which we have described is that still held by most Hindus throughout India. *Pūjā*, the domestic rites, the caste system, all survive to this day; pilgrims still bathe in their thousands in the holy Ganges, and sacred cattle still chew the cud on the street corners of the great cities. But in the last hundred years a new spirit has appeared, and it would be wrong to leave the impression that modern Hinduism was nothing more than what we have described in the preceding pages. The chief features of the new Hinduism are a deep sense of social purpose and a tendency to what may be called puritanism. Many of the more effete aspects of Hinduism are vanishing, and some have already vanished – the immolation of the *satī* came to an end over a century ago, child marriage has long been illegal, temple prostitution has been suppressed, and animal sacrifice and untouchability may soon disappear. The present Indian government has been able to do much for the untouchable, offending deep-rooted and ancient prejudices in a way in which the British régime dared not offend them. Thus temples and shops are now open to untouchables by law, and, though social pressure against them is still strong in some regions of India, actual prosecutions have already taken place to enforce their rights. Divorce and widow re-marriage are now fully legalized and polygamy is forbidden. Many of the old taboos and ideas of ritual impurity are disappearing.

Some precedents for these developments are to be found in the Hinduism of older days. The *Bhagavad Gītā*, as we have seen, inculcates ceaseless toil for the welfare of the world, though from the point of view of the author the world's welfare is intimately linked with the strict preservation of the ancient *Dharma*. Some of the devotional poetry of the Middle Ages advocates the service of the poor and suffering as a form of devotion to God. The great fifteenth-century Bengālī reformer Chaitanya, though a Brāhman, is said to have nursed the sick and aged poor of low caste, even before giving up his home for a life of asceticism when all taboos and caste restrictions cease to apply. The larger temples have always fed the hungry, and often also have cared for the sick in some measure. But the chief impetus to the great development of the social conscience in Hinduism has come from the West.

Though a few Christian missionaries, both Catholic and Protestant, worked in India in the eighteenth century, the East India Company, fearful of offending the prejudices of its Hindu and Muslim subjects, at first forbade all missionary activity in the territory which it administered. Only in 1813 the growing evangelical conscience in England forced the Company to admit missionaries. There were already in the large cities some facilities for a few Indians to obtain the rudiments of a Western education, but from this time onwards the number of missionary schools multiplied. The East India Company provided comparatively lucrative posts for Indians with a good knowledge of English, and from the point of view of the merchant it was an advantage to know something of the English language and English ways. Hence, despite caste prejudice, some middle-class Hindu fathers took to sending their sons to schools teaching English subjects in the English language. A very small group of semi-westernized intellectuals appeared in Calcutta and Bombay, and it was among these that new ideas began to stir. The first reforming leader produced by this new middle class was Rām Mohan Roy (1772–1833), a member of a Calcutta Brāhman family. As a result of the study of Christian and Muslim theology Rām Mohan concluded that originally Hinduism was a pure theism which knew no idols, and that the proliferating idolatrous polytheism of later times was a perversion of the true message. He opposed polygamy and the burning of widows and played an active part in the abolition of the latter practice. In 1828, Rām Mohan founded the first modern reformed Hindu "church", the Brāhma Samāj, which was strictly monotheist, rejected image-worship, and introduced a form of congregational worship on the Christian model. Rām Mohan's theology was very un-Indian – a cool unemotional theism of a type common in eighteenth-century Protestantism. The next leader of the Brāhma Samāj, however, Debendra Nāth Tagore, father of the famous poet, was a man of a different stamp. Where Rām Mohan's conception of divinity was rather of God transcendent, Debendra's was of God immanent, and prayer and spiritual communion were introduced into the Brāhma Samāj – already it was becoming more Indian in character. Keshab Chandra Sen, the third

great reforming leader, broke away from the Brāhma Samāj and founded in 1881 what he called "the New Dispensation", an eclectic "church", with a bible drawn from the scriptures of all the great religions of the world. Schism had already much harmed the Brāhma Samāj, and its great days were now over. In its various branches it still survives, but it has lost most of the influence it possessed in the nineteenth century. The impetus of reform moved elsewhere. The eclecticism and quasi-Christianity of the Brāhma Samāj had already ceased to meet the needs of the rising Hindu intelligentsia, which was now ready for prophets whose teaching, however much influenced by the new ideas, was firmly rooted in the traditions of Hinduism.

The first important teacher of this type was Dayānand Sarasvatī (1824–83), a *sannyāsī* of Gujarāt. After a deep spiritual crisis Dayānand came to the conclusion that the whole of Hinduism was corrupt and that its polytheism, image-worship and caste practices were false accretions upon the pure religion of the four Vedas. He rejected all sacred texts other than these, the oldest and most sacred, which he interpreted in a most fantastic manner, declaring that all the names of the many divinities to whom the hymns were addressed were in fact alternative titles of the one God, and all references to animal sacrifice were merely symbolic. Among many schools of Indian pundits there had for centuries been a tradition of adventurous exegesis, but Dayānand's interpretation of the Vedas was more daring than that of any of the older theologians. His opponents declared that he did not really believe in it himself. Dayānand's organization, the Ārya Samāj, gained many followers, and still survives as a religious force. In its social teaching it was for its time quite revolutionary, forbidding caste practices, prohibiting child-marriage, and permitting the remarriage of widows. But from the historian's point of view the most significant feature of the Ārya Samāj was that it was aggressive. Where the Brāhma Samāj was very well disposed towards non-Hindu religions, the Ārya Samāj attacked both Islam and Christianity as well as the orthodox sects. Dayānand Sarasvatī was a doughty fighter in the cause of the new "church" he had founded and made fierce polemic speeches. For the first time for centuries Hinduism took the offensive.

By the last decades of the nineteenth century pride in the Hindu heritage and resistance to the spread of direct Christian influence were growing in the Hindu middle class. The new tendency received much encouragement from a remarkable woman, Mme Helena Blavatsky, the founder of the Theosophical Society, who came to India with her faithful helper Colonel Olcott in 1877, and five years later, after travelling widely in the sub-continent, established her headquarters at Adyar, near Madras, where she remained until her death in 1891. This colourful and forceful personality is generally believed in the West to have been a charlatan, and the most charitable interpretation of the messages which she claimed to have received from the *mahātmās* of the Great White Brotherhood is that they were the work of her own subconscious mind. But, whether or not she honestly believed in the authenticity of her revelations, her effect on India was very considerable. On her travels round India she made every effort to impress the prominent Hindus whom she met with the greatness of their religion. Already a few Western scholars had publicly recognized the sublimity of the best of Hindu thought, but none of them had praised Hinduism in the terms used by Mme Blavatsky, who told the Indians that they possessed the pure Ancient Wisdom, which in the West had grown corrupt and had almost vanished. Though her earliest writings had been largely based on Kabbalism (pp. 41ff), her thought now became distinctly Indian in character, and the mysterious messages which she received from her *mahātmās* might have been culled from the Hindu and Buddhist scriptures. The Theosophical Society must be looked on as the earliest neo-Hindu sect to carry on propaganda outside India. Now of comparatively small importance, this society, especially under its second leader, Mrs Annie Besant, a woman with a personality quite as forceful as that of Mme Blavatsky, and of unimpeachable integrity, played a very big part in the Hindu revival, and its significance is often overlooked.

An even more important influence was Rāmakrishna Paramahaṁsa (1834–86), a poor Brāhman who was a devotee of the Mother Goddess at a famous temple on the outskirts of Calcutta. About 1871 this very saintly mystic began to study other religions, temporarily putting himself in the position of an earnest member of the other faith, reading only the appropriate scriptures, reciting the appropriate prayers, and following the appropriate spiritual discipline. The result of his experiments may be summed up in the slogan: "All religions are one." According to Rāmakrishna, Hinduism, Christianity, Islam, Zoroastrianism, all repeated the same message, all led back to the same truth which was perceived by the mystic – the oneness of all things in the Universal Spirit.

Around Rāmakrishna there gathered a group of able disciples who spread his message and attempted to live the life of the spirit as he led it. This gentle, semi-educated Hindu ascetic was one of those rare figures who pour out such intense spiritual power that they affect the lives of all with whom they come in contact. Keshab Chandra Sen and Dayānand Sarasvatī both met Rāmakrishna and gained something from him. His fame spread all over India, and his legacy was not only the modern Hindu sect named after him, but a deepening of the national religious consciousness and a further growth of pride in the Hindu religious tradition.

The most important of Rāmakrishna's followers was Narendranāth Datta, a well educated young Bengālī who on the master's death became a *sannyāsī* and devoted himself to the propagation of Rāmakrishna's teachings, taking the religious name of Vivekānanda. Vivekānanda was a man of strong personality and great moral earnestness, and was a very forceful speaker and writer with a good command of English. In 1893 he visited the United States to attend a parliament of religions at Chicago. America, always ready to accept new ideas and prepared for Hinduism by the sympathetic interest of a number of her literary men, took Vivekānanda to her heart. Wherever he lectured he made a very great impression on large audiences, and several Vedānta Societies were founded in the larger cities to continue his work. On his return to India, after a similar lecture tour in Great Britain, he established the Rāmakrishna Mission. Organizations for social work had already been founded by Hindus, and the Brāhma Samāj had done something in the way of famine relief, but the new society, while by no means neglecting propaganda, made relief of suffering its main duty. It marks an important stage in the growth of the Hindu social conscience. Moreover Vivekānanda's success in the West further raised the morale of Hinduism. After being subjected to the propaganda of missionaries, whether Muslim or Christian, for seven hundred years, the ancient religion of India was now at last conducting counter-propaganda on the territory of its opponents. At last a Hindu had arisen who could hold his own with the theologians and apologists of other faiths and even gain converts from them.

Nevertheless, the great wave of enthusiasm which greeted Vivekānanda's return from the West, and the foundation of the Rāmakrishna Mission, did not result in any very impressive change in the general character of Hinduism. The Mission has never been more than a comparatively small organization, and its work of relief has never removed more than a tiny drop from India's ocean of poverty and suffering. But Vivekānanda restored the educated Hindu's faith as the earlier reformers had not succeeded in doing. When he died of diabetes and overwork at the age of forty, in 1902, the new life stirring in Hinduism was quite evident. Vivekānanda

257

was a Vedāntist of the school of Śankara, in theory completely orthodox. He taught that all the institutions and practices of Hinduism were essentially good, though some had become corrupted or were misunderstood. Taking his cue from Mme Blavatsky he declared that Hinduism was the oldest and purest of the world's religions and India the most spiritual nation of the world. All that was best in the religions of the ancient world had come from India. Now India had been outstripped by the West with its practical and materialist bent. It was the duty of Indians to absorb from the West all that was good and useful in science and technology, and then once more teach the world how to live the life of the spirit in a society ordered with the furtherance of the life of the spirit as its main aim. This myth of the immense antiquity of Hinduism and of the debt of all other religions to it, and the very questionable claim that Hindu culture is essentially spiritual while that of the West is essentially materialistic, are still often to be heard in India. The old eclecticism of the Brāhma Samāj is no longer a force; the neo-Hinduism of Vivekānanda, in its many developments, is the most potent religious influence in modern India, and, adapted by the genius of Mahātmā Gāndhī, has provided the ideology of the Indian independence movement.

The Indian National Congress held its first meeting in 1885. Its early members were mainly enlightened semi-westernized Indians of the type which supported the Brāhma Samāj and the similar smaller organizations which were numerous at the time. A new intransigent nationalism soon appeared, however, and often led to riots and bomb-throwing outrages. The great nationalist leader of the early twentieth century, B.G.Tilak, was an orthodox Brāhman, willing to defend even such institutions as child marriage; but the followers of Vivekānanda also took part in this early nationalist agitation, for his teaching fostered not only the Hindu social conscience but also political nationalism.

Hitherto the new Hinduism had made little impression beyond the educated middle class of the great cities. At the beginning of this century the mass of Hindus had hardly been touched by the teachings of the reformers, and few if any of the illiterate peasants had even heard their names. It was the next of the great reformers, Mohandās Karamchand Gāndhī (1869–1948), who finally succeeded in introducing the reforms to the masses and in adapting the new ideas to the needs of the political movement which, with remarkably little bloodshed, was to drive the British from India.

Westerners are inclined to think of Gāndhī as a political leader with deep religious convictions, and sometimes he seemed to qualify for such a description; but he should rather be looked on as a religious leader with deep political convictions, for at all times his political activities were a mere by-product of his intense religious faith and experience. A further common fallacy is that Gāndhī succeeded in inspiring the ordinary illiterate Indian with a political consciousness because he appeared as the supporter of all that was sacred and orthodox. This is completely false. From the religious point of view Gāndhī was a vigorous reformer, as he himself claimed to be. His attitude to such effete aspects of Hinduism as caste distinctions, untouchability and ritual pollution was hostile; he looked on these as accretions which had corrupted the pure Hinduism of ancient days. Many of his characteristic doctrines were derived from non-Indian sources. The social equality which he propagated owed more to John Stuart Mill and the general trend of European thought than to anything Indian. Vegetarianism is certainly prescribed in Hinduism for the higher classes, but the complete non-violence which Gāndhī advocated applies only to ascetics; in the literature on the *dharma* of laymen a man is permitted to kill even his own father, if necessary, in self-defence, and righteous warfare, far from being condemned, is commended as the supreme sacrifice of the warrior. The Jain monks whom Gāndhī knew in his youth provided some inspiration for his non-violence, but probably the strongest influences came from the Sermon on the Mount and the writings of Tolstoy. Gāndhī's distaste for large-scale industry and his insistence on the nobility of manual labour have no real antecedents in the Hindu scriptures, and must be attributed to the combined influence of Tolstoy, Ruskin and William Morris. There are Hindu precedents for some of Gāndhī's chief non-violent weapons – the rent-strike, the *hartal* (cessation of all business as a form of political protest), deliberate obstruction by lying down in the way of traffic, and the "fast unto death" – but even here Gāndhī owed something to Thoreau, the British suffragette movement, and the Irish nationalists. It is as a reformer and innovator, rather than as a conservative, that he appears in the framework of India's religious history.

Gāndhī's success with the ordinary Indians was largely due to the fact that he came before them as a *sannyāsī*, adapting his new ideas to their needs and character so that they seemed perfectly natural. He was, for the simple folk, a great saint who had achieved close contact with God, and hence his utterances were thought to be divinely inspired. His voluntary ascetic poverty, in which he was followed by many of his disciples, was an earnest of his sincerity. Many people held him to be an incarnation of Vishnu, like the legendary heroes Rāma and Krishna. In his theology he was rather in the line of the medieval devotional hymn-singers than of the philosophers. Vivekānanda had been well versed in Śankaran metaphysics, and had held that behind the personal deity whom men worshipped lay the impersonal World-Spirit, the only entity which was wholly real and which could only be realized by meditation. Gāndhī appears to have had little or no interest in this rarefied concept; he was certainly a mystic, and capable of intense religious experience, but this experience was rather of a personal God than of an impersonal Absolute. His theology was simple and catholic, resembling that of Kabīr. God was a loving father, and all beings were his children. Like Rāmakrishna, Gāndhī derived much from non-Hindu religious texts – he loved the Bible and the Koran, and one of his favourite sources of inspiration was the Protestant hymn "When I survey the wondrous cross". Among his closest friends and followers were Christians and Muslims. The fanatical member of an orthodox Hindu movement who assassinated him was well aware of what Gāndhī stood for – the vigorous reform of Hinduism.

The earlier reformers had but laid the foundations – Gāndhī was the real architect of the new Hinduism. When he died Hinduism had largely reorientated itself. Caste, and the ideas of ritual pollution which go with it, are present still, but those educated Hindus who still retain the more obvious caste prejudices do so rather shamefacedly, and against their better judgment. For Gāndhī not only preached human equality, but practised it; when he persuaded his followers to perform for themselves the menial tasks normally reserved for outcastes, even to emptying latrines, he sounded the death-knell of untouchability and the whole caste system.

The spirit of the great leader is still very much alive in Hinduism. His mantle has fallen on Vinobā Bhāve (born 1895), undoubtedly the most influential Hindu leader of the present day. Living as a *sannyāsī* in the manner of his master, Vinobā journeys on foot from village to village persuading the local landlords voluntarily to give large portions of their estates to the landless peasants of the neighbourhood. The *Bhūdān* (land-giving) campaign initiated by Vinobā Bhāve has had remarkable success in many parts of India, and is only part of the neo-Hindu movement called *Sarvodaya* ("Universal Uplift"), which, independently of anything the government does, is working all over India to raise the cultural, moral and material standards of the peasant and labourer.

Modern Hinduism has produced its philosophers and theologians as well as its men of action. Most outstanding of these was probably Aravinda Ghose (1872–1950), generally known as Śrī Aurobindo according to the Bengālī pronunciation of his name. This teacher, after a turbulent youth as a nationalist leader, settled in Pondicherry, then a French possession, and became a religious teacher. The Vedānta of Śrī Aurobindo is largely that of Śankara, but it finds room for evolution and owes something to the philosophy of Bergson. The great authority on Hindu philosophy, Sarvepalli Rādhākrishnan, has also in many of his writings attempted to interpret the ancient doctrines of Hinduism in terms of the twentieth century, as have the famous poet Rabīndranāth Tagore and many lesser men too numerous to mention.

A hundred years ago, at the time of the Mutiny, there were many missionaries in India who sincerely believed that within a few generations the whole of India would become Christian. The oppressive system of ceremonial restrictions and taboos, which was the most obvious aspect of Hinduism to one who did not look below the surface, seemed bound to perish in the face of such Western innovations as railways, scientific medicine and widespread literacy, leaving a gap which could only be filled by the religion of Christ. In fact the system of caste and ritualism is rapidly perishing, but the gap is being filled by new developments in Hinduism itself. Christianity has made its mark in India, but only at second hand. Fructified by many ideas imported from the West, Hinduism has shown unexpected powers of development. We have seen that Hinduism has always tended to assimilate rather than to exclude – and in the last fifty years it has largely assimilated the principles of equality and social service. Over periods often of many generations Hinduism has also in the past quietly shed much that has lost its value. To the tribal and semi-tribal societies of Vedic times the expensive hecatombs of animals were probably socially necessary – later they gradually disappeared as they outlived their usefulness. The texts which prescribe such sacrifices are still looked on as sacred, but their prescriptions are dead letters. The same is the case with many other practices of classical Hinduism. Though all ancient texts are sacred, all are open to figurative interpretation; unlike Islam and old-fashioned Protestant Christianity, Hinduism has never depended on the letter of the scriptures. Thus there is every possibility of its adapting itself to the rapidly changing conditions of the twentieth century without formally rejecting any part of its inheritance from the past.

Hinduism has now become a world force. With

India's rise to full nationhood the thoughts and policies of men brought up in Hinduism have become matters of vital importance to every nation. And from the first visit of Vivekānanda to America, neo-Hinduism has been slowly making converts outside India. The Los Angeles branch of the Vedānta Society counts such well-known literary men as Aldous Huxley and Christopher Isherwood among its members. In many cities of Europe and America similar societies exist, and teachers of Yoga are also to be found. Through her philosophy Hinduism has long exerted a subtle but very real influence on the West, though monism of the Hindu type seems now less popular with Western philosophers than it was in the last century.

It is not as an ancient expended faith that we must view Hinduism. The old Hinduism is still there, but it is giving way to the new, not by a religious revolution, but by a steady process of adaptation. Typical of the new Hinduism is the Lakshmīnārāyan Temple at New Delhi, commonly known as Birla Mandir after the prominent industrialist who endowed it. Birla Mandir is not by any means a great work of art. Its architecture and sculpture are uninspired and largely traditional in style. But it preserves within its courts some of the wonderful mixture of ebullient vitality and mystical calm which is typical of the best of India's religious art. In Birla Mandir there is no question of excluding untouchables and non-Hindus; the temple gates are open to all who wish to enter. Here not only are the gods of Hinduism worshipped and the great saints and doctors of Hinduism reverenced, but room is found for the chief teachers of other faiths and lands also – Jesus and Muhammad, Confucius and Lao-tzü, Plato and Aristotle. The earth itself, which has mothered the millions who over four thousand years have built up the civilization of India, is revered in a shrine where a map of the Indian sub-continent replaces the usual image. Birla Mandir is symbolic of the new

Hinduism – a vigorous faith with a deep social conscience and considerable missionary zeal, willing to accept whatever it deems good wherever it finds it.

Hinduism has much to oppose it. Christian and Muslim propaganda is now no longer a serious threat to it, but scientific humanism and Communism are gathering strength in India, and the old faith of the land, despite its revitalization in the last fifty years, may yet lose ground to the new quasi-religions of the modern world. Yet its future is hardly in doubt. It will survive, continuing to change with changing conditions, its plasticity allowing it to adapt itself to fresh situations and yet in some sense to remain true to the Ancient Wisdom. The words of Mahātmā Gāndhī, with their paradoxical and typically Indian identification of true progress and return to the starting-point, might well be the words of Mother India herself:

"Consider my spinning wheel. A full turn of the wheel is called a revolution. The revolution of the stars is a revolution of light, that of the seasons of fruit and flower. A revolution in man's history should be of justice and goodness.

Those who want to mock me and my spinning wheel say, 'You want to put the clock back'.

No, my friends, I am the most advanced revolutionary, and I need only let the clock go on for it to come back to the starting point of its own accord.

A revolution is a return to the First Principle, to the Eternal. Some men cling to the forms of the past and the memory of the dead, and they live like the dead; others hurl themselves into foolish novelties until they plunge into the void. I go forward without losing my way, for I am always coming back to the most ancient traditions through a complete revolution, a total but natural reversal, willed by God and coming at its appointed time."

(Lanza del Vasto, *Gandhi to Vinoba*, p. 33.)

6. Jainism

by A. L. BASHAM

The religion of Jainism, though it is to be found only in India, has probably as much right as Buddhism to be considered as a faith distinct from Hinduism. Like Buddhism it is based on the doctrines of a heterodox ascetic, who taught in the regions now called Bihār and Uttar Pradesh in the latter half of the sixth and the beginning of the fifth century B.C. Vardhamāna Mahāvīra, the founder of Jainism, was a contemporary of the Buddha and is often mentioned in the Buddhist scriptures under the name Nigantha Nātaputta, "the Naked Ascetic of the Clan of the Jñātrikas". He is said to have been the twenty-fourth and last of the *Tīrthankaras*, the "Ford-makers" or great teachers of Jainism in this period of cosmic decline. The twenty-third of these, Pārśva, is said to have lived only 250 years before Mahāvīra, and hence may well have been a historical figure, on whose cruder teachings Mahāvīra based his more developed doctrines, and the ascetics of whose order became Mahāvīra's first followers.

Mahāvīra, like the Buddha, was the son of a chief of one of the oligarchic tribes living to the north of the river Ganges. Among the many legends told about him there are some which have the ring of truth about them, and we may believe as a minimum that he left his home at about the age of thirty to become an ascetic in search of salvation from the dreary round of birth and death and re-birth which seemed so distasteful and frightening to the more sensitive minds of the times. For some twelve years he wandered about the land, abandoning all clothing in order to be as free as possible from earthly trammels and to suffer the hardships of heat and cold, so as to work off the burden of evil *karma* (p. 225) which weighed down his soul. For some years he was associated with Gośāla, the founder of another heterodox sect, that of the *Ājīvikas*, which had a long, if not very spectacular history, surviving until the fourteenth century. But the two ascetics quarrelled, and Mahāvīra went his way alone, steadily mortifying the flesh until,

at about the age of forty-two, he found full enlightenment, at least to his own satisfaction. In the terminology of his followers he then became a "perfected soul" (*kevalin*) and a "conqueror" (*jina*). From the latter term his followers are known as *Jainas* (usually nowadays pronounced without the final *a*) or "Followers of the Conquerors". Like the Buddha, Mahāvīra soon began to gain support for his new doctrine of salvation, gathering together a band of ascetic followers, and receiving honour and alms from many lay devotees, who, like those of Buddhism, seem to have been chiefly recruited from the mercantile classes. He taught for some thirty years, dying by the rite of *sallekhana*, or voluntary self-starvation, at the age of seventy-two at Pāvā, a village not far from modern Patnā, and a great centre of pilgrimage for Jains to this day. Most modern authorities believe that the date of his death was about 468 B.C. although orthodox Jain tradition places it about sixty years earlier.

The history of Jainism, though it has much of interest to the specialist, is less spectacular than that of Buddhism. Though occasionally Jain monks may have tried to spread their teachings outside their homeland, they never made a significant impression beyond the bounds of India. Jainism has always been a purely Indian religion. Like Buddhism, Jainism has suffered a great schism. Its two branches have separate collections of sacred texts, and in the past their members have often indulged in acrimonious disputation; but the schism has not led to great developments of doctrine or philosophy, comparable to those which occurred after the division between Theravāda and Mahāyāna Buddhism, for the breach was based not on fundamental teachings but on points of ascetic discipline. The teachings of the two sects of Jainism are still virtually identical, which would point to the fact that they are authentically ancient, perhaps going back to Mahāvīra himself, with very little later alteration or development. Great Jain philosophers in the Middle Ages much elaborated the ancient doctrines and brought much dialectical skill to bear in their defence, but the fundamentals remained essentially unchanged. There is a good deal of disagreement and doubt as to what the Buddha really taught; on the other hand it is fairly certain that the basic message of Mahāvīra is that which is taught by Jains of both sects at the present day.

At times Jainism enjoyed the patronage of mighty kings and was virtually the state religion in some parts of India. Its importance declined with the growth of Hindu devotional theism in the Middle Ages, but, unlike Buddhism, it never made any real compromise with theism, and it survived in the land of its birth. Where Buddhism was dependent for its survival chiefly on the ascetic order, established in wealthy monasteries which were quickly destroyed by invading Muslims, the Jains were backed by a disciplined body of well-to-do laymen, cared for by the ministrations of their monks, and with a strong sense of solidarity in the faith. These faithful layfolk have kept Jainism alive to the present day. Jains are most numerous in Gujarāt, where the *Śvetāmbara* sect prevails, and in Mysore, the headquarters of the *Digambaras*. The basis of the schism is the question whether or not the Jain monk should wear clothes. It is said that the division arose after a great famine at the beginning of the third century B.C., when many monks emigrated to the Deccan to escape the evils of the times, and, on their return, found to their disgust that most of their fellows who had remained behind had so far forgotten their vows as to have taken to wearing robes. Both sects admit that ideally the monk should be completely naked, but the Śvetāmbaras ("white-clad") believe that owing to the degeneration of the world in the present age nudity is no longer possible; the Digambaras ("space-clad") still maintain that total nudity is right and proper for the Jain monk, but in recent centuries even they have taken to wearing robes, at least in public. There are other matters on which the two sects disagree, but none are fundamental.

The unorthodox teachers of the age of the Buddha and Mahāvīra were primarily interested in providing a means of escape from the wretched round of transmigration, but they invariably produced doctrines of a philosophical or quasi-philosophical kind to give intellectual backing to their practical systems of psychic training. Such doctrines show a striving to reach first principles and basic natural laws comparable to that which existed in the Mediterranean world at the same time, and we can find Indian counterparts for many of the philosophical systems of Greece. Early Buddhism agreed with Heraclitus in maintaining as a fundamental principle that all things were in constant flux, but, unlike Heraclitus, Buddhism also maintained as a corollary that man suffered from all the woes arising from transmigration on account of his futile attempts to enforce permanence on a universe where permanence was not to be found; and a detailed system of mental and spiritual training was devised for the purpose of bringing to an end the long chain of cause and effect which made up the specious individual.

If the axioms of Buddhism are essentially psychological, those of Jainism are rather physiological. At all times Jainism has maintained as its fundamental doctrine that the phenomenal individual consists of a soul closely enmeshed in matter; salvation is to be found by freeing the soul from matter, so that the former may enjoy omniscient self-sufficient bliss for all eternity. This view is very similar to that of the Hindu philosophical school of Sānkhya (p. 237), and it is quite possible that both Jainism and Sānkhya had a common origin in very ancient ideas ascribing living activity to matter.

For all the subtlety with which many of its doctrines have been elaborated, the primitive heritage of Jainism is very evident. It retains characteristics of a stage in the evolution of Indian thought when no entity could be conceived of except on the analogy of solid matter and when everything which moved and every object showing some degree of organization was thought of as being alive. Thus for the Jain the soul, which is identified with the life (*jīva*), is finite and has variable though definite size and weight. Moreover, primitive animistic ideas must have originally inspired the Jain's attribution of life to entities and objects not thought to be living by other Indian sects. Not only are gods, human beings, demons, animals and insects believed to be inhabited by souls, but also plants of all species, earth and stones and everything derived from the earth, rivers, ponds, seas and raindrops, flames and all fires, and gases and winds of every kind. Thus the whole universe is full of life. In every breath of wind, in every handful of earth, souls are imprisoned. When a match is struck a fire-being, the soul of which may one day become that of a man, is born, only to die again when the match is blown out. In every stone on the road a soul is locked in a prison of silent suffering, unable to escape the careless foot that kicks it or to cry out at its pain. By the fact of its incarnation the soul has suffered the loss of its pristine purity, and its pains are greater the more tightly it is bound by matter, in one of the lower forms of life. In

JAINISM

the infinitely repeated round of birth and death and re-birth the soul's agonies know no bounds:

"Helpless in snares and traps, a deer, I have been caught and bound and fastened, and often I have been killed."

"A fish, I have been caught with hooks and nets, an infinite number of times I have been killed and scraped, split and gutted."

"A bird, I have been seized by hawks or trapped in nets, or held fast by bird-lime, and have been killed an infinite number of times."

"A tree, with axes and adzes by the carpenters an infinite number of times I have been felled, stripped of my bark, cut up, and sawn into planks."

"As iron, with hammer and tongs by blacksmiths an infinite number of times I have been struck and beaten, split and filed."

"In every kind of existence I have suffered pain which have scarcely known reprieve for a moment."
(*Uttarādhyayana Sūtra*, xix. 63–7, 74.)

Thus for the Jain, even more perhaps than for the Buddhist, the universe is a place of utter misery and sorrow, and its few moments of happiness in no way compensate for the essential horror of existence. The pessimism of the Jain outlook is nowhere better expressed than in a famous parable, "The Man in the Well". A traveller was journeying through a dense and wild forest when he encountered a mad elephant which charged him with upraised trunk. As he turned to flee, a terrible demoness with a naked sword in her hand appeared before him and barred his path. There was a great tree near the track, and he ran up to it, hoping to find safety in its branches, but he could find no foothold in its smooth trunk. His only refuge was an old well, covered with grass and weeds, at the foot of the tree, and into this he leapt. As he fell he managed to catch hold of a clump of reeds which grew from the wall, and there he hung, midway between the mouth of the well and its bottom. Looking down, he saw that the bottom did not contain water, but was surrounded by snakes, which hissed at him as he hung above them. In their midst was a mighty python, its mouth agape,

waiting to catch him when he fell. Raising his head again, the man saw on the clump of reeds two mice, one white and the other black, busily gnawing away at the roots. Meanwhile the wild elephant ran up to the well, and, enraged at losing its victim, began charging at the trunk of the tree. Thus he dislodged a honeycomb which hung from a branch above the well, and it fell upon the man hanging there so precariously. Angry bees swarmed round his head and tormented him with their stings. But one drop of honey fell on his brow, rolled down his face and reached his lips. Immediately he forgot his peril and thought of nothing more than of obtaining another drop of honey.

The main purport of this story is quite obvious, but the Jain finds a parallel to each of the many horrors which beset the unfortunate traveller. The man, of course, is the soul, and his journey through the forest is *saṁsāra* (p. 225). The elephant represents death; the demoness, old age. The tree is the way to salvation, which the ordinary man cannot climb. The wall is human life, the snakes are passions, the python is hell. The tuft of reed is man's allotted span, and the black and white mice are the dark and bright halves of the month. The bees are diseases and troubles, while the honey, of course, represents the trivial pleasures of our earthly existence (*Samarāicca-Kahā*, ii. 55–80). Whether or not he taste a few more drops of honey, at last the mice will do their work and the man will fall into the jaws of the python. But here the analogy breaks down, for the python of hell must sooner or later disgorge the man and return him to the forest of the world, only to suffer further terrors of a like kind.

Every thought, word or action is liable to bring about a fresh influx of matter to obfuscate the naturally bright soul, which, when free of its material integument, is omniscient, reflecting the universe like the monad of Leibniz. The stuff which clouds the soul is not matter of the ordinary kind, but a sort of subtle matter, called *karma* in Jainism, which conditions the life of the being to which it adheres and leads to its re-birth in conditions appropriate to its former deeds. The Jain doctrine of *karma* is a further example of the survival of primitive materialism, for that which in other systems is thought to be a principle or a law of nature is in Jainism conceived on the analogy of a material substance. The cycle of transmigration is quite automatic and needs no intervention of a supernatural power of any kind. Selfish, careless or cruel actions involve the influx of much very heavy *karma*, which leads to great unhappiness for the individual who receives it. The *karma* accruing from good deeds, however, is dissipated almost immediately

263

and has no serious effects. Moreover suffering willingly undertaken has the effect of dispersing the *karma* already accumulated. To achieve salvation the soul must become free from matter of all kinds, when it will rise to the top of the universe through its natural lightness, to dwell there for ever in bliss. The souls of great sages such as Mahāvīra achieve virtual salvation while in the body; they enjoy the bliss and omniscience of the fully emancipated soul, but enough residual *karma* still clings to them to hold them to the earth; when this is exhausted by penance and fasting they die, and their naked souls rise immediately to the realm of ineffable peace above the highest of the heavens of the gods.

If he desires salvation a man must, on these premises, subject himself to rigorous hardship and pain to get rid of *karma* already acquired, and act with the utmost circumspection lest he acquire new *karma* in serious quantities. Even the unintentional killing of an ant may have very serious consequences for the soul, and injury with deliberate intention is far more serious than injury through carelessness. Directly or indirectly everyone must do some injury, at least to the lower forms of life in the Jain hierarchy of being, but all Jain ethics are directed towards the one aim of doing as little injury as possible. No other Indian sect has carried the doctrine of *ahiṁsā* (non-violence) to such extremes. To injure the higher forms of life is more serious than to injure the lower, but even the maltreatment of water and fire brings harm upon the soul, and hence must be avoided as far as possible. Even the Jain layman must be a complete vegetarian. His means of livelihood are much circumscribed. Thus he should not be a farmer, for ploughing the earth involves much injury to animal life, not to speak of injury to the earth itself; it is best that he should eat the rice grown by another, who will bear the chief burden of the harm done to plants, insects and earth in its cultivation. Even most crafts involve injury to living beings, for, as we have seen, the metal on the anvil of the blacksmith suffers excruciating tortures and the plank sawn by the carpenter is in the direst agony. Thus the safest profession for the Jain is trade, and from the earliest days of the faith Jainism has recruited most of its members from among the trading communities of India.

If the life of the Jain layman is strictly regulated in order to prevent injury to life, that of the Jain monk is even more rigidly disciplined. He should never walk along a road without carrying a little brush or a feather duster, with which gently to sweep away any insects that may cross his path. He should never walk about in the dark, lest the lower forms of life be injured. His mouth should be covered by a little veil rather like a surgeon's mask, not only to prevent injury to small insects in the air, but also to preserve the life of the air itself. His drinking water should be strained in order to avoid injury to the minute living creatures in it. He should neither light nor put out a fire. Bathing is forbidden, for it harms both the water used for washing and the vermin on the holy man's body. Lamps must never be used in the monastery, partly out of respect for the fire-beings in the flames, and partly to preserve the lives of the moths and other insects that would fly into them; the whole of the hours of darkness should be spent in meditation and sleeping.

The austere life of the Jain monk is still often terminated by the grim penance of *sallekhana* or fasting to death. When he feels that his faculties are beginning to fail and that his work in this life is complete he is advised to take this course in order to work off much evil *karma*. Very pious laymen, when they grow elderly and their health begins to fail, sometimes die by the same rite; for there is no sharp distinction between the layman and the monk; between the less earnest layman, who keeps to a vegetarian diet and renders occasional homage to the Tīrthankaras at a Jain shrine, and the unkempt, dirty and austere *sādhu* there are many gradations of pious laymen who, temporarily or permanently, adopt supererogatory vows. If the Jain layman takes his faith fully in earnest and can find time from his business activities, he will spend the days of full and new moon in a monastery living in the manner of a monk. Nowadays few Jain laymen perform this fast of *posadha* more than once a year, but the practice has had the effect of linking monk and layman. At least once annually, on the last day of the Jain religious year, which usually occurs in August, the Jain, whether monk or layman, should abstain entirely from food and drink and confess and repent all the sins which he has committed, wittingly or unwittingly, during the past twelve months, paying off all his debts and asking forgiveness of all those whom he may have injured. This great general act of penitence, called *Paryushaṇa*, is followed by a day of general rejoicing, and forms the most important feast of the Jain year. The thorough discipline of the Jain lay community is undoubtedly one of the chief reasons for the survival of the faith.

Superficially Jainism has somewhat compromised with Hinduism. Hindu gods are worshipped by the Jains, and Brāhmans are employed to perform marriage ceremonies and funerals. But though images of the gods appear in Jain temples in positions subordinate to those of the Tīrthankaras, the gods are merely finite beings capable of bestowing only temporal blessings on their worshippers. The twenty-four Tīrthankaras, the great souls who preached the true doctrine in the distant past, are now quite incapable of bestowing any blessings whatever, for they are completely separated from matter and have no attachment to the universe below them, which they survey in their timeless omniscience. But reverence to the Tīrthankaras is a most precious source of spiritual merit, and they are the real inspiration of the Jain, however worldly he may be. There has never been any compromise with theism, and the religion of Jainism remains in essence what it was two thousand years ago – an atheistic, ascetic system of moral and spiritual training, with a very pessimistic view of the universe.

The Jains developed distinctive cosmological doctrines which contain several features of interest. The universe is believed to contain an infinite number of souls, all enmeshed in matter, which, as in the Vaiśeshika school of Hindu philosophy (pp. 234–5), is thought to be atomic in structure. As the number of souls is infinite, most of them will continue to transmigrate eternally, for, however many souls may ultimately find salvation and thus be subtracted from the total, an infinite number will remain in *samsāra*, the world of birth and death and re-birth. This goes through a steady process of progress and decline, without the periodical cataclysms and cosmic nights of Hindu cosmology. At present we are in the fifth of the six periods of the stage of decline (*avasarpiṇī*). In the first of these periods men were completely without care, for all their needs were provided on demand, without labour, by the "wishing trees" (*kalpavṛksha*) which grew throughout the world; as men were spontaneously virtuous they had no need of morals or religion, and they were of enormous stature and longevity. In the second period there was some diminution of their bliss. In the third, sin and sorrow appeared in their milder forms, and the wishing trees began to wither. Then men began to feel the need of guidance and leadership. At first they looked up to natural leaders, the patriarchs (*kula-kara*), who were respected and obeyed purely by virtue of their superior wisdom; these ancient sages taught the world the various arts of civilization, which became progressively necessary as the happy state of nature gave way to more evil times. The last patriarch, Ṛshabhadeva, was also the first Tīrthankara, or teacher of the Jain religion, for by his day evil had become so prevalent that the sanctions of morality and religion were necessary to restrain it. By now men were too corrupt to live peaceably in society without coercion, so Ṛshabhadeva appointed his son Bharata to be the first emperor, and thus the state came

into being, a necessary evil in an age of increasing corruption. Further decline occurred during the fourth period, which saw the other twenty-three Tīrthankaras, last of whom was Mahāvīra. The fifth period began just after his death, and is now current; it will endure for 21,000 years, during which men will further decline in stature, longevity and virtue, and the true religion will gradually disappear. In the sixth and last period of decline, which will also last for 21,000 years, the nadir will be reached; men will live for only twenty years and will be but a cubit tall; civilization, a phenomenon only prevalent in the middle periods of the cosmic cycle, will be forgotten, and mankind will live like brute beasts, incapable even of building a hut or lighting a fire. At the end of this period a new age will commence, and conditions will slowly improve. The six periods will be repeated in reverse order until the age of gold is reached once more. Thus the universe perpetually repeats itself with complete regularity.

Jainism is not, however, a fatalistic system. The tendency to fatalism is strongly opposed by Jain philosophers, and the apparent determinism of Jain cosmology is explained by a remarkable and distinctive theory of epistemological relativity known as "the doctrine of manysidedness" (*anekāntavāda*). The details of this system are too recondite to discuss here, but its essential kernel is that the truth of any proposition is relative to the point of view from which it is made. The ebb and flow of the cosmic process is from the universal point of view rigidly determined, but from the viewpoint of the individual a man has freedom to work out his own salvation. Free will and determinism are both relatively true, and only the fully emancipated soul, who surveys the whole of time and space in a single act of knowledge from his eternal station at the top of the universe, can know the full and absolute truth.

The total number of Jains in India today is probably little more than two million. They are, as they have been for at least 2,000 years, divided into the two main sects of Śvetāmbaras and Digambaras, but a third Jain sect also deserves brief mention. This is the *Sthānakavāsī*, which appeared as an offshoot of the Śvetāmbaras in Gujarāt in the seventeenth century. The chief characteristic feature of the Sthānakavāsī sect is its rejection of image-worship. Though it is probably right in its claim that the primitive Jainism of Mahāvīra had no images, its opposition to image worship must largely be attributed to Muslim influence. The Sthānakavāsīs also reject several of the customs of the orthodox Śvetāmbaras as due to the corruption of Hindu influence, and allow little compromise with the rigorous discipline laid down in the Jain scriptures, although they do not maintain Mahāvīra's practice of complete nudity.

Though small in numbers the Jains of India are by no means uninfluential, thanks to their wealth and high standard of education, and there seems no likelihood of their disappearing into the great body of Hinduism. They have for long been very active in the promotion of works of public welfare, especially in the endowment of hospitals for men and animals, and of schools. Their rigid insistence on strict *ahiṁsā* has perhaps had a greater effect on modern India than is immediately obvious, for among the many influences which can be traced in the philosophy of Mahātmā Gāndhī that of Jainism is not the least. Born in Kāthiāwār, where Jainism is strong, he was much influenced by the saintly Jain *sādhus* whom he met in his youth, especially by a great Jain teacher of the last century, Rāīchand Bhāī, whom he mentions with much respect in his autobiography. There is no doubt that the Gandhian doctrine of non-violence owes much to Jainism.

7a. Buddhism: the Theravāda

by I. B. HORNER

INTRODUCTION

"As the great ocean has but one taste, the taste of salt, so does this Dhamma and Discipline have but one taste, the taste of freedom."
(*Vinaya-Piṭaka*, ii. 239, *Anguttara-Nikāya*, iv. 203, etc.)

Buddhism is a name given comparatively recently by Westerners to the vast synthesis of teachings, now 2,500 years old, attributed to Gotema (Sanskrit Gautama) the Buddha, the Sage of the Sakyan clan, and to much that later grew out of them as they spread from India to other lands. In his own days his Teachings were known as Dhamma (Sanskrit, *Dharma*, cf. p. 253), what is right and is as it ought to be, also as *Buddha-vacana*, the word or speech of the Buddha, or again as *Buddha-sāsana*, the message, teaching, instruction or dispensation of the Buddha. From its origin down to the present day this Teaching of peace, inner and outer, has made a triumphant appeal and now probably numbers more followers, especially in S.E. Asia, than does any other faith.

"Religion" is perhaps not a very good term to use in connection with Buddhism since it recognizes no God or godhead, no *iśvara* or Brahman in the Upanishadic sense. Life here is not regarded as a preparation for eternity, but as a discipline for governing man's attitude to the here and now, the present conditions, and, if properly and diligently carried out, will lead on gradually but surely to what is best, the highest good. "Beyond", where it is his aim to arrive and abide, is virtually the super-consciousness that was already known to the Yogīs. When a meditator or contemplative achieves this condition of the mind and is deeply and utterly absorbed, material things are so completely transcended that they cease to attract or repel or even impinge on the senses. There is no reaction to them. This is freedom, and it is peace. "Immaterial things are more peaceful than material, cessation is more peaceful than immaterial things" (*Itivuttaka*, p. 62).

Between the time the Founder entered on *parinirvāṇa*, the final termination of the countless births in which he had circled and run leaving no substratum for further birth remaining, and the writing down of these Sayings, Utterances and Discourses, four centuries were to elapse. This is partly because India at that time had no known materials suitable for writing, indeed for engraving anything more than the briefest proclamations; and partly because it was already an ancient custom to rely on human memory for the preservation and passing on of the spoken "religious" word. So, for the first 400 years or so the Sayings of the Buddha were carried in the memories of his disciples and their disciples in a long succession, or various successions of teachers and pupils. Even while the Buddha was alive, not only had attempts been made – for example by his gifted but treacherous cousin Devadatta – to wrest the leadership from him; but there had also been splits and disruptions in the order of monks in spite of machinery devised to keep it unified and harmonious. With the lapse of time and the Buddha no longer there to act as guide, law-giver and interpreter of his own sayings, divergences of opinion on this matter and that crystallized sufficiently for eighteen "schools" or sects and sub-sects to appear on the scene in the second and third centuries after his death. Because a number of these schools regarded certain aspects of the Teaching and discipline in one way and some in another, and because they stressed and developed different points, they came on the whole, though still all acknowledging allegiance to the Buddha and his teachings, to reside in different monastic centres and localities.

Alive to such possible dangers to the true Dharma, five hundred *Arhants* (those who had fully trained themselves in the development of their mental powers) gathered together at Rājagaha to hold the First Council a few weeks after the Teacher's passing from this world, with the object of reciting out loud his Dharma and *Vinaya* (monastic discipline) so as to come to agreement on the accuracy of their memory of them and so to establish them as the genuine ones to be preserved, learnt, mastered and followed. Their guiding belief and mainstay was that "Dharma is well taught by the Bhagavan (Exalted One, Blessed One); it is to be self-realized, its fruits are immediate, it is a come-and-see thing, leading onwards the doer of it to the complete destruction of anguish." Not only may a man or woman win complete confidence in it; he or she may also practise it and live it.

In the midst of the assembled *Arhants* who attended the First Council the monk Upāli answered all the questions put to him by the Elder Kassapa concerning the discipline for monks and nuns. This now forms the *Vinaya-Piṭaka*, the "basket" (*piṭaka*) containing the rules and regulations for the conduct of monastic life (*vinaya*). And after the *Vinaya-Piṭaka* had been recited the Elder Kassapa questioned the venerable Ānanda about Dharma. Dharma is now contained in the *Sutta-Piṭaka*, the Basket of Discourses, which consists of five collections of the Teachings believed to have been uttered by the Buddha and to a lesser extent by some of his monastic disciples of both sexes. To these there came to be added a third "basket", the *Abhidhamma-* (Sanskrit, *Abhidharma-*) *Piṭaka*, in which the more psychological and philosophical terms belonging to Dharma are analysed, classified and expounded. Together these three Baskets constitute the *Tipiṭaka* (Sanskrit, *Tripiṭaka*), or the three baskets of canonical texts. The version of this voluminous collection that is known sometimes as the Pali Canon, because it came to be written down in this language, is the authoritative source of the teachings for those who follow the earliest and most orthodox form of Buddhism. This goes by the name of Theravāda (Sanskrit, *Sthaviravāda*), the doctrine, speech or profession of the Elders – those Elder monks who had been the Buddha's companions and fellow-workers and some of whom convened the First Council to purify Dharma of what was not Dharma.

All accounts agree that about a century after the Buddha's passing a group of monks sought for greater laxity in ten points of discipline. The Second Council was held at Vesālī to deal with the situation, but the rebellious minority refused to abide by the decision of the orthodox majority and, splitting off from the main body, came to be known as Mahāsanghikas. These earliest seceders, the chief surviving work of one of whose sub-sects is the *Mahāvastu*, put a number of different interpretations on *Sutta* and *Vinaya* and rejected certain portions of the Pali Canon that had been confirmed at the First Council. With their conception of the Buddha as completely supermundane and appearing on the earth only in a phantom-body, they were the forerunners of the Trikāya (three Bodies) doctrine of the Mahāyāna (p. 306). Of all the eighteen schools the one that remained closest to Theravāda was the Sarvāstivādin holding that everything, past, future and present, exists, though denying any permanent substance in an individual being, but also denying the exclusively transcendental nature of the Buddha.

Other Theravāda Councils have been held at infrequent intervals, always with the object of "purifying" the records, at first spoken, later written down, and the Sixth, held in Rangoon to commemorate the Twenty-fifth Century of the Buddhist Era, has recently ended.

Though the members of the First Council had given much care and anxiety to preserving the Discourses as they remembered them, yet the Buddha had never regarded his words as sacrosanct or held that his Teachings (as distinct from his Discipline) must be believed as a whole, taken on trust or repeated faultlessly by his disciples on pain of their incurring blame or ineffectualness, as was the contemporary Brāhman view if their priests made a verbal error in reciting the sacrificial formulae. He advocated each person investigating and testing the Teachings for himself. But the whole point of this, too often overlooked by those who like to call Buddhism non-authoritarian, is that there is but the one sole Way for the purification of beings and for overcoming that covetousness and dejection, the source of which is traceable to the world of the senses, or for crushing that craving and that ignorance which bind sentient beings to the wheel of mutability and mortality from which Buddhism teaches them how to break free. Narrow and straight is the Way that must be followed for the escape into the undying and unchanging. Though Buddhas point out the Way, each discovering it anew for himself, yet "It is yours to swelter at the task" (*Dhammapada* 276) of arriving at its ending there to discard the Way like a raft once the other shore has been gained. If the aspirant goes according to his own fancy, deviates from the Way or does not put his whole energy into the struggle, he will fall short of his aim: "Sadly lives the man of sloth involved in evil unskilled states of mind, and great is the goal he fails to win. But he who stirs up energy lives happily, aloof from unskilled states of mind and great is the goal he makes perfect. Not through what is low comes the attainment of the highest, but

Photo: Khin Lay Maung

PLATE 69. The presentation of the infant Bodhisattva by his father to the seer Asita who prophesied that he would become a Buddha: terracotta and gilt relief from Pagan, Burma, eleventh century A.D.

PLATES 70 and 71. The Bodhisattva, now grown up, drives four times into the park and, in spite of his father's precautions, meets a very old man, a sick man, a corpse and then an ascetic. These represent the ills of the world and the escape from them. He decides to leave home and seek for the truth. Terracotta and gilt stelas from Pagan, Burma, eleventh century A.D.

Photo: Khin Lay Maung

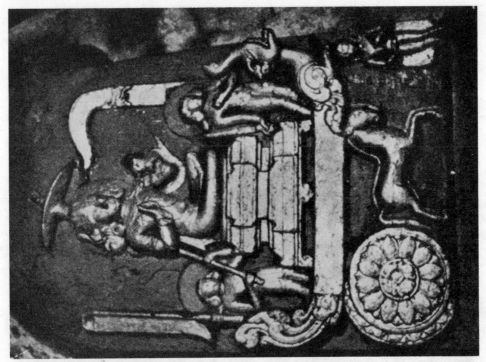

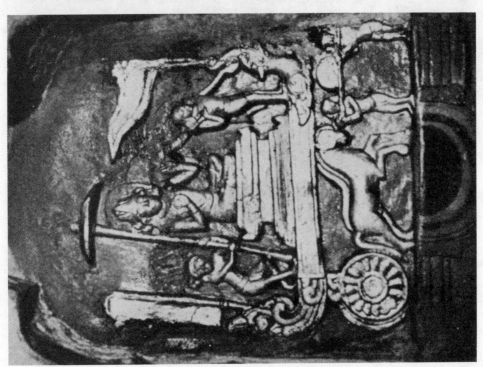

PLATE 71. *See Plate 58.*

PLATE 72. Under the Bo-tree the Bodhisattva attains Enlightenment and becomes the Buddha. *Devas* of earth and sky pay homage. The Buddha is not represented in human form in this illustration. The eight-spoked wheel symbolizes the Eightfold Way he would spend the rest of his life teaching. Sandstone sculpture from Sanchi, India, first century A.D. (*India Office Library, Commonwealth Relations Office, London*)

PLATE 73. Animals pay homage to the Buddha (here symbolized by the tree) who taught compassion and mercy to all living creatures: sandstone sculptured relief from Bharhut, India, second century B.C. (*Indian Museum, Calcutta*)

Photo: Department of Archaeology

PLATE 74. The Buddha seated cross-legged on a lotus throne with hands in the teaching gesture. Below is the Wheel of Dharma that he set rolling: sandstone sculpture from Sarnath, India, fifth century A.D. (*Department of Archaeology, Government of India*)

274

PLATE 75. Head of a standing Buddha. He taught Dharma for forty-five years: sandstone sculpture from Sarnath, India, fifth century A.D. (*National Museum of India, New Delhi*)

Photo: Brian Chirlian, Camcara Press

PLATE 76. Recumbent Buddha, or the Buddha attaining *paṭinirvāna* when he was about eighty years of age. The standing figure is either the Buddha or Ānanda, the faithful disciple who was present at the final passing away. Rock-cut statue near the ancient city of Polonnaruwa, Ceylon, eleventh century A.D.

through what is high comes the attainment of the highest. Wherefore stir up energy for the attainment, mastery and realization of what is not yet attained, mastered or realized (*Saṁyutta-Nikāya* ii. 29) . . . and train yourself by thinking: 'We will not shrink back but will struggle on . . . so that there may come to be a vortex of energy for the winning by human strength, human energy and human striving of that which is not yet won' " (*Anguttara-Nikāya* i. 50). But since no one can purify another, it is for each aspirant himself and by his own energy, effort, striving and diligence, for which Pali has many words constantly to the forefront in the Teaching, to follow and walk on the Way leading to the bliss of emancipation from the ubiquity of impermanence.

The knowledge of this emancipation is called *aññā*, profound knowledge or "gnosis". Equivalent to "arhantship" or "perfection", it does not come straightaway, but by a gradual training and course and practice (*Majjhima-Nikāya* i. 479, etc.). Often enough the inner and complete meaning of words and statements made by one who has had access to Reality or things as they really are, escapes the immediate understanding of the lesser men who follow "such a one" (*tādin*), and has to be hammered out, or explained and interpreted by teachers and preceptors and commentators before the disciple's body, speech and thought can be rightly disciplined and developed, tamed and freed by practice. This situation is further complicated for us today, far removed in time as we are from the ancient Indian Buddhist world, because we do not always know the precise meaning or even the shades of meaning, let alone the full connotation, of words and phrases used then which must have contained wider associations and subtler nuances for many of the people in the Buddha's audiences than they can have for us.

Moreover, it is not unlikely that often Dharma was given in brief – this is how Buddhas teach, they do not use expanded statements (*Majjhima Com.* v. 60) in the first instance, but will do so if they wish to or if they are requested to give the meaning in full of what they had spoken of in brief, as will also their sufficiently experienced disciples of whom Mahā-Kaccāna was ranked as the most eminent in this Buddha's dispensation for his ability to interpret his brief sayings. It is therefore sometimes held that the Pali Canon as we have it now is but a collection of elaborations, explanations and expansions of the Buddha's First Utterance or Discourse. Dharma, whether in full or in brief, was given to all who wanted to hear it, to men and women alike no matter to what clan, caste or family they belonged or what livelihood or occupation they were engaged in. It was similarly taught to members of other sects, for to understand even a single sentence would be a happiness to them for a long time (*Saṁyutta-Nikāya* iv. 314–6). There was no "closed fist" of a (Brāhman) teacher (*Dīgha-Nikāya* ii. 100), no esoteric and exoteric. Dharma was spoken in such a way that each listener understood it according to his capacity, and thought it had been spoken specially for him instead of its being, as it was, a general instruction (*Majjhima-Nikāya* i. 249). The Buddha was able to adapt himself to the general level of understanding of the audience he was about to address: "Now, I know well that when I approached various large assemblies, even before I had sat down there or had spoken or begun to teach, whatever was their sort I made myself of a like sort, whatever their language, so was my language. And I rejoiced them with a talk on Dharma, made it acceptable to them, set them on fire and gladdened them" (*Dīgha-Nikāya* ii. 109). Even so, there was occasionally a man there, such as Ariṭṭha who had been a vulture-trainer or Sāti who had been a fisherman before they had become monks, neither of whom had even a glimmering of this Dharma and Discipline (*Majjhima-Nikāya* i. 132, 258) in spite of repeated efforts to make them understand it.

Buddhism adhered to the belief, common in India at that time, that sentient beings were bound to the wheel of *saṁsāra* (p. 283) and thus circled on in birth after birth, life after life, by the operation of an unexhausted *Karma* (=Pali, *kamma*, pp. 225, 283ff.), that is to say, sewn to the process of becoming or continuity by craving, the sempstress (*Anguttara-Nikāya* iii. 400), sentient beings have in some way to go on in a series of births, for death is not the end, until the action or working of every volitional deed done either in past births or in this present one and carrying its effects forward into the future, wears to its "karmic" end. The effects then cease. A natural corollary of this belief is that mankind, though marked by no specific differences in body while the rest of "nature" varies (*Suttanipāta* 600ff), is, yet, as he must be and obviously is, characterized by individual differences in his mental and moral growth. This is a sense in which Dharma, though given in the same way, is not the same for all who hear it, for not all are able to understand, appreciate and penetrate its depths and subtleties equally.

India, in the sixth and fifth centuries B.C., had come, after long years of discussion, teaching and practice, to a stage of great religious and speculative ferment, curiosity and experimentation, combined with a remarkable attitude of tolerance, and was ever ready for the sowing and reaping, the pondering and the accepting or rejecting of some new crop of spiritual thought and discipline. Conditions were favourable for an organizer who could consolidate some of the sporadic and isolated elements into something cohesive and fruitful and for a leader, renowned for his teaching capacities, who practised what he preached and preached what he practised, to find a way out of the morass of speculation, and to present instead a teaching, the value of which and the practicability of which could be tested even in this very life. For years there had been *bhikshus*, men of the scrap-bowl, walking for almsfood; for years there had been recluses and hermits living alone in forest and jungle; men and women wanderers, great debaters who, though touring about, also had parks at their disposal; ascetics practising various forms of austerities and offering sacrifices, to the moon and the fire for example; teachers surrounded by bands of disciples, varying in size and probably in the degree of organization that held them together; and there were teachers of larger followings or groups or orders. In a word, sixty-two "heretical" sects are known to the Pali Canon where too a good deal may be learnt about the tenets of the six great leaders who were contemporaries of the Buddha: Pūraṇa Kassapa, Makkhali Gosāla, the leader of the Ājīvikas or Naked Ascetics, Ajita of the Hair-Blanket, Pakudha Kaccāyana, Nātaputta the Jain leader and head of a well organized and flourishing community of monks, nuns, men and women householders which survives in India, though regrettably in decreasing numbers, to the present day (*see* p. 261). And finally there was Sañjaya Belaṭṭhiputta, the "Eel-wriggler", so called because he had no clear-cut replies to the questions which so largely occupied men's minds, such as whether the world is finite or infinite or both or neither; whether there is another world or not, or whether there both is and is not, or whether there neither is nor is not. Nātaputta, the Jain, and Makkhali Gosāla were the most powerful rivals the Buddha encountered. These contemporary speculative thinkers, all seeking what may be described broadly as Truth, and with whom the Buddha often and definitely differed either on account of their views or their ways of putting questions, may all the same, and not unreasonably, be regarded as having made some contribution to the pattern on which the huge communities of Buddhist monks and nuns gradually took shape. Some of them, for example, recited the *Pātimokkha* rules or obligations so many times a month; in this they came to be followed by the Buddhist *Saṁgha*, or order of monks (*Vinaya-Piṭaka* i. 101). Others kept the three or four months of the rainy season in one place and did not travel about for fear of destroying the young crops or harming the minute but teeming animal

life; Buddhist monks and nuns became obliged by monastic rule to follow the example of these members of other sects and enter a residence for the rains, only leaving it in most exceptional circumstances and then for no more than a week. Jain and Buddhist, and especially the former, are ardent supporters of the age-old Indian teaching of *ahiṁsā*, harmlessness, non-injury, so ancient that its beginnings are lost in the mists of immemorial time. Even such embryonic forms of life as are "one-facultied", even such minute creatures as ants may not be destroyed by anyone following rigorously the doctrine of *ahiṁsā*.

Whatever may have been the external agencies at work modifying the organization, control and maintenance of the Buddhist Saṁgha, its numerous rules and regulations, "allowances", prohibitions and relaxations, all are ascribed to the genius of the Buddha himself no less than are the legislative powers that gradually devolved on the Saṁgha. Though the nuns have now died out, the monks remain in large numbers and are supported by the pious lay-followers of both sexes who give the gifts of faith: robe-material, almsfood, lodging and medicine for sick monks. In return the monks give the laity the best of gifts, the gift of Dharma. The Buddhist laity, though held together by no such organization as governs a monk's life or that of the Jain laity, yet have as their focal point devotion to the Buddha's supreme qualities, including his wisdom and compassion, to the Dharma he promulgated and taught, and to the Saṁgha of *Arhants* which is the repository of Dharma.

Though this chapter is concerned with some of the leading "religious" teachings found especially in the *Sutta-Piṭaka* of the Pali *Tipiṭaka*, which is the only Canon to have come down to us in its entirety, other venerable compilations also exist in Sanskrit, Chinese and Tibetan. For the Buddhism of the Buddha, as it has sometimes been called, with its affinities, depths, heights and subtleties, with its solidarity and cohesiveness, its clear pointing to something more than could actually be said in words, offered a huge field for exploration, dissection and construction; and it fell on no barren soil. Its germinal strength was responsible for the formation of the early schools or sects and, later, for its dissemination, vitally alive, far beyond India where it had originated to other Asian lands where it has proved a great blessing and a great inspiration to many visual arts. Buddhists in Ceylon, Burma, Thailand, Cambodia and Laos regard the Pali *Tipiṭaka* as the source not only for a right and skilled method of the conduct of life but of the "religious" and spiritual aspirations that grow in degree and come nearer to fulfilment the more rightly and wisely they lead their lives. And the Teaching also reached and took firm root in China, Japan, Tibet and Mongolia. Thinkers and philosophers, realizing that the Dharma (Dhamma) of the Pali Canon is characterized by depths both latent and apparent, took various of its words, points or ideas and, with these as a basis, erected a vast structure, architectonic, meditational, devotional, metaphysical, often highly intellectual and philosophical, sometimes legendary and unprovable, the great body of which came to be called Mahāyāna, the Greater Career, or the Greater Vehicle for going Beyond.

Much as Mahāyāna may have in common basically with Theravāda – the four Aryan Truths, the Aryan eightfold Way and Nirvāna (=Pali, Nibbāna), there is one point I should like to mention here where their attitudes differ. This concerns the type of being known as the Bodhisattva (Pali, Bodhisatta), a word which may be translated roughly as the Being set on Enlightenment. Thus certain Mahāyāna Sūtras recognize many Bodhisattvas, and for that matter Buddhas too, and even the Mahāsaṃghikas held that there were a number of Bodhisattvas, all of them supermundane, and able to choose the kind of birth they would enter, the better to help erring mankind to cross over the ocean of saṃsāra. For Theravāda, on the other hand, while records give the names of a varying number of Buddhas who preceded the Buddha Gautama, there is but the one Bodhisattva. This is the Great Being who took a vow aeons ago under Dīpaṃkara, one of the first Buddhas of all, one day to win complete Enlightenment by himself. Since he made that vow, which has to be made in the presence of a Buddha, the Bodhisattva has circled and run in many a birth (Dhammapada 153), often enduring terrible hardships and torments rather than abandoning his quest. In 547 stories of the Buddha's anterior births as the Bodhisattva, the Pali Jātaka relates the roles he played as animal, bird, deva (p. 294f.) or man. Other collections, for example the Mahāvastu, contain yet different stories besides some that are identical with or very similar to the Pali Stories. Incidents from these, as well as from the life of the Buddha, have been depicted in fresco, outstandingly in the caves at Ajanta, and in sculpture, for example at Bharhut, Bodh-Gayā and on the magnificent gateways at Sanchi. The Buddha's presence is indicated by symbols: a tree (enlightenment), a stūpa (various meanings), a wheel (Dharma), or by footprints, for he had feared that after his death a more personal representation might be worshipped. Yet, stylized figures came into vogue later, and show him in typical postures such as calling the earth to witness his Enlightenment, teaching,

meditation or having entered on parinirvāna, that is, final release from phenomenal existence. It was not until this birth, his last, that the Bodhisattva, born as Siddhārtha Gautama, became the Buddha by his supreme and final act of winning complete and full Enlightenment or Awakening for himself. Buddha is an epithet meaning Awakened, Enlightened or Illumined One, and strictly speaking should not be applied to this human Teacher of devas and mankind until the momentous events of the Night of Awakening had unassailably secured for him the title, unique in historical time, of sammā (fully) -sam (self) -Buddha (Enlightened One): the Wholly Self-Awakened One.

THE BUDDHA

"What was to be known is known by me, and to be developed developed is,
What was to be cast out is cast out by me, therefore am I Buddha."
(Suttanipāta 558, Theragāthā 828, Majjhima-Nikāya ii. 143, etc.)

The life of Siddhattha (Sanskrit Siddhārtha), who was to become a supreme Buddha, has often been told and I do not propose to do more here than give a brief recapitulation of it. It falls into two distinct parts which, bridged by six years spent in the practice of severe physical austerities, are divided by the Enlightenment. Siddhārtha was born about 563 B.C. (though the date is controversial) in the foothills of Nepal near Kapilavatthu and into a family called Gotama (Sanskrit, Gautama) which belonged to the proud republican clan of the Sakyas who were kshatriyas (Pali, khattiyas, see p. 253), nobles or warriors, and traced their descent from the Sun. Hence two of the many epithets later bestowed on him were "Sage of the Sakyans" and "Kinsman of the Sun". His mother died a week after he was born, and he was brought up by his aunt and foster-mother, Mahāpajāpatī, thus having two mothers as great men sometimes do. Until he was twenty-nine Siddhārtha lived in luxury, a rich young man, possessed of radiant health and adept in all manner of manly sports. He married a beautiful Sakyan girl who bore him a son, Rāhula, the "bond" – not a bond between a devoted couple, but a bond that might have held the father to the world and all the joys it could offer him, had he not been the Bodhisattva, suspecting even then that there must be peril in sense-pleasures and determined to find the escape from the pain with which, as he realized, they were closely associated. Home must therefore be abandoned in spite of its tempting delights, and Siddhārtha went forth from it accompanied only by his charioteer and his horse.

Theravādins believe that Gotama, both as Siddhārtha and as the Buddha, was a man, neither a god or creator, nor a myth or legend. As such he was, as he himself comprehended, subject to birth, ageing, decay, dying, sorrow and stain. But yet, might he not seek, might he not find, the Unborn, Unageing, Undecaying, Undying, the Sorrowless and the Stainless, each one of which he called Nivāṇa (Pali, Nibbāna)? That is what he went forth from home to find. That was the purpose of his quest (Majjhima-Nikāya i. 163).

From the night of the Great Going Forth, which was thus both from home and from the lure of sense-desires, he spent the next six years, in antithesis to the luxuries and comfort he had hitherto savoured, testing and experiencing the bodily mortifications many of his contemporaries believed would yield the goal of their spiritual aspirations. Eventually realizing that even the most extreme forms of austerity were worthless, Siddhārtha, still resolute in his quest, determined to attempt another way to Awakening. He took a little food and then remained for several solitary weeks in one posture under a Bo-tree or Bodhi-tree, the Tree of Awakening, on the banks of the river Nerañjanā in a delightful place suitable in every way for the striving of a young man bent on striving (Majjhima-Nikāya i. 167). And one night towards the dawn, even as he sat there cross-legged enjoying the bliss of freedom, he won full Enlightenment by himself alone, without the help of a teacher, that Enlightenment or Awakening from ignorance to knowledge, from darkness to light and from mortality to the Undying which, when it comes, comes in a flash and is total and complete. It was a stupendous event. Rarely do Buddhas appear in the world. According to some Pali reckonings there have been twenty-six including the Buddha Gotama, the first of whom, Dīpaṁkara, arose innumerable aeons ago; sometimes four other Buddhas are named, predecessors of Dīpaṁkara; and according to other reckonings there have been seven, the first of whom, Vipassin, arose ninety-one aeons ago (Dīgha-Nikāya ii. 2), a time during which the Bodhisattva was practising the life of a Naked Ascetic (Jātaka i. 390). The next Buddha to come, Maitreya (Pali, Metteyya), a name meaning Friendliness, whose advent has been prophesied by the Buddha Gotama (Dīgha-Nikāya iii. 76), is held to be waiting in the Tusita deva-world or world of the gods of delight until he arises here in the world to teach Dharma (p. 283 ff.) and lead an order of monks.

From the Night of Awakening onwards, therefore, the Buddha Gotama was truly a sammāsambuddha, a fully Self-Awakened One. And with his beautiful resonant voice he was superbly well equipped to teach the eternal Dharma he had penetrated and comprehended as he had sat deep in meditation under the Bo-tree. In this he had differed from another class of Buddha, known as pratyekabuddhas (Pali, paccekabuddhas), for, though these win enlightenment by their own unaided efforts, they are unable to teach and so, beyond the fact of their achievement, they carry but little weight. The Isigili Sutta enumerates the names of some of these pratyekabuddhas, now and again coupling them with some outstanding characteristic of the "private" buddha (Majjhima-Nikāya, Sta. No. 116), he who became enlightened by himself but for himself only.

After a period of hesitation, for Dharma is profound and difficult to understand and it would have been wearisome to the Buddha to teach it if he were to fail to elicit any response, he was urged forward by an unseen source of power and finally decided to give his Dharma to all who wanted to hear it. His First Discourse was delivered to the five men who had been with him during the six years of his austerities but who had left him in doubt and disgust once he had begun to take nourishment again. But now he approached them and succeeded in convincing them that "the Deathless has been found; I instruct, I teach Dharma" (Vinaya-Piṭaka i. 9). And he taught them the Discourse on the Middle Way, the mean between the two extremes of self-indulgence and self-torture. At its conclusion their doubts vanished, they plunged into Dharma and one by one asked the Buddha to let them go forth from home into homelessness in his presence. They thus came to form the nucleus of the Buddhist order of monks (bhikkhu-saṁgha) which has survived to the present day, the yellow robe of the Buddhist monk being a frequent sight in the Buddhist lands of Asia. An order of nuns (bhikkhuni-saṁgha) came into being a few years later and, though it evidently assumed large proportions, it has become extinct owing to a regrettable chain of circumstances.

The first five disciples were soon followed by fifty-five more, and so there were sixty-one Arhants in the world, inclusive of the Buddha. He then had to face temptation, the inner enemy, personified in the form of Māra, a kind of Buddhist Satan, who from this time onwards was at the Lord's side until he lay dying. But never did the Buddha give in: "Better for me were death in battle than to live defeated" (Suttanipāta 440). For him all wish and will for those sense-impressions that usually bring delight to the mind of man were past and ended and, released from their snares, freed from Māra's realm, he was liberated from great bondage (Vinaya-Piṭaka i. 21).

Māra, or Death, no longer had access to him for he no longer walked in the wrong pastures where material shapes, sounds, scents, tastes and touches are found to be either alluring or repellent. On the contrary, he had found a happiness that was not based on sense-perception.

Other events followed in quick succession. For example, a different method of ordaining those who had gone forth from home was devised, giving an earnest of the great development of the organization the Saṁgha was to undergo as the years went by. The first disciples had been ordained by the Lord himself using the simple formula: "Come, monk; well taught is Dharma; fare the Brahma-faring (see p. 295) for making a complete end of anguish." By the new regulation monks were empowered to ordain in any district by the method of making the candidate cut off his hair and beard, clothe himself in yellow robes, and then three times utter the formula: "I go to the Buddha for refuge, I go to Dharma for refuge, I go to the Saṁgha for refuge." Still later this method was supplanted by a far more formal and more complicated one, still in use, broadly speaking, in Theravāda countries.

The Buddha then set out for one of those tours on foot that were to mark at least the earlier years of his ministry – later he came to reside more and more in the Jetavana monastery near Sāvatthī that had been given to him by Anāthapiṇḍika. On the way between Benares and Uruvelā he was met by a party of thirty young men, who subsequently became his followers, worried because one of them had had his clothes stolen by a woman while they had been bathing. "Has the Lord seen a woman?" they asked him. "But what have you, young men, to do with a woman? . . . Were it not better to seek for self?" (Vinaya-Piṭaka i. 23). This counter-question is of great importance, for it brings into focus one side of the apparent contradiction that lies at the heart of all "religious" thought: it is by denying oneself, not of course of this or that small luxury, but by surrendering all that one thinks of as one's self, that self is found. And the Buddha had already virtually denied himself by indicating to Māra that impressions derived from the senses are not self, thus paving the way for the insistence that so profoundly marks his Teaching that not one of the senses is mine or I or my self.

Next, there came the conversion of a thousand matted-hair ascetics led by the three brothers Kassapa, a matter for which the Buddha is said to have exercised some of his supernormal powers. This was followed by the Second Discourse, that on Burning, a suitable topic for these fire-worshippers. The gist of it is that all the sense-

organs, of eye, ear, nose and so on, are on fire with attachment, aversion and confusion. The instructed disciple should therefore turn away from them and from the feelings to which sense-impingement gives rise. In turning away he is without attachment to them and so is freed from their lures, and is an Arhant who comprehends: "Destroyed is (saṁsāric) birth, brought to a close the Brahma-faring, done is what was to be done, there is no more of being such or so." This last phrase means, according to some of the commentaries, that there is no more of being born again either as a man or as an animal or in any of the other states of woe that in the more "popular" Buddhism are part of its cosmology.

Immediately after the conversion of the matted-hair ascetics, King Bimbisāra of Magadha gave a park near Rājagaha, his capital, to the Order of monks with the Enlightened One at their head as a place for them to reside in. This is the first gift recorded to have been offered to the Order which soon was recognized as a "great field of merit for the world". From then on all manner of other gifts continually and constantly poured in both from kings and wealthy laymen and laywomen, outstanding among whom were Anāthapiṇḍika and Visākhā, and from humbler people as well. Not only is it believed that giving and liberality confer merit on the donor in a scale related to the piety and spiritual eminence of the recipient, but this was a practical way in which the pious liked, and still like, to show their adherence and faith in those more advanced in the Way than they are themselves.

While the Buddha was still at Rājagaha, the monk Assaji, who had been one of his first five disciples, was approached by a wanderer named Sāriputta who told him that he was seeking for the Undying. As Assaji had found it already, he told Sāriputta what he could of it in brief, just its purport (attha), as he did not want a great elaboration:

"Those things which proceed from a cause, of these
    the Tathāgata [p. 282] has told the cause,
And that which is their stopping – the Great
    Recluse has such a Teaching."

Sāriputta realized that this was a Dharma that opened the way to Deathlessness, and, as already arranged, he informed his friend and fellow-wanderer, Moggallāna. They agreed to go to the Buddha as their Teacher, and set off with two hundred and fifty wanderers. When the Lord saw this concourse approaching, he welcomed Sāriputta and Moggallāna knowing that "This pair of disciples will be my chief, my eminent pair" (Vinaya-Piṭaka i. 42). All the Buddhas who had preceded him had

had two chief disciples who were monks besides another chief pair from the nuns.

The events of the subsequent years are not chronicled systematically. It must suffice to say that for about forty-five years after the Night of Awakening Gautama, now the Buddha, continued to teach and inspire an ever-increasing number of followers, men and women, lay and monastic, royal and common, while he toured North India, that land where memory is accurate and retentive and where Wisdom has never yet failed to command an answering response. Staying more and more frequently in the Jetavana monastery near Sāvat-thī, he continued to speak on all kinds of subjects, often aptly illustrated by similes, to all kinds of people who listened in groups of varying sizes.

Though the Bhagavan or Tathāgata,[1] as he was frequently called by his monks and as he frequently called himself, was incomputable after the attainment of Buddhahood, and was not to be reckoned by any of the aggregates (khandhā) as the constituents of the living body and mind came to be called (Majjhima-Nikāya i. 486), he was in no way hidden from human sight while he was alive. He was a man in a human body, not a phantom of Glory become apparent to men, far less a god or a mythological figure. This was the inspiration underlying his Teaching: what one man has done may not others do? So, "The Tathāgata's body remains though (in his life-time) he has cut off the conduit for continued becoming. As long as his body remains, devas and men shall see him; but at the dissolution of his body devas and men shall see him not" (Dīgha-Nikāya i. 46). For there were no remaining results of his karma that needed a new body and mind for their further functioning.

When he was over eighty years of age he entered on parinirvāṇa, the final waning-out and ending. Perfectly accomplished in every respect, and with all ignorance and grasping after the aggregates of existence dispelled and rooted out, no substratum for re-birth remained, no material for the future operation of karma. He was therefore freed (Samyutta-Nikāya i. 134). This body was his last. In no sense or manner could he be born again. And here it must be remembered that the attainment of parinirvāṇa is an achievement that can be won by others as well as by Buddhas. The Pali Canon contains references to disciples who in this life were able to break away from the wheel of samsāra, and achieve the final end which, whether won here or hereafter, is a "plunge into" Death-

lessness, "into the Immortal, into Nirvāṇa, into that fathomless Ocean that is at once an image of Nirvāṇa, Dharma and the Buddha himself" (Majjhima-Nikāya i. 488; Samyutta-Nikāya iv. 179, 180, 376; v. 47; Milinda-pañha 319, 346).

After the parinirvāṇa his place as Way-shower (Majj-hima-Nikāya iii. 6) was to be taken, not by any one monk (Majjhima-Nikāya, Sta. No. 108), for, being Way-followers, not one of them resembled him, but by Dharma: "Dharma is our support" (or mainstay, Majj-hima-Nikāya iii. 9), as monks are recorded to have said after the Teacher had died. This statement fully accords with the injunction the Buddha had given to Ānanda, his constant companion, shortly before this event: "The Dharma I have taught and the Vinaya I have laid down – that after my passing is to be your Teacher" (Dīgha-Nikāya ii. 154). The epithet of dhamma-kāya (Dīgha-Nikāya iii. 84), the body of Dharma, applicable only to the Lord and not even to Arhants, points in this same direction. So the Milindapañha, a later and post-canonical work, can say: "The Lord can be designated by means of the Dharma-body" (Milindapañha 75), even though he himself has entered on parinirvāṇa, has "gone home" or "set" like the Sun whose kinsman he was, and cannot be pointed to any longer as being either here or there. Thus while the unending Dharma exists the Lord exists and cannot be called extinct. And though we are here touching on a tenet that was to be developed and made much of in some of the Mahāyāna Buddhist Sūtras, its core is already apparent in the Pali writings as is practically always the case. Here there is a sense in which the Buddha and the Dharma, and the Samgha too, are re-garded as one: "Faring in the world as a man-of-naught, I am not a Brāhman or a rāja or a husbandman or anyone at all" (Suttanipāta 455). Again: "Who sees Dharma sees me: who sees me sees Dharma" (Samyutta-Nikāya iii. 120; Itivuttaka pp. 90, 91). And: "Monks, if you would tend me, you must tend the (monks who are) ill" (Vinaya-Piṭaka i. 302).

But in a less transcendental sense, though Dharma will remain as long as there is one yellow-robed monk to remember even a fragment of it, Theravādins consider that the Lord himself is now entirely extinct for he had rooted out from himself the last shred of craving for re-birth, the last remnant of pride and conceit in the thought of "I" or "mine" or "I am". In consequence his mind was utterly freed in an unshakable freedom. It is there-fore as inept to ask of him who is deep and unfathom-able as is the great ocean whether, after dying, he arises, does not arise, both arises and does not, or neither arises nor does not arise in a new body (Majjhima-Nikāya 486–

---

[1] The commentaries to the Pali Canon usually give eight meanings for the word Tathāgata. It is therefore best left untranslated. 'Accomplished One' would convey what is intended, but it has no etymological justification.

8), as it is inept to ask of a fire that has been extinguished or has gone out (*nibbuta*, same root as in *nibbāna*=*nirvāṇa*) whether it has gone in any direction. Verily is the Buddha trackless (*Dhammapada* 179, 180), the Tathāgata untraceable (*Majjhima-Nikāya* i. 140).

DHARMA

And from the night when the Tathāgata fully awakened to the supreme Self-Awakening to the night of his *parinirvāṇa* in the element of *nirvāṇa* in which none of the groups for existence remains – in that interval all that he spoke, declared and explained is exactly so and not otherwise. (*Dīgha-Nikāya* iii. 135.)

Karma

In common with other Indian thought Buddhism believes that there is "a long long faring on, both for me and for you" (*Dīgha-Nikāya* ii. 90; *Saṃyutta-Nikāya* v. 431–2; *Anguttara-Nikāya* ii. 1). Sentient beings, by their failure to awaken to and penetrate the four Aryan Truths, are bound by the operation of *karma* to the ever-turning wheel of *saṃsāra*, or constant dying followed by renewed birth and again-becoming. They have no possibility of escape from this wheel until they are able to root out from what passes as "themselves" all greed or *lobha*, all hatred or aversion (*dosa*) and all confusion or delusion (*moha*) about many things, including the fundamental truths, or better, Truth. For since "truth is Dharma" (*Saṃyutta-Nikāya* i. 169) it follows that "Truth is one, there is not a second" (*Suttanipāta* 884). These defiling mental states of *lobha*, *dosa* and *moha* are called the three roots of "unskilfulness", less satisfactorily translated as "unwholesome". They are the source and origin of all wrong deeds of body, speech and thought that are done by volition (*cetanā*) and obstruct a man from realizing the very stuff of his own-being (*evaṃ-dhammo*). *Karma* works in such a way that "one uprises (in a new birth) according to what one does," and, broadly speaking, the graver the deed the longer its effects take to wear away. These may be experienced either in this life or birth itself, or later, or in a succession of lives to be passed in Niraya Hell or as an animal, the woes of both of which are so many they are not easy to relate (*Majjhima-Nikāya* iii. 167, 169), or as a ghost (*peta*, departed one, one who has not been dead for long), or in the world of men again, or in one of the many *deva*-worlds according to the nature of the volitional deeds already done. Though birth never continues to all eternity in any of these spheres, sometimes no escape is possible for aeons. No person can "die", in the sense of finishing his *karma*-conditioned time and coming to an end of all life-spans, until the fruits of every

volitional deed he has done now or in the past, whether it was lovely or evil, have worn to their "karmic" end (*Majjhima-Nikāya* iii. 166, 183).

Karma may be regarded as an absolutely just but impersonal cosmic operation according to which the fruits, effects or ripening of a volitional act or deed of body, speech or thought are suited to that act. Actually, it is the volitional deed that is *karma*, and moreover, *karma* is volition itself, whether skilled or unskilled: "I, monks, say that *karma* is volition; when one has willed, one does a deed (*karma*) by body, speech or thought" (*Anguttara-Nikāya* iii, 415). Good *karma* and bad *karma*, which are at once the results of previous deeds and the causes of new effects, work independently of each other and are not to be balanced the one against the other in any kind of scales. "As is the seed that is sown so is the fruit that is gathered; the doer of good (gathers) good, the doer of evil, evil" (*Saṃyutta-Nikāya* i. 227). Not all the virtuous deeds a wise and compassionate person may do can affect the maturing of some evil deed done by him in the past. For example, though Moggallāna met a most savage death strangely out of keeping with what was known of his life here, the Buddha explained to the perplexed disciples that it was the appropriate outcome of his having cruelly beaten his mother and father to death in some anterior birth.

The *saṃsāra* that every sentient being undergoes has *karma* for its support or prop and stay (*Saṃyutta-Nikāya* i. 38). Because of *karma* the world revolves and creatures revolve; it keeps them bound to the wheel of *saṃsāra* as the axle holds a rolling chariot's wheel (*Suttanipāta* 654). If there were no *karma* there would be no *saṃsāra*. In a sense it is life, for it operates only where there is volition, not a characteristic of dead or inert matter any more than of an unintentional deed. The *Vinaya* shows over and over again that even a deed as grave as murder entails no offence if it is done unwittingly. Within the operation of his own *karma* a man can exercise the determination to examine, test and criticize all that he finds here and can resolve to put forth energy so as to crush the covetousness, malevolence and harmfulness leading to re-birth that he harbours in his mind. Good and evil are subjective standpoints belonging to the world of action which has not yet been supplanted by contemplation. In his active life man has the power of choice: "If it were not possible to make what is skilled come to be, I would not say to you: Make what is skilled come to be. But because it is possible, so do I say to you: Make what is skilled come to be" (*Anguttara-Nikāya* i. 58). The criterion of Buddhist morality is to ask yourself, when there is one of the three kinds of deeds that you want to do, whether it will lead to the hurt of self, of others, or of both. If you come to the conclusion that it will be harmful, then you must not do it. But if you form the opinion that it will be harmless, then you may do it and repeat it (*Majjhima-Nikāya* i. 416). A person who torments neither himself nor another is already transcending the active life, for, allayed, quenched and become cool, he lives with self Brahma-become (*Majjhima-Nikāya* i. 341, etc.), even as an epithet of the Buddha is Brahma-become (*Dīgha-Nikāya* iii. 84; *Suttanipāta* 561, etc.). Then, devoid of the three roots of unskilfulness, if a man thinks: "All this is unreal, he thereby lets go of the here and the hereafter as a snake sloughs its outworn skin" (*Suttanipāta* 10–14). This is the final liberation, and is the aim towards which the Teaching is directed.

It is considered that man is the only being who can free himself from the wheel of *saṃsāra* or that of the process of becoming. Nothing else in the world with which he is acquainted has this power, and even the *devas* must be reborn as men. He must win his freedom by dispelling ignorance and darkness and arousing knowledge and light. And he must do it by himself by following the Way that has been pointed out by the Tathāgata (p. 281. n.l.): "Buddhas point out the Way; it is for you to swelter at the task" (*Dhammapada* 276). Since he owes his origin neither to a creator-god nor to a master-puppeteer, a Thread-Spirit on whom "all this universe is strung . . . like rows of gems on a thread" (*Bhagavad-Gītā* vii. 7), it will avail him nothing to wait on destiny or for automatic purification as he fares on (*Majjhima-Nikāya* i. 81), to offer prayers or sacrifices, to perform rites and ceremonial ablutions, recite *mantras* or invocations, or implore the mercy or grace of any saviour in his efforts to get free. Nor is suicide an answer. It too is a deed, and its fruits will not necessarily come to their termination when a person takes his life. Only when such an act is accompanied by an utter lack of grasping after a new body can suicide be called "blameless" for the reason that it will then give rise to no future effects.[1]

If none but a human being can stop the revolution of the wheel, it is equally true that "few are the beings born among men; more numerous are the beings born among others than men" (*Anguttara-Nikāya* i. 35). This observation may be illustrated by the simile of the blind marine turtle who only at the end of some tremendously long

time will thrust his head through a hole in a yoke drifting on the surface of the oceans (*Majjhima-Nikāya* iii. 169; *Saṃyutta-Nikāya* v. 455). "So rare as this the chance of human birth" (*Therīgāthā* 500). Once it is achieved, its very brevity, for it seldom lasts more than a hundred years, allows of no time to waste. Wherefore, "do not let the moment pass" (*Suttanipāta* 333; *Dhammapada* 315), the "moment" for rooting out ignorance, mated as it is to craving, and thereby for reducing the domination of sense-desires. The aspirant will then be free to cross over from the hither shore of the restless sea to the other shore of meditational super-consciousness which is peaceful and pure. Better than speculating on what you were in the past or will be in the future or entertaining doubts about what you are now (*Majjhima-Nikāya* i. 8) is the acceptance of the present as an opportunity gradually to arrive at the end of the Way by developing such cardinal faculties as faith, energy, mindfulness, concentration and extra-sensory wisdom. A slightly expanded statement of the first and third Truths combined recognizes the actuality of the present, together with the possibility of transcending it: "There *is* birth, there are ageing and dying, there are sorrow and grief, and of these I lay down the suppression here and now" (*Majjhima-Nikāya* i. 430). This might be regarded as the pith and core of the whole Teaching. It is concerned with the present rather than with the past or future:

"The past should not be followed after, the future
    not desired.
What is past is done with and the future not yet
    come.
Whoever has vision now here, now there, of a
    present thing,
Knowing it to be immovable, unshakable, let him
    cultivate it.
Swelter at the task this very day. Who knows
    whether he will die tomorrow?
There is no bargaining with the great hosts of death.
Thus abiding ardently, unwearied night and day,
He indeed is Auspicious called, described as a sage
    at peace." (*Majjhima-Nikāya* iii. 87.)

Therefore, as it is even more strongly stated: "Let be the past, let be the future. I will teach you Dharma: If this is, that comes to be; from the arising of this, that arises; if this is not, that does not come to be; from the stopping of this, that is stopped" (*Majjhima-Nikāya* ii. 32). This is a universal expression of cause, *hetu*, a term almost synonymous in its implications with *paccaya*, condition, and of fundamental importance in the Teaching. It applies to the "wheel of life", of *saṃsāra*, past,

---

[1] The monk Channa (*Majjhima-Nikāya*, St. No. 144) did not grasp after another body, and his suicide was called blameless. The monk Vakkali (*Saṃyutta-Nikāya* iii. 120) did not doubt the impermanence, anguish and changeable nature of the five *khandhā* and had no desire for them. The monk Godhika (*Saṃyutta-Nikāya* i. 121) had torn out clinging with its root, and was without longing for a new life. All had reached the end of their karmic time when they committed suicide.

present and future too, unless and until the material or fuel for re-birth is withheld. Without fruitless speculation on what this past was or what the future will be, they yet have to be admitted: the past to account for the diversity among sentient beings here and now, some, for example, having a greater or quicker capacity than others for making an end of anguish; and the future to allow the powerful force of karma to work to its conclusion by finding new outlets for its exercise if the effects of the deeds a person has done are still unexpended when he dies.

It is thus believed not only that the journeying in saṁsāra may be of untold length in the future, but also that it has been going on for such innumerable aeons in the past that "incalculable is the beginning of this faring-on; the earliest point cannot be discerned of beings who are running on and faring on hindered by ignorance and fettered by craving" (Saṁyutta-Nikāya ii. 178). So remote in time was this beginning that, greater than the waters in the four oceans is the flood of tears each being has shed since then or the amount of blood he has lost when, as an animal or evil-doer, he has had his head cut off. The first Aryan Truth, in laying down that there is anguish, refers as much to all these aeons of suffering as to this one brief life-span which is being experienced here and now. As for an aeon, its length cannot be reckoned by hundreds of centuries or by thousands. It can be suggested merely vaguely by similes. Supposing, for example, there were a great solid mountain measuring seven miles in each direction and a man were to stroke it once at the end of every century with a piece of soft cloth. Sooner would that mountain be worn away then an aeon come to its end. Or again, more numerous than the grains of sand, which cannot be counted, between the source of the Ganges and where it reaches the sea, are the aeons that have passed since the incalculable beginning of this faring-on (Saṁyutta-Nikāya ii. 178–90). But nothing is permanent; not even an aeon, far less the mountains and the seas; they will crumble and dry up (Majjhima-Nikāya i. 185ff.).

Though the tremendous force of karma needs more than one life-span for its stage, yet, since it cannot be seen or handled, its precise mechanism cannot be described. When it is said: "Karma is one's own, a being is heir to karma, born of karma, kinsman to karma, the support for karma" (Majjhima-Nikāya iii, 203), there is the implication that the being who is heir to karma is heir both to his own karma and to that of other volitional beings as well. For the unexhausted force of karma has to find some "person" for the continuing fruition of its effects, and that "person" may be someone other than the

doer of the deed. But it is also sometimes true that when a man has "himself" done a deed that cannot be attributed to mother or father, brother or sister or anyone else, it is "he himself" that will experience its results (Majjhima-Nikāya iii. 180; Anguttara-Nikāya i. 139). This statement must not be taken to mean, however, as it did in the fallacious view of the Eternalists, that the man "himself" who has done the deed will survive death and be precisely what "he" is now. Equally fallacious was the Annihilationists' view which maintained that, though someone did a deed, another person would eventually experience its results, thereby implying that a painful feeling assailing one person was due to the suffering wrought by another (Saṁyutta-Nikāya ii. 19–21).

Dependent Origination

The Tathāgata taught differently. He proclaimed Dharma by a causal mean between these two dead-ends of wrong views, and also between other dead-ends (Saṁyutta-Nikāya ii. 23, 61, 76, 77). Called Paṭicca-samuppāda (Sanskrit, Pratītya-samutpāda), conditioned arising or genesis or co-production, or dependent origination, and as potent as karma, it too is a circle or wheel to which the being is bound. Each of its twelve links depends for its arising into existence on the one immediately preceding it, and itself conditions the one immediately following. The cycle of links thus comes full circle and begins again and again unless the way to stop its revolution is discovered and practised.

The Teaching on Paṭicca-samuppāda, unique to Buddhism, is very central to the whole. It is the truth the Buddha penetrated as he sat in meditation under the Bo-tree, and is regarded as lying at the very heart of Dharma: "Who sees dependent origination sees Dharma; who sees Dharma sees dependent origination" (Majjhima-Nikāya i. 190–1). If it be not understood, the escape from saṁsāra cannot be effected: "This dependent origination, Ānanda, is profound and has the appearance of being profound. It is through not knowing, not discovering, not penetrating this Dharma that this generation, become entangled like a ball of string and covered with blight like coarse grass and rushes, cannot overpass . . . saṁsāra" (Dīgha-Nikāya ii. 55; Saṁyutta-Nikāya ii. 92).

This Dharma that is dependent origination is an abstract law of contingency denying independent existence to finite things, though not denying their total reality. Such reality as they have is conditional on the occurrence of something else that has already taken place and is conditioned by it. There is therefore order in this world of relations and not anarchy. Dependent origination functions in the three modes of time as to *karma* and *saṁsāra*: past, present and future. In its forward order it is expressed as follows:

Past
- Conditioned by ignorance are the karmic formations
- Conditioned by the karmic formations is consciousness

Present
- Conditioned by consciousness is name-and-shape
- Conditioned by name-and-shape are the six sense-fields
- Conditioned by the six sense-fields is the impact on the senses
- Conditioned by the impact on the senses is feeling
- Conditioned by feeling is craving
- Conditioned by craving is grasping
- Conditioned by grasping is continued becoming

Future
- Conditioned by continued becoming is birth
- Conditioned by birth there come into being old age and dying, grief, sorrow, suffering, lamentation and despair

Such is the arising of this entire mass of anguish.

In its reverse order Dependent Origination lays down that by the stopping of ignorance the whole of the rest of the process can be stopped stage by stage. Ignorance (*avijjā*) is nescience, the unknowing of the four Aryan Truths (p. 289) in their total significance, accessible only by Wisdom; it is also the ignorance of harbouring the thoughts: "I am the doer, another is the doer" (*Udāna* 70) or of thinking "I am" (*Majjhima-Nikāya* i. 139; *Anguttara-Nikāya* ii. 216; *Vinaya-Piṭaka* i. 3; *Udāna* 10, 74 etc.). It is also the ignorance which is called the four perversions of perception, thought and view. These are to hold that there is permanence in the impermanent, anguish in non-anguish, self in not-self, and what is fair in what is repulsive (*Anguttara-Nikāya* ii. 52). Because of ignorance karmic formations operate, as they have operated in past lives, to determine the consciousness (*viññāṇa*), itself a form of ignorance, that will descend into a womb, there to take on a new bodily form (*rūpa*) and a new psychological aggregation (*nāma*). Only where there is body and mind is there awareness through the senses, the feeling consequent on this, the craving for more sense-experience and for the process of becoming to go on, which leads to grasping after birth or life (*jāti*). In this new birth ignorance remains as in earlier ones, and the process repeats itself until ignorance, the direst of

bonds (*Majjhima-Nikāya* ii. 44) and the root condition for the arising of this mass of anguish in birth after saṁsāric birth, is transcended here and now, as it can be in meditation, by the person who "stands knocking at the door of the Deathless" (*Saṁyutta-Nikāya* ii. 43) in an unresting search for freedom from the saṁsāric round.

The Fire Khandhā

Applied to man, how does this process of becoming work so that on the dissolution of the body there will still be a new arising? Death is not the end for the vast majority. It merely marks the ending of one "habitation" and the assumption of a new one. It may well be asked, as Māra asked a nun: "Who made this wooden doll? Where is its maker? Where has it arisen? Where will it perish?" The answer is that it was made neither by self nor another but that its origin is dependent on cause (*hetu*) and that by the breaking of cause it is stopped. It is only a convention to speak of a "being". As in actual fact there is no chariot apart from its constituents and their right arrangement, so it is only when there are the five *khandhā* or "aggregates" that, using ordinary parlance, we can say "There is a being" (*Saṁyutta-Nikāya* i. 134–5). These five aggregates or groups unite to form the psychophysical stuff of which a "being" consists. Physiologically, the body or material part (*rūpa*) is composed of the four great inter-related elements or primaries and derived from them: the supporting or solid, the binding or cohesive, the heating or temperature, and the motion or movement elements. They are spoken of symbolically as earth, water, heat and wind. The non-material parts (*nāma*) of a "being" are feeling, perception, the volitional activities or habitual tendencies, and consciousness. The whole psycho-physical congeries is known as *nāma-rūpa*. Its very nature is that each of the five *khandhā* of which it consists is a group of grasping: after sense-pleasures, speculative views, rites and ceremonies, and the theory of a persistent self (*Majjhima-Nikāya* i. 67). These are fetters, unreleased from which the uninstructed person is not free from birth, ageing and dying, from grief and sorrow, or from anguish (*Majjhima-Nikāya* i. 8).

Some portions of the Pali Canon indicate that it is the fifth *khandha*, consciousness or *viññāṇa*, which finds a new foothold or support for itself on the death of the body (*Saṁyutta-Nikāya* ii. 65) and enters another womb to issue forth with another set or *khandhā*. Consciousness and *nāma-rūpa* are mutually dependent for their existence (*Dīgha-Nikāya* ii. 32, 63). Where there is the one there is the other. Consciousness returns again to name-and-shape and goes not elsewhere (*Dīgha-Nikāya* ii. 32). When it has arisen it is tied to the body of a living person as are life and heat (*Dīgha-Nikāya* ii. 338). It is in this connection that the expression *paṭisandhi-viññāṇa* first appears in the Pali Canon (*Paṭisambhidāmagga*, i. 52), then to be taken up in the commentaries as the relinking or rebirth-consciousness that, when it quits its former "support", proceeds to another by means of such conditions as *karma* which were included in that former support. *Paṭisandhi-viññāṇa* is thus the source of the next life-stream but has no further identity with it. This may be illustrated by thinking of an echo. Though conditioned by sound, it does not owe its re-sound to the transmigration of the original sound. The function is transmitted but not the individual. Or again, as there is not a complete identity between milk and curds nor a complete difference, so the arising consciousness is not absolutely the same as the earlier one nor completely different from it (*Visuddhimagga* xvii). The heresy of Sāti, the fisherman who, caught in a great net of craving, misrepresented the Buddha, was to think that it was no other than this consciousness itself that circled on. For what the Buddha had taught was that "in many a figure has consciousness, generated by conditions, been spoken of by me to you, saying that apart from conditions there is no origination of consciousness" (*Majjhima-Nikāya* i. 256ff.).

In the result it must be understood therefore that deeds do not necessarily stay and rest with the doer of them. *Karma* passes on, and though in a new birth the doer is not substantially the same as he was in a preceding one nor totally different, there yet has been no discontinuity between the process of dying and that of being born again. Consciousness is a stream (*viññāṇa-sota*, *Dīgha-Nikāya* iii. 105) and the consciousness there was at the time of death (*cuti-viññāṇa*) flows on and into the *paṭisandhi-viññāṇa*, the re-birth-consciousness, without interruption. The Aryan disciple therefore does not think of "himself" as transmigrating or being re-born; he recognizes conditions dependent on which contingent personalities arise and cease to be (*Saṁyutta-Nikāya* ii. 26, 27). Therefore, since there is no "being" that passes from one "habitation" to another, it is not precisely "I" or "the man so-and-so" that fares on and circles on in *saṁsāra* or reaps the harvest of good or evil that "I" or "he" has sown in some anterior habitation. "I", "he", "being" are words used only in common parlance but in no ultimate sense. Even the Buddhas use these words however, but are not misled by them.

The Vajjiputtakas and the Sammitiyas who belonged to the sect called Puggalavādin held, in distinction to the Theravādins, that a "person" (*puggala*) was a real and ultimate fact without positing which, though it was neither the same as the *khandhā* nor different from them,

re-birth was incomprehensible. According to another sect, the Sautrāntikas, the *puggala* is a subtle *khandhā* among the five *khandhā*, and it is this that is re-born. The fact of re-birth after dying was accepted by all the Buddhist sects. They only differed in their attitude as to how it took place. In this connection the Jain belief might also be mentioned. Here it is held that each individual has an immaterial eternal soul, called *jīva* (p. 262). This is tied to matter until, by the disciple's faith, right knowledge and right conduct, the *jīva* is purified of all dross and defilements. Thus freed or won to *moksha* (release), it enters on an eternal existence and is happy.

The Not-Self

The Theravādins also classify the components of a compounded or constructed being into the six internal sense-organs of eye, ear, etc., and the six external classes of sense-data of shape, sound, etc., each corresponding to its appropriate sense-organ. Together these form the twelve *āyatanas* or sense-fields. To arrive at the eighteen *dhātus* or elements recognized by this most orthodox school of Buddhist thought, to the twelve *āyatanas* must be added the six forms of consciousness, namely the visual, auditory, olfactory, gustatory, tactile and mind-consciousness. These do not impinge on the range or pasture of one another. Over and over again it is said of each that it is *anattā*, not-self. Neither an internal sense-organ nor an external sense-object nor the cognizing of it is *attā*, self. This is, or came to be, such an important feature in the Teaching that one or two relevant passages may be quoted:

"And what is not-self? Eye (or vision) is not-self, nor are material shapes, nor is visual consciousness, nor sense-impingement on the eye, nor that feeling which arises conditioned by sensory impingement on the eye, be it pleasant or painful or neither painful nor pleasant. Ear is not-self, nor are sounds. . . . Nose is not-self, nor are smells. . . . Tongue is not-self, nor are tastes. . . . Body is not-self, nor are touches. . . . Mind is not-self, nor are mental states, nor is mental consciousness, nor sense-impingement on the mind, nor that feeling which arises conditioned by sensory impingement on the mind, be it pleasant or painful or neither painful nor pleasant. It is impermanent, it is anguish, it is not-self. Desire for it must be relinquished. By knowing and seeing its impermanence, its anguish and its not-selfness, ignorance is got rid of and knowledge arises" (*Saṁyutta-Nikāya* iv. 48–50). "Wherefore, what is not yours, put it away. Putting it away will be for a long time for your welfare and happiness. And what is not yours? Material shape, feeling, perception, the volitional activities, consciousness. Put each of them away. Now, would you say that

that man who is gathering, burning and doing as he pleases with the grass, sticks and branches in this Jeta Grove, is gathering *us*, burning *us*, doing as he pleases with *us*? You would not say so because these are not your self nor of the nature of self. Similarly, not one of the five *khandhā* is yours. Therefore put away all of them" (*Majjhima-Nikāya* i. 140–1; *Saṁyutta-Nikāya* iii, 33–4) like a useless log of wood. The instructed disciple of the Aryans therefore does not regard material shape as self, nor self as having material shape, nor material shape as being in self, nor self as being in material shape. Nor does he regard the remaining four *khandhā* in any of these modes (*Saṁyutta-Nikāya* iii. 114–5). He comprehends of each of them that "this is not mine, this am I not, this is not my self". So that when any of the *khandhā* change and alter as they inevitably do since they are all impermanent, no grief, sorrow or suffering arises in him (*Saṁyutta-Nikāya* iii. 19, etc.).

All phenomenal life, all that is constructed, structured or effected has three characteristics: it is impermanent, transient or unresting (*anicca*); it is anguish, suffering, painful (*dukkha*); and it is insubstantial (*anatta*), owing to the absence of anything that in an ultimate sense could be called "self". Everything constructed is impermanent because it is dependent or caused; its uprising is to be seen, its decaying, and also alteration in it while it persists (*Anguttara-Nikāya* i, 152). What is impermanent is anguish for the very reason that it is not permanent; and what is impermanent, anguish and of the nature to change is not-self. These three marks are features of everything we apprehend through the senses. And "these five strands of sense-activity are called 'world' in the discipline for an Aryan . . . and all of them are longed for, alluring, exciting" (*Anguttara-Nikāya* iv, 430). This "world" far from being external is internal to a man: "There where one is not born, does not age, does not die, does not pass on (from one birth) and does not arise (in another) – I do not say that that is an end of the world that one can apprehend, see or reach by walking. . . . But neither do I say that, not having reached the end of the world, an end can be made of anguish. For I lay down that the world, its uprising, its stopping and the course leading to its stopping are in this fathom-long body itself with its perceptions and ideas" (*Saṁyutta-Nikāya* i, 61–2; *Anguttara-Nikāya* ii. 47–9).

The Struggle for Freedom

This belief that the "world" is essentially of the here and now is thus balanced by the belief that its stopping or the escape from it is likewise possible here and now: "There is an unborn, unmade, not become, unconstructed; were this not so, there would be no escape for what is born, made, become and constructed here" (*Udāna* 80). It is when a man has entered on and is abiding in the ninth and final stage of meditation, where all perceiving and feeling are stopped, that he can justly be called one who, "having come to the world's end, abides at the world's end, and has crossed over the entanglement of the world" (*Anguttara-Nikāya* iv, 431–2). The world's end therefore is not to be reached by locomotion, but by meditation. Calm of mind and impassibility of body are required. The Buddha, awakened, tamed, calmed, crossed over and attained to *Nirvāṇa*, taught Dharma so that disciples might win these very states themselves (*Dīgha-Nikāya* iii. 54; *Majjhima-Nikāya* i, 235). *Nirvāṇa*, uncreate, is not a post-mortem state, nor yet has it anything to do with the world of action.

To let go of the active life by no means entails the destruction of the essential being (*Majjhima-Nikāya* i, 140). Though the senses should not be given full rein, as was the view of some of the contemporary teachers, most emphatically there should be control over them; and this was equivalent to their proper development. There was to be no atrophy of them, no atrophy of the mind, no derangement of it by seeking the goal either through such excessive sensual indulgence or such intense physical hardships as must almost inevitably lead to psychopathological states. The Buddha's experience in these two extremes in this last birth of his while he was still the Bodhisattva, not yet fully awakened, had convinced him that neither was the Way to Awakening. Victory in the struggle is to be won by the human being who resolutely refuses to injure the sense-organs, but who is neither entranced nor repelled neither affected nor distracted by anything sense-activity can convey to him, however faint and shadowy sense-awareness may become as the level of meditation gradually recedes from its influence. His attitude to the senses must be new. To watch over them can result in transcending them in the deepest meditative stage where "all is still" (*Suttanipāta* 902), and where, in the "Aryan silence", the meditator who is capable of sustained and uninterrupted meditation is so completely withdrawn from the external world and so totally irresponsive to it that only equanimity remains for him.

When a man understands something of what he is and what he is not, and of what he might be were he to strive on with diligence, he is in a better position to understand how he is kept bound to the wheel of *saṁsāra* and more ready to comprehend the escape which he should try to effect if he truly wishes for the happiness and joy that are apart from, and infinitely greater than, sensory happiness and joy. It thus comes about that the most recurrent counsel running through the Buddha's

Teaching is: "get free" (*Therīgāthā* 2), – free from the ignorance that is the fundamental cause of misery and suffering in life after life; free from untamed craving, from grasping after anything in the world; free from the taints and defilements of the mind; free from the cankers (*āsavā*) of wrong views, continued becoming and ignorance (again); free from the allurements of sense-experience; and so free from all evil unskilful states of mind. It is then that, in consequence of his freedom, the man, now a man-of-naught, will be able to enter and remain in any of the nine planes of meditation when, where and for as long as he may desire. This is the culmination of that freedom of mind and freedom through extra-sensory wisdom which, as the crown of renunciation and the casting aside of all unskills, dominates the Teaching: "Even as the great ocean has but one flavour, that of salt, so has this Dharma and Discipline but one flavour, that of freedom" (*Vinaya-Piṭaka* ii. 239; *Anguttara-Nikāya* iv. 206; *Udāna* 54), that freedom which is analogous to knowledge on the one hand and *Nirvāṇa* on the other (*Majjhima-Nikāya* i. 304; *Samyutta-Nikāya* iii. 189; v. 218), as emerges from three sets of questions and answers forming a topic of conversation between three different pairs of people. Although the wording differs to some extent in all these passages, the main points are the same: "What is the counterpart of knowledge?" (or, What is knowledge for?). "Freedom is the counterpart of knowledge." "And what is the counterpart of freedom?" "*Nirvāṇa* is the counterpart of freedom." The accent of the Teaching is on what is positive rather than on what is negative. It is on happiness, mental development, freedom and the winning of *Nirvāṇa*. When it is asked: "What is the counterpart of *Nirvāṇa*?" or, "What is *Nirvāṇa* for?" this is a question that goes too far and is beyond the compass of an answer, a commentary saying (*Majjhima Com.* ii. 370) that *Nirvāṇa* is without a counterpart. All that can be said in reply to such a question is that "the Brahma-faring is lived for the plunge into *Nirvāṇa*, for going beyond to *Nirvāṇa*, and for culminating in *Nirvāṇa*."

The Aryan Eightfold Path

The attainment of freedom or the profound knowledge that is a mark of Arhantship can be accomplished only by a gradual process of discipline. There is no sudden attainment except in a few isolated instances which, as recorded in the Pali Canon, no doubt betoken sustained resolution and energy in anterior births. Usually the disciple must first of all have faith in some teacher – for "by faith the flood is crossed . . . by faith you shall be free" (*Suttanipāta* 184, 1146) – and draw close enough to him to hear Dharma, though this was not to be whispered or spoken into his ear alone. Then he must remember what he had heard, test it and weigh it up. If he approve of it, the time is ripe for striving and effort on his part; and then, if he be self-resolute, he may realize the highest truth itself (*Majjhima-Nikāya* i. 480; ii. 173). This is *Nirvāṇa*, equivalent to the stopping of continual becoming (*Samyutta-Nikāya* ii. 117; *Anguttara-Nikāya* v. 9) and therefore of birth and therefore of anguish, as proclaimed in the statement of the third Aryan Truth. In fact the Dharma that such a disciple will hear may be summed up by and large as the four Aryan Truths which the Buddha enunciated in his First Utterance: the Aryan truth of anguish, of its arising, of its stopping, and of the course leading to its stopping.

The Aryan Truth of Anguish is that birth, ageing and dying are anguish, and also various painful states of mind; "in short, the five groups of grasping are anguish."

The Aryan Truth of the Arising of Anguish is connected with the craving for sense-experience, for the process of becoming and for more becoming.

The Aryan Truth of the Stopping of Anguish is the complete stopping, relinquishment and casting away of this self-same craving; and this is tantamount to *Nirvāṇa*.

The Aryan Truth leading to the Stopping of Anguish is the Aryan Eightfold Way itself. This Way, *magga* (from a root meaning to track or trace, and so to seek), consists of right view or understanding, right aspiration, thought or purpose, right speech, right action, right mode of livelihood, right endeavour, right mindfulness and right concentration.

These factors of the Way are all analysed and explained so that we know what the Pali Canon intends by each. There is no margin for suppositions and imaginings. Right view is the knowledge (*ñāṇa*) of the Four Truths. Right aspiration is for renunciation (of sense-desires and also, in consequence, of the household life); and it is for benevolence and harmlessness. Right speech is abstention from lying and from slanderous speech, harsh speech and frivolous chatter. Right action is abstention from stealing and wrong-doing amid the senses. Right mode of livelihood is abstention from earning one's livelihood by means that cause bloodshed, by the sale of intoxicating liquor, and by trafficking in women and slaves. Right endeavour is fourfold: to cause evil unskilled mental states that have not arisen not to do so; to get rid of those that have arisen; to cause skilled mental states that have not arisen to do so; and to maintain, increase and develop skilled mental states that have arisen. Right mindfulness is likewise fourfold: to abide contemplating the body as body, ardent, clearly conscious of it, mindful of it, so as to control the covetousness and dejection in the world (which, as we have seen, is the world of the senses); likewise to contemplate the feelings as feelings, the mind as mind, and mental states as mental states. Right concentration is again fourfold. It is expressed in the statement of the four *jhāna* or meditations belonging to the world of form, which a man can enter into if he has allayed the fivefold sense-activity and rid himself of the five hindrances (*nīvaraṇāni*), of sense-desires or covetousness, of malevolence, of sloth and torpor, of restlessness and worry, and of doubts and questionings.

These five hindrances are said to make for blindness and ignorance and for lack of profound knowledge; they obstruct Wisdom, are associated with distress and do not conduce to Nirvāṇa. But, in antithesis to them are the seven limbs of awakening (*bojjhanga*), – mindfulness, investigation of Dharma (*dhamma*) or of *dhammā*, things, mental states; energy; rapture of mind; impassibility of body; concentration; and even-mindedness. These also form part of a list of qualities or constituents that in time came to be known as the thirty-seven *bodhipakkhiyā dhammā*, that is things or states or qualities belonging to awakening. When the Buddha bade his final farewell to the township of Vesālī before he died, he charged the Order to practise these things and develop them so that the Brahma-faring should long continue for the good and welfare of mankind (*Dīgha-Nikāya* ii. 119–20). They are as follows:

(1) the four arousings or applications of mindfulness (see above, p. 289f.);

(2) the four right efforts (see above, p. 289);

(3) the four bases of psychic power: concentration of (*a*) intention ; (*b*) energy; (*c*) consciousness; (*d*) investigation, with each of which activity of striving is connected;

(4) the five cardinal virtues or controlling faculties of faith, energy, mindfulness, concentration and even-mindedness;

(5) the five powers which in name are the same as the five cardinal virtues;

(6) the seven limbs of awakening (as above);

(7) the Aryan eightfold Way (see above, p. 289). Alternatively these thirty-seven constituents of Arhantship or awakening may be reduced to thirty by counting the Way as one instead of as eight, and then adding complete purity in ethical behaviour, watch over the senses, moderation in eating, vigilance or wakefulness, and being mindful and clearly conscious of all the actions one performs in daily life.

After a person has mastered the four *jhāna* that belong to the material plane, and there are some "devices" and

"subjects" to help him focus his attention, and can pass from one to another of them at will and without difficulty, he then may be able to enter into and abide in as many as five more meditations on immaterial planes. These are the planes of infinite *ākāsa* (something like space), infinite consciousness, the plane of no-thing, that of neither-perception-nor-non-perception, and, finally, that where perceiving and feeling are stopped entirely. The trained meditator who can enter on this ultimate plane is regarded as an *Arhant*, one who is accomplished or "finished" both in the sense that he has fulfilled the Buddha's instruction and in the sense that, by having no further volition, he has broken away from all grasping and craving and hence from the wheel of *saṁsāra* and the wheel of becoming to which he had been stitched by craving, the sempstress (*Anguttara-Nikāya* iii. 400). The remainder of his actions in this life generate no more *karma*, for he now acts from Wisdom and not from volition, and therefore re-birth is at an end for him. There is no other meditational abiding higher than this one. To have gained it is to have gained unshakable freedom of mind, and this is the goal, the pith and the culmination of the Brahma-faring (*Majjhima-Nikāya* i. 197). The ninth plane therefore indicates that a man, Sāriputta for example, has attained to mastery and excellence in the Aryan Moral Habit, the Aryan Concentration, the Aryan Wisdom and the Aryan Freedom (*Majjhima-Nikāya* iii. 28–9). This is true self-conquest, the fruit of self-taming and self-development: "Though one should conquer a thousand thousand men in battle, he indeed is the greatest of conquerors who should conquer his self" (*Dhammapada* 103).

The arrogant Brāhman claims that theirs was the best and purest caste were always opposed by the Buddha. Once a man had joined the Order of monks, no matter from which of the four castes then recognized he came, all previous caste distinctions ceased even as rivers lose their names and identities on reaching the sea. There is therefore no bar depending on caste that obstructs a man from practising meditation of the most exacting kind, far less then those forms of it known as the four *Brahma-vihārā*, the abidings in the Highest or Best, the divine abidings, of friendliness or loving-kindness, compassion, sympathetic joy and even-mindedness. It is here the object of the meditator to suffuse and permeate first himself and then, in ever widening circles, the whole world including his enemies, with the potential immeasurability and far-reachingness of these four modes of meditational abiding. In the Parable of the Saw (*Majjhima-Nikāya* i. 129) it is impressed on the man who is practising the meditation on loving-kindness that even were he subjected to the direst provocation he must bear it and not retaliate. For "whoever sets his mind at enmity is for this reason not a doer of my teaching. You must train yourselves thus: 'Neither will my mind become perverted, nor will I utter an evil speech, but kindly and compassionate will I abide, with a mind of friendliness, void of hatred; and, beginning with him (the man using the saw on you), I will abide suffusing the whole world wide with a mind of friendliness that is far-reaching, widespread, immeasurable, without enmity, without malevolence'."

But these meditational practices of themselves do not lead to Nirvāṇa that changes not, but only to the Brahma-worlds where, in common with this world, nothing is permanent – worlds then, which are still "saṁsāric" in nature. Such meditations are therefore perhaps more suited to lay devotees than to monks who should have greater opportunity to meditate with other ends in view. So, it was censurable to establish a person only in the way to the Brahma-world when he was capable of something more, as can be seen from one of the three rebukes the Buddha is recorded to have administered to Sāriputta. On this occasion the "beloved disciple" had missed a rare opportunity to lift a Brāhman's mind to heights it was probably able to encompass had he been rightly taught (Majjhima-Nikāya ii. 124f.). And right teaching is not one that concentrates on re-birth in companionship with Brahmā, however dear the subject might have been to the hearts of the Brāhmans from whom the concept of the four Brahmavihārā appears to have been derived. The devas, even a Brahmā, even a Mahā-Brahmā (p. 295) are impermanent although their life-spans in the deva-worlds are so long they may forget that ultimately they will enter on a new birth. In distinction to this, right teaching is the teaching on the Middle Way that leads to the fulness of concentration in the ninth meditative plane, that where all perception and feeling are stopped, where all attachment, hatred and confusion have been burnt up, and where phenomenality, impermanence and all that is contingent and temporal have been transcended and the process of becoming has come to an end, both in the sense of the rise and fall of sense-impressions and reaction to them and in the sense of "saṁsāric" becoming.

When the seeker after Wisdom has rooted out attachment, or, as it is otherwise called, greed, when he has rooted out hatred and confusion and in consequence has begun the process of subduing unskilfulness in regard to body, speech and mode of livelihood and of making what is skilled come to be in place of what was unskilled, he is in a position to begin to realize that good ethical conduct is not only necessary, but that it leads on gradually up to the Highest (Anguttara-Nikāya v. 2). To the extent that his ethical conduct is purified and disciplined, so will the seeker after Wisdom begin to gain control over his constantly and rapidly changing thoughts which, never the same from moment to moment, are likened to a monkey busily climbing about in the jungle-trees (Saṁyutta-Nikāya ii. 95). After training in moral habit, the next step is to practise mental training. It is essential to meditation that thought be "held" and fixed on one point. Buddhist meditation is not day-dreaming or reverie, not a lazy drifting of the thoughts where they will, but an incandescent and intense activity of an absorbed mind so well directed and mastered that it can undertake uninterrupted and undeflected meditation when desired and emerge from it when desired. The Buddha thus eulogizes Sāriputta for his command in this sphere: "He has rule over mind, he is not under mind's rule; whatever attainment of abiding he wishes to abide in in the morning or at midday or in the evening, in that attainment of abiding he abides" (Majjhima-Nikāya i. 219) – just as a wealthy man would choose the clothes he would put on in the morning or at midday or in the evening.

The mind, on which practically all the emphasis in early Buddhism is laid, is held to be luminous and may be defiled by adventitious taints. Because uninstructed people do not understand this they do not develop the mind. But the luminous mind may be cleansed from the adventitious taints. Because the instructed Aryan disciple understands this, he develops the mind (Anguttara-Nikāya i. 10). No other single thing contributes so much to the arising of skilled mental states (dhammā) that have not arisen or to the decline of evil mental states that have arisen as does earnestness or diligence (appamāda, Anguttara-Nikāya i. 11). But mental states could not arise if there were no mind, and their nature depends on the quality of that mind: "Dhammā, that is feeling, perception and the habitual tendencies, have mind as forerunner, they have mind as master (over them), they consist of mind" (Dhammapada 1). It is therefore important to stabilize the mind, as can be done by the various meditational exercises Buddhism has devised, and to cleanse it of all corrupt thoughts:

"Today that mind I'll hold in thorough check,
As trainer's hook the savage elephant."
(Therīgāthā 77, 1130.)

It will therefore be seen that much of the accent of the Teaching is on what is inward and subjective. A deed done by the mind was considered by the Buddha, in opposition to his Jain contemporaries, more censurable than a deed done either by body or speech (*Majjhima-Nikāya* i. 373). The true sacrifice or the burning up of greed, hatred and confusion was, in distinction to the Brāhman view, a purification to be found in no source external to man:

"I lay no wood, Brāhman, for fires on altars.
Only within burneth the fire I kindle.
Ever my fire burns; ever composed-of-self
I, perfected, fare the Brahma-faring.

"As load of fuel, surely, is pride, O Brāhman;
The altar's smoke, anger; thy false words, ashes;
The tongue's the priest's spoon; and the heart the altar;
The flame thereon – that is man's self well tamed."
(*Saṃyutta-Nikāya* i. 169.)

The object of mind-control, or one of its objects, is the stopping of sensory reaction to what is liked, disliked or neither. The mind will then be "even", a condition praised by the Aryans who themselves are "even amid things uneven". As *sīla*, ethical conduct, is the necessary preliminary part of the training but is not an end in itself, likewise *samādhi* or *bhāvanā*, the control and development of the mind in meditation, is the essential second stage in the training but not an end in itself. The end, for the realization of which both *sīla* and *samādhi* are but preparatory instruments, is the opening of the door of the mind to unhampered comprehension in intuitive extra-sensory Wisdom (*paññā*) of the four Aryan Truths. By this opening of the door, they are to be more than comprehended; they are to be penetrated as well. Therefore, among much else that is of value to man on his quest, Wisdom gives vision of things as they really are: impermanent, of the nature of anguish, and insubstantial or empty of self, together with the bliss of emancipation from these three modes of phenomenal life.

Nirvāṇa

The aspirant who has attained the highest Aryan Wisdom and has thus come to the end of the Way, knows the complete destruction of anguish. And that freedom of his, of which he is also possessed now, is founded on truth and is unshakeable. For that highest Aryan truth is *Nirvāṇa*, beyond all suppositions, and where there is no more coming to birth and ageing and dying (*Majjhima-Nikāya* iii. 245). *Nirvāṇa* is therefore completely opposed to *saṃsāra*, the whirligig of birth and dying where life is led under the thrall of sense-desires to which a man is tied by his ignorance and his consequent incapacity to realize that neither the sense-organs nor the sense-data nor the meeting of the two in the appropriate field of consciousness are mine or I or my

self, any more than are the five aggregates of existence.

All of these are indeed not-self, *an-attā*. Though the Pali Canon frequently mentions *attā*, for example as that which should be sought (*Vinaya-Piṭaka* i. 23) as a refuge (*Dīgha-Nikāya* ii. 100, 120; *Saṃyutta-Nikāya* iii. 143, etc.), an island (*Dīgha-Nikāya* ii. 100, etc.), a lamp (*Dhammapada* 236, 238), as dear to one (*Saṃyutta-Nikāya* i. 73 = *Udāna* 47; *Saṃyutta-Nikāya* i. 140; *Anguttara-Nikāya* ii. 21), as something that can blame and upbraid one (*Anguttara-Nikāya* i. 57–8, etc.), or as dual:

"*Attā*, in thee, O man, knows what is true or false.
Indeed, my friend, thou scorn'st the lovely *attā*
Thinking to hide the evil *attā*
From *attā* that witnessed it" (*Anguttara-Nikāya* i. 149),

yet it never defines it or analyses it or gives it precision. It may be safely said however that it does not regard it either as a permanently surviving entity passing over from one birth to another, nor as any kind of a permanent core of the *santāna*, series or continuum, which is the Pali philosophical term for the individual; nor yet as transcendent or as the underlying Principle of the Universe as in Upanishadic usage. In fact, as stated in the *Dhammapada* (279), "all things are not-self", where "things" (*dhammā*) refer both to constructed phenomenal things and to the unconstructed *Nirvāṇa*. It is indeed in the doctrine of *an-attā* or "not-self" that all *Abhidhamma* thought converges and reaches its culmination, and it is to *Abhidhamma* (p. 268) that we have to turn for the interpretation of the Dharma that is regarded as authentic, especially to the *Visuddhimagga*, the "Path of Purification", compiled by the Venerable Buddhaghosa in the fifth Christian century, and to the *Abhidhammattha-sangaha*, the "Compendium of *Abhidhamma* Philosophy", compiled about the eleventh century. One passage from the former must suffice here to show why *attā* cannot be regarded as belonging to the *khandhā* or the five aggregates of existence: "They are all 'not-self in the sense of having no core',– in the sense of having no core because of the absence of any core of self conceived as a self, an abider, a doer, an experiencer, one who is his own master; for what is impermanent is painful (*Saṃyutta-Nikāya* iii, 82) and it is impossible to escape the impermanence, or the rise and fall and oppression of self, so how could it have the state of a doer, and so on? Hence it is said: Bhikkus, were any of the five *khandhā* self, it would not lead to affliction (*Saṃyutta-Nikāya* iii. 66), and so on. So they are not-self in the sense of having no core" (*Visuddhimagga* xx. 16).

The concern of the *Arhant*, the man perfected, is with neither what is *anattā* as the mark of the five groups of grasping, nor with *attā* because it is pithless and has no owner. His concern is to become uncontaminated by the world and to pass from the active to the contemplative life: "undefiled whether by good or evil, the self cast away, for such there is no more action needed here" (*Suttanipāta* 790). He, that has been born or has become or been made or constructed, is intent on seeking that which is not born or become or made or constructed(*Udāna* 90), and which is timeless and which is *Nirvāṇa*. Born neither of cause nor *karma* nor nature (*Milindapañha* 268), *Nirvāṇa* is changeless (*Saṃyutta-Nikāya* iii. 143, etc.) and deathless (*Saṃyutta-Nikāya* i. 212, etc.), not accessible by thought (*Aṅguttara-Nikāya* ii. 80) (but by meditation), without a foothold (as is necessary for consciousness, for example) (*Saṃyutta-Nikāya* i. 1) and, in contradistinction to the three roots of unskill which create limits (*Majjhima-Nikāya* i. 298), it is without limitation (*Saṃyutta-Nikāya* iv. 158; *Majjhima-Nikāya* iii. 4) and neither its emptiness nor its fulness is affected no matter how many monks attain it (*Vinaya-Piṭaka* ii. 239). These negative expressions are meant to indicate no more than that to name anything positively is at once to impose limits on it. The phenomenal may be described, analysed and confined in lists. But not so the transphenomenal (*appañca*) (*Aṅguttara-Nikāya* ii. 161ff. etc.). *Nirvāṇa* is, and it will not fail the man who has so tamed himself and developed himself that he is prepared physically, morally and mentally and in wisdom for the vision of it while he is deeply absorbed in meditation. Its unspeakable bliss cannot be described, it has to be experienced. It is for the here and now rather than a kind of heaven to be entered into by a virtuous man when he dies. Perhaps it has therefore become less difficult now to answer the question that many people find perplexing: Who is it that enjoys *Nirvāṇa* if there is not much left of the man so-and-so after he has died? The question framed thus is inept and does not fit. Rather should it be asked: Who enjoys *Nirvāṇa* here and now? The answer is the adept in meditation. For *Nirvāṇa* may be seen in this very life.

SAṂGHA

"Ah, happy indeed the *Arhants*! In them no
craving's found.
The 'I am' conceit is rooted out; confusion's net is
burst.
Lust-free they have attained; translucent is the mind
of them.
Unspotted in the world are they, Brahma-become,
all cankers gone."
(*Saṃyutta-Nikāya* iii. 83.)

When, by a conscious act of understanding, resort is made to the Three Jewels of Buddha, Dharma and Saṃgha, or refuge taken in them by the thrice repeated formula of the threefold Going for Refuge, the Saṃgha stands, ideally, for the community of *Arhants* united by their knowledge and right conduct. For in this connection Saṃgha only refers to those wearers of the yellow robe who have complete mastery in moral behaviour, concentration, wisdom, freedom and the knowledge of and insight into freedom. While the nature of this Saṃgha is transcendental or supermundane, it gives the assurance that by the "cleansing of the spirit" (*Suttanipāta* 478, 876) the ardent disciple can transcend all the things of the "world" as the *Arhants* have done. The Saṃgha therefore can be emulated, and its function is to act as an inspiration to lesser mortals to develop their faith and unwavering confidence, their resolution and comprehension. "Faith is the seed" (*Suttanipāta* 77) from which further growth will spring. Not an obediently blind faith is meant, but a conviction based on reason, on experimentation, and sometimes on observation (*Majjhima-Nikāya* ii. 120ff.) that the Way and the practice lead to unrivalled peace and happiness and, further, have been successfully pursued by these men of wisdom. Resolution will then be charged with the purposive conviction of faith, and the aspirant, developing his powers of meditation, will be serenely intent on the Four Ways of becoming perfect, all of which can be attained in this life. Comprehension, besides directing the will, controls any exuberance of faith such as might manifest itself in too emotional a way, and it controls energy. This must be "even", like the tuneful string of a lute, and neither too slack nor too taut (*Vinaya-Piṭaka* i. 182; *Aṅguttara-Nikāya* iii. 375). There is no place for worship in the Theravāda scheme, nor any place for *bhakti*, devotion to a person. The flowers and lights the devotees bring into Buddhist temples are but signs and symbols of impermanency: the flowers fade and the lamps finally go out for want of more fuel, even as the fires of attachment, hatred and aversion are extinguished when no more fuel is added to them. And the words the devotees utter are not prayers; they are meant to serve as reminders of the wonderful qualities of the Buddha, Dharma and the Saṃgha: "He is indeed the Lord, perfected, wholly self-awakened, endowed with knowledge and right conduct, well-farer, knower of the worlds, incomparable charioteer of men to be tamed, teacher of *devas* and mankind, the Buddha, the Lord. Dharma is well taught by the Lord, it is self-realized, it is timeless, a come-and-see thing, leading onwards (to *Nirvāṇa*), to be understood by the wise each for himself.

The Lord's Order of disciples is of good conduct, upright, of wise conduct, of dutiful conduct, that is to say the four pairs of men, the eight individuals. This Order of the Lord's disciples is worthy of alms, hospitality, offerings and reverence, it is a matchless field of merit for the world" (*Majjhima-Nikāya* i. 37, etc.).

The right mental attitude to *Arhants* is one of respect and honour. In reflecting on all they have accomplished complacency dies a natural death and the longing to become as they is intensified. Like all other aspirants seeking to fulfil the Buddha's instruction, *Arhants* are, or have been Way-followers. They are not Way-finders, for they are not self-awakened Buddhas. Never must one who is aiming at recluseship and all that it entails, fall short of the goal if there yet remains something further to be done. Then will his going forth into homelessness be not barren but growing and fruitful (*Majjhima-Nikāya* i. 271), again emphasizing the gradualness of attainment and the ordered progression towards it.

This gradual approach to final attainment persists even for one who is certain of eventually becoming an *Arhant*. In its technical and canonical arrangement into four stages the Way to Arhantship or *Nirvāṇa* is for "the four pairs of men, the eight individuals" who have arrived at any one of these stages and the fruits of them. In the first stage, that of entering the stream (*sotāpanna*) that flows to *Nirvāṇa*, the meditator becomes sure of attaining enlightenment. He will never be re-born in any of the sorrowful states – in Niraya Hell, as an animal, a departed one or as a demon (*asura*) because, having unwavering confidence in the Buddha, in what he taught in his Dharma, and in the Saṁgha which is the guardian of Dharma, and in the Aryan ethical precepts, he can never again and no longer commit any of the heinous offences of killing his mother or father or an *Arhant*, of wounding a Buddha (for Buddhas cannot be killed), or causing a schism in the Order. At most he will be re-born seven times as a man before he wins *Nirvāṇa* which can be achieved by none other than a human being.

The next stage, that of *sakadāgāmin*, means that because the man who is intent on self-deliverance has completely destroyed the three fetters (of wrong view as to his "own person", of doubt, and of trust in the efficacy of rites and ceremonies) and has reduced attachment, aversion and confusion to a minimum, he will return but once more to birth as a human being, then to make an end of anguish.

At the third stage, that where he is an *anāgāmin*, or never-returner to birth on earth, he has destroyed the five fetters (the three mentioned above, with sense-desire and malevolence added), and after his death here will become a denizen of one of the highest *deva*-worlds and attain *Nirvāṇa* there when the residual *karma* that led to this *deva*-birth has expended itself.

The fourth stage is that of Arhantship itself. The man who has realized by his own efforts here and now freedom of mind and freedom through intuitive wisdom, who has done all there was to be done to shed the burden of "self" and cut off the binding fetters, comes not to birth again. No fuel for birth remains in him, he no longer grasps after anything in the "world", and while he still lives here his *karma* becomes exhausted through his lack of craving for any of the five *khandhā*. This final liberation that is effected here and now confers *parinirvāṇa* on the one who is thus liberated. He will go on living here until his body dies, but then, because "such a one" (*tādin*) delights in the destruction of the three roots of unskilfulness, he is free from all becomings (*Itivuttaka*, pp. 38-9), and *saṁsāra* is at an end for him. Final liberation, though attained here and now, entails no future state. It is *anupādisesa-nibbāna*, or the state of *Nirvāṇa* that has no fuel or clinging or basis for re-birth remaining.

With his energy strung to an even pitch, he has left the hither shore of mutability and mortality, of fear and peril, and having crossed the great flood of sense-desires, the process of becoming, false views and ignorance, and having arrived Beyond on the Farther Shore which is the unborn and undying *Nirvāṇa*, he is an *Arhant* who, crossed over and gone beyond, is standing on the dry land (*Saṁyutta-Nikāya* iv. 175), the Isle of *Nirvāṇa* (*Suttanipāta*, 1094) itself.

"These are the roots of trees, these are empty places. Meditate, be not slothful; let there be no remorse later. This is my instruction to you" (*Majjhima-Nikāya* i. 46, etc.).

Various technical terms occurring in this article have a long history. Some of their salient meanings for Buddhism are briefly explained as follows:

1. *Aryan* (i) (*social*) noble, distinguished, of high birth.
(ii) (*ethical*) pure, pure one; of "noble" education. Mostly said of the Buddha's Teaching, his disciples, their discipline and practice. Hence the word has such meanings as right, good, noble, ideal.

2. *Deva*. From a root meaning to shine. To translate as "god, angel, divine or celestial being" is misleading. A *deva* is neither an animal nor a human being, but is a title attributed to beings that in certain respects are

regarded as above the human level, e.g. in their splendour, beauty, mobility, happiness or longevity. A kinship with humanity is implied, there is no complete break, *devas* and human beings can hold converse; all *devas* have been men and may become men again. Meanwhile they are in one of the twenty-six *deva-loka*, worlds, spheres or planes where *devas* have their being by reason of some outstanding merit they have performed earlier. But since no existence in a *deva-loka* is permanent, the *devas* are all still in *saṁsāra*, the circling on in life after life, and have still to get free of the unending round. In no sense is a *deva* a creator, omnipotent or omniscient, but simply a denizen of a *deva*-world.

3. *Brahmā* (i) the *deva* Brahmā, chief of the *devas*, also called Mahā-Brahmā (Great Brahmā).

(ii) the class of Brahmā *devas*, happy and blameless beings on an extra-terrestrial plane, denizens of the higher "heavens" or of a higher and better world known as *brahma-loka*, the Brahma-world. Re-birth here is the outcome of meritorious deeds, but does not endure for ever.

4. *Brahma-faring*. A distinction probably has to be made between the masculine *Brahmā* (as above) and the neuter *Brahman*. This the Pali Commentaries usually define as best or highest. Originally *brahma-cariya* (Brahma-faring) meant study or discipline. It then meant the discipline for the realization of the Best and Highest, the Walk (*cariya*) to it or with it. Hence it is the life of purity, the good life, sometimes translated as the Life Divine. Since this is principally thought of in Buddhism as the monastic life, so *brahmacariya* came to have the added meaning of chastity.

7b. Buddhism: The Mahāyāna

by E. CONZE

INTRODUCTION

The word Mahāyāna, or "Great Vehicle", is the name generally given to those ideas which dominated the second phase of Buddhist thought. One speaks of a "vehicle" because the Buddhist doctrine, or Dharma (Pali, Dhamma, *see* pp. 267, 283), is conceived as a raft, or a ship, which carries us across the ocean of this world of suffering to a "Beyond", to salvation, to *Nirvāṇa*. Its adherents called it "great" by way of praising the universality of its tenets and intentions, in opposition to the narrowness of the other Buddhist schools, which they describe as the "Hīnayāna", or the "inferior" vehicle, a term naturally not much cherished by those to whom they apply it. At present the Mahāyāna is confined to the Northern half of the Buddhist world, and the Buddhists of Nepal, Tibet, China, Korea and Japan are nearly all Mahāyānists. The South, on the other hand, is entirely dominated by the Theravādins, one of the eighteen traditional sects of the Hīnayāna, and their form of Buddhism is the national religion of Ceylon, Burma and Siam. The other seventeen Hīnayāna sects disappeared 700 years ago when the Muhammadans swept into Northern India and destroyed its flourishing Buddhist monasteries.

In point of *time* the rise of the Mahāyāna coincides with the beginning of the Christian era. It must have gathered momentum in the first pre-Christian centuries, but many of its basic ideas go back, as we shall see, to the fourth or fifth century B.C., if not to the Buddha himself. But the literature which sets out the specific Mahāyāna doctrines is attested only for the beginning of the Christian era, and this raises an interesting, and so far unresolved, historical problem. How can we account for the observation that Buddhism, just at the time when Christianity itself arose, underwent a radical reform of its basic tenets which made it much more similar to Christianity than it had been before? To show the

nature of the problem, I will mention just three parallels between the Mahāyāna and Christianity. First of all, loving kindness and compassion, subordinate virtues in the older Buddhism, are stressed more and more, and move right into the centre of the picture. This may remind us of the Christian emphasis on "love". Secondly, we hear of compassionate beings, called "Bodhisattvas", whose main claim to our gratitude lies in that they sacrifice their lives for the welfare of all. This may remind us of the Christ who died for us all so that our sins may be forgiven. And thirdly, the Buddhists of this period show eschatological interests, and fervently hope for a "second coming" of the Buddha, as Maitreya (Pali, Metteya, p. 280), the "Loving One". Thus we have at least three innovations of the Mahāyāna, of which each is as near to the spirit of early Christianity as it is to the older Buddhism.

Nor is this all. Occasionally we find close verbal coincidences between the Christian and the Mahāyāna Scriptures. Just one instance must suffice. At the time when the *Revelation of St John* was written down in Greek in the Eastern Mediterranean, the Mahāyānists produced in the South of India one of their most revered books, *The Perfection of Wisdom in 8,000 Lines*. *Revelation* (v. 1) refers to a book "closely sealed" with seven seals, and likewise the *Perfection of Wisdom* is called a book "sealed with seven seals". It is shown to a Bodhisattva by the name of "Ever-weeping" (*Sadāprarudita*), and St John "weeps bitterly" (v. 4) because he sees no one worthy to open the book and to break its seals. This can be done by the Lamb alone, slaughtered in sacrifice (v. 9). In the same way, chapters 30 and 31 of the Mahāyāna book describe in detail how Everweeping slaughtered himself in sacrifice, and how he thereby became worthy of the Perfection of Wisdom (see pp. 302–3). This parallel is remarkable not only for the similarities of the religious logic, but also for the fact that both the number seven and the whole notion of a "book with seals" point to the Judaeo-Mediterranean rather than to the Indian tradition. Here is a fruitful field for further study. At present we cannot account for the parallels between the Mediterranean and Indian developments which occur at the beginning of the Christian era. For the interpretation of the Mahāyāna they are significant and should not be ignored.

It was in fact, *geographically* speaking, in the two regions of India which were in contact with the Mediterranean that the Mahāyāna seems to have originated. On the one hand we have the South of India, which was in close trading relations with the Roman Empire, as is shown by the huge hoards of Roman coins found there in recent years. And it was in the region round Nāgārjuni-kondā, in the South, near the temple of Amarāvatī, which has rightly been called a "Dravido-Alexandrian synthesis", that tradition places the development of the first Mahāyāna Scriptures, i.e. the *Sūtras* on Perfect Wisdom, and where also Nāgārjuna (*c.* A.D. 100), the greatest philosopher of the Mahāyāna, appears to have lived. The second centre of the incipient Mahāyāna was in the North-West of India, where the successor states of Alexander the Great kept open a constant channel for Hellenistic and Roman influences, as the art found in that region amply demonstrates. Its openness to foreign, non-Indian influences was indeed one of the features which distinguished the Mahāyāna from the older forms of Buddhism.

We know little about the actual *causes* which brought about this revolution in Buddhist thought. Two, however, seem certain, the exhaustion of the *Arhant* ideal, and the pressure of the laity.

As for the first, the older Buddhism was designed to produce a type of saint known as *Arhant* – a person who has been liberated once and for all from the cycle of birth and death. Three or four centuries after the Buddha's *Nirvāṇa* the methods which had at first produced *Arhants* in profusion lost their potency, fewer and fewer monks reached the goal, and the conviction gained ground that the time for *Arhants* was over. When the expected fruits were no longer forthcoming, it was natural for a section of the community to explore new avenues, and they replaced the *Arhant* ideal by the Bodhisattva ideal (pp. 298–304).

Relations of the monks with the laity had always been precarious. Here at its base was the Achilles' heel of the whole soaring edifice. The Mahāyāna gave much greater weight to laymen. It could count on much popular support for its emphasis on active service, for its opinion that people are as important as "*dharmas*" (Pali, *dhammā*, p. 290), for its attacks on the selfishness of monks who think only of their own welfare, for its censure of "haughty" and "conceited" monks, for its stories of wealthy householders, such as Vimalakīrti, who surpassed the oldest and most venerable monks in the splendour of their spiritual attainments, and for its belief that the saints should accept a common fate with their fellow men. Popular pressure would also induce the monks to become more manifestly useful to their lay followers. They increasingly interested themselves in their daily problems, and, by acting as astrologers, exorcizers, weather makers, physicians, etc., inserted themselves into the magical side of their lives. The wishes of the dumb common people, so despised by the monkish party, in the end proved paramount.

Our knowledge of the Mahāyāna is derived from its very extensive *literature*, which was composed over about 2,000 years, most of it in Sanskrit, but some also in Chinese, in Tibetan and in Central Asian languages. Although many Mahāyāna works have been lost, the bulk of what is left is so huge that no one has ever read through it. Our views on the subject must therefore remain tentative, and future discoveries may compel their revision. This literature falls into three main classes – *Sūtras*, *Śāstras* and *Tantras*. The *Sūtras* are the most authoritative, and no follower of the Mahāyāna would wish openly to repudiate anything they contain; the authority of the *Śāstras* is more limited, and they are binding only on the members of the philosophical school which they represent; that of the *Tantras* is even more restricted, its range being confined to the few adepts of a small esoteric sect.

Sūtras claim to be sayings of the Buddha himself, and they always give at the beginning the exact place, either on earth or in heaven, where the Buddha is believed to have preached this particular sermon. In the case of Mahāyāna *Sūtras*, written more than five centuries after the historical Buddha's death, this is obviously a pious fiction. If an historian were asked to define a *Sūtra*, he would have to say that it is an anonymous document elaborated usually collectively over many centuries, which has to be significant without being controversial or sectarian. The most beautiful of all Mahāyāna *Sūtras* is the *Lotus of the Good Law*, a work of great power and magnificence. There are a few European translations, but none of them is even remotely accurate. The most instructive *Sūtras* are those on "The Perfection of Wisdom". Of that we have about thirty different recensions, composed in the course of six or seven centuries. Many other *Sūtras* are preserved, several hundred of them, but there is little point in further enumeration. The continuous, slow, and measured growth of these *Sūtras* makes them appear as more than the works of mere men, and some of their majesty is still felt in Japan, Tibet, and even in Europe.

A *Śāstra* is a treatise written by a known person, either in the form of a commentary on a *Sūtra*, or in the form of a systematic text book. When I say "a known person", I do not, of course, mean that we know the actual author, but only that it is ascribed to some actual doctor of the "Church". For there has been a tendency to simplify matters by attributing the works of many writers to a few big names. The four biggest names are, about A.D. 150, Nāgārjuna and Āryadeva, and, about A.D. 400, Vasubandhu and Asanga. The first two are the founders of the philosophical school of the Mādhyamikas, while the second two initiated the rival school of the Yogācārins (see p. 317). These two schools were engaged in constant disputes, and the works of the one have no authority for the other. The limited authority of a "doctor of the Church" is based on three factors: a saintly life, great learning, and inspiration by one of the mythical Buddhas or Bodhisattvas (p. 304ff). Wonder-working powers, though desirable, are not indispensable.

Sūtras and *Śāstras* are public documents available to anyone sufficiently interested to procure them. The *Tantras*, by contrast, are secret documents destined only for a chosen few who are properly initiated, or consecrated, by a properly initiated teacher or *guru*. To let the uninitiated into their secret is an unpardonable crime. In order more effectively to hide their contents from outsiders they employ a deliberately mysterious and secretive language. Without the oral explanations of an initiated master they are practically meaningless, and reveal nothing of any importance. *Tantras* give to the initiated instructions for the practical realization of certain Yogic practices. They were composed in profusion from about A.D. 500 onwards, and we have literally thousands of them. Their historical study has barely begun, and as outsiders we seldom have a clue to their meaning. Thousands and thousands of pages are filled with statements about "cosmic tortoises" and "sky dogs", or about gods dressed in "fur coats" or "tiger skins", living in "iron palaces" or "copper fortresses", and "holding a black trident with four heads stuck on it and a blood-dripping heart, at which two black vipers are sucking" (see R. de Nebesky-Wojkowitz, *Oracles and Demons of Tibet*, 1956). What are we to make of all that? In their desire to shock the profane, the authors of the *Tantras* are prone to the use of obscene and sexually suggestive language. Again we are at a loss to know what their jokes really meant. We can well imagine, to give a parallel case, an earnest Japanese anthropologist of the

year A.D. 3242 pondering over a choice piece of ornithological information he has found in an English soldier's letter of 1942, "Two wrens went into the sea, and four blue tits came out again". Some initiation into the lore of the British Army would soon tell him the meaning of that statement. In its absence he would have to resort to wild guesses, without having much to go on. Most of the words used in the *Tantras* can be found in our dictionaries – but then it does not help very much to know that a "red herring" is a "pink fish". We can at present form some idea of the general principles of the *Tantras* (see pp. 319-20) though the concrete detail quite passes us by. The authority of a *Tantra* is usually derived from a mythical Buddha who is said to have preached it in the remote past to some other mythical person, who transmitted it to a human teacher who stands at the beginning of a long line of initiated *gurus* who hand the secret wisdom down from generation to generation.

This ends the survey of the literary sources. In addition, we can derive much information from innumerable *works of art*, which express the spirit of the doctrine accurately and impressively. Buddhist works of art allow little scope to the arbitrary inventions of individual artists. The images are too holy for that, for they are supports, though inadequate, for meditation, as well as reservoirs of supernatural power. They are made according to formulae elaborated by the scholars and mystics, which the artist just invests with a visible form. About the mythological and ritual aspects of the Mahāyāna these works of art can teach us a great deal.

The Mahāyāna is first of all a way of life, with a clear-cut idea of spiritual perfection and of the stages which lead to it. In addition, it puts forth a number of mythological concepts and ontological doctrines. Finally, in an effort to maintain itself against hostile influences, it enlists the help of female deities and magical forces. These are the three sides of the Mahāyāna which we shall now survey one by one.

THE BODHISATTVA IDEAL

The creation of the Bodhisattva ideal and the elaboration of the doctrine of "Emptiness" are the two great contributions which the Mahāyāna has made to human thought. While the philosophy of Emptiness has proved an unfailing source of attraction to generations of scholars and intellectuals, it was to its teachings about the "Bodhisattva" that the Mahāyāna owed its success as a religion, and that it proved capable of converting the whole of Central and East Asia, and of winning, for a time, more adherents than any other religion. Here was the image of an ideal man, who could stir the hearts of all, whether rich or poor, learned or ignorant, strong or weak, monks or laymen. It could easily win their admiration, for it reflected what was best in them. It could also become a basis for immediate action, because it could be adjusted to the infinite variety of human circumstances. Put forth with self-sacrificing zeal, with all the resources of eloquence and all the refinements of art, the Bodhisattva ideal has been one of the most potent ideas of Asian thought. So irresistible was its power that even the Hīnayāna schools were prepared to incorporate it to some extent into their own systems.

What then is a "Bodhisattva"? It will be best first to explain the Sanskrit term: *bodhi* means "enlightenment", and *sattva* "being" or "essence". A Bodhisattva is thus a person who in his essential being is motivated by the desire to win full enlightenment – to become a Buddha. Destined to become a Buddha, he nevertheless, in order to help suffering creatures, selflessly postpones his entrance into the bliss of *Nirvāṇa* and his escape from this world of birth and death.

From another angle a Bodhisattva is said to be dominated by two forces – compassion and wisdom. Compassion governs his conduct towards his fellow beings, wisdom his attitude to Reality. The Mahāyāna teachings on compassion are easy, those on wisdom hard to understand. Everyone listens gladly when the talk is about himself, but gets rather bored when feeling himself ignored. So we begin with compassion, leaving wisdom for later on.

Buddhists, as is well known, regard the difference between human beings and animals as unimportant, and equal compassion should, in any case, be extended to all. Scrupulous respect for the life and dignity, for the rights and wishes of all living beings is a Bodhisattva's first and most elementary duty. During a debate with the Saskya Pandita which the Venerable Tsong-kha-pa had about A.D. 1400 his opponent, probably absent-mindedly, crushed a louse between his nails. Tsong-kha-pa interrupted him, exclaiming, "While we are here debating these abstruse metaphysical subtleties, I hear the laments of a fellow-creature rising to the sky!" The Saskya Pandita was so much taken aback by this reproof that his hat fell off, he left the tent in confusion, and victory remained with Tsong-kha-pa and his "Yellow Church" (R.Bleichsteiner, *Die gelbe Kirche*, 1937, p. 84). Likewise, it is quite usual for Bodhisattvas to sacrifice their own lives for animals. When he was a prince of Benares, the Bodhisattva who subsequently became the Buddha Gautama (=Pali, *Gotama*), threw himself down in front of a tigress who had given birth to five cubs and was exhausted from hunger and thirst. "But she did

nothing to him. The Bodhisattva noticed that she was too weak to move. As a merciful man he had taken no sword with him. He therefore cut his throat with a sharp piece of bamboo and fell down near the tigress. She noticed his body all covered with blood, and in no time ate up all the flesh and blood, leaving only the bones" (*Suvarṇa-prabhāsottama-sūtra*, ed. J.Nobel, 1937, p. 214). On another celebrated occasion, as king Śibi, the Bodhisattva ransomed a pigeon by giving a pound of his own flesh to the hawk who had caught it (E.Lamotte, *Le Traité de la grande Vertu de Sagesse*, 1944, vol. 1, pp. 255–6). This fellow-feeling for all living beings, whoever they may be, is much akin to Dr Schweitzer's "reverence for life," which, as I read some time ago, he extends to "gazelles, pelicans, ants, mosquitoes, worms and even bacilli." Even the bacteria had already been thought of by the Buddhist monks, who took special precautions against harming the invisible creatures who were said to abound in water and in the air.

And not only are all beings alike in that they dislike suffering, but they are also all capable of enlightenment. Each one of them is a potential Buddha. Hidden away within each being there exist in embryonic form the factors needed for the attainment of Enlightenment. So "the road to Buddhahood is open to all" (*Buddhist Texts through the Ages*, E. Conze, 1954, p. 181). "Even in animals the personality of a Buddha should be discerned, concealed though it be by the taints of manifold defilements" (*ibid.*, p. 183). One day these adventitious defilements will disappear, the moment they are seen to be unreal they will vanish away, and the Buddha-nature then manifests itself in its full glory. A small minority of Mahāyānists, it is true, claimed that there are some beings called the *Icchāntikas*, who are for ever excluded from enlightenment. But the overwhelming majority rejected this heresy which had crept in from Gnosticism, probably through the Manichaeans, and took their stand on the belief that every living organism has it in him to win enlightenment sooner or later. Who, then, would have the temerity to "hinder it on its upward path"?

It is the essential feature of a Bodhisattva's compassion that it is "great", i.e. boundless, and that it makes no distinctions. "He radiates great friendliness and compassion over all beings, and he resolves, 'I shall become their saviour, I shall release them from all their sufferings'" (*ibid.* No. 124). Or this is how Śāntideva, a poet of the seventh century, expresses it:

"The merit I achieved by all these pious actions,
                    may that make me
Quite able to appease the sufferings of all beings.

A medicine for the sick I'll be, their healer, and
their servant,
Until the day that sickness is a thing no more re-
membered.
With showers of food and drink I'll quench the pains
of hunger and of thirst;
In the dearth at the end of the aeon I'll turn into
food and drink.
And for the needy I'll be a source of wealth quite
unfailing,
Serving them well with all that their needs may
require.
Heedless of body, of goods, of the merit I gained
and will gain still,
I surrender my all to promote the welfare of others."
(*Buddhist Meditation*, E. Conze, 1956, p. 59.)

So far so good. The modern age, while it may deplore
the Mahāyāna tendency to hyperbole, is sure to applaud
its concern for the welfare of others. But what it has the
greatest difficulty in grasping is that compassion cannot
stand on its own feet, that it cannot do its work without
the help of wisdom, and that the Bodhisattva, instead of
doing something useful all the time, continues to push
forward to the remote, otherworldly goal of Enlightenment. I must therefore give some of the reasons which
make the Mahāyānists combine compassion with
wisdom and Enlightenment.

What then is a Bodhisattva's compassion? It is the
selfless desire to make others happy. Now (1) it is not
self-evident what is good for others, nor (2) is self-
interest easily shunned. (1) In order to make others happy,
one must have some idea of what *can* make them happy.
Being inherently foolish, the other people are not always
the best judges of that. Even if the louse had not been
crushed, it would still lead the life of a louse. Even though
the tigress was fed, she was still only a tigress. And so on.
As soon as we get down to actual details, we find it hard
to decide what is good for others, and what of real
benefit to them. Is it, for instance, an act of kindness to
kill an animal in pain, or to give whisky to a tramp? But
these are only comparatively trifling problems pertaining
to the casuistry of love. Far more fundamental difficulties
arise from the fact that one good thing can be the foe of
another. The highest good is said to be the gift of the
Dharma. In that case the gift of anything else, in so far as
it increases people's worldly welfare, may militate against
the development of their spiritual potentialities, for it
may bind them still further to this world and increase
their worries and anxieties. Should we then wish to increase the material welfare of the people, or should we

not? In the Mahāyāna texts we find a great deal of
rhetoric about this, but the actual achievements of
Buddhist countries fell far short of it. This is not surprising because social services are not only a matter of
good will, but of the productivity of labour. Before the
advent of modern technical developments there simply
did not exist the means to raise what is nowadays called
the "standard of living" of the common people to any
appreciable extent. Our attitude to these developments
is not easy to determine. On the one side our compassion
would probably make us glad to see that people are becoming less poor, that they live longer, that their sick-
nesses are treated with some care and skill, that justice is
dispensed with greater humanity, and so on. On the other
hand all these benefits depend on the technical organization of modern society, which makes a spiritual life next
to impossible. Whatever the answer, it is clear that only
a great deal of wisdom can decide a dilemma of this kind.

(2) Not only the effects, but also the motives of doing
good to others present serious problems. "Charity" has
so much fallen into disrepute because too often it was
motivated by a sense of guilt, by the desire to humiliate
the poor, or to buy them off with a few crumbs. If
others are so often ungrateful for what we have done for
them, if they hate us for the help we gave, they are in
most cases quite justified because somehow they divine
that we considered ourselves first in what we did, and
them only in the second place, degrading them into a
mere means or material of our desire to do good. The
benefits of generosity to ourselves are not in doubt. It is
the benefit to others which is in question. A very high
degree of sanctity is necessary to do good to others without harming or irritating them. Only the pure in heart can
have the vision necessary to decide what is really beneficial to others, and only they have the purity of motive.
In the Scriptures the ability really to benefit others is regarded as a very high and rare virtue, the last and most
sublime flowering of a mature development of perfect
wisdom. Eight hundred years ago Milarepa, the great
Tibetan saint, was asked by his disciples "if they could
engage in worldly duties, in a small way, for the benefit
of others". Milarepa replied: "If there be not the least
self-interest attached to such duties, it is permissible.
But such detachment is indeed rare; and works performed for the good of others seldom succeed, if not
wholly freed from self-interest. Even without seeking to
benefit others, it is with difficulty that works done even
in one's own interest are successful. It is as if a man help-
lessly drowning were to try to save another man in the
same predicament. One should not be over-anxious and
hasty in setting out to serve others before one has oneself

realized the Truth in its fulness; to do so, would be like the blind leading the blind. As long as the sky endures, so long will there be no end of sentient beings for one to serve; and to every one comes the opportunity for such service. Till the opportunity come, I exhort each of you to have but the one resolve, namely to attain Buddhahood for the good of all living beings" (W.Y. Evans-Wentz, *Tibet's Great Yogi Milarepa*, 1928, p. 271).

It is a general Buddhist conviction that ordinary life is hopelessly unsatisfactory, exposed to constant pain and grief, and in any case quite futile, since death swallows all so soon. Without the Dharma no lasting happiness is possible. But if the gift of the Dharma is the highest gift of all, one must oneself possess the Dharma in order to give it to others. And the only way to get hold of it is through Enlightenment. It is for this reason that the Bodhisattva wishes to win full Enlightenment, so that he may be really useful to others. And, of course, his usefulness to them increases as he comes nearer and nearer to Enlightenment.

What then is this Enlightenment, or *bodhi*, which is the ultimate goal of a Bodhisattva's endeavours? It is a thorough and complete understanding of the nature and meaning of life, the forces which shape it, the method to end it, and the reality which lies beyond it. Indian tradition is quite wont to see the highest achievement of man in a cognitive insight into a Reality which transcends this fleeting world, and all the beings in it. But then – and here is a definite problem – the man who has cognized this reality, which is so much more satisfactory than anything he sees around him, will want to withdraw into it and away from his fellow creatures. No more re-born, he will be lost to the world. Measuring the concerns of the world by the yardstick of true reality, he will be unable to take them very seriously. Humanity will appear to him as a mass of non-entities constantly worrying over nothing in particular. This is a specially important point in Buddhism, which has always taught that persons are not really "persons", but only imagine that they are, whereas in strict fact they *are* non-entities.

The Mahāyānists agreed that enlightenment does not automatically entail the desire to assist others. Among the enlightened they distinguished four types, of whom two do not appreciably help others, whereas the other two do. And although the Mahāyānists insist that different people must reach the goal by different ways, they regard the unselfish types as superior to the others.

The "selfish" enlightened persons are first the *Arhants* or "Disciples", who are said to represent the ideal of the Hīnayāna, and who are aloof from the concerns of the world, intent on their own private salvation alone. And then there are the *Pratyekabuddhas* (p. 280). They differ from the *Arhants* in that, independent of the instructions of a Buddha, they can gain Enlightenment by their own private efforts. But once they have gained Enlightenment, they keep their knowledge to themselves, and do not communicate it to others.

The unselfish types are the Buddhas and the Bodhisattvas. Omniscience is the chief attribute of a *Buddha*, the distinctive feature of his enlightenment. The Buddha is essential to the Buddhist religion in all its forms as the founder who guarantees the truth and reliability of the teaching by the fact that he is "fully enlightened". It was always agreed that he knew everything necessary to salvation, his own and that of others, and that therefore in spiritual matters he is a sure and infallible guide. The Mahāyāna now claims that he knows also all other things, that he is omniscient in the full sense of the term. But since it is one of the peculiarities of a Buddha's gnosis that therein the subject is identical with the object, the fact that he knows everything there is, implies that he also *is* everything there is. In consequence the Buddha becomes identical either with the Absolute, or with the sum total of existence, with the totality of all things at all times. It is only because he has merged with everything that the Buddha has cast off all traces of a separate self, and has attained complete and total self-extinction.

We can well believe in the selflessness of a Buddha conceived in this way. But when the Mahāyāna goes on to say that this Buddha – all-knowing, all-wise, all there is – is also all-compassionate, we remain slightly unconvinced. In an effort to humanize the Buddha the Mahāyānists called him a "Father" of all those who are helpless and afflicted, but this attribute never quite comes to life. Mātṛceṭa, a fine Mahāyāna poet of the second century, has this to say on the Buddha's compassion:

"Which shall I praise first, you or the great compassion, which held
You for so long in *saṃsāra*, though well its faults you knew?
Your compassion, given free rein, made you pass your time
Among the crowds, when the bliss of seclusion was so much more to your taste."
(*Buddhist Texts*, p. 192.)

The first of these verses refers to the Buddha when he was a Bodhisattva, the second to the forty-five years of his ministry on earth after his Enlightenment. It was, however, the compassionateness of a Buddha after his death, after his final *Nirvāṇa*, which has always seemed barely credible. Originally, before the Mahāyāna, the Buddha after his final *Nirvāṇa* was conceived of as totally extinct as far as this world and its inhabitants are concerned, and no longer interested in them. No amount of ingenuity could quite move Buddhism away from that original position, and really graft compassion on the Buddha who had "passed away". While it is possible to see that he helps beings by the gift of the perfect Dharma, the emotion of compassion must appear to be alien to him. The doubts which have always remained on that point are in part due to the transcendental and truly inconceivable nature of all that concerns the Buddha. Everything about him lies outside the range of our own direct experience. For selfish and limited people like us, even-mindedness and compassion seem mutually incompatible, and we are apt to think that in one vast Emptiness compassion must get lost and become inapplicable. But then what light does this kind of reasoning shed on the selfless Buddhas, who are said to have all these states to perfection – imperturbable even-mindedness, boundless compassion, and full emptiness? From our lowly perspective the transcendental world of self-extinction teems with apparent inconsistencies – but whom should we blame for that?

The *Bodhisattvas*, no the other hand, are much nearer to us in their mentality, and they take good care to remain in touch with the imperfect by having the same passions as they have, although, as distinct from them, these passions neither affect nor pollute their minds. Not yet having become everything, the Bodhisattvas are not quite beyond our ken, and we can appreciate that, while all the time intent on their transcendental goal, they remain during their struggles always aware of their solidarity with all that lives, in accordance with the famous saying:

"Can there be bliss when all that lives must suffer?
Shalt thou be saved and hear the whole world cry?"
(H. P. Blavatsky, *The Voice of Silence*, p. 78.)

But if a Bodhisattva wishes to become a Buddha, and if a Buddha is defined as the sum total of everything there is, then the distance between a given person and the state of Buddhahood will obviously be a very large one, and nearly infinite. In one life it could not possibly be traversed. Countless lives would be needed, aeons and aeons would have to pass, before a Bodhisattva can reach his goal. And yet – and this is somewhat of a paradox – only one single little obstacle separates him and us from Buddhahood, and that is the belief in a self, the belief that he is a separate individual, the inveterate tendency to indulge in what the texts call "I-making and Mine-making". To get rid of himself is a Bodhisattva's supreme task, and he finds that this is not an easy thing to do. He

takes two kinds of measures to remove this one obstacle to Buddhahood – actively by self-sacrifice and selfless service, cognitively by insight into the non-existence of a self. The latter is due to wisdom, defined as the ability to penetrate to true reality, to the "own-being" of things, to what they are in and by themselves, and held necessary to disclose the ultimate inanity of a separate self. And in this scheme action and cognition always go hand in hand, and are closely interrelated.

The self-sacrifices of Bodhisattvas are the subject of many edifying stories. By way of example I will re-tell that of the Bodhisattva "Ever-weeping" mentioned before (p. 296). I will relate it in some detail and largely in translation, because it has all the typical features of a Mahāyāna story, and exemplifies Mahāyāna mentality to perfection. It tells us how Everweeping searched for the Perfection of Wisdom, and how he found it in the end, "because he did not care for his body and had no regard for his life". He goes to see the Bodhisattva Dharmodgata, who can answer all his questions, but he feels that "it would be unseemly to come empty-handed to him". So he decides to sell his body, goes to the market place, and cries, "Who wants a man? Who wants to buy a man?" But Māra the Evil One fears that Everweeping, if he succeeds in "selling himself out of concern for Dharma, from love for Dharma, so as to do worship to Dharma", will then in due course win Enlightenment, and remove himself and others from Māra's sphere of influence. So he brings it about that no one can see or hear the Bodhisattva. Then Śakra, chief of the gods, decides to test Everweeping, and conjures up a young man who says to him that his father wants to offer a sacrifice. "For that I require a man's heart, his blood and the marrow of his bones." Everweeping, "his mind bristling with joy", agrees, and says, "I will give you my body, since you have need of it!" "He then takes a sharp sword, pierces his right arm, and makes the blood flow. He pierces his right thigh, cuts the flesh from it, and strides up to the foot of a wall in order to break the bone." Śakra "thereupon throws off his disguise as a young man, and in his proper body he stands before the Bodhisattva," applauds his resolution and asks him to choose a boon. Everweeping asks him for the "supreme dharmas of a Buddha", but Śakra has to admit that this is beyond his powers, and begs him to choose another boon. Everweeping replies: "Do not trouble your mind about the mutilated condition of my body! I shall myself now make it whole again by the magical power of my enunciation of the Truth. If it is true that I am bound to win full Enlightenment, if it is true that the Buddhas know of my unconquerable resolution – may through this Truth, through this utterance of

302

the Truth, this my body be again as it was before!" "That very moment, instant and second, through the Buddha's might and through the perfect purity of the Bodhisattva's resolution, his body became again as it had been before, healthy and whole." The story then goes on to tell how Everweeping, accompanied by a merchant's daughter and her 500 maidservants, goes to see Dharmodgata, who lives in great wealth and splendour; how they hear a sermon on Perfect Wisdom; how then they spend seven years in deep trance; and how thereafter, on meeting Dharmodgata once more, they find that "Māra the Evil One had hidden away all the water"; so, to prevent "the rising dust from falling on Dharmodgata's body", they sprinkle the earth with their own blood; and as a reward Everweeping acquires millions of trances, "sees the Buddhas and Lords in all the ten directions, in countless world systems, surrounded by their congregations of monks and accompanied by numerous Bodhisattvas". And wherever he was henceforth re-born, it was always in the presence and within the sight of a Buddha (*Aṣṭasāhasrikā Prajñāpāramitā*, ed. R.Mitra, 1888, ch. 30 and 31).

This story is not after the taste of our hard-headed age, which will condemn it as rather airy-fairy, positively puerile and out of touch with social realities. It is indeed a pure fairy-tale, showing complete disregard for commonsense and this mundane world. Everything about it is otherworldly, the excessive regard for the Dharma and its representatives, the intervention of mythological beings like Māra and Śakra, and also the almost naïve belief in the power of Truth. To the spiritually minded it nevertheless illustrates the inescapable fact that the readiness to sacrifice all is an indispensable condition for the acquisition of wisdom.

The unity of compassion and wisdom is acted out by the *six perfections*, or *pāram-itā*, "methods by which we go to the Beyond". A person turns into a Bodhisattva when he first resolves to win full enlightenment for the benefit of all beings. Thereafter, until Buddhahood, he passes many aeons in the practice of the *Pāramitās*. So important is this concept that the Mahāyāna often refers to itself as the "Vehicle of the *Pāramitās*". The six are: the perfections of giving, morality, patience, vigour, concentration, and wisdom. The terms are not really self-explicative, and require some comment.

First of all a Bodhisattva must learn to be *generous*, with everything he has, his possessions, his family, and even his own body. By *morality* is then meant the observation of the moral precepts, and the Bodhisattva will rather give up his life than offend against them by lying, stealing or killing. The Mahāyāna, in contradistinction to the Hīnayāna, has much to say about *patience*, but the word is used in a much wider sense than is usual with us. "Patience" is both a moral and an intellectual virtue. As a moral virtue it means the patient endurance of all sufferings, as well as of the hostile acts of others, without ever feeling any anger, ill-will or discontent. As an intellectual virtue it means the emotional acceptance, before one has properly understood them, of the more unpalatable, incredible and anxiety-producing ontological doctrines of the Mahāyāna, such as the non-existence of all things, which leaves us with nothing much to live for. Perfect in his *vigour*, the Bodhisattva, in spite of all discouragements and obstacles, indefatigably perseveres in his work, without ever yielding to despondency or dismay. In addition his energy is so great that he shirks no task, however difficult, however impossible:

"However innumerable sentient beings are, I vow to save them!
However inexhaustible the defilements are, I vow to extinguish them!
However immeasurable the *dharmas* are, I vow to master them!
However incomparable Enlightenment is, I vow to attain it!"

(After D. T. Suzuki, *Manual of Zen Buddhism*, 1935, p. 4).

The practice of the perfection of *concentration* then enables the Bodhisattva to gain proficiency in trances and meditations "numerous as the sands of the Ganges". These disclose to him new facets of reality unsuspected by the average worldling, and at the same time convince him of the insufficiency and unreality of all merely sensory experience. The perfection of *wisdom* finally is the ability to understand the essential properties of all processes and phenomena, their mutual relations, the conditions which bring about their rise and fall, and the ultimate unreality of their separate existence. At its highest point it leads right into the Emptiness which is the one and only Reality.

All the six perfections are dominated by the perfection of wisdom which alone makes the others into *Pāramitās*, or practices which actually lead to the Beyond. Just as blind people cannot find their way unguided into a city, so only the perfection of wisdom imparts to the other perfections an "organ of vision which allows them to ascend the path to all-knowledge and to reach all-knowledge" (*Selected Sayings from the Perfection of Wisdom*, by E. Conze, 1955, No. 36). What matters is not only what the Bodhisattva does, but the spirit in which he does it. When giving, he is constantly admonished to have no thought of what he gives, to pay no attention to the person to whom he gives, and, chief of all, to remain unaware that it is he who gives. Convinced by perfect wisdom of their ultimate unreality, he should "have no perception of self, no perception of others, no perception of a gift" (*Buddhist Texts*, No. 131). Likewise, without strong wisdom some of these virtues, such as patience, cannot possibly be practised to perfection. In the *Diamond Sūtra* the Buddha tells of the occasion when he remained unperturbed although the King of Kalinga hacked him to pieces. "At that time I had no notion of a self, a being, a soul or a person. If I had had such notions, then I would also have felt ill-will at that time" (*Vajracchedikā Prajñāpāramitā*, p. 14e). Compassion itself is capable of three degrees of perfection: at first the Bodhisattva is compassionate to living beings; then he realizes that these do not exist, and directs his compassion on the impersonal events which fill the world; finally, the compassion operates within one vast field of Emptiness. The last two stages are unattested by our everyday experience. Nevertheless, it is not necessarily absurd to speak of a compassion which "has no object at all", for we know of other emotions which arise inwardly, without the stimulus of outside objects. Under the influence of excessive adrenalin a person may feel very angry, and will then look round for an object to vent his wrath on. An elderly spinster is full of more love and tenderness than she knows what to do with, and accordingly she will not rest until she has found someone to bestow it upon, even if only a cat or a parrot. Similarly a Bodhisattva's compassion springs from the depths of his heart, and from there it spreads over to that which he knows to be illusory.

The Mahāyāna distinguishes *ten stages* through which a Bodhisattva must pass on his way to Buddhahood. This is another of its distinctive contributions which, slowly maturing over the centuries, found its final formulation before A.D. 300 in the *Sūtra on the Ten Stages*. These "stages" refer to fairly exalted conditions, for Nāgārjuna, the greatest thinker of the Mahāyāna, was a Bodhisattva of the first stage only. The first six stages correspond to the perfections, and with the sixth the Bodhisattva has by his understanding of Emptiness come "face to face" with Reality itself.

At that stage he is entitled to *Nirvāṇa*, but renounces it voluntarily. From now onwards he is always re-born miraculously, and acquires many unearthly qualities which qualify him to become a saviour of others, and raise him to the condition of a celestial being. In the course of the seventh stage he acquires "sovereignty" over the world, nothing can prevent him any longer from becoming a Buddha, he is now a "Crown Prince" of the Dharma,

and his representations in art show him as a royal personage. It is clear that the Bodhisattvas on the last four stages differ in kind from those on the first six, and in future I will speak of them as "celestial Bodhisattvas".

MYTHOLOGICAL DOCTRINES

The celestial Bodhisattvas were well suited to becoming objects of a religious cult, and soon the faithful increasingly turned to them. Many were given names and endowed with both spiritual and visible attributes. There we have Avalokiteśvara, a Bodhisattva of the ninth stage, who is governed by compassion, holds a lotus, and in his mercy helps all beings in distress, assisted by a positively Protean capacity for transforming himself into any shape desired. There is Mañjuśrī, who excels in wisdom, holds a sword, and imparts wisdom to those who implore him. There is Maitreya, the coming Buddha, now in the Tushita heaven, who represents friendliness, holds a flask filled with the elixir of immortality, and will lead many to Enlightenment at a future time. There is Kshitigarbha, a Lord of the nether world, who holds a staff and looks after the welfare of the dead, particularly in the hells. And, riding on a white elephant, Samantabhadra dispenses talismanic formulas which avert all dangers.

The conception of these Bodhisattvas often shows foreign, non-Indian, and particularly Iranian, influence. The twenty-fourth chapter of the *Lotus*, which deals with Avalokiteśvara, shows remarkable parallels to certain passages in the *Avesta*. Avalokiteśvara wears in his crown an image of Amitābha, his spiritual sire. A similar arrangement can be observed in the headdress of the priests of Palmyra and of those of the Great Goddess of Phrygia. Maitreya owes much to Mithra. His epithet is *a-jita*, "the unconquered", just as Mithras in his Roman mysteries was called *in-victus*.

The Bodhisattvas are as worthy of worship as the Buddhas, and some Mahāyānists thought that they are more so (see p. 302). In the *Lotus Sūtra* it is said that to adore Avalokiteśvara is as rewarding as the worship of countless Buddhas (*Saddharma Pundarīka*, p. 364). And elsewhere, "Indeed, O Kāśyapa, just as one worships the new and not the full moon, just so those who believe in me should honour the Bodhisattvas, and not the Tathāgatas." Or: "From the Buddha arise only the Disciples and *Pratyekabuddhas* (p. 301), but from the Bodhisattva the perfect Buddha himself is born."

The development of mythical Bodhisattvas was accompanied, and even preceded, by that of mythical Buddhas. This side of the Mahāyāna went back to within a century of the Buddha's death. It took shape in the school of the Mahāsanghikas (p. 268), the majority faction in a dispute with the so-called "Sthaviras" or "Elders", proud of their greater seniority and orthodoxy. The Mahāsanghikas were the popular and democratic party, through which popular aspirations entered into Buddhism. The conception which they formed of a Buddha is of central importance, and one cannot understand the Mahāyāna without appreciating the logic behind it.

The concept of a "Buddha" had from the very beginning contained a duality which became the starting point of far-reaching developments. The word "Buddha" itself is not a proper name, but a title, or epithet, which means the "Enlightened One". It refers to the condition of a man who is a completely unobstructed channel for the spiritual force of the Dharma. The proper name of the historical Buddha was Gautama (Pali, Gotama), or Siddhārtha (Pali, Siddhattha), or, after his tribe, he is often called Śākyamuni. The Buddha is thus on the one hand an historical individual, on the other a channel for the spiritual teachings about Dharma. This duality is normal in authoritative Asian religious leaders. In recent years we met it again in Karamchand Gāndhī, who was also the Mahātmā, the "Great-souled One". The actually observable historical effects of his actions remain a mystery to all those who cannot look through the personal mask of Gāndhī to the spiritual force which worked through him, and fail to understand that his significance lay in his Mahātmā side, for which the personality of Gāndhī was just a vessel.

In this way the individual, called Gautama or Śākyamuni, somehow co-exists with the spiritual principle of Buddhahood, which is variously called "the Tathāgata", or "the Dharma-body," or the "Buddha-nature", although the Buddhists regarded the exact relation between the individual and the spiritual sides of his being as incapable of definition. And at all times all Buddhists have also consistently opposed the tendencies of the unregenerate to put their faith in a living person, and have done everything to belittle the importance of the Buddha's actual physical existence. It is the Buddha himself who, in a Hīnayāna *Sūtra*, is reported to have said to Vakkali: "What is there, Vakkali, in seeing this vile body of mine? Whoso sees the spiritual Dharma, he sees me; whoso sees me, sees the spiritual Dharma. Seeing Dharma, Vakkali, he sees me; seeing me, he sees Dharma" (*Buddhist Texts*, No. 103).

Within the Hīnayāna the Mahāsanghika school now initiated a process, centuries before the rise of the Mahāyāna, by which the historical Buddha becomes less and less important. They regarded everything personal,

earthly, temporal and historical as outside the real Buddha, who himself was transcendental, altogether supramundane, had no imperfections or impurities whatsoever, was omniscient, all-powerful, infinite and eternal, for ever withdrawn into trance, never distracted or asleep. In this way the Buddha became an ideal object of religious faith. As for the historical Buddha, who walked the earth about 500 B.C., he was a magical creation of the transcendental Buddha, a fictitious creature sent by him to appear in the world and to teach its inhabitants. While on the one side intent on glorifying the otherworldliness of the Buddha, the Mahāsanghikas at the same time tried to increase the range of his usefulness to ordinary people. The Buddha has not disappeared into *Nirvāṇa*, but with a compassion as unlimited as his length of life, he will until the end of time conjure up all kinds of forms which will help all kinds of beings in diverse ways. His influence is not confined to those few who can understand his abstruse doctrines, but as a Bodhisattva he is even re-born in the "states of woe", becomes of his own free will an animal, or a ghost, or a dweller in hell, and works the weal of beings who have the misfortune to live in places where wisdom teaching must fall on deaf ears. Nor are Buddhas found on this earth alone. They fill the entire universe, and are to be met everywhere, in all the world systems.

The Mahāyāna took over this Buddhology in its entirety. The historical Buddha faded away, leaving the Buddha as the embodiment of Dharma as the only reality. In the *Diamond Sutra* occur the famous verses:

"Those who by my form did see me,
And those who followed me by voice,
Wrong the efforts they engaged in,
Me those people will not see.
From the Dharma should one see the Buddhas,
For the Dharma-bodies are the guides.
Yet Dharma's true nature should not be discerned,
Nor can it, either, be discerned."
(*Vajracchedikā Prajñāpāramitā*, ch. 26.)

The Buddha himself tells us in the *Lotus of the Good Law* that many Buddhists believe that "the Lord Śākyamuni, after going forth from his home among the Śākyas, has quite recently awoken to full Enlightenment on the terrace of Enlightenment, by the town of Gayā. But not thus should one see it. In fact it is many hundreds of thousands of myriads of kotis of aeons ago that I have awoken to full Enlightenment. Fully enlightened for ever so long, the Tathāgata has an endless span of life, he lasts for ever" (*Buddhist Texts*, pp. 140, 142).

As the manifestation of a type, the historical Buddha

BUDDHISM

is not an isolated phenomenon, but only one of a series of Buddhas who appear on earth throughout the ages. Knowledge of the non-historical Buddhas seems to have grown as time went on. At first there were seven, then we hear of twenty-four, and so the number grew steadily. The Mahāyāna went further and populated the heavens with Buddhas. In the East lives Akshobhya, the "Imperturbable". In the West the Buddha of "Infinite Light", Amitābha, whose cult owed much to Iranian sun worship, probably originated in the Kushāna Empire in the borderland between India and Iran, and was first brought to China, between 148 and 170, by an Iranian prince, the Arsacid Ngan che-kao. Other popular Buddhas are the "Buddha of Healing" (Bhaishajyaguru), as well as Amitāyus, the Buddha who "has an endless life-span", a counterpart to the Iranian Zurvān i Akanārak ("Unlimited Time", p. 219). Most of these innumerable Buddhas were endowed with a "kingdom", or "field", or "mystical universe" of their own, a world which is not of this world, a land which is "pure" because free from sin and the states of woe. Later on the *Tantra* added still further Buddhas, for instance Vairocana, Vajrasattva, Vajradhara, and so on. Even as an object of devotion the Buddha Śākyamuni receded into the background, and sometimes he is reduced to the status of a mere phantom body of a celestial Buddha, like Vairocana.

About A.D. 300 the Buddhology of the Mahāyāna was finally formulated in the doctrine of the *Three Bodies*. A Buddha exists on three levels: he has (1) a fictitious, conjured-up body (*nirmāṇa-kāya*), (2) a communal body (*sambhoga-kāya*), and (3) a Dharma-body. The first and third are easy to understand. The Dharma-body is the Buddha seen as the Absolute. The fictitious, conjured-up body is the one which people can see at a given time, in other words, it is an historical Buddha. In the fifteenth century this doctrine of "fictitious bodies" took in Tibet a form which has somehow stirred the imagination of the West, where everyone has heard of Dalai Lamas and "Living Buddhas" (*Tulkus=sprul-sku=nirmāṇa-kāya*). People usually misunderstand the theory behind them because they pay no attention to the essential difference between ordinary persons and accomplished saints in their manner of coming into the world. An ordinary person was someone else before being re-born here, but his re-birth was determined by his unexhausted *karma*, and he was pushed where he is more or less against his will. No such ties bind the celestial Bodhisattvas or Buddhas to this world, which they could quite easily leave behind, if their compassion would permit them to do so. Now it is a quite old tradition that perfected saints can conjure up phantom bodies which are to all intents

and purposes indistinguishable from ordinary bodies, and which they use as a kind of puppet to help to convert others. These are in no way "incarnations" of the saint in question, but free creations of his magical power, which he sends out to do his work, while he himself remains uncommitted. One might more appropriately speak of "possession", and the idea is not unlike that of St Paul who claimed that it was not he who spoke but the Christ who was in him (*Galatians* ii, 20). So it is not the Tulku who acts, but the spiritual force which directs him.

All this is common property to all Buddhists. The innovation of Lamaism in the fifteenth century consisted in teaching (*a*) that certain Bodhisattvas and Buddhas would send into certain places a certain number of phantom bodies to act as the priestly rulers of that area. In this way Avalokiteśvara would appear thirteen times as the ruler of Lhasa, Maitreya seven times in Urga, and so on. (*b*) They claimed that it is possible to discover the spiritual principle of the old ruler in the body of a child who had been conceived forty-nine days after his decease. Government by Tulkus, carefully chosen by skilled monks on the basis of rules as elaborate as those which enable the Congregation of Rites to differentiate genuine from spurious miracles, was the distinguishing feature of the Lamaist world during the last 450 years, though in the case of the highest ruler, the Dalai Lama, it was tempered by a few judicious assassinations.

All this is quite simple and straightforward. The same cannot be said of the second or "communal" body. Even the exact meaning of the term is in doubt, and "enjoyment-body" may be a better translation. It is a supernatural refulgent body in which the Buddha appears to superhuman beings and to the celestial Bodhisattvas in unearthly realms which his merit has created, and where he preaches the Dharma to them, while generating joy, delight and love for it. We must leave it at that, but may add that this glorified body provided a much-needed justification for the new Scriptures of the Mahāyāna (see p. 297), which could be traced back to its activities.

SKILL IN MEANS

And yet, if the truth be told, everything we have spoken about so far is not real at all, but is part of the vast phantasmagoria of this world of illusion. In actual reality there are no Buddhas, no Bodhisattvas, no perfections, no stages, and no paradises—none of all this. All these conceptions have no reference to anything that is actually there, and concern a world of mere phantasy. They are just expedients, concessions to the multitude of the ignorant, provisional constructions of thought, which become superfluous after having served their purpose. For the Mahāyāna is a "vehicle", designed to ferry people across to salvation. When the goal of the Beyond has been reached, it can safely be discarded. Who would think of carrying a raft along with him once he had got to the other shore?

In the *Perfection of Wisdom* the anxious gods ask the Venerable Subhūti: "Even *Nirvāṇa*, holy Subhūti, you say is like an illusion, is like a dream?" And they receive this reply: "Even if perchance there could be anything more distinguished, of that also I would say that it is like an illusion, like a dream. For not two different things are illusions and *Nirvāṇa*, are dreams and *Nirvāṇa*" (*Buddhist Texts*, No. 165). *Nirvāṇa*, as the true Reality, is one single, and it has no second. All multiplicity, all separation, all duality is a sign of falseness. Everything apart from the One, also called "Emptiness" or "Suchness", is devoid of real existence, and whatever may be said about it is ultimately untrue, false and nugatory, though perhaps permissible if the salvation of beings requires it. The ability to frame salutary statements and to act in conformity with people's needs, springs from a faculty called "skill in means", which comes to a Bodhisattva only late, on the seventh stage, after the "perfection of wisdom" has thoroughly shown him the emptiness of everything.

"Skill in means" made the Mahāyānists much more effective as missionaries outside India than the Hīnayānists. Not that the latter were deficient in missionary zeal. They were, however, handicapped by being rather inflexible literalists, whereas the Mahāyāna claimed much greater freedom in interpreting the letter of the Scriptures. This applied to both monastic rules and doctrinal propositions. The *Vinaya* books (p. 268) state that the monks must wear cotton robes. The Hīnayānists took this as a final ordinance, and in consequence they had great difficulties in establishing themselves in a cold climate, and could not efficiently operate in Tibet, Northern China, Mongolia and Japan. Mahāyāna monks, on the other hand, wear wool and felt without any qualms. Similarly, if the rules about eating meat are strictly interpreted, nomadic populations must remain without the consolations of the Dharma. Mahāyāna monks quickly found a way round unworkable rules and re-interpreted them to fit the circumstances. Of particular importance for the success of their missionary enterprises was their attitude to the *Vinaya* rule which forbids monks to practise medicine. The history of Christian missions in recent centuries shows that, violence apart, the medical missionaries effected more conversions than anyone else. The Buddhists disdained to use the sword, but the scalpel, the

herb and the potion opened to the Mahāyānists the houses of poor and rich alike. Convinced that compassion and their responsibilities to their fellow-men counted for more than a well-meant monastic rule, they zealously gave themselves over to the study and practice of medicine, which formed part of the curriculum for instance of Nalanda University, and also in the monastic institutions of Tibet.

The same easy-going attitude was practised with regard to doctrinal questions. Great care was taken to minimize the differences between Buddhist and non-Buddhist opinions, to absorb a great deal of the pre-existing views of the converts, and to effect, regardless of the purity of the doctrine, some kind of syncretism with Taoist, Bon, Shinto, Manichaean, shamanist or other views. This latitudinarianism is, of course, in danger of lapsing into laxity in the moral, and into arbitrary conjectures in the doctrinal field. The latter danger was on the whole more effectively avoided than the former, and the best Mahāyāna literature contains little, if anything, which to any fair-minded Buddhist would seem positively unorthodox.

If "skill in means" is detached from its background of a continuous and living spiritual tradition, it may well appear to amount to sheer opportunism. What then, we must ask, was it that limited and restrained the "skill in means" of these men? The first restraining factor was the belief in the inexorable force of *karma*, by which everyone "knew that he will experience the fruit of any *karma* that he may have done." For instance, it was an application of skill in means, though stretched rather far, when a monk in A.D. 842 killed the Tibetan king Langdarma who persecuted the holy religion, his ostensible motive being compassion, because he wanted to prevent the king from doing any more evil which could only result in a most unfortunate re-birth. But in spite of this high-minded motive he well knew that he had done wrong. When the persecution had abated and new monks could be ordained, he refused to officiate in the ordination ceremony, since as a murderer he had forfeited the right to do so, and would first have to be purified by a sojourn in purgatory. This kind of reasoning is quite taken for granted, and treated as self-evident. Once I had lunch with a Mongol Lama, and tried to get him vegetarian food. He declared that this was quite unnecessary, "We Mongol monks always eat meat, because there is nothing else." So I said, "Well, I only thought of the *Vinaya*," meaning the monastic disciplinary code. But he rejoined at once, "Yes, we know that by habitually eating meat we act against the ordinances of the Lord Buddha. As a result of our sin we may well be re-born in hell. But it is

BUDDHISM

our duty to bring the Dharma to the Mongol people, and so we just have to take the consequences as they come."

The Mahāyānists were further restrained by the *meditations* on traditional lines which for many years moulded and disciplined their minds, and which exert a uniform influence on all Buddhists alike. Nor did they ever swerve from the *aim* of all Buddhist endeavour, which is the "extinction of self", the dying out of separate individuality, to which all these devices are subservient. Long familiarity with the history of Buddhism reveals two further stabilizing factors, which are no less real and vital for being rather intangible, and apt to strike the casual observer as fantastic. Buddhism throughout its history has the unity of an *organism*, in that each new development takes place in continuity from the previous one. Nothing could look more different than a tadpole and a frog, or a chrysalis and a butterfly, and yet they are stages of the same animal, and evolve continuously from one another. The Buddhist capacity for metamorphosis must astound those who see only the end-products separated by long intervals of time. In fact they are connected by many gradations, which only close study can detect. There is in Buddhism really no innovation, but what seems so is in fact a subtle adaptation of pre-existing ideas. Great attention has always been paid to continuous doctrinal development, and to the proper transmission of the teachings from teacher to teacher. These are no anarchic philosophizings of individualists who strive for originality at all costs.

Furthermore, all Buddhist writings have a *flavour* of their own, and for thirty years I have not ceased marvelling at its presence in each one of them. The Scriptures themselves compare the Dharma to a taste, saying that the Buddha's words are those which have the taste of peace, the taste of emancipation, the taste of *Nirvāṇa*. Tastes can unfortunately not be described, and even the greatest poet could not tell the taste of a peach and say how it differs from that of an apple. Those who refuse to taste the Scriptures for themselves are therefore at a serious disadvantage in their appreciation of the unity which underlies all forms of Buddhism.

ONTOLOGICAL DOCTRINES

Having so far spoken about the way to the Beyond, we next turn to the Beyond itself. From the outer buildings of the palace of the Mahāyāna we now move into the inner sanctum, the wisdom teachings which concern ontology, or the nature of reality. These doctrines are extremely subtle and abstruse, and I cannot hope to expound them within the space allotted to me. It may console us to know that their true understanding is said to require not only many years but many lives even, and the Mahāyāna authors do not cease to warn their readers about the difficulties in front of them. The situation has been neatly summed up in the *Sūtra* on "Perfect Wisdom", where we read: "Thereupon the thought came to some of the gods in that assembly, 'What the fairies talk and murmur, that we understand though mumbled. What Subhūti has just told us, that we do not understand!' Subhūti read their thoughts, and said, 'There is nothing to understand, nothing at all to be understood! For nothing in particular has been indicated, nothing in particular has been explained.' " In fact, "no one can grasp this perfection of wisdom, for no Dharma at all has been indicated, lit up or communicated. So there will be no one who can ever grasp it" (*Buddhist Texts*, No. 165.) In spite of this warning I will now proceed to enumerate the chief ontological doctrines of the Mahāyāna. They will here be presented as bald dogmatic propositions, although this does violence to their true character. For they were never meant as definite statements about definite facts.

The foundations for the ontological doctrines of the Mahāyāna, as those for its Buddhology, were laid in the school of the Mahāsanghikas, who developed two philosophical theories of outstanding importance: (1) Thought, in its own nature, "own-being" or substance, is perfectly pure and translucent. The impurities never affect its original purity and remain accidental or "adventitious" to it. (2) As against the philosophical realism of the other Hīnayāna schools, the Mahāsanghikas became increasingly sceptical about the value of empirical knowledge. Some of them taught that all worldly things are unreal, because they are the result of ignorance and perverted views. That which transcends worldly things is the only reality and the absence of all of them is called "Emptiness". Others went even further, and regarded everything, both worldly and supramundane, both absolute and relative, as fictitious. They believed that nothing real ever corresponds to verbal expressions which give us a mere illusion of knowledge.

On this basis the Mahāyāna evolved the following propositions:

(1) All things are "empty". The Hīnayāna, in rejecting the "heresy of individuality", had taught that persons are "empty of self", and are in fact conglomerations of impersonal processes, called *dharmas*. The Mahāyāna now adds that also these impersonal processes are "empty of self", in the sense that each one is nothing in and by itself,

Photo: *British Museum*

PLATE 77. A Lohan from an illustrated Chinese manuscript, seventeenth century A.D. (*British Museum, London*)

Photo: British Museum

PLATE 78. Avalokiteśvara as the guide of souls: painting on silk from Tuan Hang, tenth
century A.D. (*British Museum, London*)

當麻蓮糸曼陀羅之圖 和州

PLATE 79. Amida Mandala from Japan. (*British Museum, London*)

PLATE 80. Tsong-Kha-Pa: founder of the Yellow Church of Tibet. (*British Museum, London*)

PLATE 81. Prajñāpāramitā: Ms from Nalanda, central miniature of back cover, c. 1100 A.D. (Bodleian Library, Oxford, MS. Sansk a. 7 R)

Photo: John R. Freeman and Co.

PLATE 82. Caricature of the traditional representation of Bodhi Dharma, the founder of the Zen Sect
(*British Museum, London*)

PLATE 83. Fierce demonic deity from Tibet. (*India Office Library, London*)

Photo: Exclusive News Agency

PLATE 84. Reliefs at Borobodur, Java: the top picture shows the miraculous signs at Kapilavastu heralding the Buddha's birth. Elephants and lions have come to honour his father, the king. The bottom picture shows gods worshipping Stupa.

and is therefore indistinguishable from any other *dharma*, and so ultimately non-existent.

The speculative contents of this concept of Emptiness are so rich that I must refer for further information to Professor Murti's *Central Philosophy of Buddhism*. Here it must suffice to say that "emptiness", means an absolute transcendental reality beyond the grasp of intellectual comprehension and verbal expression. Practically it amounts to an attitude of perfected even-mindedness. One should not "seize" on anything, or "grasp" at it, because that would involve an act of preference, bound up with self-interest, self-assertion and self-aggrandizement, ill-becoming to the selfless. "As contrary to the ways of the whole world has this Dharma been demonstrated. It teaches you not to seize upon *dharmas*, but the world is wont to grasp at anything" (*Perfection of Wisdom*, No. 29). The attitude of the perfected sage is one of non-assertion.

(2) This Emptiness is also called "Suchness" or the "One". It is "Suchness" if and when one takes it "such as it is", without adding anything to it or subtracting anything from it. It is the "One" because it alone is real. The multiple world is a product of our imagination.

(3) If all is the same, then also the Absolute will be identical with the relative, the Unconditioned with the conditioned, *Nirvāṇa* with *saṁsāra*. It is a practical consequence of this that the Bodhisattvas aim at a *Nirvāṇa* which does not exclude *saṁsāra*. Ordinary people choose the *saṁsāra*, the Disciples and *Pratyeka-buddhas* wish to escape into *Nirvāṇa*. The Bodhisattvas do not leave or abandon the saṁsāric world, but it no longer has the power to defile them.

(4) True knowledge must rise above the duality of subject and object, of affirmation and negation. To be is just the same as not to be, "yes" and "no" are both equally true and untrue, and everything is identical with its own negation. If statements must be made, self-contradictory propositions are the ones most likely to bring out the truth of what there actually is.

The attempt to define the exact nature of this ultimate reality led to the one serious disagreement which occurred within the Mahāyāna, otherwise singularly free from doctrinal disputes. Two philosophical schools slowly crystallized themselves, the Mādhyamikas and the Yogācārins. The Mādhyamikas maintained that no positive statement whatsoever can be made about the Absolute, that our linguistic resources are hopelessly inadequate for the task, and that the Buddha's "roaring silence" is the only medium by which it can be communicated. The Yogācārins, developing the first thesis of the Mahāsanghikas (p. 308), believed by contrast that the Absolute can usefully be described as "Mind", "Thought", or "Consciousness". The Mādhyamika philosophy is primarily a logical doctrine, which by the successive self-annihilation of all propositions arrives at an all-embracing scepticism. Kant is the nearest European equivalent. The Yogācārin philosophy is a metaphysical idealism, which teaches that consciousness can exist by itself without an object, and that it creates its objects out of its own inner potentialities. Berkeley is the nearest European equivalent. The Mādhyamikas believe that salvation is attained when everything has been dropped, and absolute Emptiness alone remains. For the Yogācārins salvation means to have "an act of cognition which no longer apprehends an object", an act of thought which is "Thought-only", pure consciousness, and altogether transcends the division between object and subject.

HELP FROM ABOVE

Many are the obstacles which beset the Bodhisattva in the course of his career. On all sides hostile forces rise up against him, not only from his own passions, but also from the powers of darkness and from adverse historical trends.

As for the powers of darkness, it was never doubted that disembodied spirits could help or hinder spiritual progress, and it is a simple matter of experience that, as they advance on the spiritual path, people become more and more sensitive to psychic, and presumably magical, influences. "For we wrestle not against flesh and blood, but against principalities, against powers, against the rulers of the darkness of this world, against spiritual wickedness in high places" (*Ephesians* vi, 12).

As for the pressure of their social environment, far from believing in progress, the Buddhist, like the Hindu, philosophy of history assumes a continuous decline in the age in which we live. Prophecies dating back to the beginning of the Christian era tell us that the Dharma will become progressively weaker, and that a decisive change for the worse will take place every 500 years. Each generation will be spiritually more obtuse than the previous one, and as time goes on the wisdom of the sages will be understood less and less. In the West Horace said nearly the same thing at the same time:

"Our father's age ignobler than our grandsires
Bore us yet more depraved; and we in turn
Shall leave a race more vicious than ourselves."

(*Odes* 3. 6.)

From A.D. 400 onwards the Buddhists of India were filled with expectations of the coming end. For Vasubandhu

> "The times are come
> When flooded by the rising tide of ignorance
> Buddha's religion seems to breathe its last."
> (*Abhidharmakosá*, ch. 9.)

Two centuries later Yüang-tsang's account of his travels breathes the same spirit, and he met with gloomy forebodings in many parts of the Buddhist world. The pressure of the times exacted many undesirable concessions, such as married monks and wealthy monasteries. The times were bad and would get worse and worse. This conviction has coloured all Buddhist thinking for the last 1,500 years.

The help which the Bodhisattva needs for his gigantic struggles comes from two sources, from personal spiritual forces and from more impersonal magical and occult powers.

The help of unseen beings had always been taken for granted. The new mythological figures of the Mahāyāna added to their number. An important innovation, which profoundly affected the whole tone of Buddhism, and which perhaps divides the Mahāyāna from the Hīnayāna more than anything else, consisted in the introduction of *feminine deities*. Religions tend normally to be either matriarchal or patriarchal. The Protestant interpretation of Christianity centres round God the Father and God the Son, and views with considerable distaste the devotion to the "Mother of God" which is accorded so much prominence among Catholics. In some schools of Buddhism the central person is the Buddha himself, a father-figure, whereas in others the Buddha is subordinated to a female force, the Prajñāpāramitā, who is the "Mother of all the Buddhas". In the older Buddhism, the higher planes of the spiritual life were considered beyond the reach of women. Even the early Mahāyāna teaches that in Amitābha's Pure Land there are no women, and in the *Lotus of the Good Law* we have the story of the daughter of a Dragon king who, the moment she becomes a Bodhisattva, automatically turns into a man (*Saddharma Pundarīkā*, pp. 226–8, tr. H. Kern, 1909, pp. 251–4).

Nevertheless, the feminine element was with the Mahāyāna from the very beginning, owing to the importance it attributed to the "Perfection of Wisdom". E. Neumann, in *The Great Mother* (1955), has recently studied all the manifestations of what he regards as the "archetype" of the "Mother", and he describes Sophia, or Wisdom, as the sublimest and most spiritual form of femininity, the last refinement of a mother-image dreamt up in remote times in the caves of Palaeolithic man. The Prajñāpāramitā is not only feminine by the grammatical form of her name, but on statues and images the femininity of her form is rarely in doubt. The Mahāyāna believed that men should in their meditations complete themselves by fostering the feminine factors of their personality, that they should practise passivity and a loose softness, that they should learn to open freely the gates of nature, and to let the mysterious and hidden forces of this world penetrate into them, stream in and through them. When they identify themselves with the Perfection of Wisdom, they merge with the principle of Femininity (Jung's *anima*), without which they would be mutilated men. Like a woman the Perfection of Wisdom deserves to be courted and wooed, and the *Sūtras* on Perfect Wisdom constitute one long love-affair with the Absolute. Meditation on her as a Goddess has the purpose of getting inside her, identifying oneself with her, becoming her. In the later *Tantra* a sexual attitude to Prajñāpāramitā is quite explicit. Disguised by the use of ambiguous terms it was already present in the older Prajñāpāramitā *Sūtras* themselves.

And it is interesting to notice that these writings show many feminine features, in which we learn to participate by their recitation, and by meditation on them: argumentations almost entirely rely on intuition, and attempts at reasoning are scanty and far from conclusive. The *Sūtras* win over by fascination, and not by compulsion. Timeless, they are not obsessed with time, but ignore it. They urge on to a contemplation of the world, and not to its conquest by manipulation. They show some of the amoralism which later on hardened into the antinomianism of the *Tantra*, and which did not fail to provoke protests from the more tight-laced monks. They are indifferent to sensory facts, and in vain do we search through thousands of pages for one single "hard fact". And in her ultimate core the Prajñāpāramitā is described as for ever elusive, not possessed by anyone, but absorbing all.

A great number of feminine deities were introduced after A.D. 400. Feminine Buddhas were, it is true, never thought of, but the Prajñāpāramitā now became a celestial Bodhisattva, and others were added as time went on. The most famous and beloved of these are the Tārās, "saviouresses" who are "the mothers of the world, born of the power of Avalokiteśvara's vow and understanding", who protect, reassure and "fulfil all our hopes". More specialized are the functions of the personifications of magical spells, like the "five Protectresses", among whom "the Great Pea Hen" is the most outstanding, or of Hārītī who gives children. A whole complicated pantheon has further been elaborated in connection with certain aspects of advanced mystical meditation, and it comprises such figures as Cundā, Vasudharā, Ushnīshavijayā, Vajravarāhī, and so on. The practitioners of the magic arts have a special devotion for the "Queens of sacred lore" and for the Dākinīs, or "skywalkers". After A.D. 700 one section of the *Tantra* further added consorts of the Buddhas and Bodhisattvas, called *Vidyās* or *Prajñās*, corresponding to the Śaktis of Śivaism (p. 232) and to the "Ennoia" and "Sophia" of Gnosticism. The cult of these Vidyās is often accompanied by an erotic ritual, which was derived from the age-old customs of non-Aryan populations, and which most Buddhists rejected as unseemly.

We must now say a few words about *magic*. Many people are astonished by the preoccupation of the later Mahāyāna with magic, and condemn it as a degeneration. I can see nothing astonishing in it, and prefer to regard it as a sign of vitality, and of a catholicity which tries to be all things to all men. Historically speaking, the spiritual and the magical, though essentially different, are everywhere inextricably intertwined. A spirituality which tries to do without magic becomes too diluted, too much cut off from the vital and living forces of the world, to bring the spiritual side of man to maturity. Protestantism is almost the only religion to cut out all magic. After first destroying the centres of spiritual contemplation, it has lately lost much of its capacity for restraining and influencing the conduct of individuals and of societies.

The Buddhists, in their turn, had never been without a belief in the occult, in magic and in miracles. But as for the dangers from evil spirits, no special measures were at first required to deal with them, apart perhaps from an occasional recourse to spells. A scrupulous observance of the rules of moral conduct as well as perseverance in meditation were sufficient to ward off dangers and secure help. But as the spiritual potency of the Dharma waned, and as history was felt to become more and more adverse, greater efforts were held to be required. First of all there was, from about A.D. 300 onwards, a great multiplication of spells (*mantras*) of all kinds, also called *dhāranīs* because they "uphold" or "sustain" the religious life. Then, after A.D. 500, all the customary methods of magic were resorted to, rituals, magical circles and diagrams, ritual gestures, even astrology. Buddhist magic does not differ from ordinary magic in any way, and all the methods employed have their parallels in numerous cultures, as the reader can verify from H. Webster's standard work on *Magic* (1948).

These magical procedures were introduced principally to guard the spiritual life of the élite. But as the Mahāyāna was also a popular religion, it was only natural that they should as well be used to give to the unspiritual multitude that which it desired. Already in the third century we are told of the virtue of pronouncing the name of Avalokiteśvara, which by itself dispels countless sufferings and troubles. For instance, when a caravan is in danger, "if then the whole caravan with one voice invoked Avalokita with the words, 'Homage, homage to the Giver of Safety, the Bodhisattva Avalokiteśvara, the great being!', then by the mere act of pronouncing that name the caravan will be delivered" (*Saddharma Pundarīkā*, p. 363). In later centuries the Mahāyānists, in order, as we said before (p. 297), to increase their usefulness to ordinary people, mobilized the whole apparatus of their magic to provide them with what they had set their hearts on – abundant harvests, good health, children, wealth and other mundane benefits. Up to then the faithful had relied on Brāhmanic rituals for obtaining these things, but now the Buddhist priests entered into competition with them in this field.

At the same time there was a natural reaction against the idea that Bodhisattvas had to go through aeons and aeons to reach Buddhahood, their last goal. For many people an aim so distant could not provide a motive for action, and they would drift into lassitude and despair. More immediate and tangible results had to be found for them to work for. Re-birth after death in some Buddha-land, say that of Amitābha in the West, or of Akshobhya in the East, became the near-term goal of the majority of the believers. Others hoped to be re-born with Maitreya, at a time when in the remote future conditions on earth will again be more promising. Those who are re-born in this way can see the radiant body of the Buddha, whose very sight has the most wonderful consequences:

"To see the Buddha, see the Lord, annuls all ills.
It helps to win the Buddha's own, the highest
gnosis."
(*Buddhist Texts*, p. 189.)

In our present age, with spirituality observably at a very low ebb, the achievement of enlightenment is by general consent normally out of the question. All we can do now is to lay the foundations for it at a future period by acquiring "merit". "Merit" is that which either guarantees a happier and more comfortable life in the future, or, alternatively, increases the scope of our spiritual opportunities and achievements. Buddhists regard our material environment as a reflex of our *karma*, or merit, and the living conditions of beings are determined by their spiritual maturity. We live in a world we deserve to live in – an awesome thought! The Bodhisattvas, by the force of their meritorious *karma*, are capable of realizing, or bringing to perfection, a "Pure Land", and by the merit of our deeds we can be transported into that more auspicious realm where, slowly matured and purified, we will in due course become Buddhas also. Faith and devotion were held to be particularly productive of merit, and great things were expected from doing worship (*pūjā*) to the Buddhas and Bodhisattvas, and bestowing flowers, perfumes, lamps, etc., upon their shrines.

The magicians went still further in their reaction against the long wait imposed upon Bodhisattvas, and claimed that magical methods could furnish an easy and quick way to Buddhahood, not in the course of three endless aeons, but miraculously in this very life, in "the course of one single thought". This theory was put forward at the very time when the Chinese Ch'an masters came to speak of a "sudden Enlightenment", and this coincidence shows that it met the needs of the Buddhists of that age.

Both the mythological and the ontological innovations of the Mahāyāna paved the way for the wholesale absorption of magical practices and beliefs. Once the Buddhist pantheon had been widened by the inclusion of new Buddhas and Bodhisattvas, the door was open to any number of new mythological figures. After A.D. 600, thousands of personifications of occult forces were at different times named, described and cultivated. Later on the Tibetans attempted to classify the resulting deities, and arranged them in ten classes, beginning with the Buddhas, and ending with godlings who inhabit mountains and rivers, with fairies, sprites, fiends, demons and ghosts. In view of the increasing sense of adversity greater and greater stress was laid on the "Protectors of the Dharma", also called "Kings of the sacred lore" (*vidyārājā*), who, though inherently benevolent, assume a terrifying appearance to protect the faithful.

The ontological thesis of the identity of *Nirvāṇa* and *saṁsāra*, of the sameness of the Absolute with the phenomenal world was easily capable of the kind of cosmic interpretation which is the philosophical basis of all magic. The Absolute, the philosophical principle behind the world, is identical with the principle of religious salvation, with Buddhahood or a personal Buddha. The Supreme Buddha pervades the entire universe, and is present in everything. Each thought, sound and action is in its true essence an activity of his saving grace. As a manifestation of the Absolute this very world contains all the mysteries of reality, and its hidden forces can be used for salvation. As a reflex of the Non-dual, it must everywhere mirror, manifest and reveal this all-comprehensive unity. If all things are fundamentally identical in one Pure Spirit, all cosmic phenomena can be conceived of as closely linked together by many invisible threads, each word, action and thought as somehow connected with the eternal Ground of the world.

The magic is this unity, as it were, in action. If Thought is the only reality, and everything material an expression of spiritual forces, then the thoughts condensed in the *mantras* could easily have power over material things. The Emptiness, in its turn, being nothing particular in itself, offers no resistance to being transformed by *mantras* into the particular form of a god or goddess, in whose powers the magician can share by identification. As long as one's own self is no longer in the way, and if one is acquainted with the secret lore of the Sages, one can without difficulty transform oneself into the One, or any of its manifestations.

This ends our survey of the Mahāyāna. In India a synthesis of all its diverse elements was effected in the Buddhist universities under the Pāla dynasty (750–1150). Then, after about A.D. 1200, Buddhism, and with it the Mahāyāna, disappeared from India, not without first having left a deep imprint on Hinduism. By then Pāla Buddhism had migrated to Tibet, which became its citadel for another 750 years. The fate of the Mahāyāna in China and Japan will be the subject of the next chapter.

7c. Buddhism: in China and Japan

by RICHARD H. ROBINSON

CHINA

The conversion of China to Buddhism is the greatest feat of Indian cultural expansion, since China is the only Buddhist country that possessed a civilization of its own before the introduction of Buddhism. Chiefly for this reason, Far Eastern Buddhism is the most vital and original provincial variant of Buddhism. No other non-Indian people assimilated the entire Indic Buddhist tradition so well, and no other contributed so much of its own. For over a thousand years Buddhism dominated the religious life of China, producing a massive pageant of devotion, a great art, and a sacred literature that embodies both the Indian inheritance and the Chinese increment. But Chinese Buddhism has been no less subject to impermanence than other conditioned phenomena, and it has gone through the common cycle of arising, flourishing and declining. At present, it is in a crisis that will either transform or disintegrate it.

The development of Chinese Buddhism was activated by tension between two divergent influences – the Indian tradition and the naturalized Chinese tradition. As long as the desire to harmonize these two persisted, the faith remained vigorous and progressive. When the accumulated tradition achieved a sort of harmony, it languished from lack of stimulus.

In general, Chinese Buddhists have not deviated willingly from Indian models. Just as in Chinese Buddhist art the central figures are Indian while the peripheral ornament is Chinese, so Chinese Buddhist writers have adapted their style to native taste, but have not generally gone against any established Indian doctrinal tradition. Even the most distinctively Chinese sects are essentially Indian in content, however Chinese their flavour may be. Chinese Buddhism has retained all the characteristic properties of Indian Buddhism – the monastic system, the rites of worship, the sacred writings and the contemplative exercises.

From A.D. 150 to 1000, when contact between India and China was significant for Buddhism, Indian Buddhism evolved considerably. As each successive Indian phase reached China, it gave rise to a cult or school. Some of these schools prospered and survived, and most of them left their deposit of literature in the canon. Thus Chinese Buddhism preserves as contemporaries schools that were successive phases in India. But the Indian intellectual environment was not transferred to China, and so debates with the Hindu schools did not sustain interest in a country where there were no Hindu schools to dispute with. Thus, though Chinese Buddhist scholars have continued to study the Indian treatises, the philosophical systems have not naturalized as successfully as the *Sūtras* (p. 297).

Chinese Buddhism evolved mainly through the study of the *Sūtras* in Chinese translation. In the early days – the third and fourth centuries A.D. – those who read and expounded the *Sūtras* were familiar with Taoist writings and "The Classics" (p. 366). Quite naturally, it was a long time before the radical differences between Buddhism and the native systems were clearly understood. Yet the interpretation of the *Sūtras* was felt to be a problem, and during the fourth and fifth centuries, the monastery schools laboured to arrive at their true meaning. Thus, by the time that the Indian systematic treatises became known, there was already a Chinese tradition based, like the Indian *Śāstra* (p. 298), on the Mahāyāna *Sūtras*, but concerned with different problems. Later, in the sixth and seventh centuries, the Chinese created scholastic systems, in imitation of the Indian ones, but deriving from the native exegetical tradition. The distinctively Chinese sects differ principally because they selected different *Sūtras* as expressing the Dharma in its quintessence.

Chinese Buddhism is entitled to a place of honour among the world's faiths for many reasons. Its devotees have been numerous and have exemplified the varieties of religious experience on a wide scale. It counts many saintly men among its followers, both past and present. Its monuments in literature and art are imposing. It is both the most distinguished offshoot of Indian Buddhism, and the parent of Vietnamese, Korean and Japanese Buddhism. And, even in its present weakness, it is in a position to contribute to the religious life of world civilization.

History

The arrival of Buddhism in China was a concomitant of the expansion of Indian culture into Central Asia at a time when Chinese political and commercial connections with that area had become important. By the first century A.D., a number of prosperous city states had arisen in the watersheds of the Oxus and Tarim rivers. The source of their prosperity was the trade between China, India and the Roman Empire. Culturally, this area was international. Some cities spoke Iranian dialects, wrote them in Indian alphabets, were ruled by Greek dynasties and issued Grecian-looking coins. Central Asian art combined Indian, Hellenistic and Iranian elements. During the first century, these states came under Chinese suzerainty. However, Indian cultural influence was dominant. Indian settlers and adventurers found their way to Central Asia, and Buddhist monks moved back and forth, travelling with the traders' caravans.

The Chinese terminus of the Central Asian trade route was the city of Tun Huang. It was an international community, where Chinese, Kucheans, Sogdians, Khotanese and Indians lived together. It is said that thirty-six languages were spoken in its market place. The two bonds between the inhabitants were trade and Buddhism. In this way, Buddhism came overland, by stages, to the frontiers of China.

The imperial annals mention Buddhism in China once or twice during the first century A.D., but there is no indication that it made any headway. The conversion of China began in earnest with the arrival of several translator-missionaries about A.D. 150.

Most of the early Buddhist missionaries in China were Central Asians. They lived in monasteries set up by imperial decree, where they were attended by Chinese disciples. Those who had grown up in Tun Huang already spoke Chinese. The others learned to speak the language before beginning their work. Apparently they did not learn to read and write it, but relied on Chinese scribes. Translation of scriptures was the most important part of their missionary labours. They were attended by Chinese monks and laymen, to whom they explained the texts, and with whom they

discussed the correct wording of the Chinese translation. They thus created a nucleus of Chinese who knew the doctrine, and a body of *Sūtras* to be read by the literati and recited publicly by Chinese monks.

At this time, China was ripe for conversion. The Han dynasty was crumbling, and warlords marched back and forth, devastating the country in their struggles. Contact with Central Asia had stimulated interest in exotic things. The old traditions were weakened, and the Chinese were not so disposed to despise things from abroad. Social disintegration turned the spirit of the times away from the manifestly perishable glories of this world and stimulated longing for an extra-mundane refuge. During the third century thoughtful Chinese returned to the long-neglected political philosophy of Chuang-tzǔ and Lao-tzǔ, and turned away from the pursuit of office and power, just as the age of Augustine and Jerome turned from the city of this world.

During the third century the Chinese Saṁgha was consolidated. In spite of the civil wars missionaries arrived and were welcomed. Buddhism spread out through the country and reached the Yangtzǔ valley. The growing community of monks acquired a translation of the *Vinaya* (p. 268), and established correct ordination procedures. In 260, a party of Chinese pilgrims set out through Central Asia in search of scriptures. They reached Khotan, practically in India, and returned with texts to augment the growing canon. Thus, by the end of the century, the nascent "Church" was at the end of its period of incubation.

During the fourth century the Buddhist "Church" expanded and became the dominant faith of China. The country was war-ridden throughout the century, and the Northern areas were overrun by barbarian chieftains. Nevertheless, missionaries converted many of these chieftains and moderated their harsh rule as much as possible. The Buddhist teaching was also influential among the cultivated gentlemen of the imperial court at Nanking. Chinese monks now lectured on the *Sūtras* and wrote commentaries. Different schools of interpretation developed as the search for the true meaning of the Scriptures progressed. Among the noted monks of the period were: Tao An, famous for his expositions of the *Perfection of Wisdom Sūtra* (p. 308), and for the first catalogue of the Scriptures; and Hui Yüan, a disciple of Tao An, who founded a community dedicated to the worship of Amitābha, and for more than thirty years directed the course of Chinese Buddhism through his timely and forceful writings.

During the fifth century Buddhism completed its domination of Chinese religious life. It was liberally patronized by the kings of the several Chinese states, and most of the population adhered to it. During the first few decades of the century a number of great translators brought important new scriptures to China. The greatest of these, and the greatest of all translators, was Kumārajīva, who arrived in 401. Three thousand monks and many eminent officials attended while Kumārajīva and his team translated. He had more than five hundred regular students in his classes, and almost all the important monks of the younger generation studied with him at some time. The ensuing period was one of intense and productive intellectual activity among the monks of China. Some studied the *Vinaya*, which was then available in a good many versions. Some specialized in expounding one particular *Sūtra*. Others worked on the problem of harmonizing the divergent teachings of the different *Sūtras*. A few thinkers, such as Seng Chao, Tao Sheng, and Hui Kuan, made independent and quite original contributions to Buddhist thought.

The earliest surviving body of Chinese Buddhist art is from the fifth century. The strongly Buddhist Northern Wei dynasty constructed the cave-shrines of Yünkang, near the Great Wall, where work continued for about a century. It is said that thirty thousand families of workmen from Tun Huang were brought to work at Yün-kang. But Yün-kang, with its dozens of caves cut out of the live rock of a cliff face and sculptures carved out of the walls, ceilings, pillars and doorways, is far from being the only surviving art of this period. There are many stone stelae and bronze figures, some of them inscribed with donors' names and dated.

Both in theme and in style early Chinese Buddhist art is a provincial variant of the North Indian (Gandhāran) tradition, modified en route through Central Asia and embellished with Chinese ornament. At this time Indian canons of sculpture were not strictly observed in China, and Chinese exaggeration and modification of the essentially Hellenistic Gandhāran style produced an effect rather close to European Romanesque. In art, as in thought, the fifth century was a period of varied individualism.

During the sixth century the individualistic religion of the fifth century was consolidated and standardized. Great systems were built by famous teachers, such as Chih-I, founder of the T'ien-t'ai Sect, and Chi-Tsang, founder of the San-Lun Sect, who attracted thousands of disciples and founded schools complete with philosophical systems, standard commentaries on the *Sūtras*, liturgies and contemplative routines. Royal favour was lavished on these teachers, who were granted large, well-appointed monasteries for their headquarters. The one

exception to this royal favour was a brief period of proscription in North China about A.D. 575, when three hundred thousand monks and nuns were forcibly returned to secular life.

After about A.D. 550 Chinese Buddhist art received fresh Indian influences, from the Gupta style. In addition standardization of technical norms gave rise to a homogeneous and polished style. Chinese feeling for linear elements was blended with Indian feeling for masses and planes. The result was the mature and robust style of the T'ang period (618–907). Thus the constructive spirit of the times was instanced in art as well as in thought and institutions.

During the seventh century, under the T'ang dynasty in its initial glory, Chinese Buddhism reached its prime. New generations of schoolmen built and refined their systems, teaching to thousands. A school of *Vinaya* masters flourished, with the laws and history of the Saṃgha as their special discipline. Hsüan-Tsang, the famous pilgrim and translator, brought the latest form of the Vijñānavāda (Yogācāra, p. 317) School back from his fifteen-year stay in India. Three outstanding masters created the Hua-yen School, the last of the great scholastic systems. The Pure Land teaching reached its definitive form and the worship of Amitābha became widespread, particularly in North China. Under the Sixth Patriarch the Ch'an movement emerged into prominence as a distinct sect. Thus the divergent tendencies that had operated since the early fifth century eventually produced the separation of distinct sectarian traditions, each with its own possibilities to work out.

During the eighth and early ninth centuries the different sects built upon their foundations. The disciples of the Sixth Patriarch spread the Ch'an teaching throughout China and even into Tibet. Among them were many colourful masters whose wit is preserved in the "old cases" on which later Ch'an students meditate. The Pure Land Sect continued to spread the worship of Amitābha, who is a popular figure in the art of the period. There were a number of eminent hymn composers among the Amitābhists of the eighth century. The Chen-yen (Tantric) Sect, last of the imported Indian sects, arrived during the eighth century and was popular for a time. This varied religious activity made its impression on T'ang culture. Many of the Emperors were Buddhist in some sense or other, and most were favourable to Buddhism. Many of the great poets of the eighth and ninth centuries were Buddhist, and some became monks. The most famous painters were Buddhist. Buddhist themes and allusions fill the art, literature and folklore of the times.

During the ninth century the T'ang regime suffered progressive impoverishment and dissension. The imperial power declined, and factions at court became more vicious towards one another. One incident in this strife was the proscription of Buddhism in 845. The motives for the imperial decision to dismantle the Saṁgha and confiscate its lands and property were a mixture of economic concern, as the state was in financial distress, and of Taoist malice, as the Emperor's ear had been lent to Taoist persuasion. Temples, images and books were destroyed. Monks and nuns were secularized and either gave up their vocations or continued their work as crypto-clerics until the proscription ended. In spite of earnest efforts at reconstruction the damage incurred during this proscription was irreparable in many ways. The destruction of libraries was a severe reverse to religious scholarship, and the destruction or temples and their furnishings weakened the prestige of Buddhism among the populace. The Ch'an and Pure Land sects suffered less than the others, as they were less dependent on libraries and "cathedrals", and consequently these sects made greater headway than the others during the late ninth century.

One result of the great proscription was to stimulate printing of the scriptures. The technique of block-printing had been known in the eighth century. However, the oldest surviving printed book in the world is a copy of the *Diamond Sūtra* printed in 868.

Under the Sung dynasty, during the eleventh, twelfth and thirteenth centuries, though all the sects and schools were practised or studied, only the Ch'an Sect continued to evolve qualitatively. It penetrated deeply into the culture of the period, which acquired a distinctively Ch'an flavour. At the same time the urbane values of the Sung court influenced the Ch'an Sect.

In this period the Neo-Confucian philosophers were busy remodelling the old secular tradition. They were markedly influenced by Buddhism, despite their antipathy to it, so that the secular tradition took on a Buddhist complexion. Nevertheless, the eventual victory of Neo-Confucianism was a setback for Buddhism, as it is essentially a secular and this-worldly philosophy.

The art of the T'ang period (618–907) was robust and vital. In the following periods iconographic Buddhist art tended more and more towards rich textures and ornament, and less and less towards basic power of line and form. Styles became lusher and less classical, and eventually the tradition stagnated.

While the iconographic tradition of Buddhist art was languishing in the twelfth and thirteenth centuries, there arose a school of painter-monks, under Ch'an influence, who practised a style derived from the secular painting tradition, rejecting the symmetry and iconography of the Sino-Indian tradition. They strove for extreme economy of means, making each line and shade suggest the maximum, and concentrating on intensity of rhythm, spatial counterpoint and tonal harmony. This austerely simple style is both forceful and rich in its aesthetic impact. In the hands of the master ink-painters painting became a contemplative exercise, and viewing paintings became a form of meditation.

This Ch'an painting school continued to flourish until the seventeenth century. Today there are still people who can paint in this idiom, but it is now an archaistic exercise rather than a live tradition.

The phases of Chinese Buddhist art correspond to the phases of the religion. The fifth and early sixth centuries were the age of free assimilation and individualistic practice of the teaching. The late sixth century was the period of transition to organized systems and sects. The T'ang period was that of the mature faith in its robust prime. The tenth to thirteenth centuries were not so productive of novelty, but were characterized by refinement, stability and vitality in certain aspects. From the thirteenth to the seventeenth century the religion lived well on its accumulated tradition, but lost impetus progressively.

The Mongols, who ruled China during the thirteenth and fourteenth centuries, adopted the Tibetan variety of Buddhism, and Lamaist establishments have since then constituted a separate sect in China. The Mongols, though tolerant of all religions, patronized Buddhism lavishly. The Ming dynasty (1368–1644), which restored native rule, looked backwards to the glorious T'ang and Sung eras. Its culture was conservative, and the power of the old ways was overwhelming. Buddhism was subject to no new stimuli and envisaged no new problems. The period from the fifteenth century to the nineteenth is predominantly an age of closed vistas. Nevertheless, there were a few outstanding thinkers and leaders in each generation of monks.

The Manchu dynasty (1644–1911) favoured Lamaism, chiefly for political reasons, and published editions of the Buddhist scriptures in Chinese, Tibetan and Manchu. At the same time it issued edicts restricting entrance into the monastic order and curtailing the activities of the monks. The purpose of these edicts was partly to keep down the amount of the national income required to support the monasteries, and partly to prevent bandits and other enemies of the regime from hiding as monks. Every monk required an official permit to leave the

PLATE 85. Buddha Amitabha Trinity and Attendants. Chinese. 593 A.D. Sui. Gift of Mrs. W. Scott Fitz. (Courtesy, *Museum of Fine Arts, Boston*.)

PLATE 86. The Bodhisattva Maitreya. Miroku, by Kaikei. Kamakura Period. A.D. 1190. Wood sculpture. (Courtesy, *Museum
of Fine Arts, Boston.*)

household life, which he had to carry with him as a passport.

There are no statistics on the number of lay Buddhists in China at any time, chiefly because the practice of taking *upāsaka* vows has never been subject to government control. However, the dynastic histories furnish statistics for the monastic system at certain periods. Between 476 and 540 the number of temples in roughly the same area of North China rose from 6,500 to 30,000 and the number of monks and nuns from 80,000 to 200,000. There were perhaps something like 500,000 monks in all China at the time in a population of about 50,000,000. In 1756, there were 5,000,000 monks in a population of perhaps somewhat less than 500,000,000. Thus, even in its lowest condition, Chinese Buddhism was still an extensive though dilapidated edifice.

Scriptures

The Chinese *Tripitaka* is a library of sacred and classical writings that comprises both an Indian legacy and substantial Chinese contributions. The composition of this library varies somewhat from edition to edition, and texts are admitted, not by decision of oecumenical councils deciding on their canonical status, but by the judgment of editors as to whether a text is worthy of preservation as a persisting part of the heritage. There is no Chinese Buddhist "Bible", and the believer is free to accept the authority of any text that he selects from the *Tripitaka*. The Mahāyāna *Sūtras* are universally accorded authoritative status, yet fewer than fifty out of the six hundred titles in this section of the *Tripitaka* have any widespread influence. Each sect selects one, two or three *Sūtras* as its basic authorities, and these are the real "Bible" of their devotees. In addition, there are some *Sūtras* that are universally read and revered.

There have been many compilations and editions of the Chinese *Tripitaka*. The first collection was made under the devout Emperor Wu of Liang, during the early sixth century. It was a manuscript edition and comprised 2,213 works. Three new manuscript editions were compiled under the Sui dynasty about A.D. 600. The earliest printed edition was produced under the auspices of the Sung dynasty in 980. This monumental work involved the cutting of 130,000 wooden printing blocks. Since then the entire *Tripitaka* has been issued in many block-print recensions, in China, Korea and Japan. Several movable-type editions have been published in Japan within the last century. The latest of these is the Taishō *Tripitaka*, published between 1924 and 1929. It has fifty-five volumes, There is a Taishō supplement of thirty-five volumes. The *Tripitaka* by no means

includes all the writings of Chinese Buddhists, and these have been published in many collectanea, some of which are larger than the *Tripitaka*.

The Chinese *Tripitaka* is a unique storehouse of information about the development of Indian Buddhism. Two-thirds of its contents are translations from Indian languages. Most of these were translated before 750, and thus were based on older versions of the Sanskrit texts than those employed by the Tibetan translators. Unlike the Tibetan *Tripitaka*, the Chinese includes the complete Hīnayāna Sūtras (*Āgamas*). In fact, about one-fifth of the Taishō *Tripitaka* consists of Hīnayāna works. Thus, though Chinese Buddhism is exclusively Mahāyāna, it has conserved the Hīnayāna tradition fully.

The two largest sections of the *Tripitaka* are Mahāyāna *Sūtras* and Chinese commentaries on the Mahāyāna *Sūtras*. This represents on the one hand the ample base of Indian scriptural authority, and on the other hand, the determined Chinese attempt to master the meaning of the Indian scriptures. Each of the "catholic sects" (see pp. 330ff.) possesses its own commentaries on the chief *Sūtras*, to the interpretation of which the sectarian doctrines are applied.

In its totality, the sacred literature of Chinese Buddhism evidences the devotion and diligence of many generations of men of letters. It bespeaks the support of Emperors who subsidized translation, publication and teaching. It also gives a measure of the devotion of multitudes of ordinary Chinese whose religious feelings made it politic for many agnostic Emperors to subsidize the production of the *Tripitaka*. The physical existence of the *Tripitaka* depends on the devout labours of countless copyists and printers such as those who carved every single sign in the block-print editions. In short, the *Tripitaka* is a monument of Chinese devotion to the Three Jewels.

Belief and Practice

Before proceeding to consider the sectarian divisions of Chinese Buddhism, it is necessary to recapitulate some central features of the common stock that underlies Buddhism in all its regional variants and degrees of sophistication. The chief terms of this common stock are *transmigration, merit, worship,* and the *worshipful personages.* They are not doctrines, but beliefs, so much taken for granted that most scriptures do not trouble to define them, and so ingrained into the popular worldview that very few Buddhists can explain them to an outsider.

Transmigration (samsāra) is the cosmological presupposition of Buddhism. The six planes of life in transmigration, or "destinies", are the stage on which the drama

327

of suffering and release from suffering is enacted. The lower destinies – hell, the realm of ghosts, the animal realm and the realm of the titans – are spheres of retribution and privation, commensurate in duration with the sins of the sufferer. The realm of the gods is a sphere of reward, enjoyed for a period commensurate with one's merit, which in this destiny can only be expended and not increased. The human plane or "destiny" is the most fortunate of all because, though it is fraught with suffering, its inhabitants alone have the power to increase their merit or sin. It is the only sphere of moral initiative and the only one in which supreme, perfect Enlightenment can be achieved. The paradises or "Buddha-lands" of the Buddhas are really a form of non-earthly human destiny, where conditions are ideal for spiritual progress. But a Buddha-land is quite different from the heavens of the gods in that it is not morally neutral, and all its inhabitants unfailingly reach Enlightenment. None of the destinies is an everlasting abode, though one may stay in a destiny for aeons before "the ripening of deeds" is completed and one migrates to another destiny.

The concept of transmigration undoubtedly played a large role in the conversion of China to Buddhism. It possesses intrinsic appeal and dramatic power. It offered a picture of man's place in the cosmos that was unrivalled by any indigenous one. Chinese Buddhists of all persuasions have always been unanimous in their belief in transmigration. Naïve ones have believed in a transmigrating soul, and sophisticated ones have understood the doctrine of no-soul (p. 292). The wide theme of the Six Destinies has been embellished colourfully in art and folklore.

Merit is a kind of spiritual credit that accrues to the doer of any good deed, word or thought. In this life or in succeeding lives, it brings good consequences to the doer or to anyone to whom he "transfers" his merit. Mundane deeds produce limited merit. Supramundane deeds produce unlimited merit. There are few human beings so deficient in goodness that they cannot do some small deed of merit. But all finite merit is minute in comparison with unlimited merit.

The multiplicity of permissible religious ways corresponds to the disparity between the capacities of living beings in the "Three Worlds". Yet there is definitely a supreme way, culminating in supreme, perfect Enlightenment, travelled by those who are equipped with boundless merit. All others are inferior to this way, and the devotees of other ways must eventually progress to it. Thus each mode of merit-seeking is good in its own kind and degree. Supreme, perfect Enlightenment is beyond the immediate reach of most human beings, yet ordinary people may progress towards it, no matter how restricted their powers and circumstances.

Among the manifold practices that earn merit certain ones have become institutionalized. Charity towards the needy and donations to the cause of the Three Jewels are encouraged by the scriptures and widely esteemed. Activities for propagating the Dharma are also highly productive of merit. Writing out scriptures was particularly important before the invention of printing. Since the advent of printing, Emperors and humble laymen alike have often paid for the publication of scriptures. Painting religious pictures and paying for them are also ways of earning merit. When a layman is in particular need of merit, in some crisis such as illness or the death of a relative or adversity in his fortunes, he often commissions monks to recite the liturgy and the *Sūtras*. This is also done on the anniversaries of a relative's death as a memorial service. Another group of practices consists of observing certain vows for a specified period of time. Abstaining from meat, wine and sexual intercourse is often undertaken on this basis. "Releasing life", another frequent deed of piety, consists of going to the market and buying fish or poultry, which are always sold alive, and releasing them. In addition all acts of worship are productive of merit.

None of these practices is peculiar to Chinese Buddhism. Whatever the doctrinal differences between sects and regions, religious practice varies remarkably little from the common stock of the Indian tradition.

Worship (*pūjā*), the act that relates the devotee to the sacred symbols and to what the sacred symbols represent, is central to Buddhism as to other religions. It consists of offering gifts and services to the Three Jewels – Buddha, Dharma and Saṁgha. The gifts are beautiful and precious objects for the purpose of maintaining the shrines and the monastic community. The services consist of chanting the liturgy and Scriptures; performing ritual acts of reverence such as pressing the palms of the hands together in the attitude of worship, and offering incense; preaching the Dharma, and listening to the Dharma. These are external acts of worship. Inner worship consists of contemplating a Buddha or Bodhisattva, focusing faith and devotion on him. Buddha-contemplation is rather like the Christian "prayer of contemplation".

It is hard to say whether Chinese Buddhists "pray" without misleading the reader. Certainly many believers petition the Bodhisattvas Kuan-yin and Ti-tsang and the Buddhas Yao-shih and Amit'o for relief from personal troubles and for personal favours. The liturgies, such as "The Daily Offices of the Ch'an Sect", include wishes for the welfare of the nation and all living beings that are rather like intercessory prayer. But in fact the fulfilment of these wishes is to be achieved through transfer of the merit arising from recitation of the liturgy, rather than through response of the Buddhas and Bodhisattvas.

The worshipful personages are the human and superhuman holy personages to whom worship is directed. Since any degree of holiness is worthy of reverence, a multitude of Indian and Chinese saints and hosts of Indian divinities who have been domesticated within the Buddhist pantheon all receive due reverence in a limited degree. True worship, however, belongs properly to the great superhuman Bodhisattvas and Buddhas, whose merit, insight and power of good means are unlimited. In practice only a very few of the Buddhas and Bodhisattvas mentioned in the *Sūtras* are the objects of cults in China. The chief ones are Śākyamuni Buddha, Amitābha Buddha (Amit'o), Maitreya Buddha (Milo), Bhaisajyaguru Buddha (Yao-shih), Avalokiteśvara Bodhisattva (Kuan-yin), and Kshitigarbha Bodhisattva (Ti-tsang). Each of these cults is based on an Indian *Sūtra* setting forth the special attributes of the holy personage.

Śākyamuni (the historical Buddha) is described as a transcendental and eternal saviour in the *Saddharma-puṇḍarīka Sūtra*, which is the most popular *Sūtra* in China. Images of Śākyamuni are exceedingly common in Chinese art of all periods. He is the chief object of worship of the T'ien-t'ai Sect. The Pure Land Sect affirms the identity of Amitābha and Śākyamuni. The Ch'an Sect traces the lineage of its special transmission of insight back to the historical Śākyamuni.

Maitreya is the future Buddha. He now resides in the Tushita Heaven, where beings may gain re-birth if they vow to seek it. The cult of Maitreya was exceedingly popular in China until the seventh century, during which period images of Maitreya were produced in greater number than those of Amitābha.

Amitābha presides over a Buddha-land (or Pure Land) named Sukhāvatī, "The Blessed Land", situated far away in the Western quarter of the universe. He was once a Bodhisattva, countless aeons ago, at which time he vowed to create the best of all possible Buddha-lands, adorned with every perfection. He vowed that anyone who called his name with sincere faith would be assured of re-birth in Sukhāvatī. A Bodhisattva, in his course towards full Buddhahood, accumulates limitless merit, and applies it to building a special Buddha-country for the benefit of living beings. A Bodhisattva's vows channel his merit through the aeons until they are fulfilled. Because of his great vows and infinite merit, Amitābha possesses unlimited power to save, and those who rely on his grace are certain to achieve full enlightenment.

The cult of Amitābha (the Pure Land cult) was known in China from the second century, but did not achieve pre-eminence until the seventh century.

Bhaisajyaguru Buddha, literally "The Master of Healing", favours his worshippers with relief from the troubles of this world. He presides over a Pure Land in the Eastern quarter. When he was a Bodhisattva, he made twelve great vows to free living beings from the bondage of *karma*. He vowed to guard their progress towards enlightenment, to help them keep the precepts, to free them from the snares of infidel faiths and Hīnayāna, to feed the hungry, clothe the naked, restore the bodies of the sick and deformed, and rescue those facing execution. To invoke his power one should call his name and recite the *Bhaisajyaguru Sūtra*. It is prescribed that this text should be read forty-nine times, with appropriate offerings of lamps and banners, to relieve illness or to avert national calamities.

Avalokiteśvara Bodhisattva (Kuan-yin) is possessed of remarkable good means. He will save the believer who calls his name, from fire, sword, poison, disease, shipwreck, wild beasts, hell, the realm of ghosts, the wrath of a king, dragons, demons and sorcery. Kuan-yin takes many forms, according to the needs of beings in trouble. Thus he (often she) appears both frequently and in many forms in sculpture and painting. The Kuan-yin cult has had a perennial vogue, though it has never become a sect. There is a vast lore about the miraculous responses of Kuan-yin to the cries of people in trouble.

Kshitigarbha Bodhisattva is specially concerned with rescuing beings from hell. He is the patron of criminals and dead children.

The problem of the relationship and jurisdiction of the various Buddhas does not trouble the unphilosophical devotee, who either worships all in turn or concentrates on the one most congenial to him. The theoretical problem is resolved by all sects in essentially the same way: the Essence Body (Dharma-body, p. 306) is free from all determinate marks such as unity and multiplicity, and the multiplicity of Buddhas belongs to the realm of appearance.

The Sects

In China the unity of the Saṁgha has been maintained well. Monks are ordained into the Saṁgha, and not into a particular sect. Certain monasteries have often been pre-empted by the adherents of one sect, but monastic corporations are self-governing and do not belong to sects. In fact there are no sectarian corporations in Chinese Buddhism.

It is evident that the divisions of Chinese Buddhism do

not conform to the usual meaning of "sect", a word that is used to translate Chinese *tsung*, which originally meant "clan shrine" and came by extension to mean the fountainhead or lineage of a tradition, since the ancestral tablets were kept in the clan shrine. In keeping with the original metaphor, sub-sects are termed "families", and the main figures in the lineage of an established sect are called "ancestors" or "grandfathers", a term generally translated as "patriarchs".

A *sect* possesses a distinctive tradition of doctrine or practice. *Sub-sects* represent lineages from the several disciples of the founder, and sometimes have minor differences of teaching. *Cults* consist of a special practice of devotion or contemplation, but do not possess a lineage of masters. For example, devotion to Maitreya was for long an important cult in China, but there was no Maitreyan sect. Devotion to Amitābha was practised for centuries before a lineage of masters founded the Amitābhist sect, and thereafter it reverted to the status of a cult. A cult commonly arises from a particular *Sūtra*. It may attract followers in all the established sects without in itself constituting a sect. The "catholic sects" deliberately include all cults within their structure.

The essential element in a sect is the heritage of a great master. This may be a philosophical system, a mystical insight, a devotional cult, a discipline or a system of rites and initiations. The sect exists as long as its lineage of masters continues. When the lineage fails, the special teachings may still be preserved and studied, and the lineage may even be revived centuries later. A sect has a centre, since a master may confer his approval on his best disciples, but it has no circumference. One can study a sect or practise its teaching, but one cannot join a sect. This absence of clear demarcation between in-group and out-group has served to keep Chinese Buddhism pansectarian.

Among the Chinese sects there are three general types. The *classical schools* have as their heritage an Indian doctrinal system, embodied in a group of *Śāstras* (p. 298). The founder of the school is the missionary who translated and expounded its fundamental treatises. The *catholic sects* classify the different Scriptures and doctrinal systems as an ascending series of accommodated teachings designed to lead beings of varying capacities upwards to the true teaching. Their fundamental texts are *Sūtras*, the true meaning of which is explained in commentaries and independent treatises by the founders and patriarchs of the sect. They possess their own liturgies and their own contemplative systems, and they harmonize all the aspects of Buddhism within their structure. The *exclusive sects* discard the classification of teachings and make no attempt to harmonize all doctrines. They deprecate other teachings, without actually declaring that they are wrong. They advocate a single path, and enjoin their devotees to follow it to the exclusion of other ways.

The principal *classical schools* are:

(1) *The Kośa School*, founded on the *Abhidharmakośa*, a compendium of Hīnayāna dogmatics translated by Hsüan-Tsang in the seventh century. This school resumed the line of *Abhidharma* studies that had flourished in the fifth century on the basis of early translations. It did not maintain a separate lineage for long after Hsüan-Tsang.

(2) *The Satyasiddhi School*, based on Kumārajīva's translation of the *Satyasiddhi Śāstra*, a compendium of dogmatics belonging to a different Hīnayāna sect from the *Abhidharmakośa*. This "Siddhi" school flourished during the fifth century.

(3) *The San-Lun (Three Treatises) School*, based on three Mādhyamika texts translated by Kumārajīva, did not arise until the early sixth century, and its lineage did not persist for many generations after Chi-Tsang (549–623), its greatest master.

(4) *The Fa-hsiang School*, based on the Indian Vijñānavāda (Yogācāra, p. 317) School, and founded by Hsüan-Tsang in the seventh century. Vijñānavāda had been known previously, through the translations of Paramārtha, about 550, on which a school had been founded. The Fa-hsiang School did not maintain an independent lineage for many generations.

The chief *catholic sects* are:

(1) *T'ien-t'ai*, founded by Chih-I (538–97), classifies the *Sūtras* according to the period of Śākyamuni's life when they were supposed to have been spoken, and again according to the audiences to whom they were addressed. The final and perfect teaching is that of the *Lotus Sūtra* (*Saddharmapuṇḍarīka*), the chief Scripture of the T'ien-t'ai Sect. Chih-I's philosophical doctrines are a combination of Mādhyamika and Vijñānavāda. He established a system of meditative exercises which are fundamentally those of the Indian texts translated in Kumārajīva's time. They consist of correct posture, correct breathing, and contemplation of the breathing; compassionate, friendly, joyful and detached thoughts; Buddha-contemplation; and contemplation of sentences from the *Lotus Sūtra*. The T'ien-t'ai Sect has its own liturgy. This sect is the only one of the "catholic sects" to survive in China until the present day.

(2) *Hua-yen*, founded by Tu-Shun (557–640) and brought to completion by Fa-Tsang (643–712), is based on the *Avataṁsaka (Hua-yen) Sūtra*, which ranks highest

in the Hua-yen Sect's classification of the "five teachings". According to the *Avataṁsaka Sūtra*, Śākyamuni, immediately after enlightenment, entered the Ocean-Seal Trance (*Sāgaramudrā-samādhi*), in which he saw simultaneously all the teachings that he later preached and all the beings to whom he preached them. However, when he preached the content of this vision as the *Avataṁsaka Sūtra*, it proved too difficult for ordinary hearers, so Śākyamuni then preached a graded series of accommodated teachings.

The *Hua-yen Sūtra* and the Hua-yen Sect's system centre about the problem of the relation of events to principles, which is rather like the Western problem of the relation between particulars and universals. The chief Buddha of the *Avataṁsaka* is Vairocana, "The Radiant One". The metaphor of radiation permeates the whole *Sūtra*. Just as light pervades space, just as reflections can be multiplied endlessly, even so the Realm of Essence (*Dharmadhātu*) is all-pervasive, infinitely multiple and constantly a unity. It is like the great god Indra's net, in which each of the gems reflects all the others.

The contemplative exercises of the Hua-yen Sect are directed towards realizing the Realm of Essence, in which all events pervade one another.

This magnificent but highly intellectual teaching did not become a popular sect, like T'ien-t'ai, and after the ninth century its lineage was broken.

(3) *Chen-yen* is the Chinese version of Indian Mantrayāna. It was introduced about 720 by three Indian missionaries, Śubhakarasiṁha, Vajrabodhi and Amoghavajra. Its chief *Sūtras* are the *Mahāvairocana Sūtra* and the *Vajraśekhara Sūtra*. The Chen-yen Sect distinguishes ten stages of the religious life, from that of the worldling up to the Chen-yen stage. Members of this sect undergo a rite of consecration that resembles baptism. Chen-yen practice consists of contemplating symbolic representations of the five chief Buddhas, of their attendant Bodhisattvas and of a multitude of lesser holy personages. The symbols are visualized in the mind. Spells are chanted, with a symbolic meaning attached to each sound. Ritual gestures are executed, again with each act symbolizing a definite concept. These are the "three secrets" of thought, speech and body. The intricate symbolism of this sect is conjoined with a philosophy of cosmic structure that is said to be meaningful only to the initiated.

The Chen-yen Sect did not maintain a lineage in China for very long. In modern times it has been re-introduced from Japan, where it prospered remarkably.

The two *exclusive sects* – Pure Land, and Ch'an – differ markedly in several ways: one is pietist, the other is mystic; one stresses faith, the other insight; one requires absolute reliance on the word of a Scripture, the other relies not on Scriptures but on a special transmission from mind to mind. The typical devotees of the two sects also differ: the Pure Land devotee commonly belongs, in the Buddhist typology, to "the tribe of lust", while the Ch'an devotee belongs to "the tribe of wrath".

But these two sects also share certain features. Both reject the gradual course and ignore grades of teachings such as those of the T'ien-t'ai Sect. Both are essentially "sudden" teachings as contrasted with the "gradual" teachings. Both proclaim a way of infinite merit, in contrast to the ways of finite merit pursued by the ordinary devotee of other sects. Both radically simplified religion and thereby made it more intense. Both teachings prospered and attracted multitudes who were confused by the multiplicity of choice offered by the catholic sects.

The Pure Land Sect emerged with the rise of devotion to Amitābha about 500. The first patriarch of the sect, T'an-luan (476–542), received imperial honours and was given a large temple in which to promulgate faith in Amitābha. The second patriarch, Tao-ch'o, gave more than two hundred series of lectures on the *Contemplation of Amitābha Sūtra*, and built up a large following. The third patriarch, Shan-tao (?–662 or 681), preached in the capital for more than thirty years, converting both monks and laity. He was eccentric and saintly. His few writings – a commentary on the *Contemplation of Amitābha Sūtra*, a treatise on doctrine, and three liturgical manuals – have exerted a vast influence. Shan-tao brought the Pure Land doctrine to its definitive form and is thus the fountainhead of authority for all Amitābhists of China and Japan.

Shan-tao distinguished the Saintly Road, the way of Enlightenment through self-power, from the Easy Road, the way of Enlightenment through other-power, through reliance on Amitābha's grace. He held that, though the Saintly Road may have been possible for people in the period of the True Law, immediately after Śākyamuni's decease, or even in the subsequent period of the Counterfeit Law, it was not possible for people in the degenerate period of the Latter Law. Consequently, they had no alternative but to rely wholly on other-power. Shan-tao maintained that right faith is produced by Amitābha's name, co-operating with his saving power. The moment that the believer places his faith in Amitābha he attains a measure of enlightenment. The inward aspect of the Easy Road is faith, and the one outward act of value is calling on the sacred name, "Namo Amit'o Fo" (Glory to Amitābha Buddha). This is not an act of self-power, and the utterer gains no merit for himself. The only merit of any avail is infinite merit, and this belongs to Amitābha, from whom the believer merely receives the gift of well-being and the assurance of re-birth in Sukhāvatī (p. 329). All good works are useless unless preceded by faith, and when preceded by faith, they are no longer done to gain merit, but as spontaneous acts of thanksgiving for the gift of Amitābha's grace.

The Pure Land Sect maintained a lineage until the ninth century, after which it had so thoroughly permeated all Chinese Buddhism except Ch'an that it ceased to have any reason for independent transmission.

The Ch'an Sect is essentially a school of *prajñā* (wisdom or intuitive insight). The special features of its tradition are summed up in four phrases:

"A special transmission outside of doctrines."
"Not setting up the written word as an authority."
"Pointing directly at the heart of man."
"Seeing one's nature and becoming a Buddha."

The Ch'an teaching is transmitted directly from master to disciple. No verbal formulation can express its meaning, which can only be realized by realizing one's own true nature or "Buddha-nature". For this reason the lineage of masters is all-important, and the sayings and deeds of the masters are valuable signposts to later students searching for the ineffable realization.

The historical origins of the Ch'an Sect are obscure, and the sectarian history contains much legend. But this semi-legendary history deserves consideration both because it is a colourful part of the sect's heritage, and because it reveals certain facets of the Ch'an view of life.

Bodhidharma, the first patriarch, is said to have come from South India in about 520. He went to Nanking, and appeared before the devout Emperor of the state of Liang, who asked how much merit he had gained by building temples, copying scriptures and supporting monks. Bodhidharma said, "No merit at all, your majesty. All these are inferior deeds, which would cause their doer to be born in heaven or on earth again. They still show the traces of worldliness. They are like shadows following objects. A deed of true merit is full of pure wisdom and is beyond the grasp of conceptual thought. This sort of merit is not to be found by any worldly works." The Emperor asked, "What is the holy absolute truth?" Bodhidharma answered, "Great Emptiness, and there is nothing in it to be called holy." The Emperor asked, "Who are you that face me?" Bodhidharma said, "I do not know."

After Bodhidharma left the court at Nanking, he travelled North to the kingdom of Wei, where he sat for nine years in "wall contemplation". When a middle-aged man named Hui K'o came to beg instruction, Bodhidharma ignored him, though he stood waiting while snowdrifts piled up around him. Finally Hui K'o cut off his right arm with a sword and presented it to Bodhidharma, who then noticed him. Hui K'o asked, "My mind is not calm. Please calm it." Bodhidharma said, "Bring me your mind, and I will calm it." – "I have sought it for many years and still cannot get hold of it." – "There! It is calmed!" said Bodhidharma. Later he passed his teaching to Hui K'o, who became the second patriarch.

Seng-ts'an, the third patriarch, received the teaching from Hui K'o. When he first came to Hui K'o, he asked, "I am suffering from a disease. Please cleanse me of my sins." Hui K'o said, "Bring your sins here and I will cleanse you of them." – "Though I seek my sins, I cannot find them." – "There! I have cleansed you of sins. You should now take refuge in Buddha, Dharma and Saṃgha." – "O Master, as I stand before you I see a representative of the Saṃgha. But tell me, what are Buddha and Dharma?" – "Mind is Buddha. Mind is Dharma. Buddha and Dharma are not two. The same is true of Saṃgha." Seng-ts'an said, "Today at last I realize that sins are neither within nor outside nor in between. Mind, Buddha and Dharma are alike and are not-two."

Tao-hsin, the fourth patriarch, lived in obscurity like his predecessor. At this time the Ch'an tradition was not yet a sect, nor even a movement.

Hung-jen, the fifth patriarch, had over five hundred disciples. His two chief pupils were Shen-hsiu, whose school flourished in North China for a while before dying out, and Hui-neng, whose lineage constituted the later Ch'an Sect.

Hui-neng (637–713), the sixth patriarch, is the most important figure in the history of the Ch'an Sect. During his lifetime it emerged from obscurity and became a distinct sect. He came to Hung-jen, the fifth patriarch, as an unlettered youth from South China. Hung-jen sent him to pound rice in the monastery granary. After a few months, Hung-jen announced that he would give his patriarchal insignia – Bodhidharma's robe and begging bowl – and the patriarchal succession to anyone who could prove that he truly understood the Dharma. Shen-hsiu, the most learned of the disciples, wrote a stanza on the outer wall of the meditation hall:

"This body is the Bodhi tree;
This mind is a bright mirror's stand.
Polish it unceasingly,
And do not let the dust fall on it."

During the night, Hui-neng had a boy write up another verse:

> "In enlightenment there is no tree;
> The bright mirror is not a stand.
> Since there is really nothing at all,
> Where could dust alight?"

Hung-jen was impressed with Hui-neng's insight. He secretly gave him his insignia and succession and sent him away from the monastery. After fifteen years in seclusion among the hills Hui-neng appeared in Kuang-tung province and commenced preaching. He acquired many disciples, and the five chief of these established lineages of their own. Two of these lineages have survived till the present day.

However uncertain the historical origins of the Ch'an Sect, the affinities of its teaching are clear. Though "Ch'an" is the Chinese form of Sanskrit *dhyāna* ("meditation"), it is not really a school of meditation, but a school of *prajñā* or intuitive insight. The lofty, paradoxical utterances of the Ch'an masters and their assertions that great merit is that which is filled with insight, are in the spirit of the *Perfection of Wisdom Sūtras*. Most ideas in eighth-century Ch'an writings are simply culled from the Mahāyāna *Sūtras*. What is distinctively Ch'an is the fresh, incisive tone and the unwavering focus of attention on the realization of insight.

The Ch'an Sect is radical in its exclusiveness, and it exhibits a manner unlike that of other sects. But it is not radical otherwise. It has kept the monastic system, though it has its own monastic rule which requires manual labour of the monks. It has not discarded rituals or any of the normal appurtenances of Chinese Buddhism.

The special Ch'an contemplative exercise, the contemplation of "old cases" or "documents", grew up several centuries after Hui-neng. The student is given some old saying. He then sits and puzzles at this riddle, and periodically returns to the master, who examines him. Here are a few of the anecdotes about old masters that form the substance of Ch'an study.

(1) Chao-chou was asked whether a dog possesses Buddha-nature. He said, "No."

(2) The master Huai-jang asked Ma-Tsu, who was sitting in meditation, "What are you doing?" – "I wish to become a Buddha."

The master picked up a brick and began grinding it with a stone. The student asked what he was doing, and the master replied, "I am trying to polish this brick into a mirror." – "But no amount of polishing will ever make a mirror out of a brick." – "And no amount of sitting cross-legged will ever make a Buddha out of you." –

"What am I to do, then?" – "It is like driving a cart. When it doesn't move, do you whip the cart or the ox? Are you sitting cross-legged to practise meditation, or to become a Buddha? If it is to practise meditation, that does not consist of sitting or lying down. If it is to become a Buddha, the Buddha has no fixed form. You cannot take hold of him or let him go. To think that you can obtain Buddhahood by sitting is simply to kill the Buddha, and until you give up the idea that you can so obtain it, you won't come near the truth."

(3) Master and pupil were out walking, when a flock of wild geese flew over. The master asked, "Where are they flying?" – "They have flown away, sir." The master seizing his pupil's nose and twisting it violently, said, "You say they have flown away, but all the same, they have been here since the very beginning." The pupil was suddenly enlightened. Next day, when the master was about to lecture to the assembly, this pupil stepped up and began to roll up the matting. The master then came down from his seat and retired from the hall. Later, he sent for this pupil and asked him to explain himself. The pupil said, "Yesterday you pulled my nose, and it hurt." – "And where were your thoughts wandering then?" – "It doesn't hurt any more."

There is nothing in these anecdotes that cannot be explained in terms of Indian Mahāyāna doctrine. Yet, on the word of the Ch'an masters, such an explanation does not constitute a solution to the riddle. This is solved only when it is "realized" in a sudden, integral illumination. In the words of Seng-ts'an, the third patriarch:

> "The more words, the more reflection, the less you
> understand the way;
> Cut off words, cut off reflection, and you penetrate
> everywhere.
> Events in the void before you all spring from
> mistaken notions;
> It's useless to seek for the true – you must just quiet
> your notions."

Buddhism in Chinese Society

Buddhism arrived in China with a world-view and a set of institutions that were incompatible with many parts of the native culture. Consequently its progress was marked by conflict with the indigenous religious tradition and with indigenous social values. The Buddhist attitude towards this conflict was complex. On the one hand, Taoism and the "Confucian" tradition were respected and acknowledged as the way fitting to those whose preconditions did not enable them to be Buddhist. On the other hand, promulgating the Dharma meant doing everything possible to convert outsiders. Yet taking refuge in the Three Jewels in no way committed the convert to renouncing his former beliefs except where they conflicted sharply with Buddhist doctrine. Within the Buddhist fold there was a great latitude of belief and practice, despite vigorous controversy between the advocates of different ways, so that no creedal formulation could divide the outsiders sharply from the insiders. Thus Buddhism demanded exclusive allegiance, but did not enforce it, with the result that it did not obliterate its rivals.

Buddhism's chief *rival* was organized Taoism. The two religions are similar in some ways. The superstitious sections of both are concerned with magic powers, miracles and spells for the fulfilment of mundane wishes. The *Tao* of the philosophers resembles Buddhist *Suchness* (p. 317) in that it is equally inconceivable and immeasurable. Both religions preach detachment and rising above worldly affairs. But the differences are great. Buddhism is a religion of universal salvation, while Taoism does not enjoin action for the benefit of others. Buddhist doctrine starts from an analysis of the mind. Taoist doctrine centres on a cosmology. In spite of extensive mutual influence the two religions are incompatible and have remained in opposition throughout the ages.

Buddhism's most dangerous *enemy*, however, has been, not Taoism, but the secular, this-worldly culture of the literate classes. The basic philosophy of the literati was an ideal of worldly happiness in a well-run state, where everyone fulfils his social duties. It is everyone's duty to raise a family and to support his aged relatives. It is the duty of the governing class to take office and work for the administration. It is the duty of the other classes to produce goods and services, and pay taxes. Buddhism ran counter to these ideals. It led people to live as celibates and leave the family circle. It led them to live a life of poverty where they produced no commodities and could pay no taxes. Furthermore, it required a substantial outlay of public funds to build temples, create works of art, publish scriptures and support monks and nuns. Buddhism was considered even more radically subversive: it made light of success in this world and turned men's thoughts away from production and administration towards spiritual realms.

The central dilemma of Chinese Buddhism has always been that its élite comes chiefly from the literate classes, who are the custodians of this tradition that is fundamentally inimical to Buddhism. In the past the educated Chinese spent his youth studying "The Classics" (p. 366). This was not merely a literary education, but a systematic moulding of character and inculcation of values. It imparted a strong sense of history and of the importance

of human affairs, but it emphasized the concrete and social at the expense of the abstract and rational. It was strongly moralistic, but intensely mundane. The Chinese who remained or became Buddhist did so in spite of this education.

Every government of China has drawn its administrators from the literati. Consequently, official support for Buddhism has depended on the goodwill of men whose tradition is antipathetic to Buddhism. The apparatus of the Chinese state remained secular even during the most religious periods, so that political careers were seldom possible for monks. The state supported but controlled the Saṃgha, so that though myriads of Chinese have been Buddhist, China has never really been a Buddhist state.

Buddhism in Modern China

The present century has seen a re-awakening of Chinese Buddhism under the stimulus of the same Western influences that provoked the rest of the Chinese revolution. This has taken the form of renewed intellectual movements, reformation of the discipline and education of the monks, formation of vigorous laymen's associations, resumption of contact with Japanese and South-East Asian Buddhism and a resurgence of the missionary impulse. Buddhist book and magazine publication has flourished. Several modern Ch'an masters are currently maintaining the old tradition. There is a Buddhist youth movement.

This renaissance, like the other achievements of twentieth-century China, has taken place in the midst of civil wars, foreign invasions, political oppression and intellectual confusion occasioned by the impact of modern knowledge. It is inevitable that its successes should be limited and that the movement should be thwarted at many points.

The career of one of the reformers gives some notion of the character of this renovation movement. T'ai-hsü (1890–1947) became a monk in his middle teens, at a time when the Manchu dynasty was crumbling. He studied, meditated and travelled, as is the custom for young monks. When he was twenty, he met a revolutionary monk, who showed him writings calling for the renovation of Buddhism and for Buddhist participation in the national renaissance. T'ai-hsü was convinced and became an associate of the revolutionary leaders in South China. After the defeat of one revolutionary army one of T'ai-hsü's fellow monks was executed by the Manchus, and he himself was sought by government soldiers. Shortly afterwards the Republic was established, and the work of the revolution began in earnest. T'ai-hsü spent

PLATE 87. Yün-Kang: interior of Cave VI, Shansi, second half of the fifth century A.D.

PLATE 88. Adoring Bodhisattva from Tun Huang, eighth century A.D.
(*Fogg Art Museum, Harvard University*)

PLATE 89. Kuan Yin: wood sculpture with colour and gold leaf, twelfth – thirteenth century A.D. (*William Rockhill Nelson Gallery of Art, Kansas City*)

PLATE 90. Maitreya Bodhisattva: first quarter of sixth century A.D.
(*Museum of Fine Arts, Boston*)

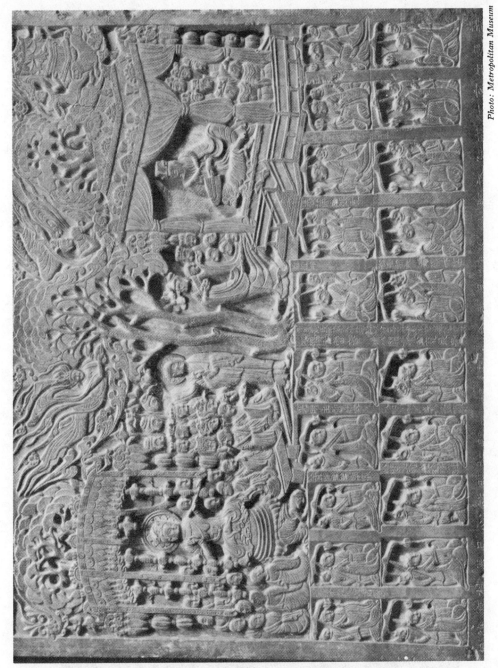

PLATE 91. Mañjuśrī goes to see Vimalakīrti: detail from Chinese Buddhist stele, Wei Dynasty, dated 533–543. (*Metropolitan Museum of Art, New York*)

Photo: Guimet

PLATE 92. Prabhūtaratna and Śākyamuni: gilt-bronze shrines.
(*Musée Guimet, Paris*)

PLATE 93. The Sixth Patriarch tearing up the Sūtras:
ink painting on paper by Liang K'ai, thirteenth century.
(*Takanaru Mitsui, Tokyo*)

PLATE 94. Amida coming over the mountain: painting on silk by an unknown artist of the Kamakura period, thirteenth century A.D.

a period of organizing lay associations and trying to revive the spirit of the monasteries. He failed and retired to a small monastery for some years of study and thinking, during which he wrote the plans for his next programme of action.

Throughout his life T'ai-hsü was both a radical and a traditionalist. He was a tireless worker in education and welfare work and contributed substantially to national life. His great hope was that the Buddhist religion could convert the world into a Pure Land. From his early twenties until his death he wrote continuously on every subject that came to his attention. His published works fill more than sixty volumes. Like other leaders of the Chinese revolution, he utilized the enormous prestige of the written word in Chinese culture.

His major concerns were:

(1) Reform of the Saṃgha – removing the gap between laity and monks, restoring discipline and improving education and morale in the monasteries. To this end he founded dozens of societies, colleges, schools, journals and leagues, many of which perished for lack of leadership and funds, but some of which survived. T'ai-hsü experimented tirelessly with ways to turn the Chinese Saṃgha into a community of Bodhisattvas.

(2) Welfare work. T'ai-hsü, with all his teaching and organizing activities, found time to work in prisons and organize a medical clinic. During the Sino-Japanese war he exhorted all Chinese Buddhists to train for civil defence, army medical work, and famine and disaster relief. The Nationalist government conferred a citation on him for his work in World War II.

(3) Saving the world through Buddhism. He came to realize that, since Western culture dominated contemporary China, he could not restore Chinese Buddhism without settling accounts with Western culture. He studied Western knowledge through Chinese translations of Western works and discussed all sorts of topics with Western-educated Chinese. He attempted to reconcile Buddhist doctrine and Western science, a task in which he was hampered by an inadequate knowledge of the latter. He approved of modern Western Buddhist studies, though on occasion they conflicted with many of his most cherished beliefs. As a means towards placing Buddhism in a dominant position in the contemporary world, T'ai-hsü ardently promoted international exchange between Buddhist countries. He went to Japan in 1924, where he established contact with many leading Buddhists. Later he arranged the exchange of Chinese and Sinhalese monks and promoted the study of Pali in China. He was also interested in Buddhist missionary work in the West, an interest which his followers still

maintain. In 1928, with subvention from Chiang Kai-shek's Nationalist government, he visited France, Germany, England and the United States, where he lectured on Buddhism and met a number of intellectual leaders. In Paris, he explained his mission in this way: "Europe is now rich in the human material for saints, but deficient in the Way of holiness. We Chinese possess the Way of the saints, but are poor in the human material. My idea in coming to Europe is to find the people with talent for saintliness and give them the Way of the saints."

(4) Reviving Buddhist scholarship. He was learned in all the traditional Chinese schools, but he did not adopt any one of them. His own teaching was a harmony of elements selected from each. He was determined to harmonize Buddhism with modern learning, with other religions and with the needs of the times, but he was not a syncretist and viewed reconciliation as a matter of finding the right place for everything. In his view Mahāyāna Buddhism should be the *religion* of China, while Taoism and the Confucian tradition should be part of culture and general ethos. His own interpretation of Buddhism remained flexible, and every few years he made a new version of his classification of sects and teachings. He encouraged the revival of the study of the Fa-hsiang School and the reintroduction of the Chen-yen Sect from Japan, though he disliked sectarianism.

T'ai-hsü died about a year before the Communist victory on the mainland. When the remnants of the Nationalist régime fled to Formosa, many of T'ai-hüs's disciples went with them. They now form part of the flourishing Buddhist movement on Formosa, where they continue to publish the magazine founded by T'ai-hsü in 1920.

The Communist régime has permitted some Buddhist institutions to function, on condition that they collaborate. They are thus forced by circumstances into some degree of compromise, like the Christian churches in the European satellites. The "Land Reform Laws" permit monasteries to keep as much of their land – the one asset that tided them through the decades of revolution – as the monks can farm. Failure to deliver their quota of crops involves forfeiture of land. The city monasteries are required to undertake light manufacturing industries. At the same time the government is spending money on exploring old Buddhist sites and has taken steps to conserve buildings and books and works of art that are national treasures. Buddhist delegations are sent to international meetings. The régime carefully fosters the impression abroad that it is well disposed towards Buddhism.

Whether Chinese Buddhism survives depends on how long the Communist régime retains its present character, and whether the Saṁgha survives. Chinese Buddhism has survived several periods of proscription when the Saṁgha was disbanded, its property confiscated and its literature and art destroyed. But none of these periods has lasted for more than about a decade, and so reconstruction has been possible. The Chinese Communists are not destroying the cultural appurtenances of Buddhism – its art and literature, but they are cutting at the economic roots of the Saṁgha and preventing the monks from carrying out the functions of the homeless life. The survival of Buddhism in Mainland China depends on a liberalization of the régime within the next two decades.

Another requisite for the survival of Chinese Buddhism is that China should get out of the grip of poverty. The maintenance and propagation of a religion requires a disposable surplus which has not been available in China for some time. Both the Nationalist and the Communist governments have worked to renovate the Chinese economy, but the problem is enormous and not amenable to rapid solutions.

No other religion is likely to take the place of Buddhism in China, and there is no reason to think that the aspirations which have prompted Chinese to follow the Buddhist course in the past will not continue to arise. Taoism as a religion would appear to be as good as dead. The old secularist tradition is dead, and the chief enemy of Buddhism is the new secular tradition. If Buddhism survives until China is freer and more prosperous, it will still have to settle with historical and natural science. Some of the Buddhist tradition would not survive this trial by science, but it is reasonable to hope that everything true and valuable would remain.

JAPAN

Though Japanese Buddhism does not differ very much from Chinese Buddhism in doctrine, in institutions and social role it is as unlike Chinese Buddhism as Japanese society is unlike Chinese society. It was intimately connected with the introduction of civilization to Japan and with the development of national institutions and values. It has shared the historical experience of the Japanese people and, thanks to the relative soundness of Japan's economy when the country was opened to westernization, Japanese Buddhism has been better preserved and has met the impact of the modern world more successfully than Chinese Buddhism.

Two features of Japanese society have conditioned the history of Buddhism in that country. One is security from foreign interference, combined with receptivity to foreign influence. Japan converted itself to Buddhism, just as it converted itself to Chinese culture. The other feature is the hierarchical social structure, in which the loyalty of vassal to lord is paramount, while the cleavages between the domains of rival lords are clear-cut and enduring. In Japan the Buddhist sects are corporations owning land and temples, conferring their own ordinations and requiring the exclusive loyalty of their followers. This allegiance is often hereditary and gives Japanese Buddhism a durability that it would not have on the basis of mere personal conviction. Sectarian traditions and properties are guarded with the kind of fidelity that was the highest civic virtue of feudal Japan.

Buddhism introduced art to Japan, and dominated the aesthetic life of the nation until the seventeenth century. A Japanese bias has been apparent from the first, a tendency towards grace and ease, colour and gaiety. Japanese Buddhist art excels in narrative and human interest. It conveys a warm and intimate mood and shuns the grotesque and discordant.

The two periods when Chinese Buddhism influenced Japan most profoundly were T'ang (approximately 600 to 900) and Southern Sung (approximately 1150 to 1250). Features of these glorious periods that have not persisted in China are preserved in Japanese Buddhism.

Buddhism first came to Japan by way of Korea. Between 550 and 600, various Korean princes sent gifts of images, Sūtras and missionaries to the Japanese imperial court. These presents were accompanied by the assurance that Buddhism was a talisman to ensure national welfare. The fortunes of the faith fluctuated for several decades according to the interpretations that were placed on such public calamities as plagues, and according to the fortunes of the noble houses struggling for power around the throne. When finally the pro-Buddhist clan won control of the imperial house, Buddhism was definitely accepted. Scriptures, art and craftsmen were brought from Korea and China, and Japanese monks were sent abroad to study. During the seventh century, under the devout and statesmanlike regent, Prince Shōtoku, and under a series of devout sovereigns, Buddhism became part of the state apparatus. Temples were founded, ordination of clergy promoted, and ceremonies performed publicly to further national good fortune. The four "classical schools" were introduced, and of these, the Fa-hsiang (p. 330, Japanese, Hossō) flourished, and acquired several magnificent temples.

During the eighth century Buddhist monks played a prominent part in the imperial administration. This was a period of political progress, during which T'ang institutions were adapted to Japanese conditions, and the imperial power reached out more and more into the provinces. Monks served as engineers in building roads, bridges, dikes and irrigation systems. They also served as scribes and clerks. In return the imperial power promoted Buddhism in the provinces, by decreeing that each should establish "a monastery for twenty monks, a convent for ten nuns and a seven-storey pagoda". Each province was ordered to possess a copy of the *Prajñāpāramitā Sūtra* and a sixteen-foot Buddha-image.

During this period the Hua-yen (pp. 330-1, Japanese, Kegon) Sect was introduced from China. It rose rapidly to an influential position. In 752 a colossal image of Vairocana, the chief Buddha of the *Hua-yen Sūtra*, was dedicated at Nara. In the political philosophy of the times Vairocana represented the all-pervasive authority of the Emperor, and the "realm-of-events-mutually-pervasive" represented the unity of Japanese society.

The "Nara" sects were rusticated when the capital was changed from Nara to Kyoto about the beginning of the ninth century. During the Heian Period (approximately 800 to 1150) influence at court accrued to two newly imported sects, *Tendai* (Chinese, T'ien-t'ai, p. 330) and *Shingon* (Chinese, Chen-yen, p. 331).

Dengyō (767–822), founder of the Tendai Sect, built a monastery in the forests of Mount Hiei, near Kyoto, while he was still a young man. Then, between 802 and 805, he studied in China, where he received the T'ien-t'ai teaching. When he returned, he built up great prestige for his sect, a feat facilitated by Mount Hiei's nearness to the new capital. When in 827 Mount Hiei received the right to ordain monks, hitherto possessed by only a few monasteries in Nara and in the remoter provinces, the Tendai Sect rapidly expanded. In its heyday Mount Hiei housed thirty thousand monks in three thousand temples. The monasteries kept armed retainers and sometimes enforced their demands on the government by threat of arms. At the same time scholarship and art flourished on Mount Hiei. Tendai was even more catholic than its Chinese parent, which accounts for the fact that all the new sects of the twelfth and thirteenth centuries were founded by Tendai monks.

Kōbō (774–835), founder of the Shingon Sect, studied in China between 804 and 807, where he received the Chen-yen teaching. On his return he founded the monastic community on Mount Koya about fifty miles south of Kyoto. He was influential at court and used his diplomatic talent to reconcile the Buddhist sects with each other and with Shintō. He set up a popular school and is said to have invented the cursive syllabary of forty-seven letters. He was also famous as a calligrapher. He is a popular figure in Japanese folklore. According to folk belief he is merely sleeping in his tomb on Mount Koya and will rise up again someday.

The Shingon Sect, with its rich ceremonies and ornate art, contributed much to the artistic life of the Heian period. Like Tendai, it was extremely catholic, so that doctrinal differences between the two sects were diminished by mutual borrowing. Shingon has prospered continuously until the present day, and it now has more than fifteen million adherents.

At the beginning of the Heian period, culture, and hence Buddhism, was the property of the court and the aristocracy, a tiny minority of the populous nation. During this period the provinces became increasingly important politically, as economic power shifted to the provincial nobility. Thus, by the middle of the twelfth century, there was a new class of gentry ready to dominate Japanese cultural and religious life.

Between 1150 and 1300 Buddhism became the religion of the Japanese people. New sects, founded by popular saint-reformers, spread rapidly throughout all classes and regions. These sects, unlike Tendai and Shingon, were exclusive and fervently propagandist. Their teachings were simple and were expressed in lively language, appealing to the hearts of soldiers, farmers and fishermen. The Buddhist art of this period conveys this earnestness. Painters now saw majesty in themes where their predecessors had seen only beauty.

Hōnen (1133–1212), the first of the saint-reformers, became a Tendai monk in his boyhood, studied on Mount Hiei, and in his early manhood went into seclusion to study and meditate. He read through the Chinese *Tripitaka* five times and became famous for his learning. Yet he continued to be troubled by a sense of his sinfulness and a conviction that he and his contemporaries could not reach Enlightenment. Eventually, at the age of forty-three, he reached the conviction that only complete reliance on Amitābha could save him. He began to teach his faith humbly and unostentatiously, but with extraordinary effect. He made converts of Emperor, Regent, noblemen, monks and commoners. The old sects opposed him, since his teaching of simple reliance on Amitābha would make their learning superfluous. At one time Hōnen was sent into exile, and some of his followers were executed. Throughout favour and disgrace his life was one of patient and kindly simplicity. As he wrote, "Those who believe in the power of calling the Buddha's name, though they may have thoroughly studied all the doctrines that Śākyamuni taught during his lifetime, should behave like a simple man of the people who cannot read a word, or like an ignorant nun, and without giving themselves airs of wisdom, should simply call whole-heartedly on the name of Amitābha."

Hōnen's chief disciples continued his teaching, and in due course his followers came to constitute the Jodo Sect ("Jodo" means "Pure Land").

Shinran (1173–1262), one of Hōnen's favourite disciples, is outstanding not only as the founder of what is now the largest sect in Japan (Jodoshinshu, the True Pure Land Sect), but because he abandoned monasticism and returned to the household life, without renouncing his religious vocation. Apparently with Hōnen's approval, he married a young noblewoman, after a vision in which Kwannon (Kuan-yin, p. 329) revealed to him that he should marry. Shinran's idea was that observing celibacy and rules of diet are marks of reliance on self-power, and that the *Vinaya* fosters pride. He was banished at the same time as Hōnen, and afterwards lived most of his long life in the provinces. His grandson carried on the lineage of his teaching, and this lineage has passed down through his descendants until the present day.

Nichiren (1222–82), founder of a "reformed Tendai" sect, the Nichiren Sect, was the son of a fisherman. He entered a monastery in boyhood, and by the time that he was thirty-one he had thought out his message and proclaimed it so militantly that he was expelled from his monastery. He declared that only the *Lotus Sūtra* should be worshipped. He sent a memorial, "Establishing Right and Making the Country Secure", to the Regent, insisting that there must be a national religion and that all other sects should be suppressed. He said: "The Pure Land Sect is the Everlasting Hell; Zen (Chinese, Ch'an) devotees are demons; Shingon devotees are ruining the nation; the Vinaya Sect are traitors to the country." The Regent's government was shocked by this intolerance, and the old sects responded by having him banished and chased from place to place. However, Nichiren predicted the attempted Mongol invasion of 1274 years before it happened. This, and his prophetic declamation of the evils of the times, attracted a substantial following. The Nichiren Sect is still quite large today and retains the pugnacious spirit of its founder.

The Chinese Ch'an Sect (Ch'an is pronounced "zen" in Japanese) was known in Japan during the ninth century, but did not take root until around 1200; Eisai (1141–1215) studied in China and brought back the Lin-chi (Rinzai) branch of Ch'an. Eisai's pupil, Dōgen (1200–53), brought the Ts'ao-t'ung (Sōtō) branch of Ch'an over to Japan. Both branches still flourish in Japan, and are reckoned as separate sects.

Zen appealed to the military class, which liked its austere tone and the forceful simplicity of its doctrine. As the great Zen temples were centres of learning and education during the period of civil wars from 1300 to 1600, this connection exerted a civilizing influence on the military at a time when they stood in need of refinement. The best painters of this period were Zen monks. Trade between Japan and China came under control of the Zen monasteries, which ran their own shipping lines. Among other imports Zen brought Neo-Confucian philosophy to Japan.

During this age of civil strife Zen was almost the only sect that did not maintain a standing army and fortify its temples. Originally the other sects took such measures for protection against marauding armies, but in time they used them to found feudal estates. Sometimes whole provinces were under the rule of a sect. This phase ended after the destruction of the fortress temples on Mount Hiei in the late sixteenth century.

The Tokugawa régime (1603–1868) attempted to eliminate civil strife by assigning all institutions a sphere and forbidding them to move outside it. Christianity, introduced in the sixteenth century, was banned as a subversive force and exterminated. The Buddhist sects were forbidden to proselytize or to contend in any way. All families were required to register at their local temple, no matter what sect it belonged to. The result was that Buddhism became an established "church", prevented from either growth or collapse. It is evidence of its deep roots that it survived this period and regained its vitality after it was disestablished by the modernizing politicians after the 1868 Restoration.

Buddhism in modern Japan has exhibited its traditional closeness to the nation's life. It has responded to Western influence by learning both from Christianity and secular scholarship. Modern welfare services are operated by the various sects. In the new Buddhist universities modern critical techniques are applied to the study of Buddhist doctrine and history. Pali, Sanskrit and Tibetan are studied, and contemporary Western currents of thought are debated. The principal old temples are museums of national art as well as centres of worship, and they draw multitudes of pilgrims. The smaller temples are in the charge of hereditary clergy; all sects now permit their priests to marry. There are all kinds of lay organizations from Sunday schools to contemplative fellowships. There are quite a few popular Buddhist magazines. The different sects publish "Bibles" containing their fundamental *Sūtras* and most esteemed sacred writings and hymns.

Modern Japanese Buddhism is strongly internationalist. Young Buddhist scholars go abroad to study Sanskrit in India or theology and philosophy in Europe and America. The dignitaries of the chief sects often tour Europe and America, encouraging the numerous congregations among Japanese immigrants in U.S.A., Canada and Brazil, and familiarizing themselves with the Western world. There has been some missionary activity in North America. Japanese missionary work in Manchuria, Formosa and China dates back to the 1870s, but was halted at the end of World War II.

In modern Japan Buddhism's rivals are the Neo-Shintō cults and Christianity. Neo-Shintō is the greater menace, since its proliferating sects all have the chauvinistic cachet of being made in Japan, and most of them require much less adaptation from the convert than Christianity does. Some have borrowed much from Buddhism, though they remain primarily faith-healing cults.

Japan is predominantly a Buddhist country. Furthermore, it is the richest and best educated Buddhist country. It has retained its classical culture and has assimilated modern civilization with outstanding skill. Though the modern manner assumed by Japanese Buddhism sometimes persuades observers that it has exchanged the otherworldliness of traditional Buddhism for a modern worldliness, the roots of the old tradition are too deep to be shaken by tactical adaptations. The ethnic trait of loyalty equals that of versatility.

At present Buddhism in Japan is about as securely entrenched as Christianity in England. There is good reason to assume that it will continue to thrive and to meet the challenge of circumstances, though its degree of success cannot be predicted.

8. Shintō

by G. BOWNAS

INTRODUCTION

It would seem certain that three racial strains have contributed to the formation of the Japanese people: one indigenous – the Ainu – and two stemming from the Asiatic mainland and the southern islands. Of the latter two, one stream seems to have emigrated by way of Korea in the north, the other from Southern China and the islands of South-East Asia. These different strands have left their mark on the culture, language, and mythology of the Japanese people and their national religion, Shintō. Thus from the outset a certain dualism appears in Shintō and its mythology which both mirrors its ritual and beliefs and forms their basis. This dualism reappears throughout the history of Shintō. Thus we find a formal, official, and national cult existing alongside an ill-assorted but often illuminating body of popular folk practices, the ordinary, everyday faith beside the hidden and the occult. Again the amalgamation of Shintō with Buddhism produced Ryōbu Shintō, which was to last for over a thousand years. Today the old-established State or Shrine Shintō rubs shoulders with new growths generally known as Sect Shintō.

Perhaps the motley origin of the Japanese is partly responsible for the eclectic nature of their thinking. Such eclecticism is apparent in many other aspects of Japanese civilization including religion. Only in certain ultra-nationalistic phases in Japanese history has eclecticism been condemned as "deviation" and charged with the crime of polluting "our own pure and sacred white with the dust and the dirt of the alien". It was fortunate that, when Buddhism came, it was in its Mahāyāna form which was then adopting an easy-going attitude on questions of doctrine, and was, wherever possible, eager to effect a syncretism.

This eclectic tendency of the Japanese mind does not always produce results. Indeed in the history of Japanese thought we rarely find any aptitude for abstract reasoning or interest in philosophical speculation. Whatever purely intellectual achievements there may be, have been due to Buddhist or Confucian influences, while the purely indigenous thinking has tended towards the practical and realistic. Its approach to any given problem has often been intuitive, and its stress has been on the simple and the natural. Jiun, an eighteenth-century Buddhist priest who also wrote authoritatively on Shintō, argued, "China is a country artificially established, whereas the way of our country is purely natural. This pure naturalness, this spontaneity, we call Shintō."[1] The Japanese is never happier than when he lives close to nature, but his mind has often been unable to correlate or develop the impressions to which this awareness of, and sympathy with, nature has made it so sensitive.

Throughout their history, the Japanese have been imitative, yet, in their way, not uninventive; they have often applied strokes of inventive genius to transform what they have borrowed, thereby producing something eminently suited to the new environment, something that is very much more than the mere sum of the borrowed components. Finally, Japan can claim a long tradition of toleration, except at such periods when an epidemic of jingoism has shortened tempers. Such tolerance is no doubt partly due to the eclectic tendencies we have mentioned, and these in turn reflect the motley make-up of the race. The two systems of thought which have most influenced Japan both have a similar tradition: Buddhism has generally shown tolerance, and Confucianism, itself at first an amalgamation of a number of streams, found few witches to hunt until the doctrinal hardening of the Sung period.

The word *Shintō* is the Chinese reading of two characters meaning "The Way of the Gods" – the way of the *Kami*, the native and indigenous spirits, as distinct from the deities of Buddhism, whose introduction from

[1] Katō Genchi, *Shintō Studies of Jiun and Motoori* (1938), pp. 9–24.

China in the middle of the sixth century is said to have created the need for a distinguishing term. The first occurrence of the term, significantly, was in the eighties of the sixth century, less than thirty years after the traditional date of the introduction of Buddhism into Japan.

The "Way", *tō* in Japanese, is the *Tao* of Taoism; *Shin* (read as *Kami* if the character occurs in isolation) is in origin related to another word *Kami* meaning "upper" or "above", according to the most generally accepted etymology. The arguments of Japanese linguists about the derivation of *Kami* have been long and varied; and it would take too much space even to summarize them here. But we should note that the word is associated by many theorists with terms meaning "awesome" or "dreadful", or again it is explained as signifying something with a "strange and mysterious power". One theory would link *Kami* with *mana*, a term common to the whole of the Pacific, a supernatural power or mysterious majesty, sensed as a result of some unusual emotional stimulus, rather than comprehended by the intellect. The very nature of the mental make-up of the Japanese as well as their physical origins would seem to favour this theory; yet, there is evidence of considerable northern influence also on Shintō belief and ritual, so that the truth would seem to lie somewhere in between. Motoori, the great eighteenth-century Shintō revivalist and scholar of the native classics (see p. 363) seems to have combined both lines of interpretation in his statement: "Anything whatsoever which was outside of the ordinary, which possessed superior power, or which was awe-inspiring, was called *Kami*. Thus, *Kami* are of many kinds: some are noble, some base; some are strong, some weak; some are good, some bad." Anything then, man or beast or plant, organic or inorganic, which was out of the ordinary – an unusually shaped tree, an especially large rock, albinism in man or animal – was invested with *Kami* capacity, because of its very unnatural quality. Such *Kami* potentiality was normally benign, for Japan's religious sentiments have mostly been those of love and gratitude rather than of fear. The purpose of religious observance was to praise and thank, and thus to ensure the continued benignity of the powers, quite as much as to placate and mollify if anger turned such normal benignity into malevolence. The great majority of these *Kami* were but vaguely conceived, just as their collective name, "superior and extraordinary beings", is less precise than our "divinity" or "deity". It is in the case of the exceptions, such as Amaterasu, the Sun Goddess, or Susanoo, the Withering Wind of Summer, that there occurs a tendency to anthropomorphism. In addi-

tion, there was no iconographical tradition to limit these vague conceptions until Buddhism, and the Chinese art that came with it, provided models to be copied and gave Shintō, although in a restricted field, an incentive to image-making.

PROTO-SHINTŌ: SOURCES AND MYTHS

Although Shintō possesses no sacred canon as such, the mythology of the "Age of the *Kami*" sections of the two earliest literary texts extant, *Kojiki* ("Record of Ancient Matters") and *Nihon Shoki* ("The Written Chronicles of Japan"), has become the broad basis of the credo of the Shintō believer, as well as an arsenal for nationalist propaganda, and the text-book which, until the occupation reforms after the Second World War, was used by every teacher for Japan's early history. *Kojiki* and *Nihon Shoki* were produced within a decade of each other in the early years of the eighth century. *Kojiki* is written primarily in Japanese and may well be a written form of an oral tradition jealously preserved among the court officials who were blind and responsible for ritual and music. *Nihon Shoki* uses the Chinese language, and this linguistic medium hides many alterations of detail made to bring the traditions into line with accepted Chinese norms: eight, for example, the Japanese "sacred" number (a greengrocer, strangely enough, is an "eight hundred shopman"), disappears frequently in favour of nine. However that may be, a long period of oral tradition preceded the actual writing down of both texts, and each of them, in the myths it records, preserves features and ideas of the earlier form of Shintō, some of which have persisted right through the long period of amalgamation with Buddhism up to the present day. Some of these features are attested in reports recorded in the Chinese dynastic histories, some five centuries before they were written down in Japan.

The first section of the creation myths is thickly overlaid with Chinese borrowings. In the beginning, heaven and earth, that is, positive and negative, were not separated. They formed a chaotic egg-shaped mass of indeterminate dimensions which contained the life principle; the purer and clearer part ascended gradually, forming heaven, while the grosser and heavier element settled down and subsequently became earth. As Motoori, keen as ever on ferreting out foreign influences, remarked, there was too much talk of abstract principles here, too much positive and negative in place of the male and female that the Japanese would prefer to use.

But the theogonic section is less tainted with such influences. "A certain thing, in form like a reed-shoot, was produced between heaven and earth. This became transformed into a god and was called Kunitokotachi no Mikoto, the 'One Who Established the Land Eternal'" (*Nihongi*, p. 2ff.). Six generations later, by spontaneous creation, came Izanagi and Izanami, the "Male Who Invites" and the "Female Who Invites", and, from this point, the creation can be explained in terms of sexual generation, for this divine creator-couple married.

Next, the islands, rivers, seas and mountains of Japan, as well as the spirits of the various aspects of Japan's climate and natural features came into being, both by spontaneous creation and by sexual generation. Two points in the narrative deserve special attention as they illustrate the organization and the beliefs of Shintō at the time when these myths were developing. Izanami was burned and died in the process of giving birth to the Spirit of Fire. Izanagi followed her into the Land of Darkness and, making a torch, looked at her. "Putrefying matter had gushed up and maggots swarmed. Izanagi was greatly shocked and said, 'Nay! I have come unawares to a hideous and polluted land!' So he speedily ran away again. When he had returned, he was seized with regret and said, 'Having gone to a hideous and filthy place, it is meet that I should cleanse my body from its pollutions.' Accordingly, he went and purified himself. . . . Deities were produced by his plunging down and washing in the bottom of the sea. Thereafter a deity was produced by his washing his left eye, which was called Amaterasu Ōmikami, the Sun Goddess. Then he washed his right eye, producing thereby a deity who was called Tsukiyomi no Mikoto, the Moon God: then he washed his nose, producing thereby a god who was called Susanoo no Mikoto, the God of the Withering Wind of Summer" (*Nihongi*, pp. 24–8).

This is a good point at which to pause and take stock, for here the legend loses its unity. Tsukiyomi is rarely heard of again, and Susanoo and Amaterasu part company, the one to become the local deity in Izumo Shintō, the other the supreme being in the Ise Shintō of the conquering people of Yamato. The Land of Darkness is the first matter for commentary: it is the land of putrefaction and pollution, the place beyond the realm of the Sun Goddess. Life and fertility, then, are a good; putrefaction and infertility are an evil. Hence the stress on rituals which will aid growth, such as harvest prayers, or which will remove the stain of the decay caused by death or the pollution of sickness. The Heaven of these myths is visualized as a "High Plain" situated above the earth and approached by a bridge which connects it with Japan. The Land of Darkness is here clearly represented as the home of horrible pollution, the home

of the decaying dead. In other contexts it will also appear as part of the land of the living with trees, houses, family quarrels and all the trappings of life before death. There seems to be no notion that *Kami* are divided or located in different abodes according to whether they are benevolent or evilly disposed, though from a description of evil spirits collectively as "like unto the flies of the fifth moon", they are clearly regarded as swarming eagerly round anything that smells of filth or decay.

From this part of the myth it will be seen that the main feature of Shintō ritual and the central pillar of Shintō belief, is purification from pollution. It is by purification and by ritual perfection that man can come near to the divine. So, in the beginning, it was often by purification or by ritual perfection that the *Kami* are said to have come into being. On the occasion of the first perambulation of the "pillar of the land", Izanami, the female, spoke first: this was ritually improper, and so ill-starred. In consequence, the first child born to the couple "was the leech whom they placed in a reed-boat and sent adrift" (*Nihongi*, p. 15). But the second perambulation was followed by a ritually correct first address by the male, and as a result of their union were born all the islands and everything under the canopy of the Japanese heaven. It was through purification by ablution after his contact with the dead and putrefying Izanami that Izanagi gave life to the three central deities of the myth of the "Age of the Spirits" in the chronicles.

The stress on purity and perfection has been a feature of Shintō, as well as of the secular life of the Japanese throughout the ages. In addition to the evidence of the eighth-century chronicles, there is that of much earlier Chinese sources. The chapter, 'The Eastern Barbarians", in the *Record of the Kingdom of Wei* (221–65) compiled by Ch'en Shou (233–97), says of the Japanese: "When death occurs, mourning is observed for more than ten days. . . . When the funeral ceremonies are over, all members of the family go into the water together to cleanse themselves in a bath of purification. When they go on voyages across the sea, they always choose a man who does not arrange his own hair, does not rid himself of fleas, lets his clothing get dirty as it will, does not eat meat and does not approach women. This man behaves like a mourner and is known as a 'fortune-keeper'. If the voyage turns out well, they all lavish slaves and other valuables on him. In case there is disease or mishap, they kill him, saying that he was not scrupulous in his duties."[1]

[1] Tsunoda and Goodrich, *Japan in the Chinese Dynastic Histories* (Pasadena, 1951), p. 11.

Photo: Harold Lindner from A. Devaney, New York

PLATE 95. The huge arch which dominates the entrance to the Heian Shrine in the center of Kyoto.

Photo: Burton Holmes from Ewing Galloway, New York

PLATE 96. Meiji Shrine Gardens, Tokyo, Japan.

Photo: Tenri Calendar, 1957

PLATE 97. The "Hand Dance" of the Tenri Sect, performed during the invocation "Cleanse the dust in us, Lord Tenri".

Photo: Tenri Calendar, 1958

PLATE 98. Crowds at the Grand Spring Festival at the Headquarters Church of the Tenri Sect.

354

Photo: G. Bownas

PLATE 99. Procession of floats along Shijō, Kyoto; from the Gion Shrine.

Photo: G. Bownas

PLATE 100. Fire Festival at Nachi: shrine virgins and torch bearers in procession from the shrine at Nachi to the base of Japan's highest waterfall. The purpose of the ritual is to ensure that the flow will not fail through the summer.

Purification after pollution by contact with the dead, then, is vital even at this early stage; the "fortune-keeper" is no doubt the forerunner of the historical "abstainer", one of the priestly classes of Shintō. The point in the "fortune-keeper" not being allowed to dress his own hair may well lie in the two meanings of the word *Kami*: "hair of the head" as well as "spirit". Such ritual puns are not uncommon in Japan.

Other examples of the overriding importance attached to purification from any form of pollution in the early part of Japan's history include the regular change of capital on the death of the sovereign. This practice continued until the foundation of Nara in 710. The contamination caused by the death of one so august necessitated a complete break with all the emblems and places associated with his authority. From this pre-Nara custom may have arisen the ritual, still performed today, of building anew, though to a plan identical in every particular with the rejected building, the Great Shrine of Amaterasu at Ise. Such rebuilding has been undertaken once every twenty years. Purgation by salt from a pollution already incurred, as well as the use of salt as a prophylactic against possible contamination, is no more than a refinement of earlier practices reflected in the myth of Izanagi plunging into the sea after his contact with the dead Izanami. So too salt is scattered in a house after a funeral; it is placed at the edge of a well; it is to be seen in a little caked cone, by the jamb of a restaurant door; and the *sumō* wrestler will scatter it as he advances to the centre of the ring to take up his ritual crouch before he grapples.

The next episode in the chronicles displays even more clearly some early characteristics of Shintō belief which were to be developed later. Susanoo, the spirit of the Withering Wind of Summer (he "caused green mountains to be withered") had "fieriness in his divine nature" and was generally unruly. This unruliness led him to commit a series of improper acts against his elder sister Amaterasu. These are catalogued as a series of crimes in *Nihon Shoki*. "The august Sun Goddess took an enclosed rice-field and made it her imperial rice-field. Now in spring Susanoo filled up the channels and broke down the divisions, and in autumn, when the grain was formed, he forthwith surrounded them with division ropes. Again, when the Sun Goddess was in her Weaving Hall, he flayed alive a piebald colt with a backward flaying and flung it into the Hall. In all these matters he behaved improperly, to the highest degree. . . . When the time came for the Sun Goddess to celebrate the feast of first fruits, Susanoo secretly voided excrement under her august seat in the New Palace. The Sun Goddess, not

knowing this, went straight there and took her seat. Accordingly, the Sun Goddess drew herself up and was sickened" (*Nihongi*, p. 47).

This list of Susanoo's offences is identical with that predicated as the so-called "Heavenly Offences", in contradistinction to earthly offences, which appear in the litany of the ritual of the Great Purification. The improper acts are either such as would be penalized in any agricultural society, or are unclean and ill-omened. Blocking irrigation channels would be a matter for the local headman: voiding excrement brought pollution and would be doubly unclean in the context of a fertility festival. A backward flaying is against the stipulations of the ritual. Perhaps Susanoo's improper behaviour is indicated once more in his choice of a piebald colt since, in China at least, animals to be offered to the spirits had to be of uniform colour.

Nowhere yet, in this list of offences, is any kind of impurity referred to other than ritual impurity or physical and external pollution. Neither in this list of Susanoo's offences nor in those styled "earthly" offences in the ritual of the Great Purification does inner or moral impurity need to be washed away: the good heart is not as yet something to cultivate or care about. The stress on externals is even more striking in the case of the earthly offences. Susanoo's crimes, the prototype for the corpus of "heavenly offences", were all deliberate and planned, but in the case of the earthly offences, some are concerned with states of uncleanliness due entirely to chance. No account is taken of the motive of the man caught up in the web of chance pollution, any more than Japan's modern legal system concerns itself with the motives of the defendant. The Ritual of the Great Purification which, from the eighth century, was celebrated twice a year at the end of the sixth and twelfth moons, was performed to secure purgation from pollutions and calamities affecting the whole population. The words of the prayer, or rather laudatory address, offered during this ritual are preserved in the tenth book of the *Engishiki*, the Ceremonial Code of the Engi Period, collected in 927. In this address it is said: "There will be a number of earthly offences, such as cutting the living skin, cutting the dead skin, being an albino, suffering from growths, a son's cohabitation with his own mother, a father's with his own child . . . cohabitation with animals, calamities caused by crawling worms, or by the spirits on high . . . and the offence of using incantations." Blood flows when a wound is inflicted; the fact of pollution through the spilling of blood, not the rights or wrongs of the case or the motives of the man who causes the blood to flow, constitutes the offence. The word for "wound" – *kega* – means a "defilement"; the man whose blood spurts causes the defilement, irrespective of whether he is the guilty party in the quarrel leading up to the infliction of the wound. The Great Purification will purge all such pollution, largely by the very perfection of the wording and the precision of the delivery of the formulae. "Then shall no offences remain unpurged. . . . They shall be carried out into the great Sea Plain by . . . the Maiden of Descent into the Current, who resides in the current of the rapid stream that comes boiling down the ravines from the tops of the high mountains and the tops of the low mountains."

Susanoo's offences so enraged the Sun Goddess that she immediately took up her abode in the Rock Cave of Heaven and fastened its Rock Door. At this point we come to the second climax of the narrative and the second point of major interest for the historian of Shintō belief and practice. The eight hundred myriad spirits took counsel on the means by which the Sun Goddess might be enticed from her hiding place, and ordained that the ancestors of the Nakatomi and Imibe clans should dig up a True *Sakaki* Tree, and hang a mirror and jewels on its upper and middle branches respectively, while from the lower branches were to be suspended "white soft offerings and blue soft offerings". Then the Nakatomi ancestor recited a liturgy "with lavish and earnest words of praise", while "The Terrible Female of Heaven", the ancestress of the ritual and purificatory *kagura* dancers, danced steps and mimed actions so obscene that the roars of interest and excitement that such lewdness stimulated on the part of the heavenly host induced Amaterasu to peep out from the Rock Door. Thus she came forth again to the world, whereupon the Nakatomi and Imibe ancestors each stretched a rope behind her, beyond which she was never again to withdraw. (*See Nihongi*, pp. 43–5.)

This section, together with the list of Susanoo's offences, clearly forms part of the myth of an agricultural people, incorporated as an ancillary episode into the creation story the earlier sections of which reflect the interests of a seafaring people. In the earlier part the emphasis was on the sea as the source of life, on Izanagi and Izanami, the last two syllables of whose names mean "quiet waters" and "waves" respectively. Again, with the switch to a theme predominantly agricultural, we find the same dualistic feature of Shintō. The Rock Cave episode is, without doubt, a portrayal of the solar eclipse, a phenomenon dire and inexplicable to a primitive people and one of the first events to be recorded once they learn the art of writing. Again, however Susanoo

be interpreted, whether as the storm wind, or as the forces of winter, or again, as has been suggested here, as the scorching summer typhoon wind, he stands for the power of destruction, for the ability to negate the fertility attributes of the sun. Hence his fight with the Sun Goddess, and her triumphant emergence from the Rock Cave, enticed forth by all the conjuratory powers at the disposal of the Shintō believer, are further evidence for the primacy of fertility and the distaste for decay in Shintō belief.

This episode in the story introduces most of the features of current Shintō ritual. The branch of the *sakaki* tree still appears today, although the strips of white and blue cloth on its branches, originally a form of offering, have been replaced by symbolic white paper strips. The mirror and the jewels remain two of the three items of Imperial Regalia, the third being the sword which, handed to her descendant Ninigi as he set forth to rule his domain, were to be emblems of his descent from the Sun Goddess and were to vouchsafe the right of her house to possess the throne from generation to generation. Each of these three treasures had all the awesome qualities requisite for ranking as *Kami*. The mirror was intended to represent the disc of the sun as soon as the Sun Goddess opened the Rock Gate. The liturgy spoken at the time included the words: "The august mirror in my hand is spotless and indescribably beautiful, as though it were thine own form."[1] Just as a child is awestruck by its reflection in a mirror, the primitive mind would imagine that here is a *Kami* which somehow has the terrible capacity to extract the life and spirit from the body and place it on the mirror's surface. In China the mirror was a revealer of demons invisible to the human eye; a mountain priest would carry a mirror on his back to keep such invisible influences at a suitable distance. "Curved" jewels of the style mentioned here were worn as a talisman against evil; and there are many stories told about swords – which can be self-wielding or which acquire a protective potency by saving life – which would warrant their ready qualification as *Kami*.

If the object of many of the prayers made through worship was purification, it follows that the greater part of the ritual of early Shintō, as well as the primary duties of the various priestly offices, was concerned with the purging of pollution. And let it be remarked once again that the pollution about which concern was felt was external; the priest prayed for the cleansing of your impure state through external contamination; neither he, nor the *Kami* whom he approached, took note of your internal or moral state. Nobody was trying to save

[1] Katō and Hoshino, *Kogoshūi* (Tokyo, 1925), p. 22.

SHINTŌ

your soul. There are variant versions in *Nihon Shoki* of the myth of the enticement from the Rock Cave. In one, the Nakatomi and Imibe ancestors recited their liturgy together; in another, while the latter was responsible for the offerings made to the Sun Goddess, the liturgy was read by the Nakatomi ancestor alone (*Nihongi*, pp. 44, 48). By whomsoever it was performed, the essential point was that the liturgy be recited earnestly, be lavish in its praise of the deity addressed, and be accomplished with absolute perfection and precision in the matter of diction, cadence and the like. This is evident from the Sun Goddesses reaction – "though of late many prayers have been addressed to me, of none has the language been so beautiful as this". The diction of another liturgy is described as "the heavenly mysterious congratulatory words". When the influence of Buddhism began to seep into Shintō, Shingon, the sect which affected Shintō the most, found a point of contact in this particular. *Shingon*, the "True Word", is a Chinese translation of the Hindu *mantra*; there was a peculiar efficacy in both the Hindu *mantra* and the Japanese *norito* to evoke the divine by virtue of the mysterious power of their words of praise.

The word *nakatomi* is explained as signifying "mediator" – the go-between for one wishing to invoke his *Kami*. Contact was made by reading *norito*, the perfect beauty of which arrested the attention of the *Kami*. The duty of the Imibe before the Rock Cave had been to make offerings; thus, in early Shintō ritual we find the Imibe (literally "the abstainer clan") securing by abstention the purity of any person or object to be employed in a ritual observance. There were three primary methods of securing ritual purity: first, *imi* was purity by abstention, the province of the priest or officiant rather than the layman. Abstention was, by and large, withdrawal – and so avoidance of anything that caused pollution; strong drink, music, food not purified by a holy flame, and relations with women were to be avoided.

Misogi, the second method of purification, is performed by the layman, the person actually involved in (usually) accidental defilement. The prototype is to be seen in Izanagi's bathing for the cleansing of his impure contacts in the Land of Darkness. Purification by ablution or by the use of salt has had its effect on all spheres of Japanese life, not only those closely connected with acts of worship. The use of salt in secular contexts has already been discussed. As has been said, the spilling of blood is in any circumstances a source of contamination. Thus, special "parturition huts" were built for women in childbirth, outside of, and away from, the actual place of residence. The practice of sending empresses

back to their paternal home for the period of their delivery, for which there is evidence in Heian times, is no doubt another aspect of this custom. Particular care was taken in the matter of the sacred places of Shintō. The holy island of Itsukushima, the vermilion *torii* (sacred gateway) to its shrine rising from the sea, is to this day safeguarded against contamination by the removal of all pregnant women to the mainland. Death and burial are likewise unknown to the island, just as the Greeks preserved Delos, sacred to Apollo, from such pollution. The Grand Shrine of the Sun Goddess at Ise was also protected, in that all women were delivered on the side of the river opposite the Shrine, in a street of temporary shacks which came to be known as Maternity Mews. Menstruation was a defilement: the authoress of *Kagerō Nikki* speaks of a five-day contamination which entailed her withdrawal from everyday activities and contacts.

The prototype of the third mode of purification, *harai*, literally "a paying", occurs in the punishment of Susanoo for his offence against his sister. After the reappearance of the Sun Goddess from the cave, "all the spirits put the blame on Susanoo and imposed on him a fine in the articles required for the ceremony of purification, one thousand tables of offerings. They further plucked out his hair as well as the nails of his hands and feet and made him therewith expiate his guilt" (*Nihongi*, p. 45). The "paying" took the form of the presentation of offerings, by way of a fine, by a priest on the offender's behalf. The priest then mouthed a purification formula, having first waved a purifying wand (*nusa*) over the offender's person. The development in the conception of this *nusa* is a good example of the way the Japanese think about magical potency; originally an offering, it soon became a symbol of the spirit to whom the offering was made, and finally came to represent and to contain within itself the mysterious powers of the *Kami*; brandished, it would avert evil influences.

At first, as in the case of Susanoo, it seems that both secular and ritual offences could be expiated by a payment of a fine to the *Kami*. Though the confusion of secular and religious categories tended to disappear with the advance of Japanese civilization, this identification of the two may not be wholly due to the same idea being commonly held at an early stage of development, though "unity of government and religion" is a phrase that has often been heard on the lips of the Japanese. The definition of political morality in terms of religious observance, and the identification of the due performances of ritual with patriotic action designed to perpetuate the spirit-born dynastic system have been features

SHINTŌ

continually recurring in the history of Shintō. Mr Hatoyama, a Christian, as a part of the ritual of his appointment as Prime Minister, visited the Grand Shrine at Ise.

Such, then, was proto-Shintō before the coming of Buddhism and Confucianism to Japan. It called for formal ritual purity, an outer cleansing that entailed no corresponding inner change of heart. Provided that the *Kami* was called on by someone outwardly clean, and that the mode of such invocation was technically perfect, the aid of the spirit's magic potency would be forthcoming, no matter how foul the heart or how evil the mind of the suppliant. *Tsumi*, the modern word for a crime and a sin, is in origin something unclean and offensive to the Japanese gods with their reflected taste for Japanese perfectionism. There was hardly any distinction made between what is unclean, what is criminal, and what is morally reprehensible. With spirits lurking everywhere, in anything awesome or unusual, everyday activities which apparently have no ritual or religious significance, or those which we should dismiss as a-moral, fall readily within the scope of actions to be measured by the yardstick of the ritual canon.

INFLUENCE OF BUDDHISM: DUAL SHINTŌ

Buddhism was introduced in the middle of the sixth century by the King of the Korean kingdom of Kudara. Although the new religion made converts very quickly, it was not until the later years of the Heian period that there arrived sects which were more suited to their new soil (both in the matter of doctrine and the demands they put on the intelligence), or which were prepared to modify and adapt their teaching to the indigenous religion. Yet, less than two hundred years after the arrival of the King of Kudara's envoys, instances are recorded which show the beginnings of the syncretism whereby Buddhist elements were incorporated into Shintō; Shintō itself was explained as a local manifestation on Japanese soil of the eternal truths of Buddhism, and its *Kami* were interpreted as local versions of the Buddhist pantheon.

Although some traditions speak of the priest Gyōji (670–749), the leader of the Hossō sect, as the author of Ryōbu or Dual Shintō, this is doubtless an example – Kōbō Daishi, the founder of the Shingon Sect, is another – of attributing a gradually developing religious process to a suitably eminent personage of the time. But while it is clear that he was not the author of the system, it seems equally evident that Gyōji did sanction and give momentum to the process by his thinking and by his actions. When it was decided to ascertain whether Amaterasu would or would not favour the construction of a giant Buddha, Gyōji proceeded to Ise with a Buddhist relic by way of a present and, in answer to his query, got an oracular response which is a masterpiece of ambiguity. However, the Sun Goddess came down in no uncertain terms on the side of co-existence when she appeared to the Emperor in a dream with this verdict: "The Sun is Birushana (*Vairocana*, p. 306). Understand this and execute your enterprise." This syncretistic tendency is more significantly confirmed in the year 765. The occasion was the ceremony of the Festival of the First Fruits, which, with its fertility connections, was an important, and hitherto distinctively, Shintō rite. Yet the Empress who celebrated the ceremony in this year and who issued the edict in question was a fervent Buddhist, so that we find these words: "My duties are first to serve the Three Treasures, next to worship the Spirits, and finally to cherish the people." If men will examine the scriptures, the edict continues, it will be found that it is proper for the spirits (of Shintō, of course) to protect and revere the teachings of the Buddha.[1]

Further evidence of Buddhist influence on Shintō rapidly follows. In the Yakushi Temple at Nikaidō, a few miles from Nara, there is an image of Hachiman, the Shintō deity of war, which is said to date from the Kōnin period (810–23); he is represented as a Buddhist priest. Shintō then is beginning to acquire iconography – though for the time being it rests on a Buddhist foundation. Hachiman's utility in the blending of Shintō with Buddhism seems to have been many-sided, for he was later held in some quarters to be incarnate in Hōnen, the founder of the Jōdo, or Pure-Land, sect (p. 331). Such co-operation benefited both sides; it was to the advantage of Buddhism to establish friendly relations with a possibly hostile and rabidly anti-foreign Shintō priesthood, while, by the introduction of images, Shintō made good a former deficiency. The introduction of image-making made Shintō's doctrines more personal and concrete and served to fill in the all-too-scanty and ill-defined outlines of its mythology.

Though this process of amalgamation was clearly in progress during the Nara period, it was not until the early years of the Heian period, when the more eclectic sects, which were less uncompromisingly Chinese and so more adaptable to the Japanese character, were introduced, that the pace began to quicken. The Tendai sect carried syncretism to extremes; it was, indeed, so comprehensive that its temples have been styled the "religious junkshops" of Buddhism. Divine Favour could be

[1] *Shoku Nihongi*. Edict No. 38.

sought by the austere discipline of the scholar – the Nara tradition – or by the simple faith later stressed in the Amidist sects, or by the meditation practised by the Zen masters. A system which allowed for approaches to the same truth from different angles was ideally suited to the Japanese temperament, and eminently appropriate at this juncture, when the trend was towards peaceful co-existence and intermingling. The Shintō traditions and rituals were only one further way of reaching the same goal and the same universal truth; they were to be welcomed, allowed to mingle in free association with all manner of other doctrines and then sent forth again, their content considerably modified. A symptom of the creativeness that Tendai engendered lies in the fact that nearly every Buddhist sect to be founded in Japan owed its origin to the influence of the temples scattered over Tendai's mountain headquarters above Kyōto. Tendai held the usual Mahāyāna doctrine that the Buddha nature is present in every human being, and that the other Buddhas are aspects of Śākyamuni: thus, with little difficulty, any Shintō spirit could be incorporated as an aspect of the Buddha. Full recognition was given to Vairocana, the Dainichi of Shingon (see p. 345), to Amida and to others; the first, in fact, was regarded in some circles as a higher aspect of Buddhahood than Śākyamuni himself.

Shingon, the Mantrayāna, a late form of Indian Buddhism which incorporated Hindu, Persian, Chinese and other elements, holds that the whole universe is a dual manifestation, divided into indestructible and material categories, of the Buddha Vairocana. In its gradual toning down of the discipline necessary for the attainment of Buddhahood, Shingon broadened the range of its appeal. However, important though the theory of the manifestation of the Buddha Vairocana in the whole universe might be, Shingon's influence on Shintō made itself felt mainly through the character of Vairocana himself – Vairocana, the Great Sun, Dainichi. The definition of the supreme and universally immanent Buddha in terms of the sun would be sure to find sympathetic ears in Shintō circles. If both Amaterasu and Vairocana were the Sun, then the way was clear for parallel identifications of Shintō *Kami* with Buddhist deities all the way down the scale. Thus, Buddhism and Shintō were but two aspects of the same belief – Dual Shintō.

The similarity existing between the Hindu *mantra*, and the Shintō *norito*, liturgies of praise, has already been discussed; the very name of this new sect, Shingon, was the Japanese reading of the Chinese translation of the term *mantra*. The union between Shintō and Buddhism

was further aided by Shingon's conception of the two aspects of cosmic life; Shingon and Buddhism were the eternal and indestructible entities, while Shintō and its spirits were partial and material phenomena, local in their influence and manifestation. This idea is expressed by the term *honji suijaku*: *honji*, the real, basic entity, is Buddhism; *suijaku*, the manifested trace, is Shintō.

The amalgamation of Buddhism with Shintō, of course, produced many outward modifications: in most Shintō shrines, for example, a special inner sanctuary was built in which the Buddhist cult was observed. But there were deeper effects which resulted in the grafting of a fresh branch of an awareness of moral considerations on to the bare trunk of Shintō's tree of purity and perfectionism. Confucianism, too, introduced (according to traditional accounts) early in the fifth century, played its part in this moral rearmament of Shintō. Yet, not even with the stimulus provided by such ethical injections, did Shintō moralists proceed beyond the point of equating and giving due emphasis to the simple ethical equivalents – "truthfulness", "sincerity" or "moral rectitude" – of their traditional a-moral purity. Thus, two years before the death in 833 of Kōbō Daishi, the founder of the Shingon sect, an edict of the Emperor Nimmyō stated: "The deity, though unseen, is ever ready to respond to prayer from a truthful heart and the divine grace is assuredly bestowed on a virtuous man." About a century later, an Imperial Prince wrote: "The gods and spirits are just and equable, for they accept only a man's religious piety. Go and pray to them with sincerity of heart and you will be sure to please them." This "sincerity" was a moral extension of an original "straight" or "right", way of performing the ritual. A thirteenth-century work attributed to priests of the Ise Shrine begins: "Divine revelation is invoked by prayer and divine providence is secured through honesty. To do good is to be pure; to commit evil is to be impure. The *Kami* dislike evil deeds because they are impure." An even clearer distinction between outer and inner rectitude is made in a fourteenth-century text also emanating from Ise: "If we wash ourselves in sea water and are cleansed of bodily filth, this is outer purity. But if we are pure in mind and body, our soul is united with the divine, and divinity in humanity is thus realized."

Although the move to amalgamate came from both sides, efforts were made to preserve such sacred centres of Shintō as the Ise and Izumo Shrines in all their Japanese purity. No Buddhist temple was to be built near, no mention of the Buddha's name was to be allowed at Amaterasu's Shrine. However, the general acceptance of the principle of amalgamation did serve to provide pre-Buddhist Shintō with a kind of headquarters in which to hibernate, where it could lie low amidst the bleak winds of the winter of Dual Shintō, to emerge unscathed when the demands of the national scholars, the politicians and the Shintō diehards coalesced into a campaign to free Shintō from its Buddhist accretions. Had co-existence not been effected – though, admittedly, given the tolerance of both religions and the traditional tendency to acceptance and integration in Japanese thinking, the outcome was never in doubt – the future for Shintō might have been very different.

ATTEMPTS TO RID SHINTŌ OF FOREIGN ELEMENTS

The impetus to rid Shintō of its foreign accretions came from many different directions. There was first the "Yuiitsu", the Unitarian Shintō movement which, in its attempt to ward off some of the attacks on Buddhism, found itself confronted with a campaign of infiltration conducted by other Buddhist sects as well as by non-Buddhist Chinese parties. This fundamentalist school, the product of fifteenth-century thinking, was in fact a combination of Shingon and Tendai mysticism as well as of Chinese philosophical elements, these latter primarily in the form of the Neo-Confucian thinking of Sung-dynasty China. Theories borrowed from yin-yang (positive and negative principles, pp. 370, 387) and five-element schools of thought loom large alongside fundamentalist statements such as: "The One God is our Kunitokotachi" (according to the early chronicles, the first Kami to come into being). That rather than to the Sun Goddess, primacy should be accorded to Kunitoko-tachi is interesting and is probably to be explained by the fact that the former, by virtue of her easy identification with Vairocana, was not entirely free from contamination.

The "Unitarians" led the way in explaining away all those foreign elements which they were unable to discard. For them Shintō was the "fountainhead of Confucianism, of Buddhism and of every religion". This was another form that the reaction from Dual Shintō took, a denial of the tenets of dualism, but a denial which borrowed its ideas and terminology from Dual Shintō itself. The Warongo, the "Japanese Analects", a mid-sixteenth-century work, the first chapter of which records over a hundred oracles attributed to various Kami, contains excellent examples of this reversal of Dual Shintō: now, instead of Shintō Kami being explained as the avatars of the celestial Buddha, the Buddhas, Bodhisattvas and all the deities of Buddhism are derived from

and viewed as local and terrestrial incarnations of primary Shintō spirits. "In India he was born as the Buddha Gotama. . . . In China, the three Sages, Confucius, Lao-Tzü and Yen Hui (Confucius' star disciple) were neither more nor less than our Kami himself. You may ask, why does one and the same deity assume such varied forms? It is simply because, being one and the same deity, he desires to preach the self-same truth and takes forms differing only in appearance from each other so that he may best adapt his teaching to the understanding of every man."

The new Shintō takes over the moral accretions and the tenets of mercy and love from its dualist partners. The Deity of Itsukushima pronounces: "Notwithstanding that I am reluctant to grant the prayers of the unjust, yet because I am the very embodiment of universal and unconditioned loving-kindness, I frequently do so." This is a far cry from concern only with ritual purity and correctness. In the same vein, the Daimyōjin of the Kasuga Shrine, in Nara, declares: "Even though a man provides me with a nice clean room, offering me rare and precious treasures of the land. . . . I am unwilling to favour a house with my presence whose owner is dishonest, harsh or greedy. But even though one, by reason of deep mourning for a deceased parent, is polluted and therefore cannot invite me, yet if he be always kind-hearted towards others, he may expect me to appear in his dwelling, because I, the Kami, am truly the very incarnation of Mercy."

In certain respects, the influence of Shingon doctrine is still very apparent: "Our Sun Goddess is believed to manifest herself as Sūrya (the Hindu god of the sun) or Mahā Vairocana in Buddhist doctrine. The same Sun Goddess, however, also manifests herself in the form of the dragon god of the sea; . . . all other things in the universe . . . are after all but different manifestations of the one Supreme Being." Such pantheistic trends, very different from the thorough-going polydaemonism of proto-Shintō, are paralleled in Amidist thinking. The seventh Patriarch of the Jōdo (Pure-Land) Sect had argued that Amida is omnipresent, while theologians of the Shin Sect who always had a greater feeling for monotheism than other Buddhist sects, were even more outspoken: "The gods, Buddhas and Bodhisattvas are numerous, but since all these are branch bodies of Amida . . . it is sufficient to worship the one Buddha Amida and not necessary to worship these many deities separately."[1]

However, as a result of the labours of the eighteenth-century scholars of the "National Learning", Shintō

[1] Elliott, Japanese Buddhism, p. 380.

revival was no longer dependent on Buddhist or Confucian models for its interpretation of Shintō ideas. All such foreign elements could be purged, once the triumvirate – Kamo Mabuchi, Motoori Norinaga and Hirata Atsutane – had, by their research into Japan's classics, provided both the scraper for removing the layers of foreign lacquer, and the key to open the Japanese treasure box that lay beneath. Both Motoori and Hirata argued that as Japan was the land of the gods, as she was ruled by an unbroken line of Sun-born Emperors in perfect harmony of thought and feeling with the Sun Goddess herself, both ruler and people were naturally endowed with the knowledge of what they ought to do and what should be avoided. Japanese hearts are always pure – and a pure heart needs no moral laws or teaching. Mabuchi had come very near to Taoism in his advocacy of the "way of nature"; this Motoori corrected, for it was, after all, yet one more aspect of Chinese contamination: "Lao Tzü honoured naturalness – but he did not know that the gods are the authors of every human action."

In face of this Shintō revival, Buddhism, though it was in its Amidist form almost the established "church" of the Tokugawa Shōgunate, found little energy to combat the charges of the Shintō revivalists or to supply the faith which the emergent merchant and artisan classes were seeking. Socially, the age was exciting; there was a new-found consciousness and confidence in the man in the street – but all that Buddhism came up with was an unimaginative new sect, a branch of Zen, a dull copy of a Chinese prototype. We never hear of any spirited defence of Buddhism in these years to counter the charges and the splinter movements of Shintō thinkers, nor any realization that in fact, by divorcing itself from Buddhism, Shintō was impoverishing itself, since it was precisely the borrowed elements that provided its power of attraction. But parallel with the effort to purify Shintō of its doctrinal dualism, there was another trend towards a new kind of dualism – the growth of new sects which once again provided Shintō with the nearness, the comfort and the appeal of an all-embracing panacea to the farmer or the artisan which the purged and formal established State or Shrine Shintō had rejected.

SECT SHINTŌ: TENRI

Many of the "big thirteen" branches of the so-called Sect Shintō have only a very tenuous relationship with Shintō proper in the matter of belief: it merely happened that at the time they were seeking recognition, in the early years of the Meiji period (1868–1911), the trend of the period was strongly anti-Buddhist, and a campaign for incorporation waged under the banner, and with an outward veneer, of Shintō, was the more likely to succeed.

To conclude this survey of Shintō belief, I shall review very briefly some of the tenets of the most flourishing of the sects, Tenri-kyō, the Religion of Divine Wisdom, centred in the newly-created city of Tenri, some six miles to the south of Nara in the heart of Yamato. The organization of Tenri owes much to Buddhism – the hierarchy of the churches, for example – as do many aspects of its ritual such as the tradition, quite foreign to Shintō, of congregational worship and the very formula of such worship, "Namu Tenri Ō no Mikoto", with the Buddhist repetition of this formula. Many of the beliefs of Tenri stem from the place of its origin and the peculiar circumstances of its Foundress, Nakayama Miki, in whose family the Patriarchate of the sect has descended. Miki herself was a devout Pure-Land Buddhist before she received her revelation in 1839; the church she founded was attached for a brief period to a Shingon foundation; Miki's maternal ancestors used by tradition to provide their eldest daughter as a virgin purificatory dancer at the local shrine, the Ō-Yamato Shrine. This was of early foundation and ranked high among the shrines under the patronage of the Yoshida house at the time of the revival of Shintō, and so would subscribe to Yoshida Shintō beliefs with their heavy overlay of Sung Neo-Confucian ethics. There is ample scope here, then, for the employment of the broad native eclecticism.

First, in the matter of the traditional Shintō creation myth and the related problem of the lack of a true sacred canon, Tenri accepts, by and large, the stories as they appear in the early Chronicles, but provides them with an overlay of peculiar details, the majority of which can be traced to the influence of local lore.

Much of the doctrine concerning Tenri's deity, Tenri Ō no Mikoto, is influenced by both Pure-Land and Shingon thinking. The term employed in Tenri's sacred canon (Miki's writings constitute its major part) changes from the vague and ill-defined Kami in the first place, via Tsukihi, "The Moon and Sun" – a newly coined word – to the nearer and more personal term Oya – "Parent". Tsukihi (the term used mainly in metaphysical contexts) is manifested in the other deities which go to make up the Tenri godhead and which are revelations and aspects of this supreme godhead – in much the same way as in some Jōdo or Shin Sect thought, every deity was a branch body of the omnipresent Amida. There is similarly in Tenri thought some Shingon and Dual Shintō influence in the equation of each of the ten manifestation deities with a Buddhist divinity: Dainichi, for example (Shingon's

Vairocana), becomes now a manifestation of Kashikone, one of Tenri's ten deities, and a traditional Shintō *Kami*, and loses the time-honoured connection with Amaterasu.

It is in its doctrine of evil that Tenri shows its affiliations with Shintō most clearly. Man is created by the *Kami*; his body is on loan from the god. Only his mind and heart are at his own free disposal. Man was originally born good ("I have looked over the world and all ages, but can find no evil there", *Ofudesaki*, i. 52) but it is in his heart that evil, in the form of the eight lapses of the heart, the eight dusts, comes into being. Illness and disease, the impurities of proto-Shintō, are the outward indications, sent by heaven, of inner dust on the heart. "All forms of illness are no more, for now there are 'heart-lapses'. There are niggardliness, greed, desire and

bias, lust and pride" (*Ofudesaki*, iii. 95–6). The cure of such disease is simple – man should go deeper and wipe the dust from his heart. This latter is to be accomplished by a wholehearted performance of the Tenri service of praise and a sincere acceptance of the Parent deity. "If you perform the service, dust will disappear. If God truly accepts man's heart, all dust is swept away" (*Ofudesaki*, xiii. 22–3).

The removal of dust and dirt, then, is one of the primary considerations, which, when you discount the ready acceptance of a theory of evil in Tenri, is not very far removed from proto-Shintō. Closely akin to it too is the stress its rituals place on fertility. The pervasiveness of beliefs which have come to be regarded as typically Shintō indicates to what degree the "Way of the *Kami*" is "natural" to the Japanese.

9. Confucianism

by A. C. GRAHAM

INTRODUCTION

When we speak of "living faiths", we generally think of religions and philosophies. But in every society the standards by which most people judge conduct in practice, and the way they conceive their place in the world, are only partly derived from the religion they profess and often directly contradict it. It is sometimes supposed that this situation is modern and European, due to the decline in the influence of religion over the last few centuries; but the codes obeyed in practice in Christian countries, such as the aristocratic codes of honour which permitted adulterous intrigues within rigid conventions of their own, and prescribed the duel even when duellists were excommunicated, have always clashed with Christianity. The ordinary Christian does not simply fail to live up to the moral teaching of Jesus, on many points he has always implicitly rejected it; he believes that it is improvident not to take thought for the morrow, swears in a court-of-law with a good conscience and regards anyone who turns the other cheek as a coward. Nor can we take it for granted that the view of life reflected in a religion is typical of the people who, with part of their minds, believe in it. Buddhism is a "Nay-saying" religion, rejecting all life as suffering and promising release from it; yet whenever one is actually in a Buddhist country it is hard to resist the impression that one is among the liveliest, the most invincibly cheerful, the most "yea-saying" people on earth.

We must distinguish between the customary codes which the majority of a people, or class within a people, accept in practice, and the international religions which in certain civilizations influence, without permeating, these codes. In China this distinction is much more striking than in Europe, where the true nature of the beliefs on which a man acts may be hidden from him by the Christianity which overlays them. What is called in the West "Confucianism" is not a religion, but the tradi-

tional view of life and code of manners of the Chinese gentry for two thousand years up to the Revolution of 1911. Confucius was not the founder of a religion, nor was he a philosopher; he was a gentleman whose sense of what is done and what is not done has been taken as standard ever since. The Chinese who ask deeper questions than how to behave as a filial son and as a loyal minister, and who require a mystical philosophy or a religion, turn to Taoism or Buddhism. This does not mean that they cease to be "Confucians"; unless they retire from the world, they continue to direct their public lives as "Confucians" and their private lives as Taoists or Buddhists. This condition will seem surprising if one imagines that it is like being a Christian and a Muslim at the same time; but it is much more like being both a Christian and a gentleman.

Buddhism entered China from India at about the time that Christianity was spreading from Palestine over the Roman Empire, and for many centuries seemed likely to be equally successful. But unlike Christianity in Europe, Buddhism never quite submerged the traditional moral code of the Chinese ruling class, and after the Confucian revival led by Han Yü (768–824) the gentry recovered its self-consciousness as a group with values opposed to Buddhism. The essentially secular and this-worldly attitude of orthodox Confucianism can be seen in this polemic against Buddhism by Hu Yin (1098–1156):

"Man is a living thing; the Buddhists speak not of life but of death. Human affairs are all visible; the Buddhists speak not of the manifest but of the hidden. After a man dies he is called a ghost; the Buddhists speak not of men but of ghosts. What man cannot avoid is the conduct of ordinary life; the Buddhists speak not of the ordinary but of the marvellous. What determines how we should behave in ordinary life is moral principle; the Buddhists speak not of moral principle but of the illusoriness of sense-perception.

It is to what follows birth and precedes death that we should devote our minds; the Buddhists speak not of this life but of past and future lives. Seeing and hearing, thought and discussion, are real evidence; the Buddhists do not treat them as real, but speak of what the ear and eye cannot attain, thought and discussion cannot reach."

It must be emphasized that "Confucianism" was so named by Westerners who supposed that it was a religion founded by Confucius, as Christianity was founded by Christ and Muhammadanism by Muhammad. But when "Confucians" wish to distinguish themselves, they do not call themselves after their supposed founder, but by a word of uncertain origin, *ju*; and they speak of their principles by such phrases as "the way of the sages", "the way of the ancients". This "Way" (*Tao*), which is first of all a system of government and of rules of behaviour for members of the governing class, is assumed to have existed from time immemorial. In ancient times it was perfectly realized by the sages, such as Yao and Shun, Yü the founder of the Hsia dynasty (the traditional dates of which are 2205–1767 B.C.), T'ang, founder of the Shang dynasty (?1766–?1123 B.C.) and Kings Wên and Wu and the Duke of Chou, founders of the Chou dynasty (?1122–256 B.C.), under whom the Empire enjoyed ideal government. Since the decline of the Chou dynasty and the emergence of the feudal lords as rulers of virtually independent states, the Way has never been completely practised. The last of the "sages", the perfectly good and wise men, was Confucius (?551–?479 B.C.), a scholar from the small feudal state of Lu who wandered over the Empire seeking without success a ruler willing to apply the Way. Thus no originality is claimed for Confucius; and if he receives more attention than the other sages, it is only because more is known about him, his predecessors being rather shadowy figures even in legend.

THE CLASSICS

The scriptures of Confucianism are the "Classics", of which there were originally six, comprising all the surviving books believed to have existed in the time of Confucius. These are the *Odes*, an anthology of early songs; the *History*, a collection of documents ascribed to Emperors and ministers from Yao down to the early Chou dynasty; the *Rites*, a compendium of ritual; the *Music*, now lost; the *Changes*, a manual of divination with philosophical appendices; and the *Spring and Autumn Annals*, a chronicle of the state of Lu. According to the tradition, rejected by modern scholars, Confucius

edited some of the Classics and himself wrote the *Spring and Autumn Annals* and the appendices to the *Changes*. The authority of the Classics is thus that of the whole succession of the sages from Yao to Confucius. By the time of the Sung dynasty (A.D. 960–1279) the six Classics had grown to thirteen by the addition of works ascribed to the late Chou dynasty, including the *Analects*, the sayings of Confucius, and the *Mencius*, the sayings of the most prominent of his successors, Mencius (?371–?289 B.C.). These works formed the basis of the education of a ruling class which prided itself on learning, and the set texts of the examinations by which the bureaucracy was recruited. It is characteristic of Confucianism that, while the canon of the Bible was fixed by the Church Synods (p. 60), that of the Classics was established by Imperial decree.

ORIGINS

The conviction of the Chinese gentry that its code of behaviour had come down unchanged from the remotest past does not, of course, settle the question of its origin for us. Although Chinese civilization is the most stable in the history of the world, it has undergone, not only gradual transformation, but violent upheavals, notably the transition from a feudal to a bureaucratic system in the third century B.C. The traditional beliefs of the ruling class developed slowly from the beginnings of Chinese history without any break comparable, for example, to the Christian break with Judaism; but they were modified almost imperceptibly by original thinkers who read back their discoveries into ancient texts. Although Confucius did not claim originality for himself, and none was claimed for him by his followers, there is no doubt that he was the greatest of these innovators, and that until the victory of his own school in the second century B.C. no ruler ever attempted to follow the Way which he supposed to have been practised by the ancients.

The traditional history of China before the foundation of the Chou dynasty (?1122 B.C.) is almost entirely legendary, although some information about the preceding Shang dynasty is being recovered by archaeology. The beliefs reflected in the early Chou literature contained in the Classics do not differ in any very sensational way from those of Confucius; but when we turn from them to the *Analects* of Confucius, we are at once aware of a more developed morality and of a shift of attention from the divine to the human. It seems clear that Confucius himself was not aware of these differences. He considered himself "a transmitter and not an originator, trusting in and loving the ancients" (*Analects*, vii. 1), whose mission was to bring to light the neglected teaching of the Duke of Chou and the founders of the Chou dynasty by the study of old books, traditions, rituals and music. We find him, for example, reading moral lessons into love songs from the *Book of Odes*, as Jews and Christians have done with the *Song of Solomon*.

It would be a mistake to think of Confucius either as a prophet, appealing to divine revelation, or as a philosopher, appealing to reason. He makes no claim to supernatural authority and he seldom gives reasons; he presents himself simply as a gentleman whose sense of fitness has been matured by conscientious study of the best models. A customary morality needs no justification except "This is how it has always been done"; and one who like Confucius refines a moral tradition without breaking with it only needs to say, "This is how it was done in the Golden Age, although in these degenerate times most people do it differently."

It was some time before the Confucian re-interpretation of the past came to be generally accepted. Between the fifth and the third centuries B.C. a variety of conflicting schools appeared, most of which claimed the authority of the ancients, and quoted earlier works such as the *Odes* and the *History* in the same way that Confucius did. This was a period of constant war; the great fiefholders in the Chou feudal system, already virtually independent in the time of Confucius, were taking the title of king and fighting for control of the Empire. Each of the rival schools promised that political order could be restored by the practice of its own methods – according to Confucians such as Mencius and Hsün-tzǔ, by returning to the supposed moral standards of the ancients; according to Mo-tzǔ, by universal love; according to the Taoists, by rejecting both the artificial wants created by civilization and the morality which restrains them, and returning to the natural Way or *Tao*; according to the Legalists, by putting law within the state and war between states in the place of morality. The unification of the Empire by the victory of the state of Ch'in in 221 B.C., and the replacement of the feudal system by a centralized bureaucracy, was achieved by the ruthless practicality of the last school. But during the Han dynasty (206 B.C.–A.D. 220) Confucianism quickly won an ascendancy within the bureaucracy which it retained for two thousand years. Thus a moral code which originated in a hereditary feudal nobility, devoted to war and open-air sports, finally took root in a very different kind of landed gentry, sedentary, book-learned, without hereditary titles or political control over tenants, exercising power by way of office in a centralized administration.

The Confucian way of life can only be practised within one type of society, and it assumes that the natural world is a reflection of that society. All that happens on earth is due to the "decree of heaven", and all things have regular courses to follow, the "way of heaven" – the succession of day and night, the sequence of the four seasons, the harmonious conduct of father and son, ruler and minister, husband and wife, elder and younger, friend and friend. All under heaven (the world, that is China) is under the Emperor, the "Son of heaven", who owes his power to the "decree of heaven". Within this all-embracing harmony the moral power of the Emperor and his conduct of ritual have immediate, magical effects on the natural and social order. The sage Emperors of antiquity did not need to govern at all, since the moral influence which emanated from them was enough to bring about peace and prosperity. Thus Confucius says in the *Analects* (xv. 4):

"Was not Shun one who ruled without action? For what action did he take? He did nothing but sit reverently facing due south."

When someone asked Confucius about the meaning of an ancient sacrifice, he replied:

" 'I do not know. Could not one who knows its meaning deal with the Empire as though he were turning it over here?' – He pointed at the palm of his hand" (*Analects*, iii. 11).

This conception of the place of man in the world goes back as far as the history of China can be traced, and underlies Taoism (which stresses the natural rather than the social aspect of the Way or *Tao*) as well as Confucianism. It seems clear that in its more primitive phase the Emperor was conceived as a purely ritual head who reigned "without action" (*wu-wei*, a phrase prominent in Taoist literature and used above by Confucius), ensuring the regularity of the seasons and the fertility of the land by his ritual functions, while the practical work of government was left to his ministers. In most parts of the world where such ceremonial kings are found it is the custom to kill them at regular intervals in order to prevent the waning of their powers in old age from affecting the fertility of the land. Although there is no direct evidence of such a custom in China, it is tempting to suppose that some memory of it may lie behind the belief that when an Emperor rules badly his subjects have the right to rebel and institute a new dynasty.

It is assumed that as long as government follows the way of heaven, as long as the proper sacrifices are performed by the Emperor to heaven and earth, by his magistrates to the mountains and rivers, by families to their ancestors, there is peace within the Empire and natural conditions favourable to the harvest. But flood, famine, rebellion, omens in the sky, are signs that the Emperor no longer deserves to rule and that heaven has withdrawn the decree by which he reigns. This theory was used by the founders of the Chou dynasty to justify their overthrow of the last Shang Emperor (whose name is also spelled "Chou" in English, although pronounced and written differently in Chinese). When Mencius was asked by the king of Ch'i whether this implied that a subject has the right to murder his ruler, he replied:

"A robber and ruffian should be called a commoner. I have heard that they punished the commoner Chou, but I have not heard that they murdered their ruler" (*Mencius*, xvi. 8).

Chinese dynasties are not, like the royal houses of England, branches of a single line. The founder of a new dynasty does not claim Imperial descent and, although usually a member of the gentry, may come from the people. (Examples are the founders of the Han and Ming dynasties.) His success in building an orderly and lasting government is enough to prove that he rules by the decree of heaven; survivors of the old dynasty are not accorded any right to the throne and soon cease to claim it. Sir James Frazer noticed in his *Golden Bough* the startling contrast between the semi-divine honours accorded to primitive ceremonial kings and the profoundly democratic conviction that they must be killed off as soon as they cease to be useful to the people; and something of this contrast persists in the Confucian attitude to the Son of Heaven.

By the time of Confucius the political impotence of the Chou Emperor was already taken as proof that he no longer ruled by the decree of heaven, and that one of the feudal lords would sooner or later unite the Empire and rule in his place. The Confucians insisted that a feudal lord who conquered his rivals by force alone would not be the legitimate successor of the Chou; the true heir would be one to whom the people turned voluntarily because he ruled his domains according to the Way. This idea, at first ritual and magical, was gradually moralized and rationalized. Confucius himself seems to have thought that the Empire would fall at the feet of the ruler who observed the proper rituals. When asked how a state should be governed, he gave this (to us) surprising answer:

"Follow the calendar of the Hsia dynasty; ride in the coach of the Shang dynasty; wear the Chou ceremonial cap; for music take as model the Shao dance and get rid of the tunes of Chêng" (*Analects*, xv. 10).

But two hundred years later Mencius declares that the way to become the heir of the Chou is to govern in the interests of the people:

"With no more than a hundred square miles of land you can be heir to the Empire. If Your Majesty governs the people with benevolence, is sparing with punishments, reduces taxation, and encourages agriculture, so that adults have time to cultivate filial piety and fraternal duty, loyalty and good faith, serving their fathers and elder brothers at home and their elders and superiors abroad, your subjects will be ready to fight with sticks against the strong armour and sharp weapons of Ch'in and Ch'u.

"The rulers of those states snatch their people from the land at the seasons when they should be ploughing and weeding to support their parents. Their parents are cold and starving, their brothers, wives and children are scattered. Such rulers ruin their own people. If Your Majesty goes to punish them, who will be a match for you?" (*Mencius*, ia. 5).

Sacrifices to the ancestors are performed within the family, other sacrifices by the Emperor and his officials. (The priests in Confucian shrines are little more than caretakers.) These sacrifices are addressed, not to personal gods, but to natural phenomena and to men of the past. Although heaven is spoken of in semi-personal terms, it is the superior member of the pair "heaven and earth", the sky itself rather than a person living in the sky. In early Chou literature there are references to a certain Shang-ti, the "Supreme Emperor" or perhaps the "Primordial Ancestor", but afterwards the name is treated as no more than a metaphor for heaven. There are sacrifices to the mountains and rivers and to the heavenly bodies, but the spirits to whom they are addressed are hardly detached from the natural objects themselves. The word *shên*, usually translated "spirit", refers to a vague numinous influence, conceived almost as a property of the thing in which its potency is felt: thus the stalks used in divination are *shên*, and so is the sage, whose mind sees through all things and whose inward power influences everything around him for good. In Confucianism (although not in popular religion) *shên* is impersonal and devoid of proper names and mythology. The only personal beings to which sacrifices are made are men such as the legendary inventors of the crafts, the sages, one's own ancestors.

In Europe and Western Asia this kind of nature-worship has been replaced by the worship, first of gods with elaborate mythologies, then of a single absolutely good God; and moral development has been accompanied by increasing differentiation between the divine and the devilish and by the idea of supernatural reward and punishment. But Eastern Asia has developed in quite different directions. Thus in India some types of mysticism have, so to speak, by-passed religion. It is still assumed that the gods exist, but only in the sense that existence can be asserted of the world as it appears to the senses, from which the mystic is trying to liberate himself; the service of gods is a duty only for the uninitiated, and the gods themselves need illumination. For us, the supreme importance of God, if he exists, is common ground for Christians and atheists, and we are surprised to find anyone treating gods, not as imaginary, but as irrelevant. But Confucianism also by-passes religion. The short-lived rival school of Mo-tzŭ (fifth century B.C.) claimed that heaven and the spirits reward the good and punish the wicked on earth: and personal gods, myths, and later the Buddhist idea of reward and punishment in the next world took root among the common people. But the Confucians simply turned their backs on religion and developed their moral code without any appeal to religious sanctions, assuming that man has no business with spirits except to pay them the sacrifices which are their due. The old religious order in which all things follow the "Way of heaven" was either taken for granted, or rationalized as a philosophical order, without any intervening stage of personal religion.

We read in the *Analects* (vii. 20) that "the Master did not speak of marvels, feats of strength, irregular happenings, and spirits". When asked for a definition of wisdom, Confucius said:

"Devotion to one's duties as a subject, and respect for the spirits while keeping them at a distance, may be called wisdom" (*Analects*, vi. 20).

Mencius said:

"The people are the most important; the spirits of the soil and the grain come next; the ruler is the least of all" (*Mencius*, viib. 14).

The most striking illustration of the attitude of Confucianism to the supernatural is its approach to the problem of survival after death. Many Confucians explicitly denied survival; but a more typical view is that men have no business except with the living and should not concern themselves with what happens after death. According to the *Analects* (xi. 11):

"Chi-lu asked about the service of spirits. The Master said, 'Until you can serve men, how can you serve spirits?' When he said, 'I should like to ask about death,' the Master replied, 'Until you understand life, how can you understand death?' "

It might be supposed that sacrifice to one's ancestors takes for granted their survival, and this argument was indeed used against the Confucians by Mo-tzŭ and later by the Buddhists. But the Confucians regard sacrifice principally as a means of expressing reverence for the ancestors; what matters is that the reverence should be sincere, not that the spirit addressed should exist. Confucius, we are told, "sacrificed to spirits *as though* they were present". Hsün-tzŭ (third century B.C.), the most sceptical of the earlier Confucians, observed that "to pay attention to your parents when they are alive but not when they are dead is to reverence them while they are conscious of you and slight them *when they are not*", and also: "It is said: 'The motives of sacrifice are remembrance and longing. By it loyalty, faith, love and reverence reach their utmost, and the emotions moderated and refined by ritual are most fully expressed. No one except the sage can understand it.' The sage clearly understands it; knights and gentlemen confidently practise it, officials treat it as a duty, the people acquire it as a custom. Among gentlemen it is regarded as a human practice, among the people as a service to the spirits" (Dubs, *Works of Hsüntze*, pp. 227, 244).

There is a story that in 265 B.C. a queen of Ch'in (the state in the far North-West which eventually unified China in 221 B.C.) ordered that when she died her lover should be buried alive in her grave. She changed her mind when it was pointed out that if, as she believed, the dead have no consciousness, there would be no point in taking her lover with her; and if they have, her late husband would be waiting for her. The custom of burying retainers with a dead prince had already been given up in the central states of China, and Confucius is said by Mencius to have been shocked even by the practice of burying images in their place (*Mencius*, ia. 4). That this archaic custom should exist side by side with a denial of survival after death illustrates the manner in which China leapt straight from a primitive stage of religion to a sceptical humanism.

The most influential of the later Confucian philosophers, Chu Hsi (A.D. 1130–1200) pronounced that consciousness ends at death. He made, however, a couple of qualifications which are of some interest. He could not reject all stories of angry ghosts since there are some in the Classics; so he declared that if a man is killed before his life-span is complete, his vital spirit is not yet exhausted and may survive for a time as a ghost. But this is highly undesirable; the sage lives out his full span and his spirit disperses with the death of the body. As for sacrifices, when a man's descendants pray to him with perfect sincerity his dispersed spirit temporarily re-assembles to attend the ceremony and afterwards disperses again.

Confucians rejected the popular Buddhist doctrine of reward and punishment after death as an attempt to back morality by self-interest which could deceive only the ignorant. Similarly, they dismissed the Taoist appetite for personal immortality (p. 387) as a selfish refusal to accept the natural rhythm of things, by which death follows life as night follows day and autumn summer. For them, the question of survival mattered only in connection with the duties of the living to their ancestors. Perhaps the most instructive illustration of their attitude is this saying, ascribed to Confucius in a work given its present form in the third century A.D., the *Chia yü*:

"If I say that the dead have consciousness, I am afraid that filial sons and obedient grandsons will burden their lives in order to send off the dead. If I say that they have not, I am afraid that unfilial sons will abandon their parents and refuse to bury them. Do not ask to know whether the dead have consciousness or not. There is no urgency at present, and afterwards you will know for yourself" (*Kramers*, ii. 10b).

Thus belief or disbelief is judged solely by its effect on human conduct; and the best effect is achieved by balancing on a fine edge of scepticism.

THE NEO-CONFUCIANS

The transformation of the old Confucian world-view into a philosophy was completed during the Sung dynasty (A.D. 960–1279) by the Neo-Confucians, the chief of whom, Chu Hsi, we have just had occasion to mention. The Neo-Confucians accepted the old conception of a world-order in which public sacrifices have a place and in which the moral power of the sage directly influences nature and society; their purpose was to systematize the traditional beliefs in order to defend them against Buddhism, which had brought from India a coherent philosophy more formidable than anything hitherto known in China. Like Confucius himself, and every other great innovator in China before the nineteenth century, Chu Hsi did not claim to be original; he read back all his discoveries into the Classics, and the official recognition of his teaching took the form of prescribing his commentaries on the Classics for students taking the civil service examinations.

The Neo-Confucian philosophy has two basic terms, for which rough English equivalents are Principle and Ether. The material universe is composed of ether (more literally, "breath"), out of which solid things condense and into which they dissolve. The ether alternately moves and returns to stillness, like breathing out and in; moving, it is called *Yang*; becoming still, it is called *Yin*. In each pair of opposites, light and darkness, man and woman, ruler and minister, the ether of the active member is *Yang* and of the passive member *Yin*. Principle (a word which also has the concrete meaning "veins in jade") is a

grain running through all things, which it is easy to follow and hard to go against. It is by thinking along the vein which runs from one thing through other things that we are able to infer from the known to the unknown. The old world-order thus begins in Neo-Confucianism to be conceived as a rational order. Principle is present inside man as moral principle, which he does not always follow because it is obscured for him by the density of the ether of which he is composed; but by moral education the ether is gradually refined until it becomes easy to act according to principle.

For the Neo-Confucians the Way and heaven are simply names for principle. The two kinds of spirit, *shên* and *kuei* (traditionally explained as meaning "stretching" and "returning"), are identified with the expansion and contraction of the ether. As we have seen, the tendency had been to conceive spirit as a sort of impersonal potency; in spite of their scepticism about the spirits of the dead, Confucians generally did not question that "spirit" in this sense is active in the heavenly bodies and the mountains and rivers, even when they opposed the popular belief in personal spirits. The rationalization of spirit as a kind of natural force is thus understandable.

THE CARDINAL VIRTUES

Confucianism recognizes five cardinal virtues, for the names of which it is difficult to find exact English equivalents. These are *jên*, "benevolence", which shows itself, according to Mencius (*Mencius*, iia. 6), in the feeling of sympathy for others; *yi*, "duty", reflected in the feeling of shame after a wrong action; *li*, "manners", propriety, good form, reflected in the feeling of deference; *chih*, "wisdom", reflected in the sense of right and wrong; and *hsin*, good faith, trustworthiness, for which no corresponding feeling is given by Mencius. The moral code based on these five virtues may be described as secular rather than religious, having no religious backing except the general assumption that by following it one follows the "Way of heaven". A Confucian who offended against it felt ashamed – not only before others, but in his own eyes when there were no witnesses – but he did not experience a religious sense of sin. Confucianism did not provide for private worship or prayer, nor for rites of atonement, confession and self-mortification to take away sin. (The sacrifices, as we have seen, were performed by the State and the family.) In the case of the instinct which in Europe has most to do with the sense of sin, Confucians were ashamed, to the point of prudery, of exposing the body or talking about sex; but they did not regard the flesh as sinful, had no ascetic tradition, and considered it a binding duty to provide sons to continue the ancestral sacrifices.

Of the five virtues, "duty" is the ordinary term for what is morally right in situations where right and wrong are definitely laid down ("benevolence", on the other hand, leads us to help others even when there is no specific obligation). "Wisdom" implies practical as well as moral knowledge, and its inclusion illustrates the fact that the gentleman is expected to possess the practical as well as the moral qualities needed in a ruler or minister, although it is on morality that the stress is always laid. "Good faith" implies keeping promises, but as in most codes which whole communities actually try to obey in practice, there is no obligation to tell the truth in all circumstances. The following anecdote has shocked missionaries who have made the mistake of judging Confucius as the founder of a religion rather than as a gentleman:

"Ju Pei wished to visit Confucius. Confucius excused himself, saying that he was unwell. But as Ju Pei's messenger was going out of the door, Confucius took his lute and began singing before the messenger was out of hearing" (*Analects*, xvii. 20).

Benevolence

The highest of the five virtues is *jên*, a word related to the ordinary Chinese word for "man", also pronounced *jên*. In the early feudal period the latter seems to have been used only of members of the aristocratic clans, and even in later Chinese it tended for a long time to be confined to civilized men (that is, Chinese), excluding barbarians as well as birds and animals! The moral term *jên* seems to be a collective name for the qualities which distinguish, first the polite classes from the vulgar (compare "noble", "gentle"), and later, civilized men from savages and men from beasts (compare "humane", "human"). *Jên* first becomes prominent in the *Analects*, and this emergence of the word marks the stress laid by Confucius on moral rather than ritual and magical considerations. Since he uses it to embrace his whole moral ideal, it is no more possible to confine its meaning to a single virtue than it would be in the case of such English words as "noble" and "civilized". Thus on one occasion (*Analects*, xvii. 21) he accused a questioner who wished to reduce the period of mourning, of lacking *jên*; on another, declared that "those who have *jên* necessarily have courage" (*Analects*, xiv. 5); on yet another, when asked for a definition of *jên*, gave a list of five qualities (which are, it may be noticed, qualities suitable for a ruler):

"Confucius said: 'He who can practise five things in dealing with the Empire may be accounted *jên*.' When his questioner asked what they were, he said: 'Politeness,

liberality, good faith, diligence, generosity. Being polite, you will not be slighted; being liberal, you will win the people; having good faith, you will be trusted by others; having diligence, you will be successful; being generous, you will be worthy to employ others'" (*Analects*, xvii. 6).

There are, however, passages in which we find Confucius searching for a single principle behind *jên* and therefore behind morality itself:

"Fan Ch'ih asked about *jên*. The Master said, 'The *jên* love others'" (*Analects*, xii. 22).

"Jan Jung asked about *jên*. The Master said, 'Behave in office as though you were receiving an important guest. Employ the people as though you were conducting an important sacrifice. What you do not like yourself do not do to others. Then there will be no resentment against you either in the state or in your own family'" (*Analects*, xii. 2).

"'The *jên*, wishing to stand themselves, help others to stand; wishing to arrive themselves, help others to arrive. An ability to appreciate the needs of others by comparing them with one's own may be said to be in the direction of *jên*'" (*Analects*, vi. 28).

Two hundred years later Mencius was insisting that this concern for the well-being of others must be absolutely disinterested; and that such a disinterested concern is present in all men by nature, whether or not they allow it to develop:

"Now if anyone suddenly notices a child on the point of falling into a well, he will have a feeling of alarm and distress. It is not that he hopes to gain the favour of the child's parents, nor that he expects to be praised by his friends and neighbours, nor that he dislikes earning a bad reputation" (*Mencius*, iia. 6).

Thus from the time of Mencius *jên* is identified with the altruistic principle. The accepted English equivalent of *jên* in this sense is "benevolence", made standard by the great nineteenth-century translator of the Classics, James Legge (an admirer of the moral philosopher Bishop Butler, who used "benevolence" for the altruistic principle in contrast with "self-love"). Benevolence is often associated, and even identified, with love; thus Han Yü, the leader of the Confucian revival in the ninth century A.D., declared that "Universal love is what is meant by benevolence." Confucians, however, with their strong concern for the family and filial piety, do not believe that one should love all men equally, and are generally careful to use a term for "universal love" slightly different from that of Mo-tzŭ, the great Chinese advocate of indiscriminate love for all.

Although some Confucians speak loosely as though

benevolence and love were the same, in practice they use "benevolence" as a moral term, not as the name of an emotion. Thus Confucians hold that a benevolent man loves his own family more than strangers, but it would be a misunderstanding of the word to ask whether he is more benevolent to his family than to strangers. The Neo-Confucians, from the eleventh century onwards, laid great stress on this distinction, treating benevolence as one aspect of the ultimate principle which unites all things, love as an emotion which accompanies benevolent action. Ch'êng Hao (1032–85) gives the following description of benevolence:

"When there is perfect benevolence, heaven and earth are regarded as one body, and the different things and innumerable forms within heaven and earth as the 'four limbs and hundred members'. How can any man regard his four limbs and hundred members without love? . . . Some medical books describe paralysis of the hands and feet by saying that the limbs are 'unfeeling' (literally, 'not *jên*'), because pain in them does not affect the mind. What better term could there be for unawareness of pain in hands and feet which are part of oneself? The self-injury of the callous and merciless men in the world is no different from this."

Rites and Music

Of the other Confucian virtues the one which deserves most attention is *li*, "manners". Like the English word, it covers both the customary rules of polite behaviour and the inner attitude of respect and deference which informs them. However, the former aspect of *li* is much more comprehensive than the English "manners", including rituals, customs, conventions, at every level from the sacrifices to heaven and earth down to details of dress and etiquette. In this sense, *li* is commonly translated "rites". Three ancient manuals of such customary observances are included in the Thirteen Classics, the chief of which is the *Book of Rites*, which assumed its present form about the first century A.D., but contains much older materials. The great importance attached to the three hundred major and three thousand minor rules of *li* is a reminder that Confucianism is in the first place the code of behaviour of a leisured class.

The Confucians greatly disliked the view of the Legalist school of the third century B.C., that the social order must be maintained by law, by punishments imposed by the ruler. In their view social order should be preserved as little as possible by force, as much as possible by customary rules defining the relation between father and son, ruler and minister, husband and wife, elder and younger, friend and friend; and right up to the present

century statute law had a very small place in China compared with customary law. Confucius said:

"If you govern them by regulations and keep them in order by punishments, the people will avoid trouble but have no sense of shame. If you govern them by moral influence, and keep them in order by a code of manners, they will have a sense of shame and will come to you of their own accord" (*Analects*, ii. 3).

"In judging law-suits I am the same as other men, but we must bring it about that there are no law-suits!" (*Analects*, xii. 13).

According to the *Rites of the Elder Tai*:

"If you rule the people by a code of manners and duties, they will become more and more well-mannered and dutiful; if you rule them by punishments, you will need more and more punishments. If punishments multiply, the people will resent it and rebel: if manners and duties are increasingly respected, they will be harmonious and friendly."

Confucianism attached great importance to the music and dancing which accompanied the rites. The ancient Chinese were intensely conscious of the power of music over the emotions, its possibilities as a social force, its capacity to refine or corrupt its audience; and, as in the case of rites, they conceived music to act magically, contributing to or disturbing the harmony of the universe. According to Confucius:

"Education begins with the Odes, is confirmed by practice of the rites, and is completed by music" (*Analects*, viii. 8).

We have already noticed how Confucius considered that one of the most pressing needs of government was to get rid of the lascivious airs of Chêng, and there are several sayings which illustrate his preoccupation with music and its moral effects:

"The Master said that the Shao dance was perfectly beautiful and also perfectly good, while the war dance was perfectly beautiful but not perfectly good" (*Analects*, iii. 25).

"When the Master was in Ch'i he heard the Shao music, and for three months did not notice the taste of his meat. He said, 'I never imagined that music had reached this height'" (*Analects*, vii. 13).

The purpose of rites and music is to prevent the conflict between desires from producing anarchy, within the mind of the individual as well as in society. Music harmonizes the passions, while ritual and etiquette confine the desires within limits set by age and rank. According to the *Book of Rites*:

"Music makes for community, the rites make for distinction. When there is community there is mutual

PLATE 101. Illustration to a sacrificial hymn from the *Book of Odes*, traditionally supposed to have accompanied the offering of red bulls by King Ch'êng (?1115–?1079 B.C.) to the spirits of his father King Wu and grandfather King Wên: by an artist of the Ch'ing dynasty (1644–1911 A.D.)
(*Victoria and Albert Museum, London*)

Solemn the hallowed temple,
Awed and silent the helpers,
Well purified the many knights
That handle their sacred task.
There has been an answer in heaven;
Swiftly they flit through the temple,
Very bright, very glorious,
Showing no distaste towards men.

A Book of Songs, No. 214, translated by Arthur Waley.

373

PLATE 102. Illustration to a sacrificial hymn to King Wên; by an artist of the Ch'ing dynasty
(*Victoria and Albert Museum, London*)

> The charge that Heaven gave,
> Was solemn, was for ever.
> And ah, most glorious
> King Wên in plenitude of power!
> With blessings he has whelmed us;
> We need but gather them in.
> High favours has King Wên vouchsafed to us;
> May his descendants hold them fast.

A Book of Songs, No. 215, translated by Arthur Waley.

PLATE 103. Illustration to a hymn to King Wên; by an artist of the Ch'ing dynasty
(*Victoria and Albert Museum, London*)

Clear and glittering bright
Are the ordinances of King Wên.
He founded the sacrifices
That in the end gave victory
That are the happy omens of Chou.

A Book of Songs, No. 216, translated by Arthur Waley.

PLATE 104. The Temple of Heaven at Peking in which the Emperors sacrificed.

PLATE 105. The three-tiered altar at the Temple of Heaven, Peking, at which an account of the past year was delivered.

PLATE 106. Confucius: from a stone rubbing of the Yüan period, 1280–1368
(School of Oriental and African Studies, University of London)

西王母

Photo: Universal Drawing Office

PLATE 107. Hsi-wang-mu, the "Western Royal Mother" (*see* page 389).
(*School of Oriental and African Studies, University of London*)

張道陵

PLATE 108. Chang Tao-ling (*see* page 391).
(*School of Oriental and African Studies, University of London*)

affection, when there is distinction there is mutual respect. When music predominates, differences are blurred; when the rites predominate, differences lead to alienation. It is the task of rites and music to co-ordinate the passions and to ornament appearances. . . . Music issues from within, the rites act from outside. Serenity is the result of music issuing from within, refinement is the result of the rites acting from outside. Great music must be simple, great rites must be easy. When music is at its best there is no resentment, when the rites are at their best men do not contend. It is to rites and music that this saying refers: 'By bowing and giving way one could set the world in order' " (*Sacred Books of the East*, vol. xxviii. pp. 98f.).

Among the "ten thousand things" between heaven above and earth below man is supreme, "making a trinity with heaven and earth". Heaven is round, earth is square: the special position of man is shown by the fact that, unlike birds and animals, his head is round like heaven and his feet square like earth. By the harmonious interaction of the *Yang* ether descending from heaven and the *Yin* ether ascending from earth, all things are born, grow, wither and die through their natural cycles. Rites and music *are* – it would be an understatement to say that they represent – this natural order. The distinction between heaven above and earth below is the distinction between father and son, ruler and minister, realized in their prescribed forms of behaviour; the harmony between *Yin* and *Yang* is the harmony of sound and gesture in music and the dance. The following extract from the *Book of Rites* is typical:

"Heaven being honourable and earth lowly, the positions of ruler and minister are fixed. When high and low are set forth, noble and mean are in place. Having a constant rule that one should move and the other be still, great and small are separated. The grouping of animals in classes and the division of plants into families shows that their natures and destinies are not the same. In heaven things take form as images (the heavenly bodies, less solid than the shapes on earth), on earth they take form as shapes. This being so, the distinctions made by the rites are the distinctions of heaven and earth.

"The ether of earth ascends, the ether of heaven descends; the *Yin* and *Yang* interact, the forces of heaven and earth co-operate. They are drummed on by thunder, stirred by wind and rain, kept in motion by the four seasons, warmed by the sun and moon; from all this the innumerable transformations arise. This being so, music is the harmony of heaven and earth" (*Ibid.*, pp. 103f.).

DESTINY

The morality of Confucianism is closely connected with its view of destiny. A sharp distinction is drawn between heaven and man, the "decree of heaven" and "human action". Whether I am a filial son and loyal minister depends on myself; whether I enjoy riches and long life or suffer poverty and early death is decreed by heaven. Although the decree of heaven is beneficial in the long run (for example, by the removal of degenerate dynasties), it does not necessarily reward or punish the individual. Thus Confucius himself was a sage who, had he become Emperor like Yao and Shun, could have restored good government throughout the world; but by the inscrutable decree of heaven he spent most of his life out of office in a small feudal state. The Confucian does not question that riches and long life are unmixed blessings, but neither does he expect them as a reward for living rightly. He accepts the alternation of good fortune and bad as part of the natural rhythm of things; he does not, like the Buddhist, regard all life as suffering, nor does he, like many Western humanists, support himself by faith in a future Utopia on earth. So long as he fulfils his duty, failure and adversity should not trouble him, since they are due to heaven, not to any fault of his own.

It is interesting to note, however, that Confucius himself did not always live up to this view of destiny. A couple of his sayings suggest a faith that his own mission to restore the way of the sages could not be in vain, that its success was decreed by heaven:

"Heaven gave birth to the moral power within me. What can Huan T'ui do to me?" (*Analects*, vii. 22).

"Since the death of King Wên, has not the responsibility for this culture rested on me? If heaven intended to destroy this culture, later mortals such as I would not have been able to share in it. If heaven is not going to destroy this culture, what can the men of K'uang do to me?" (*Analects*, ix. 5).

But on another occasion when he was in danger we find him rising to a complete acceptance of destiny:

"Whether the Way will be practised depends on destiny; whether the Way will be abandoned depends on destiny. What can Kung-po Liao do against destiny?" (*Analects*, xiv. 38).

About 400 B.C. the Confucian view of destiny was strongly attacked by Mo-tzǔ, founder of a rival school whom we have encountered already. Mo-tzǔ felt that morality requires the ultimate sanction of reward and punishment by heaven and the spirits, and that to recognize that the righteous may suffer and the wicked prosper undermines the motives for moral action. The

Confucians held that, on the contrary, one who understands destiny knows that it is mere accident if selfish action is followed by material success, and can therefore prefer right to self-interest with an undivided mind. Confucian fatalism does not deny free will, and, after all, the objection that such a philosophy weakens the motives for action does not apply even to certain doctrines which do deny it, such as Calvinist predestination and Marxist determinism. Confucius regarded his understanding of destiny as one of the decisive steps in his moral development:

"At fifteen I resolved to learn: at thirty I had a firm foothold; at forty I had an undivided mind; at fifty I understood the decree of heaven; at sixty my ear was obedient; at seventy I could follow the desires of my heart without transgressing the rule" (*Analects*, ii. 4).

Was it at fifty that Confucius learned to dispense with the faith that his mission was under the special protection of heaven?

HUMAN NATURE

What man cannot alter is decreed by heaven. This includes not only outside events which are beyond our control, but also everything in ourselves which belongs to us by nature, such as the need for food and for sexual intercourse. Is human nature good or evil? Is morality a fulfilment of man's nature, or is it something which must be followed against the grain of one's nature? This is the one abstract problem which has always profoundly interested Confucians, and every possible solution has been proposed and defended by one or another Confucian philosopher. Confucius himself, according to the *Analects* (v. 13), refused to discuss this or any other speculative problem; but between his time and that of Mencius the theories that human nature is neutral, that it is a mixture of good and bad, and that it is good in some men and bad in others, were all being discussed by his school.

In the fourth century B.C. Mencius took the view that man's nature is good. Every man, he says in a passage we have already had occasion to quote, will be moved at the sight of a child about to fall into a well; and this proves that moral education merely develops impulses which are in us by nature. The same view is reflected in the *Doctrine of the Mean*, a chapter of the *Book of Rites* which opens with the words:

"That in man which is decreed by heaven is what is meant by 'nature'; to follow his nature is what is meant by the 'Way'; cultivation of the Way is what is meant by 'education'."

This later became Confucian orthodoxy, and in the

twelfth century A.D. Chu Hsi grouped the *Mencius* and the *Doctrine of the Mean* with the *Analects* and the *Great Learning* (the latter also taken from the *Book of Rites*) as the "Four Books" in which Confucian doctrine was most fully expressed. But for about fourteen hundred years the Mencian theory had scarcely any advocates. Amid the increasing anarchy of the third century B.C. such an optimistic view of man became less and less plausible. Hsün-tzŭ took the opposite position, that human nature is evil. The most rationalistic of the early Confucians, he held that the principles followed by natural phenomena are morally neutral, and that morality is not the Way of heaven but a human invention – a conception almost without parallel in the history of Confucianism. In his view, the desires implanted in us by heaven are dangerous unless restrained by the morality which the sages invented to save us from the consequences of the primeval war of all against all. Hsün-tzŭ, as a Confucian, still believed that men can conquer their natural inclinations by educating themselves in the rites; but his distrust of human nature influenced and was carried further by the Legalist school, which asserted that few men are capable of altruism, and that the majority can be kept in order only by laws imposed by force from above.

Between 200 B.C. and A.D. 1100 the two extreme theories had very few followers, and most Confucians adopted one or another of the intermediate explanations already current before the time of Mencius. Thus Yang Hsiung (52 B.C. – A.D. 18) regarded human nature as a mixture of good and bad, while Han Yü (A.D. 768–824) argued that some men have a good nature which can be realized by education, others a bad nature which can be restrained only by punishments, the rest a mixed nature capable of development in either direction. Finally Ch'êng Yi (A.D. 1033–1107) and Chu Hsi (A.D. 1130–1200), the founders of the Neo-Confucian philosophy of Principle and Ether, revived the Mencian theory in a qualified form. Every man can discover moral principle inside him without being taught, but the extent to which he can see and follow it depends on the transparency or opaqueness of the ether of which he is composed. The moral principle within him is his true nature, which is therefore good; the endowment of ether received at birth, which determines his innate personal characteristics, is his "physical nature", which varies with different individuals and is alterable by education. The victory of the Mencian doctrine in this form was permanent, and later philosophers who modified Chu Hsi's dualism in the direction of idealism or of materialism did not question it.

FILIAL PIETY

The strongest of Confucian duties is filial piety. A son must obey his father absolutely, not only in childhood, but until his father's death, upon which event he is expected to retire from office and live in a hut near the tomb, abstaining from wine, meat, and sexual intercourse for twenty-five months – a term of mourning which seems to have no parallel anywhere in the world. From this centre his duties extend outwards in diminishing circles; beyond the outer limit of those connected with him by blood, by friendship, or by position in the official hierarchy, he has only the vaguest responsibilities. As we have noticed already, the idea that one should love all men equally, strangers as much as parents, is anathema to Confucians; Mencius even considered Mo-tzŭ's universal love to be as dangerous as the amoral egoism of another philosopher of the same period, Yang Chu (*Mencius*, xxxvi. 9). It is on this point that Confucian morality differs most from our own. The Confucian is horrified by the neglect of old people in the West, the Christian is equally appalled at the open nepotism of Chinese public life, and at the assumption of Chinese that it is none of their business to come to the help of a stranger who is being murdered in the street.

The difference between the Confucian point of view and our own is however one of degree only. The European who believes in equal love and equal justice nevertheless has a Confucian strain in him which distrusts anyone who betrays his family or his friends out of a disinterested passion for the good of humanity. The Confucian recognizes the same conflict between public and private loyalties when it comes to such an issue as private revenge, the rights and wrongs of which have often been discussed. The same fundamental moral issue can be seen in this passage from the *Analects*, in which Confucius takes what many Europeans would consider the wrong side:

"The Duke of Shê told Confucius: 'In my country there was a certain honest Kung who, when his father stole a sheep, bore witness against him.' Confucius said: 'The honest men of my country are different from this. The father covers up for his son, the son covers up for his father ... and there is honesty in that too'" (*Analects*, xiii. 18).

Collisions of principle of this sort on the whole do not worry Confucians as much as they worry us. Confucian morality depends less on consistent obedience to absolute standards than on a sense of timeliness and an instinct for the mean which lies between extremes. In a phrase from the *Doctrine of the Mean* (a section of the

Book of Rites), the gentleman "strikes the mean according to the times". In spite of the importance attached to punctilious observance of rites, conventions and etiquette, Confucius himself was well aware that the manners of Chou were not those of earlier dynasties, and that in the future they too would change with the times (*Analects*, ii. 23). A man who, because it is improper for him to touch her, refuses to pull his drowning sister-in-law out of the river, would be a wolf rather than a man, to quote Mencius (*Mencius*, iva. 18). The sage Shun married without informing his father, normally the height of unfilial conduct; but had he informed him, his father would have forbidden him to marry, and not to have descendants to carry on the ancestral sacrifices would have been still more unfilial (*Mencius*, iva. 26). The idea of timeliness runs through all Confucian thought; the right to overthrow a degenerate dynasty is the extreme illustration of it.

In its emphasis on the mean, as in so much else, Confucianism reminds one less of the moral teachings of the world religions than of secular moralities such as Aristotle's, and of modern liberalism. According to Confucius (*Analects*, xi. 15), "to exceed is as bad as not to reach", and the word for "excess" is also the ordinary Chinese word for "error" in general. Confucius often reminded his disciples of the narrow margin which separates certain virtues from certain vices, of how courage can easily pass over into turbulence, wisdom into cunning, uprightness into harshness. As Arthur Waley has noticed (*Analects*, p. 37), one of the most striking achievements of Confucianism was to give the idea of moderation an emotional force which did not spend itself for over two thousand years, while European liberalism has never succeeded in giving it a drive equal to the fascination of extremes.

SOCIAL CLASS

Confucianism is not a body of ideas to which an unbeliever can be converted, but a way of life which could be practised only within traditional Chinese society. A *ju* (the nearest equivalent in Chinese to our word "Confucian") was not simply a believer in Confucian ideas, but a scholar educated in the Confucian Classics. He was satisfied that the barbarians on the four sides of the "Middle Kingdom" would benefit by coming under the rule of the Son of Heaven, becoming civilized, and learning to follow the Way of heaven; but the idea of missionary activity to convert them would never have occurred to him. A European who wished to become a Confucian would have had to go to China and live the life of a Chinese gentleman. Some Confucian ideas may well survive the present social revolution and influence the direction taken by Communism; but unless a counter-revolution gives it new life, Confucianism itself is now dead in China, since there is no room in a Communist society for a leisured class educated to practise it.

One who lives successfully by Confucian standards is a *chün-tzŭ* (literally "lord's son"), often translated "superior man"; the word combines social and moral implications in much the same way as the English "gentleman". His opposite is the *hsiao-jên* (literally "small man"), the knave, churl or villain. Since good manners, book-learning and adminstrative ability are essential features of the *chün-tzŭ*, one cannot hope to become a sage (as one can become a Christian saint) without the benefits of leisure and education. As for the common people, the Confucian was on the whole content that they should combine some Confucian virtues (such as filial piety) with a nature-worship overlaid with Taoism and Buddhism which he himself regarded as superstition. In the words of Confucius (speaking of the Way), "the people can be made to follow it, but they cannot be made to understand it" (*Analects*, viii. 9).

This does not mean that the upper classes were considered to be innately superior to the lower, for the tendency in China, at any rate since the decay of the feudal system, has been to explain merit by environment rather than by heredity, by education rather than by a mystique of blood. Until quite recently it was assumed in Europe that the moral qualities inherent in noble blood would show themselves even in one who by some accident was brought up by humble parents, although a person who believed this also believed as a Christian

that the noble might go to hell and the commoner to heaven. The former assumption is as alien to Confucianism as the latter is. Confucius declared that "by nature we are near to each other, by practice we draw far apart" (*Analects*, xvii. 2) and taught anyone who came to him, irrespective of wealth or class, saying, "I have never refused instruction to anyone, even if he could bring no better present than a bundle of dried meat" (*Analects*, vii. 7). On one occasion he thought of going to live among the barbarians, and when it was suggested that he would find their boorishness intolerable, replied: "Would they be boorish if a gentleman lived among them?" (*Analects*, ix. 13).

After the feudal period the Chinese ruling class, although, like all others, largely self-perpetuating in practice, did not usually bear hereditary titles and prided itself on education rather than descent. The Confucian conviction that the qualities of the gentleman may be latent in the members of any class is reflected in the examination system by which the bureaucracy was recruited. Admission to the examinations, at first limited to the landlord class, was gradually extended to all except a few special pariah professions. Although the history of this process has not yet been fully explored, there is no doubt that during the last five hundred years of the Imperial regime a continuous, if narrow, stream of candidates was rising from the merchants and peasantry into the ruling class. It may be noted also that, although a few Confucians have held that some men are good and others bad by nature, most discussions of human nature assume that natural inclinations are either good or bad, and either developed or suppressed by education, in all men alike. In the words of Mencius, "every man can become a Yao or a Shun" (*Mencius*, vib. 2).

10. Taoism

by WERNER EICHHORN

Taoism is a religion as well as a philosophy. It came gradually to the fore during the period of the Warring States (453–221 B.C.), arising from an ancient undercurrent of a magico-shamanistic character and can, up to a point, be described as a revival of the religious mentality of the Shang dynasty (about 1558–1102 B.C.). Its rise was probably encouraged by the coming forward of lower social classes and other great changes in the structure of Chinese society.

THE TAOIST SCHOOL OF THE CHI-GATE

The name for "Taoism" was not coined until the first Han dynasty in the second century B.C., by which time some of the main currents of the Taoist creed had been merged into one. One of these currents is linked with the mythological Yellow Emperor (Huang-ti) and can be traced to the state of Ch'i, that is to say, the Northern part of modern Shantung and the Southern part of Hopei. The rulers of this state like others considered themselves to be descendants of the Yellow Emperor, and his cult was practised at their court. But they also inaugurated an academy of philosophers, called the academy of the Chi-gate, that is, the gate of the god of agriculture, which flourished during the later part of the fourth century B.C. One of the most prominent figures of this academy was the famous Tsou Yen, who was the first to formulate a Chinese "scientific" view of the universe in a system based on two universal energies – *Yin* (dark, female, etc.) and *Yang* (light, male, etc., cf. p. 370), combined with the five moving forces or elements (*wu-hsing*). But the majority of the scholars of this academy belonged to several Taoist schools. Most prominent amongst them were Sung Hsing and Yin Wên. Their doctrines, however, seem to stem from the philosophy of an older thinker, Yang Chu, who advocated what can be described as individual salvation. His teachings were in direct opposition to those of the well-known Mo-tzǔ

(Mo Ti), whose works appear in the Taoist canon. The doctrine of this latter is based on the ancient Chinese ideal of the king and leader who, like the holy Yü, sacrificed himself for his people. Whereas the trend of thought of Mocius leads up to the ideal of "universal love", Yang Chu was unwilling "to pluck out a single hair even if it might have benefited the whole world" (*Mêng-tzǔ*, viia. ch. 26). To keep one's own person out of harm and to live as long as possible were the main tenets of his school.

Within the academy of the Chi-gate the teachings of Yang Chu, mixed with old physical theories, were developed into a theory culminating in what they called the "fine parts". These "fine parts" are closely connected with another basic notion, Ch'i, which means air or breath. Apparently there existed ancient Chinese views that air was the physical basis of the universe acting through the agency of the "fine parts". These, the subtlest parts of the air, were believed to be the essence of all life. They were, for instance, in the five species of grain and by being eaten they were taken into the human body. It was, of course, very important to accumulate these fine parts within one's body in order to preserve and prolong life. So we read in old Taoist texts: "Those things which possess the fine parts (of the air) produce the five grains below (on earth) and the stars above (in the sky). When they flow between heaven and earth they are called spirits. Those who can store them within their breasts are called the saints" (*Kuan-tzǔ*, ch. 49, unpublished). "While the fine parts remain and grow, one's exterior will flourish. When they are stored within, they will become a source, they will become profuse, harmonious, and balanced so as to form the spring of the breath" (*ibid*). The fine parts in man are the product of heaven, while his body is the product of earth. They are the imperishable part of our body, and by fostering and accumulating them life can be prolonged.

385

According to the varying conceptions of the true nature of the fine parts, numerous practices were developed in Taoist circles in order to accumulate them in the body and so obtain immortality. The problem of safeguarding and prolonging human life is fundamental in all Taoist beliefs and practices. Taoism is therefore closely linked with medicine, the military art of defence, charity and welfare.

THE SCHOOL OF LAO-TZŬ AND CHUANG-TZŬ

The school of Lao-tzŭ, Lieh-tzŭ, and Chuang-tzŭ, well known in Western circles, also gives an answer to this problem. These teachers developed the theory of Tao, the fundamental basis of all being. As such, however, it cannot itself *be* being but must rather be not-being. This not-being can be described as emptiness or oneness. Therefore Tao was universal, all-pervading, all-embracing, and indestructible. To avoid death and annihilation, then, nothing was more efficacious than to become like Tao or to unite oneself with Tao. Because Tao was emptiness, it was also silent, retiring and clear. Therefore if one wanted to be like Tao one had to become silent, to retire from worldly affairs and empty oneself of all personal desires. Not to be involved in any hustling business by day and to have no dreams by night was the ideal pursued by the sages of this school, which was mainly represented by hermits and scholars living in rural retirement. Their distinctive belief was that unification with Tao could be brought about by deep thinking and meditation, and that diet and breathing practices alone did not suffice. All through Chinese history the more advanced thinkers were attracted by the philosophy of this kind of Taoism.

TAO, "THE WAY"

The basic conception of the Tao of the Taoists certainly stems from an old popular religion which possibly flourished during the Shang dynasty and of which we know little. We read, for instance, in the *Tao-tê ching*, the "Classic Book of the Tao and the Tê", which shows many traces of a transition from religion to philosophy, that the "gate of the dark female" is the origin of all things. This evidently is a quotation from an older work and may point to an ancient earth or water goddess, who gave birth to all beings and took them back after death. The rising from the orifice of this goddess was interpreted as the passing from not-being to being. That from which being originated was therefore not-being, and the conclusion was reached that all

beings must finally revert into not-being. So this ancient goddess was replaced by the conception of a silent, unmoving background from which all movement and existence originates and to which it inevitably returns.

Motion can only be conceived as motion if it is compared with something at rest, and existence can only become manifest against the background of its opposite. "Everybody recognizes beauty as beauty and thus ugliness is known" (*Tao-tê ching*, ch. 2). But one of the two things confronting each other in antithesis must be prior to the other. According to Taoist philosophy rest is prior to motion, tranquillity to action, and so on. Furthermore tranquillity, silence and humility are the characteristics of the Earth and the *Yin* (the dark, the female, the watery) in ancient Chinese belief, and so, in the old Taoist literature, we meet with a marked preponderance of *Yin*, often represented by the element water. The goodness of water consists in this, that it benefits the "ten thousand beings" without ever striving to do so; it stays in the lowest place which all men despise, and in this it comes near to Tao. This preferential position of *Yin* is one of the main characteristics of Taoism during the pre-Christian era.

The ground from which movement originates is charged with every kind of potential motion, and in it all actual movement is implicit. Therefore, when seen from the point of view of existence, this ground is in an eternal state of change and motion, but in so far as it is the origin of the actual existence of motion and change, it must at the same time be unmoving and unchanging. And so it can be likened to a "Way", that is "Tao", because, though motionless in itself, it nevertheless offers itself as a basis for every possible movement.

By such reasoning the old goddess and "progenitor of all beings" is gradually supplanted by the philosophical term "Tao". Thus we read in the *Tao-tê ching*: "There was a living thing, a mixture of all potentialities but perfect in itself, before the skies and the earth were formed. It was tranquil and empty . . . and may be regarded as the mother of the universe. I do not know its proper name, but choosing a written character for it, I take the character Tao, the Way" (ch. 25). Whereas the *Tao-tê ching* preserves the reflection of this old goddess, Tao appears within the philosophy of Chuang-tzŭ and Lieh-tzŭ as a definable term: "That which creates the creating cannot be created: that which changes the changing cannot be changeable in itself" (*Lieh-tzŭ*, ch. 1). The *Tao-tê ching*, then, may be regarded as holding the middle way between an ancient popular religion and the Taoist philosophy of later days.

TÊ, OR "VIRTUE"

Although Tao is emptiness, not-being, and above all non-action, it is not without its efficacy, which is called *Tê*, "Virtue". *Tê*, we may say, is the *mana* or mysterious power of Tao and shows that although Tao may be not-being, it is not for that reason nothing, but rather the potentiality of all being. It only appears to be not-being when looked at from the position of being. And so we read in the *Tao-tê ching* (ch. 51) that "Tao produces and *Tê* rears all beings". *Tê* can be defined as the prolongation of Tao into the actual existence of each individual thing. It is by *Tê* that Tao becomes manifest as the unifying One, the unity behind the multiplicity of beings. Or in other words Tao through the agency of *Tê* causes all existing beings to be linked in an underlying unity. The *Tê* in things is always that which turns from outward to inward: it is introvert, retiring and weak. Thus we read: "The movement of Tao is to turn backward. The function of Tao is to be weak" (ch. 40). To exist means "to embrace the *Yang* principle (the light) and turn one's back on the *Yin* (the dark)". To change this by reverting to *Yin* means, in the sense of the *Tao-tê ching*, to return to the dark and mysterious source of life. But the actual process of living depends on the harmonious blending of the *Yin* breath with the *Yang* breath. About the end of the fourth century A.D. this theory was changed under the influence of Manichaeism and a decided preference was then given to the light, or *Yang* principle. The *Yin* principle was henceforward considered to be the source of death and had to be kept down, whereas the *Yang* principle had to be increased. This controversy, however, was never decided, and even as late as the Ming dynasty (1368–1644) we find two schools of Chinese medicine, one stressing the importance of the *Yin* and the other of the *Yang* energy.

IMMORTALITY

Immortality to the ancient Chinese always meant physical immortality. The Western conception of spiritual immortality was unknown to them before they came in closer contact with Buddhism. Physical immortality was believed to be a change into a body made of more durable or lighter material than the one we have in normal life. Therefore we meet with a creed, stemming from the ancient state of Ch'i in North-Eastern China, and quickly spreading through all parts of the Empire during the fourth and third centuries B.C., that man after death leaves his old body, as a cicada or snake sloughs off its old skin, and soars off to the spheres of happiness. This creed was most willingly taken up in the state of Ch'in in the North-Western part of China, where the ground had been well prepared for it by a notable influx of shamanistic-ecstatic religion from the ancient Shang dynasty. The first Emperor of this Ch'in dynasty, Shih-huang-ti (221–210 B.C.), especially went to great lengths in order to become an immortal (*Hsien*) and for this purpose he collected a host of magicians at his court.

PRACTICES USED TO OBTAIN LONGEVITY

Allusions to life-prolonging practices can already be found in the *Tao-tê ching*, which may be considered as a general guide to the Taoism of the period of the Warring States (453–221 B.C.). We read for instance: "By concentrating one's breath, one may become pliable and soft. Could one not then be like an infant?" (*Tao-tê ching*, ch. 10). Life is strongest in infants "because the 'fine parts' in an infant have attained the utmost potency" (*Ibid.* ch. 55). This quotation shows clearly the link connecting the *Tao-tê ching* with the above-mentioned school of the Chi-gate.

Life-prolonging practices may be classified as follows:

(*a*) religious: the observation of commandments, moral conduct, prayer, incantations, etc.,

(*b*) physical: diets, medicines, chemicals, breathing methods, gymnastics, etc.

There were many schools which combined both religious and physical means. As these practices are one of the main features of Taoism it may be convenient to enlarge upon them a little. Apparently there were two very old methods of obtaining longevity in China. One was to foster the body, that is, to store as much vitality as possible by excessive eating and drinking and thus to stave off death. The other was to change the body by replacing its destructible materials by indestructible ones. It is this second method which we find in Taoist circles in the fourth and third centuries B.C. The most ancient version of this latter method is perhaps a short-cut proceeding, probably introduced from Tibetan tribes and designed to replace the material of the body by the essential material of fire. Thus we hear about adepts of longevity who threw themselves into fire in order to ascend into the sky as a flame! But this somewhat painful proceeding was soon abandoned for gentler methods. In order to ascend into the air one had to cleanse one's body from all impure and heavy material. This could be attained by living on a diet of gold, cinnabar, jade, and certain flowers. All these were believed to cleanse the human body from any kind of impurity and therefore make it light. Best of all was, of course, to live on air ... but not simply on any kind of air. In springtime one had to take the morning mist, in autumn the sinking *Yin*-clouds, in winter the midnight mist, and in summer the sun's rays. In between, one had to take the dark air or the upper sky and the yellow air near the earth. The inhaling of different kinds of air had to be assisted by certain gymnastic exercises during which one had to move like a bear or a bird. The inhaled air had to be conducted to certain parts of the body and stored there. It seems that one could choose one's sphere in the world of immortals. This method of eating air enabled one to ride on clouds, use dragons for horses, and ramble through the remotest corners of the air – in short, to become an immortal of the skies. But one could also become an immortal of the earth by building up a body from the hardest and most durable of all materials, and live as a hermit in the depth of the mountains. Furthermore one could take medicines which enabled one to walk upon and under water and thus become an immortal of the water.

DEITIES

Tao, itself beyond cognition, is apprehended through its emanation as the One, that is, the antithesis to the countless multitude of existing things. Because Tao was the originator of all life, that by which it became cognizable could not be a lifeless abstraction but must be filled with life. Thus it suggests itself that the One became the first personification of Tao emanating itself into being. He is the first and greatest god of Taoism. As such this "Greatest One" was introduced into the official worship during the first Han Dynasty (206 B.C. – A.D. 8) and placed on top of the five legendary emperors. Later he received the honorific designation of *Yüan-shih t'ien-tsun*, "Celestial Venerable of the Mysterious Origin". During the Sung dynasty (A.D. 960–1229) this was replaced by the title "Pure August" (*Yü-huang*).

He was then enlarged into a Trinity at the beginning of the third century A.D. (Some would take this to show the influence of the Christian Trinity.) The underlying idea of this Trinity was that Tao emanated itself into creation in three stages. Each stage came to be personified as a god. The first was the "Celestial Venerable of the Mysterious Origin" (*Yüan-shih t'ien-tsun*), the second the "August Ruler of the Tao" (*T'ai-lao tao-chün*), and the third the "August Old Ruler" (*T'ai-shang lao-chün*). Lao-tzŭ, the prominent saint of Taoism, was supposed to be an incarnation of the third. Besides this Trinity there was a great variety of Taoist gods and saints,

continuously increased during the ages, who even in a larger treatise could not be exhausted.

POLITICAL THEORIES

The Taoist school of the Chi-gate and the Lao-tzŭ school, however, developed also a political theory mainly in accordance with the basic demand of their doctrine to abstain from activity (*Wu-wei*). According to this the Emperor had to refrain from all governmental affairs, and occupy himself with meditation and the purification of his person in order to bring about unification with Tao. He was given every opportunity to obtain Taohood and to become the first saint of his people. The government, on the other hand, was under the guidance of an old and wise Prime Minister well versed in all the ways of Tao and, in fact, an embodiment of it. About the leading principle of his government we read for instance: "Therefore the saint, in exercise of government, empties their hearts and fills their bellies, weakens their will and strengthens their bones, thus constantly ensuring that the people are ... without desires. ... He practises non-action and consequently there is nothing that is not well governed" (*Tao-tê ching*, ch. 3). The government of the people should be such that "one did not even know there were rulers". At some periods of Chinese history attempts were made to put this Taoist policy into practice. The Han government, for instance, in its initial stage, was very much under its influence. And when the Confucians, after a long struggle and much intrigue, ousted Taoism from its influential position, they had to take over some of the ideas of their opponents. One of these apparently was to prevent the Emperor as much as possible from interfering in the administration of the Empire. Under the tutelage of the Confucians he became, as we know, the central figure of an elaborate state cult of official rites and ceremonials.

HUANG-LAO SCHOOL

We have already mentioned the legendary Yellow Emperor who was the outstanding saint of the Taoist school of the Chi-gate and in consequence became a prominent figure of Chinese medicine. The saint of the other pre-eminently philosophical and ethical Taoist school was Lao-tzŭ. Very little is known about him. He is supposed to have been a contemporary of Confucius and a keeper of records in the capital of the Chou dynasty (*c.* 1050–255 B.C.). But in Taoist circles his life has become a myth which was built up and gradually enlarged during the ages. When these two schools were more and more blended into one there emerged the designation of Huang-Lao as a name for the combined Taoism in the first Han and antecedent period (the third and second centuries B.C.).

THE T'AI-P'ING RELIGION

In many of the Taoist works we can find evidence that Taoism reached down into the lower strata of Chinese society – in contradistinction to Confucianism which reflected the mentality of feudal lords and government officials. In the rural population outside the city walls we find communities headed by religious leaders practising certain kinds of magic in order to ensure the loyalty of their followers. The spiritual outlook of those leaders can be traced back to Mo-tzŭ and his school. We also mentioned that the teachings of this philosopher were modelled after the holy Yü, who exhausted himself in unceasing toil on behalf of his people. Originating from this basic concept we find many features in those Mohist creeds which remind us of some typical aspects of Christianity such as the idea of universal love, mutual help, and so on. Another feature of Mohism was the firm belief that the world surrounding the living was densely populated by gods, spirits, demons, and filled with all sorts of good and evil influences. It was the task of the religious leaders to deal with all such powers by propitiating them or warding them off. The ancient shamanistic undercurrent of religious life in China can easily be traced back to these Mohist communities. Under the influence of the rhythmical changes in the correlation of *Yin* and *Yang* the Mohist-shamanistic group developed a doctrine of the periodical return of times of great calamities and disasters followed by intervals of universal peace and prosperity. These latter were called "*T'ai-p'ing*" ("Universal Peace"), and this was the name by which this creed became known in Chinese history. It was the duty of the religious leaders of such communities to exercise all their magical power in order to see their followers safely through the dangers caused by fire, water, war and pestilence till they reached the happy time of *T'ai-p'ing*. Therefore we can consider this a kind of collective salvation in contradistinction to the individual salvation of the other schools.

PARADISES

Linked up with the doctrine of how to become an immortal was the belief in certain abodes where the immortals lived in bliss. As immortality was physical, those abodes were also believed to be within the physical world. So we read about the blessed islands, P'êng-lai, Ying-chou, Fu-sang and others that were situated in the sea off the coast of Shantung. On these islands everybody was immortal. All animals and birds were pure white, and the palaces and gates were made of gold and silver. The faith of the first Ch'in Emperor in tales about such islands was so strong that he sent out a fleet of ships with young men and girls to find them. But like all other similar expeditions they never reached their goal but pretended to have seen those abodes of the immortals from afar without being able to approach them. Another of these abodes was on the summit of the K'un-lun mountain in the west of China. The belief in this mountain paradise evidently became more prominent during the first Han period and may have been one of the motives which impelled the Emperor Wu-ti to send his minister Chang Ch'ien on his famous mission to the West in the second century B.C. One of the deities presiding over the genii dwelling on the K'un-lun was the "Western Royal Mother" (*Hsi-wang-mu*). She is sometimes represented as having a human form, a panther's tail, a tiger's teats and dishevelled hair. She lived in a palace of massive gold ornamented by precious stones. In her garden was a peach-tree which put forth leaves once every three thousand years, and it required three thousand years after that for the fruit to ripen. But these peaches were endowed with the virtue of conferring longevity on anybody who had the good fortune to taste them. Therefore all the immortals assembled there in order to eat of these fruits and preserve their immortality. The Western Royal Mother also became a deity of medicine presiding chiefly over pestilences and the like. Corresponding to the Western Royal Mother there was the "Eastern Royal Duke" (*Tung-wang-kung*) in the East. He had a human form, but a bird's face and a tiger's tail. His palace was in the misty heavens: violet clouds formed its dome, and blue clouds its walls.

REVOLUTIONARY TAOIST TENDENCIES

Many of those Taoist paradises clearly show a spirit of protest against the existing feudal society. So we read in Lieh-tzŭ: "This kingdom was without commanders or elders: it simply went on itself. Its people were without desires or cravings: they simply followed their natural instincts" (*Lieh-tzŭ*, ch. 2). "Old and young lived pleasantly together, and there were no princes nor lords. Men and women wandered freely about in company; marriage-plans and betrothals were unknown"

(J. Needham, *Science etc.*, vol. ii, p. 142). This latter quotation especially shows that in rural communities there existed a spirit of strong antagonism to the established customs of official Chinese society according to which girls were considered to be human beings of a minor value and in many cases drowned immediately after birth. Wives were practically the slaves of their mothers-in-law and their husbands. Taoist sects made vigorous propaganda against the drowning of female infants and seemingly aimed at a society in which men and women would be on a more or less equal footing. This accounts for the great number of women followers and even leaders in the ranks of popular Taoism.

Certain Taoist sects, especially the sect of Universal Peace (*T'ai-p'ing*) were, generally speaking, the hotbed of political opposition, ready to burst into open rebellion at any provocation – by maladministration, oppressive taxation, natural disasters and the like.

THE YELLOW TURBANS

The biggest Taoist rebellion occurred in the year A.D. 184 under the leadership of Chang Chio. He was a representative leader of the T'ai-p'ing sect. Making use of the widespread discontent among the rural population caused by ever-worsening economic conditions, he collected huge bands of followers and formed them into a large organization. The missionaries and priests of Chang Chio were clad in yellow robes and his followers wore yellow head-gear as a distinctive mark. They are therefore usually known as the Yellow Turbans.

The creed of Chang Chio was based on a revelation received in his early life that the happy age of *T'ai-p'ing*, Universal Peace, would arrive when the present "Blue Heaven" would be replaced by the "Yellow Heaven". This event would take place at the end of the current sixty years' cycle in the year A.D. 184. The last ten years before the arrival of *T'ai-p'ing* were to be filled with an incessant sequence of devastating political and natural catastrophes as well as pestilences. Chang Chio was believed to be the great magical leader who would steer his flock safely through all these dangers into the happy period of *T'ai-p'ing*. According to his teaching all misfortune was caused by sin. Sins consisted in misconduct against the gods, spirits and demons surrounding mankind, and misdeeds against the community or one of its members. His method of salvation began with both a private and a public confession of all sins committed by the new aspirant, who was then given a drink of water which had been sanctified by the ashes of a charm. After that he was magically protected against all dangers

from gods, demons, nature and men. If, after all, he perished in one of the current catastrophes his death was attributed to lack of faith in the magical leader or secret sins which he had not included in his confession.

The main god of this special *T'ai-p'ing* belief was the "Yellow-Old Ruler" (*Huang-lao-chün*) or "Central Yellow-Old Ruler" (*Chung-yang Huang-lao-chün*) already worshipped in the rural Taoist communities of the third century B.C. He was the younger brother of the "Highest and most Subtle Heavenly Emperor and Ruler" (*T'ai-shang t'ai-wei t'ien-ti-chün*). Like most Taoist gods, he was a god of the external macrocosm as well as a god of the exact counterpart of this outside world in the interior of man, and in consequence had his abode somewhere in the heavens as well as in the centre of the human head. From this latter abode he probably supervised the human body, and became thereby one of the most important gods for the healing of diseases. And as plagues and pestilences were one of the most terrible dangers of those times it can be easily imagined that the prophet of this god, Chang Chio, met with a tremendous success. The roads of the Eastern and central part of the Han empire became obstructed by people who had given up their homes and property in order to follow him. From this we may perhaps deduce that these Taoist groups operated on a principle of mutual help and the communal use of goods. Furthermore we read in the *History of the Later Han Dynasty* (A.D. 25–220) that some Taoists distributed their property to the poor, established homes for orphans, built roads and bridges by voluntary labour and performed other similar good works. Chang Chio's movement had originally been planned as a peaceful demonstration of unarmed people. But, on the information of a traitor, the government attacked him and his followers at the end of the year A.D. 183. Although Chang Chio died a few months after the outbreak of armed intervention, the fight against his followers dragged on for about twenty years. Except for the T'ai-p'ing rebellion in the nineteenth century this was the greatest religious rebellion in Chinese history.

A TAOIST STATE

Another famous representative of a similar Taoist creed was Chang Lu, who founded a little Taoist state in the valley of the upper course of the Han river between Shensi and Szuchuan. This state flourished from approximately A.D. 188 to 215. It was administered by a Taoist hierarchy, and the whole system was characterized by integrity, probity, mildness and tolerance. An offence, for example, could be repeated three times before action was taken against the offender and the punishment for lesser offences was to repair a hundred paces of road. From time to time the priest-administrator requested his subjects to hold a kind of self-examination of sins which might have passed unnoticed. A special feature of this state was the free hostelries, where travellers could spend nights and eat meals free of charge. In front of these places dishes were set out with food for the use of needy passers-by. The misuse of these institutions was punished by diseases inflicted by the spirits.

CHANG TAO-LING AND THE WU-TOU-MI TAO

The tradition of this Taoist group goes back to the grandfather of Chang Lu, the famous Chang Tao-ling, who became one of the most prominent figures of Taoism. He emigrated from East China to Szuchuan in the West and established himself as a magician in a community of mainly Tibetan natives. The great Lao-tzǔ in person honoured him with a visit and, through his instruction, he was enabled to conclude a universal treaty by which all the demons and spirits in the world were brought under his power. This enabled him to produce protective charms, and charms of exorcism, that is to say, magical characters written on any kind of material. These became one of the main features of this school and were the height of fashion during the second and third centuries A.D. and later. By his power over ghosts and other preternatural beings Chang Tao-ling became the protector of his followers against all evil influences. He transmitted this power to his son Chang Hêng, and through him it was passed on to Chang Lu. From then on, the transmission of the power of Chang Tao-ling became hereditary among the descendants of the Chang family (or so the legend goes) who eventually took their abode on the Dragon and Tiger mountain (*Lung-hu shan*) in Kiangsi in A.D. 1016. This is supposed to be the beginning of the so-called Taoist "papacy" which (so it seems) was officially set up in the eleventh century and was carried on until quite recently. It ended in 1930 when the Red Army of Kiangsi broke all the jars in which the "Celestial Master" had imprisoned the evil spirits. Because of this the Taoist sect of Chang Tao-ling is often mentioned as the Taoism of the Celestial Master (*T'ien-shih Tao*).

The firm belief in ghosts and demons and in the power of the religious leader to keep them under control was the spiritual basis of Chang Lu's state. He collected a tax in kind of five pecks of rice from his followers, and so the whole sect is known as the "Taoism of Five Pecks of Rice" (*Wu-tou-mi Tao*).

This was in fact the usual levy of the Chinese government collected from Tibetan and other natives, and from this we can already deduce that the majority of Chang Lu's subjects were Tibetans. The influence of these natives made itself felt in the emergence of certain rituals in the cult of this Taoist sect which showed a markedly ecstatic and orgiastic character. There were rituals of repentance during which the participants rolled in mud and smeared their faces with dirt, indulged in communal sex practices, and much more besides. When the Taoism of Chang Tao-ling became the predominant Taoist creed during the third and fourth centuries A.D., such rituals were practised in rural communities all over the Empire.

REFORM TAOISM

The crudity of the rituals of the Taoism of Chang Tao-ling was probably one of the main reasons why the Buddhists separated themselves from the Taoists. The original status of Buddhism in China was, properly speaking, that of just another Taoist sect advocating a special method of obtaining immortality. The Taoists even circulated a legend that Lao-tzǔ emigrated to the West and became the Buddha. Buddhism, by its rational and highly developed philosophy and moral standards, found a firm foothold in circles which detested the absurdity of Taoist superstition and the primitive crudity of its rituals. Furthermore it took advantage of the powerful organization of the Buddhist "church" to establish members of the rich and powerful families as abbots in monasteries and similar high positions. Therefore, in the course of the fourth and fifth centuries A.D., Buddhism developed into a formidable spiritual and economic power threatening to bring the whole of Chinese society under its control. The Taoists, who were being increasingly ousted from their posts as official exorcists and religious advisers at the imperial or feudal courts, tried to counteract this by taking over from the Buddhists everything that would secure their own position, especially their ecclesiastical organization. In the wake of this anti-Buddhist movement of the Taoists, the great reformer K'ou Ch'ien-chih came to the fore. He had a revelation in A.D. 415 in which "the guardian spirit of Mount Sung, chief of the palace of the assembled immortals", entrusted him with the dignity of "Celestial Master" (*T'ien-shih*) and the mission to purify and rectify instruction in the Tao. His first action was to banish the false doctrine of the three Changs (Chang Tao-ling, Chang Hêng and Chang Lu), in other words to bring the Taoist ecclesiastical and monastic life (of which he probably was the originator) up to the level maintained by the Buddhists and to make it acceptable to the higher classes of Chinese society. According to his teaching the chief requirement for obtaining immortality was moral conduct and, in the second place, dieting and exercises pursued in secret. He claimed that the Buddha was one of the Taoist saints and said about Buddhism: "Because it is a doctrine of hardship and suffering, the disciples all shave their hair and dye their clothes, and do not follow normal human life," thus formulating one of the main propaganda objections of the Taoists against Buddhism.

K'ou Ch'ien-chih's success, brought about by obtaining the favour of the third Toba-Wei Emperor (424–458), did not last long. Shortly after his death in 448 the violent persecution of the Buddhists instigated by him and his followers was stopped, and they quickly regained their former influence. This was the first attempt of the Taoists to oust the Buddhist "church" *en bloc* and take over their economic and spiritual power.

A further attempt of K'ou Ch'ien-chih to establish a Taoist "papacy" was no more lasting. He himself was the first and the last of this line. He did, however, succeed in mitigating and refining the shocking rituals of the three Changs. Their cruder forms, nevertheless, were preserved for a long time in a rebellious Taoist undercurrent of Chinese society, which must be clearly distinguished from the Taoism practised in the leading Taoist monasteries and by its official representatives at the imperial court of the various dynasties. At the court they mainly functioned as advisers on auspicious days for any kind of political or private enterprise. They even determined the right time for the Emperor and Empress to start the continuation of the imperial lineage. Besides, they practised all sorts of Taoist exorcisms, magic and healing methods in the palaces.

THE SECRET OF IMMORTALITY

The Taoist preoccupation with finding means of prolonging individual life and of becoming an immortal was continued in the third and fourth centuries A.D. But, instead of the long and rather difficult method of keeping a certain diet or practising breathing exercises over many years, their main concern was now to find the miracle drug, the arcanum, by which the transformation of the body could be effected in a moment. Although this line of research had already been pursued in previous centuries, it now came very much into fashion. So we read: "As for transforming gold, melting jade, using talismans,

and preparing water, efficacious recipes and marvellous formulae exist by the thousands and tens of thousands. The best formulae are said to produce feathers for flying to heaven; the next best are said to dissipate calamity and exterminate disaster. Consequently, lovers of the marvellous are the ones who usually respect and practise them." The chief representative of this school was Ko Hung, better known as Pao-p'u tzŭ, who can rightly be called the greatest alchemist in Chinese history. Although he had a Confucian education and was well versed in the Classics, he spent all his life experimenting with cinnabar to produce the drug which could prolong life. Evidently his conviction was based on the fact that human life, in some cases, was short and in others long. Therefore there must be more durable ingredients in the physical structure of those who lived longer which enabled them to do so. And these ingredients, the essence of which he believed to be cinnabar, he tried out on himself. Cereals, formerly believed to contain the very essence of life, were now considered the most destructive of foods, a real carrier of death. This speaks volumes for the rivalries and struggles going on in the different schools of this creed. On the other hand Ko Hung was firmly convinced that the consumption of drugs alone would never produce immortality. It was equally essential to acquire merit by doing good works. Hence it was that a strong ethical trend was introduced into his teachings. The belief that the physical structure of the human body could be so changed as to become more or less imperishable was so strong during this period that the first Emperor of the Toba-Wei dynasty in 398–404 established a large academy for the concoction and preparation of such medicines, which were tried out on criminals found guilty of capital offences. "But, since it was not their original intention to obtain immortality, many died without proving the efficacy of the potion." It is furthermore of interest to see how this belief in physical immortality led to many fantastic stories widely circulated and firmly believed in those times. So we learn, for example, that immediately after death the body of K'ou Ch'ien-chih shrunk from eight feet three inches to six inches after his immortal part had left it.

TAOIST PHILOSOPHY

The philosophical thought of the *Tao-tê ching* and Chuang-tzŭ was carried on and developed in the third and fourth centuries. It became known as *Hsüan-hsüeh* or "Mysterious Learning". In 470 when one of the Emperors of the Liu-Sung dynasty created a new "Academy of General Learning" it was introduced as one of the main subjects of study. As the representatives of this school were themselves literati their Taoist philosophy was closely linked with the Confucian thought traditionally carried on in those circles. It is, in fact, the continuation of the tendencies of a Taoist sect, traces of which can be found in certain chapters of Chuang-tzŭ, where Tao is placed second, after *T'ien*, "Heaven". "If therefore somebody is going to explain the great Tao, he first explains *T'ien* and then follows the explanation of Tao and *Tê*" (*Chuang-tzŭ*, ch. 13). This group which tried to combine Taoism and Confucianism was prominent in the first Han dynasty. It was now represented by Wang Pi (226–249), the well-known commentator of the *Tao-tê ching*, and Kuo Hsiang (died in 312), the equally famous commentator of Chuang-tzŭ. It is one of the characteristic features of their doctrine that they acknowledged Confucius to be the greatest sage of all ages but interpreted the meaning of "sage" in a Taoist way. According to their opinion Confucius, as the sage, was identical with "not-being". Therefore he "realized that not-being could not be made the subject of instruction and so felt bound to deal with being. Lao-tzŭ and Chuang-tzŭ, however, not yet having completely escaped from the sphere of being, constantly spoke of not-being in which they were themselves deficient" (*see* Fung Yu-lan, *History of Chinese Philosophy*, vol. ii, p. 170).

This revival of Taoist philosophy presents itself mainly as a new way of interpreting the ideas of the Classic *Book of Changes* (*I-ching*), which always formed a link between Taoist and Confucian thought, as well as those of the *Tao-tê ching* and Chuang-tzŭ. The new interpretations, of course, were tinged with the general spirit of the period and the class-mentality of the literati. Stress was laid on "oneness" as the natural justification of monarchy and monarchic leadership. So we read: "The many cannot be governed by the many. It is the supremely solitary (i.e. the sovereign) who governs the many. Activity cannot be controlled by activity. It is he who is stable and single who controls the world's activities. Therefore in order that the many may be all equally sustained, the ruler must to the highest degree maintain his oneness" (*Ibid.*, p. 180).

Tao cannot produce anything because it is not-being. "It does not cause the gods to be divine, but they are divine of themselves" (*Ibid.*, p. 208).

"Not only is it that not-being cannot become being, but also being cannot become not-being. . . . Being eternally exists" (*Ibid.*, p. 209).

All things "spontaneously produce themselves" and do not issue from anything else. "This is the Way of Heaven (*T'ien tao*)" (*Ibid.*, p. 209).

"Hence we may know that the relative positions of ruler and subject, superior and inferior, hand and foot . . . conform to a natural principle of Heaven and are not really caused by men. . . . Let the servants simply accept their lot and assist each other without dissatisfaction" (*Ibid.*, p. 227).

This sounds very different from "in ancient time there were no lords and officials" of the anarchist Pao Ching-yen who put into words the mentality of other strata of Chinese society of the third and fourth centuries.

We also meet with a new interpretation of the old Taoist insistence on non-activity (*Wu-wei*). It is not reached "by folding one's hands in silence amidst the mountains and forests" as the hermits of Chuang-tzŭ's times would have it. "It simply means allowing everything to follow what is natural to it, and then its nature will be satisfied" (*Ibid.*, p. 216).

NATURALISM

This new Taoist philosophy gave the impulse to a movement of "following Nature" among the literati of this epoch. In the attempt to abandon themselves to their nature some let their hair grow or refused to talk, expressing themselves rather by strange actions or by whistling. Some indulged themselves in wine, took off their clothes or lay sprawled on the ground. In short, they did everything to flout correct Confucian manners and behaviour. They said this was the way to obtain the origin of the great Tao.

This movement did, however, provide the inspiration of a school of great artists who, inspired by wine and the beauty of Nature, produced outstanding works of poetry and painting.

The poet Hsi K'ang (223–262), founder of the circle of the "Seven Sages of the Bamboo Grove", could be quoted as the initiator of this artistic movement born out of the Taoist spirit of the time. One of his many later admirers was the great painter Ku K'ai-chih (344–405). This art, inspired by a Taoist view of life, reached its apogee in the poetry of the T'ang period (618–906) with such famous names as Li Tai-po, and in the painting of the Sung dynasty (960–1279). It was during this latter period that the trend of philosophical thought originally stemming from Taoism was definitely merged with Confucianism into what is known as Neo-Confucianism (p. 370).

TAOISM DURING THE T'ANG DYNASTY

Under the T'ang dynasty (618–906) the Taoist "church" was strongly supported by the government.

This can be attributed to the fact that the reigning house had the same surname Li as Li Êrh, or Lao-tzŭ, who was good enough to appear in person in order to make this known to the first T'ang Emperor. It is possible that Lao-tzŭ owes much of his eminent position in the Taoist hierarchy to this relationship of the T'ang rulers, who bestowed on him more and more honorific titles. But the real reason for this favour was probably the intention of the government to use the Taoist "church" to counter-balance the economic power of the Buddhists. This rivalry eventually led to a very severe persecution of the latter, instigated by the Taoists, in 845. It was a blow from which the Buddhist "church" never entirely recovered. This event was preceded in 843 by a persecu-tion of the Manichaeans, which drove them underground and forced them to merge with the underground Taoist current that originated from the defeated Yellow Turbans.

The Taoism of the T'ang period is characterized by the great development of Taoist monastic life which now became fashionable. So we read that in 711 even imperial princesses became Taoist nuns. At the beginning of the eighth century there were, in the capital Changan, ten Taoist monasteries and six nunneries (compared with sixty-four Buddhist monasteries and twenty-seven nun-neries). The monastic rules for Taoist monks and nuns were closely modelled on the *"Vinaya"*-rules of the Buddhists. The initiate had to sacrifice to the images of the highest Taoist gods and to hand in an application to them for acceptance into the monastic circle. Then he was pledged to keep the following commandments: not to kill, not to eat meat or drink alcohol, not to lie, not to steal, and to live in chastity. These commandments were steadily increased when he rose to higher monastic rank.

TAOIST PURITANISM

On the other hand, it seems that the Taoists of the T'ang period endeavoured to become paragons and arbiters of puritan morality. One of the outstanding figures in this respect was Lü Yen, better known as Lü Tung-pin (755–805), who set up a kind of account-keeping of merits and demerits. According to his calculation a merit redeemed a demerit, and a demerit annulled a merit. At the end of a month, one had to add up each column, subtract the smaller from the larger total, and to add the remainder, positive or negative, to the amount brought forward from the preceding month. He gave a detailed list of merits and demerits. Among the first we find: "Bearing with troublesome parents (100 merits), not believing gossip of one's brother's wife

or servant (10 merits), properly controlling the concu-bines of inferior rank (1 merit), preventing a wife or daughter from lounging about outside (10 merits), keeping promises made to friends (1 merit each time), saving a female child who was to be drowned (50 merits), reuniting two separated married persons and their dispersed children (100 merits), saving the life of an insect (1 merit), restoring an infant slave gratis to its parents (1 merit per 100 copper coins of its venal value), not fixing one's eyes on a pretty person (5 merits)" (Lü-Yen, *Fên-lei kung-kuo ko,* tr. L. Wieger), etc. On the other hand we learn about demerits: "Soiling a piece of paper with written characters on it, urinating or spitting towards the celestial luminaries (Sun, Moon and Great Bear, old Taoist divinities), pressing a poor debtor, staying naked in one's house for comfort during the hot season, uttering an obscene word," etc. (*Ibid.*).

Apart from the fact that this list represents what we might call bourgeois morality, it clearly leads up to the *Book of Rewards and Punishments* (*Kan-ying p'ien*), a very famous treatise on popular Taoist morality widely circulated during the Sung dynasty. The introduction to this little tract gives us an idea of popular Taoism in those days: "The Most High (*T'ai-shang*) says: Misfortune and fortune have no door (through which they would enter by themselves) but are called by men. As the shadow follows the form, so are good and evil deeds requited. Therefore Heaven and Earth have spirits acting as judges, who, according to the lightness or gravity of a sin, make deductions from the number of one's years. . . . There are also the divinities of the Great Bear and the Dipper who keep a record of men's sins from above, and pronounce sentence. . . . Within there are the three spirits of the body (i.e. in the head, the chest and the belly) who report on every fifty-third day to the heavenly court of justice on offences committed. On the last day of each month also the God of the Kitchen (*Tsao-wang*) hands in a similar report. In all cases, a grave fault is punished by a deduction of twelve years, a light offence by the deduction of one hundred days of one's life." We here meet with the tail end of certain doctrines of Chang Lu and the puritan tenden-cies of K'ou Ch'ien-chih. As many laymen tried to keep all those detailed regulations in their daily life, Taoism got the general reputation of being superior to Buddhism in the matter of religious discipline.

TAOISM DURING THE SUNG DYNASTY

During the Sung dynasty the Taoists likewise enjoyed the protection and favour of some of the Emperors. But, in general, it can be said that the religious impetus of Taoism was giving out. Much of it melted away into the different Buddhist creeds, since the belief that physical death could be postponed for an indefinite period by diet, breathing exercises or a secret, had become weaker and weaker, and people were more interested in bringing their souls safely into Sukhāvatī (p. 322) or some other Buddhist paradise. Although the ancient life-prolonging practices were still privately carried on by some individuals and circles, only a minority of the educated class really believed in them. The main trend of Taoist philosophical thought was absorbed into Neo-Confucianism, coming to the surface only sporadically, either in the system of a thinker of the later dynasties or as an occasional fashion amongst the intelligentsia and literati. The emotional impulses of Taoism were transformed into the poetry and painting of Chinese romanticism.

ATTEMPTS TO REANIMATE TAOISM

Official Taoism, supported especially by the third and the eighth Sung Emperors, tried to revive its vanishing attraction by borrowing from Amidism (the religion of Amitābha, pp. 304, 331–2), which had become the fashionable religion of the middle classes in the towns of the Empire. So a new god, the "Pure August" (*Yü-huang*), was introduced by the Taoists and installed by the third Sung Emperor. He was made the supreme god of the official Taoist pantheon and considered to be the equivalent of the "Sovereign on High" of ancient Chinese theism and of the Amitābha of Amidism. The liturgy of this new god was copiously borrowed from the latter. Under the patronage of this same Emperor the finding of letters and tracts dropped from heaven, a very frequent occurrence during the T'ang period, was resumed. These events were usually foreshadowed by a vision of the Emperor, during which he was informed by supernatural messengers that he would receive a message from Heaven. This message was, shortly afterwards, found wrapped in a yellow scarf dangling from the cornice of a city gate and solemnly collected by the Emperor in person. It was mostly written in the style of the *Tao-tê ching* and gave great praise to the Emperor and his good government.

THE TAOIST CANON (TAO-TSANG)

The Sung epoch was a time of great publishing activity in Taoist as in all other kinds of literature. It was then that, thanks to imperial patronage and the rapidly spreading art of printing, most of the works incorporated into the Taoist canon, the *Tao-tsang*, were produced. The *Tao-tsang* itself was published in the first half of the fifteenth century. It consists of 1464 works arranged in three sections in imitation of the Buddhist *Tripitaka*. These three sections correspond to the "Three Domains of Purity" (*San-ch'ing ching*), that is, the domain of the saints or the "Jade Purity", the domain of those who became really united with Tao or the "Highest Purity", and the domain of the immortals or the "Greatest Purity". The presiding rulers of the three domains together formed the highest Taoist trinity. Each of these rulers is considered to be responsible for the contents of the section over which he presides. The *Tao-tsang* is the most important source work for all aspects of Taoism.

POPULAR TAOISM

By far the greater part of the old Taoist faith was absorbed in the vast sea of popular religion, a complex of superstitious beliefs and practices sprinkled all over the countryside. Most of these cults had been branded as heretical and were outlawed. Therefore they split up into hundreds of little groups "assembling at dusk and dispersing at dawn", hidden in the mountainous regions of the vast country. Many of these societies, especially those in Fukien and Che-kiang, were Manichaean in outlook and were strongly influenced by the old sectarianism of Chang Chio (p. 390), who was considered by them to be a saint and whose name was treated as taboo. In 1120 these heretical communities burst out into open revolt under the general leadership of a disgruntled local bully, Fang La. It is significant of the mentality of the provincial Sung population that the badly armed rebels were able to put the government troops to flight, simply by painting their eyebrows red and pretending to be demons or possessed by spirits. The rebellion was one of the main reasons for the fall of the first Sung dynasty.

It was in this atmosphere of half-creeds and superstitions prevalent among the rural communities and lower social strata of the towns that popular Taoism was kept alive till recent years, when the drive of the government to exterminate superstition finally did away with the very thing on which it thrived. Small cult societies sprang up here and there wherever a person became possessed by a spirit or had revelations. As often as not they ended in small-scale rebellions. As an example we may quote the uprising of the sorceress T'ang Sai-êrh who, in 1420, pretended to have received a magic sword and a book on magic warfare. This enabled her to

TAOISM

become the central figure of a local religion and eventually of a sedition which was crushed in a few months.

SECTARIANISM AND SECRET SOCIETIES

Since the end of the thirteenth century there is a noticeable difference between the Taoism of the South and that of the North. The main group in the region South of the Yangtse was the "Principal-One" (*Chêng-i*) sect. The belief of this sect, which came to the fore at the beginning of the twelfth century, was built on the legend of the dignity, position and power of the "Celestial Master" ostensibly handed down from Chang Tao-ling (p. 391). It was alleged that his sword which could kill demons at a distance of thousands of miles, his seal which could not be broken by evil spirits, as well as many secrets connected with magic charms, had been preserved and passed on through the ages. This so-called Celestial Master was in fact the head of a troop of sub-magicians furnished by him with diplomas in the magic art. This practice consisted for the most part in making charms against rain, drought and devils, in exorcizing evil spirits, and in acting as mediums. They lived as Taoist laymen among the people and were married, differing in this respect from the Taoist monks, who lived as celibates in monastic communities and practised Taoist asceticism and meditation. Already during the T'ang and Sung dynasties these master sorcerers had been summoned to court to deal with floods, high tides, comets and droughts, and had been decorated for their services.

The most outstanding group in the North was the "Perfecting the True" (*Chüan-chên*) sect. It was founded by Ch'iu Ch'ang-ch'un, who in 1280 was invited by the Emperor to reside with eight disciples in the Temple of the White Cloud near Peking. This temple subsequently became the centre of the sect. Its teaching was to be in harmony with Nature: one should be calm, tranquil, simple and at peace with oneself. This was achieved by an asceticism resembling that of the Manichees in some respects. The followers of this sect were hard workers, producing their own food, and striving for social independence. They were all regular Taoist priests who had renounced their homes and adopted a vegetarian diet, and who lived in monasteries. They fasted on certain occasions, did not marry, and abstained from alcoholic drinks. Another feature of this school is the tendency to combine the three religions, Taoism, Confucianism and Buddhism into one.

Besides these two, there existed a number of other sects, for the most part of minor importance. Some

measure of mutual tolerance existed among all these Taoist groups, as did some degree of co-operation among their leaders. These societies furnished a bulwark of a sort against the Tartars and Mongols, and played a role in the resistance movements and rebellions against the conquerors.

Taoism, of course, also played a leading part in the secret societies in which political opposition found its expression under the Manchus (1644–1911). And if we look beneath the superficial Christian veneer of the T'ai-p'ing rebels and their leader we can find much of the spirit of the old *T'ai-p'ing* messiah Chang Chio.

At the beginning of the present century we find Taoist religious beliefs and practices still carried on by numerous and mostly secret sects. Among these was the society of the "Pervading-Unity Tao" (*I-kuan Tao*). This sect believed that the One is the root of all things and, as a principle, penetrates through and pervades all existence. The universe will pass through a number of great catastrophes marking the end of cosmic periods. According to this belief we are at present in the midst of the third catastrophe, but will be saved by the "Old Mother transcending Life" (*Wu-shêng Lao-mu*) whose cult was already developing during the Ming dynasty, and who later became an important deity of most of these religious societies. Followers of the *I-kuan Tao* were much addicted to the use of charms, planchette, the practice of the "three secrets" of finger signs, and magic phrases and incantations. They also abstained from meat, tobacco and alcohol. They worshipped images of all religions and recited both Buddhist and Taoist *Sūtras*. During the Second World War this society was very active especially in North China.

Another of these sects was the "Hall of the Tao" (*Tao yüan*) or the "Society of the Tao and Tê" (*Tao-tê shê*). It was started in Tsinan about 1921 when a revelation was received through the planchette. Thence it spread over North China and the Yangtse area and even opened a branch in Japan. In 1927 it claimed thirty thousand members. Its building contained five halls, one each for worship, scripture reading, meditation, preaching and charity. The sect worshipped the ancient Taoist god, the "Greatest One" (*T'ai-i*). Below his altar were the names of Confucius, Lao-tzŭ and Buddha, as well as the symbols of Christianity and Islam. They emphasized the community of Heaven and man in matters of the spirit, and the spirit of world brotherhood on earth. Because this society placed great stress on charity, it later assumed the name of the "Universal Red Swastika Society", and carried on Red Cross work.

There was also a secret sect in Shantung, whose

PLATE 93. Detail of "The Lord of the Northern Dipper" fresco from a Taoist Temple in the Shansi Province, China, fourteenth century. (*Royal Ontario Museum, Toronto*)

東王公

Photo: Universal Drawing Office

PLATE 94. Tung-wang kung, the "Eastern Royal Duke" (*see* page 389).
(*School of Oriental and African Studies, University of London*)

Photo: Karsh of Ottawa

PLATE 95. Dr Carl Gustav Jung, the Swiss psychologist, on his eighty-third birthday, July 1958.
(*Camera Press, London*)

Photo: Exclusive News Agency

PLATE 96. Friedrich Engels (1820–95): co-founder of Communism and theoretician of dialectical materialism.

members had to give up all their private property to the society. From this we may assume that communism, as practised in the first Christian communities, may have been carried on by little Taoist societies in some corner of China all through history.

After the revolution of 1911 which terminated the Manchu dynasty there was a period when secret societies seemed to hold the real power in China. They developed and practised gangsterism on a large scale, filling important posts with their partisans and terrorizing the people. When Mao Tsê-tung came into power one of his first measures was to exterminate these degenerate heirs to the tradition of resistance to foreign conquerors or social injustice. In 1949 the leaders of the *I-kuan Tao* society were arrested, and in 1951 the survivors, taking advantage of a general amnesty, apostatized in large numbers. Some of the secret societies were linked with partisans of Chiang Kai-shek or former landlords, and this, of course, provided sufficient reason for their liquidation.

The last head of the *Chêng-i* sect, the sixty-third Celestial Master, Chang Ên-pu, left the mainland of China in 1949 and became a refugee in Formosa. With him this degenerate form of Taoism which subsisted on the traffic in charms and magic formulas, as well as the "worship firms" which carried on a regular business in "masses" for the dead and exorcisms by piercing shrieks and the sound of shrill instruments or ram's horns, will most probably disappear for ever.

TAOISM OF TODAY

Taoism as a religion, however, is by no means defunct. It is as much alive as ever. But because it has always been a peculiarly Chinese religion and was never propagated among non-Chinese peoples, little is known of its present condition outside the borders of China. Nevertheless, it was, is, and probably always will be an integral part of the Chinese way of life. It makes a direct appeal to the innate love of the Chinese for the beauty of their landscape and the spirit of veneration which the reflec-

tion of this beauty calls forth in the Chinese soul. In its fundamental conception Taoism was always a worship of Nature without and within man and an attempt to bring both into harmony with each other. Perfection according to the Taoists was not to obstruct the way of Nature, but to give oneself completely to it. Thus it reached a very high ethical standard and brought out the best qualities in the Chinese character. The peaceful life of the temples, the architecture of which was, with consummate artistry, fitted into the Chinese landscape, and the quiet struggle for purification and union with Nature by meditation will never lose their attraction for the true Chinese mind.

Because it was linked up with secret societies, Taoism was exposed to persecution for a number of years during which much damage was done to shrines and temples. But all this has been stopped now. The temples are being repaired and the cult images placed under protection. Taoism has once more been granted the standing of a state religion by the present government. On 12 April, 1957, the China Taoist Association was officially founded in Peking at the closing session of a conference attended by Taoist priests and nuns from all over the country. Yüeh Chung-tai, abbot of the T'ai-ch'ing-kung monastery in Shenyang and a member of the National Committee of the Chinese People's Political Consultative Conference, was elected president of the association. The aims of the association are to unite the Taoists throughout the country, to promote the traditions of Taoism, to support the Socialist construction of the country, to participate in the movement for the protection of world peace, and to assist the government in the thorough implementation of the policy of religious freedom. Taoism, by its tradition, is certainly in an excellent position to promote peaceful coexistence and fair social conditions for everybody. Above all, Taoism will provide a stronghold for the Chinese mind by which it will be protected from becoming a spiritual satellite of any of the other spiritual powers of the present-day world.

11. A New Buddha and a New Tao

by R. C. ZAEHNER

In the introduction to this work, when we were discussing the nature of religion and what common factors could be found in the various world religions, we came to the conclusion that the only thing that was common to all of them in the religious rather than in the ethical sphere was that they were in some way connected with "the eternal", whether this is understood as an eternal Being outside man – God, or as the eternity of man's own being – immortality. We saw that it is quite possible for a religion to be strictly godless, as in the case of primitive Buddhism, which recognizes neither God nor Absolute, yet is nonetheless a religion and generally recognized as such. So it is when we come to consider the gropings of the religious instinct of modern man in this so-called post-Christian age.

Loss of faith in a given religion does not by any means imply the eradication of the religious instinct. It merely means that that instinct, temporarily repressed, will seek an object elsewhere. Any reader who has carefully perused the articles in this book, will perhaps have come to the conclusion that in all religions there are, in different proportions, three main ingredients – faith, a desire to "belong" and a desire for "escape".

Faith means either belief in the "mission" of a certain individual or group – prophet, incarnate god or church – or assent to a particular interpretation of existence, which enjoys the authority of antiquity or of human sages of proved experience. Faith in a personal god expresses itself in practical worship; faith in a given interpretation of existence finds its practical application in the schooling of mind and body in an effort to realize the spiritual state which this interpretation of existence claims is man's spiritual goal. In Indian religion this goal is called "release" or "emancipation", and by this is meant the enjoyment of an eternal mode of existence here and now.

The desire to "belong" is not, of course, a specifically religious phenomenon, but it *is* present, to a greater or lesser degree, in all religions. It may manifest itself in all

kinds of ways. At its simplest it is the desire to be incorporated into a spiritual society and to become integrated within it, as a part of the body is in the body itself. Alternatively, as in nature mysticism, it may express itself as a merging in the "all". In its extreme form, as in the Indian Vedānta (pp. 237–9), this merging in the "all" is transcended, and the individual, by the mere act of casting off individuality, becomes, or believes he becomes, *identical* with the "all"; or, in Tennyson's words, "out of the intensity of consciousness of individuality, individuality seems to dissolve and fade away into boundless being".

The desire to "escape" too is present in all religions – strongest in the Indian tradition and weakest in Islam. It is on the matter of that from which release is sought that religions so profoundly disagree. The Christian seeks release from the bondage of sin; the Buddhist seeks release from human existence as such. Islam, on the other hand, which accepts this world as God's creation and field of operation, was nevertheless unable wholly to resist the pressure of its own mystics who turned their backs on this world entirely.

In this chapter we shall be discussing two modern manifestations of the religious instinct, which, though they are not generally recognized as being specifically religious, nonetheless contain these three ingredients which may be considered as essential to religion. The one is esoteric, the other exoteric. The first is Jungian "depth psychology", the second Marxian Communism. The first deals with individual souls, the second claims all humanity as its subject-matter. Let us see how far faith, the desire to belong, and the desire to escape, fit into these two widely differing phenomena.

The patient of a Jungian psycho-analyst cannot hope to make any progress until he has complete faith in his analyst. Only then can he hope to "escape" from his neurosis which itself is due to the warfare of the "opposites" in his soul, and achieve "integration" and harmony with himself; for until he fully "belongs" to himself, he cannot belong to society. The Marxist too must have un-swerving faith in the original "revelation" of dialectical materialism in Marx and Engels, and in the absolute com-petence of the Communist Party to interpret these oracles. His desire to "belong" finds its fulfilment in the Party itself and, through the Party, in the society of the future and in the whole grand sweep of Nature herself triumphantly surging forward to her own fulfilment in the classless society. This hope is accompanied not only by a desire to "escape" from the old society, now ripe for destruction, but by a positive will to smash that outmoded thing.

Modern industrial civilization has, by separating man from his roots in nature, also deprived him of his tradi-tional religious roots; for religions, with very few excep-tions, in their popular form, conform to a certain degree with the natural order of things. Christianity is perhaps fortunate in that it was the first of the great religions to face up to the enormous social changes that industrializa-tion brought in its wake: it has had nearly two hundred years in which to adapt itself to the scientific age. It has had time to prepare its defence against the forces of scientific materialism and to meet the challenge that science seemed to present to religious belief. It has got used to the fact that a new civilization based on technology has come to stay and that Christianity, so far from seeking to oppose the inevitable, must welcome it and adapt itself to it.

For the other religions the testing time has come only now; for this century is characterized by two movements of immense force – Communism and the awakening of Asia. The Asiatic countries have at last realized that, if they wish to speak to the West on equal terms, they can only do so if they are materially as well equipped as they. This means industrialization and, since they lag so enor-mously behind the West in this respect, industrialization at breakneck speed. This is the purely outward aspect of Asia's awakening. On the religious side we find a new self-confidence among an élite and a strong desire not only to assert the values of their own religion but to propagate those values in the West. This is particularly true of Hinduism and Buddhism, both of which conduct vigorous propaganda in Western lands.

JUNGIAN DEPTH PSYCHOLOGY

Coincident with the popularization of Hindu and Buddhist ideas in the West is the rise of the Jungian school of psychology. Freudian psychology was basically anti-religious; Jungian psychology not only takes cognizance of religion but regards it as essential to psychological health. For Jung the religious instinct in man is of over-whelming importance, and the unprecedented violence and cruelty which have been released in this deplorable century only reflect a deep psychological illness consequent on the loss of traditional religious values. Whatever the truth of this may be, the fact remains that Jungian psycho-logy itself seems to be fast developing into a religion – an esoteric religion, it is true, but a religion nonetheless. It would scarcely be an exaggeration to say that Jungian psychology is a re-emergence of some aspects of Budd-hism and Taoism in modern dress; it is nature mysticism made respectable for the modern mind by the jargon of psychology.

Jung himself is, of course, fully conscious of his debt to Asiatic thought; and he has, in the author's opinion, done more to interpret Eastern religion to the West than any other man. In the following passage he re-asserts the Buddha's own view of religion as being simply a tech-nique for achieving a deathless state of consciousness, to which metaphysics of any kind is irrelevant.

"To be specific in this matter", Jung writes, "I can say that my admiration for the great Eastern philosophers is as great and as indubitable as my attitude toward their meta-physics is irreverent. I suspect them of being symbolical psychologists, to whom no greater wrong could be done than to take them literally. If it were metaphysics that they mean, it would be useless to try to understand them. But if it is psychology, we can not only understand them, but we can profit greatly by them, for then the so-called 'meta-physical' comes within the range of experience. If I accept the fact that a god is absolute and beyond all human experience, he leaves me cold. I do not affect him, nor does he affect me. But if I know, on the other hand, that God is a mighty activity of the soul, at once I must concern my-self with him" (*Secret of the Golden Flower*, 1931, p. 129).

Through the practice of depth psychology Jung has done in the twentieth century A.D. what the Hindus did in perhaps the eighth century B.C.; he has discovered empiri-cally the existence of an immortal soul in man, dwelling outside time and space, which can actually be experienced. This soul Jung, like the Hindus, calls the "self"; and the concept of the "self" is central to his psychology and gives it religious content. By the self he does not mean the "ego", the ordinary experiencing agent, or the conscious mind; he means something altogether different and ex-tremely difficult to describe in words. Hence his "self" is as hard to grasp as the Indian *ātman* (pp. 227-8, 238). Most basi-cally it is the entity in man which reconciles the opposites in the psyche and which transcends time and space. It is exactly what the Hindus understand by *ātman*, but devoid of the metaphysical apparatus which became attached to the latter. "It includes the totality of the psyche in so far as this manifests itself in the individual. [It] is not only the centre, but also the circumference that encloses consciousness and the unconscious; it is the centre of this totality, as the ego is the centre of consciousness" (*Integration of the Personality*, 1939, p. 96). It is, then, both the totality of the human psyche in which opposing characteristics, such as good and evil, are seen as reconciled and united, and the "deep centre" of that personality: it is the uniting principle where good and evil, male and female, and all the opposites in the world are seen to be really one. "In the self good and evil are indeed closer than identical twins" (*Psychology and Alchemy*, Collected Works, xii, p. 21), for Jung's self, like the Hindu *ātman*, is beyond good and evil as it is beyond all the other polarities. This self is, indeed, bisexual; for, according to Jung, every human soul is androgynous; every man has his *anima* or female counterpart within himself, and every woman has her *animus* or male counterpart. "This self is the total, *timeless* man and as such corresponds to the original, spherical, bisexual being who stands for the mutual integration of conscious and unconscious" (*Psychology of the Transference*, Collected Works, xvi, p. 311).

Timeless: that is the point. Empirically the human soul *is* immortal and can be experienced as such. "As a transcendental idea," indeed, "immortality cannot be the object of experience, hence there is no argument either for or against. But immortality as an *experience of feeling* is rather different. A feeling is as indispensable a reality as the existence of an idea, and can be experienced to exactly the same degree. On many occasions I have observed that the spontaneous manifestations of the self, i.e. the appearance of certain symbols relating thereto, bring with them something of the timelessness of the unconscious which expresses itself in a feeling of eternity or immortality. Such experiences can be extraordinarily impressive" (*Ibid.*, p. 310): and so the Hindus and Buddhists have always taught us, but it needed a Jung to make Western man take them seriously. Moreover, just as the Hindus tended to identify this "self", experienced as immortal, with the ground of all things that are – with God, that is to say – so does Jung conversely see in the gods of all religions what he calls the "archetype of the self".

Jung does not deny the ontological existence of the Judaeo-Christian God as creator and sustainer of the universe, for this is an unverifiable metaphysical question with which he is not concerned. As a "psychological fact", however, God or the God-archetype exists and can be experienced as a content of the so-called collective unconscious or as the symbol of the "self". "God is our own longing to which we pay divine honours," he had said as early as 1919 (*Psychology of the Unconscious*, p. 52). God, in other words, is simply another term for the collective unconscious or for some content of it.

Jungian psychology, as everyone knows, regards the soul as being composed of three layers – the conscious mind, the individual unconscious, and the collective unconscious. The latter is Jung's own discovery, and he owes it as much to his study of Asiatic religions as he does to the practice of psychotherapy. The collective unconscious is the great unknown, the chaotic "primal matter" of the alchemists, whereas the ego is the rational, divisive, classifying and formative principle. Consciousness and the unconscious should work harmoniously together, but they rarely do so. When harmony is established the "self" is born, that is to say, an immortal spirit which had formerly been hidden, manifests itself, harmony is established outside time, and man realizes with wonderment that he is indeed an immortal soul, he realizes himself as "God". This is "integration of the personality", the goal of Jungian psychology.

"Integration", however, is quite distinct from what the Indians call *samādhi*, an ecstatic condition which modern Vedāntins tend to speak of as being "superconscious", "universal consciousness", or in Mr Aldous Huxley's phrase "Mind at Large". "The Yogis," Jung says, "wind up with *samādhi*, an ecstatic condition that seems to be equivalent to an unconscious state. The fact, that they call our unconscious the universal consciousness, does not change things in the least: in their case the unconscious has devoured the ego-consciousness. They do not realize that a 'universal' consciousness is a contradiction in terms, since exclusiveness, selection, and discrimination are the root and essence of all that can claim the name of consciousness. A universal consciousness is, then, 'identical with unconsciousness' " (*Integration of the Personality*, p. 26). Integration, on the other hand, is to realize the totality of the self without the loss of ego-consciousness: it is the realization of a timeless being in oneself without at the same time losing consciousness of time. It is a godlike condition.

God, then, or at least the God of mystical experience, is, for Jung, probably identical with the collective unconscious, or rather with the "self" which is at the same time its totality and its centre. The collective unconscious itself is that part of the unconscious which is common to all men, "deeper than, prior to, and more fundamental than the individual personality . . . in the sense that as something generically present in man, it is collectively held by all men. Most essentially what Jung intends to convey by his concept is not that the unconscious is held in common as a collective inheritance, but rather that the unconscious contains materials which are held collectively by all men *because* they have a psychic reality which is *prior to personal experience*" (Ira Progoff, *Jung's Psychology and its Social Meaning*, 1953, pp. 53–4). God, then, for Jung, is part of man's inherited psychological equipment: he is in fact man's immortal soul.

This brings us right back to the old question of whether God and Nature are identical or different; for in Jung's system the unconscious in man, the microcosm, is the reflection of Nature or the universe, which is the macrocosm. Is God simply another word for the collective unconscious or not? On this all-important question Jung is best left to speak for himself:

"It is only through the psyche," he writes, "that we can establish that God acts upon us, but we are unable to distinguish whether these actions emanate from God or from the unconscious. We cannot tell whether God and the unconscious are two different entities. Both are border-line concepts for transcendental contents. But empirically it can be established, with a sufficient degree of probability, that there is in the unconscious an archetype of wholeness which manifests itself spontaneously in dreams, etc., and a tendency, independent of conscious will, to relate other archetypes to this centre. Consequently it does not seem improbable that the archetype of wholeness occupies as such a central position which approximates to the God-image. The similarity is further borne out by the peculiar fact that the archetype produces a symbolism which has always characterized and expressed the Deity. These facts make possible a certain qualification of our above thesis concerning the indistinguishableness of God and the unconscious. Strictly speaking, the God-image does not co-incide with the unconscious as such, but with a special content of it, namely the archetype of the self. It is this archetype from which we can no longer distinguish the God-image empirically. We can arbitrarily postulate a difference between the two entities, but that does not help us at all. On the contrary, it only helps us to separate man from God, and prevents God from becoming man.... The religious need longs for wholeness, and therefore lays hold of the images of wholeness offered by the unconscious, which, independently of the conscious mind, rise up from the depths of our psychic nature" (*Answer to Job*, pp. 177–8).

Jungian psychology, then, would appear to be almost identical with nature mysticism in that it sees the goal of life as being the bringing of the "self", that eternal substance which lives in an everlasting "now", right up into consciousness and in integrating this "divine child" with consciousness and with our ordinary world of space and time. This constitutes an "awareness on the one hand of our unique natures, and on the other of our intimate relationship with all life, not only human, but animal and plant, and even that of inorganic matter and the cosmos itself. It brings a feeling of 'oneness', and of reconciliation with life, which can now be accepted as it is, not as it ought to be" (F. Fordham, *An Introduction to Jung's Psychology*, 1953, p. 63). This is, in essence, the teaching of the Upanishads in modern dress. Yet Jung, like the Buddha, draws no metaphysical conclusions from the ineffable experiences of his patients nor from the mythological material that he utilizes. He is, therefore, careful to regard the identification of the "God-image" with the "self" purely as a psychical experience, not, as the extreme form of the Indian Vedānta does, when it identifies *Brahman* or the "divine ground" with the *ātman* or "self", as the highest metaphysical truth. It is a psychical condition verifiable by experience, but it is not a metaphysical truth. The experience always brings with it a sense of universal validity – of absolute truth therefore – for no better reason than that itself derives "from the universality of the collective psyche" (*Two Essays*, Collected Works, vii, p. 149). Yet though Jung condemns "sundry natures of feeble instinct" for "affecting Indian philosophy and the like" (*Ibid.*), there can be no doubt that basically his psychology agrees with the Vedānta except that – and the exception is enormous – he speaks of the God-image *in* man only and nowhere seeks to identify this image with the transcendent God of prophetic religion; for such a God, if he exists, must be unknowable by the mere fact of being transcendent. Jung's integrated man is almost certainly what the Buddha understood by *Nirvāṇa*; and it is quite fair to assume that the Buddha never made any definite statement on this subject simply because he knew the fatal tendency of those who have achieved such spiritual liberation to interpret it as a state of identity with the Supreme Spirit.

The importance of Jungian psychology, then, is that it in fact introduces Indian religion to the West in a form in which it can be assimilated. In so far as Jung teaches that there is an immortal soul in man which can and may be actually experienced, he is teaching a psychological truth which is basic to all Indian religion. He is reviving a mystical tradition in Europe that had seemed dead since Meister Eckhart and, after him, Angelus Silesius spoke of the birth of the Son of God in the soul of man. Jungian psychology is essentially mystical, but it is a mysticism which refuses to draw metaphysical conclusions that are wholly at variance with all rational experience, from the preternatural experiences which he analyses. He regards all religions as being more or less accurate maps of the contents of the collective unconscious; and since his own map tallies so very much more closely with the immanentist religions than with the prophetic ones, he is very much more in sympathy with the first. Among the varieties of Christianity he finds that Catholicism reflects the human psyche very much more completely than does Protestantism, and he even goes so far as to describe the Papal definition of the dogma of the Assumption of the Virgin as being "the most important religious event since the Reformation" (*Answer to Job*, p. 169), since for him this means that the Catholic Church has, albeit unconsciously, recognized that male and female are both present in the human soul of which the Godhead is only the image. His attitude to religions, then, is again almost identical with that of the great Asiatic religions themselves: all religions contain elements of "psychic truth", and Jung is therefore anxious that his patients should return to their various religions, not because they are in any sense revealed truth, but because they all give healing to the sick soul simply by being repositories of collective "psychic truth". With the exclusive claims of any of the religions he has no patience at all.

It is plain that Jungian psychology must, from the religious point of view, be an esoteric cult. It is no more suitable to the average modern man than the esoteric cults of India. There can be no doubt, however, that it will be pressed into the service of the Neo-Vedāntin and Zen Buddhist causes in so far as these are making themselves felt in the West, though Jung himself sees nothing but danger in such a proceeding. He does not believe that you can "transplant the spirit of a foreign race *in globo* into our own mentality without sensible injury to the latter" (*Two Essays*, p. 149).

Jungian psychology is a religious technique for achieving what the Hindus call "liberation" and the Buddhists *Nirvāṇa*. As such it is purely the affair of the individual: it cannot develop into an organized religion. There is, however, one great movement which, despite its atheism, must be regarded as being, in some sense, a religion: I mean, of course, Marxian Communism.

MARXIAN COMMUNISM OR DIALECTICAL MATERIALISM

"There was something formlessly fashioned
That existed before heaven and earth"
(*Tao-tê ching*, tr. Waley, 25).
"Being and Not-Being grow out of one another"
(*Ibid.* 2).
"Heaven and Earth are ruthless" (*Ibid.* 5).

Marxian Communism differs from Nazism, which too could be regarded as a type of religion, in that it has an ideological basis which is fundamental to it. In Nazism the Party satisfied that desire to belong which we saw was an irreducible component of the religious instinct, while the Führer himself provided the idol at whose feet the German people were called to worship. Nazism was, however, a wholly irrational movement, so entirely founded on and fed by emotion that, even if it had succeeded, it could not have lasted as a creed because it lacked any kind of theoretical background. Nazism has been compared to Islam, and Islam did, of course, develop and flourish both as a religion and as a social system after fighting a series of victorious wars. But Islam from the beginning had basic dogmas about God and his transcendence which were capable of inspiring a lasting fanaticism. Hitler may have had many qualities, but he was still no adequate substitute for Allah. The appeal of Hitlerism was crudely racial: the appeal of Communism is far more subtle, and we propose to devote the remainder of this chapter to the religious content of Marxian Communism or rather "dialectical materialism", the ideology on which Communism is based.

Jung's psychology, like some forms of Taoism (p. 386), is based on the theory of opposites and their resolution in the "self": dialectical materialism is based on the theory of "contradictions" and their final synthesis in a classless society. What Jung sees in the microcosm, man, Marxian Communism sees in the macrocosm, the universe. This is less surprising than might at first sight appear, for Jung re-discovered Asiatic immanentist religion via psychology, though he refused to draw any philosophical conclusions from the psychological data, whereas Marx and Engels inherited the "dialectic" of Hegelian idealism which has long been recognized as the nearest European equivalent to Indian monism, and applied it to the material world. Jung applies the Vedānta to the human soul, whereas Marx and Engels transform its Hegelian equivalent into an all-embracing theory of matter.

Dialectical materialism is the ideological foundation on which Marxian Communism is built; yet the working out of the system as a philosophy rather than as a social science was due not so much to Marx as to his friend and collaborator Friedrich Engels. The classic text-books of philosophical dialectical materialism are *Anti-Dühring* and the unfinished *Dialectics of Nature*, both by Engels. The theory was, however, first adumbrated in one of the earliest joint works of the co-founders of Communism, *The Holy Family*. In this work Marx for the first time applies the Hegelian dialectic to capitalist society. A classic "pair of opposites" stares him in the face: "Proletariat and wealth are opposites" (*The Holy Family*, 1956 ed., p. 51):
"Private property as private property, as wealth, is

compelled to maintain *itself*, and therefore its opposite, the proletariat, *in existence*. That is the *positive* side of the contradiction, self-satisfied private property.

"The proletariat, on the other hand, is compelled as proletariat to abolish itself and thereby its opposite, the condition of its existence, what makes it the proletariat, i.e., private property. This is the *negative* side of the contradiction, its restlessness within its very self, dissolved and self-dissolving private property."

Proletariat and private property "form a single whole". They are the positive and negative tensions in human society; in Chinese terms they are *Yang* and *Yin* (pp. 370, 386-7). They are opposite aspects of a single thing at war with itself. Once the tension becomes intolerable there must be an explosion, "a revolution of the mode of production and distribution *must* take place" (*Anti-Dühring*, 1934 ed., pp. 176-7), the contradictions must resolve into synthesis. So the proletariat, "*through the very nature of things*", "executes the sentence that private property pronounced on itself by begetting the proletariat. ... When the proletariat is victorious, it by no means becomes the absolute side of society, for it is victorious only by abolishing itself and its opposite. Then the proletariat disappears as well as the opposite which determines it, private property" (*The Holy Family*, p. 52).

In this short passage Marx sowed the seed of dialectical materialism. In the contradiction between proletariat and private property and their "negation" by proletarian revolution Marx was applying the Hegelian principle of thesis, antithesis and synthesis to nineteenth-century society. Engels was later to apply the same principle to the whole of life, indeed to the whole of existence: he was to proclaim it as an absolute law of Nature inherent in all things.

Hegelian idealism is notoriously akin to the Eastern idealisms of the Vedānta and Taoism. In the Vedānta all opposites are reconciled in the One; in Taoism the *Yang* and the *Yin* are reconciled in the Tao. For Hegel thesis and antithesis are resolved in the synthesis. All these systems are generally considered to be mystical; and, in developing the system of dialectical materialism, Engels himself realized that his pet theory of the "transformation of quantity into quality" would be interpreted "as mysticism and incomprehensible transcendentalism" (*Dialectics of Nature*, 1954 ed., p. 91), a description of his thought that he found far from flattering. Yet even he was prepared to admit that "the transformation of attraction into repulsion and *vice versa* is mystical in Hegel, but in substance he anticipated by it the scientific discovery that came later" (*Dialectics of Nature*, p. 324). Moreover, Marx himself, in formulating his theory of the eternity of matter and

motion, appeals to the authority of the German mystic, Jakob Boehme, who speaks of "the throes of matter" (*The Holy Family*, p. 172), and Engels too cites the Buddhists as being proficient in "dialectical thought" (*Dialectics of Nature*, p. 296). Thus the co-founder of dialectical materialism was not unaware of the likeness of his thought to that of the great Eastern systems; and, as if to confirm this little understood fact, Communist China is now reported to have proclaimed Taoism an official religion of the land (p. 401).

For Engels the precursors of dialectical materialism were above all the pre-Socratic Greek philosophers and among them, particularly Heraclitus (*Anti-Dühring*, p. 27), whose conception of the world was "intrinsically correct"; for, according to him, "everything is and also is not, for everything is in *flux*, is constantly changing, constantly coming into being and passing away" (*Ibid.*, cf. *Ludwig Feuerbach*, 1946 ed., p. 52; *Dialectics of Nature*, pp. 249-56, 266). This was an ancient truth which had become obscured, and subsequent materialism had degenerated into something static and "mechanical" (*Dialectics of Nature*, p. 335). This had been the great error of the French Encyclopedists.

By applying the Hegelian dialectic to matter, Marx and Engels brought matter to life and made it a living and thinking thing. "The first and most important of the inherent qualities of *matter* is *motion*, not only *mechanical* and *mathematical* movement, but still more *impulse, vital life-spirit, tension,* or to use Jakob Boehme's expression, the throes (*Qual*) of matter" (*The Holy Family*, p. 172). "And the Lord God formed man of the dust of the ground, and breathed into his nostrils the breath of life; and man became a living soul" (*Genesis* ii, 7). What the Lord God had done for man, Marx did for matter.

What do Marx and Engels understand by "dialectics"? "Dialectics", says Engels, "is nothing more than the science of the general laws of motion and development of Nature, human society and thought" (*Anti-Dühring*, p. 158). "Dialectics, so-called *objective* dialectics, prevails throughout Nature, and so-called subjective dialectics, dialectical thought, is only the reflection of the motion through opposites which asserts itself everywhere in Nature, and which by the continual conflict of the opposites and their final passage into one another, or into higher forms, determines the life of Nature" (*Dialectics of Nature*, p. 280; cf. *Ludwig Feuerbach*, p. 15). Attraction-and-repulsion is the basic "dialectical" duality which manifests itself throughout the whole domain of matter – in the universe, in society, and in the thinking of the individual. Duality, however, is not absolute, "positive and negative" do not "absolutely exclude one another" (*Anti-Dühring*, p.28; cf. *Ludwig Feuerbach*, p.52); on the contrary "every organic being is at each moment the same and not the same", for at all moments and in all places the opposites meet and coalesce: all is in flux always. Thought only reflects motion, and man is therefore the image not of God, but of living matter. No wonder Engels recognized his kinship with the Buddhists!

The Three Laws

Dialectics is "the science of inter-connections" (*Dialectics of Nature*, p. 83). "It is, therefore, from the history of nature and human society that the laws of dialectics are abstracted. For they are nothing but the most general laws of these two aspects of historical development, as well as of thought itself. And indeed they can be reduced in the main to three:

"The law of the transformation of quantity into quality and *vice versa*;

"The law of the interpenetration of opposites;

"The law of the negation of the negation" (*Ibid.*).

Let us study these laws in turn. The transformation of quantity into quality means that quantitative change reaches a point when the changing substance turns into something quite different. This is called the "qualitative leap" (*Anti-Dühring*, p. 54), and the simplest example of it is the transformation of ice into water, and water into steam, by the quantitative increase of heat. Chemistry, however, is the typical field in which such changes occur, and the example Engels is particularly fond of quoting is that of oxygen and ozone; for "if three atoms" of oxygen "unite into a molecule, instead of the usual two, we get ozone, a body which is very considerably different from ordinary oxygen in its odour and reactions" (*Dialectics of Nature*, p. 88). Similarly, as we have seen, Communist revolution produces a complete qualitative change in society: class society is transformed into a classless state. This first law is perhaps the least satisfactory of the three, and Engels draws most of his examples from chemistry where it is most obviously applicable.

The Interpenetration of Opposites

The second law is the interpenetration of opposites; and it gives Engels enormous scope. Things are at the same time the same and not the same. "Every organic being is at each moment the same and not the same; at each moment it is assimilating matter drawn from without, and excreting other matter; at each moment the cells of the body are dying and new ones are being formed; in fact within a longer or shorter period the matter of its body is completely renewed and is replaced by other atoms of matter, so that every organic being is at all

times itself and yet something other than itself. . . .The two poles of an antithesis, like positive and negative, are just as inseparable from each other as they are opposed, and . . . despite all their opposition they mutually penetrate each other" (*Anti-Dühring*, pp. 28–9). The opposites, then, of which positive and negative are the most fundamental, and which correspond exactly to the Chinese *Yang* and *Yin* are merely aspects of moving and living matter – the Chinese Tao.

So too there is no ultimate dualism between mind and matter. Both derive from nature. Thought and consciousness "are products of the human brain and . . . man himself is a product of nature . . . ; whence it is self-evident that the products of the human brain, being in the last analysis also products of nature, do not contradict the rest of nature but are in correspondence with it" (*Anti-Dühring*, pp. 44–5, cf. *Dialectics of Nature*, p. 243). Nature is the womb and origin of all things, and mind devolves naturally from nature itself. Hegel had turned the whole relationship of mind and matter the wrong way up by making matter the reflection of mind rather than the reverse; for "the dialectics of the mind are" really "only the reflection of the forms of motion of the real world, both of nature and of history" (*Dialectics of Nature*, p. 271; cf. *Ludwig Feuerbach*, pp. 15, 35). Thought, then, is necessarily determined by nature, and nature, on its side, is both reasonable and conscious: "Nature cannot be unreasonable or reason contrary to nature" (*Dialectics of Nature*, p. 294). "The truth is," Engels says, "that it is the nature of matter to advance to the evolution of thinking beings, hence this always necessarily occurs wherever the conditions for it . . . are present." Because thought is a reflection of matter and the nature of matter is "dialectic", it follows that thought *must* be dialectic too, that is to say, polarized (*Dialectics of Nature*, p. 283). The fact that it so rarely is does not seem to have worried Engels much; but it does explain why he and Communists in general attach such overriding importance to "correct" thinking and the Party line. To think incorrectly means that one has dropped out of the stream of Tao or nature, that one is senselessly opposing the laws according to which matter operates. To think correctly is to be in harmony with nature, for the "laws of thought and laws of nature are necessarily in agreement with one another, *if only they are correctly known*" (*Dialectics of Nature*, p. 299; cf. p. 352). Error, then, is sinful because it is unnatural: hence the rigour with which the Communists chastise "incorrect" thinking.

Contradictions are always relative (*Ludwig Feuerbach*, p. 52) as is everything else: so too is equilibrium (*Anti-Dühring*, p. 73) and the two are inseparable (*Dialectics of*

Nature, p. 326), "there is motion in equilibrium and equilibrium in motion: ... the individual motion strives towards equilibrium, the motion as a whole once more destroys the individual equilibrium" (*Ibid.*). But, for Engels in his *Dialectics of Nature*, the fundamental pair of opposites is attraction and repulsion, the "love and strife" of Heraclitus, the "desire and anger" of both Hinduism and Muslim philosophy. The interpenetration of these two is a fundamental law of nature.

"All motion consists in the interplay of attraction and repulsion. Motion, however, is only possible when each individual attraction is compensated by a corresponding repulsion somewhere else. Otherwise, in time, one side would get the preponderance over the other and then motion would finally cease. Hence all attractions and all repulsions in the universe must mutually balance one another. Thus the law of the indestructibility and un-creatability of motion is expressed in the form that each movement of attraction in the universe must have as its complement an equivalent movement of repulsion and *vice versa*: ... the sum of all attractions in the universe is equal to the sum of all repulsions" (*Dialectics of Nature*, pp. 95–6). For "dialectics has proved from the results of our experience of Nature so far that all polar opposites in general are determined by the mutual action of the two opposite poles on each other, that the separation and opposition of these poles exist only within their mutual connection and union, and, conversely, that their union exists only in their separation and their mutual connection only in their opposition" (*Dialectics of Nature*, p. 96).

Engels says: "Dialectics has *proved* from the results of *experience*...." By this he means that the "dialectical" laws of Nature can be proved by the physical sciences. Scientific discoveries, however, do not necessarily conform to the Marxian dogma of the uncreatability and indestructibility of matter, and Engels seems to have taken the line that, in that case, judgment should be reserved until further discoveries negate this particular negation (cf. *Dialectics of Nature*, p. 374). In theory, however, science, which reveals the laws of nature in *detail*, *cannot* conflict with correct dialectical thinking, which itself is a product of Nature and its reflection. Thus when science had reduced matter to little more than electricity or energy, Lenin was not alarmed. He merely re-defined matter as "*nothing but* objective reality existing independently of the human mind and reflected by it" (V.I.Lenin, *Materialism and Empirio-Criticism*, p. 270). Matter, then, equals objective reality.

"Correct" thinking, then, is the direct consequence of the operation of Nature itself; incorrect thinking is due, in some way, to chance. But, like all opposites, necessity and chance are relative terms, and chance itself "is summed up in necessity" (*Dialectics of Nature*, p. 295; cf. *Ludwig Feuerbach*, p. 53). Nature, like Allah, leads astray whomsoever she will, and even man's intellectual sins, his incorrect thinking, are predetermined by natural necessity which blinds him to any true reading of a given situation, Necessity, like the *māyā* of the Hindus (p. 238), both reveals *and* conceals. There is no such thing as freedom from necessity, that is, the immutable laws that inhere in Nature: freedom, rather, can only be understood as "the appreciation of necessity" and "necessity is blind only in so far as it is not understood" (*Anti-Dühring*, p. 128), "Freedom of the will therefore means nothing but the capacity to make decisions with real knowledge of the subject. Therefore the *freer* a man's judgment is in relation to a definite question, with so much the greater *necessity* is the content of this judgment determined; while arbitrary choice between many different and conflicting possible decisions, shows by this precisely that it is not free, that it is controlled by the very object it should itself control. Freedom therefore consists in the control over ourselves and over external nature which is founded on knowledge of natural necessity; it is therefore necessarily a product of historical development" (*Ibid.*). Freedom, in fact, is to act and think in accordance with an historical necessity which, in the present time, is bound to explode "in a revolution which will put an end to all class divisions" (*Anti-Dühring*, p. 177).

If, as seems obvious, Marxism is a religion in the sense that primitive Buddhism and Taoism are, we should expect it to have something to say on the subject of the human soul and the meaning of life and death. Like all the opposites, life and death interpenetrate each other. "Death", says Engels, is "an essential element of life, the *negation* of life as being essentially contained in life itself, so that life is always thought of in relation to its necessary result, death, which is always contained in it in germ.... For anyone who has once understood this, all talk of the immortality of the soul is done away with. Death is either the dissolution of the organic body, leaving nothing behind but the chemical constituents that formed its substance, or it leaves behind a *vital principle, more or less the soul*, that then survives *all* living organisms. Here, therefore," Engels glibly concludes, "by means of dialectics, simply becoming clear about the nature of life and death suffices to abolish an ancient superstition. Living means dying" (*Dialectics of Nature*, pp. 387–8). Matter, it will be remembered, is uncreated and indestructible. Moreover, it is a moving and therefore a living thing. Hence there must be a "vital principle, more or less the soul" in matter into which all individual souls dissolve just as all dead bodies dissolve into their chemical components. The soul, then, at death, merges into the Soul of the All. This is the mysticism of "matter" or nature – nature mysticism – with a vengeance.

The last of the opposites we have to consider, which is, from the practical point of view, the most important, is that of good and evil. These, like all other opposites, must be relative, and there can, therefore, be no such thing as absolute morality. Morality, according to Engels, is purely relative, it is only a historically determined collection of "unstable opinions and sentiments" which, of themselves, are of purely transitory value. Christian morals serve the interests of the governing class; and proletarian morals can, thus, only mean that which furthers the cause of proletarian revolution. "Men ... derive their moral ideas in the last resort from the practical relations on which their class position is based" (*Anti-Dühring*, p. 107). We are by now fully familiar with Communist morality which is quite consistent with the opinions of the founders of the Party. However, even Communists are beginning to question whether the interests of proletarian revolution are in fact identical with those of the ruling class in the Soviet Union.

The Negation of the Negation

The third law of dialectical materialism laid down by Engels is that of the "negation of the negation". The supreme example of this is, of course, the negation of private property by the proletariat and the consequent negation of the proletariat itself in the classless society. This is the goal with which all Nature has been travailing since life first emerged on earth: it is the final negation and the final synthesis in so far as human class relationships are concerned. This does not seem to be very consistent with the pure relativism preached by Marx and Engels (*see* especially *Ludwig Feuerbach*, pp. 14–15); but it is this teleological or eschatological element in Marxism that gives it its strength. Engels was a German and a Hegelian: Marx was a Jew, a member, then, of that race which brought prophetic religion into the world. Engels worked out dialectical materialism as a semi-mystical system, the centre of which might be said to be the "immanent will" of Nature; and this finds an exact parallel in the *Prakṛti* or "Nature" of the Sānkhya system in India (p. 237) and the Tao in China. The great defect of all the great Asiatic immanentist religions is that, by concentrating so exclusively on the other world, they drain this world in which we live of all meaning. Dialectical materialism, by adding a sense of purpose to what is, after all, a system of immanentist monism in which matter or Nature takes the place of the One, *Brahman*,

Dharma, or the Tao, and by investing matter with all the qualities of mind, soul and spirit, combines, for the first time since Christianity, the prophetic and eschatological type of religion with the mystical. Not only does it teach, like the Asiatic religions, that the basic opposites of life and death merge in the Soul of the All, but it teaches also that life on earth, impelled by the necessary laws of Nature, is moving inexorably to an earthly paradise where all men will be equal, all classes will be done away with, where man will no longer be exploited by man, where the state will wither away, and a true, because a necessary, freedom will at last be realized. In striving towards this goal man is co-operating with the purpose of Nature itself: he is swimming in the stream of the Tao. What Marx had not foreseen, however, was that the negation of the negation which leads to the establishment of the classless society, must inevitably, in accordance with his own dialectic, lead to the appearance of new contradictions – to the contradiction between the new bureaucratic ruling class and the once more enslaved working masses.

Starting from Marx's "negation of the negation" as applied to social classes, Engels makes it a universal law of dialectics, applicable in "the animal and plant kingdoms, in geology, in mathematics, in history and in philosophy" (*Anti-Dühring*, p. 157). Speaking of a grain of barley as an example of the negation of the negation, he says: "If it falls on suitable soil, then under the influence of heat and moisture a specific change takes place, it germinates; the grain as such ceases to exist, it is negated, and in its place appears the plant which has arisen from it, the negation of the grain. But what is the normal life-process of the plant? It grows, flowers, is fertilized and finally once more produces grains of barley, and as soon as these have ripened the stalk dies, is in its turn negated. As a result of this negation of the negation we have once again the original grain of barley, but not as a single unit, but ten, twenty or thirty fold" (*Anti-Dühring*, p. 152). This again is strangely reminiscent of the purely religious idea of dying to self, or, in Jungian parlance, of negating the ego in order to find the "self". Once again we find that what Jung declares to be true of the human psyche, Engels claims to find in the external world.

Matter and Motion

All that exists is matter, and "motion is the mode of existence of matter" (*Anti-Dühring*, p. 70). This principle had already been announced by Marx in *The Holy Family* (p. 172). It is the "scientific basis of dialectical materialism. Matter without motion is as unthinkable as motion without matter. Motion is, therefore, as uncreatable and indestructible as matter itself." Matter is in fact used by Engels to mean anything that moves, and by movement or motion he does not understand merely change of place, but all kinds of change. Matter and change are therefore inseparable and the ultimate source of all that has existence. Matter, then, which is undergoing qualitative as well as quantitative change the whole time, is eternal, because indestructible (cf. *Dialectics of Nature*, pp. 51, 93); and because thought and mind are simply evolutes of matter, matter itself must be, in some sense, conscious and rational, as well as alive. Because it can be neither created nor destroyed, the quantity of matter existing in the universe must always be the same: it is a unity, and, for Engels, "the unity of all motion in Nature is no longer a philosophical assertion, but a natural scientific fact" (*Dialectics of Nature*, p. 264). In matter there is "universal action and interaction, in which causes and effects are constantly changing places, and what is now or here an effect becomes there or then a cause, and *vice versa*" (*Anti-Dühring*, p. 29). The law of change is an infinite one "including itself in itself" (*Dialectics of Nature*, p. 315); for matter, like time, is infinite, and, being infinite, it is its own final cause (*Dialectics of Nature*, p. 337), that is to say, its purpose and destiny are identical with itself. In other words it is God.

There is nothing haphazard about matter or Nature, for it follows its own immutable laws. The law of Nature, unlike Nature itself, does not change; it is eternally the same. "The form of universality in Nature is law, and nobody talks more of the eternal character of the laws of Nature than natural scientists" (*Dialectics of Nature*, p. 310). It follows, then, that "all true knowledge of Nature is knowledge of the eternal, the infinite, and hence essentially absolute". This, sure enough, is the *sanātana dharma*, "the eternal law" or "perennial philosophy" of the Hindus. The good life consists in knowing the laws of Nature and in living "in harmony with" them (*Anti-Dühring*, p. 129); for "we, with flesh, blood, and brain, belong to Nature, and exist in its midst . . . and all our mastery of it consists of being able to know and correctly apply its laws" (*Dialectics of Nature*, p. 242). This, obviously only the Communist can do, and a perfectly harmonious life is only possible in the classless society which is Nature's goal, in "a state of society in which there are no longer class distinctions or anxiety over the means of subsistence for the individual, and in which for the first time there can be talk of real human freedom and of an existence in harmony with the established laws of Nature" (*Anti-Dühring*, p. 129).

For Engels, then, the Absolute, that is to say, that

which is changeless in a world of flux, is natural law. With this Absolute man can live in harmony, and he can even gain some knowledge of it – knowledge which consists "in seeking and establishing the infinite in the finite, the eternal in the transitory" (*Dialectics of Nature*, p. 310), in penetrating to the "form of the universal" **via** the particular. "The form of universality, however, is the form of self-completeness, hence of infinity; it is the comprehension of the many finite in the infinite" (*Ibid.*). And "just as the infinity of knowable matter is composed of the purely finite things, so the infinity of thought which knows the Absolute is composed of an infinite number of finite human minds, working side by side and successively at this infinite knowledge. . . . And that fully suffices us in order to be able to say: the infinite is just as much knowable as unknowable, and that is all we need" (*Dialectics of Nature*, p. 311; cf. *Anti-Dühring*, p. 100). The human race, then, is regarded as partaking of the infinite knowledge that belongs to the Absolute, each man knowing according to his measure. Thus Engels postulates "Absolute Mind" as well as "Universal Soul" in a sense that seems to be distinct from simply the totality of human minds and souls in time past, present, and yet to come.

All things are many yet one; transitory, yet eternal; finite, yet infinite. There is identity, yet "difference within identity" (*Dialectics of Nature*, p. 284). Natural scientists who have not grasped the "eternal law" of Nature are foolish enough to imagine that "identity and difference are irreconcilable opposites, instead of one-sided poles which represent the truth only in their reciprocal action, in the inclusion of difference *within* identity" (*Dialectics of Nature*, p. 286). All things are one in Nature; but Nature is not an absolute monad, as with Parmenides and the extreme Indian monists of Śankara's school (p. 237-8): it is a unity in difference; and this, according to Engels, is a scientific fact. "The unity of all motion in Nature", he says, "is no longer a philosophical assertion, but a natural scientific fact" (*Dialectics of Nature*, p. 264). "Difference in identity" would appear in Sanskrit as *viśishtādvaita* or "differentiated nonduality", and this, precisely, is the term used to describe the philosophy of Rāmānuja and his followers (p. 239); but for Rāmānuja the One is God, whereas for Engels it is Nature. For Spinoza God and Nature were interchangeable terms; and it is therefore arguable that, in Spinozan terms, Rāmānuja and Engels do not differ in any essential respect.

In a memorable passage Engels describes the whole, grand, infinite sweep of Nature in all its superb contradictoriness:

"It is an eternal cycle in which matter moves, a cycle which certainly completes its orbit in periods of time for which our terrestrial year is no adequate measure, a cycle in which the time of highest development, the time of organic life and still more that of life of beings conscious of Nature and of themselves, is just as narrowly restricted as the space in which life and self-consciousness came into operation; a cycle in which every finite mode of existence of matter, whether it be sun or nebular vapour, single animal or genus of animals, chemical combination or dissociation, is equally transient, and where nothing is eternal but eternally changing, eternally moving matter and the laws according to which it moves and changes. But however often, and however relentlessly, this cycle is completed in space and time; however many millions of suns and earths may arise and pass away; however long it may last before, in one solar system and only in *one* planet, the conditions of organic life develop; however innumerable the organic beings, too, that have to arise and to pass away before animals with a brain capable of thought are developed from their midst, and for a short space of time find conditions suitable for life, only to be exterminated later without mercy – we have the certainty that matter remains eternally the same in all its transformations, that none of its attributes can ever be lost and therefore, also, that with the same iron necessity that will exterminate on the earth its highest creation, the thinking mind, it must somewhere else and at another time again produce it" (*Dialectics of Nature*, p. 54).

Of such is dialectical materialism.

The theoretical working out of dialectical materialism was done entirely by Engels, and if the *Dialectics of Nature* (which he did not live to finish) was the only work of Marx and Engels that survived, it would be difficult to see what makes Communism so vital a creed. The answer is that social revolution, culminating in the establishment of a classless society here on earth, is represented as part of Nature's law, as the fulfilment of Nature's purpose, indeed, on this small earth of ours. To oppose the revolution is to fight against Nature, and that is criminal lunacy. Engels has laid down the three basic laws of Nature which we quoted above. The question, however, remains as to who is to interpret those laws. The problem is very similar to that which separates Catholics and Protestants over the interpretation of the Bible. Is there room for private judgment or does the correct interpretation lie with the Church? and if with the Church, does it lie with the whole body of the faithful, or only with the bishops, or with the Pope?

Yet even Catholics admit the infallibility of the Pope only in matters of faith and morals when he is speaking *ex cathedra* (p. 161). For Marxists, since there is a "correct" interpretation of the laws of Nature, and since these determine every possible sphere of activity, and since Communism is primarily a political movement which seeks to conquer the whole world, plainly it is of paramount importance to know what authority can be relied on to give the "correct" interpretation in any given set of circumstances. Stalin saw, quite rightly, that since the laws of Nature manifested themselves in the tactical vicissitudes of day-to-day politics with no sort of clarity, even the most orthodox Marxists were bound to go astray. It was, therefore, necessary that some one man whose authority was absolute, should be found to pronounce *ex cathedra* what the correct reading of historical necessity was. Such a man he found in himself. In the Stalinist era, then, dialectical materialism combined a philosophy of Oriental nature mysticism with both a typically Jewish eschatology of a new heaven and a new earth and a hierarchical system which reflected the hierarchy of the Roman Catholic Church. The "perennial philosophy" at last received a sense of purpose and a mission on this earth, and the mission itself was directed by an infallible leader and guide. The present rulers of the Soviet Union make a mistake, from the point of view of dialectical materialism, in abolishing the "cult of personality", by which they mean the absolute dictatorship and the absolute infallibility of the semi-divine person; for by admitting that the workings of Nature are not necessarily reflected "correctly" in any human mind, they are striking at the roots of the whole elaborate edifice of dialectical materialism itself.

The religious possibilities of Communism are enormous, as the Chinese seem to realize in granting Taoism official status. By doing this they recognize that Taoism, and with it Buddhism and many forms of Hinduism, are one and all assimilable to dialectical materialism. But whereas all these religions fall short of perfection in that they tend to turn their backs on this world – and the transformation of Hinduism in a more "activist" sense during the last century and a half rams in this point – dialectical materialism gives point, purpose and tremendous drive to a type of religion that had hitherto been content to seek its One, its Tao, and its *Nirvāṇa* in a world that lay outside space and time. Dialectical materialism brings down the kingdom of heaven on to this earth of ours; but the kingdom of heaven as now established is far other than that foretold by Marx and Engels, the prophet and the seer.

Conclusion

by THE EDITOR

We have now reviewed the principal faiths by which men still live today. The picture that results is confusing since the mere collocation of the various faiths of mankind only brings out into relief the sharp differences between them. In this final section we will try to make some sense of the differences and also to assess the prospects of the various religions in the modern age of technology when all of them will have to face up to the challenge of an overwhelmingly secular civilization.

Hitherto the great religions have also provided the social framework of the society they dominated. Everywhere this purely religious framework is breaking down and giving way to a system of social ethics that derives in fact largely from that Christianity which, as a dogmatic religion, the West has in part abandoned. The clearest evidence of this is the changing attitude of both Muslims and Hindus to polygamy and child marriages. However, in the Christian world itself, Christian ethics, as well as Christian beliefs, are increasingly questioned; and whereas in India and the Muslim world polygamy is no longer quite respectable, in the West and particularly in the United States successive polygamy in the shape of easy divorce is becoming increasingly common.

Christianity was the first religion that had to face up to the purely secular idea that found its expression most completely in the French Enlightenment. The Church's right to provide the framework in which men should live out their lives was questioned, and man was invited to live by the unaided light of reason. The Enlightenment was a necessary and a salutary influence, for it forced the Christian churches to reconsider their positions and to hold their own not by the *vis inertiae* of a dying tradition but by boldly facing up to the challenge. Though it is probable that the number of professing Christians is still declining, it is very questionable whether the number of *believing* Christians is doing the same. The increased vitality of the Catholic Church and the increasing awareness among Protestants of the necessity of drawing closer together shows that both great branches of the Western Christian Church are very much alive.

What of the other religions? and how will they face up to the challenge of the modern world? Everywhere in re-awakening Asia the "intellectuals" are turning away from religion as they largely did in Europe in the eighteenth century. Asia's very backwardness is seen as a result of an unquestioning subservience to religion, and the amazing growth of science in the West and the mastering of the means of production are seen against a background of scientific man's defiance of religion. This is, of course, an over-simplification, since basically there is no contradiction between science and Christianity. This, however, does not alter the fact that the Asiatic equates scientific advance with the rejection of religious belief. In actual fact it can be argued that scientific progress was only possible in a civilization whose religion firmly stressed the reality of the world and considered that reality to be expressly confirmed by God's incarnation as man. If the world is in fact an illusion as an important school of Hindu philosophy believes (p. 238), or is re-created ever anew as the Muslim atomist theory has it (p. 200), there would appear to be singularly little incentive to engage in scientific research.

The old conflict between religion and science, however, is largely played out since it was based on a misunderstanding. A very much more serious challenge faces organized religion in the shape of the growth of materialism, both in its crude and in its Marxist form. We tried to analyse the latter in our last chapter and saw how it too, by blurring the distinction between matter and mind, and deifying mind-bearing matter, was very near to becoming an immanentist religion. Dialectical materialism can meet the purely immanentist religions on their own ground: they can all be regarded as more or less fumbling prefigurations of the Marxist analysis of the nature of this universe in which we live. Marxist materialism can be seen as completing the immanentist world-views of

413

Indian and Chinese religion; the gods are done away with but the eternal laws of Nature remain. This cannot but remind the Hindu or Buddhist philosopher of his own great insights, that of an eternal *Brahman* revealing itself in ever-changing forms or of the wheel of *saṁsāra* set over against the eternal and changeless *Nirvāṇa*.

Much closer to Hinduism and Buddhism, however, is Jungian psychology which interprets much that is essential in these two religions in purely psychological terms. When Jung equates the "God-image" with the archetype of the "self", he is expressing in his own psychological terminology the old Hindu identification of the *ātman*, the human soul or self, with the *Brahman*, the ground of the entire universe. He confirms this central Hindu doctrine, but in terms that deal no longer with objective being but with subjective psychological states: he reduces all religions to so many techniques of achieving psychic integration. His attitude is classically Indian and is most succinctly expressed in Rāmakrishna's "All religions are true" (p. 257), which is equivalent to saying that none of them are.

Jung's attitude towards religion is typical of the secular reaction of the West to its long domination by a religion that lays claim to absolute and exclusive truth. No less typical is the reaction of another great modern thinker, Arnold Toynbee. For him the religions are all expressions of essential truths: their differences are concerned merely with non-essentials. These truths are according to him:

(1) "Man himself is certainly not the greatest spiritual presence in the Universe."

(2) "There is a presence in the Universe that is spiritually greater than Man himself."

(3) "In human life, knowledge is not an end in itself, but is a means to action."

(4) "Man's goal is to seek communion with the presence behind the phenomena, and to seek it with the aim of bringing himself into harmony with this absolute spiritual reality."

(5) "A human self cannot be brought into harmony with absolute reality unless it can get rid of its innate self-centredness. This is the hardest task that Man can set himself."

(6) "Absolute reality has both an impersonal and a personal aspect."

(7) "The personal aspect or 'God' must be good as well as omnipotent" (*An Historian's Approach to Religion*, 1956, pp. 273–4).

Yet even these broad generalizations, which Toynbee regards as the essential "truths" of religion, are not common even to the seven religions with which he deals, as anyone who has read through the present volume will very soon realize. For the non-dualist Vedānta as well as for the Theravādin Buddhists and the Jains, man, in his eternal essence, *is* the greatest spiritual presence in the universe. Again his second "truth" is not accepted by the same three schools of thought. His fourth point is not true of orthodox Islam, for it was only the Ṣūfīs who sought communion with the "presence behind the phenomena" and they were never fully accepted by the orthodox (p. 204). Again it is doubtful whether any Jew outside Kabbalistic circles would agree that God has an impersonal aspect: the God of the Old Testament could scarcely be more personal. Nor, for that matter, would most Christians concede that there is such a thing as an "impersonal aspect of absolute reality" since this would make nonsense of the fatherhood of God on which Christianity lays such tremendous emphasis, for in Christianity God the Father, as fountain-head of all godhead, *is* the "absolute reality". Again the Yahweh of the Old Testament who "creates evil" (p. 31) and the God of Islam who "leads astray whom he will" (p. 189) can scarcely be said to be absolutely good. Professor Toynbee's "essential truths" unfortunately do not coincide with the facts: he is making the great religions say what he personally thinks they ought to say.

Toynbee seems to think that it is possible to arrive at some sort of "higher synthesis" of essential truths and that ideally the great religions should concentrate on these to the exclusion of "non-essentials". In this he is at one with the modern syncretizing tendency in Hinduism but with no other trend discernible in the religious situation today. However much he may bewail what he calls the "group selfishness" of the great religions, this "group selfishness" is inherent in any religion which believes itself to be true, and is, in fact, what gives it life. That each of the prophetic religions believes itself to be uniquely true has been pointed out in the Introduction. It is, however, equally true that the Buddha claimed that "there is one sole way for the purification of beings" (p. 268), and that "truth is one, there is not a second" (p. 283). Buddhism, then, as originally propounded, is as exclusive as are the three great monotheistic religions of Semitic origin. But between the latter and it there is a quite fundamental difference; for what is in dispute between the three Semitic religions is the validity of later *revelations*, the Jews denying the Messianic claims of Christ as well as the prophetic claims of Muhammad, and the Christians denying the latter. What is in question is the authenticity of Christ's claim to be the Son of *God* and Muhammad's claim to be the "Seal of the Prophets" sent by God. About the existence of God as an objective reality and his intervention in human history there is no dispute at all. With

Buddhism, on the other hand, the existence or non-existence of God is simply irrelevant; for whereas the theme of the Semitic religions is God's relations with man, the theme of Buddhism is the way to achieve deliverance from this world of coming-to-be and passing-away. There is no conflict here because the Semitic religions and Buddhism are dealing with quite different problems. Religion, indeed, in Miss Horner's words, "is not a very good term to use in connection with Buddhism" (p. 267): rather it might much more aptly be described as "depth psychology".

It is, then, methodologically quite wrong to treat the great religions of the world as parallel phenomena and to saddle all of them, as Professor Toynbee does, with purely subjective "essential truths", of a number of which many of them are innocent. It is also unhistorical, since it makes no attempt to distinguish between the essentials of any given religion and the subsequent accretions. Thus, enormous though the differences between the Theravāda and the Mahāyāna appear to be, Dr. Conze can quite rightly say of the Mahāyānists: "Nor did they ever swerve from the *aim* of all Buddhist endeavour, which is the 'extinction of the self', the dying out of separate individuality" (p. 308). This alone of Toynbee's essentials is the essence of Buddhism. Such an ideal is quite foreign to Judaism, Christianity and Islam except in their more unorthodox manifestations.

To make any sense of the general pattern of the world's faiths the premisses from which each starts must be clearly understood. The Judaic premiss concerning the nature of man is that he is a creature composed of soul and body indissolubly united. Thus, though the soul may survive death, it is still only half a man, the nobler half, but still only a half. Salvation, then, means the making whole again of man in body and in soul in "the New Era of God's Kingdom" (p. 34). This is diametrically opposed to the Indian conception of man, since for the Indians man's body is either totally distinct from the soul (p. 237), though temporarily joined to it, or it is, together with the whole world of space and time, "little different from a dream, a figment of the imagination; it is like the deceptive appearance produced by a conjuror" (p. 238). When the nature of man is thus diagnosed, salvation can only mean the final release of the soul from the body and from matter: the nature of divinity ceases to be of prime importance, "it is not a question of great concern whether a man believes in one god or several or in no god at all" (p. 241).

Similarly, in the Mahāyāna, the sublime idea of the Bodhisattva who, "destined to become a Buddha, nevertheless, in order to help suffering creatures, selflessly post-pones his entrance into the bliss of *Nirvāṇa* and escapes from this world of birth and death" (p. 299), is somewhat vitiated by the opposite and more fundamental truth that "in actual reality there are no Buddhas, no Bod-hisattvas, no perfections, no stages, and no paradises" (p. 306). Both the Hindu gods and the Bodhisattvas of the Mahāyāna, however deeply they may touch the popular imagination, nevertheless can never take the place of the God of prophetic religion because their own ultimate reality is always in doubt when seen against the dominant monist philosophy of both creeds. Of these gods Voltaire's aphorism that, if God did not exist, it would be necessary to invent him is surely true.

"Classical" Hinduism and Buddhism are both essentially religions of escape, and there is no doubt that they make a powerful appeal to a certain type of mind, to all, indeed, who have lost their sense of purpose, for they consider that "ordinary life is hopelessly unsatisfactory, exposed to constant pain and grief, and in any case quite futile" (p. 301). Such religions, though a useful antidote to the prevalent materialism, would seem to be ultimately unsatisfactory psychologically because they deprive human existence as we know it of all meaning. The "reform" which has taken place within Hinduism itself during the last century and a half is proof enough that the old philosophy of classical times has in the long run been found wanting. The classical Judaic view, moreover, that man is not just his soul or a deathless something, finds support in the more down-to-earth philosophy of the Chinese. In his criticism of Buddhism the Confucian Hu Yin says:

"Man is a living thing; the Buddhists speak not of life but of death. Human affairs are all visible; the Buddhists speak not of the manifest but of the hidden. After a man dies he is called a ghost; the Buddhists speak not of men but of ghosts. . . . What determines how we should be-have in ordinary life is moral principle: the Buddhists speak not of moral principle but of the illusoriness of sense-perception. It is to what follows birth and precedes death that we should devote our minds; the Buddhists speak not of this life but of past and future lives. Seeing and hearing, thought and discussion, are real evidence; the Buddhists do not treat them as real, but speak of what the ear and eye cannot attain, thought and discussion cannot reach" (pp. 365–6).

If this is how the Chinese mind sees Buddhism, it is not surprising that Marxian Communism gained so easy a victory in China, for Communism *both* has an oriental metaphysic which discerns an eternal *dharma* beneath the ever-changing flux of things, *and* a positive this-worldly remedy for the evils of *saṁsāra*. Whereas Buddhism offers individual salvation in the total extinction of individuality in the "unborn and unbecome", Marxism offers collective salvation here and now in a "monolithic" society in which the individual is asked to identify himself not with a *Brahman* or a Tao but with the living and toiling collectivity.

Yet philosophically Marxian Communism and Mahāyāna Buddhism are closely akin. "If all is the same," as Dr. Conze writes, "then also the Absolute will be identical with the relative, the Unconditioned with the conditioned, *Nirvāṇa* with *saṁsāra*" (p. 317). For Engels the "eternal", which is for the Buddhist *Nirvāṇa*, is the Law of Nature (p. 411) which is "the infinite and hence the essentially absolute" (*ibid*): but the finite and the infinite do not exclude each other, they are "poles which represent the truth only in their reciprocal action, in the inclusion of difference *within* identity" (*ibid*). Philosophically the two systems are not dissimilar, since they both equate *Nirvāṇa* with *saṁsāra*, mind with matter, but the equation works out in opposite directions; for whereas *Nirvāṇa* is the only important "pole" of the opposites for the Buddhist, *saṁsāra* or matter is all-important to the Marxist. For him the opposite pole is not simply an eternal something which forms the backcloth to the saṁsāric puppet-show but the eternal law which regulates all change. To live in accordance with this Law is to live in accordance with Nature itself; it is to achieve one's *Nirvāṇa* here and now in space and time. Seen in this light the triumph of Communism in China represents the triumph of the claims of *saṁsāra* over against *Nirvāṇa*, of matter over against spirit; it is the quite natural assertion of the material world to its due place in the created order, for the indiscriminate identification of matter and spirit inevitably leads to the deification of one or the other; and the Mahāyāna identification of the two must in turn be seen as the natural revolt against the view that matter is no more than the prison-house of the soul.

Even so it would appear that the Indian view of the nature of man must be true; for what Indian religion asserts is that while the physical death of the body is an uncontrovertible fact, the eternal essence of the soul can equally be experienced in Yogic trance. This experience is, of course, not confined to India, but re-appears at all times and in all places in the nature mystics. It is this experience which accounts for the hatred and contempt that classical Indian religion feels for the body and all its works. For the body dies and cannot be revived. Yet the belief that the body was once immortal is an almost universal primitive belief, and the complementary belief that it can once again be made so is best illustrated by the

pathetic attempts of the Taoists to achieve physical immortality in this life (pp. 387–8).

The Semitic and Zoroastrian doctrine of the resurrection of the body is not very popular nowadays and is much derided, but it is the only way that the typically Semitic (and Zoroastrian and Taoist) conception of man could be preserved. If to be a man is to be an ensouled body, then, though the soul may in some sense survive, the man does not unless his body is resurrected too. Neither Judaism, Zoroastrianism nor Islam can at all justify their belief in the ultimate resurrection of the body except by faith; but in the Resurrection of Jesus Christ the Christian can see the firstfruits of his own immortality in body and in soul. This is why the Eastern Orthodox lay such immense stress on the Resurrection, for it is God's promise to man that he will share in the full life of the risen Christ, who is not only man but God. The Christian and the Buddhist points of view are diametrically opposed, for whereas the Christian agrees with the Buddhist that in order to achieve eternal life man must deny himself and hate "the life of this world" (*John* xii, 25), by doing so he does not simply disappear into a "trackless" and "untraceable" (p. 283) form of existence, but, on the contrary, starts life as a "new creation" destined to share in the life of the risen Christ in body as well as in soul.

The two views of salvation correspond to the two views on the nature of man; and each view represents a different attitude to life and death. The Semites and the Zoroastrians see eternal life as an everlasting existence of body and soul in which there must be something at least corresponding to space and time, the Indians see it as a form of existence in which time and space are transcended, as an eternal "Now". For the Indians the body is "evil" simply because it is mortal and transient: evil is equated with *saṁsāra*, the world of change, good with *Nirvāṇa* or *Brahman*, the world that does not change. For the Semites the body is not evil because it is transient, but transient because it has become evil as a result of sin. Thus while a Christian would not deny the validity of the Hindu or Buddhist experience of the eternity of the human soul which they call *Nirvāṇa*, he would deny that this represents man's ultimate bliss; for as the Hindu theists themselves, who reacted against Śankara's rigid monism, realized, the soul's realization of its own timelessness and isolation is not the final purpose of human existence, which is rather that soul's union and communion with God and its re-union with a transfigured body.

Christianity teaches that Jesus Christ rose from the dead, his sacrifice on the Cross having re-established man's relationship with God which is said to have been broken off by Original Sin. At the same time the incarnation of God as man signifies the sanctification of all matter, as the Orthodox particularly emphasize, and the resurrection of the God-Man foreshadows the redemption of the whole man in body as well as soul and his incorporation into Christ and, through Christ, into God. The recent definition of the dogma of the Assumption emphasizes precisely this; for by declaring that the Blessed Virgin Mary was carried up into heaven in body and soul, the Catholic Church re-emphasizes the fact that the redemption achieved on Calvary is the redemption of the whole man, not only the redemption of his soul. Mary is thereby seen as the first purely human creature to enter in her full creatureliness into eternal life.

Professor Toynbee's equation of Christianity with Mahāyāna Buddhism thereby completely misses the point. Buddhism in all its forms is a religion of escape – of escape from the world of *saṃsāra* where all is pain and suffering: Christianity is a religion which sanctifies matter and elevates it to the realm of spirit, or, to put it into Indian terms, which causes *saṃsāra* to partake of the nature of *Nirvāṇa*. At the same time it bids us accept this world with all its transient joys and sorrows, to grasp the nettle of this world of pain, to take up our cross, not to try to discover how we can rid ourselves of it either by our own efforts or by seeking the succour of a compassionate Bodhisattva. It is no part of the editor of a book such as this to say which he considers to be the nobler ideal: the reader will either have to choose for himself or else reject all the solutions to the problem of human existence which the great religions offer him. One thing, however, seems certain, and that is that the differences that separate the great religions will not, in the foreseeable future, suddenly evaporate into any "higher synthesis", but will continue to preach their different messages, seeking to save and comfort souls according to what they believe to be the truth; "for what is needed in the present time of world-encounter of religions," as Hendrik Kraemer rightly says (*Religion and the Christian Faith*, 1956, p. 134), "is not to be as sweet as possible with each other, but to learn the art of being as true as possible with each other, in spiritual emulation."

Meanwhile all the religions will be faced with the twin challenges of materialistic secularism and Marxian Communism with which Christianity alone is now fully familiar. How far the purely immanentist religions which originate in India will be able to meet this challenge remains to be seen, for there is so much in dialectical materialism that is akin to much of the "dialectical" thought of the Hindus and Buddhists that their wholesale conversion to this new religion which puts Nature in the place of God cannot be altogether ruled out. Further, if the Marxists ever saw fit to come to terms with Jungian psychology, they might find that whereas the thought of Engels is in harmony with the *Tao-tê ching*, that of Jung is no less in line with the psychological theories of the Buddhists and Hindus. The combination of the two might well prove irresistible, for both of them have succeeded in re-creating ancient doctrines in a modern and "scientific" form.

Against such a combination, it would seem, only the three great monotheistic religions which uncompromisingly affirm the reality, omnipotence and absolute sovereignty of God over against Nature and all the created order, are likely to prove effective. Throughout the centuries Jewry has shown that no amount of savage persecution can tear it away from the faith of its fathers: Christianity too has shown its power to face up to the challenge even unto death: for Islam, the last of the great monotheistic religions, the time of testing is yet to come.

For Further Reading

CH. I. Judaism or the Religion of Israel

TEXTS

The Bible (Soncino Books of the Bible, Hebrew text and English translation and commentary, 14 vols., London and Bournemouth, 1943–52. Editor: Rev. Dr A. COHEN).

The Babylonian Talmud, transl. into English with notes, glossary and indexes under the editorship of ISIDORE EPSTEIN; 34 vols. and index volume, London, 1935–52.

The Midrash, transl. into English with notes, glossary and indexes under the editorship of H. FREEDMAN and M. SIMON, 10 vols., London, 1939.

The Zohar, transl. by H. SPERLING and M. SIMON, 5 vols., Soncino, London, 1949.

GENERAL

The Jewish Encyclopaedia, 12 vols., New York, 1901–6. (Antiquated in some respects but still excellent.)

The Universal Jewish Encyclopaedia, 10 vols., New York, 1939–43. (Modern but inferior to the preceding.)

The Jews: Their History, Culture and Religion. (Ed. L. FINKELSTEIN), 2 vols, 2nd edition, New York, 1950. (Concludes with an excellent chapter by L. FINKELSTEIN on "The Beliefs and Practices of Judaism"; ch. 35, vol. ii, pp. 1327–87.)

HISTORY

A Social and Religious History of the Jews, by S. W. BARON, 2nd edition, Columbia, New York, 1952. (The modern standard work.)

A Short History of the Jewish People, by CECIL ROTH, 1st edition 1936, and many subsequent editions, East & West Library, London. (A convenient and well-written account.)

RELIGION (Biblical and early Rabbinic)

From the Stone Age to Christianity, by W. F. ALBRIGHT, 2nd edition, Johns Hopkins, Oxford, 1946.

Hebrew Religion, Its Origin and Development, by W. O. E. OESTERLEY and T. H. ROBINSON, 2nd edition, S.P.C.K., London, 1937. (Follows the older "critical" view rather too closely.)

Inspiration and Revelation in the Old Testament, by H. WHEELER ROBINSON, Oxford, 1946.

Judaism in the First Centuries of the Christian Era, by G. F. MOORE, Cambridge, Mass., 1927–30.

The Pharisees, by R. TRAVERS HERFORD, Allen & Unwin, London, 1924.

MODERN ACCOUNTS OF JEWISH RELIGION AND BELIEF
Descriptive

A Handbook of Judaism as Professed and Practised Through the Ages, by M. WAXMAN, New York, 1947.

The Jewish Religion, by M. FRIEDLANDER, 3rd edition, London, 1913.

Philosophy and Mysticism

The Philosophy of Judaism, by J. GOTTMAN, Meridian Books, New York, publication due 1960.

Major Trends in Jewish Mysticism, by G. SCHOLEM (2nd edition New York, 1946, 3rd edition, Thames & Hudson, London, 1956).

Hasidism

Tales of the Hasidim, by M. BUBER, Thames & Hudson, London, 1956.

The Hasidic Anthology, by L. I. NEWMAN, Bloch, New York – London, 1934.

Modern Theologies

Jewish Theology, Systematically and Historically Considered, by KAUFMAN KOHLER, New York, 1918. (Suffers from its slavish imitation of nineteenth-century liberal Protestant theology.)

The Jewish Way of Life, by ISIDORE EPSTEIN, Pardes, London, 1946.

The Faith of Judaism; An Interpretation for Our Times, by ISIDORE EPSTEIN, Soncino, London, 1954. (Orthodox. Both works are fluently and well written but show no acquaintance with the real problems of modern theology and religion.)

The Essence of Judaism, by L. BAECK, Schaeken, New York, 1948. (The point of view of "Progressive Judaism"; by far the best publication of its kind.)

Man is not Alone: A Philosophy of Religion, by A. J. HESCHEL.

God in Search of Man: A Philosophy of Judaism, by A. J. HESCHEL, Farrar, Straus, New York, 1955. (Both works may be said to represent the mystical, "neo-Hasidic" trend in modern Judaism.)

Judaism and Modern Man: An Interpretation of Jewish Religion, by WILL HERBERG, Farrar, Straus, New York, 1951. (Written under the obvious influence of Reinhold Niebuhr.)

CH. 2a. Christianity: the Early Church

The Primitive Christian Catechism, by P. CARRINGTON, Cambridge, 1940.

Early Christian Worship, by O. CULLMANN, S.C.M., London, 1953.

The Spirit, the Church and the Sacraments, by J. G. DAVIES, Faith Press, London, 1954.

Paul, by M. F. DIBELIUS, Longmans, London, 1953.

The Shape of the Liturgy, by G. DIX, Dacre, Black, London, 1945.

The Apostolic Preaching and its Development, by C. H. DODD, Hodder, London, 1936.

The Mission and Achievement of Jesus, by R. H. FULLER, S.C.M., London, 1954.

Paul and his Predecessors, by A. M. HUNTER. S.C.M., London, 1940.

The Eucharistic Words of Jesus, by J. JEREMIAS, Blackwell, Oxford, 1955.

Early Christian Creeds, by J. N. D. KELLY, Longmans, London, 1950.

Early Christian Doctrines, by J. N. D. KELLY, Black, London, 1958.

The Teaching of Jesus, by T. W. MANSON, Cambridge, 1931.

God in Patristic Thought, by G. L. PRESTIGE, Heinemann, London, 1936.

Doctrines of the Creed, by O. C. QUICK, Nisbet, London, 1938.

The New Testament Doctrine of the Christ, by A. E. J. RAWLINSON, Longmans, London, 1926.

A Study in Christology, by H. M. RELTON, S.P.C.K., London, 1917.

The Miracle Stories of the Gospels, by A. RICHARDSON, S.C.M., London, 1941.

The Council of Chalcedon, by R. V. SELLERS, S.P.C.K., London, 1953.

The Formation of the New Testament, by H. F. D. SPARKS, S.C.M., London, 1952.

The Patristic Doctrine of Redemption, by H. E. W. TURNER, Mowbray, London, 1952.

The Pattern of Christian Truth, by H. E. W. TURNER, Mowbray, London, 1954.

An Approach to Christology, by A. R. VINE, Indep. P., London, 1948.

CH. 2b. Christianity: the Eastern Schism and the Eastern Orthodox Church

Byzantine Empire

Byzantium, its Triumphs and Tragedy, by RENE GUERDAN, Allen & Unwin, London, 1956.

The Schism

The Byzantine Patriarchate, by G. EVERY, S.P.C.K., London, 1947.

The Eastern Schism, by S. RUNCIMAN, O.U.P., Oxford, 1955.

History of the Eastern Church

The Waters of Marah (The Present State of the Greek Church), by P. HAMMOND, Rockliff, London, 1956.

The Russians and their Church, by NICOLAS ZERNOV, S.P.C.K., London, 1954.

Teaching and Worship

The Orthodox Church, by S. BULGAKOV, Centenary Press, London, 1935.

The Eastern Orthodox Church, by R. FRENCH, Hutchinson, London, 1951.

The Church of the Eastern Christians, by NICOLAS ZERNOV, S.P.C.K., London, 1942.

Mysticism and Spiritual Life

A Treasury of Russian Spirituality, (ed. by) G. FEDOTOV, Sheed, London, 1950.

Eastern and Western Reunion

Vision and Action, by L. ZANDER, Gollancz, London, 1951.

The Reintegration of the Church, by NICOLAS ZERNOV, S.C.M., London, 1952.

CH. 2c. Christianity: St Thomas and Medieval Theology

Selected Texts of St Thomas

St Thomas Aquinas: Theological Texts, by THOMAS GILBY, O.U.P., Oxford, 1955.

St Thomas Aquinas: Philosophical Texts, by THOMAS GILBY, O.U.P., Oxford, 1951.

Selected Writings (Thomas Aquinas), ed. M. C. D'ARCY, Everyman, No. 953, Dent, London, 1939.

General

Mediaeval Religion and Other Essays, by C. DAWSON, Sheed & Ward, London, 1934.

The Christian Philosophy of St Thomas Aquinas, by E. GILSON, Sheed & Ward, London, 1957.

History of the Christian Philosophy of the Middle Ages, by E. GILSON, Sheed & Ward, London, 1955.

The Spirit of Mediaeval Philosophy, by E. GILSON (Gifford Lectures), Sheed & Ward, London, 1936.

Thomas Aquinas, by M. C. D'ARCY, Clonmore, London, 1930.

Aquinas, by F. C. COPLESTON, Penguin, London, 1955.

A History of Philosophy, by F. C. COPLESTON, Vol. 2, *Augustine to Scotus*, Burns, Oates, London, 1953.

CH. 2d. Christianity: Protestantism

Documents on Christian Unity, by G. K. A. BELL (Three Series), O.U.P., Oxford, 1924, 1930, 1948.

Dividend Christendom, by Y. M. J. CONGAR, Geoffrey Bles, London, 1939.

The Worship of the English Puritans, by HORTON DAVIES, Dacre, Black, London, 1948.

Protestant Christianity, by J. DILLENBERGER, and C. WELCH, New York, 1955.

German Protestantism Since Luther, by A. L. DRUMMOND, Epworth, London, 1951.

Billy Sunday Was his Real Name, by W. G. McLOUGHLIN U. of Chicago, 1955.

The History and Character of Calvinism, by J. T. McNEILL, O.U.P., Oxford, 1954.

A History of the Ecumenical Movement, by R. Rouse and S. C. Neill, S.P.C.K., London, 1954.

The Righteousness of God, by E. G. Rupp, Luther Studies, Hodder, London, 1955.

The Church of South India. The Movement Towards Union, by B. G. M. Sundkler, Lutterworth Press, London, 1954.

The Story of Religion in America, by W. W. Sweet, New York, 1950.

The Crisis of the Reformation, by N. Sykes, Bles, London, 1946.

A New History of Methodism, by Townsend, Workman and Eayrs, Hodder, London, 1909 (2 vols.).

Let God be God. An Interpretation of the Theology of Martin Luther, by P. Watson, Epworth, London, 1947.

Northern Catholicism, by N. P. Williams, ed., S.P.C.K., London, 1933.

Ch. 2e. Christianity: the Catholic Church Since the Reformation

Catholic Encyclopedia, New York, 1907–12 (15 vols.).

Dictionnaire de théologie catholique, Paris, 1903–50 (15 vols.).

Dictionnaire apologétique de la foi catholique, Paris, 1913 (4 vols.).

A Catholic Commentary on Holy Scripture, Nelson, London, 1953.

Theology and Sanity, by F. Sheed, Sheed and Ward, London, 1952.

The Faith of the Roman Church, by C. C. Martindale, Methuen, London, 1927.

Catholicism, by M. C. D'Arcy, Clonmore, London, 1955.

Roman Catholicism, by T. Corbishley, Hutchinson, London, 1952.

Origin of the Jesuits, by J. Brodrick, Longmans, London, 1940.

Progress of the Jesuits, by J. Brodrick, Longmans, London, 1946.

St. Peter Canisius, by J. Brodrick, Sheed and Ward, London, 1935.

Vatican Council, by C. Butler, Longmans, London, 1930.

Ch. 3. Islam

The Koran Interpreted, by A. J. Arberry, 2 vols., Allen & Unwin, London, 1955.

Mohammed, The Man and his Faith, by Tor Andrae, Allen & Unwin, London, 1936.

Muhammad at Mecca, by W. M. Watt, O.U.P., Oxford, 1953.

Muhammad at Madina, by W. M. Watt, O.U.P., Oxford, 1956.

The Social Laws of the Qoran, by R. Roberts, Williams & Norgate, London, 1925.

The Preaching of Islam, by T. W. Arnold, second edition, London, 1913, and reprints.

The Muslim Creed, by A. J. Wensinck, Cambridge, 1932.

Development of Muslim Theology, Jurisprudence and Constitutional Theory, by D. B. Macdonald, Semitic Series, London and New York, 1903, and reprints.

The Religious Life and Attitude in Islam, by D. B. Macdonald, Chicago, 1906, and reprints.

Muslim Theology, by A. S. Tritton, Luzac, London, 1947.

Introduction à la Théologie Musulmane, by L. Gardet and M. N. Anawati, Paris, 1948.

The Shi'ite Religion, by D. M. Donaldson, Luzac, London, 1933.

The Social Structure of Islam, by R. Levy, Cambridge, 1957.

Outlines of Muhammadan Law, by A. A. A. Fyzee, O.U.P., London, 1949.

Law in the Middle East, (eds.) M. Khadduri and H. J. Liebesny, vol. i, Washington, D.C., 1955.

Revelation and Reason in Islam, by A. J. Arberry, Allen & Unwin, London, 1957.

Sufism: an account of the Mystics of Islam, by A. J. Arberry, Allen & Unwin, London, 1950.

Studies in Islamic Mysticism, by R. A. Nicholson, Cambridge, 1951.

The Mystical Philosophy of Ibnul 'Arabi, by A. E. Affifi, Cambridge, 1939.

The Dervishes, by J. P. Brown, ed. H. A. Rose, O.U.P., Oxford, 1927.

Islam and Modernism in Egypt, by C. C. Adams, O.U.P., Oxford, 1933.

Modern Trends in Islam, by H. A. R. Gibb, O.U.P., Chicago, 1947, and reprints.

Indian Islam, by Murray Titus, Oxford, 1930.

La Cité Musulmane, by L. Gardet, Paris, 1954.

Shorter Encyclopaedia of Islam, (eds.) H. A. R. Gibb and J. H. Kramers, Leyden, 1953.

The Legacy of Islam, T. W. Arnold and A. Guillaume (eds.), Oxford, 1931.

Ch. 4. Zoroastrianism

TEXTS IN TRANSLATION

Gāthās: the best translations in English are: *The Hymns of Zarathustra*, by J. Duchesne-Guillemin, London, 1952, and *Early Zoroastrianism*, by J. H. Moulton, London, 1913, pp. 344–90.

Avesta: in *Sacred Books of the East*, vols. iv, xxxi, and xxxiii.

Pahlavi Texts: Selections in the two books by R. C. Zaehner listed below.

GENERAL WORKS

The Persian Religion according to the Chief Greek Texts, by E. Benveniste, Paris, 1929.

Zoroastre, by J. Duchesne-Guillemin, Paris, 1948.

Ormazd et Ahriman, by J. Duchesne-Guillemin, Paris, 1953.

The Foundations of the Iranian Religions, by L. H. Gray, Bombay, 1925.

Zoroaster, Politician or Witch-doctor?, by W. B. Henning, Oxford, 1951.

Zoroastrian Studies, by A. V. W. Jackson, New York, 1928.

The Religious Ceremonies and Customs of the Parsees, by J. J. Modi, 2nd edition, Bombay, 1937.

Early Zoroastrianism, by J. H. Moulton, Williams & Norgate, London, 1913.

FOR FURTHER READING

The Teachings of the Magi, by R. C. ZAEHNER, Allen & Unwin, London, 1956.

Zurvan, A Zoroastrian Dilemma, by R. C. ZAEHNER, O.U.P., Oxford, 1955.

CH. 5. Hinduism

GENERAL OUTLINES OF HINDUISM AND HINDU CULTURE

Hinduism and Buddhism, by SIR C. ELIOT, 3 vols., Routledge, London, 1922.

A Primer of Hinduism, by J. N. FARQUHAR, Probsthain, London, 1912.

The Wonder that was India, by A. L. BASHAM, Sidgwick & Jackson, London, 1954.

Living Religions of the Indian People, by N. MACNICOL, London, 1934.

SPECIAL ASPECTS OF HINDUISM

Religion and Philosophy of the Vedas and Upanishads, by A. BERRIDALE KEITH, Cambridge, Mass., 1925.

Indian Philosophy, by S. RADHAKRISHNAN, 2 vols., Allen & Unwin, London, 1923-7.

History of Indian Philosophy, by S. N. DAS GUPTA, 5 vols., C.U.P., Cambridge, 1923-55.

Hindu Social Institutions, by P. H. VALAVALKAR, 2nd edition, Baroda, 1942.

The Hindu Ideal of Life, by B. K. GHOSH, Calcutta, 1947.

Caste in India, by J. H. HUTTON, C.U.P., Cambridge, 1946.

Popular Hinduism, by L. S. S. O'MALLEY, C.U.P., Cambridge, 1934.

Theism in Medieval India, by J. ESTLIN CARPENTER, Williams & Norgate, London, 1921.

The Sikhs, by KHUSHVANT SINGH, Allen & Unwin, London, 1953.

Modern Religious Movements in India, by J. N. FARQUHAR, Macmillan, London, 1929.

The Gandhi Sutras: the Basic Teachings of Mahatma Gandhi, by D. S. SARMA, New York, 1948.

Social Ethics in Modern Hinduism, by R. W. SCOTT, Calcutta, 1953.

Gandhi to Vinoba, by L. DEL VASTO, Rider, London, 1956.

TRANSLATIONS OF HINDU RELIGIOUS TEXTS

The Wisdom of India, (ed.) LIN YUTANG, Michael Joseph, London, 1949.

The Indian Heritage, by V. RAGHAVAN, Bangalore, 1956.

Thirteen Principal Upanishads, by R. A. HUME, O.U.P., Oxford, 1921.

The Laws of Manu, trans. G. BÜHLER (*Sacred Books of the East*, vol. xxv), Oxford, 1886.

The Mahabhārata and Rāmāyana (abridged), by R. C. DUTT, London, 1917.

The Bhagavad Gītā, by W. D. P. HILL, O.U.P., Oxford, 1928.

The Vedānta Sutrās with the Commentary of Sankarācārya, by G. THIBAUT (*Sacred Books of the East*, vols. xxxiv, xxxviii), Oxford, 1890-6.

The Vedanta Sutras with Ramanuja's Commentary Sribhāsya, by G. THIBAUT (*Sacred Books of the East*, vol. xlviii), Oxford, 1904.

Śivajñāna Siddhiyār, by J. M. NALLASWAMI PILLAI, Madras, 1913.

Hymns of the Tamil Śaivite Saints, by F. KINGSBURY and G. E. PHILIPS, Calcutta, 1921.

One Hundred Poems of Kabir, by RABINDRANATH TAGORE, London, 1921.

Psalms of the Marāthā Saints, by N. MACNICOL, Calcutta n.d.

CH. 6. Jainism

Jaina Scriptures trans. H. JACOBI (*Sacred Books of the East*, vols. xxii and xlv), Oxford, 1884-95.

Outlines of Jainism, by J. JAINI, 2nd edition, C.U.P., Cambridge, 1940.

Outlines of Jaina Philosophy, by M. L. MEHTA, Bangalore, 1954.

The Heart of Jainism, by MRS S. STEVENSON, O.U.P., Oxford, 1915.

Studies in Jaina Philosophy, by N. TATIA, Benares, 1951.

Jainism, by H. WARREN, Madras, 1912.

CH. 7a. Buddhism: the Theravāda

Hinduism and Buddhism, by A. K. COOMARASWAMY, New York.

Time and Eternity (Chapter on Buddhism), by A. K. COOMARASWAMY, Ascona, 1947.

Buddha and the Gospel of Buddhism, by A. K. COOMARASWAMY, Indian edition, Bombay, 1957.

Introduction to Living Thoughts of Gotama the Buddha, by A. K. COOMARASWAMY, and I. B. HORNER, London, 1948. Indian edition, Bombay, 1956.

The Meaning of Life in Hinduism and Buddhism, by H. FLOYD ROSS, London, 1952.

La Vie du Bouddha d'après les Textes et les Monuments de l'Inde, by A. FOUCHER, Paris, 1949.

Buddhist India, by T. W. RHYS DAVIDS, 3rd Indian edn., Calcutta, 1957.

Manual of Buddhism, by MRS RHYS DAVIDS, S.P.C.K., London, 1932.

Poems of Cloister and Jungle, by MRS RHYS DAVIDS, J. Murray, London, 1941.

Indian Religion and Survival, by MRS RHYS DAVIDS, London, 1934.

The Buddha and Five After Centuries, by S. DUTT, London, 1957.

Hinduism and Buddhism, by C. ELIOT, 3 vols., Routledge, London, 1921.

Doctrine of Awakening, by J. EVOLA, trans. H. E. MUSSON, Luzac, London, 1951.

History of Pāli Literature, by B. C. LAW, 2 vols., London, 1933.

Fundamentals of Buddhism, by NYANATILOKA MAHĀTHERA, Colombo, 1949.

Guide through the Abhidhamma-piṭaka, followed by an Essay on Paṭṭica-samuppāda, by NYANATILOKA MAHĀTHERA, Colombo, 1957.

Indian Philosophy, by S. RADHAKRISHNAN, vol. I, 2nd edition, Allen & Unwin, London, 1929.

Introduction to Dhammapada, by S. RADHAKRISHNAN, O.U.P., Oxford, 1950.

A Manual of Abhidhamma, by Nārada Thera, 2 vols., Bangalore, 1956, 1957.

History of Buddhist Thought, by E. J. Thomas, Routledge, London, 1933.

Life of Buddha as Legend and History, by E. J. Thomas, 3rd edition, Routledge, London, 1949.

Philosophies of India, by H. Zimmer, ed. J. Campbell, Bollingen Series XXVI, New York, 1951.

Myths and Symbols in Indian Art and Civilization, by H. Zimmer, ed. J. Campbell, Bollingen Series VI, New York, 1946.

Ch. 7b. Buddhism: the Mahāyāna

Śantideva, *Śikshāsamuccaya* (Compendium of Training), trans. C. Bendall and W. H. D. Rouse, London, 1922.

Selected Sayings from the Perfection of Wisdom, by Edward Conze, The Buddhist Society, London, 1955.

Buddhism, by Edward Conze, 3rd edition, Faber, London, 1957, pp. 119–99.

Buddhist Texts Through the Ages, ed. Edward Conze, Faber, London, 1954, pp. 119–268.

The Bodhisattva Doctrine, by Har Dayal, London, 1932.

The Tibetan Book of the Dead, by W. Y. Evans-Wentz, 3rd edition, O.U.P., Oxford, 1957.

The Lotus of the True Law (Sacred Books of the East, vol. xxi), trans. H. Kern, Oxford, 1884.

The Central Philosophy of Buddhism, by T. R. V. Murti, Allen & Unwin, London, 1955.

Lankavatara Sutra, trans. D. T. Suzuki, Routledge, London, 1932.

Mahayana Buddhism, by B. L. Suzuki, 2nd edition, London, 1948.

Ch. 7c. Buddhism: in China and Japan

History of Japanese Religion, by Masaharu Anesaki, Kegan Paul, London, 1930.

The Jewel in the Lotus, by John Blofeld, Buddhist Society, London, 1948.

Chinese Buddhism, by Joseph Edkins, Kegan Paul, London, 1879.

Japanese Buddhism, by Charles Eliot, Edward Arnold, London, 1935.

The Path of the Buddha, by Kenneth W. Morgan, The Ronald Press, New York, 1956.

The Pilgrimage of Buddhism, by James Bissett Pratt, New York, 1928.

Essays in Zen Buddhism, by D. T. Suzuki, London, 1927 (First Series), 1933 (Second Series), 1934 (Third Series). Reprinted by Rider & Co., London, 1949, 1950.

The Essentials of Buddhist Philosophy, by Junjiro Takakusu, University of Hawaii, Honolulu, 1947.

Ch. 8. Confucianism

The Chinese Classics, trans. James Legge, 2nd edition O.U.P., Oxford, 1893.

Sacred Books of the East, vols. iii, xvi, xxvii, xxviii, trans. James Legge.

Analects of Confucius, by Arthur Waley, Allen & Unwin, London, 1938. (The numbering of sections is often one or two more or less than Legge's.)

Three Ways of Thought in Ancient China, by Arthur Waley, Allen & Unwin, London, 1939.

Works of Hsüntze, trans. H. H. Dubs, Probsthain, London, 1928.

K'ung tzü chia yü, trans. R. P. Kramers, Leiden, 1950.

A History of Chinese Philosophy, by Fung Yu-lan, trans. Derk Bodde, 2 vols., Princeton, 1953.

Translations in the article are the author's, and do not necessarily agree with the version to which the reference is given. No references are given to untranslated works.

Ch. 9. Taoism

Religious Trends in Modern China, by Wing-tsit Chan, New York, 1953.

Researches into Chinese superstitions, by Henri Doré, trans. D. J. Finn, vols. i–x, 1914–33.

Taoist teachings from the book of Lieh Tzŭ, trans. Lionel Giles, J. Murray, London, 1912.

The Religious System of China, by J. J. M. de Groot, vols. i–vi, Leyden, 1892–1910.

Science and Civilisation in China, by J. Needham, vol. ii. 'The Tao Chia (Taoists) and Taoism', C.U.P., Cambridge, 1956.

T'ai-Shang Kan-Ying P'ien, Treatise of the Exalted One on Response and Retribution, trans. Teitaro Suzuki and Dr Paul Carus, Chicago, 1906.

The Way and its Power, by Arthur Waley, Allen & Unwin, London, 1937.

A History of the Religious Beliefs and Philosophical Opinions in China, by Léon Wieger, trans. by E. C. Werner, Tientsin, 1927.

Chuang-tzü, a new selected translation with an exposition of the philosophy of Kuo Hsiang, by Feng Yu-lan, Shanghai, 1931.

A History of Chinese Philosophy, by Fung Yu-lan, trans. Derk Bodde, 2 vols., Princeton, 1953.

Ch. 10. Shintō

History of Japanese Religion, by Masaharu Anesaki, London, 1930.

Shintō, The Way of the Gods, by W. G. Aston, London, 1905.

Ancient Japanese Rituals, by Karl Florenz, Transactions of the Asiatic Society of Japan, 27, 1 (1900) pp. 1–112.

Les Religions du Japon in *Histoire des Religions*, 2, by A. Hauchecorne, Paris, 1954.

The National Faith of Japan: a study in Modern Shintō, by D. C. Holtom, London, 1938.

The Outline of Tenrikyō, by Takahito Iwai, Nara, Japan, 1932.

A Study of Shintō, the Religion of the Japanese Nation, by Genchi Katō, Tokyo, 1926.

Religions in Japan, SCAP Civil Information and Education Section, Tokyo, 1948.

Shintō, Der Weg der Götter in Japan, by Georg Schurhammer, Bonn und Leipzig, 1923.

Shintoism, by A. C. Underwood, Epworth, London, 1934.

CH. 11. A New Buddha and A New Tao

I

A good introduction to JUNG's work is: *An Introduction to Jung's Psychology*, by FRIEDA FORDHAM, Pelican, London, 1953.

The Collected Works of Jung are now being published by Pantheon Books in the United States and by Routledge in England.

INDIVIDUAL WORKS by C. G. JUNG

Two Essays on Analytical Psychology, by C. G. JUNG, Routledge, London, 1953.

The Secret of the Golden Flower, by C. G. JUNG, London, 1931.

Psychology and Religion, by C. G. JUNG, O.U.P., London, 1938.

The Integration of the Personality, by C. G. JUNG, New York, 1939, Routledge, London, 1940.

Answer to Job, by C. G. JUNG, Routledge, London, 1954.

II

Anti-Dühring, by F. ENGELS, Lawrence & Wishart, London, 1955.

Dialectics of Nature, by F. ENGELS, Lawrence & Wishart, London, 1955.

Ludwig Feuerbach, by F. ENGELS, Lawrence & Wishart, London, 1946.

The Holy Family, by K. MARX and F. ENGELS, Moscow, 1956.

Materialism and Emperio-Criticism, by V. I. LENIN, Lawrence & Wishart, London, 1950.

References in this chapter to *Anti-Dühring* are from the 1934 edition and to *Ludwig Feuerbach* to the 1946 Moscow edition.

Acknowledgments

We are indebted to the following publishers who have given us permission to reproduce passages from the books specified below:

TEXT:

40 *Selected Poems of Jehudah Halevi*, tr. Nina Salaman.
53 *The New Testament Doctrine of Christ*, by A.J.Rawlinson, Longmans, Green & Co. Ltd, London, 1926.
54 *The Teaching of Jesus*, by T.W.Manson, Cambridge University Press, London, 1931.
59 *Christianity according to St John*, by W.F. Howard, Gerald Duckworth & Co. Ltd, London, 1943.
59 *Interpretation of the Fourth Gospel*, by C.H.Dodd, Cambridge University Press, London, 1953.
60 *The Gospel according to St John*, by C.K. Barrett, S.P.C.K., London, 1955.
108 *The Christian Philosophy of St Thomas Aquinas*, by Etienne Gilson, Sheed & Ward Ltd, London, 1957.
118 *Comments on Epistle to Galatians*, ed. Watson, S.P.C.K., London, 1953.
119, 131 *Northern Catholicism*, by N.P. Williams, S.P.C.K., London, 1933.
120 *Luther's Letters of Spiritual Counsel*, ed. T.G.Tappert, S.C.M. Press Ltd, London, 1955.
120 *Ways of Worship*, ed. F.R.Maxwell, S.C.M. Press Ltd, London, 1952.
122 *The Nature of the Church*, ed. R.N.Flew, S.C.M. Press Ltd, London, 1952.
127 *Divided Christendom*, by Yves M.J. Congar, Geoffrey Bles Ltd, London, 1939.
128 *Arthur Stanton*, by G.W.E.Russell, Longmans, Green & Co. Ltd, London, 1917.
128, 129 *Received with Thanks*, by H.A. Wilson, A.R.Mowbray & Co. Ltd, London, 1940.
129, 130 *Memoirs of G. C. Ommanney*, ed. F.G.Belton, Geoffrey Bles Ltd, London, 1936.
132 *Billy Sunday was his Real Name*, by W.G.McLoughlin, Jr., University of Chicago Press, Chicago, 1955.
134, 135 *Report to the Convocation of Canterbury*, S.P.C.K., London, 1907.
144 *Amsterdam 1948: an account of the first assembly of the World Council of Churches*, H.G.G.Herklots, by S.C.M. Press Ltd, London, 1948.
153 *Religion Since the Reformation: Bampton*

Lectures, by L.Pullan, Oxford University Press, London, 1923.
239, 240 *Kabir's One Hundred Poems*, tr. Rabindranath Tagore, Macmillan & Co. Ltd, London, 1938.
240 *The Heart of India*, by L.D.Barnett, John Murray Ltd, London, 1938.
240, 241 *Psalms of Maratha Saints*, tr. Nicol Macnicol, Oxford University Press, London, 1919.
241 *Gandhi to Vinoba*, by Lanza del Vasto, Rider & Co., London, 1956.
299, 300 *Buddhist Meditation*, by E.Conze, Allen & Unwin Ltd, London, 1956.
299, 301, 304, 306, 307, 308, 319 *Buddhist Texts Through the Ages*, ed. E.Conze, Faber & Faber Ltd, London, 1954.
300, 301 *Tibet's Great Yogi Milarepa*, by W.Y.Evans-Wentz, Oxford University Press, London, 1951.
302 *The Voice of Silence*, by H.P.Blavatsky, Theosophical Book Co, Surrey, 1953.
303 *Manual of Zen Buddhism*, by D.T. Suzuki, Rider & Co., London, 1935.
303 *Perfection of Wisdom*, by E.Conze, J.M. Watkins, London, 1955.
362 *Japanese Buddhism*, by Sir C.Eliot, E.J. Arnold & Sons Ltd, Leeds, 1935.
369 *Works of Hsuntze*, by H.H. Dubs, Arthur Probsthain, London, 1928.
372 *Sacred Books of the East*, tr. James Legge, Oxford University Press, London, 1952.
385 *Chuang-Tzu*, by Feng Yu-Lang, Commercial Press, Shanghai, 1931.
403 *Secret of the Golden Flower*, by C. G.Jung, Routledge & Kegan Paul Ltd, London, 1931.
404 *Psychology of the Unconscious*, by C. G. Jung, Routledge & Kegan Paul Ltd, London, 1917.
404 *The Integration of the Personality*, by C. G. Jung, Routledge & Kegan Paul Ltd, London, 1940.
404, 405 *Collected Works*, by C. G. Jung, Routledge & Kegan Paul Ltd, London.
405 *An Introduction to Jung's Psychology*, by F.Fordham, Penguin Books Ltd, London, 1953.
404, 405 *Psychology and its Social Meaning*, by Ira Progoff, Routledge & Kegan Paul Ltd, London, 1953.
406 *Two Essays on Analytical Psychology*, by C. G. Jung, Routledge & Kegan Paul Ltd, London, 1933.
405, 406 *Answer to Job*, by C. G. Jung, Routledge & Kegan Paul Ltd, London, 1954.

407, 411 *Dialectics of Nature*, by F. Engels, Lawrence & Wishart Ltd, London, 1955.
406, 407 *The Holy Family*, by Marx and Engels.
407 *Anti-Dühring*, by F. Engels, Lawrence & Wishart Ltd, London, 1955.
414 *An Historian's Approach to Religion*, by Arnold Toynbee, Oxford University Press, London, 1956.

We are indebted to the following:

MONOCHROME PLATES:
2 *The Jewish Chronicle*, London.
4 Miss Ruth P. Lehman, Jews' College, London.
16 *Byzantine Legacy*, by Cecil Stewart, Allen & Unwin Ltd., London.
18 D.M.Nicol, Dublin.
22 Edinburgh International Festival Society Ltd, London.
35 The Reverend Kenneth Ross, All Saints' Church, London.
37 The Society of Friends, London.
42 Father Valentin Arteta, S.J., *Hechos y Dichos*, Zaragoza, Spain.
44 *The Observer*, London.
49 *A Survey of Persian Art*, by A. Upham Pope, Oxford University Press, London.
54, 62, 101, 102, 103 Victoria and Albert Museum. Crown copyright.
56 *The Rock Sculptures and Inscription of Darius at Behistun*, by R.C. King, and L.W.Thompson, The Trustees of the British Museum, London.
69, 70, 71 Khin Lay Maung, Rangoon.
72, 83 India Office Library, Commonwealth Relations Office, London.
83 Professor Seiichi Mizuno, Research Institute of Humanistic Science, Kyoto University, Japan.
93 Takananu Mitsui, Tokyo.
97, 98 Tenrike Headquarters, Tenri City, Nara Prefecture, Japan.
107, 108, 110 School of Oriental and African Studies, University of London.

CAPTIONS:
Plates 101, 102, 103 *Book of Songs*, translated by Arthur Waley, Allen & Unwin Ltd, London.

Notes on the Contributors

A. L. BASHAM, B.A., PH.D., Professor of the History of South Asia, School of Oriental and African Studies, University of London. Publications include: *History and Doctrines of The Ājīvikas*, Luzac, 1951; *The Wonder that was India*, Sidgwick & Jackson, 1954.

G. BOWNAS, M.A., Lecturer in Chinese and Japanese Studies, University of Oxford. Publications include: *Confucius*, translation from the Japanese of Shigeki Kaizuka, Allen & Unwin, London, 1956.

EDWARD CONZE, PH.D., Lecturer for the Extra-mural Department, University of London. Publications include: *Buddhism*, Oxford, 1951; *Buddhist Meditation*, Allen & Unwin, 1956; *The Buddha's Law Among the Birds*, Faber & Faber, 1956.

T. CORBISHLEY, S.J., M.A., Superior of Farm Street Church, London. Formerly Master of Campion Hall, Oxford (1945-1958). Publications include: *Agnosticism*, C.T.S., 1935; *Roman Catholicism*, Hutchinson, 1950.

J. G. DAVIES, M.A., D.D., Senior Lecturer in Theology, University of Birmingham. Publications include: *Daily Life in the Early Church*, Lutterworth Press, 1952; *Social Life of Early Christians*, Lutterworth Press, 1954; *He Ascended into Heaven, A Study in the history of Doctrine*, Lutterworth Press, 1958.

H. FRANCIS DAVIS, M.A., D.D., Recognized Lecturer in Theology, University of Birmingham. Publications include contributions to: *John Henry Newman*, Burns Oates, 1945; *Centenary Addresses on Newman's Idea of a University*, London, 1953.

WERNER EICHHORN, D.Phil., Librarian Assistant, School of Oriental and African Studies, University of London. Publications include contributions to: *Zeitschrift der Deutscher Morgenlandischera Gesellschaft; Muterlungen des Instituts fur Orientforing Deutsche Akamie der Wissenscharten, Berlin.*

H. A. R. GIBB, Kt., F.B.A., M.A., University Professor of Arabic and Director of the Center for Middle Eastern Studies, University of Harvard; formerly Laudian Professor of Arabic, University of Oxford. Publications include: *Travels of Ibn Battúta, 1324-54*, Routledge, 1929; *Mohammedanism, An Historical Survey*, Oxford, 1949, Mentor Books, New York, 1955; *Shorter Encyclopaedia of Islam*, Luzac, 1953; *Islamic Society and the West*, Vol. I, part 1, 1950, part 2, 1957.

A. C. GRAHAM, M.A., PH.D., Lecturer in Classical Chinese, School of Oriental and African Studies, University of London. Publications include: *Composition of the Gongsven Long tzyy*, Asia Major, 1957; *Two Chinese Philosophers*, Lund Humphries, 1958.

I. B. HORNER, Secretary of the Pāli Text Society. Editor and Compiler of Pāli texts; translator of *Book of Discipline*, Luzac, 1940-52.

JOHN KENT, M.A., PH.D., Ranmoor Professor in Church History at Hartley Victoria College, Manchester.

R. H. ROBINSON, D.D., Lecturer, University of Toronto. Publications include: *Chinese Buddhist Verse*, John Murray, 1954.

R. J. ZWI WERBLOWSKY, B.A., D.ÈS.L. (Geneva), Lecturer in Comparative Religion, The Hebrew University, Jerusalem. Publications include contributions to: *The Hibbert Journal; The Journal of Jewish Studies; Judaism; The Listener.*

R. C. ZAEHNER, M.A., Spalding Professor of Eastern Religions and Ethics and Fellow of All Souls College, Oxford. Publications include: *Zurvan, A Zoroastrian Dilemma*, Oxford, 1955; *The Teachings of the Magi*, Allen & Unwin, 1956; *Mysticism, Sacred and Profane*, Oxford, 1957; *At Sundry Times*, Faber, 1958.

NICOLAS ZERNOV, M.A., D.Phil., F.R.S.L., Spalding Lecturer in Eastern Orthodox Culture, University of Oxford. Publications include: *The Church of the Eastern Christians*, S.P.C.K., 1942, *The Russians and their Church*, S.P.C.K., 1945; *Re-integration of the Church*, S.C.M., 1952.

Index

INDEX

Vaiśeshika, 234, 237, 265
Vaishṇava, 230
Vaisya, 253
Vajjiputtakas, 287
Vallabha Sect, 241
Vardhamāna Mahāvīra, 261–6
Varuṇa, 226, 228, 233
Vedānta, 18, 234, 237–8, 257–60, 402, 407, 414
Vedas, 226–7, 231, 237–8, 243, 253, 256
Vedic period, 227–8, 231, 241–3, 259, 237
Vemana, 229
Vēmana, 240
Vendetta (tha'r), 183, 186, 189
Vidēvdāt, 209
Vinaya Sect, 346, 394
Viśākhā, 281
Vishnu, 226, 228–9, 230–3, 240–2, 254, 259
Viśishṭādvaita, 239
Vivahvant, 211
Voltaire, F.M.A. de, 159

Wahhābīs, 205–6
Waley, Arthur, 383
Welfare State, 143

Wesley, Charles, 123
Wesley, John, 123, 132, 145, 147
Wesleyan Movement, 123, 145 (*See also:* Methodism)
Weston, Bishop Frank, 128, 146
Whitefield, G., 124
"Wholeness", 213–14, 220–1
Will of God, 17, 18, 24, 29–33, 200
Will of Man, 30, 31
Wisdom, 369–70
Wise Lord, 210–14, 219
Word Incarnate, 72
Word of God, 30, 58–9, 148 (*See also: Logos*)
World Council of Churches, 107, 120, 144, 147
World-religions, 16, 19
Worship, 16, 17, 24, 31
Worship, Buddhist doctrine of, 328
Wu-wei (without action), 367, 388, 393
Wyclif, John, 164

Yahweh, 31, 57, 212
Yamato, 350, 363
Yang Chu, 383–5
Yao, 366, 381, 384
Yashts, 209–10

Yasna, 209, 222
Yathrib, 178–80
Yazatas, 210
Yehudah Halevi, 39
Yen Wên, 385
Yezīdīs, 205
Yi (duty), 370–1
Yima, 211
Yoga, 226, 231, 237, 260
Yogācārins, 317
Young Men's Christian Association (Y.M.C.A.), 133
Yü, 385–9
Yüang-tsang, 318
Yüan-shih t'ien-tsun, 388
Yugas, 229–30
Yü-huang, 388, 395

Zaidī Sect, 201, 202
Zāwiya, 202–3
Zen Buddhism, 15, 346, 361–3, 406
Zinzendorf, Count N.L. Graf von, 121
Zionism, 24, 49
Zoroaster (Zarathustra), 209, 209–22
Zoroastrianism, 16, 17, 19, 180, 205, 209–22, 231, 257
Zwingli, Ulrich, 121

431

REL STUDIES 35-260

DATE DUE

DATE DUE